Graceful Reason

Joseph Owens, CSSR

PAPERS IN MEDIAEVAL STUDIES 4

GRACEFUL REASON

Essays in Ancient and Medieval Philosophy
Presented to

Joseph Owens, CSSR

on the Occasion of his Seventy-Fifth Birthday
and the Fiftieth Anniversary of his Ordination

edited by

LLOYD P. GERSON

PONTIFICAL INSTITUTE OF MEDIAEVAL STUDIES

CANADIAN CATALOGUING IN PUBLICATION DATA

Main entry under title:
  Graceful reason

(Papers in mediaeval studies, ISSN 0228-8605 ; 4)
Bibliography: p.
Includes index.
ISBN 0-88844-804-X

1. Philosophy, Ancient - Addresses, essays, lectures.   2. Philosophy, Medieval
- Addresses, essays, lectures.   3. Owens, Joseph, 1908- - Bibliography.
I. Owens, Joseph, 1908-   II. Gerson, Lloyd Phillip, 1948-   III. Pontifical
Institute of Mediaeval Studies.   IV. Series.

B73.G72   180   C83-098146-2

© 1983 by

Pontifical Institute of Mediaeval Studies
59 Queen's Park Crescent East
Toronto, Ontario, Canada M5S 2C4

PRINTED BY UNIVERSA, WETTEREN, BELGIUM

Contents

Contributors

Vernon J. Bourke is professor emeritus of philosophy at St. Louis University.

Jacques Brunschwig is professor of philosophy at the Université de Paris X, Nanterre.

W. Norris Clarke, sj, is professor of philosophy at Fordham University.

William Dunphy is professor of philosophy and Principal, St. Michael's College, University of Toronto.

Cornelio Fabro, css, is professor at the Università di Perugia.

Walter Leszl is professor of philosophy at the Università di Pisa.

Ralph McInerny is Grace Professor of Philosophy and Director of the Medieval Institute at the University of Notre Dame.

Giovanni Reale is professor of philosophy at the Università del Sacro Cuore di Milano.

L. M. de Rijk is professor in ancient and medieval philosophy at the Rijksuniversiteit in Leiden.

John M. Rist is Regius Professor of Classics at the University of Aberdeen.

Kenneth L. Schmitz is professor of philosophy at Trinity College, University of Toronto.

Leo Sweeney, sj, is research professor of philosophy at Loyola University of Chicago.

Edward A. Synan, frsc, is professor of philosophy and Fellow, Pontifical Institute of Mediaeval Studies.

Fernand Van Steenberghen is professor emeritus of philosophy at the Université de Louvain.

Henry B. Veatch is professor of philosophy at Georgetown University and the University of St. Thomas, Houston.

Gerard Verbeke is professor emeritus at the Katholieke Universiteit Leuven and Permanent Secretary of the Royal Academy of Sciences, Brussels.

W. J. Verdenius is professor emeritus of ancient Greek at the Rijksuniversiteit in Utrecht.

Cornelia J. de Vogel is professor emeritus of ancient and patristic philosophy at the Rijksuniversiteit in Utrecht.

James A. Weisheipl, OP, is professor of philosophy and Fellow, Pontifical Institute of Mediaeval Studies.

Norman Wells is professor of philosophy at Boston College.

John F. Wippel is professor of philosophy at the Catholic University of America.

Acknowledgments

I would like to thank Professor Barry F. Brown, Professor Janine Langan, the Reverend P. Osmund Lewry, OP, Mr. Jack Marler, the Reverend Armand Maurer, CSB, and the Reverend Christopher Ryan for their generous and astute advice in the preparation of this volume. I am particularly grateful to Professor James P. Reilly for his great assistance in every phase of this project. I would also like to note with sadness the absence in this volume of one planned contribution, that of Professor Suzanne Mansion, who died only a matter of days after she had expressed to me her eagerness to contribute to a *Festschrift* for Fr. Owens.

Lloyd P. Gerson
St. Michael's College,
University of Toronto

Preface

Edward A. Synan, FRSC

Pontifical Institute of Mediaeval Studies

Among the memories of graduate students from my time at the Pontifical Institute of Mediaeval Studies and the University of Toronto, none is more vivid than is that of the defense made by Joseph Owens, CSSR, of his dissertation for the Institute doctorate. His erudition had long been the object of awe-struck rumor on the campus; with that ceremony it ceased to be rumor and became attested fact. Owens faced a board of examiners calculated to strike awe in any student. To name only those who spoke that day for philosophy, Etienne Gilson and Anton C. Pegis were members of his jury. Awe, however, ran in the opposite direction. This formidable board voted Owens his doctorate *summa cum laude* and the world of learning has been confirming that judgment ever since. The dissertation Owens defended has merited publication in three revisions and four printings.

The very title of this dissertation, along with its sub-title, serves as a convenient rubric for the long career in research, in teaching, and in publication then inaugurated: *The Doctrine of Being in the Aristotelian Metaphysics. A Study in the Greek Background of Mediaeval Thought.* Greek philosophy, on its own terms to be sure, but also in its consequences for the Middle Ages and above all for the thought of Thomas Aquinas and John Duns Scotus, has dominated Owens' work from the day on which we witnessed the cut and parry of his defense until this present writing. His bibliography abundantly documents the point.

Research and publication have given depth to, and received vitality from, his teaching role. It will be conceded that the University of Toronto is not the least among the universities of North America; Joseph Owens has served her for decades as professor of philosophy. During those years too he has been a Fellow of the Pontifical Institute of Mediaeval Studies. More than forty years ago Owens began the first of three periods of seminary teaching. Nor has his teaching on the university level been confined to Toronto. The Academia Alfonsiana of the Lateran University in Rome, Assumption University in Windsor, and Purdue University in Indiana have welcomed him as visiting professor.

For nearly three decades Owens has been a Fellow of the Royal Society of Canada. Learned journals in his field, *The Monist* and *The New Scholasticism*, have been glad to profit from his collaboration as editor; The Metaphysical Society, The Canadian Philosophical Association, The Society for Ancient Greek Philosophy, and The American Catholic Philosophical Association have chosen him in turn as President. The last-named has awarded him its prized Aquinas Medal.

An account of Owens' academic career must include mention of his Herculean labors as a dissertation supervisor. Both philosophy and mediaeval studies have long been held in high esteem on the Toronto campus and the two disciplines have drawn students from afar in impressive numbers. Not one of us in those special fields will contest the claim that Joseph Owens has accepted and has seen through a disproportionately large number of supervisions. Nor is it a secret that the recurrent extension of his appointment as teacher and supervisor reflects the conviction of University authorities that we can ill-afford to lose the drawing power of his name with prospective students.

All these accomplishments and honors are worn lightly by our friend and colleague. For us who see him day by day other characteristics stand between us and his merely academic background. Why, for instance, does this *professor emeritus* appear to be fifteen or twenty years younger than his dossier asserts him to be, born, so those documents say, on the 17th of April, 1908? Perhaps the stiff daily walk, to the campus from his residence and back, provides a part of the answer, perhaps his custom of swimming frequently and of playing pick-up hockey (for ice marks our Toronto winters) must be called into evidence. No philosopher, however, would neglect the role played by a serenity arising from principles engendered in "upright reason" and lived without anxiety because they have become for him as second nature. The Aristotelian dictum κατὰ τὸν ὀρθὸν λόγον πράττειν might have been formulated to describe his flexible, but rigorous, way of life. Neither agressive nor retiring, Joseph Owens fits smoothly into the activities of the interlocking communities of which he is a member.

This moves us to advert to the massive fact that Joseph Owens is not only a most distinguished scholar, and one whose physical vigor supports work that Augustine would have likened to a *sarcina*, to the heavy backpack of a Roman legionary; he is also and primarily a man of lived faith. Generally speaking, his religious Order (commonly known as "the

Redemptorists") is dedicated to pastoral service. It is a tribute, not only to this Redemptorist, but also to his superiors in the Order, that since 1936 Owens has been free to serve the apostolate of intellect. Neither he nor his religious superiors have thought that a child-like faith and urbane scholarship are in conflict and still less that either one might substitute for the other.

Such is the friend whose friends join hands to honor with this volume. Diversity of philosophical or of religious conviction is here transcended by the joy that all hands feel in knowing Joseph Owens and by their shared esteem that cries out for a public and permanent expression. What could please a scholar more than one more scholarly book, planned in his honor and written by his fellow-citizens in the republic of letters? If Diogenes Laertius was right, Aristotle held that friendship entails "a single soul dwelling in two bodies," μία ψυχὴ δύο σώμασιν ἐνοικοῦσα. Here a troop of friends constitute a community with Joseph Owens and their unifying soul is the love of wisdom to which he and we have dedicated our lives.

1

L'argomento contro i molti in DK 29 B 1
e il procedimento di Zenone

Walter Leszl

Università di Pisa

Gli argomenti di Zenone concernenti il rapporto uno-molti non godono della popolarità che continuano ad avere quelli contro il movimento, perché i paradossi che pongono paiono essere legati ad una concezione della realtà, quella eleatica, che non è accettabile, e per di più comportare fallacie di facile soluzione. Tuttavia gli argomenti del primo tipo non riflettono minore ingegnosità degli altri e sicuramente meritano una particolare attenzione da parte di chi voglia arrivare a definire la posizione di Zenone nella storia del pensiero antico, a partire da una considerazione del suo metodo e delle sue intenzioni. Infatti le testimonianze antiche rilevanti si attagliano, almeno principalmente, al creatore di tali argomenti; ed è solo nel loro caso che possediamo delle citazioni dall'originale.

Di questi argomenti è molto discusso quello che viene desunto dai primi due frammenti rimastici dell'opera di Zenone e dal contesto al quale appartengono nell'opera di chi li cita, il commentatore aristotelico Simplicio.[1] Il lavoro di ricostruzione dell'argomento compiuto dagli studiosi si è strettamente intrecciato allo studio della sua logica e del suo

---

[1] *In Aristotelis Physicorum libros quattuor priores commentaria*, ed. H. Diels (Berlin 1882), p. 139 e p. 141.

Graceful Reason: Essays in Ancient and Medieval Philosophy Presented to Joseph Owens, CSSR, ed. Lloyd P. Gerson. Papers in Mediaeval Studies 4 (Toronto: Pontifical Institute of Mediaeval Studies, 1983), pp. 1-27. © P.I.M.S., 1983.

ruolo nel pensiero zenoniano.[2] In effetti l'interpretazione dell'argomento è al centro di tutte le valutazioni che sono state date dell'attendibilità di quella che è la testimonianza più ampia e più antica che abbiamo sugli intenti di Zenone nell'opera che, secondo ogni probabilità,[3] conteneva tutti i suoi argomenti contro la pluralità e contro il movimento, e cioè la testimonianza offerta da Platone nella parte iniziale del suo dialogo *Parmenide*.

Secondo la presentazione che ivi (126A-128E) troviamo dell' opera di Zenone questa conteneva argomenti tutti rivolti contro la pluralità, con i quali il loro autore metteva in luce le "impossibilità" (ἀδύνατα) che conseguono all'ammissione dei "molti" (πολλά), in tal modo difendendo la tesi parmenidea che "tutto è uno" (ἕν τὸ πᾶν). Si sarebbe trattato, insomma, di argomenti confutatori delle concezioni pluralistiche, i quali, per questo fatto stesso, vengono in soccorso alla concezione monistica della realtà elaborata da Parmenide.

Questa presentazione degli intenti di Zenone (che è ripetuta, quasi *verbatim*, da Simplicio)[4] ha lasciato poco persuasi diversi studiosi i quali, quando non sono arrivati a contestare completamente l'attendibilità della testimonianza di Platone, hanno per lo meno espresso il dubbio che

---

[2] Fra i contributi più significativi cito: G. Calogero, *Studi sull'Eleatismo* (Roma 1932; Firenze 1977²); H. Fränkel, "Zeno of Elea's Attacks on Plurality," *American Journal of Philology*, 63 (1942), pp. 1-25 e 193-206, rist. con revisioni in *Studies in Presocratic Philosophy*, ed. R. E. Allen e D. J. Furley (London 1975), 2: 102-142 (donde cito); G. Vlastos, rec. di H. Fränkel, *Wege und Formen frügriechischen Denkens* (include trad. ted. del precedente), *Gnomon* 31 (1959), pp. 193-204 (le pp. 195-199 su Zenone sono rist. in *Studies*, cit., 2: 177-183); dello stesso "A Zenonian Argument against Plurality," in *Essays in Ancient Greek Philosophy*, ed. J. P. Anton e G. Kustas (Albany, N. Y. 1971), pp. 119-144; dello stesso la voce "Zeno of Elea," in *Encyclopaedia of Philosophy*, ed. P. Edwards (New York, 1967), 8: 369-379; G. E. L. Owen, "Zeno and the Mathematicians," *Proceedings of the Aristotelian Society* 1957-58, pp. 199-222, rist. in *Studies*, cit., 2: 143-165 (donde cito); D. J. Furley, *Two Studies in the Greek Atomists* (Princeton, N.J. 1967); M. C. Stokes, *One and Many in Presocratic Philosophy* (Cambridge, Mass. 1971); F. Solmsen, "The Tradition about Zeno of Elea Re-examined," *Phronesis* 16 (1971), pp. 116-141; W. E. Abraham, "The Nature of Zeno's Argument against Plurality," *Phronesis* 17 (1972), pp. 40-53; K. von Fritz, voce "Zenon von Elea" in *Pauly-Wissowa Realencyclopädie der classischen Altertumswissenschaft*, vol. 10A (1972), coll. 53-83; dello stesso "Zeno of Elea in Plato's *Parmenides*," in *Serta Turyniana*, ed. J. L. Heller (Chicago 1974), pp. 329-341; W. J. Prior, "Zeno's First Argument concerning Plurality," *Archiv für Geschichte der Philosophie* 60 (1978), pp. 145-156; J. Barnes, *The Presocratic Philosophers* (London 1979), vol. 1.

[3] Sull'unicità dell'opera cfr. G. Vlastos, "Plato's Testimony concerning Zeno of Elea," *Journal of Hellenic Studies* 95 (1975), (pp. 136-163) p. 136 e nn. 2-5.

[4] Che questa testimonianza (*in Phys.* 134.2 sgg. = DK 29 A 23) dipende da quella platonica è stato mostrato in modo convincente da Solmsen.

l'intento dell'Eleate non fosse poi del tutto così positivo o costruttivo. I loro dubbi e le loro riserve si sono fondati, oltre che su altre testimonianze (come quella dello stesso Platone nel *Fedro*, 261D, che fa di Zenone un "antilogico"), la cui conciliabilità con essa non è del tutto ovvia, su illazioni suggerite dall'esame dei testi.

Così è significativo che Fränkel, a conclusione del suo importante studio sugli argomenti contro la pluralità (in Furley-Allen, p. 126, e cfr. p. 117), fosse indotto a sostenere che Zenone, pur essendo consapevole dell'importanza e della profondità dei problemi da lui affrontati, non aveva resistito alla tentazione di condurre un gioco di abilità verbale allo scopo di ingannare i suoi lettori od uditori. Non del tutto dissimile da questa caratterizzazione è quella di J. Barnes che attribuisce un intento distruttivo e di *mockery* a Zenone e arriva ad affermare che egli "è il primo dei 'sofisti' " (*Presocratic Phil.* 1: 294). Non mancano affermazioni simili a queste in altri studiosi.[5] Più sfumata è la posizione adottata da von Fritz, che riscontra in Zenone bensì una difesa della concezione parmenidea, ma una difesa che è "aporetica."[6] Prima di tutti questi Calogero aveva visto in Zenone colui che, sebbene involontariamente, finisce col portare alla sua dissoluzione il monismo eleatico, colpendolo al cuore.[7] Come si vede, lo studioso italiano non pretende così di smentire totalmente l'immagine che Platone dà di Zenone nel *Parmenide* – questa rimane valida per comprendere ciò che l'Eleate consapevolmente si prefiggeva – ma la inserisce in un quadro dello sviluppo del pensiero eleatico nel quale il ruolo di Zenone è di fatto (cioè come conseguenza necessaria degli argomenti da lui usati) del tutto distruttivo. Chi più decisamente ha contestato la stessa fondatezza storica della testimonianza di Platone è stato Solmsen (nel suo articolo sulla questione), il quale vede in Zenone un puro dialettico (o "antilogico"), cioè un pensatore che aveva senz'altro intenti distruttivi, in quanto le sue argomentazioni erano volte a rigettare non soltanto la pluralità ma anche l'uno eleatico. All'estremo opposto è invece la posizione adottata da Vlastos nell'articolo "Plato's Testimony," il quale non solo ribadisce la sua tesi[8] della serietà di intento dell' Eleate, ma difende la sostanziale attendibilità storica della testimonianza di Platone nel *Parmenide*: Zenone non è il puro dialettico che

---

[5] Alcune sono citate da Vlastos, "Plato's Testimony," p. 139, n. 16.

[6] Voce "Zenon," col. 78, cfr. col. 58; inoltre *Grundprobleme der Geschichte der antiken Wissenschaft* (Berlin 1971), pp. 42-43.

[7] *Studi*, cit. (1977), p. 112; cfr. anche *Storia della logica antica. 1. L'età arcaica* (Bari 1967), pp. 178-182.

[8] Espressa per esempio in "Zenonian Argument," pp. 135-136, e nella recensione a H. Fränkel (*Studies*, p. 182).

argomenta in modo del tutto distruttivo, ma uno che difende la concezione parmenidea della realtà.

Nonostante le divergenze che ci sono nel presentare la figura di Zenone s'è stabilito un consenso generale sulla ricostruzione, anche se non su tutti i punti di interpretazione, di quell'argomentazione, attestata da B 1 e B 2, che è cosi importante per la determinazione degli esiti (intenzionali o meno) del procedimento zenoniano. Tutti gli studiosi, compreso il "dissenziente" Solmsen, accettano la proposta avanzata e difesa nella forma più ampia ed approfondita da Fränkel nello studio citato, che sta nel riconoscere che quei frammenti (presi nell'ordine inverso di quello adottato da Diels e Kranz) sono le attestazioni di un *unico* argomento articolato in tutta una serie di passaggi. Ma nel saggio stesso di Solmsen come anche nei contributi di altri studiosi (particolarmente in quelli di Abraham, di von Fritz e di Owen) si trovano degli elementi per una ricostruzione differente, abbondonando quella corrente, che non era parsa sempre del tutto logica ed inevitabile, come mostrano le interpretazioni che dell'argomento in B 1 erano state offerte a suo tempo da Tannery e da Heath.[9]

I

Comincio con un'esposizione della ricostruzione corrente dell'argomento e delle considerazioni che la giustificano, trascurando certe differenze di opinione che ci sono fra gli studiosi su punti di dettaglio (mentre certe scelte in fatto di traduzione saranno giustificate più oltre):

(A) "Niente (οὐδέν) ha grandezza, perché ciascuno dei molti è identico a se stesso e uno."

(B) "[Ma] se ciò che è non possiede grandezza (μέγεθος), sarà non esistente." *Ovvero:* (B¹) "Cio che non ha né grandezza né spessore (πάχος) né massa non è nulla (μεθείς ἐστιν)."

(c) "Infatti (1) se [qualcosa che non ha grandezza] venisse aggiunto ad un altro essere, non lo renderebbe maggiore per nulla. Poiché (2) non ha grandezza, se viene aggiunto [a qualcos' altro], non può servire per nulla ad accrescerne la grandezza. Ne consegue che (3) ciò che viene aggiunto

---

[9] P. Tannery, *Pour l'histoire de la science hellène* (Paris 1887), pp. 254-255; T. L. Heath, *History of Greek Mathematics* (Oxford 1921), 1: 275 (cfr. la discussione in Vlastos, "Zenonian Argument," pp. 125-126 e nn. 32-34). – La ricostruzione adottata da Fränkel era già stata anticipata da E. Zeller, *Die Philosophie der Griechen in ihrer geschichtlichen Entwicklung*, ed. 6ª, ed. W. Nestle (Leipzig 1919), 1.1: 749-752, e riproposta con delle giustificazioni da Calogero, *Studi*, p. 119, n. 13 (come riconosce Fränkel in n. 38).

non sarebbe niente. Se invero (δὲ) (4) quando [qualcosa è] sottratto ad un altro questo [ultimo] non diminuisce per nulla, e neppure esso [quest'ultimo] aumenta se [il primo] viene aggiunto ad esso, è chiaro che ciò che viene aggiunto oppure che viene sottratto non è nulla."

(D) "Ma se è (εἰ δὲ ἔστιν), è necessario che ciascuna [cosa, entità] abbia una certa grandezza e spessore e che di essa [cosa] una [parte] stia separata (ἀπέχειν) dall'altra. E lo stesso discorso (λόγος) vale per la [parte] restante [dopo la divisione]: anche questa avrà grandezza e qualcosa (= una parte) di essa si troverà avanti (= resterà). Ma è lo stesso dire questo una volta e dirlo sempre: nessuna cotale [parte] di essa sarà l'ultima e non sarà mai che non sia qualcos'altro rispetto ad altro."

(E) "Così se soni [i] molti (εἰ πολλά ἐστιν), è necessario che questi siano piccoli e grandi ad un tempo: (1) così piccoli da non avere grandezza affatto, (2) così grandi da essere infiniti."[10]

È manifesto, in questa successione, che (C) contiene la dimonstrazione di (B) ovvero di (B¹) e che (D) contiene la dimostrazione – tutta o in parte – di (E). Manca la dimostrazione di (A), per la quale non pare esserci niente di rilevante nella nostra documentazione su Zenone. Per la ricostruzione di questa dimostrazione mancante prima Fränkel e poi Vlastos[11] hanno utilizzato il fr. 9 di Melisso, che mostra che dagli Eleati era riconosciuto che, se qualcosa è uno (ἕν), non può avere parti (cioè essere divisibile), perché altrimenti sarebbe "molti." Questa loro proposta mi pare plausibile ed è confermata dal fatto che Aristotele connette l'argomento in (C) alla tesi dell'indivisibilità.[12] La dimostrazione che di (B)

---

[10] Ho messo fra virgolette semplici (A) perché la citazione è leggermente modificata per accordarla col resto. I testi sono i seguenti: (A) = Simpl. 139.18-19 (contesto del fr. 2 in DK, p. 257.3-4); (B) = Simpl. 141.1-2 (contesto del fr. 1 in DK, p. 255.14; n. 10 Lee); (B¹) = Simpl. 139.10 (contesto del fr. 2 in DK, p. 256.8-9; n. 9 Lee); (C) = Simpl. 139.11-15 (fr. 2 DK; n. 9 Lee); (D) = Simpl. 141.2-6 (fr. 1 DK; n. 10 Lee); (E) segue immediatamente a (D) = Simpl. 141.6-8 (parte rimanente del fr. 1 DK e di n. 10 Lee). – Rispetto alle suddivisioni del materiale introdotte da Fränkel e riprese da altri studiosi ne ho aggiunto una per maggiore chiarezza, per cui valgono le seguenti corrispondenze: (A) = (a); (B) + (C) = (b); (D) = (c); (E) = (d); inoltre ho citato (B¹) come variante di (B).

[11] Cfr. Fränkel, p. 111 e n. 40; Vlastos, "Zenonian Argument," pp. 119-120, e voce "Zeno," p. 369b.

[12] L'argomento, come vedremo, giustifica (B) inteso come una conseguenza di (A). L'affermazione di Aristotele è la seguente: "Inoltre, se l'uno in sè è indivisibile, secondo il principio di Zenone, non sarebbe niente. Infatti ciò che né se è aggiunto né se è sottratto rende maggiore o minore nega che abbia esistenza, poiché è chiaro che per lui ciò che esiste ha grandezza. Ora se ha grandezza è corporeo ..." (Metaph. B 4, 1001b7 sgg.; trad. Pasquinelli). L'assunto qui è evidentemente che l'uno è indivisibile perché non ha grandezza – altrimenti non sarebbe qualcosa che risulti essere non esistente. Varrà dunque anche il principio che ciò che ha grandezza (μέγεθος) è divisibile.

ovvero di (B¹) è offerta in (c) non è molto chiara. A questo proposito Vlastos[13] riprende il suggerimento di von Fritz[14] di intendere il δέ che precede la suddivisione (4) (= Simpl. 139. 14 inizio) nel senso di "perché," considerando cioè questa parte come quanto giustifica la conclusione tratta in (3) a partire da (1) e (2), tenuto conto che uno dei due casi prospettati in (4), quello della sottrazione, è lasciato sottinteso (oppure è omesso da chi cita) nell'argomentazione che porta a (3). Anche questa proposta mi pare plausibile[15] e comunque da dare per accettata, dal momento che non fa gran differenza per la trattazione seguente. L'interpretazione esatta di (D) e, in particolare, la risposta da dare alla questione se questo passo *da solo* giustifica (E), è un punto cruciale per la ricostruzione stessa dell'argomento nel suo complesso e va affrontato più oltre.

Gli studiosi recenti, con alcune eccezioni (Owen, Solmsen, von Fritz e Abraham), danno la seguente interpretazione dell' argomento nel suo complesso (sulla base della ricostruzione sopra riportata): tutta la successione (A) - (D) viene a giustificare la conclusione che viene tratta in (E), cioè che se i molti sono, essi sono (1) piccoli al punto da non avere grandezza affatto, (2) grandi al punto da essere infiniti (cioè da avere grandezza infinita). Più precisamente, la proposizione (E) (1) trova la sua giustificazione in (A) (insieme, ovviamente, alla sua dimostrazione andata perduta); la proposizione (E) (2) trova invece la sua giustificazione in (D), insieme (come vedremo) a qualche assunto tacito.

Nel proporre un'interpretazione di tal fatta si incontra subito la difficoltà che si deve considerare come parte di quest'unica argomentazione un pezzo tutt'altro che trascurabile, e cioè (B) + (C), il quale, almeno *prima facie*, non contribuisce alla conclusione in (E). L'argomentazione è infatti che i molti, dato che per esistere (e dunque essere molti) debbono avere grandezza – questa è l'affermazione con la quale inizia (D) – sono piccoli al punto da non avere grandezza affatto e grandi al punto da averla infinita; ora la contradditorietà reciproca delle due proposizioni che costituiscono la conclusione invalida l'assunto iniziale che essi hanno grandezza e che questa loro grandezza è finita, per cui l'argomento diventa una *reductio ad absurdum* della postulazione iniziale dei molti. Invece in (B) + (C) viene dimostrata l'inesistenza di ciò che *non* ha grandezza, il che

---

[13] Cfr. "Zenonian Argument," pp. 121-123; voce "Zeno," p. 370a.
[14] Rec. di G. Calogero, *Studi sull'Eleatismo, Gnomon* 14 (1938), (pp. 91-109), p. 105.
[15] Certamente più di quella di Fränkel, che ritiene che Zenone sfrutti un'ambiguità del greco (pp. 113-115 e 117).

ovviamente non può fare parte di un'argomentazione riguardante cose che la grandezza l'hanno.

Tuttavia diversi studiosi ritengono di poter ugualmente mostrare che questa parte contribuisce a quella conclu sione almeno in maniera indiretta, in quanto (D) dipenderebbe da (B) + (C) . Secondo questa proposta (avanzata per primo da Fränkel) tutta la parte (A) - (C) costituisce una *reductio ad absurdum* della tesi che i molti sono, perché viene mostrato prima, in (A), che essi non hanno nessuna grandezza, poi, in (B) - (C), che essi hanno grandezza; ma questa seconda dimostrazione contribuisce pure all'argomentazione in (D), perché qui il punto di partenza è la conclusione della parte precedente (ma in questa non tratta esplicitamente) che l'affermazione che le cose senza estensione non hanno esistenza rende necessaria la postulazione di cose ("i molti") dotate di estensione.

Questa proposta però può essere intesa in due modi alquanto differenti. Se si insiste, come fa lo stesso Fränkel (pp. 116-117), che questa prima antinomia è indipendente da quella sviluppata in (D) - (E), cioè costituisce una *reductio* per conto proprio, diventa allora più naturale trovare soltanto in (D) la giustificazione della seconda coppia di proposizioni in reciproca contraddizione, cioè di (E); ma in questo caso viene meno un motivo importante per considerare il tutto come un argumento unico. Se d'altra parte si insiste (come mi pare faccia Vlastos) sulla continuità di tutti questi passaggi, si va incontro ad una curiosa incongruenza, che sta nel fatto che Zenone, anziché fermarsi all'antinomia data da (A) e (B) - (C), cioè che, se i molti sono, essi (1) non hanno nessuna grandezza, (2) hanno grandezza, introduce con (D) - (E) una dimostrazione della proposizione che, se i molti hanno grandezza, ne hanno una infinita (= conclusione (E) (2)), mentre si limita, sempre in (E), a ripetere la proposizione (1). Così lo scopo della nuova parte sarebbe solo quello di rendere più grave un'antinomia comunque letale, peraltro modificando solo una delle due proposizioni incompatibili.

Se poi Fränkel è indotto a sottolineare la indipendenza della prima parte è perché (D) ha tutta l'aria di partire non semplicemente dalla premessa "se i molti hanno grandezza" ma piuttosto dalla premessa "se i molti sono, hanno grandezza," la quale non è una semplice ripresa di (B) - (C), anche ad adottare l'interpretazione da lui data di questa parte. E c'è l'ulteriore difficoltà, riconosciuta dallo stesso Fränkel, che (A) non giustifica la conclusione precisa di (E) (1) che i molti sono *piccoli*, e *piccoli* così da (μικρὰ ὥστε) non avere grandezza affatto – una conclusione che ha tutta l'aria di essere un'allusione a quanto risulta da una divisione all'infinito –, ma giustificherebbe piuttosto la pura e semplice conclusione che non hanno grandezza per nulla (e ciò che non ha grandezza per nulla *non* può

essere piccolo). È vero che rimane artificioso parlare di piccolezza a
proposito di ciò che viene dimostrato non avere grandezza per nulla anche
nel caso che si ammetta che la dimostrazione si trova in (D); ma che
dell'artificio sia responsabile Zenone stesso è reso probabile dal modo in
cui è sottolineata l'opposizione "piccoli – grandi" come parte dell' antinomia complessiva prospettata in (E), perché questo tradisce la sua intenzione di desumere l'antinomia dalla premessa che, se i molti sono, *hanno*
grandezza.[16]

A questi rilievi c'è da aggiungere che (E) ha tutta l'aria di contenere la
proposizione che i molti sono *sia* grandi *che* piccoli (μιχρά τε εἶναι χαὶ
μεγάλα), e che questo risponde al procedimento di trarre conclusioni in
mutua contraddizione che è attribuibile a Zenone sia sulla base del fr. 3
("se i molti sono, sono *sia* limitati – di numero – *che* infiniti") che sulla
base della presentazione che Platone nel *Parmenide* (127E) dà di un
argomento zenoniano ("se i molti sono, sono *sia* simili *che* dissimili").
Anche questo esito è poco giustificato, come Fränkel riconosce (p. 122), se
si ammette che le due conclusioni (E)(1) ed (E)(2) sono dimostrate in modo
indipendente.

Va infine osservato che l'interpretazione che questi studiosi propon-
gono per (B) - (C) non è affatto suggerita dal testo zenoniano, che parrebbe
piuttosto sviluppare una conseguenza necessaria di (A), cioè argomentare
che, se i molti non hanno grandezza, non hanno neppure esistenza. Ad
adottare la loro interpretazione ci sarebbe la complicazione che una delle
due proposizioni che sono le conclusioni della *reductio ad absurdum* della
tesi "che i molti sono" è essa stessa stabilita mediante una *reductio* della
proposizione opposta (cioè la tesi che i molti hanno grandezza è stabilita
per esclusione della tesi che non hanno grandezza, in quanto questa porta
all'affermazione della loro non esistenza), il che pare piuttosto artificioso.
In effetti l'interpretazione è suggerita solo dal commento di Simplicio in
139.16-18 ("e questo Zenone lo dice non con l'intento di negare l'uno, ma
per il fatto che ciascuno dei molti e infiniti esseri ha grandezza..."). Date le
incertezze che questi mostra circa le intenzioni di Zenone e data la sua
preoccupazione di difenderlo dall'accusa di "negare l'uno" (= l'Uno par-

---

[16] Vlastos, "Zenonian Argument," p. 129, contesta che ci sia questa incongruenza, ma
l'uso stesso, per di più insistito, della parola "piccoli" la rende inevitabile: non si dice solo
che qualcosa è così piccolo da non avere grandezza, ma che è piccolo *simpliciter*.
L'artificio sarebbe eliminato adottando la traduzione di Calogero "piccoli *fino a* ...," con
allusione ad una condizione di grandezza decrescente risultante da un processo di
divisione ancora in corso (cfr. *Studi*, pp. 120 sgg., specialm. p. 128), ma non si vede come
trarre questo dal testo greco (dove è usato ὥστε e, in un'occasione, cioè Simpl. 139.9, οὕτως
ὥστε).

menideo), non può certo trattarsi di una testimonianza utile per la comprensione del significato dell'argomento in (B) - (C).[17]

Lo stesso Fränkel deve ammettere che l'argomento, in base alla sua ricostruzione e interpretazione, risulta "tortuoso" (p. 122); ora questa tortuosità non sembra tipica degli argomenti zenoniani in genere, e gli altri argomenti contro la molteplicità paiono rispondere perfettamente allo schema: se i molti sono, ne segue necessariamente ... (e quanto segue si traduce in due proposizioni mutuamente contraddittorie circa i molti). Se un tale schema si lasciasse estendere con coerenza alla parte (D) + (E), ciò diventerebbe di già una considerazione molto forte a favore di questo tipo di interpretazione, che tratta questa parte come un argomento autonomo.

II

È comprensibile che, di fronte a questa situazione, Solmsen fosse indotto a contestare l'interpretazione corrente dell'argomento.[18] Egli tuttavia non arriva a contestare la stessa ricostruzione di questo, cioè l'ammissione che la successione (A) - (E) costituisce un argomento unico, pur ammettendo che essa presenta degli "aspetti problematici" (p. 132). La sua proposta di interpretazione è in conformità con l'intento che si prefigge di mostrare che Zenone era un dialettico puro, cioè uno che argomenta *in utramque partem* (secondo la descrizione che si può desumere dal *Fedro*, 261D): la prima parte del nostro argomento, cioè (A) - (C), è un attacco contro l'uno (che coincide senz'altro con l'Uno eleatico), mentre la seconda parte di esso, cioè (D) - (E), è un attacco contro la pluralità. Così inteso l'argomento nel suo complesso conserva la caratteristica di συνάγειν τὰ ἐναντία e questo nella maniera comprensiva di prima demolire l'ἕν, aprendo così la via ai πολλά, e poi di demolire questi a loro volta (p. 137).

Solmsen stesso riconosce (nella n. 62) che secondo la sua proposta la confutazione dell'"Uno" non risulta avere la forma di dimostrare i contrari (ἐναντία) per esso, ma si domanda: "yet why should all of Zeno's arguments be cast in the same mold?" Tuttavia l'obiezione è più seria di quanto qui egli voglia ammettere, perché nessun autore antico ci attesta che gli argomenti zenoniani si conformavano alla semplice generica esigenza di "mettere insieme" o "accoppiare" i contrari, ma le testi-

---

[17] Sulla posizione di Simplicio cfr. la trattazione di Solmsen, e cfr. più oltre, sez. III.

[18] Nel saggio più volte citato, peraltro senza riconoscere espressamente tutte queste difficoltà, ma solo quella dell'irrilevanza di (B) - (C) per (E) (cfr. p. 136), sottolineando invece altre difficoltà suggerite da considerazioni linguistiche, il cui valore è un po' opinabile (cfr. le critiche di Prior, "Zeno's First Argument," pp. 249-251).

monianze sono tutte del tenore di quella di Simplicio, cioè che gli argomenti di Zenone venivano a provare "che chi ammette i molti è obbligato
pure ad ammettere i contrari";[19] e mentre ci sono delle esemplificazioni
del procedimento così descritto, non ce ne sono del primo. Un'altra
obiezione è che, ad accettare la proposta di Solmsen, avremmo comunque
un'asimmetria fra il modo in cui Zenone argomenta contro i molti nella
seconda parte dell'argomento, cioè in (D) - (E), e il modo in cui egli
argomenta contro l'uno nella prima parte, cioè in (A) - (C), che non è un
reductio fondata sulla deduzione di contrari, e questo pure la rende poco
plausibile (almeno: a dare per scontato che si tratta di un unico
argomento).

A Solmsen è stato pure obbiettato (da Prior, p. 250) che, dal momento
che egli ammette che l'argomento in (A) - (C) è rivolto contro ogni unità
concepibile (si esclude che questa possa avere dimensioni spaziali e quindi
che possa esistere), esso finisce col demolire non soltanto l'Uno eleatico
ma anche le unità che costituiscono i molti, dunque qualsiasi tipo di entità,
per cui non si tratta affatto di un argomento che "apra la strada" ai molti:
non solo il monismo ma anche il pluralismo sarebbe da esso smentito.
Questa obiezione è certamente pertinente, ma non si vede come essa possa
valere solo come obiezione *ad hominem* contro Solmsen, a meno che non
si riesca a mostrare che l'Uno eleatico era concepito in maniera del tutto
differente dall'"uno dei molti" (una distinzione fra i due difficilmente può
essere fatta se si concede che anche il primo occupa spazio).[20] Non ci basta
certo che Simplicio dichiari che l'intenzione di Zenone era quella di
colpire solo l'"uno dei molti"! In realtà, non ci basterebbe neppure
un'indicazione più sicura che questa era l'intenzione di Zenone stesso,
perché ciò non cambierebbe il fatto che la sua argomentazione ha
comunque la conseguenza di colpire anche l'Uno eleatico: questo al
massimo confermerebbe la tesi di Calogero che gli esiti del tutto distruttivi
della sua dialettica non rispondono alle sue intenzioni. Non credo
comunque che l'argomento di (C) (= fr. 2; n. 9 Lee) sia rivelativo

---

[19] ὅτι τῷ πολλὰ εἶναι λέγοντι συμβαίνει τὰ ἐναντία λέγειν, 139.6-7. – Questa obiezione a
Solmsen è avanzata anche da Prior (p. 251).

[20] Non posso qui giustificare questa che mi pare rimanga l'interpretazione più
plausibile della descrizione che dell'essere dà Parmenide nel suo poema; mi limito a notare
che nei vv. 26-33 del fr. 8 viene negato che l'essere si muova, cioè, come conferma il
v. 41, che cambi di luogo, mentre la questione se si muove o meno neppure si porrebbe se
si trattasse di un'entità puramente ideale; naturalmente ritengo che per lui, come per
Melisso, la spazialità non porta con sè la corporeità (condivido l'interpretazione che
Furley, *Two Studies*, pp. 60-61, dà del fr. 9 di Melisso, mentre non condivido, come si
vedrà, la sua interpretazione della posizione di Zenone su questo punto).

dell'intenzione di colpire unicamente l'"uno dei molti" (come pretende Prior, p. 250), per il fatto che prospetta l'esistenza di *più* (almeno due) entità, giacché questo viene fatto in maniera del tutto ipotetica, all'unico scopo di mostrare che (come dice Simplicio, 97.15-16; la formulazione è del tutto generale anche in 139.10) "ciò che aggiunto non aumenta e che sottratto non diminuisce non ha esistenza," in quanto (così si può riformulare la tesi) esso non fa nessuna differenza.

Solmsen prospetta pure (p. 136), come possibilità subordinata, che l'argomento di Zenone fosse bensì tutto rivolto contro i molti – dunque che questi partisse già in (A) dalla ipotesi "se i molti sono" – ma che venisse pure a colpire l'"Uno" nel corso dell'argomentazione stessa. Questa che per lui è una possibilità subordinata in realtà diventa obbligatoria, una volta rifiutata la possibilità principale che egli aveva prospettato senza abbandonare la ricostruzione complessiva dell'argomento; ed è una possibilità obbligatoria anche per coloro che sostengono che gli argomenti di Zenone erano tutti rivolti contro i molti.

III

La ricostruzione ormai tradizionale dell'argomento di Zenone (quella riportata e discussa nella prima sezione) si fonda, oltre che sulla considerazione che non è logicamente possibile desumere (E) unicamente da (D), sulla persuasione che Simplicio offre delle indicazioni chiare ed univoche per l'intera successione (A) - (E) come parti di un unico argomento. In questa sezione mi propongo di mostrare che quelle indicazioni si prestano invece ad essere intese in maniera differente, permettendoci di considerare i due gruppi (A) - (C) e (D) - (E) come due argomenti autonomi; nella sezione successiva cercherò di difendere la proposta di giustificare (E) unicamente con (D).

Fränkel (e gli altri studiosi con lui) ravvisa nel testo di Simplicio le seguenti tre indicazioni per la successione (A) - (E), come successione senza soluzioni di continuità:

(I) La prima sta nel passo 139.5 sgg. (= fr. 2 con contesto; n. 9 Lee), che egli intende sostanzialmente come segue: "tuttavia in questo libro (ἐν μέντοι τῷ συγγράμματι), che contiene molti argomenti, egli (sc. Zenone) mostra in ciascuno di essi che (καθ' ἕκαστον δείκνυσιν) chiunque dica che ci sono i molti si trova costretto ad affermare cose (tesi) contrarie. Uno di questi argomenti è quello in cui mostra che (ὧν ἕν ἐστιν ἐπιχείρημα, ἐν ᾧ δείκνυσιν ὅτι) 'se i molti sono, sono sia grandi che piccoli: grandi al punto da essere infiniti per grandezza, piccoli al punto da non avere grandezza

affatto' (139.7-9). In questo argomento egli mostra *pure* che (ἐν δὴ τούτῳ
δείκνυσιν ὅτι) ciò che non ha grandezza né spessore né massa non poù
nemmeno esistere. 'Se infatti venisse aggiunto ad un altro essere...'
(= (c))." Evidentemente Fränkel intende l'ultima formula per la quale ho
riportato il greco nel senso di: "nel corso di questo stesso argomento," con
allusione a quello formulato in 139.7-9, che è chiaramente un'altra
formulazione di (E) (= 141.6-8), donde l'ovvia conclusione che (c) precede
(E) nel corso di uno stesso argomento.

(II) Qui il riferimento è a quanto Simplicio afferma a commento
dell'argomentazione in (c) (quindi il passo è di seguito a quello citato in (I),
dove ho riportato solo l'inizio di (c), cioè del passo 139.11-15): "Zenone
dice queste cose non perché vuole eliminare l'uno, ma per il fatto che
ciascuno dei molti e infiniti esseri ha grandezza in quanto c'è sempre
qualcosa prima di ciò (= della parte) che si prende, per via della divisibilità
all'infinito. Egli mostra questo avendo prima mostrato che (ὃ δείκνυσι
προδείξας ὅτι) niente ha grandezza perché ciascuno dei molti è identico a se
stesso e uno" (139.16-19). Secondo Fränkel anche questo passo, in quanto
suggerisce la continuità fra (A) e (D), mostra che i due tronconi principali
dell'argomento (come da lui ricostruito) sono congiunti.

(III) Un'ulteriore attestazione è data da Simplicio, 141.1 sgg. (= contesto di B 1; n. 10 Lee): "avendo infatti mostrato prima che (προδείξας γὰρ
ὅτι) 'se ciò che esiste non ha grandezza, neppure esiste', egli aggiunge
(Fränkel traduce: "he continues": ἐπάγει): 'ma se è, è necessario che
ciascuno...' (= (D) + (E))." Anche questo passo, dato l'evidente riferimento
all'argomento in (B) - (C), attesterebbe la continuità fra i due tronconi
dell'argomento.

In realtà, non c'è molto bisogno di sottolineare che, nel caso delle
considerazioni (II) e (III), quanto Simplicio dice attesta sicuramente la
successione (A) + (B) + (C) e (D) + (E), ma non la *continuità* completa fra
questi due gruppi. (Indubbiamente avere reso chiaro che c'è questa
successione è in se stesso in risultato importante.) Simplicio usa cor-
rentemente ἐπάγει quando si tratta di collegare citazioni distinte, per
esempio di associare versi derivanti da parti differenti del poema di
Parmenide;[21] e il participio προδείξας attesta semplicemente che *prima*
aveva offerto un certo argomento, non che ciò fosse fatto immediatamente
prima e che si trattasse dello *stesso* argomento.

---

[21] Così a p. 78 egli cita il fr. 7 v. 2 e poi passa, con un ἐπάγει, al fr. 8 v. 1, omettendo
7.3-6.

La tesi della continuità (non della semplice successione degli argomenti nell'originale in quell'ordine) si fonda dunque soltanto su (I), il che è in effetti quanto lo stesso Fränkel afferma espressamente (pp. 111-12), ma favorendo l'impressione (per esempio ponendo (I) alla fine della serie di attestazioni, come se ne costituisse il culmine) di una maggiore omogeneità fra queste tre considerazioni. Ora, se si esamina il passo citato in (I) nel suo contesto, si constata che neppure esso dimostra tanto.

Nella sua esposizione (a commento di Aristotele, *Phys.* 1.3, 187a1), a cominciare da 138.29, Simplicio rileva che l'opinione di Alessandro, che Zenone avrebbe offerto un argomento per eliminare l'uno (ὡς ἀναιροῦντος τὸ ἕν, linea 30), risale ad Eudemo (che il riferimento sia ad un *argomento* è suggerito dall'affermazione attribuita ad Alessandro in 138.3 sgg., che Zenone avrebbe *dimostrato* [δεικνύντος] che 'l'uno non è nessuno degli enti'). Simplicio prosegue citando Eudemo, il quale, dopo aver alluso al problema se l'uno c'è, avrebbe aggiunto: "dicono che anche Zenone asserisce che, se qualcuno fosse riuscito a spiegargli che cos'è l'uno (τὸ ἕν ... τί ποτέ ἐστιν), sarebbe stato in grado di menzionare [parlare di, postulare: λέγειν] gli enti (τὰ ὄντα). La sua aporia, a quanto pare, dipende dal dire che ciascuna delle cose sensibili è molti categoricamente e per divisione, mentre faceva del punto [matematico] un niente.[22] (139.2-3:) Infatti ciò che non produce un accrescimento quando è aggiunto né una diminuzione quando è tolto egli non lo giudica [pone, ammette come] facente parte degli enti." Dopo questa citazione Simplicio concede che Zenone poteva avere argomentato *in utramque partem* con intento "ginnastico" (139.3-5, con allusione a *Parmenide*, 136c) e aggiunge subito quanto riportato precedentemente, in (I) (= 139.5 sgg.).

E' molto chiaro che, secondo questa esposizione di Simplicio, sia Alessandro che Eudemo alludono ad un argomento di Zenone e che l'argomento al quale fanno allusione è quello riportato in 139.2-3, in una formulazione (apparentemente quella usata da Eudemo) che è evidentemente un riassunto di (c), usato sempre a giustificazione della proposizione (B). Ma allora è molto naturale che Simplicio, dopo aver rilevato che il libro di Zenone include molti argomenti tesi a mostrare che la postulazione di una molteplicità di cose comporta l'affermazione di proposizione "contrarie," e dopo aver esemplificato questo con l'argomento di cui (in quel contesto) riporta solo la conclusione (= (E)), *ritorni*

---

[22] Questa spiegazione, di chiaro marchio aristotelico (come sottolinea anche Solmsen, pp. 128-129), appartiene sicuramente ad Eudemo. (Notare che la citazione di Eudemo ricorre in Simplicio, 97.13 sgg. = n. 5 Lee).

all'argomento che è tutto il tempo (cioè a cominciare da 138.3) in discussione, cioè appunto all'argomento (B) + (C). E' di *questo* argomento che si tratta di mostrare, come Simplicio tenta di fare in 139.16-18, dopo averlo citato per esteso, che esso, contrariamente alle apparenze, e contrariamente al modo in cui lo intendono Alessandro ed Eudemo, non elimina l'uno, se concepito come l'Uno parmenideo. (Per questa motivo è da preferire, per la frase ἐν δὲ τούτῳ δείκνυσιν, una lezione con il δέ avversativo, anziché attenersi a quella dei MSS. con δή, che Fränkel intende, ma non senza qualche dubbio, nel senso di "pure" (*also*). Il senso complessivo è: "argomenti come quello ora citato (= (E)) sono chia- ramente rivolti contro i molti; però quello in discussione, e che ora cito, fà difficoltà ....") Insomma, è solo trascurando il contesto nel suo complesso che si è potuto creare l'impressione che, nell'usare l'espressione: "in questo argomento," Simplicio intendesse alludere a quello da lui appena citato, chiaramente rivolto contro "i molti" (nel corso del quale dunque si sarebbe svolta pure la dimostrazione apparentemente rivolta contro "l'uno"), e non a quello del cui significato stava discutendo in tutta la parte precedente, perché era la causa di un non piccolo rompicapo per lui.

Si potrebbe obbiettare che Simplicio riporta il passo (D) iniziando con la formula "ma se è" (εἰ δὲ ἔστιν, 141.2), che pare fare parte della citazione dal testo di Zenone a lui disponibile. Si tratta infatti di una formula che tende a suggerire una continuità con quanto precedentemente argomentato, che secondo le indicazioni di Simplicio è rappresentato da (A) - (C).[23] In risposta c'è da dire che è indubbiamente vero che tale formula comporta un richiamo a quanto è stato argomentato in precedenza, ma che essa non indica necessariamente che si tratta di *parti* di uno *stesso* argomento anziché di argomenti differenti, esposti in successione. E' una formula di transizione che può essere intesa in maniera "gorgiana," cioè concessiva- mente: "anche se si ammettesse che qualcosa esiste, ne segue ugualmente che ...." Zenone aveva dimostrato che niente esiste (in quanto una qualsiasi cosa che esista deve essere una, ma se ha grandezza – altra condizione di esistenza – non può esserlo), ed ora dimostra che, anche ad ammettere che qualcosa esista – e dunque abbia grandezza – si va pur sempre incontro a delle conseguenze spiacevoli, allo stesso modo come

---

[23] L'obiezione può valere indipendentemente dal modo in cui si intende esattamente la formula, punto sul quale non c'è un consenso fra gli studiosi: c'è chi, come Vlastos ("Zenonian Argument," p. 123), l'intende come equivalente a "se i molti sono"; altri, come von Fritz (voce "Zenon," col. 70), l'intendono come equivalente a "se questo è cosi" (cioè: se ciò che non possiede grandezza non può affatto esistere).

Gorgia, dopo aver mostrato che l'essere non esiste, argomenta pure che, *se anche esistesse* (εἰ καὶ ἔστιν),[24] non sarebbe conoscibile, e così via.

Non si tratta dunque di un unico argomento, ma di una serie di argomenti ciascuno dei quali è fondato su di un' "ipotesi" che viene smentita mettendo in luce le sue implicazioni negative (è chiaro il carattere ipotetico dell'intera formula all'inizio di (D): εἰ ... ἀνάγκη ...). Indubbiamente c'è una forte probabilità, allora, che nel testo che Simplicio aveva di fronte (A) - (C) precedessero immediatamente (D) - (E), il che può essere significativo per la comprensione di (B) - (C); ma trattandosi di due (o forse tre) argomenti distinti, non di due tronconi di uno stesso argomento, Zenone non è il responsabile di tutte le illogicalità che comporta il passaggio dal primo al secondo troncone!

IV

Se le parta (D) - (E), ovvero il contenuto del fr. 1, costituisce un argomento autonomo, è inevitabile che la conclusione tratta in (E) trovi la sua completa giustificazione in (D). Questo era il modo in cui intendevano l'argomento Tannery e Heath, ma nei contributi più recenti prevale la tendenza ad escludere questa possibilità perché la conclusione (E) (1), cioè che i molti sono piccoli così da non avere grandezza affatto, non può essere tratta in tal modo senza una qualche fallacia o "logical gaffe" (come la chiama Vlastos, "Zenonian Argument," p. 135). In (D) infatti Zenone aveva ammesso che, delle parti che emergono dalla divisione, dal momento che questa è all'infinito, nessuna è l'ultima (ἔσχατον) e senza rapporti con le altre – dunque (si implica) nessuna è senza grandezza; in (E) è invece ammesso che qualcuna di esse è senza grandezza affatto, dunque (si implica) che la divisione all'infinito è stata completata.

Tuttavia, anche se tale inferenza fosse davvero fallace, ci sarebbe da osservare che pure nel caso dell'altra conclusione, (E) (2), cioè che i molti sono grandi fino ad avere grandezza infinita, si concede generalmente che essa è ottenuta a partire da (D) solo compiendo un'altra fallacia, che è quella di non tener conto del fatto che le parti ottenute mediante la divisione si riducono gradualmente di grandezza, per cui la loro somma non dà una grandezza infinita (la somma di una serie convergente infinita ottenuta per divisione non supera la grandezza di partenza; per esempio $1/2 + 1/4 + 1/8 + 1/16 + 1/32... = 1$), e questo per avere invece assunto che ci

---

[24] La differenza fra questa formula, che si trova nello scritto *Sul non-essere* (nella versione di Sesto, *Adv. math.* 7: 65),e quella zenoniana è minima.

deve essere una grandezza minima per tutta la sequenza.[25] Sarebbe dunque pertinente l'osservazione di Solmsen (pp. 135-36) che Zenone, nel procedere sempre da (D), avrebbe dato prova di una certa logica, nel commettere delle "illogicalità" parallele; lo è ancora di più, s'intende, l'osservazione che le illogicalità non si evitano adottando l'interpretazione alternativa.

Tuttavia questa questione merita una nuova riflessione: non si può ovviamente giudicare la "logicalità" delle inferenze zenoniane a partire da sviluppi probabilmente assai successivi nella teoria dell'infinito; quello che ci dobbiamo domandare è se abbiamo a che fare o no con errori grossolani, che non avrebbero dovuto sfuggire ad un pensatore sofisticato della prima metà del v° sec. a.C.[26]

Prendiamo in considerazione il testo del fr. 1. La parte (D) è stata piuttoso discussa dagli studiosi, soprattutto per via dell'uso dei verbi ἀπέχειν e προέχειν, che sono stati spesso intesi (rispettivamente) nel senso di "avere distanza" o "trovarsi ad una (certa) distanza da" e nel senso di "stare oltre," "essere proiettato in avanti." Questo ha fatto pensare (con qualche elaborazione ingegnosa, soprattutto da parte di Fränkel) ad un processo di aggiunta o di accrescimento oltre la cosa data inizialmente. Tuttavia questa idea del "trovarsi ad una certa distanza da" non è facilmente giustificabile comunque, cioè neppure a prospettare un processo di accrescimento piuttosto che uno di divisione, perché è più naturale ammettere che la cosa che si aggiunge, comunque concepita, sia ad immediato contatto con l'entità inizialmente postulata, se questa è il punto di partenza del processo additivo. C'è poi la considerazione che il processo di aggiunta è più artificiale (perché si tratta dell'aggiunta di qualcosa che prima non c'era per nulla) di quello di divisione, che è quello normalmente attestato per Zenone. È dunque preferibile intendere quei verbi in un senso un po' diverso (dell' "essere distinto o separato da" e del "trovarsi avanti" = "avanzare," "rimanere"), dunque come riferentesi a ciò che rimane indiviso a ciascun stadio in un processo di divisione, cioè a ciascuna delle due parti in cui si trova divisa la cosa data inizialmente oppure in cui è stata ulteriormente divisa una parte precedentemente divisa in essa.[27]

---

[25] Sulla questione cfr. specialmente Vlastos, "Zenonian Argument," pp. 130-133, e voce "Zeno," pp. 370b-371a.

[26] Il criterio qui enunciato è sicuramente accettato da Vlastos e da altri studiosi, ma c'è dissenso nel valutare ciò che avrebbe dovuto essere riconosciuto da un pensatore al corrente degli sviluppi della matematica del tempo; cfr. più oltre e la n. 38.

[27] Su questa linea sono le proposte presenti nei contributi di Vlastos, Abraham, von Fritz e di altri.

Ebbene, se Zenone ha in mente il processo di divisione all'infinito di una cosa che ha grandezza spaziale, com'è che arriva alla conclusione che i molti (dove questi "molti" debbono essere sia le molte parti in cui la cosa è supposta essere divisa sia l'insieme delle cose di cui questa che viene divisa è una)[28] sono così piccoli da non avere grandezza affatto, così grandi da avere grandezza infinita?

La spiegazione della prima conclusione non può essere data che dal riconoscimento che Zenone assume che la divisione, per quanto infinita, abbia trovato il suo completamento, per cui non rimane più nessuna grandezza (anche infinitesimale) da dividere. Ora ci è attestato indipendentemente dal nostro testo, sia da Aristotele (*De generatione et corruptione* 1. 2, 316a14 sgg.) sia da Porfirio (riportato da Simplicio, *in Phys.* 139.27 sgg. = n. 2 Lee) sia ancora da Filopono (*in Phys.* 80.23 sgg. = n. 3 Lee)[29] che Zenone prospettava appunto questa possibilità e riteneva che, finché c'è qualcosa dotato di grandezza, la divisione non è stata portata a termine, mentre una volta che questa sia stata compiuta ci saranno cose senza grandezza, le quali ovviamente non possono costituire cose ("i molti") con grandezza.[30]

Si può trovare da ridire sulla tesi che una divisione all'infinito possa trovare il suo completamento, perché è sufficiente, perché essa sia all'infinito, che si possa proseguire con essa ad ogni punto al qaule si sia precedentemente arrivati, mentre ad affermare che non c'è più nulla che possa essere diviso si entra in contraddizione con l'implicita definizione (introdotta in (D)) della divisione all'infinito come quella che esclude un ultimo membro della serie.[31] Ad adottare questa posizione dunque Zenone

---

[28] Fra i due casi non c'è sostanziale differenza dal punto di vista della concezione eleatica dell'essere, che fa di esso un tutto omogeneo dotato di spazio (cfr. von Fritz, voce "Zenon," coll. 71-72 e 77-78).

[29] Che quanto Aristotele riporta risale, in ultima istanza, a Zenone, non a Democrito (come hanno sostenuto Hammer-Jensen, Luria, Furley e altri, donde l'inserimento del testo fra le testimonianze democritee in DK 68 A 48b), ho cercato di mostrarlo nell'Introduzione, sez. IV.3, al vol. *I Presocratici* da me curato per le ed. "Il Mulino" (Bologna 1982); ma sarebbe necessario un confronto analitico fra queste varie versioni per mostrarne la comune origine, la quale, nonostante certe innegabili differenze, è assai probabile (era stata contestata da Vlastos nell'art. "Zenonian Argument," pp. 126-129, ma non più nella sua voce "Zeno," cfr. p. 371b).

[30] L'argomento è dunque (come rileva anche Vlastos, voce "Zeno," p. 371b) questo: se qualcosa è divisibile all'infinito, non c'è contraddizione ad ammettere che è stato diviso esaustivamente (o totalmente: πάντῃ); ma una divisione completa ridurrebbe la cosa ad elementi o parti di estensione nulla; questo è impossibile, perché nessuna cosa dotata di grandezza (e ogni cosa che esista è dotata di grandezza) può essere costituita da parti senza grandezza, che sono quelle che risulterebbero dalla sua divisione all'infinito.

[31] Sulla questione cfr. anche Vlastos, "Zenonian Argument," p. 132; voce "Zeno," p. 371a.

si sarebbe trovato ad un tempo ad escludere che la divisione di una grandezza possa mai aver termine (non c'è motivo per fermarsi ad un punto piuttosto che ad un altro)[32] e ad ammettere che tutta la divisione infinita sia stata completata. Tuttavia si può suggerire che questa contraddizione poteva essergli sfuggita perché aveva adottato inavvertitamente due prospettive differenti: la prospettiva di chi considera la divisione mentre è in corso, dove il fatto stesso che essa sia in corso porta all'esclusione di un ultimo membro risultante dalla divisione; e la prospettiva di chi guarda non più al processo della divisione ma al risultato al quale si perviene ammettendola compiuta, che è precisamente che non c'è più niente da dividere, dunque più niente che sia rimasto. Nel passaggio dalla prima alla seconda prospettiva c'è sì un errore, che sta nell'assimilazione di un processo senza fine ad uno finito, ma questa assimilazione era facile per un pensatore greco che avesse ritenuto inconcepibile un processo senza nessun completamento, nessun *telos*.

Mi pare che un'analisi dell'argomento contro la pluralità del fr. 3 confermi questa spiegazione: anche qui c'è una transizione fra l'affermazione che, data l'esistenza dei "molti," fra (in mezzo: $\mu\varepsilon\tau\alpha\xi\acute{\upsilon}$) ogni coppia di tali esseri ve ne sarà sempre ($\dot{\alpha}\varepsilon\acute{\iota}$) un altro, e poi nuovamente ($\pi\acute{\alpha}\lambda\iota\nu$) un altro per ciascuna di queste nuove coppie, e così via, e la conclusione che in questo modo ($o\ddot{\upsilon}\tau\omega\varsigma$) gli esseri saranno un'infinità (di numero). Questa conclusione infatti dà il processo ormai come compiuto, perché altrimenti avremmo una *crescita* degli esseri all'infinito, ma non un'infinità data di essi, mentre è questo che Zenone deve aver voluto suggerire nel porre la conclusione in antitesi a quella che, data l'esistenza dei molti, gli esseri sono di numero finito essendo tanti quanti sono.[33]

Quanto ora detto è rilevante pure per chiarire il rapporto fra il nostro argomento contro la pluralità e gli argomenti contro il movimento, perché è manifesto che di questi ultimi almeno l'"Achille" e quello della dicotomia comportano l'assunto che il processo di divisione non può essere completato (ad ogni progresso di Achille ne corrisponde uno della tartaruga, senza mai arrivare ad un termine, che sarebbe quello in cui Achille raggiunge la tartaruga).

---

[32] Cfr. *De generatione et corruptione* 1.8, 325a8-12 (e cfr. i miei commenti nell'Introd. al vol. cit.).

[33] Vlastos, quando osserva che "here too the argument would have been ruined if Zeno thought that this process *could* be completed" ("Zenonian Argument," p. 129), sfrutta solo l'affermazione iniziale. Concordo con lui invece nell'escludere (come egli fa a pp. 130-131) la proposta di Fränkel di intendere $\ddot{\alpha}\pi\varepsilon\iota\rho\sigma\nu$ in questi casi nel senso di "indeterminato," "senza limite" (cfr. "Zeno of Elea's Attacks on Plurality," pp. 119-120).

Vlastos vede un'incompatibilità fra questo assunto degli argomenti contro il movimento e l'assunto sul quale il nostro argomento *sarebbe* fondato, se la conclusione che i molti sono piccoli al punto da essere senza grandezza si fondasse sulla dimostrazione del fr. 1 (cioè se (E) (1) si fondasse su (D)), e ritiene che mostri che quella conclusione deriva invece dalla proposizione precedentemente stabilita che niente ha grandezza (cioè da (A)). Tuttavia vedremo che l'assunto che la divisione abbia trovato un termine è alla base pure della conclusione (E) (2), cioè che i molti sono grandi al punto da avere grandezza infinita, della quale né Vlastos stesso né altri dubitano che derivi da (D). Invece Owen, che è uno dei pochi studiosi a derivare entrambe le conclusioni (E) (1) ed (E) (2) da (D),[34] riconosce che Zenone ricorre sempre a tale assunto, ma ritiene che esso sia da lui ammesso *per impossibile*, con l'intento appunto di mostrare (traendo quella antinomia) l'assurdità che sta nell'assumere che, se qualcosa è divisibile all'infinito, questa divisione può essere completata. La strategia di Zenone è di escludere prima questa possibilità e poi, ricorrendo all'argomento dell'"Achille," la possibilità rimanente che la divisione all'infinito proceda senza mai trovare un termine. Secondo questa interpretazione, allora, tutti gli argomenti di Zenone (non solo questi, ma anche altri, dalla cui analisi qui debbo prescindere) vengono ad infirmare la tesi dell'infinita divisibilità delle cose intesa come conseguenza necessaria dell'affermazione della loro pluralità, dunque sono tutti argomenti rivolti – ma rivolti *indirettamente* – contro la pluralità. Per quanto ingegnosa sia questa proposta, non mi pare plausibile, in primo luogo perché la formulazione effettivamente usata nei fr. 1 e 3 (εἰ πολλά ἐστιν, ἀνάγκη ...) mostra che si tratta di argomenti rivolti *direttamente* contro la pluralità (mentre l'assunto che la divisione all'infinito ha trovato il suo completamento non è resa esplicita in questi passi, ma solo nella versione di Aristotele e di Porfirio alla quale ho fatto prima riferimento, e anche qui non è certo formulata come un'"ipotesi" che deve essere invalidata); in secondo luogo perché c'è troppa differenza fra questi argomenti contro la pluralità e quelli contro il movimento, perché si possa presumere che siano stati esposti a coppie con un argomento del primo tipo e uno del secondo che procedono come argomenti contrari e simmetrici.[35]

---

[34] Cfr. "Zeno and the Mathematicians," p. 146 (per quanto segue pp. 145. sgg. e n. 10).

[35] Riserve all'impostazione di Owen sono avanzate, oltre che da J. Barnes, *The Presocratic Phil.* 1: 233-234 (e cfr. n. 5 per riferimenti ad altri tentativi del genere), soprattutto da M. C. Stokes, *One and Many*, pp. 189 sgg., la cui discussione include un contributo interessante all'analisi dei procedimenti di Zenone (i miei suggerimenti nella sez. V non si sostituiscono ad esso, anche dove dissento, perché sono più circoscritti).

Mi pare che si debba dunque riconoscere che la dualità di prospettiva che ho rilevato non è presente solo all'interno degli argomenti contro la pluralità, ma riguarda pure il loro rapporto con gli argomenti contro il movimento: in questi ultimi (o almeno nell'"Achille" e nell'argomento della dicotomia) è presa in considerazione *solo* la situazione nella quale il processo di divisione è *in corso*, il che, mi pare, è reso necessario dalla connessione che viene istituita fra questo processo di divisione spaziale e la temporalità.[36]

Per passare ora alla seconda conclusione del nostro argomento, dunque alla proposizione (E) (2), c'è da osservare, prima di tutto, che se vale (come mi pare inevitabile sostenere) che essa è derivata da (D) e se vale pure che essa è vista come una conseguenza, altrettanto necessaria della prima conclusione, dell'ipotesi che ci sia qualcosa che ha grandezza e dunque può essere diviso, non si può trattare, come di solito si assume, di una possibilità prospettata in alternativa alla precedente. Lo stesso linguaggio usato nelle citazioni conferma che l'esito dell'argomentazione è che i molti sono *sia* così piccoli da non avere grandezza affatto *sia* così grandi da essere di grandezza infinita.[37] Ma com'è possibile questo esito?

Anche in questo caso bisogna pensare che Zenone supponeva che la divisione infinita si sia verificata tutta, abbia trovato un termine, e che i risultati di questa, cioè le parti dotate ciascuna di una certa grandezza (per quanto modesta sia), siano stati messi in fila: trattandosi di una serie infinita di grandezze, anche la grandezza che ne risulta, egli riteneva, deve essere infinita. Anche questa è una conclusione la cui fallacia non è tanto ovvia, in quanto l'assunto (legato all'ammissione di un termine ultimo della serie) che c'è una grandezza minima nella serie (per cui la serie tutta ha una grandezza almeno pari a quella di questo *minimum* moltiplicata per un'infinità di volte) è giustificato dalla considerazione che *ogni* membro della serie ha una grandezza superiore alla grandezza zero, e non viceversa.[38]

---

[36] Dall'esposizione di Aristotele (*Phys.* 6, 9, 239b14 sgg. = test. 25) risulta che c'era un riferimento espresso al tempo già nel caso dell'argomento della dicotomia; per un'analisi di entrambi gli argomenti cfr. Vlastos, voce "Zeno," pp. 372-374.

[37] La difficoltà, come s'è indicato sopra, sez. I, era già stata riconosciuta da Fränkel. Non mi convince il tentativo di von Fritz (voce "Zenon," col. 72) di mostrare che, nonostante la formulazione usata ($\tau\varepsilon$ ... $\varkappa\alpha i$ invece di η ... η, cfr. Simpl. 141.7 e 139.8), Zenone aveva in mente un *aut-aut*.

[38] Come sostiene Vlastos, voce "Zeno," p. 370b. Si può ipotizzare che Zenone avrebbe considerato una seria convergente del tipo: $1/2 + 1/4 + 1/8 + ...$, *qualora* la sua somma dia 1, dunque un numero finito, come una serie che *procede* all'infinito, ma non come una serie infinita *data* (nella sua completezza); ed è perché intende la serie in quel modo e non per un errore di logica o di calcolo, che la sua posizione differisce da quella dei matematici

Ma a questo punto diventa pure comprensibile come mai Zenone poteva ritenere che entrambe le conclusioni del suo argumento risultano dall'ammissione che la divisione all'infinito è stata completata: essendo appunto una divisione all'infinito essa per definizione dà luogo ad una serie infinita di grandezze (anzi, poiché per ogni nuova parte che si ottiene in una divisione per due inizia un'altra divisione all'infinito, dà luogo ad un'infinità di serie infinite di grandezze), la cui somma è una grandezza infinita; ma essendo stata completata, si è arrivati ad un termine, che è in qualche modo trans-infinito, cioè al di là della serie, il quale non ha più grandezza (anzi, si arriva ad un'infinita molteplicità di tali termini, per il solito motivo). Zenone evidentemente ritiene che c'è contraddizione fra il primo risultato, che è che i molti hanno grandezza infinita (manifestamente: ciascuno di essi, perché ciascuno di essi è costituito da un'infinità di parte dotate di grandezza), e il secondo risultato, che è che i molti sono senza grandezza (di nuovo ciascuno di essi, perché ciascuno di essi è costituito da parti senza grandezza), in quanto si viene ad attribuire proprietà incompatibili (ἐναντία) alle stesse cose, cioè ai molti (più esattamente: a ciascuno di essi). Non si tratta però di conclusioni che comportino contraddizione indipendentemente dall'applicazione ad uno stesso soggetto, dunque che rivelino una contraddizione nel metodo adottato per pervenire ad essi. Infatti l'aggiunta di termini senza grandezza, non più appartenenti alla serie infinita di grandezze ottenuta con la divisione all'infinito (perché oltre ad essa), all'infinita grandezza che si ottiene sommando tali grandezze, non modifica il risultato complessivo: $\infty + 0 = \infty$. Dunque *entrambi* questi termini, sia zero che infinito, sono il risultato di una divisione all'infinito così come la concepisce Zenone!

V

C'è ormai la conferma della conclusione che l'argomento (o la coppia di argomenti?) contenuto in B 2, cioè l'insieme da (A) a (C), è del tutto autonomo rispetto all'argomento contenuto on B 1, cioè (D) - (E), anche se

---

odierni. Secondo Vlastos, "simple arithmetic, well within Zeno's reach, would have shown him that any partial sum of this sequence would be less than 1;" ma Zenone non si accontenta di "any *partial* sum," vuole la somma *totale* della serie infinita, e questa, se la si potesse davvero ottenere, non sarebbe finita. L'errore da lui commesso è dunque un altro (questo giustamente diagnosticato da Vlastos, ivi, p. 371a, e "Zenonian Argument," p. 132), ed è quello di aver ritenuto che una serie che procede all'infinito possa avere una fine, dunque è quello di assimilare una tale serie ad una finita (Aristotele invece, coll'ammettere nel caso della divisione un infinito che è solo *potenziale*, evita questo errore).

probabilmente lo precedeva immediatamente (almeno: nel testo che Simplicio aveva a disposizione), in quanto la formula ipotetica εἰδὲ ἔστιν con cui comincia (ᴅ) pare presupporre una conclusione negativa circa l'esistenza delle cose nella parte precedente. Con ciò ci troviamo da capo di fronte al problema di determinare il significato dell'argomento e il ruolo che esso aveva nell'opera di Zenone, e se questo era un rompicapo per Simplicio, lo è ancora più per noi, che ne sappiamo meno di lui[39] e ci dobbiamo basare largamente sulle sue indicazioni che oltre tutto non sono né chiare né univoche). Ma non è fra i miei propositi tentare qui di affrontare questo problema in modo approfondito: questo richiederebbe un altro articolo. Mi limito invece ad alcune osservazioni che servano a completare l'esame precedentemente condotto dell'argomento di B 1, cercando di chiarire quale connessione ci può essere stata fra questo e l'argomento di B 2 e di trarre pure qualche conclusione generale circa le tecniche di argomentazione adoperate da Zenone.

Si potrebbe sostenere che rimane valido il suggerimento di Solmsen – anche se applicato ormai a due argomenti distinti, ma in immediata successione – che Zenone argomentava prima contro l'uno (senza escludere l'Uno di Parmenide) e poi contro i molti. Per la tesi contraria, infatti, cioè che egli argomentava unicamente contro i molti, ci si deve fondare sulle attestazioni di Platone e di Simplicio;[40] ora quasi certamente la seconda non è fondata su di un conoscenza, se non parziale, dell'originale, ma dipende largamente da quella platonica, mentre la prima non è esente dal sospetto di dare dell'opera di Zenone una presentazione conforme alle preoccupazioni dello stesso Platone nel dialogo. Come ha sottolineato von Fritz ("Zeno of Elea in Plato's *Parmenides*," p. 333) è ben possibile che Platone vedesse negli argomenti di Zenone degli argomenti rivolti esclusivamente contro la pluralità, e non anche contro l'Uno, perché questo è per lui del tutto non spaziale, del tutto ideale, e l'eliminazione dell'uno dotato di grandezza ai suoi occhi fa parte dell'eliminazione dei molti (perché è un "uno dei molti," cioè facente parte delle cose empiriche) a favore della postulazione dell'Uno inteso a quel modo. Che questo è quanto gli importa è mostrato dal fatto che per ben due volte nel *Parmenide*[41] è sottolineata l'esigenza di elevarsi al di sopra

---

[39] Quando egli stesso, com'è stato sottolineato da più studiosi (per esempio da Vlastos, "Zenonian Argument," p. 137, n. 7), probabilmente aveva di fronte a sè solo un estratto dell'originale zenoniano, date le incertezze che tradisce a proposito dei contenuti di questo.

[40] Per Platone cfr. il passo già menzionato del *Parmenide*; per Simplicio cfr. quanto afferma in 139.5-7.

[41] In 128ᴇ-130ᴀ e 135ᴇ (cfr. specialmente, in 129ᴇ-130ᴀ, la contrapposizione ἐν αὐτοῖς τοῖς εἴδεσι ... ἐν τοῖς ὁρωμένοις).

del piano del sensibile, abbandonando in tal modo il procedimento espressamente attribuito agli Eleati: evidentemente egli ritiene (come farà poi anche Aristotele)[42] che il riconoscimento che qualcosa ha grandezza implica il riconoscimento che esso è corporeo o sensibile. E non è superfluo sottolineare, a questo proposito, che Platone neppure pretende di esporre un'intenzione che Zenone avesse formulato espressamente nel suo libro, perché altrimenti non avrebbe sentito il bisogno di ricorrere alla finzione di un interrogatorio rivolto da Socrate a Zenone per accertare quali fossero le sue intenzioni reali.[43]

Tuttavia, a voler sostenere, come Solmsen pare voler fare, che Zenone aveva argomentato *sistematicamente* sia contro l'uno che contro i molti (per esempio alternando, nella sua esposizione, un argomento contro l'uno e un argomento contro i molti), non solo si dovrebbe ammettere che c'è stato il curioso accidente storico che l'estratto di Simplicio (per sua affermazione, in 139.5-7) conteneva soltanto argomenti del secondo tipo, ma si dovrebbe pure sostenere che la presentazione di Platone nel *Parmenide* non è semplicemente distorta ma è un vero e proprio falso. (Notare ugualmente che, dei rimanenti argomenti, noi conosciamo solo argomenti contro il movimento e non anche argomenti contro la quiete.) La logica stessa dell'argomento in discussione non favorisce una conclusione del genere, perché, se non si vede come esso potesse colpire l'"uno dei molti" senza colpire l'Uno parmenideo, non si vede neppure come esso potesse colpire soltanto il secondo.

Non mi pare neppure ammissibile stabilire una connessione fra (A) - (C) e (D) - (E) al modo in cui lo fa Owen ("Zeno and the Mathematicians," pp. 145-146), cioè sostenendo che (A) viene a mostrare che le unità che costituiscono una molteplicità non possono avere grandezza (altrimenti avrebbero parti e non sarebbero unità ma esse stesse molteplicità o collezioni di unità), (B) viene a mostrare che, al contrario, non ci può essere qualcosa che non abbia nessuna dimensione (perchè altrimenti, come viene argomentato in (C), sarebbe non-esistente), e che questo secondo corno dell'alternativa viene sviluppato in (D) - (E), di nuovo elaborando un'alternativa. (Come si può constatare, egli segue Fränkel nell' analisi della parte (A) - (C), facendo però della parte (D) - (E) un intero argomento, che tuttavia non è autonomo ma dipende alla parte

---

[42] A proposito di Zenone alla fine del passo citato sopra, n. 12.

[43] Vlastos stesso, nella sua difesa della fondamentale attendibilità della presentazione platonica, non può negare la presenza in essa di distorsioni, particolarmente nel focalizzare il pensiero parmenideo sull'uno anziché sull'essere e nell'ignorare gli argomenti zenoniani contro il movimento ("Plato's Testimony," pp. 143-146).

precedente, perché riduce all'assurdo uno dei due corni dell'alternativa ivi elaborata.) Per lui, poi, come abbiamo già visto, tutto questo blocco costituisce (o fa parte di) uno dei due corni dell'alternativa che si pone circa la divisibilità delle cose (che la divisione all'infinito sia stata completata; che non si lasci mai completare).

Ho già espresso delle riserve su alcuni punti di questa costruzione, in particolare escludendo che (B)-(C) possa costituire altro che lo sviluppo di una conseguenza di (A); ovviamente anche le obiezioni da me rivolte all'interpretazione che Fränkel dà della parte (A) - (C) sono pertinenti, con l'aggiunta che l'argomento in (C), peculiare com'è, neppure si inserisce bene all'interno di un'alternativa complessiva circa la divisibilità delle cose. Più in generale c'è da dire che, se è vero che tutti gli argomenti contro la pluralità dei quali abbiamo cognizione (cioè, oltre a quello del fr. 1, quello del fr. 3 e quello riportato sommariamente da Platone nel *Parmenide*, con la possibile eccezione di quello del fr. 2 se era un argomento contro la pluralità) elaborano ciascuno un'antinomia , tuttavia lo scopo di questa tecnica è evidentemente quello di ottenere una *reductio ad absurdum* mostrando che le due conclusioni sono in contraddizione l'una con l'altra; invece non c'è niente che faccia pensare che questi argomenti stessi costituissero i corni di alternative elaborate indipendentemente da questo scopo.[44]

È importante soffermarsi ulteriormente sul significato delle tecniche di *reductio* adottate da Zenone. È manifesto che un suo procedimento standard, applicato in quegli argomenti contro la pluralità, sta nel dedurre, dalla comune premessa "i molti sono," coppie di proposizioni in contraddizione l'una con l'altra ("i molti sono simili e dissimili;" "i molti sono limitati di numero e infiniti;" "i molti sono grandi e piccoli – grandi al punto da essere di grandezza infinita, piccoli al punto da essere di grandezza nulla").[45] Tuttavia proprio nel caso dell'argomento di B 1 questo procedimento presenta una variante significativa, perché esso comporta non solo che le due conclusioni siano incompatibili – fra di loro, ma che esse siano pure *assurde* ciascuna per conto proprio (ovviamente, in relazione alla premessa: perché è impossibile "comporre" o ricostituire un ente finito, cioè quello che all'inizio viene diviso, mediante un insieme di parti che costituiscono una grandezza infinita oppure che sono ciascuna del tutto priva di grandezza). Infine, è manifesto che, nel caso degli

---

[44] In breve, Zenone elabora antinomie, non dilemmi (cfr. anche Stokes, *One and Many*, pp. 201-202; è vero che la distinzione fra i due casi non è sempre del tutto netta).
[45] Dunque la forma di questi argomenti è (come nota anche Vlastos, "Zenonian Argument," p. 136): "Se P, allora Q e non-Q [perciò, non-P]."

argomenti contro il movimento, la *reductio* adottata è "lineare" (o semplice), cioè non comporta l'elaborazione di nessuna antinomia, ma c'è un'unica conclusione che è assurda (in relazione alla premessa). Siamo dunque di fronte a tre tecniche di *reductio*: la *reductio* lineare; la *reductio* antinomica; la *reductio* mista (quella adottata in B 1, che è una combinazione delle altre due).[46] Se poi Zenone applicasse dei criteri per ordinare gli argomenti nel suo libro a seconda della tecnica di *reductio* adottata in ciascuno di essi, non lo sappiamo proprio.

Di fronte a questa situazione c'è indubbiamente la possibilità che l'argomento in B 2 fosse una *reductio* lineare della postulazione della molteplicità, perché niente sappiamo della elaborazione di un'alternativa ad esso (e non è neppure facile prospettarsi un'alternativa alla dimostrazione adottata in (c), che porti alla conclusione contraria). Non è affatto improbabile che Zenone, nell'argomentare contro la pluralità, facesse uso di tutte le tecniche possibili che gli permettessero di ottenere lo scopo di ridurre all'assurdo la sua postulazione. E non c'è dubbio che nel caso del nostro argomento questo scopo è pienamente raggiunto mostrando che le unità che costituiscono la molteplicità, per il fatto di non poter possedere grandezza, neppure esistono: una molteplicità costituita da

---

[46] Trovo curioso il tentativo di J. Barnes, *The Presocratic Phil.*, 1: 236, di contestare la tesi generalmente accetta che Zenone aveva fatto un uso cosciente della tecnica logica della *reductio*, suggerendo invece che questo è solo quanto Platone ed altri attribuiscono a Zenone. Secondo lui nel *Parmenide* "Socrates is bringing to fictional consciousness what was at best latent in historical reality. Zeno's surviving fragments contain no *reductio*: he takes an hypothesis and infers an absurdity from it; but he never makes the characteristic move of *reductio*, the inference to the falsity of the hypothesis. He argues 'If P, then Q,' where Q states some absurdity; but he does not explicitly infer the falsity of P. In other words, he does not use *reductio ad absurdum* as a technique for disproof." In risposta c'è da dire, in primo luogo, che se è vero che le citazioni dall' originale fatte da Simplicio non contengono l'affermazione della falsità della premessa, tuttavia sia lui (anche nel constesto stesso di una tale citazione, cfr. 139.5 sgg. = B 2) che altri commentatori sono concordi nell'attribuire questa intenzione a Zenone, per cui non è affatto impossibile che egli l'avesse affermata espressamente, per esempio all'inizio o alla fine del suo libro, senza sentirsi obbligato ad introdurre quell'inferenza in ogni singolo caso (e le domande di Socrate nel *Parmenide* partono dalla citazione sommaria di un singolo argomento). In secondo luogo, egli poteva dare per scontato da parte del lettore od uditore intelligente che questi avrebbe compreso il senso dell'argomentazione; se no per qual motivo al mondo dedurre assurdità dalla premessa "i molti sono," e questo adottando sistematicamente una formulazione di tipo condizionale, alle volte sottolineando la necessità della conseguenza (p. es. in Simpl. 141.6-7 = (E)? Nel caso poi dell'argomento del fr. 2, cioè di (B) - (C), che ho considerato una *reductio* di tipo lineare, è estremanente evidente che la conclusione ("questo neppure esisterebbe") è una riduzione all'assurdo della premessa ("qualcosa non ha grandezza"). Bisogna certamente andare cauti nell'identificare premesse e inferenze che rimangono tacite, ma se non lo si fa la storia del pensiero antico diventa del tutto impossibile.

non-entità è essa stessa una non-entità.[47] Quanto all'argomentazione in
B 1, questa presumibilmente veniva in immediata successione, per
mostrare che, anche ad ammettere i molti – ammettendo insieme che essi
hanno grandezza – ne risultano delle conseguenze non meno letali per la
postulazione della loro esistenza di quella tratta nel primo argomento.

Rimane tuttavia la complicazione che, quale che fosse l'intento di
Zenone nell'elaborare questo argomento, esso finisce col colpire anche
l'uno parmenideo, in quanto anche questo è dotato di grandezza spaziale.
Non credo che la complicazione sia evitata sottolineando, col Furley,[48] che
l'aggiunta del termine πάχος sia in (b[1]) che in (c) non può essere
accidentale, ma mostra che le unità che Zenone rigetta sono dotate non
semplicemente di grandezza ma anche di quest'altra caratteristica (la
densità fisica?): è sufficientemente chiaro che in (A) la divisibilità è vista
come una conseguenza di già del possesso della sola grandezza (il che è
confermato dalla testimonianza di Aristotele considerata sopra, n. 12).
Pare dunque che su questo punto Zenone dissentisse, almeno implicita-
mente, sia da Parmenide che da Melisso, con conseguenze gravi per la
concezione eleatica dell'essere, che richiede la sua unità e indivisibilità.

È possibile che Zenone non si fosse accorto di queste conseguenze?
Non è una domanda alla quale sia facile dare una risposta, ma credo
di non essere l'unico a provare qualche riluttanza ad abbracciare la
tesi calogeriana dell'involontarietà di questo colpo dato da Zenone
all'eleatismo. Non vedo poi come si possa parlare, come fa il von Fritz, di
una difesa "aporetica" dell'eleatismo, quando si tratta di ben di più di una
semplice aporia.[49] Certo è che della totale distruttività di questo suo
argomento si accorsero ben presto altri,[50] ed è molto probabilmente questa
loro constatazione che gli creò la fama, nell'antichità, del dialettico puro,
dell'"antilogico" (cioè di colui che argomenta in utramque partem) – una
fama della quale il passo già menzionato del Fedro è una delle

[47] Una conferma di questa interpretazione può essere trovata nelle attestazioni di
Filopono (in Phys. 80.23-29 Vitelli = n. 3 Lee; e 42.9 sgg., specialm. 42.31-43.6 = DK
A 21 = n. 8 Lee) che paiono riguardare l'argomento in B 2, e nel modo in cui Gorgia (Sul
non-essere, versione di Sesto, Adv. Math. 7: 74) ricalca l'argomentazione zenoniana (cfr.
anche Stokes, One and Many, p. 214).
[48] Furley, Two Studies, pp. 66-68, che suggerisce che la posizione di Zenone è simile a
quella di Melisso (nel fr. 9).
[49] Cfr. anche le osservazioni di Vlastos, "Plato's Testimony," p. 159, n. 52.
[50] Se ne accorse di già Gorgia, che non si limita ad argomentare (nel passo citato in
n. 47) contro la molteplicità dell'essere, evidentemente ricalcando Zenone, ma argomenta,
pure espressamente (nel passo immediatamente precedente, cioè in sez. 73) contro il suo
essere uno.

attestazioni.[51] Ma se anche egli fosse stato un "antilogico" consapevole, deve esserlo stato con la riluttanza di chi si accorge delle conseguenze negative di una scoperta fatta perseguendo scopi positivi. Per lo meno si può dire che l'analisi dell'argomento di B 1 non ha offerto nessun elemento per pensare che egli avesse l'intento sofistico di trarre in inganno i propri uditori e lettori.

---

[51] Non posso qui esaminare queste testimonianze, ma debbo dire che non mi persuade il tentativo di Vlastos (nell'art. cit.) di sminuirne il peso: non mi pare dubbio che quello ora detto è il senso più ovvio della parola ἀντιλογικός usata nel *Fedro* per Zenone; e la contraddizione con la testimonianza platonica del *Parmenide* è per lo meno molto attenuata interpretando quest'ultima secondo le indicazioni di von Fritz sopra menzionate.

2

Did Parmenides Reject the Sensible World?

L. M. de Rijk

Filosofisch Instituut, Leiden

In his excellent *A History of Ancient Western Philosophy* Father Joseph Owens remarks that there is in fact little exaggeration in saying that without a sufficient grasp of the way in which the problem of being was originally placed by Parmenides, the subsequent long-drawn-out controversies upon the subject become impossible to understand.[1] One may assume that the well-known author of the magistral thesis on Aristotle's doctrine of being can best be honoured by a short paper[2] on that important predecessor of the Stagirite.

Two camps of scholars interpreting Parmenides' poem have recently been distinguished and labeled as the Majority and the Minority. The former holds that, unlike the Alêtheia part, the Doxa part presents an altogether untrue account of things that properly speaking have no real existence. According to the Minority, however, the Doxa was put forward as possessing some kind or degree of cognitive validity.[3] I shall

---

[1] J. Owens, *A History of Ancient Western Philosophy* (New York, 1959), p. 76.

[2] Of course I am much indebted to modern research, especially the fundamental works of W. Verdenius, *Parmenides* (Groningen, 1942); H. Fränkel, *Wege und Formen frühgriechischen Denkens*, 2nd ed. (München, 1960); J. Mansfeld, *Die Offenbarung des Parmenides und die menschliche Welt* (Assen, 1964); L. Tarán, *Parmenides* (Princeton, 1965); and A. P. D. Mourelatos, *The Route of Parmenides* (New Haven and London, 1970).

[3] W. J. Matson, "Parmenides Unbound," *Inter. Philos. Quarterly*, 2 (1980), 345.

Graceful Reason: Essays in Ancient and Medieval Philosophy Presented to Joseph Owens, CSSR, ed. Lloyd P. Gerson. Papers in Mediaeval Studies 4 (Toronto: Pontifical Institute of Mediaeval Studies, 1983), pp. 29-53. © P.I.M.S., 1983.

try to show that both these two positions are ambiguous and accordingly
fail in giving a clear insight into what Parmenides intends to tell us. They
both seem to need correction to the extent that Parmenides does
distinguish the Alêtheia route from the Doxa route(s), but there is nothing
in the text to tell us that he makes a distinction between two separate
domains, one true and the other untrue. As any genuine philosopher he
was concerned about the sensible world, *our* world and it was *that* which
he wanted to truly understand.

Let us examine more closely what he tells us in the most relevant parts
of his poem.

I. The Route of Truth as Giving True Information
About the Appearances

We are told by the famous poem that "the youth" (κοῦρος, Parmenides)
was transported to a divine region. There it is "by right and justice"
(b 1.28) that he is set upon the right route "far from the beaten track of
men" (b 1.27) and a goddess urges him to travel upon it and on no other
one (b 2).

Right in the proem the decisive lines are found to settle the dispute on
the poet's attitude to the sensible world – the description of the purport of
the route commended by the goddess:

> It is right that you should learn everything: on the one hand the un-
> wavering temper of trustworthy truth and on the other the opinions of
> mortals in which there is no true reliance. (b 1.28-30)

The opinions of mortals are not excluded beforehand and the goddess
explains why opinions should be learned though they are not truly
reliable:

> But nonetheless this too you shall learn: how the things as they are taken to
> be (τὰ δοκοῦντα) would have had to *be* trustworthy (χρῆν δοκιμῶς εἶναι) in
> spite of (περ) their being continually (διὰ παντός) manifold (πάντα = παντοῖα).
> (b 1.31-32)

Some remarks on my translation. For the rendering of δοκοῦντα, see
Heraclitus, b 28 and Mourelatos, p. 203 n. 28. I take χρῆν ("had to be") as
referring to what Mourelatos happily calls "intrasystematic necessity."
However, unlike him and others, I think of a necessity within the system
of the route commended. Travelling on this route one learns indeed not
only unshaken truth but also how things ought to be deemed to be
trustworthy, that is, how one could succeed in perceiving their true nature

(of "being," as will be clear from в 2.3 onwards), once their manifold disguises have been seen through (notice the νοεῖν [νόημα] of в 2.2, в 3, в 6.1, в 7.2, в 8.8, в 8.34 ff., etc.). I read with the better manuscripts περ ὄντα (instead of περῶντα which cannot mean "pervade" [= "to pass through *and then occupy*"] as has been rightly pointed out by Mourelatos, pp. 213 f.) and take πάντα in the sense of παντοῖα,[4] as, e.g., in Homer, *Iliad* 5.60; *Odyssey* 4.417, 9.19.

So the particles ἠμὲν – ἠδὲ in в 1.29-30 articulate *two* things as coordinate, viz. truth *and* opinions. The ἀλλ' ἔμπης καὶ of в 1.31 does not introduce a third member (against Mourelatos[5] and others) nor does it make an element subordinate to the second member (opinions). Instead, it explains the use that there still is in learning opinions in spite of their unreliability as well as how to achieve such useful learning. It tells how things, in spite of their many shapes disguising their true nature of "being," would be taken *to be* genuinely – δοκιμῶς. So в 1.31-32 does not contain any concession to mortal opinions nor suggest something like "just make some corrections and human opinion will be all right." On the contrary, the goddess still takes the opinions of mortals as completely deceptive, but denounces the "manifoldness" of the things as their deceitful ontological failure that disguises their true nature ("be-ingness"). At the same time our corresponding epistemic failure is exposed to the extent that our opinions are always concerned just with those manifold disguises. Therefore a total conversion to faithful truth still remains needed. Within the intrasystematic necessity of the first route the δόξαι too are introduced as within the system of Truth and the goddess needs not confine herself to just warning us against deceptive opinions but is eager to teach us, along the lines of the same route of Truth, the *why* and *how* of the deceitful state of both sensible things and our opinions about them. It should be borne in mind that like the English "appearances" or "the world as it appears," τὰ δοκοῦντα stands at the same time for our opinions about the world and that world itself.

---

[4] Mourelatos' explanation of πάντα περ' ὄντα as close to the later formula τὸ ὂν ᾖ ὂν is ingenious but somewhat far fetched. Besides, the location of περ is not in favour of his interpretation. For that matter, it does have the usual concessive sense and sets off the previous πάντα: "although they are so *many* (= 'manifold')."

[5] The strong adversative ἀλλ' ἔμπης καὶ cannot be taken with Mourelatos (p. 209) as just introducing a third member and needs a clearer point of contrast. Tarán, p. 211, is right in referring the phrase to the untrustworthiness of δόξαι ("the opinions of men *in spite* [ἀλλ' ἔμπης] *of the fact that they are false*"). He is right in rejecting any tripartition on this account.

So the only true route that there is (that is, the Alêtheia route), may teach mortals first to understand What Is or Being-ness as such, and second to see *how* hopelessly deceitful sensible things and our opinions are. So people will see through deceptive appearances and never "be outwitted by mortal wisdom" (cf. B 8.61), not only in being acquainted with human cosmology, but als seeing through it. (See also below, p. 47).

The other fragments seem to confirm that there is one true route which is concerned with both the truth and the true evaluation of the doxa. It is put in strict contrast to the opposite way (B 2) including its perverse variant (B 6.4-9) which leads to anything but Truth and is open only to the sensible world because unlike the route of Truth, it adheres to the "likely-seeming" (the term is Guthrie's) appearances of the sensible world.

II. THE TWO MAIN ROUTES AS OPPOSED IN B 2

Our second fragment contrasts the only true route recommended in B 1.28 ff. with its opposite:

> I shall tell you ... which are the only routes of inquiry for thinking (νοῆσαι); the one < conveying at > "that is" and "that impossibly is not" is the course of Persuasion (for she is the faithful companion of Truth); the other < conveying at > "that is-not" and "that rightfully is-not," this I point to you as being a path that does not bestow any information (παναπευθέα); for you could neither come to know what is-not (such is unreachable, indeed) nor could you single it out. (B 2)

Mourelatos[6] is quite right in taking νοῆσαι in B 2.2 as epexegetic of "inquiry" (διζήσιος; so: "route of inquiring") and in referring to Empedocles, B 3.12. Thinking and the routes are identified materially; the latter are "routes of thinking." I follow Mourelatos also in taking παναπευθέα (B 2.6; with which compare the ideal of πάντα πυθέσθαι in B 1.28) in the active sense, rather than as "unknowable" (as does Tarán among others), which does not fit the context since the wrong route *is* described by the goddess. The word is to be compared with the epitheton πολύφημον assigned to the right route: "resounding" = "from which much information comes," "that bestows knowledge."

The core of this text lies in the ὅπως ἔστιν (B 2.3) and ὡς οὐκ ἔστι (B 2.5) formulas. There is general agreement among modern scholars[7] on the absence of a subject for ἔστι (and the εἶναι of the polar tournures in the

---

[6] Mourelatos, p. 55, n. 26.
[7] See ibid., p. 47.

second hemistiches of B 2.3 and B 2.5) which is regarded as intentional and is not to be emended away nor should in their view a subject be mentally supplied.

However, there is some confusion in the interpretative practice of most students of the Parmenidean texts. Mourelatos[8] has already pointed to Tarán's inconsistency on this account when he rejects Fränkel's proposal that ἔστιν is impersonal but writes on the same page that ἔστιν and οὐκ ἔστι are used as impersonals.[9] For that matter, Mourelatos[10] who takes the ἔστι in B 2.3 and B 2.5 as an "enriched" copula indicating what he calls "speculative predication" still has himself to explain what the speculative predicate is predicated of. He has in mind predications of the "what is it?" type[11] but what does the "it" refer to? I think that one cannot help mentally supplying as the subject of the ἔστιν and οὐκ ἔστι whatever in our sensible world makes the object of one's inquiry (διζήσιος) and νοεῖν.[12] Anything in our world may be such a "*material* object" of the quest realized by the first route (as well as by every false route). However, the "*formal* object" of each quest as well as of νοεῖν is just a thing's "what-is" or being-ness.[13] This may be clarified by strictly esteeming the metaphysical relationships which Parmenides ever maintains between ἐόν on the one hand and νοεῖν, "quest," and their cognates or coordinates, on the other.

III. Νοεῖν AND Φράζειν AND THEIR IMPACT ON THE CHARACTER OF THE TWO ROUTES

Mourelatos[14] rightly links up the problem of the ὡς (οὐκ) ἔστι formulas with the exact meaning of νοεῖν and refers to the rich results of the pioneering study on this account by Kurt von Fritz. Von Fritz has clearly shown that as early as in Homer the hard core meaning of νοεῖν is the "recognition of the true nature or essence of a thing against its surface

---

[8] Ibid., p. 47, n. 2.
[9] Tarán, p. 36.
[10] Mourelatos, pp. 56-61.
[11] Ibid., p. 57.
[12] Cf. G. E. L. Owen, "Eleatic Questions," *Classical Quarterly*, 54 (1960), 94-95; Verdenius, p. 32; and Jonathan Barnes, *The Presocratic Philosophers*, I; *Thales to Zeno* (London, 1979), p. 163. See also below, pp. 33-35, 42 ff.
[13] Mourelatos is quite right in saying (p. 74) that the ἐόν is whatever answers to the δίζησις (quest) of the positive route, but his statement should be further qualified in the way I have just tried to do.
[14] Mourelatos, pp. 68-70.

appearance."[15] In the early period there is nothing philosophical about this; it just concerns "seeing through" a situation (or person), not being misled by any surface appearance.[16] For Parmenides, however, von Fritz thinks he finds[17] "a very real difficulty" in that in some instances Parmenides seems to assert (e.g., B 8.34-37) that νοῦς and νοεῖν are always and necessarily connected with εἶναι and ἐόν and therefore with the truth, which seems to imply that the νοῦς cannot err, while in others (e.g., our B 2.2-8, B 6.6) it is asserted or implied that a wrong νοεῖν is also possible. He tries to solve the problem – conceding at the same time that it perhaps does not admit a perfect solution (p. 237), one in the realm of human logic (p. 239) – by assuming that even the erring νοεῖν of the mortals "cannot fail to be linked up inextricably with the ἐόν (p. 239). I should like to correct von Fritz's solution to the extent that both series of texts clearly show that νοεῖν is bound to ἐόν and always imply one's aiming for "what-is," the real nature of a thing (in von Fritz's words, "a thing's true nature or essence") and his claim that he is successful in doing so.[18] So the proper meaning of νοεῖν is "to see as (or to consider) the real nature of x" rather than "to see actually the real nature of x."[19] So the wrong routes are not excluded from being a "νοεῖν-route."

The same holds true for such terms as quest (δίζησις) and "speaking" (λέγειν, φάναι), the latter especially in the φράζειν and φατίζειν variants. The word δίζησις has the connotation of seeking information about the object which we want to reach and to possess securely; it means "investigation in depth."[20] For Heraclitus δίζησις is "directed to that which is hidden and inaccessible to unthinking mortals"; for Parmenides it is a quest for ἀλήθεια.[21] Φράζειν is rightly taken by Mourelatos[22] as connoting the

[15] K. von Fritz, "Nous, Noein and Their Derivatives in Homer," *Class. Philol.*, 38 (1943), 90.

[16] Cf. K. von Fritz, "Nous, Noein and Their Derivatives in Presocratic Philosophy Excluding Anaxagoras," *Class. Philol.*, 40 (1945), 223, where he points to the etymology of νοεῖν, deriving it from a root meaning "to sniff" or "to smell."

[17] Ibid., p. 237 ff.

[18] Gabriel Nuchelmans (*Theories of the Proposition, Ancient and Medieval Conceptions of the Bearers of Truth and Falsity* [Amsterdam, London, 1973]) is right in pointing (p. 10) to the important distinction between "intending to think of something or to refer to something" and "succeeding in these endeavours." Indeed, Parmenides seems to have overlooked this distinction. For the rest I do not agree with him (p. 9) that Parmenides concentrates upon only one sense of the verb εἶναι.

[19] Cf. Mourelatos, pp. 175-177.

[20] See ibid., pp. 67-68.

[21] Ibid., p. 68.

[22] Ibid., p. 20, n. 28.

attention of an audience. It does not have the trivial sense "to tell" but rather "to exhibit, to explain, to make evident for all to see." The basic idea in φράζειν and φράζεσθαι ("to think," "to attend to") as well is that of selective attention and focus.[23] Φατίζειν seems to have a similar connotation of "making plain," "declaring" and "revealing" what might be unclear or somehow disguised. So the verb seems to connote essential or relevant information. He who φατίζει something does justice to it in setting off clearly the core of the matter. To my mind λέγειν and φάναι do not as such possess the same connotation as φράζειν and φατίζειν but it should be noticed that Parmenides pairs them most often with νοεῖν (and δίζησις) and then they share in its connotation of deep penetration into the matter under inquiry to the extent indeed that νοεῖν καὶ λέγειν comes to mean "to really understand and name something's nature."

Fragment B 2 should be interpreted along these lines. The goddess describes the only two possible routes of quest, the νοεῖν ... "that is" and the νοεῖν ... "that is-not." Their number (two) is implied in the logical dichotomy found in B 2.3-5.[24] This pair of routes actually consists of the right route that understands a thing's being as its true nature (asserting of it essentially that it is: ἐόν) and the wrong one that understands a thing's not-being as its true nature (asserting of it essentially that it is-not). The first route is that of Truth and its maid Persuasion. The goddess hits the mark (φράζω, B 2.6) in describing the wrong route as bestowing no information about the matter under inquiry.

That a thing's true nature aimed for by the first (i.e., positive) route is its "what-is" (τὸ ἐόν) is to be gathered not only from the formula ὅπως ἔστιν (B 2.3) but also from the explicit mention of "what is-not" (τὸ μὴ ἐόν) as the awkward product of the negative (rather, "destructive") route in B 2.7.

So fragment B 2 is in substance a further description of the Alêtheia route recommended in B 1.27ff. and its contradistinction to its perverse counterpart, the negative (destructive) route. In fact good and bad νοεῖν are contrasted. In B 2.7 the perversity of bad νοεῖν is shown by the impossibility of its illocutionary correlate. So fragment B 2 dictates the understanding and qualification of things as ἐόν ("be-ing," in German "seiend," in French "étant," in Dutch "zijnd").

---

[23] Ibid. Compare πολύφραστοι ἵπποι ("well-discerning mares") in B 1.4 and φράζεσθαι ("to attend to," "to ponder") in B 6.2.

[24] Once and for all the reader is referred to the excellent analyses of Parmenides' ways of reasoning in Jaap Mansfeld, *Die Offenbarung des Parmenides* (Assen, 1964), esp. pp. 42-121.

IV. Fragments 4-7

Fragment в 3 will be discussed below together with в 8.34-41(see pp. 42 ff., 45). In fragment в 4 the goddess asks Parmenides to see (λεῦσσε, в 4.1) things which are far off as nevertheless firmly present to the νοῦς. The operation proper of the νοῦς is explained in в 4.2-4:

> For it will not cut off "what is" from holding fast to "what is," either by scattering it all in every manner all over the universe, or by bringing it together [as if it were dispersed].

The πάντηι πάντως ("in every manner") seems to have some affinity with the πάντα (= πάντοῖα "manifold") of в 1.32. I take the χατά in χατὰ χόσμον distributively in в 1.3 (χατὰ πάντ' ἄστη, "in each and every place"). The first line of this fragment in fact asserts that what the νοῦς aims for is firmly present to it and therefore reachable, whereas the remaining lines explain this by describing its operation. However, given the close correlationship of νοεῖν and its specific object ἐόν it implicitly describes at the same time Being as continuous and holding together, as is done more explicitly by в 8.23-25. One should notice the opposition of the plural ἀπεόντα and παρεόντα to the singular forms τὸ ἐόν and τοῦ ἐόντος. The former refer to the appearances, the latter to their unique essential feature – "being-ness."[25]

It is possible (but far from certain) that fragment в 5 ("And it is indifferent to me from where I should start; for there I shall come back again") is to be taken with Mourelatos[26] as expressing the revolving of the νοῦς around "what-is" that always is firmly present to it (в 4.1).

The sixth fragment seems to be most vital to our understanding of Parmenides' doctrine. The first line certainly expresses the explicit command of the goddess to choose the first route (i.e., the positive or Alêtheia route) and so reinforces what has been suggested earlier (в 1.28-32; в 2.6-8 which sets off the second route as nonsensical; в 4.1). The text runs as follows:

> It is right that < your > asserting and thinking aim for "what-is" < in the object of inquiry > ; indeed, it *is* and its being what is-not is impossible.

[25] There seems to be no cogent reason to relegate в 4 (with Mansfeld, p. 208) to the Doxa part of the poem, as its main purport is to give an explicit recommendation of the First Route which is only implicitly involved in the pejorative description of human practice in the Doxa part, e.g., at в 8.53-59. Besides, the Alêtheia part of в 8 contains (38-41) a similar discussion of human opining and linguistic practice as opposed to the correct attitude toward Alêtheia.
[26] *The Route*, p. 193.

To begin with my rendering of the second part of the quotation, I reject the clumsy construction ἔστι γὰρ εἶναι, "there is to-be," which has no more sense than Tarán's incorrect "for there is *Being*." [27] Εἶναι should be construed with μηδὲν[28] and so our text nicely parallels 2.3.

As for the opening line of в 6, it seems to be far more difficult to construe than to catch its meaning. It must rephrase the earlier idea of the relationship of νοεῖν (and λέγειν) with be-ing (ἐόν), not doctrinally this time but in the shape of a command concerning our actual asserting and thinking. The most plausible construction seems to be to take ἐόν as the formal object of λέγειν τε νοεῖν τε (see below, pp. 42-45), and to understand the line as "it is right that one's (τὸ) asserting and thinking is < an assertion and thinking > of 'what-is'." Thus most properly the first route is commended and the second one forbidden. The pregnant construction seems to underline the specific relationship of νοεῖν and its quasi-internal object ἐόν which may be compared with the later situation when its proper internal object (νοητόν) is fully identical with Being or What-Is.[29] As a matter of fact Simplicius[30] has the same interpretation: ὅπερ ἄν τις ἢ εἴπῃ ἢ νοήσῃ τὸ ὄν ἔστι – "whatever one asserts or thinks, is Being."

Next follows the phrase "this I bid you ponder" (в 6.2) which is commonly taken as referring to the previous line, which is quite possible. However, I like to connect it with what follows in в 6.3ff. and take the γὰρ in в 3 as explanatory (after the *verbum cogitandi*).[31]

> This I bid you ponder: first of all I bar you from *that* route of quest, and then again from this one along which wander mortals who know nothing, two-headed; indeed helplessness in their bosoms steers their thought adrift: they are carried along deaf and blind at the same time, stupified, a horde

---

[27] *Parmenides*, p. 54.

[28] For the particle δέ postponed, see Denniston, *The Greek Particles* (Oxford, 1934), pp. 185f. A remarkable parallel is found in Heraclitus, fragment в 2: τοῦ λόγου δ ἐόντος. Another nice example is found in Simplicius, *In Arist. Phys.*, 86.31: καὶ τὰ ἐπαγομένα δὲ. So the words μηδεν εἶναι are put into a stronger connection. Besides, the usual translation seems to require οὐδεν rather than μηδεν. For the sense of μηδεν in Parmenides, see Mourelatos, p. 85, n. 29.

[29] Hermann Fränkel, *Dichtung und Philosophie des frühen Griechentums* (Munich, 1968), 3: 458, and Untersteiner (see Tarán, pp. 56, 58) follow the same construction but seem to take ἔμμεναι as existential instead of copulative. Fränkel has: "Es ist erförderlich dass ein Aussagen und Denken dessen was Ist, Ist." However, the reality of thinking and asserting is not under discussion. To give full weight to ἔμμεναι ("... that that which is, *is*") should be rejected since ἔμμεναι always functions as a copula in Parmenides (see below, pp. 48-49) whereas ἐόν, which is a very important word to Parmenides, never acts as a copula (see also Fränkel, *Wege und Formen*, p. 192). See also below, pp. 48-51.

[30] *In Arist. Phys.*, 86.29.

[31] For this use see Denniston, p. 59, and also в 8.53.

without discernment by whom To Be and Not To Be are considered the
same and not the same, and the course of all of them is a boomerang course
[= self-contradictory for returning on one's "yes"]. (B 6.3-9)

Tarán[32] thinks that ταύτης in B 6.3 can only refer to the first (i.e.,
Alêtheia or positive) route mentioned in the first line and he has to take
the "I bar you" as a "momentary abandonment." [33] But his translation of
πρώτης is certainly wrong (πρώτης ... ὁδοῦ ταύτης would be clumsy Greek
for "that first way"). Of course πρώτης is to be taken predicatively: "the
first way from which I debar you." [34] In fact it *is* the second, negative
route of B 2.5-8.

To what route do B 6.4-9 refer? Tarán[35] excludes any reference to a
third route. However, it is introduced by the goddess as a route distinct
from the negative route already known. This route, however, cannot be
labeled "third route" except secondarily since it is just an awkward
combination of elements of the first and second routes. It not only
combines "what-is" and "what-is-not" but it even fails to distinguish
between "what-is" and "what-is not," which was exactly the main motive
of Parmenides' doctrine (see B 2 and B 8.15-16) and therefore, after closer
inspection, it is better that this way should not even be called a "route." [36]

Are the lines B 6.4-9 more specifically directed against some thinker or
thinkers or some other people? Tarán[37] rightly remarks that the plurals do
not exclude an allusion to a particular person as the plural may be used to
express contempt. Surely Parmenides does not refer to all mortals in
general because the πάντων of B 6.9 is qualified by the context; Parmenides
speaks of all *those* fools who are unable even to distinguish in a consistent
way between two opposites, *in casu* between Being and Non-Being. Well,
B 8.53-59 discuss the opinions of mortals who do distinguish sharply
between two opposite forms. This excludes him speaking in B 6.4-9 of all
people in general.

The lines B 6.4-9 most probably contain a contemptuous description of
Heraclitus and other people following him.[38] They are depicted as double-

[32] *Parmenides*, pp. 60f.
[33] Ibid., p. 61.
[34] Kathleen Freeman, *Ancilla to Presocratic Philosophers* (Oxford, 1948), p. 45 gives
the correct translation; Mourelatos strangely gives the correct one alongside the wrong
one (p. 77 n. 7).
[35] *Parmenides*, p. 72.
[36] Taking "route" in the strict sense of "a directed, one-way course, or an itinerary"
(Mourelatos, p. 275).
[37] *Parmenides*, pp. 61f.
[38] Cf. Tarán, pp. 61-72.

headed, deaf and blind, stupified (= "not knowing what to choose") and devoid of discernment. Hence they resort continually to evading the decisive choice prescribed in B 8.15-16 (cf. the κρίσις of B 8.15 with ἄκριτα φῦλα of B 6.7). The portrayal of a wavering Heraclitus who tries to run with the hare and hunt with the hounds is extremely malicious and fully unjustified, of course. Indeed, Parmenides must have considered him his most powerful rival.[39]

The purport of fragment B 7 brings it rather close to B 6.[40] In fact, Parmenides is asked to avoid the perverse mixture of the right and the wrong routes denounced in B 6.4-9, and not to let himself be forced toward it by much inured habit (B 7.2-3). Again that route is described as a [false] "route of quest" or "route of νοεῖν." It should be noticed that both the negative Persuasion-Alêtheia Route that brutally asserts that things that *are* not *are* (B 7.1-2) and the Doxa alternative of this route of casting an aimless eye, an echoing ear and tongue (B 7.3-5a) are rejected. Instead the rational choice or disjunction (κρίσις) (that the ἄκριτα φῦλα of B 6.8 are unable to make), recommended by the goddess implicitly in B 2.2ff. and explicitly in B 8.15-16, should be made (B 7.5-6): "judge by rational account the much contending refutation < of the false route > delivered by me [in B 2.6-8]." As is well known, the Greek verb κρίνειν has the connotation of judging by discerning the right from the wrong ("to sift out").[41] It is most significant that in the *Sophist* Plato reports "that pronouncement of father Parmenides" as denying that "what is not" *is* and conversely that "what is" *is not* (241D6-7; cf. 237A-B, 258D5). For that matter the "parricide" which the Eleatic Visitor is going on to commit (241D) consists precisely in rejecting this Parmenidean thesis.

V. THE PURPORT OF FRAGMENT B 8

In this fragment the goddess further elucidates the radical choice for the first route of quest that makes us "perceive a thing's true nature" (νοεῖν) either by assigning the only right appellation ("what *is*") to it or by discerning what exactly is wrong about human beliefs. So the program announced in B 1.28-32 is carried out. The fragment has two parts: the first, B 8.1-49, contains the goddess' trustworthy account (πιστὸς λόγος) concerning Truth where in clarifying the Route-ὅπως ἔστι she discusses

---

[39] See below, pp. 52-53.
[40] Cf. Verdenius, pp. 54ff.
[41] Cf. P. Chantraine, *Dict. étym.*, p. 585.

the investigation of "being(ness)" as the true nature of things (or, "things in their be-ingness"), whereas the second part, B 8.53-61, shows "where mortals have gone astray" (B 8.54), that is, it argues that their failure consists of using the improper ("un-real") appellations (names) that cannot help but conceal the things' unique characteristic of being(ness).

The Three Clusters of Signposts Discussed in B 8.2-49

The opening lines tell us that "the sole account that remains of the route < of quest > is that < it is the route qualifying a thing > as 'be-ing' (literally, as 'that it *is*');" of course, the first route mentioned in B 2.3 and B 6.1 is meant. Quite fortunately "there are quite a number of signposts along this route" (B 8.2-3) which may show us that we are still on the right track (rather than prevent us from going astray which was the aim of the goddess' warning in B 7.3-5). So the signposts all are indicative of equivalents of "being" and reducible into four clusters: (1) "not involved in any process of coming into being or passing away"; (2) "indivisible and cohesive"; (3) "motionless-changeless"; and (4) self-identical, self-sufficient, not incomplete but completed – the last of which provokes the comparison of ἐόν with a sphere. The characteristics ("signposts") are at the same time proofs that we are on the right track, and signs significative of ἐόν (there is possibly a hint of σημαίνειν in Parmenides' use of σῆμα here).

Each of the four clusters of characteristics are proved. B 8.6-21 gives a proof of the first cluster that concerns the fact that Being is not involved in any process. In B 15-21 this first cluster is most clearly reduced to the fundamental characteristic of "beingness":

> And the decision (κρίσις) about these lies in this: *is* or *is not*. Well, it has been decided, as is the constraint, to leave the one < course of thinking > unpracticed [literally, "left without thinking and naming"] – for it is not a true route – the other in its truth. Indeed, how could "what *is*" be lying in the future, and how could it be in a process of *getting* to be. For if it were in such a process then it *is* not, nor if its being lies somewhere in the future.[42] In this manner coming to be and obliterative perishing are radically ruled out.[43]

---

[42] "Being can be expressed at any moment by 'estin'" (Tarán, p. 114). The purport of these lines seems to be the radical contradistinction of *being* and *becoming* and to underline the actuality of Beingness. See below, pp. 48-51. So there is no crux in B 8.20 (against Mourelatos, pp. 102-103, whose disposal of the supposed crux is far from convincing).

[43] Literally, "stifled." They are now out of scope once we have found the Route of Truth (to take the verb in its literal sense would contradict Parmenides' doctrine). This verse is referred to in B 8.27b-28: "since coming-to-be and passing away strayed far and wide, driven off by trustworthiness (πίστις ἀληθής; cf. B 1.30).

So the first main characteristic is closely connected with the third one already announced in B 8.5-"Nor lies Being (ἐόν) somewhere in the past, nor in the future, since it is *now*, altogether" – where Being's actuality is also stressed. It should be noticed that to admit "*was*" or "*will be*" to the characteristics of Being amounts to the introduction of ὄλεθρος and γένεσις as belonging to the true nature.

The second cluster is concerned with Being's cohesiveness, continuity and homogeneity that do not allow any distinction or division. It is elaborated in B 8.22-25:

> Nor is What-Is divisible since It is all alike. Nor is It somewhat more here and somewhat less there, which might prevent It from cohering, but everything is full of What-Is. Therefore, all is continuous, for What-Is consorts with What-Is.

The third cluster (elaborated in B 8.26-31) concerns Being's immunity to change and motion and its impassiveness and complete independence ("self-sufficiency") which are founded on the exclusion of any form of process.[44]

The fourth cluster is about Being's completeness and plenitude.[45] It is noticeable that this characteristic gets the bulk of the goddess' attention and takes up no less than eighteen lines (B 8.32-49). The completeness of Being is inferred from its radical independence:

> Wherefore it is not right that What-Is should be incomplete; indeed, it is in no need; otherwise[46] Being would be in need of everything. (B 8.32-33)

But, the goddess continues, you will find Being everywhere and nothing but Being (B 8.33-41 – discussed below). Next the completeness is illustrated by the famous image of the sphere. In fact this image involves a neat interweaving of several characteristics mentioned before: completeness, homogeneity, equal intensity and sameness:

> And so since there is an outermost bound, it is rounded off (τετελεσμένον): like the expanse of a ball nicely circular from every side, from the center

---

[44] B 8.27b-28 (see the previous note). Mourelatos is wrong in finding (p. 117) the argument for Being's changelessness in B 8.6-21 since there *radical actuality* is given as its characteristic and the argument there clearly is against coming-to-be and passing away, not against change and motion as such.

[45] To be well distinguished from the fact that the All is full of Being (B 8.24).

[46] For this use of ἄν (κεν) see R. Kühner, *Ausführliche Grammatik der griechischen Sprache*, 3rd ed. by B. Gerth (1898), 1: 214 (who mention *Iliad*, 3.56-57). The usual taking of ἐόν as a hypothetical participle seems unnecessary. My preference for taking ἐόν for τὸ ἐόν is based on the high degree of technicality of the term ἐόν in Parmenides. See above, p. 37, n. 29 and below, pp. 48-51.

equally advanced in every direction. For this (i.e., Being) may not be somewhat bigger nor somewhat smaller here or there. For neither is there what-is-not which might stop it from reaching homogenity, nor is it in any way possible that what-is should be here more than what-is and there less, since it is all inviolate. For being from every side equal to itself it is present (κύρει) within its bounds equally. (B 8.42-49)

The Meaning of B 8.33-41: Mind's Commitment to "What-Is"

These lines are commonly regarded as containing the central issue in Parmenides' metaphysical doctrine. Indeed, they give a basic discussion of the relationship of mind to the things there are, more properly of that between νοεῖν and true Being. The passage is mostly considered a digression or recapitulation on Thought and Being. However, Moure-latos[47] rightly links it up with the previous argument on the completeness of Being. For that matter, that argument is continued after our passage.

Although nearly all critics read the first line as confirming thought's commitment to Being, both the interpretation of this view and the most plausible construction of the verse have been eagerly debated so far. In accordance with what has been said about B 6.1 (above, p. 37), I take B 8.34 to mean that what is aimed at by correct νοεῖν is "being-ness." As to the construction, ταὐτόν must be the predicate, not the subject (against Mourelatos),[48] and the sentence asserts the "sameness" of aiming at something by νοεῖν and the "be-ing" of the object of thought (νόημα).

The construction is not quite clear. Some critics take οὕνεκεν as "where-fore" which (in maintaining ταὐτόν as predicate) gives: "the same is thinking and the object of thinking." But this seems to be rather weak for if the "sameness" is explained as Parmenides himself does, the line says nothing but the co-occurrence of thinking and its object, but such is not peculiar of thinking (the same can be said of "to beat" or "to eat," it seems). Therefore one should take οὕνεκεν as "that" (= ὅτι; it may be used instead of ὅπως of B 2.3 and B 8.9 for metrical reasons). But then the

[47] *The Route*, p. 165.
[48] Ibid., pp. 165ff. He renders it as: "And the same thing is to be thought and (is) wherefore is the thinking" (p. 166). There are three strong arguments against Mourelatos' construction. First he takes ταὐτόν as referring back to τὸ ἐόν (discussed in the previous lines), but this use of it is late (see Liddell and Scott, s.v.). Besides, in his interpretation, fragment B 8.34 is tautological (cf. Tarán, p. 121; in spite of Mourelatos' attempt to refute Tarán: *The Route*, pp. 167-169). Finally, because of the explanation given in B 8.35-37 ταὐτόν must refer to the "sameness" of two distinct things and, therefore, cannot mean some one thing.

construction defended by Tarán and some other scholars,[49] who all take
νόημα to govern the that-clause, is not possible since the that-clause must
follow the conjunction; otherwise the renderings "for the sake of which,"
"wherefore" or "because" seem to be unavoidable. That is why I take
νόημα (basic sense: "that which is thought"; see Liddell and Scott, s.v.) for
"the *thing* which is thought of" [50] and supply a repetitionof the preceding
νοεῖν (τε καὶ < νοεῖν > οὕνεκεν ἔστι νόημα) – "and to think that the object of
thought *is*" – that is, νοεῖν always aims at the "being-ness" of its object.
(For the meaning of *is*, see below, pp. 48-51.) For the rest, all critics who
take οὕνεκεν as "wherefore" (including Mourelatos) come to give the same
purport to в 8.34: *being* and νοεῖν are most intimately connected.[51]

The crucial point is the meaning of the phrase "the same." Most
fortunately Parmenides himself explains it in в 8.35-37:

> For not without what-is in which thinking is substantially worded[52] will
> you find thinking. For nothing is, or will be, something different from (ἄλλο
> πάρεξ) what-is.

"What-is" ("Being," ἐόν) is the inalienable element in each and every
thing since nothing *is* or will ever *be* something different from be-ing (ὄν).
Well, since correct νοεῖν is nothing else but searching for and touching
"being-ness" that is present in each and every thing, and in which νοεῖν
finds its essential expression, it actually grasps a thing *just as be-ing* rather
than in its being endowed by (or concealed with) some inessential (= "not
being-like") form. The passage on mortals' practice of giving names goes
smoothly along the same line of thought; in fact, all names are given to
ἐόν, that is, in spite of their pluriformity they all refer to ἐόν after all:

> Well, since[53] it is just *this* (i.e., ἐόν) that Fate shackled to be whole and
> unchanging, to this (i.e., ἐόν) all names are given[54] such as mortals have

---

[49] So L. Woodbury, "Parmenides on Names," *Harvard Studies in Classical Philology*,
63 (1958), 150ff., and Tarán, p. 122 (who, however, gives quite a different interpretation),
among others. It was first advanced by W. A. Heidel, "On Certain Fragments of the Pre-
Socratics," *Proceedings of the American Academy of Arts and Sciences*, 48 (1913), 722-
723.

[50] For "thought" and "name" as equivalent to "thought" and "name" including its
referent, see L. M. de Rijk, "On Ancient and Mediaeval Semantics and Metaphysics,"
Vivarium, 19 (1981), 35, 44 and 115, n. 74; 20 (1982), 111, n. 15.

[51] Cf. Mourelatos, pp. 165-177.

[52] For the sense of φατίζειν, see above, pp. 34-35; see also Woodbury, nn. 31 and 32.

[53] I prefer to connect the ἐπεί sentence with what follows, transposing the usual
punctuation marks after ἐόντος (line 37) and ἔμεναι (line 38). For ἐπεί read *in apodosi*; see,
e.g., в 8.42, в 9.1.

[54] For πάντα as internal object of ὀνομάζειν (so πάντα = all *names*), see Woodbury,
p. 149, Mourelatos, pp. 182-185, and Matson, pp. 353-356. Cf. de Rijks, "Semantics and
Metaphysics," p. 113, n. 70.

posited trusting that they are correct viz. "coming-to-be," "being and[55] not be-ing," "altering its place," and "transmuting its bright surface."[56] (ʙ 8.37b-41).

One should bear in mind that in the ancient view the practice of giving names is far more than just designating things. Rather things are really described as such-and-such.[57]

The Close Affinity between B 3, B 6.1-2 and B 8.38-41

The crux in ʙ 8.34 and ʙ 3 as well seems to lie in the meaning of ταὐτόν ("the same"). To take it as referring to a formal or material identity in the strict sense between Thought and Being would lead to some insurmountable difficulties, especially in ʙ 3 where at first glance such an identification seems to be conveyed which, for the rest, still admits of quite different interpretations.[58] However, ʙ 8.35-36 contains a clear clue; the "sameness" is explained there as a coincidence. It should be noted all the same that in ʙ 8.35-36 the coincidence (co-occurrence) is said to be between "thinking" and "be-ing" whereas in ʙ 8.34 the relation of "sameness" is between "thinking (x)" and "thinking that (x) is." So there is no assertion to the extent that thinking and Being should be the same, but that "thinking" is coextensive with "thinking that is."[59]

We have already found an interpretation of ʙ 6.1-2 along the same lines (see above, pp. 36-37). There too the fundamental idea of an intimate correlation between νοεῖν with being (ἐόν) as its internal object is conveyed. But again the relation is in point of fact that of the coextensiveness of "thinking (and asserting) (x)" and "thinking (and asserting) that (x) is." That is why I prefer the translation "it is right that one's thinking and asserting is of 'what is'," to the one proposed by others:[60] "it is right to think and to assert that Being is." The latter rendering takes ἐόν for "a

---

[55] The use of τε καί shows that the composite appellation "being and not being" is meant, such as mentioned in ʙ 6.8-9.
[56] See Mourelatos, p. 184, n. 45. For two remarkable parallels in Empedocles (DK 31, ʙ 8-9) see Mourelatos, pp. 188-189.
[57] See Mourelatos, p. 184 and the paper quoted above in note 50.
[58] See Tarán, pp. 41-44.
[59] One may compare such expressions as "to see this girl is to love her," "to put the choice is to make the choice," but the Parmenidean case is much stronger since in "νοεῖν is νοεῖν Beingness." Beingness acts so to speak as an internal object of the verb (cf. "to dream is to dream a dream"). No wonder that with later philosophers (especially Neoplatonists) the internal object of νοεῖν, viz. τὸ νοητὸν is synonymous with τὸ ὄν.
[60] See Tarán, pp. 54-58.

being" (a "thing") but then this technical term loses its specific meaning which it always had in the poem, viz., "just what-is."[61]

Finally fragment B 3: Mourelatos rightly speaks of an "undeniable syntactic ambiguity" in the case of B 3, and thinks it gratuitous to make any attempt to obtain from this line positive information regarding Parmenides' philosophical doctrine, whereas it is not likely that this passage should contain information which is not available from other fragments.[62] However, this may induce us to endeavour to give an interpretation of B 3 along the lines sketched above.

Well, a similar ταὐτόν formula is found in B 8.34 where the "sameness" is in fact a most intimate relationship of thinking and Being which is further described in terms of coextensiveness. It seems quite plausible to see B 3 in the same light and to paraphrase "for the same is thinking and being" with "for thinking cannot be found [cf. the explanation of ταὐτόν in B 8.35-6] unless as involving Being."[63]

The Remainder of B 8: On Doxa vs. Alêtheia

So far the goddess has taught the κοῦρος about the strict and un-compromising course of the First Route, viz. to understand (νοεῖν) all phenomenal things as be-ing (ἐόν) and to assert (λέγειν φράζειν φατίζειν) of each of them that it *is* (ἔστι, εἶναι). Indeed, the ἐόν is a thing's "what is" and the εἶναι is all-inclusive, in need of nothing (B 8.32-33) and so there is nothing beyond Being (B 8.12-14) and all is full of Being (B 8.24-25). Therefore, the only real choice is between *is* and *is-not* (B 8.15-16), the second alternative being awkward (B 2.5-7; B 8.17-18).

Then she continues along the same line of thought and explains to us how the arrangement (διάκοσμον, B 8.60) designed by mortals is and in what respect it differs from the trustworthy account (πιστὸς λόγος, B 8.50), namely, by distinguishing *two* contrary forms instead of arranging the world according to the only true and trustworthy principle, Be-ing (ἐόν or ὡς ἔστι). So the remainder of B 8 surely belongs to the Alêtheia approach to the world (the First Route). The mortal beliefs are not yet expounded as such in B 8.53-59 but are only exposed as offending against the principle

---

[61] See above, p. 37, n. 29 and below, pp. 48-51.

[62] Mourelatos, Preface, pp. xv f.

[63] Tarán's rendering (p. 41) "for the same thing can be thought and can exist," and that given by Mourelatos (p. 75, n. 4) "the same is there to be thought of and to be," both suffer from the difficulty of taking the epexegetic infinitive νοεῖν in the passive sense and εἶναι in the active. Besides, it seems most unlikely that an epexegetic infinitive should be found *preceding* the *verbum finitum*. The grammars do not give any examples of an epexegetic infinitive preceding whatever it intends to specify.

of the First Route of quest. So there is not "a transition from Truth to Doxa"[64] in the warning statement of в 8.52, no more than such a transition could be found in в 8.38-41 where human name-giving is criticized. The goddess does not start her exposition of δόξα ("human opinion") until в 8.60 where she describes men's actual opinions. Her trustworthy account ends at в 8.49 and in в 8.50-59 she prefaces the account of the human opinions by judging them in the light of the First Route and condemning (and clarifying!) their deceptive character:

> Here I end my trustworthy account and thought concerning Truth. From now on learn you the opinions of mortals, listening to the deceptive arrangement evoked by my words. They came namely by lack of resolution[65] to use *two* forms as names[66] one of which [viz. Night] it is not right < to use as a name >, and that is where[67] they have gone astray. As opposite in frame they have distinguished them [viz. those forms][68] and marked them off from one another in giving them different signs: on one side the etherial Flame of fire, mild and very light, in every way the same with itself and not the same with the other; but that one too < they have posited > as by itself and opposite < to the former one >, dark Night, dense in frame and heavy. – Well, this likely-seeming ordering I declare to you in all detail (πάντα) so that no mortal opinion may outstrip you.

Obviously the goddess is willing to teach Parmenides a detailed human cosmogony/cosmology in order that he may not be outwitted by the "likely-seeming" learned talk of his fellow men, but she attaches much value to first pointing out the basic mistake in those mortal opinions to the extent that, in search of the true nature of things, men posited *two* forms instead of understanding (νοεῖν) the unique characteristic, "be-ing" (ἐόν). They came to gauge two essential names, Fire and Night, and were not aware that in the last analysis all names refer to ἐόν (в 8.34-41), so that their introduction of *two* essential characteristics which they so drastically marked off from one another is really deceptive. Quite ironically the first form, Fire, is described in the same terms of self-identity in which the

---

[64] Mourelatos, p. 226.

[65] For an ingenious and elegant explanation of the syntactic scramble in в 8.53, see Mourelatos, pp. 228-231, where he points to the intended ambiguity and *double entendre* in this verse.

[66] The usual rendering ("to name two forms") is not correct. Just as in в 8.38 the object of ὀνομάζειν is the name used, not the thing designated by it. See also, above, p. 43, n. 54.

[67] Is there possibly a joke intended in the phrase: "where" = "in the Dark of the night..." etc.?

[68] For the easy transition from the name to the thing named, see above, p. 43, n. 50.

nature of ἐόν was revealed (Β 8.43 ff.). This may explain why the goddess says (Β 8.54) that it is not right to assign one of the two appellations as a characteristic name to things.

Finally it should be noticed that in revealing the basic mistake in human opinions about the world (Β 8.51-59), the goddess has fulfilled what she had promised in Β 1.30-32. Indeed, she has clearly shown how the apparent pluriformity bestowed on things by human opinion and laid down in name-giving, which, no doubt, is an essential part of the κόσμον ἐπέων ἀπατηλόν (Β 8.52), should be seen as concealing the unique characteristic, "Be-ing." No doubt Parmenides will be acquainted with human cosmology and so never be outstripped by other people, but at the same time be wiser than they are in understanding in what respect every beautiful cosmology falls short.

VI. The Fragments Β 9, Β 16 and Β 19

Fragment Β 9 starts from the deceptive human understanding of things as essentially Light and Night and the corresponding semantic practice, and argues that, accordingly (ἐπεί), everything is full of Light and invisible Night together, both equal since nothingness partakes in neither.[69] Again, a characteristic of the unique ἐόν (Β 8.24) is ascribed to the deceptive products of men, this time to the combination of the two forms. For that matter, once *two* characteristic features are posited, one cannot help but assign them to all things since all and every thing cannot be deprived of what is considered to be an essential characteristic.

Fragment Β 16 teaches the dependence of actual thinking upon the actual condition of the human body:

> For such as is the state of mixture at each moment of the much wandering limbs, even such mind (νόος) has occurred to men. For it [viz. mind] is just the same as what the nature of the limbs apprehends among men, both all and each. Actual thought, indeed, is what preponderates < in the mixture > .

Fragment Β 19, which is usually regarded as the concluding lines of the poem, says that in the light of human opinion the phenomenal world originated thus and will expand and finally end. Quite far from understanding the real nature of things ("be-ing," τὸ ἐόν) men have attached a distinctive name to each of the appearances.

---

[69] Cf. Mourelatos, pp. 85-86.

VII. PARMENIDES' DOCTRINE OF BEING

The foregoing analysis of the fragments has shown that the Route of Truth is connatural with the unique characteristic of things – "being-ness" (τὸ ἐόν) – and accordingly is also concerned with True Being ("Beingness") that is concealed in the "many shaped" sensible world. In other words, the Route of Truth is there to lead us correctly through the sensible world and it serves to reveal the core of Being-ness residing (as the unique real feature) in each and every thing in our world.

I have argued earlier (pp. 33 ff.) that one should not hesitate to supply *mentally* things (inquired) of our world as the material subject of the pregnant ὡς (or ὅπως, οὕνεκεν) ἔστι formula. Father Owens seems to be quite right in assuming[70] that to the ordinary hearer of Parmenides'verses, the "(what) is" could hardly refer to anything else than the world of sense experience, the world that preceding thinkers from Thales onward had studied and described. In the very beginnings of philosophic speculation some bold spirits startled their contemporaries with direct pronounce-ments such as "It's all water," "It's all air," etc.[71] Parmenides stands in this tradition at a more developed stage. He relegates all particular instances of φύσις (water, air, etc.) to sensible appearances and focusses on "beingness" only: "It's all Be-ing(ness)." Well, the "*it*" still refers to (particulars of) our sensible world as had been the case with all his predecessors. Like all of them Parmenides is in search of some steady "entity" in all the things there are.[72]

However, as with the hearers of Parmenides' day modern readers "have drastic interpretation to make about the meaning of 'is'."[73] Indeed we have.

The Specific Sense of "is" in Parmenides

Our analysis of the fragments has shown that Parmenides points to "Being-ness" (τὸ ἐόν) as the true nature of things. But what exactly does he understand by "*is*"? Of course, one should first recall the essential characteristics of τὸ ἐόν which Parmenides gives in B 8: ungenerable, imperishable, indivisible, continuous, changeless, unique and perfectly

---

[70] Owens, p. 62.
[71] Cf. Mourelatos, pp. 216f.
[72] Even Heraclitus says of the κόσμος: "... it was always and is and will be *ever living* Fire, kindled in measure and quenched in measure" (fr. 30).
[73] Owens, p. 62.

self-identical. However, this obviously does not suffice, for modern critics have still eagerly debated the precise meaning of "*is.*"[74]

Let us start with the different grammatical uses of εἶναι, *cum annexis*, in the poem. Two main types should be distinguished:

(A) non-technical uses (for which no other word could be substituted):
1. copulative: ἔμμεναι, в 6.1, 6.2, 8.38; ἔστι, в 6.9, 8.33, 8.34 (first), 8.42, 16.4; ἔστιν, в 8.3, 8.9, 8.22 (bis), 8.24, 8.25, 8.27, 8.35, 8.48, 9.3, 16.3; εἶναι, в 8.18, 8.32, 8.39; πελέναι, в 8.45; εἴη κεν, в 8.47; εἰσίν, в 8.54; ὄντα (in my interpretation), в 1.32; ἐόν (the usual interpretation), в 8.33.
2. presentative (εἶναι = "to be there"): εἰσι, в 1.11, 2.2; ἐστίν, в 1.27, 8.15, 8.47; χρεών ἐστι, в 8.45; ἔασι, в 8.2, 19.1; ἀπέοντα, в 4.1; παρέοντα, в 4.1; χρεών ἐστιν, в 8.11; ἔστι, в 8.46; χρεῶν ἐστιν, в 8.54; cf. χύρει, в 8.49.
3. οὐκ ἔστιν (= "it is not possible"): в 2.3, 6.2.

(B) technical uses:
1. ἔστι/ν: в 2.3 (first), 2.5 (first), 8.2, 8.9, 8.16 (bis), 8.20, 8.34, 8.36; cf. ἦν, в 8.5, and ἔσται, в 8.5, 8.36.
2. εἶναι: в 1.32, 2.3, 2.5, 3, 6.8, 7.1, 8.40; cf. πέλειν, в 6.8, and πελέναι, в 8.11.
3. ἐόν: в 6.1, 8.3, 8.24, 8.25 (bis), 8.33 (in my interpretation), 8.47 (bis).
4. τὸ ἐόν: в 4.2 (bis), 8.19, 8.32, 8.35, 8.37.
5. μὴ ἐόν: в 8.7, 8.12.
6. οὐκ ἐόν: в 8.46.
7. τὸ μὴ ἐόν: в 2.7.
8. μὴ ἐόντα: в 7.1.

It is striking that unlike εἶναι the form ἔμμεναι is only used as a copula and ἐόν (τὸ ἐόν) is only used technically for Parmenides' "what is."

It is obvious that when used technically εἶναι and its cognates stand for the unique decisive "property" of things that are, which can only be paraphrased by such epithets as "ungenerable," "imperishable," etc. Surely the worst rendering would be "exist" (unless some unusual sense is given to this verb). Nor is there much use in modern distinctions such as "copulative," "identifying," "veridical," etc. They are all quite anachronistic. However, let us be on our guard against the opposite mistake of charging the ancients with some "primitive confusion." Indeed, we ought

---

[74] See Mansfeld, pp. 51-55; Tarán, pp. 33-40 and 175-201; Mourelatos, pp. 47-61 and 269-276.

to stop short of speaking of confusion or fusion in such cases.[75] In point of fact there could not possibly be in ancient thinking such a "fusion" of elements which were never separated out until modern times. Nor has a general meaning covering distinct sub-meanings *per se* anything to do with primitive thinking. Is Greek a primitive language because with its particle δέ it confuses (sic) such diverse meanings as "*but*" and "*for*"? Parmenides apparently was not in want of differentiating among existential, copulative, identifying, and other uses of εἶναι; his use of this verb does not exclude nor single out any of them. The only thing we can do is try to paraphrase that over-all meaning of εἶναι.

To my mind, of the modern labels, "veridical" (Charles Kahn) and "speculative" come closest to it. But the former is too reflexive in relating Being to human apprehension ("it is true [the case], that ...") and because of its connection with states of affairs instead of things (somebody or something *is* but is not the case). Mourelatos' label "speculative" is clearly related to predication (he speaks of "speculative predication")[76] and, in fact, is a special case of the copulative use.

First of all we should get rid of any connotation of syntax; the verb's *semantic value* is under consideration, not its syntactic use. This semantic value must be somehow opposite to that of φαίνεσθαι and δοκεῖν (see B 1.30-32) both of which have some subjective flavour about them. To my mind εἶναι is best rendered by "to be given," "to present itself," "to occur." This basic meaning covers all other meanings. But we have to start from the technical term ἐόν rather than from the ambiguous εἶναι which is also used in its harmless grammatical sense (see above, p. 49). Well, the substantivated participle ἐόν is used as a *name* (not as a predicate); it is said of *things*: "presenting itself," "being there," "occurring in our world," "existing." It could also be said of *states of affairs* – "being the case" – but in point of fact it is not used this way in Parmenides. Well, the *name* (or appellation) "ἐόν" (= "*what is*") can also be attached predicatively to a thing; then the formula is "**it is ἐόν*" is replaced by "it *is*" (ὅπως [or ὡς] ἔστιν).

Thus the finite form ἔστιν and the infinite εἶναι come up for consideration. They signify

(A)   absolutely, "to present itself"
  1. said of things: "to be there," "to occur in our world," "to exist"
  2. said of states of affairs: "to be the case"
  3. said of an account: "to be true"

---

[75] Cf. Mourelatos, p. 195, n. 5.
[76] Ibid., pp. 56-61.

(B) in a qualified sense, "to present itself *as* (*qua*) something," "to be
   something," "to be of some quality." The verb, then brings in its
   absolute meaning as part of a sememe in which it is mixed up with a
   property ("be-φ"), "being-φ."
   1. "speculative" ("essential predication"): e.g., Thales' "It's all
      water" ([the] true nature is designated)
   2. "identifying": e.g., "she is my mother" (a thing's identity is clari-
      fied)
   3. in a weak copulative sense: e.g., "she is glad" (an incidental
      quality is given).

It should be now noted that what Mourelatos calls "speculative
predication," however close it is to what Parmenides intends to clarify,
still is only part of the essential (and unique) qualification ("being-water,"
"being-air," etc.) whereas Parmenides, *is* (as standing for "is $\dot{\varepsilon}\acute{o}\nu$") is itself
the complete (and unique) qualification.[77] It needs no further determina-
tion ("water," "air," "being-φ") but is itself complete, rounded out,
unique, etc. It is all-inclusive, that is, inclusive of all properties and for
that reason perfect. Being is by definition full Being (hence "*plenitudo
entis*"), and so Non-Being is impossible as it is absolute Emptiness (в 2.5).
   So Being is itself a nature, in fact the unique all-inclusive nature.[78] That
is why the only names allowed are $\dot{\varepsilon}\acute{o}\nu$ and its unique counterparts
("ungenerable," etc.; see above, pp. 40-42). All other names or
appellations which mortals use refer to particularizations of the unique
perfect Being and as such are contradictions in terms. In fact they all refer
(not intentionally, it is true) to $\dot{\varepsilon}\acute{o}\nu$. The famous pair, "Light" and "Night,"
are not an exception; they are just one too many (в 8.54) and in their
exclusivity all the more dangerous.

Alétheia versus Doxa

   As has been argued before (pp. 33-35) Being is the counterpart of $\nu o \varepsilon \tilde{\iota} \nu$,
$\varphi \rho \acute{\alpha} \zeta \varepsilon \iota \nu$ and $\varphi \alpha \tau \acute{\iota} \zeta \varepsilon \iota \nu$, all of which as verbs connote "reaching a thing's true

---

[77] I think that there is some confusion in Mourelatos' account (pp. 56-60) of the
matter. It is as correct to say that "speculative predication" "makes better contact with the
metaphor of the routes of questing" (p. 59) than Kahn's "veridical usage," as it is no less to
say that the copula functions precisely as "the conveyer to the true nature of a thing."
However, not the conveyer is under consideration but *what is conveyed* by it. So the "*is*"
as what is being conveyed should be focused on, rather than the copula "is" as conveyer
that completely hides itself in the mixture *is* ("is $\dot{\varepsilon}\acute{o}\nu$").
[78] For *being* as "all embracing Nature" in Plato's *Sophist*, see de Rijk, "Semantics and
Metaphysics," pp. 42ff.

nature," "arriving at its essence." This implies a penetration of the
disguises of the manifold forms and shapes with which the world is
endowed. Whoever succeeds in seeing through all the disguises walks
along the Route of Alêtheia, but those who let themselves cheat follow a
false course. The routes all lead through the sensible world, the only one
that is given to mortals. So there are two main routes (with the perverse
deviance of the negative one – see above, p. 32), but only one single world
is given: ours. It is highly misleading, accordingly, to speak as many
critics have done[79] of "the world of Doxa" as opposed to the "world of
Alêtheia." Not until Plato did the distinction of Doxa and Alêtheia imply a
χωρισμός of two ontic worlds,[80] and those found in Parmenides' writings
are just mental – Conviction-Trust versus Opinions, or "the world as
really understood" versus "the world as appearing to mortals." This is a
tremendous distinction from the formal point of view, solid enough,
indeed, for Parmenides to build his system on. But materially speaking
there is only one world, that of sense experience, the world that includes
all of us and all and every visible and tangible thing. The doxai are *the*
world as it is presented to mortals.[81]

Parmenides' Position in the History of Philosophy

The older physicists had intended to reduce the appearances to the inner
nature residing in them, so they could say "It's all water," "It's all air," or
"The world is essentially water (or air)." In Parmenides' view, however,
in doing this they just singled out *some* feature of the sensible things and
sublimated it into the status of "inner nature." Like those who reduced all
to Light and Night they were missing the point. The decision (κρίσις) is not
between "being Light and Night" and "not-being Light and Night" (or
"being Water" and "not-being Water," etc.) but between "Be-ing" and
"not-Be-ing."

The critical attitude, introduced by Xenophanes, is most certainly found
also in Heraclitus (Frag. B 123: "the real constitution of things is

---

[79] So Tarán, passim. E.g., p. 198: "He (Parmenides) denies that anything else except
Being exists" and so *he denies the existence of the phenomenal or sensible world itself*. To
my mind one should say: so he states that the only real thing in the sensible world is
Being(ness). Tarán also joins (p. 175) most strangely the ontic "necessity of existence" to
the epistemic "impossibility of conceiving non-Being." His statement (p. 202) that "the
sensible world in which we live can have no existence whatsoever" is largely due to his
view of ἔστι = "exists," but it is still rather strange.

[80] See also Tarán, p. 187.

[81] "Die Welt, so wie sie für die Menschen da ist" – H. Schwabl, "Sein und Doxa bei
Parmenides," *Wiener Studien*, 66 (1953), 59, as quoted by Fr. Owens, *A History of Ancient
Western Philosophy*, p. 59.

accustomed to hide itself"). By his doctrine of opposites he was opposed to all unjustified reductions: in our sensible world there is a perpetual change from opposite to opposite (Frag. B 126), so that it is basically wrong to name one (or two) steady form(s) as the inner nature of things. The unity of the opposites is hard for mortals to see since "they do not understand how < the universe > being at variance (yet) is self-identical: harmony consists of opposing tension, as in the bow and lyre" (Frag. B 51).

One cannot deny that Heraclitus faced the primitive approach of the physicists in a radical way. So Parmenides in defending another steady inner nature ("Be-ing") sees in him his most dangerous rival. No wonder that his offences against Heraclitus are the most bitter. And indeed he tries to bring Heraclitus into the company of those who, two-headed as they are, are not able to make the great decision.

Subsequent thinkers had to take into account Parmenides' doctrine and in fact could not help digesting its rigidity. Plato was the first to take the big decision so seriously that he left the idea of one world as approached by mortals along two different Routes and settled on the assumption of two separate worlds, one of Unshakable Being, the other of Unreliable Becoming. Aristotle, for his part, thought it possible to dispose of Plato's χωρισμός and find the inner nature of things right in themselves. No doubt it is Parmenides, cited by Fr. Owens as "one of the truly great philosophic geniuses in the history of Western thought," [82] who was the catalyst of all subsequent metaphysics.

[82] Owens, p. 76.

3

The Meaning of Potency in Aristotle

Gerard Verbeke

Katholieke Universiteit, Leuven

The concept of potency is at the very heart of Aristotle's thought; it plays a decisive role in his philosophy of nature, where it is involved in the explanation of movement and the demonstration of the existence of a prime mover. It is constantly present in the development of his metaphysics where it enables him to disclose the basic structure of sensible reality as well as the unique position of the first act, free from any kind of potency.[1] It is a key term in Aristotle's psychological teaching where it is utilized in the interpretation of sensible and intellectual knowing and in the explanation of the relationship of body and soul. As for the ethics, the concept of potency permeates the whole doctrine of moral behaviour; it dominates the teaching about ethical virtue and the definition of human perfection or happiness.

Why did Aristotle introduce that notion? What exactly did he expect from it in his philosophical inquiry of reality? Dealing with the relationship between act and potency, the Stagirite declares that, with respect to their concept and knowability, act is prior to potency.[2] This

---

[1] Book ix of Aristotle's *Metaphysics* is almost entirely dedicated to the study of act and potency; the same topic is also investigated in Book v, chapter 12. Some thirty years ago A. Smeets made a careful analysis of these texts both from a literary and philosophical viewpoint (*Act en Potentie in de Metaphysica van Aristoteles* [Leuven, 1952]).

[2] *Metaph.* ix, 8, 1049b10-17: the concept of act is prior to that of potency because this latter involves the concept of act and could not be understood without it. Does the concept of act necessarily include that of potency? Not according to the Stagirite; act means perfection, it can exist without potency. But when act comes to be, then it refers to potency: in this sense act and potency are correlative concepts.

Graceful Reason: Essays in Ancient and Medieval Philosophy Presented to Joseph Owens, CSSR, ed. Lloyd P. Gerson. Papers in Mediaeval Studies 4 (Toronto: Pontifical Institute of Mediaeval Studies, 1983), pp. 55-73. © P.I.M.S., 1983.

sentence could mean that act represents a higher degree of intelligibility, what is certainly true in the framework of Aristotle's thought. A universal is more knowable than particular things, what is immutable and uncompounded is also more intelligible than what is changing and compounded, and finally, what is necessary is more knowable than what is contingent. Hence, the highest level of intelligibility is represented by what is universal, unchangeable, uncompounded, and necessary.[3] That is what Aristotle calls the most intelligible in itself: in this respect act is undoubtedly more intelligible than potency. The situation is different, however, when knowability with respect to us is envisaged: the most immediately and directly knowable for us is sensible reality, which is compounded and constantly changing. We have to start from what is immediately given in sensible experience in order to reach what is in itself the most intelligible. Although pure act is the most intelligible object, it could not be directly attained by human knowledge, but only on the basis of an argument starting from sensible knowledge.[4] In Aristotle's view act is in itself more knowable than potency; is it also more knowable for us? Our author believes it is: potency is not immediately given in sensible experience. It is not directly noticeable, and may only be known through act.[5] The potency of a given being is gradually displayed in the process of actualization. It is impossible to grasp directly the hidden possibilities of a particular thing if they remain at the level of mere potency. Aristotle wants us to start from experience, which corresponds to his general theory of knowledge: one notices that things ceaselessly become what they were not, without being able, however, to develop into anything else, no matter what. The potency of a being is not unlimited, it is confined within the boundaries of a particular area. This is already obvious in the field of technical activity: the materials to be used depend on the product that is intended. The same obtains in biological evolution: the development of a germ is determined by the kind of seed under consideration. The range of possibilities of a human being is very broad with respect to

---

[3] *Metaph.* xii, 3, 1078a9: in this passage Aristotle explains that what is logically prior to something else possesses a higher degree of intelligibility and is more ἀκριβές. This term has an ontological meaning: some objects are more "accurate" (intelligible) than others. In Aristotle's opinion the ultimate object of metaphysics is the most intelligible (*Metaph.* i, 2, 982a25-b4).

[4] Cf. G. Verbeke, "Démarches de la réflexion métaphysique chez Aristote," in *Aristote et les problèmes de méthode* (Louvain-Paris, 1961), pp. 107-129.

[5] *Metaph.* ix, 8, 1049b16. Aristotle states: ὥστ' ἀνάγκη τὸν λόγον < τοῦ λόγου > προϋπάρχειν καὶ τὴν γνῶσιν τῆς γνώσεως. The knowledge of act must precede that of potency: of course in the evolution of an individual being potency comes first, since the development proceeds from potency to act (*Metaph.* xii, 6, 1072a3).

learning, moral life, skillful activity and other performances, but they also are limited, and we have to wait until their actualization before we can be sure that they are present.

The concept of potency seems to be closely connected with that limited scope of possibilities which are present in a particular being. Everything is endowed with a certain amount of possibilities and it is able to evolve within these frontiers. Hence, Aristotle concludes that the development of a being is not from mere absence to the presence of an act, but from a potential presence to an actual presence.[6] If the evolution were from mere non-being to actualization, it would be hard to explain why a process of becoming is possible in some cases and not in others. So the potency present in individual beings could not be denied because they are able to develop in one sense, but not in another. As for knowing whether a particular potency is present or not, one has to rely on its actualization. Of course, with regard to individual beings of a certain kind, one can expect that they will be gifted with the same possibilities as other individuals belonging to the same species. And yet it still remains true that our knowledge of a potency is attained as a result of its actualization.

Since potency is not directly observable, it must be known in an analogical way.[7] What kind of analogy? Aristotle does not fully specify his teaching: potency is not a univocal notion; it has various meanings.[8]

---

[6] In Aristotle's opinion a development never proceeds from a mere non-being or a total emptiness, but from a potential presence to an actual realization: ἀεὶ γὰρ ἐκ τοῦ δυνάμει ὄντος γίγνεται τὸ ἐνεργείᾳ ὂν ὑπὸ ἐνεργείᾳ ὄντος (Metaph. IX, 8, 1049b24). In the field of knowing this potential disposition is also required: learning could not start from nothing; in order to be able to learn something, one must already possess some initial knowledge (Metaph. IX, 8, 1050a1). Aristotle is cautious and adds "probably" (ἴσως): he does not hesitate about the necessity of some previous knowledge to be there, but about the kind of knowledge that is required. According to him human learning in general could never start if there is not at least some antecedent knowledge already there (Anal. Post. I, 1, 71a1-17).

[7] Metaph. IX, 6, 1048a35: δῆλον δ' ἐπὶ τῶν καθ' ἕκαστα τῇ ἐπαγωγῇ ὃ βουλόμεθα λέγειν, καὶ οὐ δεῖ παντὸς ὅρον ζητεῖν ἀλλὰ καὶ τῷ ἀνάλογον συνορᾶν. Dealing with the notion of potency Aristotle rightly points to the fact that it is not always necessary to look for a definition, but that it may be adequate to proceed in an analogical way, starting from individual cases; this process is an inductive one and had been used frequently by Socrates. Starting from an actual case of building we may understand what it means to be able to build; the same obtains with respect to being awake and asleep, to seeing and having the eyes shut, to matter already shaped and mere matter, to a ready product and something unwrought. In all these instances the comparison between two terms suggests the meaning of potency. In his Physics (I, 7, 191a7) the Stagirite also declares the substratum to be known through analogy (κατ' ἀναλογίαν).

[8] Phys. VIII, 4, 255a30; Metaph. IX, 1, 1046a4. The various meanings of potency refer to a first kind or meaning, a basic significance which is found everywhere where potency is involved: it is a principle of change in something else or in the same being insofar as it is other (Metaph. IX, 1, 1046a9-11).

What potency means exactly has to be clarified by comparing different cases of becoming in which it is involved. Potency may be an active principle of movement produced in something else or even in itself insofar as it is distinct from what is moved; it may also be a passive ability to be moved by something else or by itself inasmuch as it is different from the moving cause.[9] In both cases there is a distinction between the mover and what is moved. This kind of potency may be called kinetic (κίνησις) and is related to all sorts of change, becoming, and movement.[10] If a movement or change takes place, Aristotle concludes that, before it began, the potency to that kind of becoming was already present in the being concerned. Of course, there are many sorts of transformations and some of them affect things much more deeply than others.[11] There is a variety of accidental changes, which are rather superficial and do not touch the substance of things; but there are also substantial transformations, e.g., the assimilation of food by a living being. In this latter case inorganic matter becomes part of a living organism. In all these changes, the kind of potency involved is still kinetic potency. From these various levels of transformations our author arrives at the notion of non-kinetic potency, belonging to the structure or composition of beings. In order to secure the continuity of change some substratum will always be required.[12] When the transformation is merely accidental, the substratum will be substance. So the same substance may be changed in various ways without losing its identity; it is in potency to accidental changes. When, however, the transformation occurs at a deeper level, there will be a substantial change. Here again some continuity has to be guaranteed. That means that a substratum is needed, and in this case it will be prime matter, which is merely potential, without any formal determination.[13] Dealing with the origin of human potencies or powers Aristotle states that some of them are inborn, belonging to the natural equipment of an individual; others are acquired by repeating frequently the same acts. In this way one may get some technical skills or moral habits. Finally, some of them are the result of study and learning: due to the study of grammar one becomes able to write his language without mistakes.[14] By comparing these various cases in which potency is involved, one realizes the general features charac-

---

[9] *Metaph.* IX, 1, 1046a10-13; V, 12, 1019a15.
[10] *Metaph.* IX, 3, 1047a30: Aristotle states that the name ἐνέργεια has been shaped in connection with ἐντελέχεια and was originally applied to movement.
[11] *Phys.* I, 7, 190a31: Πολλαχῶς δὲ λεγομένου τοῦ γίγνεσθαι.
[12] *Phys.* I, 7, 190a31-b3.
[13] *Phys.* I, 7, 191a8-13.
[14] *Metaph.* IX, 5, 1047b31-35.

terizing this basic concept. Our author repeatedly stresses the fact that potency is unable to be actualized by itself. We shall later come back to this important aspect.

Aristotle's doctrine of potency is the result of a critical dialogue with former philosophers. The position of our author differs clearly from that of Parmenides: the latter rejects firmly change or becoming because it is not liable to any rational interpretation. Whatever the information of sensible experience about the physical world may be, if it is contrary to the teaching of intellectual insight, it must be repudiated.[15] This view of Parmenides about the value of perception is radically different from that of the Stagirite, who teaches that all intellectual knowledge originates from sensible experience. Aristotle starts from accepting the information of the senses concerning becoming and movement and then he endeavours to explain philosophically these data. In this context he appeals to the notion of potency. As to the criticism of Parmenides against movement, Aristotle believes it to be worthless although it is true that being could not proceed either from being or from non-being.[16] Our author agrees that from absolute non-being nothing could ever originate. But change never means a beginning from absolute nothingness. In Aristotle's view change is a passage from potency to act under the impact of something else. In this doctrine potency is not absolute non-being; it is the possibility of a particular being to be transformed in a certain way under the influence of an external cause. As it has already been stated, the continuity of movement and change always implies some potential principle, which is the substratum.[17] If previous philosophers had already

[15] *Phys.* I, 8, 191a23-33. When Aristotle deals with the philosophers who reject multiplicity and change he tries to explain why they went astray. They endeavoured to disclose the truth (τὴν ἀλήθειαν) and nature (τὴν φύσιν) of all beings. The term "truth" probably refers to the first part of Parmenides' philosophical poem, the way of truth, which reveals the authentic nature of things. The term φύσις in this context corresponds to "truth": it is not taken in its original meaning, which points to growth and development. These philosophers did not uncover the true nature of reality. They erred through lack of experience (ὑπὸ ἀπειρίας). Instead of relying on the data of experience, they repudiated them on behalf of the requirements of reason. Basically, Aristotle criticizes these thinkers because they appeal to theoretical speculations instead of grounding their considerations on the teaching of sensible knowledge.

[16] *Phys.* I, 8, 191a27-31.

[17] *Phys.* I, 8, 191a31: ὑποκεῖσθαι γάρ τι δεῖν; cf. *Metaph.* VIII, 1, 1042a32. Is matter a component of all beings? Not according to the Stagirite: all sensible substances are compounded of a material principle, and this material subject is οὐσία although in a different sense from the substantial form. Matter is not an individual being in act, but only in potency, whereas the formal principal is a τόδε τι and may be conceived of as something independent (*Metaph.* VIII, 1, 1042a25-29). Our author even declares that matter is in itself unknowable (*Metaph.* VII, 10, 1036a8), but it is postulated in order to ensure the continuity of change (cf. *Metaph.* VIII, 5, 1044b27).

understood the concept of substratum and the role it has to play in the explanation of change, they would not have gone astray. Change could not be adequately interpreted either by the concept of otherness, or by that of inequality, or by that of non-being. It means an actualizing process that is incomplete since it is going on.[18] In this process potency and act are both incomplete; potency is incomplete because it extends beyond what has already been realized; act is also incomplete because the development does not stop, but goes further. Thus change is not a passage from absolute non-being to being.

Aristotle's interpretation of movement differs strongly from the one put forward by Heraclitus. In his opinion all things are in a permanent conflict, not only among each other, but even with themselves. Conflict is the father and king of everything because it is the stimulating and propelling force of all change that occurs in the world.[19] Why do things become, why do they not remain in the situation in which they happen to be? To this question the general reply of Aristotle would be that things are not only act, but also potency. Insofar as they are potency, they are able to evolve beyond the boundaries of their present situation; if they were only act they would be definitively fixed in the state in which they are. This development occurs whenever the conditions for the actualization of a potency are fulfilled.[20] According to Heraclitus becoming never stops because the internal conflict is never stabilized. There is never a definitive supremacy of one of the opposing powers, which continue struggling against each other, never being eliminated for ever. Day and night, life and death, peace and war oppose each other in a permanent battle and they will alternately oppress the adversary power, but never extirpate it.[21] So the indestructible conflict of adversary forces produces the permanent evolution that takes place in the world and never comes to an end. In

---

[18] *Phys.* III, 2, 201b19-24. Some philosophers appeal to the notions of otherness, inequality and non-being, because change is something undetermined (ἀόριστον). It is unsteady, fluctuating, passing from one situation to another. In Aristotle's view change is undetermined, neither potency nor act, but an incomplete act corresponding to an incomplete potency (III, 2, 201b31).

[19] H. Diels, *Die Fragmente der Vorsokratiker*, 6th ed. rev. W. Kranz, 3 vols. (Berlin, 1952), 22: Herakleitos, B53.

[20] *Metaph.* IX, 7, 1049a8-18.

[21] Diels-Kranz, *Die Fragmente*, 22, Herakleitos, B10: καὶ ἐκ πάντων ἓν καὶ ἐξ ἑνὸς πάντα; cf. B50: σοφόν ἐστιν ἓν πάντα εἶναι. Nature as well as technical activity brings opposing components together. In the area of human performances Heraclitus refers to painting, music and grammar. Contrary constituents are put together and amalgamated into a unity. According to fr. B67: "God is day-night, winter-summer, war-peace, satiety-famine" (transl. K. Freeman).

Heraclitus' doctrine there is no real development, no pregress and nothing new. Things remain for ever what they are, namely, conflicting powers which alternately oppress their opponent. If death follows after life, it is because it was present in life from the very beginning. In Aristotle's view things are really transformed due to the impact of external factors. If beings develop and change, it is because they bear within themselves the potency of becoming different, but it is also because they have been influenced by something else that actualized their potential disposition.[22] In Aristotle's opinion, too, there is nothing radically new that is introduced. A potency could only be actualized by an already existing act. But at least something new is realized with respect to a particular being. The actualization of a potency is something new, although it could not take place without the influence of an act that already exists.[23]

Dealing with the notion of potency Aristotle also has to face the teaching of the Megarians. According to them potency coincides with the actual exercise of a technical skill; a craftsman is only a craftsman when he is practising his art. A man has the potency to build when he is building; on the contrary, when he is not building, he apparently does not possess the potency to do it.[24] This probably refers to one of the most vulnerable aspects of the Aristotelian doctrine on potency, namely, its knowability. As we have stated, potency is not immediately knowable. It can be grasped only indirectly through the act, that is, through the process of actualization. When a particular act has been realized, one may conclude that, before it was there, the potency to receive it was already

---

[22] Aristotle always stresses the distinction between the mover and what is moved, even when both belong to the same being (*Metaph.* ix, 1, 1046a10; ix, 2, 1046b4; ix, 8, 1049b7; v, 12, 1019a15 and 1020a4; *De caelo* iii, 2, 301b17). As for animals the question arises whether or not they move themselves. In a sense they do, but here again a distinction has to be made between what is moving and what is moved. It is quite certain that whatever changes is moved by something; it might, however, be difficult to draw a clear distinction within an animal between the moving principle and what is moved (*Phys.* viii, 4, 254b28-33).

[23] In this respect Aristotle agrees with the Eleatic school which held that nothing could ever originate from non-being (*Phys.* i, 8, 191a30). Could the first act produce something without using some material cause? The question is not raised and is clearly foreign to the Aristotelian mind.

[24] *Metaph.* viii, 3, 1046b29-32; viii, 3, 1047a19-20. The account of the Megarian doctrine is rather elliptical. Do these philosophers claim potency to be certainly absent when the process of actualization is not going on? This would not be in conformity with the eristic trend of their thought. Besides, their attack would be very weak; they could hardly demonstrate that the potency was not there before the actualization started. What they probably assert is that nobody could ever prove the potency to be there when it is not being actualized.

present. The Megarians strongly opposed this view and pushed their criticism to its extreme consequences. Whereas Aristotle concludes that potency must have been present *before* the actualization process started, the Megarians state that potency can only be known to be there when the actualization is occurring. A man who is actually building a house certainly possesses the potency to do what he is doing. Could one ever know that he already possessed the capacity to do this before he started his activity? Not according to the Megarians; in their view potency manifests itself in the actual exercise of an act only. Do the Megarians totally deny the existence of potency? Not properly; they simply deny the possibility to know that a particular potency is present, when it is not actually realized.

The answer of Aristotle to this objection is closely linked to some basic aspects of his philosophical system. According to him the special capacity of a craftsman is the result of a gradual process in which similar acts have been repeatedly performed. These acts, when they have been performed, do not completely disappear without leaving any trace in the acting individual. By repeating frequently the same acts a man becomes able to perform them more easily and in a more adequate way, progressively acquiring a special competence with respect to this activity.[25] A human being does not live in the present only. The past is constantly present in the development of man's existence. An individual is not only responsible for his behaviour, he is also the outcome of his acts. To some extent he makes himself what he is. In Aristotelian language it means that by performing frequently the same acts a man acquires gradually a particular habit, a stable propensity to perform these acts and a growing capacity to achieve them with competence.[26] This occurs primarily in the area of

---

[25] *Eth. Nic.* II, 1, 1103a26 sqq. Aristotle makes a distinction between inborn and acquired capacities. The former are not the result of previous activity. Thus, the faculty of sight is not the outcome of some acts of seeing, for it belongs to the natural equipment of a human being. But in the field of technical work and in moral life, habits are acquired by repeatedly performing similar acts: ἃ γὰρ δεῖ μαθόντες ποιεῖν, ταῦτα ποιοῦντες μανθάνομεν (1103a32). One becomes a skillful builder by exercising this activity. The same rule applies to moral behaviour. An individual becomes just or temperant or courageous by frequently accomplishing acts belonging to these virtues. The nature of the habits is also the result of the preceding acts. One will become a capable builder if the former acts have been performed adequately.

[26] In Aristotle's opinion education has to start from early childhood (εὐθὺς ἐκ νέων: *Eth. Nic.* II, 1, 1103b23). Lawgivers are quite conscious of this necessity. The laws of a political society are the embodiment of a moral ideal. They have to be imposed on young people in a compulsory way in order to bring them to moral praxis and then to ethical knowledge, which enables them to judge correctly moral values in the changing situations of life (*Eth. Nic.* II, 1, 1103b2-6; x, 9, 1179b32 sqq.).

technical skills, but also in that of moral conduct. Moral virtues are also habits. They are not inborn, nor do they belong to the natural equipment of an individual; rather, they are the result of human behaviour. Each individual is the creator of his habits in the area of technical skills as well as in moral life. A habit is not something that suddenly arises and then after a while totally disappears. As the result of previous actions, and having been acquired gradually, it is characterized by its stability and the competence of its performances.[27] When a man is able to build a house with competence and facility, it must be because he had accomplished this activity many times before and had already acquired a special capacity for doing this work. And when such a craftsman stops building, he does not lose immediately the habit he possesses. He may lose it of course after a long period of inactivity, but not immediately.[28] So the answer given by Aristotle to the Megarians is that the capacity of a craftsman neither suddenly arises nor suddenly disappears. Looking at the work performed by a craftsman, one may conclude that he possesses in a stable way the potency of his art as a result of former acts. Of course, the Megarians could insist that only during the actual exercise of an activity is the capacity to do it manifested. The difference between the two opponents may be summarized as follows: in Aristotle's opinion the exercice of an activity may display the presence of a steady capacity, whereas in the opinion of the Megarians it only reveals the actual presence of a potency, at the moment and for the time of the performance.

The same line of thought is expressed in the other arguments of the Megaric school. Is it possible to assert that something is perceptible when it is not actually perceived? Not according to the Megarians: the potency to be perceived manifests itself within the act of perception and the

---

[27] *Metaph.* ix, 3, 1046b33-1047a4. The question has been raised whether the Aristotelian doctrine of act and potency primarily springs from the observation of biological processes or from the experience of technical work. W. Jaeger rightly maintains against H. Meyer (*Der Entwicklungsgedanke bei Aristoteles* [Bonn, 1909], pp. 66-83) that this important theory stems from the activity of craftsmen and the way they proceed in realizing a product (*Aristoteles. Grundlegung einer Geschichte seiner Entwicklung*, 2nd ed. [Berlin, 1955], pp. 410-411). A similar paradigm has been chosen by Aristotle when he elaborated his ethical treatise.

[28] *Metaph.* ix, 3, 1047a1-2. Aristotle does not deny that it is impossible to lose some habit that has been acquired. This may be caused by oblivion or illness or even by time, when the activity was not exerted during a long period. Then our author adds: οὐ γὰρ δὴ τοῦ γε πράγματος φθαρέντος, ἀεὶ γὰρ ἔστιν. Technical skills could not develop without the necessary material; if this material were missing, they could not be exercised anymore. Our author, however, immediately adds that matter will never perish, but it will always be available. So what man needs for his technical performances will never be lacking.

temporal limits of this act. It is impossible to state that something is cold, warm, sweet, or in general that it is perceptible, when it is not actually known as such.[29] The intention of the Megarians is not to point to the subjective character of sensible qualities, which would depend upon the dispositions of the knowing individual. What they want to stress is that sensible qualities could not be attributed to things without the act of perception. One could not even declare that those things are endowed with the potency to be perceived. In Aristotle's view, on the contrary, the nature of things does not vary from one instant to another. Things in the physical world are perceptible because of their natural structure. They are composed of matter and form,[30] they are included in a specific category of reality, and they present some accidental features, which may be either connected necessarily with the substantial nature (properties) of things or be linked to them in a contingent way.[31] This latter category may vary under the influence of external factors without affecting the substantial nature. In his criticism of the Megarians Aristotle refers to the teaching of Protagoras who believes man to be the measure of everything:[32] if "man" is understood as an individual, then the doctrine amounts to epistemo-logical relativism, when, however, it is understood as referring to the whole of mankind, the connection with Megarian doctrine is closer. Then it means that things exist insofar as they are perceived, which is decidedly contrary to the Aristotelian view.

Another argument of the Megarians is related to perception. The presence of a faculty could only be asserted when it actually exercises its activity. When is it possible to state that an individual is endowed with the power of seeing, hearing, or smelling? Only when he is actually seeing, hearing, or smelling. When an act is being performed, the Megarians agree that there must be a principle able to execute it. But when this activity is not exerted, it is impossible to show the power to be there.[33]

---

[29] *Metaph.* IX, 3, 1047a4-6.

[30] *Metaph.* VIII, 1, 1042a25-31.

[31] Cf. G. Verbeke, "La notion de propriété dans les Topiques," in *Aristotle on Dialectic, the Topics,* ed. G. E. L. Owen (Oxford, 1968), pp. 257-276.

[32] *Metaph.* IX, 3, 1047a6: Aristotle believes the Megarians to side with Protagoras when they claim things to be perceptible only if they are actually perceived. The view of Protagoras, however, seems to be more radical. He declares that things exist or do not exist insofar as they are perceived or not perceived. It is true the method of arguing is the same in both cases: if things are not actually perceived, one could not know, according to the Megarians, that they are perceptible or even, according to Protagoras, that they exist.

[33] *Metaph.* IX, 3, 1047a7-10. Here again Aristotle's account of the Megaric doctrine seems to be summarized and simplified. Did the Megarians assert that an individual suddenly becomes blind or deaf when he has finished a particular act of perception? That

Here again the reaction of the Stagirite is quite negative. Aristotle agrees that one can only conclude the existence of a perceiving power from the activity that is displayed. This, however, does not entail that the power comes to be when the perceiving act starts and passes away when it stops. In his view man is equipped with some cognitive faculties which belong to his being in a permanent way. It is absurd to hold that the same individual becomes blind and deaf several times a day. By means of the activity that is accomplished we are able to discover the presence of a permanent faculty which belongs to the nature of a human being.[34] Man is considered by Aristotle to be a rational animal. In Aristotle's view this rational ability is not something transitory that suddenly arises and afterwards disappears. To be a rational animal is a distinctive characteristic of human beings that is always present. Man does not lose his faculties when he ceases exercising them.

A final argument of the Megarians concerns the process of becoming. Only what is actually becoming may be said to have the potency of becoming. Without this actual process nothing can be declared to possess that potency. It reveals itself only within the development, neither before nor after it.[35] But if a being does not possess this potency, it will always remain in the condition in which it happens to be and not change. A man who is sitting or standing will constantly remain sitting or standing, which is in Aristotle's view totally contrary to sensible experience.[36] According to the Stagirite a change that actually occurs is only possible if, before it starts, the potency for that change is already present; if it is not there, change will never take place. The Megarians agree that the potency must

---

does not make sense and is not in conformity with our information about the school. The position of the Megarians is quite understandable and sharp if they simply declare that it is impossible to demonstrate the presence of any power or faculty without the process of actualization.

[34] According to the Stagirite the faculty of seeing or hearing is inborn; it is not the result of former acts, like a moral or technical habit. It is thanks to the presence of these inborn perceptive powers, that man is able to perform the corresponding acts (*Eth. Nic.* II, 1, 1103a26-31).

[35] *Metaph.* IX, 3, 1047a10: ἔτι εἰ ἀδύνατον τὸ ἐστερημένον δυνάμεως, τὸ μὴ γιγνόμενον ἀδύνατον ἔσται γενέσθαι. Aristotle starts from the concept "impossible": what is devoid of potency is impossible, in the sense that it could not become something. If the potency of becoming manifests itself only during the actual process of evolution, nothing could be said to have that potency without the process of change. Hence one may conclude that outside the changes actually going on nothing could be said to be able to evolve. Does this view entail that what is not actually changing is unable to change? That is the interpretation of Aristotle, which again seems to be a simplification of the Megaric doctrine.

[36] *Metaph.* IX, 3, 1047a12-17.

be there, when the change is taking place, but in their view it is impossible
to show the presence of any potency without the process of actualization.
In Aristotle's teaching the potency for change is a permanent feature of
the physical world. It belongs to the nature of sensible things. In this
sublunary world things come to be and pass away, they are permanently
in a process of evolution and change, they move from one place to
another, and they exist in time, which means that they constantly pass
from one situation to another. Time has an extatic character, which means
that it constantly propels things out of the situation in which they happen
to be.[37] Change and becoming are not accidental and superficial features
of the physical world; rather, they must be rooted in the deepest structure
of things. All sensible things include in their nature a material principle
that is in all respects potential. This substantial structure does not arise
when a particular motion or change takes place, but it is always there as
long as these things exist.[38]

   We have already mentioned that in Aristotle's opinion the Platonic
notion of alterity or otherness does not enable one to explain adequately
movement and change.[39] It must, however, be acknowledged according to
Aristotle that alterity or relative non-being offers a valuable answer to the
main objection of Parmenides against motion and multiplicity. According
to Plato between being and non-being there is an in-between, which is
relative non-being. Is it possible to predicate of being that it is not? It is
possible, indeed, provided some specification be added.[40] To say that a
particular being is not something else involves no contradiction. Each
particular being is much more non-being than it is being. With respect to
all other things existing in the world it is non-being because it does not
coincide with them. As for becoming, here again otherness is involved.
Things can only become what they were not before the change started.[41]

   [37] *Phy.* IV, 13, 222b16. According to Aristotle the notion of time is directly connected
with that of movement and change. When movement is grasped as a multiplicity of before
and after, awareness of time arises. Every change is by nature extatic: μεταβολὴ δὲ πᾶσα
φύσει ἐκστατικόν; cf. IV, 12, 221b3: ἡ δὲ κίνησις ἐξίστησιν τὸ ὑπάρχον. Sensible things always
exist in time, they are temporal by nature, and they never stop becoming and changing.
Consequently, a permanent potency for change must be present in physical reality.
   [38] *Metaph.* IX, 5, 1044b27: all beings that are inserted in becoming and change include
a material component.
   [39] *Phys.* III, 2, 201b20. Before Aristotle the term δύναμις frequently occurs in the
dialogues of Plato (cf. J. Souilhé, *Étude sur le terme δύναμις dans les dialogues de Platon*
[Paris, 1919]).
   [40] *Phys.* I, 8, 191b13-27.
   [41] *Phys.* I, 8, 191b15-17. In this context Aristotle introduces the notion of privation
which refers to relative non-being. Things are able to become something else insofar as

Here also the area of non-being is much larger than that of being. Things may evolve in many different ways and on various levels, whereas the portion of being they represent is limited. The error of the Eleatic school consequently springs from the fact that these thinkers simply oppose being and non-being without any qualification.

On the other hand, Aristotle is dissatisfied with the notion of otherness. In his view it could not adequately explain the possibility of change. Otherness means relative non-being. It simply indicates that things are not yet what they are going to be. Consider the assimilation of food: before its integration food is not yet a part of a living organism. Otherness represents in a changing thing a mere absence of the feature it will acquire. According to the Stagirite that mere absence is not sufficient to explain the process of becoming. Things are not able to become anything else, no matter what, as we already explained. The potency that exists in a particular thing is limited.[42] Hence, at the origin of change there is something more than relative non-being or mere absence of a perfection. Potency, although it could not be actualized without some external impact, is more than a mere absence, it is a positive orientation towards certain kinds of evolution, whereas others are excluded. Such an orientation quite obviously stems from the nature of things. In this sense things are more than what they are at a given instant, because they are fit for adopting a way of being which they do not yet possess.

Aristotle could not have been acquainted with the Stoic teaching concerning seminal reasons. It may be fruitful, however, to compare this doctrine with the notion of potency in order to reach a better understanding of the Aristotelian view. Endeavouring to interpret the development of the cosmos as a whole as well as that of the individual beings, the Stoics appealed to a biological paradigm: the world springs from an original germ in which logos and undetermined matter are

---

they are deprived of what they are going to be (191b9: τὸ ἐκ μὴ ὄντος γίγνεσθαι τοῦτο σημαίνει, τὸ ᾗ μὴ ὄν). In the *Sophist* (256D) Plato declares that movement is really non-being (ὄντως οὐκ ὄν ἐστι), although it is also being, since it participates in being. This statement means that movement does not coincide with being; it is different from being. In the same context (256E) the author maintains that around each form there is a multiplicity of being, but also an infinite quantity of non-being, since each form is distinct from the others. Hence, when Plato deals with the basic categories of thought, he accepts otherness to be one of them.

[42] *Metaph.* IX, 3, 1047a24-26. Aristotle deals with the concept δυνατόν: he wonders what may be said to be possible. In his answer he declares that something is possible with respect to some perfection, if nothing impossible follows when the perfection, towards which it was in potency, is realized. Something indeed may be devoid of a particular perfection, without being able to adopt it. From the mere absence of a perfection in a particular being, one could not conclude that it is possible to bestow it on it.

combined.[43] Due to a gradual process of evolution the four elements are generated first and then progressively the variety of individual beings.[44] The world as a whole is a living organism and is permeated everywhere by divine reason, the immanent creative principle of the universe. The same theory applies to the development of each individual in which a particle of the divine spirit is present and active. Human soul also is considered to be a portion of that creative Reason. As a result the Stoics emphasize the organic unity of the cosmos as well as the rational character of its development. The power that governs the world is not blind fate, but creative reason.[45]

What is the difference between this pattern of thought and Aristotle's notion of potency? The Stagirite, being the son of an outstanding physician, has always been interested in biology, anatomy and physiology, and yet he never adopted the view that the world is one gigantic living organism. He makes a distinction between organic and inorganic nature, as he draws a line between plants and animals, although in some cases it may be difficult to discern whether a particular being is a plant or an animal. As to the notion of potency, although it is universally applied by the Greek master, it seems to originate primarily from technical activity: potency is not a seed in which the elements of further evolution are present from the very beginning; such an evolution is a kind of self-development in which the hidden components of an initial germ are gradually displayed, whereas in the work of a craftsman matter is used in order to realize a particular product. Potency is more passive than a seminal reason and requires a more active intervention of an external

---

[43] According to Zeno, the founder of the Stoic school, God is the seminal reason of the universe (Diog. Laert. vii, 136): τοῦτον σπερματικὸν λόγον ὄντα τοῦ κόσμου. What is the origin of this germ? In this account Diogenes teaches that in the beginning God was by himself; but He transformed the whole substance through air into water and thus constituted the seed from which the cosmos gradually could develop. At this stage God is working as an immanent logos within the material principle of the world.

[44] Diog. Laert. vii, 136; in this context the author refers not only to Zeno (Περὶ τοῦ ὅλου), but also to Chrysippos' first book of the Physics and to Archedemos (Περὶ στοιχείων).

[45] Zeno elaborated several arguments in order to show that the world is a living, animated and rational being. One of these arguments was that nothing is more perfect than the cosmos; if it were devoid of life and reason, other beings would be at a higher level of perfection (Sextus Empir., Adv. math. ix, 107 and 104; Cicero, De natura deorum ii, 21, SVF i, 110-111). Zeno also points to the fact that the world produces animated and rational beings. How could it generate such beings, if it is not itself animated and rational? (Sextus Empir., Adv. math. ix, 110; Cicero, De nat. deorum ii, 22; SVF i, 113). Moreover, the cosmos includes some animated and rational beings. A part could not be more perfect than the whole (Sextus Empir., Adv. math. ix, 85; Cicero, De nat. deorum ii, 22; SVF i, 114). In all these arguments the cosmos is considered to be a coherent unity.

cause.[46] Moreover, the process from potency to act is much more comprehensive than the corresponding one from seminal reason to maturity. In Aristotle's view the cosmos is also a coherent whole in which individual beings constantly influence each other.[47] Of course, a particular change may be superficial, but in other cases it will be profound and modify even the substantial structure. Without the reciprocal influence of individual beings acting on each other, everything would remain in the situation in which it happens to be without being able to change it. In Stoic philosophy individual existence is less emphasized, since every being is incorporated in an organic whole. Even man is inserted into that organic unity; hence, the question arises as to what extent a human being may be the principle of his own life. The Stagirite, however, stresses the individual nature of beings existing in the world. Each of them has his proper features, belongs to a particular species, and possesses its own individuality due to the material substratum. Things evolve constantly under the influence of external factors.[48] The coherence of the universe is not jeopardized, nor is the individual consistency of each being endangered. The evolution of things depends much more upon the ceaseless impact of other beings than it is believed to be by the Stoics.

In Aristotle's teaching there is a correspondence between potency and act. Does this doctrine imply that all potencies are necessarily actualized? In other words, is it impossible that a potency be never actualized, neither in the past nor in the future? This question is not merely speculative. It is important to know whether all the possibilities of the world have been

---

[46] Aristotle always stresses the fact that no potency could be actualized by itself, but only by something that already possesses the act which it will communicate. When things are moved against their natural tendency, that could only occur under the influence of an external actor. But even when they are moved according to their nature, an external cause is required. The interpretation of the process of thinking is a characteristic instance of this doctrine: the potential intellect could only be actualized by an object that is intelligible in act (De anima III, 4, 429b29-31). Sensible data by themselves are unable to actualize this potential power. They have to be transformed and made intelligible thanks to the intervention of a creative principle which Aristotle calls ποιητικόν (De anima III, 5, 430a14-18). In this process the interference of an external factor is twice needed.

[47] Phys. III, 1, 201a22: πολλὰ ἤδη ποιήσει καὶ πείσεται ὑπ' ἀλλήλων.

[48] Phys. VIII, 4, 255b29: ὅτι μὲν τοίνυν οὐδὲν τούτων αὐτὸ κινεῖ ἑαυτό, δῆλον. In the framework of the argument developed in Phys. VIII the notion of potency plays a decisive part. Movement could never start, because any movement has to be produced by something else. If this external factor did not move before, it must have changed in some way in order to move. Hence, there could not be a first movement, for any movement implies a previous one. On the other hand, not everything could change. There must be one exception, an unmoved mover. Without this principle any movement will depend upon an infinite number of subordinate causes, which is impossible. There must be a first cause that makes the working of all the subordinate causes possible.

already or will be actualized. The alternative would be that some of them remain at the stage of sheer potentialities. Moreover, the question should be asked whether it does not depend upon the beings existing in the world that some potentialities are actualized or not. With respect to human beings it is quite obvious that they have to realize their proper perfection through their own efforts and activity. Could one state that the level of actualization of the potentialities present in the world depends on the activity of the individual beings or is it a kind of necessary process?

Let us first look at the individual beings taken separately. In the sublunary world they all are inserted in a process of coming to be and passing away. Although the world exists from eternity, these individual beings last only during a limited period, which is very different from one case to another. It could hardly be asserted that all potencies present in individual beings will some day be actualized. The clearest instance is that of human beings. In his ethical works Aristotle outlines the essential features of human perfection. He describes carefully the nature of the various virtues which belong to a moral person and shows what is the highest level of perfection that may be attained by a human being. He is quite conscious of the fact that not all humans reach the ideal of moral life and he carefully describes how it is possible to deviate from it and to go astray.[49] That means that not all men actualize the potencies they possess. This may be extended to other individual beings, animals, plants and inorganic things. Of course, everything is attracted by the good, for all things bear within their nature a teleological inclination. This does not mean, however, that in each case the highest degree of actualization is attained. What about the world as a whole? Does it include some hidden potencies that will never be realized? The answer of the Stagirite is

---

[49] Even if a man knows what is right, he may do wrong. In this respect Aristotle disagrees with Socrates; somebody may know in a universal way that what he is doing is wrong without applying this knowledge to his particular situation. It is possible also to possess some habitual knowledge of what is right and wrong without actualizing it. In some cases actual moral intuition may be prevented by all kinds of causes like emotions, passions, drunkenness and many others. It may also happen that the starting point of a deliberation on what should be done is uncertain because one may hesitate concerning the value to be attributed to some fundamental factors of human life, like honour, pleasure, wealth, political power, or moral conduct (*Eth. Nic.* vii, 3, 1146b31-1147b20). Hence, moral faults are not merely the result of ignorance; to some extent an individual may act against his moral knowledge. On the other hand, Aristotle believes man to be responsible for his ethical intuition which is closely linked to his moral behaviour (*Eth. Nic.* iii, 5, 1114a32-b3; 1114b22-24). In spite of all moral deviations Aristotle believes moral perfection to be largely diffused (πολύχοινον). Many people participate in it and it is actually accessible to all those who are not deprived of normal human capacities (*Eth. Nic.* i, 9, 1099b18-20). This view is quite understandable since man is by nature a moral being.

negative and must be negative: the world exists from eternity and will always exist in the future. There is a ceaseless interaction of beings, due to which potencies are actualized. Could there be in that everlasting process a potency that was never actualized in the past nor will be actualized in the future? That is impossible. Nature does nothing without purpose. Of course there may be exceptions, but in the great majority of cases nature attains the intended aim. The other cases are due to chance, and are connected with the fact that nature, using a material principle, may convey some by-products which were not intended.[50] Let us take again the case of human beings. If during the course of history not a single individual ever attained the moral ideal as it has been outlined by Aristotle, that would mean that man does not possess the potency to reach it.

In his *Metaphysics* our author states that, if all beings have the possibility of not existing, at some stage in the future nothing will exist.[51] The reason behind this statement is obvious. If all beings have the potency for not existing, then the whole of existing things has the potency for not existing, and this potency could not be a real potency without being realized. Hence, the conclusion that at least one being must exist necessarily without having the potency for not existing. If there is at least one such being, there could never be in the future a total collapse of existing things. Thus, the everlasting permanence of reality is guaranteed. This, however, does not imply that the one necessary being is the efficient cause of all other beings. Such a perspective is not envisaged by the Stagirite.[52]

In Aristotle's teaching there is only one substance without potency; all other beings are both act and potency. Let us look more closely at this doctrine, which is directly connected with the object of our inquiry. In

---

[50] *Phys.* ii, 5, 196b10 sqq.

[51] *Metaph.* xii, 6, 1071b13; 1071b24: ἀλλὰ μὴν εἰ τοῦτο (namely, if potency is prior to act), οὐθὲν ἔσται τῶν ὄντων · ἐνδέχεται γὰρ δύνασθαι μὲν εἶναι μήπω δ᾽ εἶναι. Could a being always exist, without beginning or end, and still have the potency of not existing? Not in Aristotle's view. If something has the possibility of not being, it will some day cease to exist. In the framework of free divine creation the answer to this question would be different. Something that by nature is perishable, may always exist due to the creative power of God.

[52] In this respect there is an agreement between the teaching of Aristotle and that of Diodoros, a well-known dialectician who lived at the time of Ptolemaios Soter (Diog. Laert. ii, 111) with regard to the κυριεύων λόγος. Diodoros accepts the first and second sentences to be true: whatever belongs to the past is necessarily true, and nothing impossible could follow from what is possible. Therefore he rejects the third sentence (possible is what is not true and will never be true) and declares that nothing is possible that is not true and will never be true (cf. G. Verbeke, *Kleanthes van Assos* [Brussels, 1949], p. 114).

Aristotle's opinion a potency can only be actualized by something else that already possesses the act that corresponds to the potency concerned. A teacher must already possess the knowledge that he wants to convey to his pupils. If change were a process of mere self-development, it would not be necessary to appeal to a first act entirely free from potency. This possibility is unequivocally denied by the Stagirite. A germ could not be the first principle, because every germ springs from something perfect. Only the perfect could be the first principle.[53] The highest substance is immutable;[54] if it were changeable, it would possess potency, which could only be actualized by something else. Not being the creator of the world, the divine principle would in that case undergo the influence of something that is actually independent of him. That of course is impossible. Immutability does not mean absence of activity or of life; it refers strictly to the impossibility of being influenced from outside. Does immutability imply this first substance to be indifferent towards the world and its history? Aristotle could not avoid denying the traditional notion of divine providence, which would entail some passivity in the first act. On the other hand, the first principle is the final cause of all movement that occurs in the universe. Could it be unaware of the activity it exercises? The first act is object of love in everything that exists which means that all things which are a combination of act and potency crave for a perfection that is devoid of any incompleteness.[55] This pure act, being the fullness of perfection and permanent activity, could not be unaware of itself and of the role it constantly plays in the development of the world.[56] If the notion of potency is excluded, is there any progress in the divine substance? The answer will depend on the concept of progress: if it involves some enrichment afforded from outside, that kind of progress is to be rejected; if it means the constant exercise of the highest activity, also with respect to the universe, that progress is not incompatible with the perfection of the

---

[53] *Metaph.* xii, 7, 1072b35: πρῶτον οὐ σπέρμα ἐστὶν ἀλλὰ τὸ τέλειον οἷόν τε πρότερον ἄνθρωπον ἂν φαίη τις εἶναι τοῦ σπέρματος, οὐ τὸν ἐκ τούτου γενόμενον ἀλλ' ἕτερον ἐξ οὗ τὸ σπέρμα. A germ springs from a mature being, so it could not be the first principle of everything. What is perfect is prior to what is imperfect.

[54] *Metaph.* xii, 6, 1072a10: δεῖ τι ἀεὶ μένειν ὡσαύτως ἐνεργοῦν.

[55] *Metaph.* xii, 7, 1072b3: κινεῖ δὲ ὡς ἐρώμενον.

[56] *Metaph.* xii, 9, 1074b33: αὐτὸν ἄρα νοεῖ, εἴπερ ἐστὶ τὸ κράτιστον, καὶ ἔστιν ἡ νόησις νοήσεως νόησις. The self-consciousness of the divine act involves an awareness of the fundamental fact that this highest perfection is the final cause of whatever exists. It is also the "mover" of all thinking, since it represents the supreme degree of contemplation, a permanent contemplation without passivity. According to Aristotle a wise man is θεοφιλέστατος (*Eth. Nic.* x, 8, 1179a24 and 30): he comes closest to the divine perfection, since he dedicates his whole life to intellectual activity.

divine. So pure act undoubtedly excludes passive potency, but it is not incompatible with self-awareness, including also awareness of the activity exerted in the world.

*
* *

The notion of potency, as it has been elaborated by Aristotle, has a deep philosophical meaning. It is the expression of a world-view that, far from being static, is essentially dynamic and teleological. According to this view things are more than what they are at a particular time; they are open to something new, to an act they do not yet possess. Of course, this openness is not a creative power. It is a capability to receive from outside a perfection or disposition to which things are orientated. In the totality of being this new act is not completely new. It is new with respect to this particular being, but it must already exist so that it may actualize the potency in question. The doctrine of potency is also the expression of a coherent universe in which things constantly act upon each other. The evolution of the world is the result of this uninterrupted interaction. Finally, it is closely connected with Aristotle's teaching on universal teleology. The striving of things is immediately directed towards their own good and ultimately to the supreme perfection of the first act. In Aristotle's universe there is only one supreme perfection. It is the basic condition for all other beings which are both act and potency. So we may conclude that potency is present almost everywhere.

4

A Non-Cartesian Meditation upon the
Doctrine of Being in the Aristotelian Metaphysics

Henry B. Veatch

Georgetown University and University of Saint Thomas

I

What is it if not a veritable part of our proverbial wisdom that the cat may look at the king! And suppose the cat to be a Cheshire cat, might he not be permitted perhaps a grin at the king as well! Accordingly, on the occasion of this *Festschrift* for Father Owens, I wonder if I might be permitted a bit of a critical look, to say nothing of a grin, at "the modern Aristotle," as Father Owens has not infrequently been referred to. For with respect to one of his recent publications, I find myself inclined somewhat timidly to take issue with the redoubtable scholar and philosopher whom this volume is designed to honor! It was on the occasion of a symposium devoted to the theme, *One Hundred Years of Thomism: Aeterni Patris and Afterwards*,[1] that Fr. Owens delivered a most interesting paper on "The Future of Thomistic Metaphysics." Facing up directly to the now widespread indifference to St. Thomas that is manifested by contemporary philosophers, Father Owens recommended three areas, or three topics, in Thomistic metaphysics, that in his judgment particularly call for renewed study and reflection in the present day. First, there is the area of our "human knowledge of the existence, nature, and providence of God."[2]

[1] Edited by Victor B. Brezik, CSB (Houston: Center for Thomistic Studies, 1981).
[2] Ibid., p. 146.

Graceful Reason: Essays in Ancient and Medieval Philosophy Presented to Joseph Owens, CSSR, ed. Lloyd P. Gerson. Papers in Mediaeval Studies 4 (Toronto: Pontifical Institute of Mediaeval Studies, 1983), pp. 75-100. © P.I.M.S., 1983.

Then "a second enduring need for Thomistic metaphysics regards the human soul." [3] And finally, "the third need concerns the destiny of man, the purpose of human living." [4]

Now how could anyone disagree with recommendations such as these, particularly if one is oneself devoted to the advancement of Thomistic metaphysics? One can't, of course! And yet where I would take issue with Father Owens is over the question of what possible good it does to make recommendations like this to contemporary philosophers – yes, even contemporary metaphysicians! Not only are they likely to pay no attention to you; in addition, they will scarcely even know what you are talking about! For I wonder if there be not something in the very condition and situation of contemporary philosophy that practically precludes today's philosophers from even looking at, much less taking seriously, such topics in Thomistic metaphysics as Father Owens specifies, viz. our knowledge of God, of the soul, and of the destiny of man.

And suppose that one should counter by saying that even in that mammoth new best-seller, *Philosophical Explanations*, by Robert Nozick,[5] one finds the entire first part devoted to "The Identity of the Self," and the concluding section entitled, "Philosophy and the Meaning of Life." Not only that, but in that concluding section even God himself manages to slip in, albeit as it were through the back door, and being allotted but a scant 50 pages out of nearly 750, in a section devoted to "God's Plan." [6] Despite all of this, however, I wonder if there may not be a certain radical disability that attaches to nearly the whole of contemporary philosophy, and that renders it largely incapable of appreciating topics such as those of God, the soul, and man's destiny, in anything like St. Thomas' sense – or in Father Owens' either, for that matter. Yes, I don't doubt that this holds even in cases when the very terms that many contemporary philosophers find themselves using tend faintly to echo the terms used by St. Thomas, or by Aristotle, or by Father Owens. That's why it is my inclination to say that before one can very well address oneself to topics of the sort Fr. Owens would suggest need to be addressed, with a view to reviving and

---

[3] Ibid., p. 151.
[4] Ibid., p. 154.
[5] Cambridge, Mass.: Harvard University Press, 1981.
[6] It perhaps needs to be added that God does do rather better, so far as the index is concerned, having earned some 25 or more references! Still, some might be captious enough to think that such evidence of God's coming into His own again is at least somewhat marred by the fact that God wins a place only in the Subject Index and not in the index of Persons Mentioned. But then Nozick may have theological reasons for supposing that maybe God is only a subject and not a person.

insuring the future of Thomistic metaphysics, it is first incumbent upon us to try to diagnose that radical disability that would seem to permeate so much of current philosophy and that makes for its seemingly impenetrable non-comprehension of anything like either Aristotelian or Thomistic metaphysics.

What, then, is it that, as it would seem to me, is no less than the very source of that structural disability and incapacity in contemporary philosophy, which tends to render it incapable of appreciating the sort of message that Father Owens would send to our contemporaries? Well, if I be not mistaken there is no little irony in this question itself, particularly when it is put as a kind of challenge to Father Owens. For I believe that at the root of that incapacity on the part of so many contemporary philosophers for appreciating just such metaphysical issues as Father Owens is wont to raise is that these same philosophers have just never bothered to read *The Doctrine of Being in the Aristotelian Metaphysics*! Or supposing that some of them have read it, then all one can say, in the words of the old *Book of Common Prayer*, is that they have somehow failed to "read, mark, learn, and inwardly digest" what they read! After all, was it not Pascal who said, "Had Cleopatra's nose been shorter, the whole history of the world would have been different?" Very well, I am tempted to say that had only the Wittgensteins or the Heideggers, the Russells or the Quines, the Sartres or the Merleau-Pontys of this world, but read Father Owens' book contemporary philosophy would have been a very different affair from what it is today.

Still, to sustain my thesis that the peculiar metaphysical illness or *malaise* of contemporary philosophy is due to its not having accepted the medicines and ministrations of the *Doctrine of Being*, I must first give a preliminary characterization of what that illness is, before going on to suggest just why it is that it is nothing if not just Father Owens' medicine that contemporary philosophy so mightily needs. Now the way I like to characterize this diagnosis of mine as to the present unhappy condition of contemporary philosophy is to say that now-a-days philosophy has pretty much made "the transcendental turn." Instead of supposing with the better part of classical and traditional philosophy – certainly with Aristotle and Aquinas – that the business of philosophy is with a knowledge of being, and of things as they really are in themselves, the current fashion would appear to be to consider that the business of the philosopher – and doubtless of the scientist as well – is not at all to know reality as it is, so much as it is to project various all-embracing categorial schemes, or over-arching hypotheses, or perhaps even ingenious world-views, through which reality can come to be ordered and structured for purposes of our better human manipulation and control of it, and as a result of which anything and everything that as human beings we are able to know will come through to us as inescapably "theory-laden," or as but appearance rather than reality, or as a reality cut to the specifications of our human organizing schemes, rather than reality as it is in itself.

Moreover, it strikes me as not a little curious, not to say even frightening, what the implications of making this transcendental turn must presumably turn out to be, so far as human liberty and freedom are concerned. For could not one say that the basic implication of this transcendental turn is that mankind and even human individuals thereby come to be invested with what is no less than a freedom unlimited? After all, Robert Nozick and other Libertarians have now made us familiar with the contrasting pair of terms, *archism* vs. *anarchism*. Accordingly, why may it not now-a-days be said that, in view of philosophers having made the transcendental turn, we human beings now no longer need to regard ourselves as being subject to what can only be designated as a veritable metaphysical *archism* of a God-given order of being and reality? No, the prospect now seems to be one of nothing less than a metaphysical *anarchism* of literally staggering proportions: there just is no order of nature or of being, but what it has somehow to be imposed or bestowed upon things by hypothesis-generating, or world-view generating, human beings. And there being presumably no "laws," either natural or moral, that can very well be thought to govern or determine our transcendental generation and projection of hypothetical world-views, why not say that basically our entire enterprise and activity as human beings – our very human being, indeed, even to our activity of cognition and knowing – this is all nothing if not an exercise in an ultimate, or literally metaphysical, freedom or liberty?

Is it surprising, then, that with this kind of framework, or, shall we say, mind-set or behavior-pattern, afflicting contemporary philosophers, they can hardly be expected to be either in a mood or of a mind to consider questions as to our knowledge of God, or of the human soul, or of our human destiny? Nor is it any more surprising that under such circumstances Father Owens' recommendations as to what needs now to be done by way of assuring a future for Thomistic metaphysics must somehow seem wide of the mark. Instead, what rather needs doing, I would think, if contemporary philosophers are ever to be got to give a hearing to Thomistic metaphysics, is to get them first to read, mark, learn, and inwardly digest *The Doctrine of Being in the Aristotelian Metaphysics*!

"But just why this last?" someone might ask. And in answer I would like to propound the thesis that at the root of any number of the manifold troubles and disabilities that afflict contemporary philosophy is the strange and sorry fact that any number of today's philosophers, whether they be conscious of it or not, just don't seem to be able to understand how anything – or, if you will, how any being or entity or substance – can ever be what it is. Recall how in chapter 6 of Book A of the *Metaphysics*, Aristotle remarks on how Plato in his youth had become familiar with Cratylus and the Heraclitean doctrines, and that "he continued to believe these even in his later years. Now Socrates was engaged in the study of ethical matters, but not at all in the study of nature as a whole, yet in ethical matters he sought the universal and was the first to fix his *thought* on definitions. Plato, on the other hand, taking into account the *thought* of Socrates, came to the belief that, because sensible things are always in a state of flux, such enquiries were concerned with other things and not with the sensibles. ... He called things of this other sort 'Ideas' and believed that sensible things exist apart from Ideas and are named according to Ideas. For the many sensibles which have the same name exist by participating in the corresponding Forms." [7]

No, I don't think that it can be inferred from this that contemporary philosophy has had the problem of trying to free itself from any sort of Heracliteanism exactly; and yet it has been seriously troubled by, and has never managed to solve, the problem of how what Plato called Ideas or Forms can ever – to put it crudely – really be brought down into sensible things. And so the result has been that such sensible things tend to be thought not either to have or to be the very Forms or Natures or Essences [8] that they would quite patently seem to have to be judged either to have or to be. Call this, if you will, just the problem of "essentialism." After all, that is a term in some currency today. Moreover, is it entirely without significance that that particular variety of analytical philosophy that immediately preceded the new fashions of the later Wittgenstein was the

[7] *Metaphysics* A6, 987a33-b10 (Apostle translation). It must be admitted that in this, as in other quotations from Aristotle, my choice of translations will be determined not by faithfulness to the original (of which I am afraid I am a rather poor judge), but solely by considerations of which serves best to bring out the sense I think the passage in question needs to be given. Nor that I would presume to defend such a practice. Instead, I will simply admit that by scholarly standards it is quite unconscionable!

[8] No, I fear that throughout this essay I make no apology for my failure to follow Father Owens' recommended conventions respecting translations of key Aristotelian terms – e.g., "Entity" rather than "substance," or "the what-is-being" rather than "essence," etc. Undoubtedly, if such conventions should come to be generally accepted, they would be an improvement. But until they come to be so accepted, the more feckless among us will probably just go along using the more customary, but uncritically determined, English translations such as "substance," "essence," etc.

sort of thing that one associates with "the logical atomism" of Bertrand Russell, and later with Gustav Bergmann?[9] And was it not Bergmann's constant insistence that what he called "particulars" are absolutely and in principle "unnatured"? In other words, it is simply impossible to consider that natures or essences (or, if you will, forms) are ever the natures or essences or forms of anything. In other words, what is this if not just the problem of essentialism, which has tended to plague modern analytical philosophy almost from its very early days, and to plague it oftentimes unbeknownst to the more naive of the philosophical analysts themselves!

Nevertheless, however much contemporary analytical philosophy has had an undeniable legacy of unhappiness and embarrassment as regards the problem of essentialism, it needs never to be forgotten that for all of their just not knowing how to handle such things as the natures or essences of things, contemporary analytical philosophers have never for a minute doubted that the things of the world – i.e., "sensible things," as they are termed in the above-quoted Apostle translation of Aristotle – were perfectly well able to be talked about or discoursed about in language. Quite the contrary, one might almost say that contemporary analytical philosophy is nothing if not a philosophy precisely of logic or language; and this just in the sense that for analytical philosophy the very business of philosophy is primarily, if not ultimately, simply a business of the analysis or logic or language. Hence whatever difficulties the analysts may have had with trying to comprehend how the things of the world could ever *be* what they are essentially, it must never for a minute be supposed that analysts were at a loss to propound theories as to how we come to *talk about* things in terms of what they are essentially, or to make what at least would appear to be essential predications. It's almost as if an understanding of predications were supposed to do duty for an understanding of being.

Consider, though, what the consequences must almost inevitably be, when it comes to such a shift of interest on the part of analytical philosophers from how things can possibly ever be their essences to how they can be talked about in terms of what they presumably are essentially. Instead of its being supposed that forms or natures or essences are what sensible things either have or are in reality and in themselves, it is rather

---

[9] Although it is our underlying thesis that nearly all varieties of contemporary philosophy make the transcendental turn – analytical philosophy, existential phenomenology, French structuralism, Frankfürter School Marxism, *et al.* – in this particular paper we must confine our illustrations and arguments simply to analytical philosophy, and even then to only a chosen few from among the analytical philosophers.

supposed that so-called forms or essences are but the characters or natures that we human beings come to bestow upon things in speaking and discoursing about them. And what is this if not to have made the transcendental turn?

Oh, it's true, of course, that contemporary analytical or linguistic philosophy differs in all sorts of ways from the particular kind of transcendental philosophy that one finds in the First Critique. And yet what is the thrust of Kant's transcendental deduction of the categories, if not that unless our experience be somehow structured and ordered and categorized by what might be called forms or essences, or natures supplied by the mind, then we human beings would have no experience at all, and our experience of a sensible world would not be an experience of a world at all, but of no more than a "booming, buzzing, confusion," if even that! Besides, so far as the transcencental character of such a philosophy is concerned, it would seem to make no very appreciable difference whether the ordering and categorizing of experience be the work of human minds, or of a transcendental unity of apperception, or maybe of no more than articulated linguistic behavior on the part of human language-users. In any and all of these cases the natures and forms and essences which sensible things come to have in the context of our experience will in no wise represent what these things really are in themselves, but only what they are made to appear to be as a result of what can only be described as literally a kind of transcendental activity – be this activity that of a so-called transcendental logic, or merely that of human linguistic behavior that articulates our experience for us in various ways.

II

With this as a kind of forerunner, then, why do we not now turn to a brief consideration of *The Doctrine of Being in the Aristotelian Metaphysics*? For if I am right, Father Owens succeeds brilliantly in showing just how Aristotle, in his account of substances and their essences, managed to obviate that particular problem, which, as I have been suggesting, was largely responsible for contemporary philosophers feeling constrained to make the transcendental turn. This was the problem of how a being could possibly be what it is. Or recalling the earlier quotation from Aristotle regarding Plato, we might say that the problem is that of how "sensible things" could possibly be what ostensibly they are, viz. their Ideas or Forms. How, then, is it that Father Owens represents Aristotle as having, not so much resolved, as dissolved, this problem?

At this point, though, I must crave the reader's – and also Father Owens' – indulgence, if I undertake not just to summarize, but to summarize presumptuously and in my own words, what I take to be the salient features of Father Owens' interpretation of Aristotle in this regard. (May I just add parenthetically that while I may have some hope of winning the reader's indulgence on this score, I know that no such indulgence would ever be forthcoming from the redoubtable Father Owens himself – and that as a matter of principle!) To begin with, then, we are all familiar with how, in Chapter 1 of Book *Γ*, Aristotle declares that metaphysics or first philosophy is "a science that investigates being *qua* being and what belongs essentially to it." [10] But what then is being? Or perhaps we might put it: what is being, or what does it take, or what is requisite for a thing to be a being? And to this question, we all know Aristotle's celebrated answer in Chapter 1 of Book *Z*, viz. that to be a being is to be a substance. "And indeed the question which was raised of old and is raised now and always, and is always subject of doubt, viz. what being is, is just the question, what is substance?" [11]

This, however, serves but to raise the further question, "What is substance?" And here we know how, in determining Aristotle's answer to this question, Father Owens leads us through the tortuous course of Book *Z*, eliminating, as candidates for the role of substance, the universal and the genus of course, and also matter or the substratum, in order finally in chapter 17 to settle upon form or essence as being what substance is. In other words, what any substance is is simply its form and essence.

Such, then, is a summary account of how, according to Father Owens, Aristotle is led eventually, as it were, to equate or identify any being or substance with its form or essence. Moreover, if Aristotle is successful in thus bringing off such an equation or identification of substance with its form or essence, then it would seem that he would thereby need to be adjudged no less successful in obviating both Plato's problem of participation, as well as the problem that we have suggested afflicts so many contemporary philosophers – of just how a thing can ever be what it is.

Still, some of you may not be altogether convinced that Aristotle does really manage to bring off such an equation of beings or substances with their forms or essences; or if you are convinced that Aristotle does succeed

---

[10] *Metaphysics Γ*, 1, 1003a22 (Apostle).
[11] Ibid., *Z*, 1, 1028b3-4 (Oxford).

in this, you may not be too confident as to just how he does so. Nevertheless, if I have understood Father Owens correctly in *The Doctrine of
Being*, it is in terms of two major moves or ploys that Aristotle manages to
effect such an equation. Thus in his initial ploy it is as if Aristotle sought
to imply, if not actually to specify, certain evident criteria of being; and
then, having shown that only substances are able to meet all of these
criteria, it must therefore be substances that are the fit candidates for the
role of beings. Following this, Aristotle's second move might be
interpreted as being one of showing that the several criteria of being are all
of them compatible with one another; and that, therefore, in meeting these
criteria, the notion of substance will not find itself suddenly in danger of
being convicted of internal inconsistencies or self-contradictions.

First, then, what are these so-called criteria of being that I am
suggesting are implicit alike in Aristotle and in Father Owens' exposition
of Aristotle? Well, I would say that there are at least four such criteria,
which I would designate somewhat crudely and roughly as follows:
(1) the independence criterion; (2) the determinacy criterion; (3) the non-
predicability or individuality criterion; and (4) the unity criterion. Thus
what I am here calling the independence criterion simply points up the
fact that, to be a being in the true sense, a thing must be "independent,"
just in the sense in which substances may be said to exist *in se*, whereas
accidents of substances must needs always exist *in alio*. Or again, it is in
virtue of what I am calling "independence" that Aristotle is able to say of
primary substances: "Thus everything except primary substances is either
predicated of primary substances, or is present in them, and *if the last did
not exist, it would be impossible for anything else to exist*." [12]

Very well, then, proceeding to the determinacy criterion, this signifies
no more than that to be a being a thing must be something or other. That
is to say, it must be the kind of thing that it is. In other words, nothing
could possibly be a being without being anything at all – i.e., without
being this, that, or the other. Moreover, as for the individuality criterion,
or non-predicability criterion, this but articulates the sorts of things that
Aristotle would seem to be getting at, alike in the *Categories* chapter 2,
and in Book *Z*, chapter 13. Thus in *Categories* 1b6, Aristotle declares that
"that which is individual and has the character of a unit is never
predicable of a subject" (Oxford); and in *Metaphysics Z*, 13, Aristotle
seems to be saying that substances, and, for that matter, any and all
beings, must be individual; they cannot be universal.

---

[12] *Categories* v, 2b3-6 (Oxford). Stress added.

Finally, then, the unity criterion in effect says no more than that to be a being, a being must be *a* being – i.e., it must be one, and not more than one. Nor, surely, do we need to take time to show how, given these criteria of being, it presumably must be substances (in Aristotle's sense), and only substances, that meet all four of these criteria. Or perhaps, it might be more accurate to say that it is not so much substances in Aristotle's sense that meet the criteria, as it is these criteria that really serve to give the sense of the fundamental kind of things that Aristotelian substances are.

And now let us get on with Aristotle's second move or ploy, by way of showing that what a being or substance is is simply its form or essence. For no sooner do the two criteria – that of the determinacy of all beings, as well as that of the individuality of all beings – come to be laid down, than they threaten to turn out to be embarrassingly inconsistent with one another. Or rather it is not so much that these two criteria themselves are inconsistent with one another, as rather that the two of them together seem hardly reconcilable with the unity criterion. Thus if any individual being or substance is necessarily and at the same time a certain kind of being or substance, does this not tend somehow to split that being's unity, and irrevocably so? Yes, it's as if even on mere linguistic or logical grounds alone, it would seem that there were an inevitable, not to say irreparable, distinction or division that breaks out, within the very unity of any individual thing or substance, between the substance itself and the determinations that make it to be the kind of being it is. Thus we cannot help both saying and thinking that there must always be an "it" or a something that is the subject of the determinations that come to be predicated of it. Nor can there be any understanding of what a thing thus is without its being an understanding of "what" some "it" is. In other words, this inevitable division between subject and predicate – between the "it" in question and "what" we consider it to be – just cannot seem to be overcome in any way.

Or to put this a little differently, is there any possible way in which we can even so much as speak or think of the determinations of a thing, without thinking of them as being the determinations of something? Nor would it seem in any way conceivable how the two sides, or the two parties, as it were, to this "of"-relationship could ever be erased or eradicated – i.e., the distinction between the determinations of a thing, on the one hand, and the individual thing that comes to be determined by them on the other; Must it not then be Plato who was right after all: no individual thing or being could possibly ever simply *be* what it is; instead, it can only "participate" in its essence or form or Idea!

But now, do we need more than remind ourselves of the first five chapters of the *Categories*, to realize that Aristotle was nothing if not at least threatened with embarrassment on the score of this seeming insuperable separation of individual things, or beings, on the one hand, and their own very determinations, in virtue of which they are the things or beings that they are, on the other? Thus primary substances are said to be never "predicable of a subject," primary substances being individuals, and "that which is individual and has the character of a unit is never predicable of a subject" (1b6. Oxford). In contrast, "in a secondary sense those things are called substances within which, as species, the primary substances are included; and also those which, as genera, include the species" (2a13-15. Oxford). Very well, dispensing with further quotations, why could we not sum up Aristotle's teaching by saying that substances in the primary and most proper sense are individuals, and as such cannot be predicated of anything else; on the other hand, secondary substances are inescapably universal just because they are predicable of other things, viz. of primary substances? But, then, by virtue of what we have been calling the non-predicability or individuality criterion, to be a being a thing must be individual and non-predicable. Accordingly, secondary substances cannot then rightly be considered to be beings at all.

Yes, but while this is all very well, so far as it goes, we must be careful not to lose sight of the fact that however much it might seem that secondary substances cannot be beings in any proper sense at all, still without secondary substances the primary substances just could not possibly be the beings that they are – which is to say that by the determinacy criterion they could not even be beings! And now consider just how this simultaneous application of the non-predicability and the unity criteria thoroughly shatters the unity of the substance. Thus so far as primary substances go, they are radically and in principle individual and not predicable of many. Yet by the determinacy criterion any primary substance cannot but be something or other: it has got to be the kind of thing that it is, which is to say that it must be what it is. But what is this if not to say that what in predication we cannot but pronounce any primary substance to be is just a secondary substance, which, of course, is universal and predicable of many. In other words, any primary substance, as individual and not predicable of many, cannot possibly be other than universal and predicable of many! Is it any wonder, then, that Plato's seemingly intolerable notion of so-called "participation" would appear to be somehow unavoidable after all: no individual, no particular, no "sensible thing," can ever be what it is – i.e., it cannot possibly be the Idea or form or essence in virtue of which it is what it is.

Now, of course, we all know what Aristotle's solution of this problem was. Or rather, if I may speak in a more personal vein, and express therewith my own sense of gratitude, I am inclined to say that none of us would ever have known – or at least I would never have known – what Aristotle's solution is, had it not been for Father Owens' magisterial exposition and exegesis in Part III, A, chapters 8-13 of *The Doctrine of Being*. Moreover, if I might be permitted a rendering of this solution in more or less Thomistic language,[13] it consists in simply recognizing that the forms, or natures or essences of things need to be "absolutely considered" – i.e., no form or essence or nature considered as such and just in itself is either universal and thus predicable of many, or individual and thus not predicable of many. At the same time, even though in itself a form or essence is neither, it nevertheless can become either or both. And so it is that the essence of any individual thing or being is itself individual just in its being the essence of that individual. At the same time, so far as logic and language are concerned, when we want to say what that individual is essentially, the predicate through which the essence comes to be predicated of it is of course universal and predicable. And yet the essence that thus comes to be predicated, when we thus say what that individual is, is of course not universal. For if it were, then it would be valid to infer: "The individual man, Socrates, is a human being; but being human is, of course, predicable of many; therefore the individual Socrates is predicable of many." (Cf. *On Being and Essence*, chapter III.)

But of course, it is not only with reference to issues arising out of the distinction between primary and secondary substance that Aristotle finds himself compelled to deal with the question of how an individual thing or substance can ever be said to be what it is. In addition, as we know, Aristotle seeks to deal with the same question, not simply as it emerges in the context of logical predication, but also as it emerges in the context of the physical, or metaphysical, composition of substances out of matter and form. Thus with reference to the latter context, it is obvious that any

---

[13] By this, of course, I do not mean to suggest St. Thomas' disposition of the realism-nominalism issue is to be read back into Aristotle, or even that Aristotle should be taken to have anticipated the later Thomistic solution in every respect. Oh, it's true that at one point in my ill-fated career I did have the ignorance and the temerity to suggest just such anachronisms. The occasion was the appearance of the first edition of *The Doctrine of Being*, which Father Owens was kind enough to suggest that I review, and which I was fool enough to undertake to do. The result was my commission of just those historical enormities regarding Aristotle and St. Thomas that I mentioned above. Is it any wonder that I was roundly and rightly chastised for my follies by Father Owens in the second edition of the book! *Mea culpa*!

individual substance is more than just its essence. For example, Socrates, in addition to being human, was also bald, snub-nosed, married to Xantippe, etc. Accordingly, may it not therefore be said that, besides his essence or substantial form, Socrates was also composite of what might be called a material potentiality which was the source of his being open to all of his various accidental determinations, in addition to just his essence or substantial form as such?

With this, though, we are immediately up against those same vexatious issues that Aristotle faced in chapter 3 of Book Z, and that many of us think he seemed to dispose of almost too summarily in that same chapter. For given that a substance is composite of matter and form, one cannot possibly identify the substance simply with its matter, "for to be separable and to be a *this* is thought to belong most of all to a substance" (1029a28-29. Apostle). (In other words, Aristotle is here invoking the criteria of independence and of determinacy with respect to substance.) With this, Aristotle then continues, "Accordingly, the form or the *composite* would seem to be a substance to a higher degree than matter. The composite substance, that is, the composite of matter and shape, may be laid aside for it is posterior..." (1029a29, 30-32. Apostle). In other words, the only alternative left would seem to be that of considering a substance to be nothing if not simply its form or essence.

And yet how can this be? Here again, it is Father Owens who, as it would seem, comes to Aristotle's rescue. Or better were it to say perhaps that here Father Owens comes to the rescue of those of us dull-witted readers of Aristotle who have found that while we may be able to read the master, it is only Father Owens who makes sense of him for us! In any case, as we all may recall, it is by invoking the notion of πρὸς ἕν equivocation that Father Owens is able to explain how Aristotle manages to make good on his suggestion that a substance is simply to be identified with its substantial form or essence. In other words, what is a substance, if not simply its very "what" or essence? Yet this is not to deny that a substance has a material component. Rather it is but to insist that such a material component is but a potentiality to be that kind of substance. Indeed, it is because of this element or component of matter as potentiality for form, or as that which takes on substantial form, that not only enables us to say, but even requires us to say, of any substance, that *it* is the kind of thing it is. There is always, in other words, that ineradicable distinction between what the substance is and the "it" that thus is what it is.

Nevertheless, such an "it," considered simply as a material potentiality to be what it is, is not any independent being or entity in its own right; instead, it is only as a potentiality or ability to be something, or to be what it is, that this "it" is at all. Accordingly, it – i.e., the material component of any substance – can only be said to be, or to be a being, by equivocation. Yes, this case of the being of such a material component or substrate of a substance is not unlike the case of the so-called being of accidents in Aristotle. Thus Aristotle certainly says that to be a being is to be a substance. But does that mean that accidents, being other than substances, are not beings at all? Hardly. Instead, accidents, like the material component or substrates of substances, may be said to be beings by πρὸς ἕν equivocation: they are beings, and yet only by reference to substance.

And so by this means the unity criterion in respect to substances gets upheld after all. Recall the famous passage from the *De anima*, Book II, chapter 1: "That is why we can wholly dismiss as unnecessary the question whether the soul and body are one: it is as meaningless to ask whether the wax and the shape given it are one, or generally the matter of a thing and that of which it is the matter. Unity has many senses (as many as 'is' has), but the most proper and fundamental sense of both is the relation of an actuality to that of which it is the actuality." (412b6-9. Oxford.)

III

But what now of contemporary philosophy? For recall that the earlier accusation which we levelled against contemporary philosophers was that nearly the whole lot of them have signally failed to understand what Aristotle (at least in terms of Father Owens' exegesis) succeeded so well in making clear – viz. how individual things, beings, or substances can ever actually manage to be what they are, i.e., to be their very forms or essences or Ideas. Moreover, having failed to understand this, it is as if contemporary philosophers had resorted to what I would call "the transcendental turn." And that way, it seems to me, spells disaster! It commits us irrevocably to a knowledge of only appearances, and not reality. Or as Kant would say, it limits us to a knowledge of *phenomena*, to the exclusion of *noumena*. And it certainly precludes us from seriously considering any future for Aristotelian or Thomistic metaphysics, such as Father Owens would recommend.

However, there is neither time nor space left in this paper, nor do I have the scholarly resources, to make good on my rather sweeping charges against practically the whole of contemporary philosophy! Instead, as I remarked earlier, I must confine myself to but a couple of illustrations drawn from what might be called the two seemingly rather dramatically different periods within the so-called analytical philosophy of the English-speaking world. And first, let us consider that earlier period of which a typical example might be Russell's philosophy of logical atomism, particularly as this was later developed and made far more precise and rigorous by Gustav Bergmann. The program of such a philosophy was not infrequently characterized as being that of a metaphysics or ontology, although, so far as I know, the logical atomists might have been reluctant to characterize their metaphysical undertaking exactly in Aristotelian terms as being the study of being *qua* being. Rather they said that their preoccupation was with the analysis of language or logic:

> The reason that I call my doctrine *logical* atomism is because the atoms I wish to arrive at as the sort of last residue in analysis are logical atoms and not physical atoms. Some of them will be what I call "particulars' – such things as little patches of color or sounds, momentary things – and some of them will be predicates or relations and so on. The point is that the atom I wish to arrive at is the atom of logical analysis, not the atom of physical analysis.[14]

At first blush, this might seem to be rather odd as a program, particularly one in metaphysics! For how by an analysis of logical propositions – and this was precisely what Russell had in mind – should it ever have been supposed that one could arrive at a knowledge of reality? But this was exactly what Russell envisaged. Starting with logical propositions, Russell notes that of course when it comes to molecular propositions, these can be analyzed down into atomic propositions. Then, in turn, any atomic proposition may be seen to be analyzable into one or more subject terms, on the one hand, and a predicate term, on the other. Moreover, as the passage quoted above makes clear, in the final analysis any subject of a proposition must turn out to be a particular (or, in Aristotle's language, a thing not predicable of many). Still, all of this would seem to have to do with no more than subjects and predicates of logical propositions. And what can that possibly tell us about the real world?

Presumably, Russell's answer to this was that, after all, propositions are such things as are susceptible of truth or falsity. And what else is a true proposition but one that somehow reflects or represents or mirrors a true state of things in reality? Thus using the sort of example that is a favorite with Bergmann, suppose that in experience I am presented with a visual datum of a red patch that is, say, round, a half-inch in diameter, etc. Will not the propositions, "This is red," "This is round," "This is a half-inch in

---

[14] Bertrand Russell, "The Philosophy of Logical Atomism," in *Logic and Knowledge*, edited by Marsh (New York: The Macmillan Company, 1956), p. 179.

diameter," but reflect an actual state of things in which there is, in reality, a particular or individual entity, referred to by the "this," as well as a property or a character of that same individual, referred to by "red" or "round" or whatever? Again, as Russell says:

> ... in a logically correct symbolism there will always be a certain fundamental identity of structure in the world between a fact and a symbol for it; and ... the complexity of the symbol corresponds very closely with the complexity of the facts symbolized by it. Also, ... it is quite directly evident to inspection that the fact, for example, that two things stand in a certain relation to one another − e.g., that this is to the left of that − is itself objectively complex, and not merely that the apprehension of it is complex. The fact that two things stand in relation to each other, or any statement of that sort, has a complexity all of its own. I shall therefore in future assume that there is an objective complexity in the world, and that it is mirrored by the complexity of propositions.[15]

Very well, suppose that for purposes of argument, we accept this Russellian version of the picture theory of meaning, there then is no denying that what one will arrive at through an analysis of logical propositions will be no less than an insight into the structure of actual facts in the world. And what is this structure of atomic facts? It is clearly a structure involving at least one individual or particular, together with an attribute or a character of that individual; which, of course, cannot be other than universal.[16] Or as an alternative, it might be a case of several individuals standing in a certain relation to one another. For it will be recalled that Russell thought he had greatly amplified, not to say revolutionized, the old Aristotelian notion of predication: instead of there having to be but one subject in a proposition, which stands to its predicate as a thing to its property, there can very well be two, three, four, or any number of subjects that are correlated with one another in the proposition through a dyadic, triadic, or n-adic relational predicate. In fact, one can exhibit the possible forms or structures of propositions (and also of facts) in terms of a series of one-place, two-place, three-place or n-place functions.

$$f(x)$$
$$f(x, y)$$
$$f(x, y, z)$$
etc.

[15] Ibid., p. 197.
[16] Of course, it is possible that one might have a proposition involving the "is" of identity, rather than the "is" of predication. But this need not concern us in this present context.

Accordingly, by this supposedly smooth and easy route of logical analysis, the logical atomist supposes that he has thereby got to metaphysics or ontology. Not only that, but he confidently proclaims that he can now be said to know, in general, the way the world is – at least in terms of the the structure of so-called atomic facts: reality is simply made up of particulars and universals in conjunction or connection with one another. "Yes," but one might respond at this point, "doesn't this very business of the 'conjunction' or 'connection' of particulars with universals, or of individual things with their attributes, simply beg the major question of our entire paper thus far: how is it possible for things ever to be, or to have, or to 'participate' in, the forms or attributes or character that they do have? Yes, wasn't that just Plato's problem: what kind of a 'conjunction' or 'connection' can it possibly be that 'sensible things' have with their Ideas or Forms? And what, then, is the logical atomist, now become metaphysician, to say about this?"

Before we attempt directly to answer this question, however, we had better first say a word more about the logical atomist's understanding of those "particulars" or "individuals" that turn out to be the ultimate subjects of logical propositions, as well as one of the ultimate components of the atomic facts of the world. "For why," one might ask, "could not universals function as the subjects of propositions, no less than particulars?" To this, Russell would make rejoinder – and all modern logicians would go along with him – that, in so far as any universality attaches to the subject term of any proposition, the proposition has not been fully analyzed; and that further analysis will disclose how any and all of the universal elements or features attaching to subject terms need to be analyzed out and relegated to the predicate-place in the propositions of which they are a part.

For instance, if one says, "All men are mortal," it is misleading to suppose that the term "men" can properly be the subject. For "man" is clearly a universal, and as a universal it is predicable of many. But whatever is predicable of many is properly a predicate, and not a subject at all. In fact, why not tear a leaf from Aristotle's book and say that just as a primary substance is never predicable of a subject, so likewise a primary or ultimate subject must needs be such as cannot possibly be predicated of a subject? And so, on the basis of considerations such as these, we get the familiar analyses and recasting of propositions that are demanded, if one is ever properly to operate with the so-called Lower Functional Calculus of modern logic. For example, a sentence like "All men are mortal" gets rendered as "For any x, if x is a man, then x is mortal." Or as another example, recall Russell's way of handling definite descriptions. Thus,

"The present King of France is bald" comes to be rendered as, "There is at least one x, such that x is pesently a King of France, and x is bald, etc." Yes, Quine has even suggested that one needs to carry out a comparable analysis with respect to proper names occurring as subjects of propositions, since ordinary proper names tend to have universal characters or attributes associated with them. Accordingly, for Quine, "Pegasus is a winged horse" would be rendered as "There is an x, such that x is a winged horse, and x Pegasizes, etc."

Very well, if such be the way particulars and individuals need to be treated, in order to function as the subject terms of propositions – i.e., they need to be stripped bare of any and all of their universal features and elements – what implications does this have for those metaphysical individuals or particulars that are the counter-parts in atomic facts of those same particulars that function as subjects in atomic propositions? Surely, this can only mean that, as existing in the real world, these atomic particulars have to be regarded as literally "bare" of any attributes or characteristics whatever. In fact, Bergmann calls them "bare particulars," in precisely the sense that one cannot say that they are anything, or have any features or characters of any kind, by virtue of which they can be said to be this, that, or the other. They are, as Bergmann says, "unnatured"; they literally have no essences; and although they are beings or entities, all right – yes, even items in "the ultimate furniture of the world" – they none-the-less in their being constitute a standing repudiation of the Aristotelian determinacy criterion.[17]

---

[17] Perhaps we might note in passing still another factor that would seem quite to militate against the possibility of any analytical philosopher's being ever able to conceive of how any particular being or entity could ever be what it is. This factor is simply the so-called relational character of predication, which is fundamental to the entire Lower Functional Calculus in modern logic. Already we have seen how Russell had insisted that predicates needed to be construed relationally, rather than in the manner of the older Aristotelian type of predication. Thus, for exmple, in a case of a one-place predication, the subject is considered to be related to the predicate as a thing to its quality (or in the language of Aristotle's *Categories*, in the manner of a substance to its accidents). Likewise, in the case of a two-place predicate, two things are considered to be related to each other; in the case of a three-place predicate, three things to each other, and so on.

But notice how, the minute one construes predication in this way, it becomes quite impossible to think of an ordinary predicate as stating or signifying what its subject or subjects are. For example, take a two-place predicate, as in "a is the father of b;" or a three-place predicate, as in "a is between b and c." By no stretch of the imagination can one consider that in the case of the two-place predication what is being affirmed is that a and b are fathers, or a father of, or the father of, or anything else for that matter. Likewise, in the three-place predication, in no wise can it either be said or thought that what one is affirming of the supposed three subjects, a, b, and c, is that what they are is between ! Yes, even in the case of the one-place predicate, one cannot possibly suppose that what the

But then, of course, this notion of metaphysical ultimates such as bare particulars – viz. existing particular things, and yet things that aren't anything – such a notion could hardly have had any other effect but that of creating almost intolerable difficulties for a metaphysics such as that of Bergmann. For if the particulars that are the necessary parts of the atomic facts of the world are bare particulars, then what must be this connection or relation or conjunction with such universals as are also components of the same atomic facts – the very universals which, as Bergmann says, must needs be regarded as being the "characters" of such particulars? Indeed, in just what sense can such particulars be said "to have" or "to be" the characters that are thus attributed to them? Well, Plato, be it recalled, was constrained to admit that sensible things only "participate" in the Forms or Ideas; and in a not dissimilar vein Bergmann insists that bare particulars merely "exemplify" the relevant universals, which are supposed to be the "characters" of those particulars. Nor would Aristotle's rather caustic comment about the Platonists in this connection seem any less applicable to Bergmann and the logical atomists: "But as to what the participation or the imitation [and now let us add, the exemplification] of the Forms could be they left an open question" (987b12-13. Oxford).

All right, suppose, then, that even our very brief sketch of this earlier version of analytical philosophy – call it "logical atomism" – suffices to show that such a metaphysics simply flunks the test of what we earlier designated as being the unity criterion, at least as this applies to beings or entities in the real world. That is to say, Russell and Bergmann, no less than Plato – albeit in a somewhat different way than Plato – show themselves to be pretty well bankrupt, when it comes to explaining how beings or substances can at one and the same time be individuals, and hence non-predicable, and yet at the same time meet the determinacy

---

thing that is being referred to by the subject is simply its quality. Thus the quality of a particular leaf that one happens to be referring to may be the color green. And yet surely, in one's proposition one can never assert that the leaf simply is its color. Thus as Aristotle might have put it, no substance could possibly be said to be its accident. If it were, it would not then be a substance!

Now so far as I know, no contemporary logician or philosopher has ever been particularly sensitive to this fact that apparently, on grounds of modern logic alone, any such thing as essential predication becomes quite impossible! Little wonder that a Bergmann should insist that particulars can only be "bare particulars," that they have no natures! It's true that in a rather insignificant book of my own some years ago, I sought to call attention to this curious incapacity of modern logic for any such thing as essential predication. But that book, it would seem, no one has ever read. Surely, though, that need not preclude me from recommending it yet again! It is: *Two Logics* (Evanston: Northwestern University Press, 1969), esp. Chapter ɪ.

criterion.[18] But for all of that, it needs to be noted that all of these types of metaphysics – Russell's and Bergmann's, no less than Plato's – both purport to be, and are, metaphysics, pretty much in the classical sense of Aristotle: they all of them are concerned (each in his own way, to be sure, and although no one of them might want to express it in quite such Aristotelian language) with the examination and investigation of beings – yes, of being *qua* being, if you will.

In contrast, once the transcendental turn is made, there can be no knowledge of being *qua* being, but only of appearances; not only that, but the very subject matter of metaphysics then tends to shift from a study and investigation of being to a study of the transcendental conditions of our very knowledge of being. And indeed, if I am right, it is just such a shift from what we might call an older realistic metaphysics to a metaphysics of the transcendental type that characterizes so-called analytical philosophy in more recent years, as contrasted with that older type of analytical philosophy, as exemplified by Russell, Bergmann, and perhaps even the Wittgenstein of the *Tractatus*. Not only that, but I would also wonder if perhaps the principal factor that may well have operated, be it consciously or unconsciously, in the minds of the later analysts, and that led them to discredit the earlier type of analytic metaphysics, may not have been just that same total incapacity on the part of this earlier type of metaphysics to account for beings, substances, ultimate entities – call them what you will – ever being able to be what they are.

Yes, on even a mere *prima facie* consideration of the matter, why would it not be plausible to suppose that for an analytical philosopher confronted with this problem, a transcendental turn might easily recommend itself as a possible way out of such difficulties? For suppose that our analyst might wish to avoid trying to break his head over the problem of how a thing can ever be what it is. And after all, we have already supposed that our analyst has never read Father Owens, and so has not been informed of how the problem is indeed readily resolvable along Aristotelian lines! Might it not then be an obvious turn for our

---

[18] It is perhaps not entirely without irony that in his very insistence that his particulars aren't anything – i.e., have no natures – Bergmann would seem rather to contradict himself. For however much his particulars are said not to be anything, and thus to be without any determinate nature, it at the same time cannot be denied that they are particulars – i.e., they are not universals, or *nexūs* of exemplification, or anything else in the Bergmann roster of ultimate metaphysical entities. In other words, they just are particulars. And why should it not thus be said that that is just what their nature or essence is, viz. to be particulars? This very telling line of criticism of Bergmann is due to John Peterson. See his *Realism and Logical Atomism* (University, Alabama: The University of Alabama Press, 1976), esp. Chapter IV.

analyst to take to suppose that while he of course could not hope to explain how any thing or being could ever be what it is, he at least might be able to explain how, as human logic- and language-users, we might very well come to think about things and talk about them, as if they indeed are what they are?

After all, Kant never succeeded in explaining how in fact and in reality there could ever be such things as necessary connections, as opposed to mere constant conjunctions, between events or happenings in the real world. On the other hand, Kant did manage to explain, by his two supposed deductions of the categories, how human beings could not do other than to think of things as thus causally connected. And so it was that the transcendental solution that Kant provided for the problem of causation was a solution that involved explaining how things must inevitably appear to us as causally connected, even though we have no way of knowing whether, in fact and in reality, and so far as things-in-themselves are concerned, events are really causally connected or not. Why, then, might not analytical philosophers avail themselves of a transcendental solution as regards the problem of essentialism, much as Kant availed himself of a transcendental solution with respect to the problem of causation? True, it need not necessarily be a solution exactly along Kantian lines, with, say, the apparatus of both a metaphysical and a transcendental deduction of the categories; but still it could be a *bona fide* transcendental solution for all of that.

With this, then, may we take it that a so-called transcendental solution to the problem of essentialism could well have suggested itself to latter-day analytical philosophers as something that could possibly provide them with "a happy issue out of all their afflictions"? Indeed, that such a solution did not merely suggest itself, but actually became the solution adopted by Quine and others, let us now consider but briefly and by way of conclusion. Thus we all recall how Quine even in his earlier essays made it clear that he just could not stomach the extreme realism with respect to universals that was characteristic of Russell and Bergmann and other such earlier analysts. True, Quine never questioned the customary analyst's way of analyzing propositions in terms of the lower functional calculus: all descriptive or universal elements need to be analyzed out of the subjects of propositions, and relegated to the predicate place, thus leaving ultimately nothing but the bare x's over which quantifications may be made by way of rendering them the proper subjects of propositions.

At the same time, though, that Quine agrees with such a rendering of propositions, he is no less determined in his repudiation of anything like the picture theory of meaning. And after all, it was just such a theory of meaning that presumably was the generative source of the extreme realism of the earlier logical atomists. Thus if there must necessarily be a one-to-one correspondence between the structures of atomic propositions and the structures of the corresponding atomic facts, then given that in atomic propositions the subjects can only be particulars and the predicates universals, then quite undeniably the structure of the corresponding facts can be none other than one of particulars exemplifying characters. Nor could such characters be other than universals, and universals actually existing *in rerum natura*! All this would seem to be no more than a necessary consequence of the picture theory, or referential theory, of meaning.

Why, though, assume any such picture theory of meaning? After all, Ryle poked fun at it, calling it "the 'Fido'-Fido fallacy": just because a name "Fido" occurs in a proposition, it surely need not follow that there must necessarily be a thing named, viz. Fido, existing in reality. Or as a better example, just because the universal, "red," occurs in a proposition such as "The rose is red," does it have to be assumed that, if the proposition be true, there must be in reality a real universal, viz. red, that is presumably named by the predicate in the proposition? Still, even more telling than just this rather general challenge was the ploy that Quine and others have resorted to of drawing a distinction between "meaning" and "naming," or "sense" and "reference" (Frege's *Sinn* and *Bedeutung*) of the terms contained within a proposition.

Thus just because a term such as "red" in the above proposition is meaningful, it does not follow that it must therefore also refer to or name – i.e., designate as actually existing – an attribute of redness existing as such *in rerum natura*. No, Quine insists, the only real or existing entities in the world that a true proposition may be presumed to name or refer to are just those individual x's over which one quantifies in the subject term of one's proposition. Accordingly, Quine concludes, a pro-position like "'Some dogs are white' says that some things that are dogs are white; and in order that this statement be true, the things over which the bound variable 'something' ranges must include some white dogs, but need not include doghood or whiteness." Oh it's true, Quine adds, "when we say that some zoological species are cross-fertile we are committing ourselves to recognizing as entities the several species themselves, abstract though they are." [19] However, Quine takes care of this possible exception

---

[19] See the essay "On What There Is" in *From a Logical Point of View* (Cambridge, Mass.: Harvard University Press, 1953), p. 13.

as regards the reality of universals, by saying that in his own logical practice, he, Quine, will always be careful never to quantify over species or universals of any kind. And so we may take it that that is indeed something Quine does not do, and never has done!

But just where does such a program in logic leave Quine, so far as his metaphysics is concerned? For remember that it is a principle with all analytical philosophers that the key to any analysis of being must be the analysis of language and/or of logic. And so we find Quine, in his own analysis of logical propositions, insisting that while the universal predicate terms that function in propositions are meaningful, they do not refer − i.e., one does not in the use of such universal terms either name or refer to anything as actually existing. Instead, the only things that the ordinary proposition should be taken to name as existing would be the bare x's − i.e., the individuals over which one quantifies in one's enunciation of the proposition. Does this not, though, sound as if Quine were like Bergmann, after all, in asserting that the individuals that exist in the world are nothing more than "bare particulars" − i.e., particulars of which it cannot be said either what they are, or even that they are anything? True, Quine strikes out that other component of atomic facts, which Bergmann had insisted exist in their own right in the real world, and which are exemplified by the particulars, viz. universals. However, Quine having insisted, like any analytical philosopher, that it must be by an analysis of sentences or logical propositions that we must find our key to an understanding of what the world or reality is like, and having now denied that the universals which function as predicates in propositions need have any counterparts in reality, must not the consequence be for Quine's metaphysics that nothing whatever may be held to exist − i.e., nothing that is capable of being named or referred to in propositions − other than bare, individual x's?

Yes, that would certainly seem to be a necessary consequence for Quine's metaphysics. And yet that is not quite all there is to it either. For remember that in his insistence that universal terms, while meaningful, do not refer, Quine immediately goes on to the somewhat puzzling addendum: "The words 'houses,' 'roses' and 'sunsets' are true of sundry individual entities which are houses and roses and sunsets, and the word 'red' or 'red object' is true of each of sundry individual entities which are red houses, red roses and red sunsets; but there is not, in addition, any entity whatever, individual or otherwise, which is named by the word 'redness,' nor, for that matter, by the word 'household,' 'rosehood,' 'sunsethood'." [20] For just how is one to understand Quine's confident

---

[20] Ibid., p. 10.

assurance that while there are no such entities as redness, household, rosehood or sunsethood, there nevertheless are entities – yes, individual entities such as red houses, red roses and red sunsets? If universal predicates in no wise refer to entities in the real world, then how does the mere meaningfulness, as it is called, of such predicates justify one in supposing that they can be used to refer after all, even though their reference be confined exclusively to individuals, albeit to individuals as supposedly characterized by universal predicates?

Does this mean that Quine would deny that the particulars that are quantified over, and that therefore may be considered to exist in the real world are not bare particulars? For how can they be otherwise than bare, at least metaphysically or ontologically? After all, from Quine's stand-point, particulars cannot be said to exemplify universals, in the way Berg-mann thought, because Quine has denied that there are any such universals in reality for the particular to exemplify. On the other hand, nowhere in Quine does one find any treatment – comparable to Aris-totle's, as interpreted by Father Owens – of how individuals can actually be what they are, certainly not essentially, or presumably not accidentally either. What, then, can Quine possibly mean by his seemingly confident assertions that determinate or "charactered" individuals do actually exist in the world and are actually named or referred to in propositions? In other words, it would seem to be altogether unintelligible how in any Quinean universe particulars or individuals could in any sense be what they are, or have the determinations that Quine seems to assert that they do have.

Accordingly, it is our suggestion that the only way Quine could possibly give any sense to his own assertions that there are such things as red houses and red roses and red sunsets is by his having either unwittingly or surreptitiously availed himself of the transcendental turn. Thus suppose one asks Quine: "Descriptive terms are meaningful, you say, even though they do not name anything at all. But then, just what ontological status is to be given to those 'meanings' that you seem to imply that descriptive terms have?" But, of course, we all know how Quine goes up in smoke at the mere suggestion of such a question! For he wants to deny any ontological status of any kind to meanings in any sense. But then, what are meanings? Or since Quine does not like such a way of posing the question, just what does the meaningfulness of descriptive predicates and attributes after all amount to? When confronted with such a question, Quine's only recourse is to consider that meaningfulness has no status of any kind apart from the conceptual or linguistic activities of human beings. It is for that reason and in that sense that he wishes to deny it ontological status altogether.

But with this has not Quine already made the transcendental turn, be it willy-nilly or not? The x's or the bare particulars that are quantified over in propositions in the lower functional calculus do not have any natures or characters, really or as they are in themselves; no, they only have a character given them or bestowed upon them by us language users, who give color and character to the individuals of the world by our logical and linguistic actions of predicating and describing or simply talking about them.

Of course, if there were either time or point to doing so, we could go further and trace the development and the ramifications of Quine's transcendentalism in his later writings – his so-called holism, his accounts of the use of hypotheses in both science and metaphysics, according to which the world comes to appear to us in various guises, but beyond which it is futile for us to press further with a view to finding out what reality is really like, as opposed to what it only appears to be in the light of our various theories and hypotheses and conceptual schemes. All of this would be but just so much further confirmation of the extent to which the transcendental turn has been made by contemporary analytical philosophy.

Nor is it only analytical philosophy that has thus effected such a displacement of a traditional realistic metaphysics like that of Aristotle or St. Thomas, in favor of what we have been designating as being a transcendental type of metaphysics. No, a comparable transcendental displacement, I believe, may be found to characterize almost the whole of contemporary philosophy – on the Continent, no less than in the English-speaking world; among existential phenomenologists and structuralists, no less than among analysts; among Frankfurt school Marxists, no less than among Libertarians. You have scarcely to name the area, and transcendentalism may surely be found to be rampant in it! But also, I am far from able to demonstrate this here and now, or perhaps even ever, life being short and my wits dull!

Still, as a final message to Father Owens, I wonder if I could not humbly suggest that maybe it does behoove him in his continuing concerns with the future of Aristotelian and Thomistic metaphysics perhaps to pause a bit and to direct his attention to that seemingly well-nigh impossible roadblock of transcendentalism that now lies athwart the path of contemporary philosophy, and that bids fair to blocking any and all advances in the direction of either an Aristotelian or a Thomistic metaphysics. After all, that roadblock would never have been there, had our contemporary philosophers but read Father Owens' *The Doctrine of Being in the Aristotelian Metaphysics*. Why, then, is not Father Owens just the man to be clearing that roadblock away, considering that he is a living testimony to the fact that there need never have been such a roadblock in the first place!

5

Hylozoism in Aristotle

W. J. Verdenius

Rijksuniversiteit, Utrecht

Aristotle's attitude towards the Presocratics shows a curious ambivalence: on the one hand he is eager to point out their mistakes, on the other hand he seldom omits prefacing his own view of a problem with a survey of earlier doctrines. This paradoxical method is to be explained by his conviction that the views of famous men of old must contain some truth, and this conviction is based on his idea that a long tradition is akin to what exists by nature. His conclusion is that we may adopt what has already been sufficiently expressed and try to discover what has been neglected.[1]

One of the oldest and most persistent traditions of Greek thought has been labelled "hylozoism," i.e., the view that matter is endowed with a kind of life,[2] and it may be expected that traces of this view are to be found in Aristotle. We shall see that even his main tenets show the influence of a hylozoistic tradition.

These traits of his thought are commonly ascribed to his biological and medical interests. It is true, for instance, that a field naturalist sees an individual object almost immediately as a specimen.[3] On the other hand

---

[1] Cf. *EN* 1.8, 1098b27-29; *Rh.* 2.9, 1387a16-17; *Pol.* 7.9, 1329b33-35. See further my article "Traditional and Personal Elements in Aristotle's Religion," *Phronesis*, 5 (1960), 56-70, esp. 56-59; G. Verbeke, "Philosophie et conceptions préphilosophiques chez Aristote," *Rev. philos. Louvain*, 59 (1961), 405-430.

[2] Cf. my article "Hylozoism in Early Greek Thought," *Janus*, 64 (1977), 25-40.

[3] Cf. M. Grene, *A Portrait of Aristotle* (London, 1963), pp. 108-109. She also points out (pp. 55-56, 212) that for a biologist it is self-evident that a thing's nature is determined by its form.

Graceful Reason: Essays in Ancient and Medieval Philosophy Presented to Joseph Owens, CSSR, ed. Lloyd P. Gerson. Papers in Mediaeval Studies 4 (Toronto: Pontifical Institute of Mediaeval Studies, 1983), pp. 101-114. © P.I.M.S., 1983.

the framework of biology is too narrow to explain the principles of Aristotle's physics and metaphysics.[4] In this field hylozoism offers a wider perspective and promises a more fruitful approach. I shall try to show that this point of view may help us to understand some difficult aspects of (1) his picture of the world as a whole, (2) his doctrine of the four elements, (3) the transition from potentiality to actuality, (4) the connection between matter and form.[5]

I. THE WORLD AS A LIVING BEING

Aristotle calls the universe[6] ἔμψυχος (*Cael.* 2.2, 285a29). This is obviously inspired by Plato's statement (*Tim.* 30в) that the world is a ζῷον ἔμψυχον. Aristotle avoids the term ζῷον probably because in his vocabulary this usually means "animal." The term ἔμψυχος is explained[7] by the fact that the universe has a principle of movement within itself. Movement is not conceived by Aristotle in purely mechanical terms: the heavenly bodies are said to possess πρᾶξις καὶ ζωή (*Cael.* 2.12, 292a21), and at 292b1-2 we read: δεῖ νομίζειν καὶ τὴν τῶν ἄστρων πρᾶξιν εἶναι τοιαύτην οἵα περ ἡ τῶν ζῴων καὶ φυτῶν. It has been suggested that these phrases are metaphorical ways of hinting at properties transcending the sphere of human imagination[8] but it appears from 292a23-24 that Aristotle assumes a real analogy between the activities of the stars and those of the sublunary world. This conclusion is corroborated by the fact that he ascribes an "innate urge to change" (ὁρμὴν μεταβολῆς ἔμφυτον) to natural objects as contrasted with

---

[4] Cf. D. M. Balme, "Development of Biology in Aristotle and Theophrastus: Theory of Spontaneous Generation," *Phronesis*, 7 (1962), 94: "His metaphysical arguments befit a potential biologist; but they do not reflect the actual biology of his biological works." See also Balme's inaugural lecture *Aristotle's Use of the Teleological Explanation* (London, 1965), pp. 19-20, and H. Happ, *Hyle* (Berlin, 1971), pp. 73-75, who observes (n. 325) that "ὕλη ist kein vitalistisch sprossender 'Wald', sondern Holz als Rohstoff, Material technischer Prozesse."

[5] I do not pretend to give a complete explanation, but will tentatively draw some outlines.

[6] For οὐρανός used in the sense of "universe" cf. *Cael.* 1.9, 278b20-21; 1.10, 280a22; Bonitz, *Ind.* 541b56.

[7] For the specifying force of καί at *Cael.* 2.2, 285a30 cf. *Ph.* 2.1, 193a10: ἡ φύσις καὶ ἡ οὐσία τῶν φύσει ὄντων (W. K. C. Guthrie, "Notes on Some Passages in the Second Book of Aristotle's *Physics*," *Classical Quarterly*, 40 (1946), 70, rightly translates "nature, that is the substance of natural things"); *GC* 2.11, 338a18-19: ἡ κύκλῳ κίνησις καὶ ἡ τοῦ οὐρανοῦ; and my "Notes on Menander's *Epitrepontes*," *Mnemosyne*, 27 (1974), 25.

[8] P. Aubenque, *Le problème de l'être chez Aristote* (Paris, 1962), pp. 352-353. Cf. his remarks on the Unmoved Mover at pp. 353-355, 359 n. 2, 364.

artefacts (*Ph.* 2.1, 192b18-19), and calls their movement "a kind of life" (*Ph.* 8.1, 25ʹb14-15).[9]

Plato called the principle of universal movement ψυχή (e.g., *Leg.* 896β), but Aristotle prefers to speak of φύσις[10] and he apparently does so for two reasons: in the first place he is inclined to regard ψυχή as a characteristic of animals and men,[11] and in the second he consciously adopts the original meaning of φύσις, "growth," to express the immanent dynamism of nature: cf. *APo.* 2.11, 94b37-95a1, where φύσις is equated with ὁρμή,[12] and *Ph.* 2.1, 193b12-17, where the statement ἡ φύσις ἡ λεγομένη ὡς γένεσις ὁδός ἐστιν εἰς φύσιν is explained by τὸ φυόμενον ἐκ τινὸς εἰς τί ἔρχεται ᾗ φύεται.[13] The double meaning of φύσις – "process of growing" and "result of growth," "being full-grown" – explains the fact that φύσις is the principle both of movement and rest (*Ph.* 2.1, 192b13-14). In a state of perfect rest the thing's "life" is going on for it manifests the thing's ἐνέργεια (*Met.* 7.15, 1154b27), a word which still carries the connotation of "being at work" derived from the sphere of social life (see below, Part III).

From this point of view it is not surprising that Aristotle does not draw a sharp distinction between organic and inorganic nature.[14] Together they form the one φύσις who, as a kind of person, leads everything to its end. Such phrases as "Nature does nothing in vain" (*Cael.* 1.4, 271a33) and "Nature always has the best in view" (*MA* 8, 708a10-11)[15] are no poetic

---

[9] Cf. also *Cael.* 1.9, 279a29-30, where εἶναι and ζῆν are used as synonyms. See further J. L. Le Blond, *Logique et méthode chez Aristote* (Paris, 1939), p. 351; J. Mansfeld, *The Pseudo-Hippocratic Tract Περὶ ἑβδομάδων Ch. 1-11 and Greek Philosophy* (Assen, 1971), pp. 73-75.

[10] Cf. F. Solmsen, *Aristotle's System of the Physical World* (Ithaca, NY, 1960), pp. 92-99.

[11] Plants are ἄψυχα: cf. *PA* 4.5, 681a12-17; *HA* 8.1, 588b4-7.

[12] Similarly *Met.* 4.23, 1023a9; *EE* 2.9, 1224a18.

[13] Cf. *Met.* 5.4, 1015a10-11, where the form and essence of a thing is called τὸ τέλος τῆς γενέσεως. See also Le Blond, p. 350. The fact that Aristotle (*GC* 2.6, 333b13-15; *Met.* 5.4, 1014b36-1015a1) misunderstood Empedocles β 8.1 φύσις as "essence" may be connected with his conception of essential nature as the result of growth. See further J. Owens, "Aristotle on Empedocles Fr. 8," in R. A. Shiner and J. King-Farlow, *New Essays on Plato and the Pre-Socratics* (Guelph, Ont., 1976), pp. 87-100.

[14] At *Ph.* 2.1, 192b9-11 Aristotle enumerates the things existing "by nature" (φύσει): animals, plants, and the four elements. At *HA* 8.1, 588b4-7 he suggests that there is a continuous transition from non-living things to plants and animals. See further H. Happ, "Die *scala naturae* und die Scheidung des Seelischen bei Aristoteles," in *Beiträge zur Alten Geschichte und deren Nachleben: Festschrift F. Altheim* (Berlin, 1969), pp. 220-244, esp. pp. 224-225 and 234-235. For the connection between biology and cosmology cf. M. Nussbaum, *Aristotle, De Motu Animalium* (Princeton, 1978), Essai 2, and the critical comments made by H. B. Gottschalk, *AJP*, 102 (1981), 91.

[15] See further Bonitz, *Ind.* 836b28. Grene (p. 134) seems to me wrong in calling these phrases "misleading" and in thinking that in Aristotle's view "there is no Nature, but each

images but they reflect the close connection between teleology and hylozoism. This also explains the comparison drawn by Aristotle between the organizing activity of Nature and that of a manager or a craftsman.[16]

II. THE FOUR ELEMENTS

Aristotle (*Meteor*. 2.3, 357a24-28) blames Empedocles for calling the sea "the sweat of the earth" (B 55) and he adds the remark that metaphors belong to poetry, not to science.[17] His own conception of the elements, however, is not so far removed from the views of the Presocratics as he himself suggests: the comparison with living beings is less explicit but it is never absent. For instance, the fact that an organism grows by assimilating food is explained by Aristotle (*GC* 1.5, 322a10-13) by referring to the fact that fire "takes hold of" (ἁψάμενον) inflammable

---

kind has *its* nature." Similarly Balme, *Teleological Explanation*, p. 24, who further maintains (p. 10): "Nor is there any question, in his philosophy, of providential design in nature." See, however, my remarks in "Traditional and Personal Elements," pp. 60-61.

[16] E.g., *PA* 2.9, 654b29-32; 4.10, 687a10-12; *GA* 1.22, 730b29-30; 2.6, 744b16-17. Nature, just as a writer or a physician, sometimes makes mistakes (*Ph.* 2.8, 199a33-b1), and there are "superfluous" by-products (*PA* 4.2, 677a10-15). For the analogy between φύσις and τέχνη cf. also *Ph.* 2.8, 199a12-14 and *GA* 1.22, 730b19-22. See further Solmsen, pp. 115-116; G. E. R. Lloyd, *Polarity and Analogy* (Cambridge, 1966), pp. 285-294; W. Kullmann, *Die Teleologie in der aristotelischen Biologie* (Heidelberg, 1979), esp. pp. 22-26; H. Wagner, "Einiges über die Naturteleologie des Aristoteles," in *Dialogos: Festschrift H. Patzer* (Wiesbaden, 1975), p. 109: "Wie aber Aristoteles überhaupt noch keine prinzipielle Naturgesetzlichkeit kennt, so auch keine, welche für die Tatsache regelmässiger Zweckmässigkeit aufkommen würde. Und darum bleibt für ihn notwendigerweise als die Alternative zum Zufall, der nichts erklärt, nur die Teleologie der Natur, einer Natur, die nach Zwecken *tätig ist*" (my italics).

Kullmann (p. 24) argues that such passages as *PA* 4.10, 687a11: καθάπερ ἄνθρωπος φρόνιμος and *GA* 2.6, 744b16: ὥσπερ οἰκονόμος ἀγαθός are metaphorical phrases: "Da Aristoteles nicht müde wird, die Ewigkeit der Arten zu betonen, kann ein Herstellen von Arten und eine Zuteilung von Organen an einzelne Arten nicht wörtlich gemeint sein." But the context of these phrases shows that Nature's planning does not aim at the creation of new kinds but at the preservation of the existing order. Kullmann (pp. 25-26) further points out that Aristotle does not consider man to be the ultimate object of creation, but this does not imply that the passage *Pol.* 1.8, 1256b15-22, where it is observed that Nature has made the animals for the sake of man, should have no more than a dialectic value, as is held by Kullmann (similarly p. 48). It is a pity that Kullmann does not discuss *Met.* 12.10, 1075a16: πάντα δὲ συντέτακταί πως and a18-19: πρὸς μὲν γὰρ ἓν ἅπαντα συντέτακται in this connection. Cf. A. Mansion, "Le dieu d'Aristote et le dieu des Chrétiens," in *La philosophie et ses problèmes: Recueil ... R. Jolivet* (Paris, 1960), pp. 21-44, esp. 41-43, and J. Owens, "Teleology of Nature in Aristotle," *The Monist*, 52 (1968), 159-173, esp. 168-171.

[17] See further D. Bremer, "Aristoteles, Empedokles und die Erkenntnisleistung der Metapher," *Poetica*, 12 (1980), 350-376, esp. 363-375.

material. This phrase shows that fire is imagined as a living being just as in the *Iliad* (23.183) fire "devours" (δάπτει) a corpse.[18] It is true that Aristotle (*An*. 1.5, 411a14-15) rejects the supposition that fire or air might be a ζῷον, but here ζῷον has the restricted sense of "animal." [19]

The other elements, too, behave like living beings. They all have their special properties, but these are called δυνάμεις, and this word still carries its original meaning of "power" which it has in the Hippocratic writings. In the tract *Regimen*, for instance, the human body and the whole world are assumed to consist of fire and water: fire has the power to move, water has the power to nourish. Every change is caused by the fact that each element alternately masters the other. Their interaction gives rise to the existence of organisms: thus an embryo is formed when fire dries the moisture in the sperm so that it is solidified into bones and tissues, while at the same time water provides fire with its necessary nourishment. But also winds have their δυνάμεις: a dry wind, for instance, feeds itself by withdrawing moisture from animals and plants.[20] Similarly Aristotle takes dry and moist, hot and cold to be the δυνάμεις of the elements on which all further properties depend (*PA* 2.1, 646a14-20).[21] For instance, the hot associates things of the same kind but the cold brings together both things of the same class and of different classes (*GC* 2.2, 329b26-30).[22] Hot and cold are more active, moist and dry more passive qualities (*GC* 2.2,

---

[18] This is no metaphor, for fire, just as man, has μένος (*Il*. 6.182; 17.565; *Od*. 11.220). Heraclitus generalizes this idea in his πῦρ ἀείζωον (B 30).

[19] Lloyd (p. 264) concludes from this passage that Aristotle "did *not* believe that the four sublunary elements are alive, and he clearly recognised that the analogy between their natural movements and those of living things is *only* an analogy." But Aristotle treats the similarity between the elements and living beings as a real one and never uses such qualifications as "only an analogy."

[20] See further H. W. Miller, "The Concept of *Dynamis* in *De victu*," *TAPA*, 90 (1959), 147-164. Cf. also G. Plamböck, *Dynamis im Corpus Hippocraticum* (Wiesbaden, 1964), and Solmsen, pp. 346-347 and 359-360.

[21] He emphasizes the fact that cold is no στέρησις, but has its proper φύσις (*PA* 2.2, 649a18-19). A. L. Peck in the Loeb edition of *PA* (p. 31) translates δύναμις by "strong substance of a particular character" and argues that "there is no notion here of the substance *having* power in the sense of power to affect an external body in a particular way. (This meaning developed later.) If any effect did result, it would be described simply as the presence of the strong substance." But *PA* 2.1, 646a15-16 refers to *GC* 2.2, where the notion of power is prominent (see below). See also Solmsen, pp. 337-338. It is misleading, however, when he maintains (p. 82) that Aristotle's contraries "are no longer 'powers'" and that "their active role, their life and death struggle ... are gone." It is true that at *Ph*. 1.6, 189a22-24 and *GC* 1.6, 322b16-18 Aristotle defines qualities as abstractions, but elsewhere (e.g., *GC* 2.3, 330b25-26: τὸ δὲ πῦρ ἐστιν ὑπερβολὴ θερμότητος, and *GA* 4.6, 775a18: πέττει δὲ ἡ θερμότης) he treats them as active substances.

[22] Cf. Solmsen, p. 362 n. 38.

329b24-26).[23] More generally all change is the result of "acting" ($\pi o \iota \varepsilon \tilde{\iota} \nu$) and "suffering" ($\pi \acute{a} \sigma \chi \varepsilon \iota \nu$).[24]

Every element is dominated by one of the four powers: earth is dry (and cold secondarily), water is cold (and moist), air is moist (and hot), and fire is hot (and dry) (GC 2.3, 331a4-6). The elements change into one another when their dominant qualities are overpowered by the opposite qualities of other elements (Meteor. 4.1, 379a11-12): for example, fire will become air if the dryness of fire is overpowered by the moisture in water (GC 2.4, 331a26-29).[25] If the powers of the elements are not completely dominated by their opposites, the result is mixture (GC 1.10, 328a28-31). It is interesting to note that these relations are not conceived in mechanical terms: Aristotle simply assumes that a small quantity of some quality is assimilated by its opposite (GC 1.10, 328a24-26) and that in the case of a mixture of two elements "there is a kind of balance between their powers," but still writes that "each changes from its own nature into the prevailing quality ($\varepsilon i \varsigma \tau \grave{o} \varkappa \rho \alpha \tau o \tilde{\nu} \nu$), but does not become the other" (a28-30). This paradox[26] can only be solved if we take the use of the verb $\varkappa \rho \alpha \tau \acute{\varepsilon} \omega$ literally: the meeting of two elements is like a contest of boxers, one excelling in resisting power the other in striking power; both powers are "prevailing," but both have to give way one to another, either completely, which means the defeat, i.e., the disappearance, of one of the parties, or partly, which means that the trial ends in a draw (a31 $\mu \varepsilon \tau \alpha \xi \acute{\nu}$).[27] In that case the powers are balanced but each of them is still "prevailing," for in a mixture "each ingredient is still potentially what it was before they were mixed" (GC 1.10, 327b25-26).

---

[23] Cf. Solmsen, pp. 350 n. 54, 358 and 361. The texts quoted above clearly show that G. A. Seeck, ed., Die Naturphilosophie des Aristoteles (Darmstadt, 1975), p. xiii, is completely wrong in maintaining that "Aristoteles geht es nicht um diese Qualitäten an sich, sondern er benutzt sie nur, um ein System mit rein formalen Merkmalen aufstellen zu können."

[24] Cf. Solmsen, ch. 18; Th. Tracy, Physiological Theory and the Doctrine of the Mean in Plato and Aristotle (The Hague-Paris, 1969), pp. 163-178.

[25] Cf. W. J. Verdenius and J. H. Waszink, Aristotle, On Coming-to-Be and Passing-Away, 2nd ed. (Leiden, 1966), p. 51.

[26] G. A. Seeck, Über die Elemente in der Kosmologie des Aristoteles (Munich, 1964), p. 54, thinks that $\varepsilon i \varsigma \tau \grave{o} \varkappa \rho \alpha \tau o \tilde{\nu} \nu$ "ist hier ganz sinnlos" and should be bracketed. He is followed by I. Düring, Aristoteles (Heidelberg, 1966), p. 382 n. 247.

[27] H. Carteron, La notion de force dans le système d'Aristote (Paris, 1923), p. 67, observes that "l'image dominante qui préside à l'explication de l'interaction des éléments est celle de la lutte." He continues: "Nous disons que c'est une image parce qu'Aristote ... n'a pas rendu compte du principe de vie qu'anime cette activité," but it would be more correct to say that what for us is an image was a reality for Aristotle. Cf. also Solmsen, pp. 357 n. 18, 361 and 374.

Each of the four elements has its own kind of movement. We have already seen (above, Part I) that these movements are defined as "a kind of life" and that they are based on an innate ὁρμή, which is more than a tendency or impulse for the word is properly used for an "urge" or "desire" in living beings.[28] This "urge" aims at reaching the element's natural place where it settles down and where its φύσις, "growth," attains its fulfilment (see above, Part I).[29] In other words movement is equivalent to development and it has a qualitative rather than a quantitative character.[30] This doctrine has been called "astonishing," [31] but in the context of hylozoism it is only natural. This also appears from the remark that the question why fire moves upwards and earth downwards is just as superfluous as the question why the curable progresses towards health and not towards whiteness (Cael. 4.3, 310b16-19).

The idea of natural movements and natural goals also determines Aristotle's doctrine of weight.[32] The essence of lightness and heaviness is that the former has an upward, the latter a downward tendency (Ph. 8.4, 255b14-17). Hence Aristotle assumes the existence of the absolutely light whose nature is to move always upwards, and the absolutely heavy whose nature is to move always downwards (Cael. 4.4, 311b14-15), and he even concludes that a larger quantity of fire always moves upwards more quickly than a smaller quantity, and a larger quantity of earth downwards more quickly than a smaller quantity (Cael. 1.8, 277b4-5). Here his qualitative point of view becomes most conspicuous: lightness and heaviness are powers similar to those of living beings.[33]

The inconsistencies in Aristotle's conception of coming-to-be are most easily understood if they are viewed in the perspective of hylozoism. On the one hand Aristotle argues that coming-to-be cannot be a movement, on the other hand he often treats it as a kind of movement.[34] In a world

---

[28] Homer uses it of fire and of waves, but these are conceived as living beings: for fire see above, Part II; for waves, cf. Il. 1.481-482: κῦμα ... ἴαχε and 17.264: βέβρυχεν μέγα κῦμα.

[29] Accordingly, rest (στάσις) is said to be better than movement: Top. 4.6, 127b16.

[30] Cf. Carteron, p. 21: "La force reste une émanation de la substance;" p. 24: "la force est comme une quantité d'énergie qui ne se transmet pas, à proprement parler, mais s'éveille;" p. 44: "La force est donc de nature essentiellement qualitative."

[31] Solmsen, p. 255.

[32] For particulars see D. O'Brien, "Heavy and Light in Democritus and Aristotle," JHS, 97 (1977), 64-74, esp. 71-73.

[33] Cf. also GC 1.10, 328a34 and 2.4, 331a22-23, where "quicker" is associated with "easier." See further Carteron, pp. 15-17, who rightly concludes that the whole theory is based on "la notion vulgaire de force, dont le type est la force du corps humain."

[34] Cf. Solmsen, pp. 80, 82 and 178-179.

considered to be permeated by life the beginning of anything new is naturally seen as a special manifestation of life, and so as due to an inner movement.[35]

Aristotle added a complication to his doctrine of motion when he realized that the four elements do not move themselves, because "this is a characteristic of life and peculiar to living things" (Ph. 8.4, 255a5-7).[36] This might seem to affect the principle of hylozoism but it does not mean a real breakthrough. The natural objects still have a principle of movement in themselves, but this is the capacity of being moved (Ph. 8.4, 255b29-31): their own movements are inspired by the desire to imitate a divine Unmoved Mover which is the ultimate source of all natural movement. This imitation shows two stages of perfection: the continual trans-formation of the elements into one another imitates the eternal being of the cyclical movement of the stars (GC 2.10, 336b32-337a7)[37] and this cyclical movement is the nearest approach to the active rest (Met. 7.15, 1154b27) of the Unmoved Mover (Ph. 6.9, 240a29-31). The Unmoved Mover has "the best kind of life" (Cael. 1.9, 279a21; Met. 12.7, 1072b28) and the world's desire to imitate it is denoted by the verbs ἐράω (Met. 12.7, 1072b3) and ὀρέγω (Met. 12.7, 1072a26; GC 2.10, 336b27-28). This shows that hylozoism is not abandoned, but perfected and refined: the Unmoved Mover is a superstructure imposed on Nature but it does not destroy its life for Nature's "urge" to move is now based on a desire to imitate the principle of eternal life.[38]

---

[35] Solmsen (p. 342) points out that Aristotle interprets coming-to-be as a kind of qualitative change. Cf. also J. Stallmach, Dynamis und Energeia (Meisenheim, 1959), p. 34 and n. 24.

It is significant that Aristotle assumes a parallelism between the drawing of a conclusion and the generation of natural entities (Met. 7.9, 1034a30-32), so that hylozoism extends to his logic. See further L. Robin, "Sur la conception aristotélicienne de la causalité," in La pensée hellénique, 2nd ed. (Paris, 1967), pp. 423-485, and Le Blond, pp. 103-104, who quotes a remark made by O. Hamelon: "C'est la vie même du rapport causal qu'Aristote a voulu représenter par ce syllogisme" (viz. the syllogism of the διότι).

[36] Similarly, at Cael. 2.9, 291a23 he denies that the movement of the stars is ἔμψυχος.

[37] Cf. also Met. 9.8, 1050b28-29. See further Solmsen, pp. 386-389 and 426. D. C. Williams, "Form and Matter," Philos. Rev., 67 (1958), 312, seems to me wrong in thinking that "Aristotle has no evidence ... that things can achieve their own forms by aiming at superior forms."

[38] Cf. W. K. C. Guthrie in the introduction to the Loeb edition of De Caelo (London, Cambridge, Mass., 1935), p. xix: "The internal source of motion is not annihilated by the external mover, but subordinated to it." Similarly Lloyd, p. 261. See also Solmsen, pp. 101-102 and 244-245; Aubenque, pp. 355-368; B. Effe, Studien zur Kosmologie und Theologie der Aristotelischen Schrift 'Über die Philosophie' (Munich, 1970), pp. 102-109. H. Happ, "Weltbild und Seinslehre bei Aristoteles," Ant. u. Abend., 14 (1968), 74, observes that "Aristoteles intendiert ein unräumliches Göttliches, den unbewegten Beweger," but "das Anderssein, also die Transzendenz, wird sachwidrig mit den

III. POTENTIALITY AND ACTUALITY

Modern readers of Aristotle might get the impression that the use of the formula "potentially - actually" hardly explains anything: "A becomes B because potentially it was already B." [39] The phrase is much less artificial, however, within the framework of hylozoism. It should be borne in minde that "potentially" (δυνάμει) is still clearly connected with the original meaning of δύναμις, "power" (see above, Part II). This appears, e.g., from GA 1.19, 726b15-19 where the sperm is said to be δυνάμει the future organism because ἔχει τινὰ δύναμιν ἐν ἑαυτῷ. [40] It is also significant that Aristotle (Met. 9.6, 1048a32-35) mentions a piece of stone destined to become a statue and a man capable of studying as examples of potentiality without noting any difference between the two cases.

The primary function of potentiality is to explain change (Met. 5.12, 1019b35-1020a1). A thing changes when it is acted upon but such action presupposes the potency, within the very thing acted upon, of being changed (Met. 9.1, 1046a11-13). For instance, water can be changed into air because it is potentially air (Ph. 4.5, 213a2-4). Such a potency is not pure passivity but an inner directedness towards actualization. [41] This implies that qualitative change, just as movement (see above, Part II), is a kind of self-development. In the case of living beings the power of self-development is an accepted fact and in the world-picture of hylozoism this self-evidence extends to any kind of change. [42]

Kategorien der raumzeitlichen Dingwelt gedacht und dadurch aufgehoben." The contradiction arises from the fact that an object of desire cannot be strictly transcendent.

[39] Cf. Carteron, p. 223: "On ne peut donc pas dire que l'on comprenne, à la rigueur, le passage de la puissance à l'acte."

[40] For more examples cf. Stallmach, pp. 39-40 and 50. Solmsen (p. 376) writes: "It is startling to see how easily Aristotle's concept of potentiality can change back into that of power." But there is no real "change back," because the notion of "power" always forms the background of potentiality. Cf. also W. D. Ross, Aristotle's Metaphysics (Oxford, 1924), 2: 240-241.

[41] Cf. Bonitz's phrase "patiendi nisus" quoted by Le Blond, p. 366. See also S. Moser, "Der Begriff der Natur in aristotelischer und moderner Sicht," Philos. nat., 6 (1960-1961), 278-279, who rightly argues that Nicolai Hartmann was wrong in thinking that the Aristotelian δύναμις and ἐνέργεια mark only the initial and final stages of a natural process, and observes: "Das der Dynamis nach Seiende ist nach Aristoteles positiv geeignet und dienlich zu etwas und nicht bloss potentiell im Sinn der leeren Möglichkeit."

[42] Stallmach (pp. 42-44) rightly emphasizes the aspect of self-development, but seems to me wrong in thinking (p. 44) that this view is incompatible with the δυνάμει ὄν "im eigentlich aristotelischen Sinn." He argues (pp. 25-27) that Aristotle tried to transform the dynamic sense of δύναμις into a modal sense but the former remains the background of the latter as appears, e.g., from Met. 9.3, 1047a24-26 (called by Stallmach, p. 27, an "Inkonsequenz").

The term for actuality, ἐνέργεια, properly means "the state of being at work." Aristotle himself (Met. 9.3, 1047a30-31) notes that it stems from the sphere of movement. The nature of this movement is defined in another passage (Met. 9.8, 1050a16-23) where ἐνέργεια is said to be derived from ἔργον, a statement which is preceded by the following explanation: "just as teachers have achieved their end when they have exhibited their pupil at work (ἐνεργοῦντα), so it is with nature ... for the end is action, and action is actuality." [43] The word ἔργον is often translated by "function," but in connection with δύναμις ἔργον always means "action" or "activity": e.g., at GA 1.2, 716a23-24 ἔργον is immediately followed by ἐργασία.[44]

In living beings "power" is so closely connected with "action" that the transition from the former to the latter is accepted as self-evident: a power usually functions to some degree before it comes into full action. This observation is generalized by Aristotle when he states (Met. 8.6, 1045b20-21) that "the potential and the actual are in a sense one." The same view is expressed in the seemingly circular definition (Met. 9.3, 1047a24-26) "A thing is capable of doing something if there is nothing impossible in its having the actuality of that of which it is said to have the potentiality." [45] In this case, just as in the cases of change and movement, the basic principle of the theory is the notion of vital development.

IV. MATTER AND FORM

Aristotle (Met. 1.3, 984a27-29) criticizes the Milesians because they naively ascribed movement to the substrate of the universe: in reality matter is always passive (GC 2.9, 335b29-31).[46] But passivity is not an absolute notion: a thing's specific matter is identical with its form in that the former is potentially what the latter is actually (Met. 8.6, 1045b18-19)[47] so that the dynamism of the form must have its counterpart in the

---

[43] The common translation of the last words, "actuality is the action," seems to me wrong. In Greek sentences the predicate is often put before the subject for the sake of emphasis: cf. Verdenius-Waszink on GC 1.3, 319a32, and my note on Cael. 2.8, 289b27 in Naturphilosophie bei Aristoteles und Theophrast, ed. I. Düring (Heidelberg, 1969), p. 279. The connection between ἐνέργεια and ἔργον ("activity") is also emphasized at EN 9.7, 1168a7. See also Stallmach, p. 53; and Le Blond, pp. 358-360.

[44] Cf. also Pol. 1.1, 1253a20-24; Meteor. 4.12, 390a10-11; Met. 7.10, 1035b16-18.

[45] Similarly at Met. 8.6, 1045a30-34 Aristotle argues that there is no special cause of the potential sphere to become an actual sphere, but that becoming actual is the very essence of potentiality.

[46] Similarly GC 1.4, 320a2-3; 1.7, 324b18. Cf. A. Mansion, Introduction à la Physique Aristotélicienne (Louvain-Paris, 1946; rpt. Paris, 1974), p. 243 n. 23, and Stallmach, p. 49 n. 35.

[47] Similarly Ph. 2.1, 193b19-20. Cf. Stallmach, pp. 37-38.

thing's matter. Matter is called a "joined-cause" (συναιτία) of form, "like a mother" (*Ph.* 1.9, 192a13-14);[48] it has a natural longing (πέφυκεν ἐφίεσθαι καὶ ὀρέγεσθαι) for actuality and form as the female longing for the male (192a18-23). This implies that matter has some innate activity. Thus an embryo originates when the sperm imposes form and movement on the female matter (*GA* 1.20, 729a9-11). The latter is παθητικόν (729a29-30) but not in an absolute sense: copulation, just as the meeting of the elements (above, Part II), is a trial of strength, the result of which is determined by the degree to which the male element (the hot) succeeds in dominating (κρατεῖν) the female.[49] Both elements, sperm and menses, have their own power (δύναμις): in the case of the former this derives from the blood which has a natural moving power (*GA* 1.19, 726b9-12, 18-19); the menses are a "residue" of the blood and as such have a similar power but in an analogous way (727a2-4).[50]

It may be concluded that matter in Aristotle's system, even when it functions as a principle of resistance, has its proper activity which cannot be completely changed by form.[51] This is to be explained from the fact that the resistance exercised by matter is not pure negation but is always coordinated with the directive power of form.[52] On the other hand form is not completely free from change[53] for it is closely connected with matter: sperm as an acting power is form but at the same time it is a kind of matter (*GA* 1.18, 724b5-7). This has been called "a puzzling passage"[54] but

---

[48] Aristotle was obviously inspired by Plato's *Timaeus*, where the materials used by the demiurge are called συναίτια (46CD) and the receptacle is compared to a mother (50D).

[49] There is a degrading scale of boys resembling their fathers, girls, monstrosities. For particulars cf. *GA* 4.3 and Happ, *Hyle*, pp. 748-750 and 770-771. It is misleading to call the influence exercised by the sperm on the menses "ein physiologisch-chemischer Vorgang," or even "physikalisch-chemische Vorgänge" (Kullmann, pp. 56, 58).

[50] See further Kullmann, pp. 52-53.

[51] As is rightly observed by Happ, *Hyle*, pp. 763, 771.

[52] Cf. Happ, *Hyle*, p. 762, who remarks that matter can only be determined by form "wenn eine in ganz bestimmter Weise auf die betreffende Form hin präformierte Materie vorliegt." See also pp. 749, 754. Th. A. Szlezak in his review of Happ, in *Göttingische Gelehrte Anzeigen*, 225 (1973), 215, disregards the intentional aspect of matter's resistance. He thinks it to be significant ("bezeichnend," n. 48) that the passage *Ph.* 1.9, 192a18-23 quoted above occurs in a book in which the motive cause is not mentioned, but Aristotle does use the term συναιτία (a13). Similarly, W. Wieland, *Die aristotelische Physik* (Göttingen, 1962), p. 140 n. 29, is wrong in dismissing the dynamic interpretation of matter by observing that *Ph.* 1.9, 192a14ff. forms part of a discussion with Platonists (cf. pp. 211, 265-266).

[53] Cf. Solmsen, pp. 83, 89. Before sperm becomes a human being it has to change (μεταβάλλειν): *Met.* 9.7, 1049a15. H. Tredennick, tr., *The Metaphysics of Aristotle* (London, New York, 1933), ad loc., wrongly thinks this to be inconsistent with the role of sperm as the formal element in reproduction.

[54] Grene, p. 36.

matter and form are "virtually relative terms" [55] just as there is no sharp distinction between activity and passivity. Vagueness in the use of these terms seems to be characteristic of our observation of living beings: in a plant matter and form are less easily distinguished than in a stone, and it is equally difficult to say where in life action ends and reaction begins.[56]

It should be added that if the doctrine of power ascribed to both matter and form is taken seriously, hylozoism in Aristotle is associated with "morphozoism." This also appears from the fact that form embodies the directive tendency of nature more strongly than matter (*Ph.* 2.1, 193b17-18) and is equated with ἐνέργεια (e.g., *Met.* 8.2, 1043a26-28; 9.8, 1050b2).

V. THE RELEVANCE OF HYLOZOISM

It has often been observed that modern science has dissociated itself from its classical origin by substituting systems of relations for the ancient substances and their inherent powers.[57] From time to time, however, dissenting voices are to be heard. C. F. von Weizsäcker[58] emphasizes the

---

[55] Balme, *Teleological Explanation*, p. 18. Cf. *Ph.* 2.1, 193b19-20: ἡ στέρησις εἶδός πώς ἐστιν, and Carteron, pp. 204-208, who concludes (p. 208): "Ce désir de la matière qui a pour fin la forme lui vient de sa propre nature; or, qu'est cette nature si ce n'est une forme, inférieure à la forme que le changement a pour but de réaliser, mais forme cependant et qui permet d'appeler la matière une substance ou presque?" See also Mansion, *Introduction*, pp. 241-242; Solmsen, pp. 283, 332-333 and 362; E. E. Ryan, "Pure Form in Aristotle," *Phronesis*, 18 (1973), 209-225.

[56] Aristotle may also have been influenced by the fact that in Greek the meanings of ποιεῖν and πάσχειν often overlap one another: cf. my observations in "Plato, *Republic* 409ab, and the Meaning of ὁμοιοπαθής," *Mnemosyne*, 20 (1967), 296; and P. T. Stevens, *Colloquial Expression in Euripides* (Wiesbaden, 1976), p. 41.

[57] See my article "Science grecque et science moderne," *Rev. Philos.*, 87 (1962), 319-336, esp. 332-336. Cf. also K. von Fritz, *Grundprobleme der Geschichte der antiken Wissenschaft* (Berlin, New York, 1971), pp. 102-111. Williams (p. 295) regrets the fact that Aristotle "cannot with good grace admit relational pattern into the very core and essence of things."

[58] E.g., in his book *Die Geschichte der Natur*, 2nd ed. (Göttingen, 1954), p. 89, he writes about a candle-flame: "Niemand leugnet, dass wir sie physikalisch-chemisch verstehen. Aber sie hat Stoffwechsel bei gleichbleibender Form, sie stellt ihre Gestalt nach äusserer Störung wieder her, sie vermehrt sich, wenn man andere Kerzen mit ihr anzündet, ja man kann das Driesch'sche Seeigelexperiment mit ihr anstellen: spaltet man den Docht, so entstehen zwei ganze, aber schwächere Kerzenflammen. ... Mit Grund ist das Feuer seit der Urzeit das Symbol des Lebens. Sollten zwei so ähnliche Erscheinungen im Wesen so verschieden sein?" Cf. his book *Zum Weltbild der Physik*, 4th ed. (Zürich, 1949), p. 21, where he observes that a virus which exists in living tissues can be crystallized. In his work *Die Einheit der Natur* (Munich, 1971), p. 315, he suggests that "Bewusstsein und Materie sind verschiedene Aspekte derselben Wirklichkeit" (cf. pp. 365-366).

similarities between organic and inorganic nature. W. Stegmaier[59] argues that processes of growth and the survival of species cannot be understood without assuming the real existence of substances. H. B. Veatch[60] calls Bertrand Russell's interpretation of the individual as "a series of occurrences" and as "a logical construction out of sense data" a case of "tomfoolery" and praises Aristotle as the champion of "common sense" for whom substance is "an ultimate fact of nature." J. H. F. Umbgrove[61] suggests that matter and life are the complementary aspects of one and the same entity.

Such considerations are connected with the fact that some fundamental problems of science are still unsolved. E. Meyerson[62] admits that the essentially new factor in a chemical compound cannot be explained and E. J. Dijksterhuis[63] complains that this very problem is commonly ignored.[64] K. Hummel[65] observes that in biology qualitative differences cannot be reduced to quantitative relations; The most baffling difficulty in modern science is the fact that the manifestation of light as a stream of particles cannot be coordinated with its manifestation as a wave, and that the position and the velocity of the particles cannot be measured at the same time.[66]

It is interesting to note that these and similar problems have led to a kind of rehabilitation of hylozoism. The elementary particles are credited with "elementary acts" which are "completely free" although they somehow cooperate in building a "figure" ("Gestalt") which cannot be explained, however, by purely mechanical laws.[67] This recognition of

---

[59] *Grundbegriffe der Metaphysik* (Stuttgart, 1977).

[60] *Aristotle: A Contemporary Appreciation* (Bloomington, London, 1974), pp. 13-25.

[61] *Leven en materie* (The Hague, 1943), esp. pp. 118-122.

[62] *Identité et réalité*, 3rd ed. (Paris, 1926), p. 252.

[63] In his inaugural lecture *Doel en methode van de geschiedenis der exacte wetenschappen* (Amsterdam, 1953), p. 17.

[64] R. A. Horne, "Die Chemie des Aristoteles," in *Die Naturphilosophie des Aristoteles*, ed. Seeck, pp. 339-347, praises Aristotle for drawing a distinction between a chemical compound and a mixture (*GC* 1.10, 328a7-14), but he blames him for spoiling the explanation by introducing the idea of a balance of powers (pp. 343-344) instead of investigating the laws governing the grouping of atoms (p. 346). He does not seem to realize that Aristotle would never have accepted such a formal description as a real explanation.

[65] "Der Begriff des Lebenden bei Aristoteles und in der wissenschaftlichen Biologie von heute," *Studium Generale*, 14 (1961), 419.

[66] Cf. F. Schmeidler, *Alte und moderne Kosmologie* (Berlin, 1962), pp. 66-67, who concludes: "eine wirklich überzeugende Klärung dieser Probleme liegt bis heute nicht vor."

[67] Cf. B. Bavink, *Die Naturwissenschaft auf dem Wege zur Religion* (Basel, 1948), pp. 105-106, 122 and 129-130. Similarly von Weizsäcker, *Geschichte der Natur*, pp. 60, 93.

spontaneity in nature accords well with Aristotle's doctrine of natural powers. It even seems to bring about a *rapprochement* between the modern concept of energy and the original ἐνέργεια. In spite of its mathematical connotation energy is described as a productive substance which materializes in the formation of new creations.[68] Similar ideas have been expressed by A. N. Whitehead in whose view spontaneity is charac-teristic of the whole of nature, inorganic nature being distinguished from organic nature by its more rigid structure. He tries to replace the notion of "thing" by that of "process," [69] but if these processes are differentiated by their specific "order" [70] he seems to need some principle of form. White-head rejects the Aristotelian idea of natural substances as a hypostatized linguistic category,[71] but he might have profited by considering the possibilities of a modern use of morphozoism, i.e., the conception of form as a dynamic entity.[72]

---

[68] Cf. W. Heisenberg, *Physik und Philosophie* (Frankfurt, 1959), p. 132: "so kann man sagen, dass die Materie des Aristoteles, die ja im wesentlichen 'Potentia', d.h. Möglichkeit war, mit unserem Energiebegriff verglichen werden sollte; die Energie tritt als materielle Realität durch die Form in Erscheinung, wenn ein Elementarteilchen erzeugt wird. ... Eine klare Unterscheidung zwischen Materie und Kraft oder zwischen Kraft und Stoff kann in diesem Teil der Physik nicht mehr gemacht werden." Although Heisenberg (pp. 151-152) warns his readers that "potency" is an image rather than a precise description, it seems to me significant that he uses the term "erzeugt" in a physical context. See further Moser, pp. 281-283, who rightly points out the weak points in Heisenberg's comparison of Greek and modern physics. For the interpretation of substance as a unity of matter and energy see also von Weizsäcker, *Einheit der Natur*, pp. 344-346, and D. Dubarle, "L'idée hylémorphiste d'Aristote et la compréhension de l'univers," *Rev. sc. philos. théol.*, 36 (1952), 3-29, 205-230 and vol. 37 (1953), 3-23, esp. vol. 37, p. 16: "L'énergie physique ne vient pas de l'actualité formelle de l'individu: elle est bien plutôt une ressource immanente à cet en-soi matériel de l'organisme. Ce que la forme apporte, ce qu'elle est de quelque manière, c'est l'acte même de la régulation imposée aux énergies physiques à l'œuvre dans l'organisme individuel." Grene in her chapter (VII) on "The Relevance of Aristotle" does not have an eye for the regulating power of dynamic form. She believes (p. 232) that "the hazards of mutation, of environmental change, of inter- and intra-specific competition, all these and more furnish a background of contingency" and that, correspondingly, scientific construction is "a hazardous venture" (p. 238), even "a gamble."

[69] Cf. e.g., *Process and Reality* (New York, 1929), p. 327: "each actual entity is itself only describable as an organic process."

[70] Cf. his ch. III "The Order of Nature."

[71] *The Concept of Nature* (Cambridge, 1920), pp. 16-18.

[72] von Weizsäcker, *Einheit der Natur*, p. 361, concludes: "Materie ist Form. Bewegung ist Form." Cf. also p. 362: "Materie ist, aristotelisch gesprochen, Möglichkeit von Form."

6

Aristote et le statut épistémologique
de la théorie de l'arc-en-ciel

Jacques Brunschwig
Université de Paris X, Nanterre

Dans une remarquable thèse, encore inédite, sur "Les sources et le contexte historique de la théorie aristotélicienne de l'arc-en-ciel," [1] un jeune chercheur français, M. Guy Picolet, a démontré avec une parfaite clarté l'importance et l'intérêt de cette théorie apparemment marginale du Stagirite, sur le double plan de l'histoire des sciences et de l'épistémologie. Au cours de son étude, il examine de fort près un passage plus connu sans doute de la moyenne des aristotélisants que les difficiles chapitres 2-5 des *Météorologiques* 3, où Aristote traite *ex professo* de l'arc-en-ciel: à savoir, ce passage des *Seconds Analytiques* (1.13, 79a10-13) où il mentionne la théorie de l'arc-en-ciel, afin de préciser les relations épistémologiques entre la physique, l'optique et la géométrie. La discussion très probe et très minutieuse que M. Picolet présente de ces quelques lignes m'a paru aboutir à ce résultat (d'autant plus remarquable qu'il n'était pas recherché) que les interprétations traditionnelles que l'on en donne se heurtent à de considérables difficultés. Je me propose ici, sur la lancée du travail de M. Picolet et avec son autorisation, très généreusement accordée,[2] de repren-

---

[1] Cette thèse de 3e cycle a été soutenue à l'Université de Paris X - Nanterre le 6 mai 1982; elle avait été préparée sous la direction du Professeur Jacques Merleau-Ponty.

[2] M. Picolet pense en effet faire publier sa thèse, ce qui est très souhaitable à tous égards.

Graceful Reason: Essays in Ancient and Medieval Philosophy Presented to Joseph Owens, CSSR, ed. Lloyd P. Gerson. Papers in Mediaeval Studies 4 (Toronto: Pontifical Institute of Mediaeval Studies, 1983), pp. 115-134. © P.I.M.S., 1983.

dre l'examen de ce passage, et de suggérer une solution possible de ces difficultés. Comment mieux témoigner de la continuité des études aristotéli-
ciennes qu'en offrant à un vétéran, unanimement admiré et respecté, le
fruit d'une réflexion suscitée par les travaux d'un jeune et talentueux
chercheur, lorsqu'on se trouve soi-même, par la grâce de l'état-civil,
quelque part entre les deux ?

I

Le passage qui va nous occuper se situe dans le chapitre 1.13 des *Seconds
Analytiques*, où Aristote étudie la différence entre la connaissance du *fait*
(ὅτι) et celle du *pourquoi* (διότι), ou plus exactement, comme le fait
remarquer avec juste raison Jonathan Barnes dans son brillant commentaire,[3] entre la connaissance d'un fait sur une base autre que celle de son
explication et la connaissance d'un fait sur la base de son explication. La
différence peut se situer entre des connaissances appartenant à une seule et
même science;[4] elle peut aussi se répartir entre deux sciences distinctes.[5]
Dans ce dernier cas, les deux sciences en cause peuvent n'entretenir
aucune relation particulière;[6] mais la situation qui intéresse le plus Aristote, et à laquelle il consacre le plus long développement, est celle où la
science dont relève la connaissance du fait est *subordonnée* à celle dont
relève la connaissance du pourquoi. Ce thème des rapports de
subordination entre certains couples de sciences, qui atténue la rigidité de
l'interdit porté contre la μετάβασις εἰς ἄλλο γένος, est récurrent, comme on
le sait, dans les *Seconds Analytiques*;[7] il est de grande importance au point
de vue épistémologique, puisqu'il aménage une passerelle entre mathématiques et physique.[8] Les rapports de subordination entre deux sciences
s'analysent en diverses relations, dont les unes paraissent pointer plutôt
vers le rapport d'une science appliquée à une science pure, et les autres

---

[3] *Aristotle's Posterior Analytics*, translated with notes by Jonathan Barnes (Oxford, 1975), p. 149.

[4] 78a22-23: πρῶτον μὲν ἐν τῇ αὐτῇ ἐπιστήμῃ.

[5] 78b35: τῷ (τὸ codd.) δι' ἄλλης ἐπιστήμης.

[6] Le cas est fréquent (πολλαί, 79a13); il est illustré par l'exemple de la médecine, qui constate que les blessures circulaires guérissent plus lentement, fait que la géométrie explique.

[7] Cf. le relevé des textes dans J. Barnes, p. 129, *ad* 75b6. On peut y ajouter, en dehors des *Analytiques*, *Phys.* 2.2, 194a7-12; *Métaph.* M.3, 1078a14-16.

[8] Dans le passage de la *Physique* cité à la note précédente, Aristote dit que l'optique, l'harmonie et l'astronomie (qui dans les *Analytiques* constituent ses exemples majeurs de sciences subordonnées) sont "celles des connaissances mathématiques qui sont plutôt physiques (τὰ φυσικώτερα τῶν μαθημάτων)."

plutôt vers le rapport d'une science d'observation à une science explicative;[9] les exemples régulièrement allégués par Aristote vont tantôt dans un sens (harmonie, arithmétique; optique, géométrie),[10] tantôt dans l'autre (astronomie "nautique," astronomie mathématique; harmonie acoustique, harmonie mathématique); dans ce second cas, et seulement dans ce second cas, précise Aristote, les sciences ainsi couplées sont "presque synonymes."[11]

C'est dans le courant de cette analyse qu'Aristote introduit la remarque suivante, que je donne d'abord dans le texte, la ponctuation et la traduction qu'adopte M. Picolet: "Or une autre science est à l'optique dans le même rapport que cette dernière à la géométrie, à savoir l'étude de l'arc-en-ciel: car la connaissance du fait relève ici du physicien, tandis que celle du pourquoi relève de l'opticien, considéré en tant que tel d'une façon absolue ou bien suivant la discipline mathématique" (ἔχει δὲ καὶ πρὸς τὴν ὀπτικήν, ὡς αὕτη πρὸς τὴν γεωμετρίαν, ἄλλη πρὸς ταύτην, οἷον τὸ περὶ τῆς ἴριδος · τὸ μὲν γὰρ ὅτι φυσικοῦ εἰδέναι, τὸ δὲ διότι ὀπτικοῦ, ἢ ἁπλῶς ἢ τοῦ κατὰ τὸ μάθημα, 79a10-13).

Avant d'entrer dans l'examen des problèmes que pose cette phrase, je noterai, en guise d'observation générale, qu'Aristote souligne ici lui-même, à propos des notions de science subordonnée et de science subordonnante qu'il vient de dégager, un trait caractéristique de beaucoup de ses concepts fondamentaux:[12] ce sont très souvent des concepts *fonctionnels*, qui désignent, non pas des choses ou des classes de choses, mais des rôles définis et interchangeables, que certaines choses jouent par rapport à certaines autres, et qui peuvent varier, pour une seule et même chose, selon les rapports que l'on prend en considération. Ainsi, comme il

---

[9] Cf. les analyses de J. Barnes, pp. 151-155. Quand une science x est "sous" une science y, les démonstrations de y s'appliquent au genre spécifique d'objets dont traite x; les démonstrations de x empruntent leurs principes à y.

[10] Ce dernier exemple, qui nous concerne particulièrement, apparaît en 75b16, 76a24, 78b37.

[11] 78b39: σχεδὸν συνώνυμοι. Le mot de "synonyme" est probablement à prendre dans un sens qui n'est pas le sens technique aristotélicien (cf. *Cat.* 1, 1a6-7); ce dernier ne se laisse pas aisément atténuer par un σχεδόν. Il est plus simple de comprendre que l'astronomie mathématique et l'astronomie nautique, par exemple, sont "presque synonymes" en ce sens que leurs noms sont partiellement identiques. Lorsque la "science" subordonnée est purement observationnelle (79a2-3), on ne voit guère, en effet, comment elle pourrait avoir un nom totalement différent de celui de la science qui explique les faits qu'elle-même se borne à relever; c'est cette dernière qui est, à proprement parler, la science de l'objet qui leur est commun. Lorsque l'objet des deux sciences est "différent", elles ne sont pas "synonymes" (cf. 76a12 et 23, avec les exemples donnés dans le contexte).

[12] Cf. en particulier Wolfgang Wieland, *Die aristotelische Physik* (Göttingen, 1962), notamment pp. 173-187.

est bien connu, de la forme et de la matière, de l'acte et de la puissance: telle chose est forme ou acte selon tel rapport, matière ou puissance selon tel autre. Ainsi encore, ici même, de la science supérieure et de la science inférieure: il existe une science qui est à l'optique ce que l'optique elle-même est à la géométrie, à savoir science subordonnée par rapport à sa science subordonnante. L'optique est donc science subordonnante sous un certain rapport, et science subordonnée sous un certain autre rapport.[13]

Après cette remarque préliminaire, abordons maintenant, sur les traces de M. Picolet (dont je commencerai par résumer les analyses), les difficultés que comporte ce texte. Une première question, assez facile à résoudre, se pose à propos des mots ἄλλη et ταύτην, dont les référents ne sont pas immédiatement évidents. Un moment de réflexion suffit cependant pour s'assurer que ταύτην ne peut se rapporter qu'à ὀπτικήν, et que ἄλλη se rapporte au substantif sous-entendu ἐπιστήμη. Les autres difficultés du texte sont plus sérieuses, et le désaccord des commentateurs anciens en témoigne. On peut en distinguer deux principales:

(1) Quel est le sens précis de l'expression τὸ περὶ τῆς ἴριδος ? Cette expression est manifestement destinée à préciser, d'une manière ou d'une autre, le mot ἄλλη, par lequel est introduite cette science anonyme qui est subordonnée à l'optique; mais le contexte ne permet pas de déterminer quel mot, du genre neutre, il faut sous-entendre pour compléter l'article τό.

(2) Que signifie au juste le membre de phrase ἢ ἁπλῶς ἢ τοῦ κατὰ τὸ μάθημα ? La disjonction ne peut guère se rapporter qu'à ὀπτικοῦ; elle revient donc à introduire une distinction entre deux sortes d'opticiens, ou entre deux aspects du savoir de l'opticien: l'opticien ἁπλῶς et l'opticien κατὰ τὸ μάθημα. Mais c'est le sens même de cette distinction qui est loin d'être clair.

Les commentateurs anciens ont consacré beaucoup d'attention à la première de ces difficultés. Alexandre d'Aphrodise, dans son commentaire

---

[13] Il n'est pas tout à fait exact de dire, avec Jonathan Barnes (p. 152), que le couple (étude de l'arc-en-ciel, optique), établi en 79a10, rapproché (par le lecteur ou l'interprète) du couple (optique, géométrie), établi en 75b16, 76a24 et 78b37, engendre, du fait qu'il possède un terme commun avec lui, la triade (étude de l'arc-en-ciel, optique, géométrie). En fait, Aristote lui-même, dans la phrase citée, établit explicitement une analogie à trois termes: le rapport que l'optique entretient avec la géométrie, une autre science (qui n'est pas formellement identifiée avec l'étude de l'arc-en-ciel) l'entretient avec l'optique elle-même. Il ne fait rien de tel concernant l'harmonie et l'astronomie; on préférera donc prendre acte de cette dissymétrie, plutôt que d'essayer de construire des triades correspondant à ces deux derniers cas.

perdu sur les *Seconds Analytiques*, dont quelques citations ont été préservées par Philopon,[14] identifie la science anonyme, qui est à l'optique ce que l'optique elle-même est à la géométrie, avec "celle qui examine la question de l'arc-en-ciel" (ἡ ἐπισκεπτομένη τὸ περὶ τῆς ἴριδος θεώρημα), donc avec une discipline scientifique spécifique, à laquelle il ne donne cependant pas de nom précis, et dont on ne peut savoir s'il la conçoit comme strictement limitée à l'étude de l'arc-en-ciel, ou comme regroupant cette étude avec celle d'autres phénomènes de la même espèce ou du même genre. Thémistius, au contraire, considère que cette science n'est autre que la physique, identification qui s'accorde avec la dernière partie du texte, puisque Aristote y déclare que c'est le physicien qui a compétence sur le ὅτι dans l'étude de l'arc-en-ciel, alors que l'opticien est compétent sur le διότι.[15] Proclus, enfin, dont l'exégèse ne nous est connue, elle aussi, que par des citations de Philopon,[16] adopte une troisième solution: la science qu'Aristote a en vue est selon lui la catoptrique, discipline spécialisée dans l'étude des rayons (lumineux ou visuels) brisés par la réflexion ou la réfraction; en effet, selon Aristote lui-même, l'arc-en-ciel est un phénomène engendré par la réflexion des rayons visuels sur les gouttes de pluie.[17] Ces trois solutions ont chacune leurs inconvénients, qu'il est inutile ici de détailler; M. Picolet estime que celle de Thémistius est encore la plus proche du texte, bien que l'expression οἷον τὸ περὶ τῆς ἴριδος reste étonnante, de son propre aveu, dans cette perspective. Peut-être, suggère-t-il, préférera-t-on encore se résigner à laisser ce problème sans réponse.[18]

[14] Cf. Philopon, *In Ar. Anal. Post.*, 181.11-19 Wallies. Ce passage est le fragment 20, pp. 43-44, dans l'édition de Paul Moraux, *Le Commentaire d'Alexandre d'Aphrodise aux "Seconds Analytiques" d'Aristote* (Berlin, New York, 1979) (l'une des très rares lacunes de la bibliographie de M. Picolet).

[15] Cf. Themistius, *Ar. Anal. Post. Paraphr.*, p. 29.24-26 Wallies. Cette identification avec la physique est reprise par Waitz, *Organon*, t. 2 (Leipzig, 1846), p. 337; mais, par une aberration curieuse, il interprète ἴρις comme signifiant l'iris de l'œil, et non l'arc-en-ciel. Pour désigner l'iris, Aristote dit τὸ μέλαν (cf. Bonitz, *Index aristotelicus*, 451a60); ἴρις en ce sens n'apparaît, semble-t-il, que chez des médecins tardifs (cf. LSJ s.v.).

[16] Cf. Philopon, 181.19-182.7 Wallies.

[17] Cf. *APo.* 2.15, 98a25-29 (l'arc-en-ciel est ici rapproché de l'écho et du miroir; dans les trois cas, nous avons affaire à une réflexion, ἀνάκλασις; le problème est identique génériquement, bien que spécifiquement différent); *Météor.* 3.2, 372a17-19; 4, 373a32. M. Picolet a d'ailleurs établi de façon absolument convaincante qu'en ceci Aristote est tributaire d'une longue lignée de devanciers.

[18] M. Picolet cite Th. Heath, *Mathematics in Aristotle* (Oxford, 1949), p. 60, à l'appui de cette résignation: "When Aristotle mentions the theorem of the rainbow (79a10) as an illustration of another science related to optics, in the same way as optics is related to geometry, he need not be taken quite literally." – Il est assez étrange qu'à l'exception de Paul Moraux (p. 45), aucun commentateur ancien ou moderne n'ait désigné la météo-

De toute façon, quelle que soit l'identité exacte de cette science anonyme, son rôle est parfaitement clair: c'est à elle qu'il appartient d'établir le ὅτι concernant l'arc-en-ciel. Peut-on cependant préciser les limites de cette sphère de compétence? Elle comprend à coup sûr tout ce qui relève des faits observables, concernant la couleur, la forme, les conditions d'apparition du phénomène. Mais, selon Thémistius,[19] il appartiendrait encore à la connaissance du fait de savoir que l'arc-en-ciel est une réflexion de la vue vers le soleil, à partir d'un nuage constitué et disposé d'une certaine façon; ce savoir relèverait aussi, par conséquent, de la compétence de la science subordonnée à l'optique. Cette répartition des compétences pourrait s'autoriser de la disposition de l'exposé d'Aristote dans les *Météorologiques*: il semble bien, en effet, qu'Aristote y range la nature catoptrique[20] de l'arc-en-ciel parmi les faits d'observation qui concernent ce phénomène, et considère que l'on ouvre le chapitre de l'explication au moment seulement où l'on rend compte de la nature et des causes de la réflexion qui produit l'arc-en-ciel.[21] Il ne faudrait donc pas hésiter à dire, en dépit des indications apparemment formelles de notre passage des *Analytiques*, que la découverte de la cause (ou du moins de la cause principale) de l'arc-en-ciel relève du physicien, et non de l'opticien; ce que l'on pourrait d'ailleurs inférer aussi du passage du livre 2 des *Seconds Analytiques* (15, 98a25-29) où la cause commune de l'écho, de la vision dans les miroirs et de l'arc-en-ciel est désignée comme un phénomène de réflexion. Cette désignation ne peut relever de la compétence des

---

rologie comme étant cette science qui étudie l'arc-en-ciel (entre autres choses) et qui est subordonnée à l'optique. Cette solution n'est, bien évidemment, en contradiction ni avec la proposition de Thémistius, ni avec le texte des *Seconds Analytiques*, puisque la météorologie est la dernière partie du cours de physique d'Aristote, d'après le célèbre début des *Météorologiques* (1.1, 338a20-b1).

[19] Cf. Thémistius, 29.26-27 Wallies.

[20] Plus exactement: anaclastique (cf. les textes cités n. 17). Jonathan Barnes (p. 152), qui estime que l'étude de l'arc-en-ciel est probablement à prendre comme un exemple de ce qu'étudie la science subordonnée à l'optique, affirme qu'Aristote "n'avait pas de terme pour désigner la catoptrique," ce qui est littéralement exact; mais M. Picolet fait remarquer qu'il a pu connaître un terme équivalent, formé sur le substantif ἔνοπτρον, synonyme de κάτοπτρον, s'il est vrai que son contemporain Philippe d'Opunte a rédigé une *Enoptrique* en deux livres (ἐνοπτικῶν codd., ἐνοπτρικῶν edd.; cf. Leonardo Tarán, *Academica: Plato, Philip of Opus and the Pseudo-Platonic Epinomis* [Philadelphie, 1975], test. I). M. Picolet a établi, par ailleurs, l'importance décisive de l'œuvre de Philippe d'Opunte pour Aristote savant, notamment en optique et en météorologie.

[21] Cf. la transition du début du chapitre 3.4 (373a32-34): "Que l'arc-en-ciel soit une réflexion, on l'a dit auparavant (*sc.* 372a17). Mais de quelle nature (ποία δὲ τις) est cette réflexion, et comment ainsi que par quelle cause (καὶ πῶς καὶ διὰ τίν' αἰτίαν) arrive chacun des faits d'expérience (τῶν συμβαινόντων) constatés à son propos, il nous faut maintenant l'expliquer (λέγωμεν νῦν)."

spécialistes de chacun de ces trois phénomènes (l'acousticien, le catoptricien, le théoricien de l'arc-en-ciel), puisqu'elle repose sur leur rapprochement; et l'on ne voit guère que le physicien qui puisse ainsi regrouper dans un même genre les objets d'étude propres de ces trois spécialistes, et leur assigner une explication commune.

Concernant maintenant la discipline de laquelle relève le διότι de l'arc-en-ciel, le texte d'Aristote la désigne sans ambiguïté comme étant l'optique. Mais Aristote établit, on s'en souvient, une distinction entre l'opticien ἁπλῶς ("simplement," "au sens absolu," "sans autre distinction") et l'opticien κατὰ τὸ μάθημα ("selon la discipline mathématique"); et cette distinction soulève la seconde des deux difficultés signalées plus haut. En s'appuyant sur des indications de Thémistius et de Proclus, ce dernier cité par Philopon,[22] M. Picolet explique cette disjonction comme celle de deux disciplines ou de deux aspects de la discipline optique, en la mettant en correspondance avec la distinction de deux catégories de faits relatifs à l'arc-en-ciel. Les uns sont de nature géométrique (forme, grandeur); leur explication relève donc de l'opticien en tant qu'il suit les principes et les modes de raisonnement de la discipline mathématique dénommée optique, c'est-à-dire de l'opticien qu'Aristote appelle ici κατὰ τὸ μάθημα. Les autres faits constatables relativement à l'arc-en-ciel tiennent plus parti-culièrement au fonctionnement de notre appareil visuel; ce sont notamment les couleurs de l'arc, mais aussi le "fait" qu'il n'est rien d'autre qu'une réflexion du rayon visuel. L'explication de cette classe de faits relève donc d'une optique plus "physique" que "géométrique," s'occupant d'une manière générale des divers phénomènes visuels qui restent réfractaires à la géométrisation; cette optique est celle de l'opticien ἁπλῶς. Il faut, en conséquence, admettre que, dans le texte qui nous occupe, Aris-tote emploie le mot "optique" en deux sens différents, une fois (en 79a10) dans le sens de "science mathématique, subordonnée à la géométrie, et traitant géométriquement d'un certain nombre de questions relatives à la vue," une autre fois (en 79a12) dans le sens plus général de "science des questions relatives à la vue."

La pensée d'Aristote, toujours selon M. Picolet, se résumerait donc de la manière suivante. L'établissement d'une théorie adéquate de l'arc-en-ciel comporte principalement deux étapes: une étape "essentiellement descriptive"[23] qui fournit la connaissance du fait, puis une étape d'expli-

---

[22] Cf. Thémistius, 29.27-28 Wallies; Philopon, 181.22-25 Wallies.

[23] Dans cette expression de M. Picolet, l'adverbe est destiné à corriger l'adjectif dans une mesure suffisante pour que l'assignation de la réflexion comme "cause principale" de l'arc-en-ciel puisse encore tomber à l'intérieur de cette étape. Il est permis de douter que cet élargissement suffise à supprimer le paradoxe.

cation "proprement dite" [24] qui fournit celle du pourquoi. Mais chacune de ces deux étapes se subdivise encore en deux phases distinctes. La connaissance du fait, tâche du savant qui est le plus directement en contact avec la réalité sensible, c'est-à-dire du physicien, s'effectue en deux temps: des observations répétées permettent d'abord de dégager un certain nombre de données d'expérience universelles sur le phénomène; des comparaisons méthodiques avec d'autres phénomènes du même genre, comme l'écho et la vision dans les miroirs, permettent ensuite de remonter à la cause principale de l'arc-en-ciel et des phénomènes analogues, en l'espèce la réflexion. L'explication "proprement dite" des phénomènes ainsi collectés relève de l'optique, dont l'intervention doit également se subdiviser pour répondre à la diversité des propriétés de l'arc-en-ciel: ses propriétés "optiques" générales seront traitées par l'opticien en tant que spécialiste de tout ce qui touche à la vue, alors que ses aspects proprement géométriques seront expliqués par l'opticien en tant que spécialiste de l'optique mathématique, qui est une forme de géométrie appliquée.

L'exposé même de la théorie aristotélicienne de l'arc-en-ciel, dans les *Météorologiques*, paraît répondre parfaitement à cette répartition des tâches entre physicien, opticien *simpliciter* et opticien-géomètre. En effet, dans une première partie de cet exposé (3.2), Aristote se cantonne dans un rôle "essentiellement descriptif," se bornant à exposer les faits et circonstances entourant la production de l'arc-en-ciel (et d'autres phénomènes apparentés), ou bien à affirmer que l'arc est un phénomène de réflexion, au même titre que les autres météores lumineux, comme le halo. Dans une seconde partie (3.4-5), au-delà d'un chapitre consacré au halo, il se livre à l'explication "proprement dite" des faits précédemment énoncés. La partie descriptive comporte elle-même une distinction nette entre les données d'expérience proprement dites (2, 371b21-372a17) et l'affirmation que l'arc et les phénomènes similaires sont des effets de la réflexion (372a17-b11). La partie explicative est également subdivisée en deux: dans toute la section initiale de l'exposé (4), il n'est fait pour ainsi dire aucun usage des notions géométriques, alors que, dans la section suivante (5), Aristote se sert pour ainsi dire exclusivement de notions et de raisonnements mathématiques (d'un niveau technique élevé) pour expliquer les propriétés géométriques de l'arc-en-ciel.[25]

---

[24] Cette expression, toujours de M. Picolet, constitue la contrepartie de celle qui a fait l'objet de la note précédente. Elle appellerait la même observation.

[25] L'authenticité de ce chapitre a été parfois contestée, en raison précisément d'un niveau technique jugé hors de proportion avec les connaissances mathématiques d'Aristote, et aussi parce qu'il est omis dans certaines traductions anciennes des *Météorologiques*. M. Picolet plaide avec beaucoup de force, au contraire, la thèse de l'authenticité.

Ce scénario quadripartite peut d'ailleurs se simplifier, si l'on veut bien considérer qu'il appartient au seul physicien de relever et de décrire toutes les propriétés de l'arc-en-ciel, qu'elles soient ou non géométriques. Il est alors possible de réduire à une division tripartite la classification des disciplines qui entrent en jeu dans la constitution d'une théorie complète de l'arc-en-ciel; et l'on rejoint par là le texte des *Seconds Analytiques*. Cette théorie fait nécessairement recours à trois sciences, subordonnées entre elles deux à deux: la physique, l'optique *simpliciter* et l'optique géométrique (celle-ci étant subordonnée, à son tour, à la géométrie pure).

II

Telle est l'interprétation à laquelle on parvient lorsqu'on déroule rigoureusement et méticuleusement, comme l'a fait M. Picolet, les conséquences des lectures traditionnelles de notre passage des *Seconds Analytiques*. On aura peut-être remarqué, chemin faisant, les difficultés intrinsèques de ces conséquences, difficultés assez considérables, à mon sens, pour obliger à remettre en question les prémisses sur lesquelles elles reposent. J'essaierai maintenant de dégager clairement ces difficultés.

(1) La première est que l'on est contraint, en suivant M. Picolet, d'attribuer à Aristote l'idée d'un dédoublement de l'optique en deux disciplines discernables, alors qu'Aristote, ni dans les *Seconds Analytiques* ni ailleurs, ne souffle mot d'une telle distinction (en dehors de notre passage tel qu'on l'interprète habituellement). L'optique (tout court) est régulièrement présentée par le Stagirite comme une discipline unique, suffisamment située, au point de vue épistémologique, par sa relation de subordination à l'égard de la géométrie.[26] Dans notre texte même, il en est tout d'abord ainsi: il y a une science, dit Aristote, qui est à l'optique ce que celle-ci (αὕτη) est à la géométrie; rien absolument n'indique que l'optique puisse, par une partie ou par un aspect d'elle-même, échapper à cette subordination. Le moyen le plus commode d'attribuer malgré tout ce dédoublement au Stagirite est d'extrapoler à l'optique ce qu'il dit (en *APo.* 1.13, 78b39 sqq.) de l'astronomie et de l'harmonie, subdivisées chacune en deux disciplines "presque synonymes," l'une purement observationnelle, et l'autre mathématique.[27] Mais on peut tout aussi bien tenir pour

---

[26] Cf. les textes cités ci-dessus, notes 7 et 10.

[27] Cette extrapolation est explicite dans le commentaire de Ross, *Aristotle's Prior and Posterior Analytics* (Oxford, 1949), p. 555, *ad* 79a12-13. M. Picolet la juge également légitime. Il est indiscutable que l'optique est souvent associée, dans les textes d'Aristote, avec l'harmonie et/ou l'astronomie (cf. *APo.* 1.7, 75b16; 13, 78b37-39; *Phys.* 2.2, 194a8; *Métaph.* B.2, 997b20-21; M.3, 1078a14). Mais cf. la note suivante.

remarquable qu'Aristote n'ait pas procédé à cette extrapolation, et se soit abstenu de nommer l'optique dans ce contexte.[28]

(2) Ce dédoublement, dira-t-on, est cependant clairement imposé par notre texte: Aristote n'y distingue-t-il pas sans ambiguïté l'opticien ἁπλῶς et l'opticien κατὰ τὸ μάθημα ? Admettons provisoirement que cette disjonction concerne bien deux disciplines optiques, ou deux aspects distincts du savoir de l'opticien; nous ne serons pas au bout de nos peines, car le modèle de dédoublement que ce texte (ainsi conçu) implique est incompatible avec ceux auxquels d'autres textes paraissent conduire. Si l'on cherche à se représenter avec quelque précision les relations entre deux hypothétiques branches de l'optique, on peut distinguer, je pense, au moins quatre schémas concurrents:

(i) Une optique ἁπλῶς et une optique κατὰ τὸ μάθημα s'opposent, non pas comme deux espèces d'optiques, mais comme l'optique en général (ἁπλῶς = "tout court," "sans autre qualification")[29] et l'une de ses parties spécifiées, l'optique mathématique; le terme d'optique *simpliciter* ne pourrait alors désigner que l'*ensemble* que cette optique mathématique formerait avec une optique résiduelle, non mathématisée. Il n'y a aucune raison d'appeler cette dernière du nom d'optique *simpliciter*: elle est tout aussi spécifiée que l'autre, encore que ce soit d'une façon négative.

(ii) L'exposé des *Météorologiques*, au moins tel que l'interprète M. Picolet, conduit en revanche à distinguer deux disciplines optiques *coordonnées*, toutes deux *explicatives*, mais à l'égard de deux ordres de faits différents: l'une, "qualitative" et "plutôt physique," est censée rendre compte des aspects non géométrisables, ou en tout cas non géométrisés, d'un phénomène comme l'arc-en-ciel, alors que l'autre, "mathématique"

---

[28] Pour comprendre que l'optique ne partage pas en tous points le statut épistémologique de l'astronomie et de l'harmonie, on peut invoquer des raisons historiques: elle ne faisait pas partie du *quadrivium* pythagoricien (arithmétique, géométrie, astronomie, harmonique); elle n'apparaît dans le *cursus* mathématique ni chez Platon (*Rép.* 7), ni chez un encyclopédiste comme Hippias d'Élis (cf. Platon, *Protag.* 318e). Elle fait au ive siècle, semble-t-il, une entrée beaucoup plus brusque sur la scène scientifique que l'astronomie et l'harmonie, sans traîner derrière elle, comme celles-ci, les lambeaux d'une préhistoire pythagoricienne. Aussi son nom peut-il n'avoir jamais couvert une discipline purement observationnelle et non encore mathématisée. Dans son *Dictionnaire historique de la terminologie optique des Grecs* (Paris, 1964), Charles Mugler, à l'article ὀπτικός, ne mentionne rien de ce genre. Il cite un texte de Geminus, qui dit que l'optique n'est pas une discipline physique (οὔτε φυσιολογεῖ ἡ ὀπτική), et un autre de Proclus, qui établit une tout autre distinction entre "l'optique proprement dite," qui "explique les raisons des apparences trompeuses faussant la vraie distance des objets de la vue" (perspective, illusions d'optique), et la catoptrique, "qui a pour objet les réflexions de tout genre"; il s'agit de deux disciplines toutes deux explicatives.

[29] Cf. Bonitz, *Index aristotelicus*, 77a33 sqq.

ou "géométrique," a pour tâche d'expliquer les propriétés géométriques de ce même phénomène.

(iii) Si l'on prend maintenant comme modèle de dédoublement le rapport de subordination explicitement posé par Aristote entre l'optique et la géométrie d'une part, entre une science subordonnée à l'optique et l'optique elle-même de l'autre, en identifiant ce dernier couple comme celui d'une optique inférieure et d'une optique supérieure, on est amené à se représenter ces deux branches de l'optique comme *subordonnées* l'une à l'autre et comme *explicatives* l'une et l'autre, mais selon un ordre hiérarchique: les théorèmes explicatifs fournis par la branche inférieure sont à leur tour expliqués par la branche supérieure; celle-ci donne les raisons des raisons que donne celle-là. Il en résulte que l'optique géométrique est considérée comme capable d'expliquer ce que l'optique qualitative énonce sans en dire le pourquoi; autrement dit, l'autonomie au moins relative de l'optique inférieure ne saurait reposer sur l'irréductibilité de certains aspects des phénomènes optiques à la géométrisation, puisque ce que par principe elle ne peut pas expliquer géométriquement, l'optique supérieure peut l'expliquer géométriquement.

(iv) Enfin, le modèle de dédoublement "synonyme" offert par l'astronomie et l'harmonie, si l'on se croyait autorisé à l'appliquer par induction à l'optique, conduirait encore à une autre représentation des choses: en effet, dans leur cas, la discipline inférieure est limitée à l'observation empirique, sensorielle, et sa compétence est strictement bornée au ὅτι;[30] seule la discipline supérieure, mathématique, est une connaissance du διότι, c'est-à-dire une connaissance explicative. L'assignation d'une fonction purement constative à l'une des branches de l'optique paraît d'ailleurs en contradiction formelle avec le texte de 79a12, qui attribue sans ambiguïté à l'opticien (fût-ce sous deux aspects différenciés) la connaissance du διότι dans le cas de l'arc-en-ciel.

Ces divers modèles de dédoublement sont donc clairement irréconciliables entre eux: l'on ne peut amalgamer des distinctions entre (i) le tout de l'optique et l'une de ses parties, (ii) deux optiques explicatives coordonnées, (iii) deux optiques explicatives subordonnées l'une à l'autre, et (iv) deux optiques subordonnées l'une à l'autre, la première constative, la seconde explicative. L'hypothèse d'une subdivision de l'optique ne parvient pas à trouver une assise stable et conséquente à travers les divers textes qui paraissent militer en sa faveur.

(3) Une troisième difficulté concerne le statut de la physique, et le rôle qui peut être considéré comme laissé au physicien dans la théorie de l'arc-

---

[30] Cf. 79a2-3.

en-ciel, si l'on admet, en suivant la lecture traditionnelle de 79a10-13, que la connaissance du pourquoi de ce phénomène relève *tout entière* de l'optique, dédoublée éventuellement en ses deux branches. Le texte dit expressément qu'il appartient au physicien de connaître le ὅτι de l'arc-en-ciel. Faut-il penser que c'est *la seule chose* qui lui appartienne en l'occurrence? Bien que le texte ne comporte pas d'expression limitative, on est contraint de le penser, s'il est vrai que l'optique accapare toutes les fonctions explicatives à l'égard du phénomène de l'arc-en-ciel. Pourtant, il paraît difficile de penser que le rôle de la physique (qui est une science, est-il besoin de le rappeler?) soit uniquement, s'agissant de l'arc-en-ciel, de noter sa forme, ses couleurs, les circonstances de son apparition. Bien plus: la découverte d'une identité générique entre les problèmes de l'arc-en-ciel, de l'écho et de la vision dans les miroirs, qui permet de voir en tous ces divers phénomènes des effets de la réflexion,[31] ne peut être attribuée, comme nous l'avons vu, qu'à un savant qui surmonte les limitations des divers spécialistes de ces phénomènes, donc, en particulier, celles de l'opticien; et ce savant à la science moins étroite ne peut guère être que le physicien. Partant de toutes ces considérations, on est conduit à tenter d'étoffer le rôle de ce dernier dans la théorie de l'arc-en-ciel. Mais plusieurs contraintes s'exercent alors en des sens contraires: si l'on veut maintenir ensemble l'idée que le physicien n'est compétent que relativement au ὅτι de ce phénomène, et l'idée qu'il lui appartient de déterminer la réflexion comme sa cause principale, on arrivera à des formulations extrêmement paradoxales, comme de dire que la théorie de l'arc-en-ciel comporte deux phases, dont la première, celle du physicien, est "essentiellement descriptive," ce qui ne l'empêche pas de contenir l'identification de la "cause principale" du phénomène,[32] alors que la seconde, celle de l'opticien, apporte "l'explication proprement dite" des faits mis à jour par le physicien, tout en étant dispensée d'en rechercher la "cause principale," puisque le travail a déjà été fait au cours de l'étape

[31] Cf. 98a25-29.
[32] À cet égard, il paraît difficile de considérer l'ensemble du chapitre 3.2 des *Météorologiques* comme "descriptif." Vers le milieu du chapitre en question, Aristote passe explicitement de l'examen des propriétés (συμβαίνοντα) des météores lumineux (halo, arc-en-ciel, parhélies, colonnes solaires) à l'exposé de leur cause (αἴτιον, 372a17-18). On remarquera aussi qu'un peu plus loin, il s'appuie sur "ce qui a été démontré au sujet de la vue" (ἐκ τῶν περὶ τὴν ὄψιν δεικνυμένων δεῖ λαμβάνειν τὴν πίστιν, 372a32). Les traducteurs interprètent généralement cette expression comme se référant aux "démonstrations de l'optique" (cf. la traduction de J. Tricot [Paris, 1955], p. 188, et celle de H. D. P. Lee, Loeb Classical Library [1952], p. 245); je pense que le mot d'*optique* n'est pas évité sans raison, et qu'ici Aristote pense plutôt à la physiologie des sensations (cf. ἐν τοῖς περὶ τὰς αἰσθήσεις δεικνυμένοις, 372a9-10, qui paraît reprendre l'expression citée ci-dessus).

précédente. Mais comment admettre que la discipline qui fournit "l'explication proprement dite" puisse être une autre que celle qui énonce la "cause principale"? Que celle qui est officiellement cantonnée dans la connaissance du fait soit aussi celle qui est capable d'en découvrir la "cause principale"? Et que celle qui a pour fonction d'en dire le pourquoi soit, pour l'essentiel, déchargée de ce dernier office? Nous sommes ici, il faut l'avouer, en pleine aporie.

(4) Une dernière difficulté, plus ponctuelle, va nous remettre sur la voie d'un examen plus approfondi du texte dont nous sommes partis. L'interprétation de M. Picolet, on l'a vu, oblige à penser qu'à deux lignes d'intervalle (79a10 et 12), Aristote emploie le mot "optique" en deux sens différents, d'abord étroit, ensuite plus large. Certes, le cas ne serait pas sans exemple dans les textes d'Aristote, dont on sait assez que le vocabulaire est loin d'être stable; cependant, s'agissant d'un terme technique (et récent)[33] de la science de son temps, on doit hésiter à admettre un pareil glissement, à moins d'avoir vérifié qu'il n'existe absolument aucune autre issue à la difficulté d'interprétation que ce glissement est censé résoudre.

III

Revenons donc à notre texte initial, et complétons d'abord son analyse par quelques observations supplémentaires.

(1) Le mot οἷον, qui introduit la mention de l'arc-en-ciel à la ligne 79a11, est compris par M. Picolet, comme par d'autres avant lui, dans le sens de "à savoir."[34] Lu de cette manière, le mot établit un lien fort étroit entre ἄλλη (sc. ἐπιστήμη) et τὸ περὶ τῆς ἴριδος; en d'autres termes, cette lecture conduit à identifier la science qui a pour objet l'arc-en-ciel avec cette science qui est à l'optique ce que celle-ci est à la géométrie. Cette identification se heurte cependant à plusieurs objections: (a) si le mot ἐπιστήμη restait sous-entendu devant περὶ τῆς ἴριδος, on devrait avoir l'article féminin ἡ, non l'article neutre τό à cette place; (b) il ne peut être évidemment question qu'une discipline scientifique soit consacrée tout entière à l'étude exclusive de l'arc-en-ciel; il faut donc comprendre que l'arc-en-ciel n'est qu'un *exemple* de ce qu'étudie la science subordonnée à l'optique;[35] mais pour signifier "à savoir celle qui étudie par exemple l'arc-

---

[33] Le mot ὀπτικός ne semble pas attesté avant Aristote; il ne figure notamment pas chez Platon.
[34] Cf. les traductions de J. Tricot ("savoir"), Mure ("namely"), J. Barnes ("viz.").
[35] Cf. J. Barnes, p. 152.

en-ciel," il faudrait une expression grecque plus complexe que οἶον τὸ περὶ τῆς ἴριδος; (c) enfin et surtout, il serait tout à fait étrange, et maladroit au dernier degré, de la part d'Aristote, d'utiliser l'arc-en-ciel pour désigner, par son objet ou l'un de ses objets, la science (*unique*) qui est subordonnée à l'optique; en effet, la suite montre précisément que la connaissance de l'arc-en-ciel exige la collaboration de *deux* sciences distinctes; aucune science singulière ne peut donc être adéquatement décrite comme celle qui s'occupe de l'arc-en-ciel. Ces divers arguments conduisent à comprendre οἶον comme signifiant "par exemple," [36] plutôt que "à savoir"; le cas de l'arc-en-ciel permet d'illustrer la situation de l'optique et de la science qui lui est subordonnée, il ne peut servir à définir une science particulière.

(2) Le neutre τό, dans l'expression οἶον τὸ περὶ τῆς ἴριδος, peut être considéré comme la preuve qu'Aristote ne songe pas à identifier l'étude de l'arc-en-ciel avec la science subordonnée à l'optique. Convient-il de lui chercher un autre référent? On pourrait le comprendre comme n'ayant qu'une référence très vague, et traduire "par exemple, < considérons > le cas de l'arc-en-ciel"; peut-être aussi est-il permis d'y voir une anticipation des expressions neutres qui vont se rencontrer immédiatement après, à savoir τὸ ὅτι et τὸ διότι. On arriverait alors à la traduction, ou paraphrase, suivante: "par exemple, le < fait et le pourquoi > de l'arc-en-ciel < illustrent cette relation entre l'optique et une science qui lui est subordonnée > ."

(3) Dans la phrase explicative (γάρ) qui suit, 79a11-13, il est d'abord dit qu'il appartient au physicien de connaître le ὅτι de l'arc-en-ciel. Puisque le thème fondamental de tout le paragraphe est de montrer que, dans certains cas, le ὅτι et le διότι d'un même objet sont du ressort de deux sciences distinctes,[37] et que celui de cette section particulière est de montrer que, dans certains (seulement) de ces cas, les sciences en question sont subordonnées l'une à l'autre,[38] il n'y a pas lieu d'hésiter à identifier la physique avec la science ici subordonnée à l'optique.[39] Mais il faut ajouter que cette identification peut ne valoir que pour l'exemple de l'arc-en-ciel (et des phénomènes du même genre); elle n'implique, ni bien sûr que la physique soit tout entière subordonnée à l'optique, ni qu'elle soit tout entière une science de simple observation. Il n'est même pas dit, comme on a déjà eu l'occasion de le noter, que, s'agissant de l'arc-en-ciel lui-

---

[36] Cf. les traductions de Ross ("e.g.") et G. Colli ("ad esempio"). Tel est d'ailleurs le sens premier de οἶον (cf. Bonitz, *Index aristotelicus*, 502a1 sqq.).

[37] Cf. 78b34-35.

[38] Cf. 78b35-37, 79a13-16.

[39] Cf. ci-dessus, n. 18.

même, le physicien n'ait aucune autre compétence que celle qui consiste à observer les phénomènes; il est seulement dit que si quelqu'un a cette compétence, c'est lui.

(4) La disjonction ἢ ἁπλῶς ἢ τοῦ κατὰ τὸ μάθημα, qui suit l'assignation à l'opticien de la connaissance du pourquoi de l'arc-en-ciel, est, comme on l'a vu, le principal appui textuel que l'on puisse invoquer en faveur de l'hypothèse d'un dédoublement de l'optique en deux branches, coordonnées ou subordonnées. Il faut cependant remarquer que cette lecture de l'expression est loin d'être la plus naturelle, puisqu'elle revient à interpréter une disjonction au sens d'une conjonction. Supposons qu'Aristote ait voulu dire que le διότι de l'arc-en-ciel relève à la fois, sous deux rapports distincts, d'une optique I et d'une optique II: il aurait sans doute employé des liaisons comme μέν/δέ, καί/καί ou τε/καί.[40] La disjonction ἢ/ἢ, il est vrai, peut à la rigueur s'interpréter comme une disjonction non exclusive (*ou bien ... ou bien ... ou les deux*), dont il ne faudrait encore retenir, pour obtenir le sens requis, que le dernier membre; mais elle s'interprète beaucoup plus naturellement comme une disjonction exclusive (*ou bien ... ou bien ... mais non les deux*), et notamment, avec ἁπλῶς dans le premier membre, dans le sens d'une atténuation (*ou bien ... ou du moins*)[41] ou d'une correction (*ou bien ... ou plus exactement*).[42] Il serait imprudent de négliger ces possibilités alternatives, qui ont été adoptées par plusieurs commentateurs.[43]

(5) Le seul écart que mentionnent les apparats critiques, par rapport au texte de notre passage, est une variante présentée par l'édition Aldine;[44] mais elle intéresse très directement notre propos. Cette édition omet en effet l'article τοῦ, dans l'expression ἢ ἁπλῶς ἢ τοῦ κατὰ τὸ μάθημα. Or cet article est, en somme, le seul élément textuel qui contraigne à considérer que la disjonction en cause se rapporte à l'opticien, ὀπτικοῦ, référent de l'article τοῦ; c'est donc lui seul qui invite à subdiviser, d'une manière ou d'une autre, l'unité de la discipline optique. Si l'on acceptait le texte de

---

[40] Cf. l'emploi de cette dernière conjonction en 78b40-79a2.

[41] Cf. Bonitz, *Index aristotelicus*, 313a26 sqq.

[42] Ibid., 77a32 sqq.

[43] Cf. Ross, p. 552 ("the fact is the business of the physicist, the reason that of the student of optics, *or rather* of the mathematical student of optics"); J. Barnes, p. 152 ("when he talks of 'optics *simpliciter* or mathematical optics' (79a12) he means that *we should call* the second member of < the pair 'study of the rainbow, optics' > mathematical optics since 'optics' without qualification might include both members of < that pair > "). Les italiques sont de moi.

[44] C'est l'*editio princeps* des œuvres d'Aristote, publiée à Venise, en six volumes, de 1495 à 1498.

l'Aldine, sans l'article, une tout autre construction deviendrait possible: au lieu de se rapporter à l'opticien, la disjonction pourrait se rapporter à l'ensemble de l'énoncé τὸ δὲ διότι ὀπτικοῦ ("la connaissance du pourquoi < de l'arc-en-ciel > relève de l'opticien"). En conservant l'interprétation corrective de la disjonction, on arriverait ainsi au sens suivant: la connaissance du pourquoi de l'arc-en-ciel relève, soit purement et simplement, soit du moins sous le rapport mathématique, de l'opticien. La portée de cette rectification pourrait se comprendre de la manière suivante: si l'on disait, sans autre précision, que l'optique est la discipline qui livre le pourquoi de l'arc-en-ciel, cette affirmation serait inexacte en toute rigueur, parce que le terme d'"optique" désigne de façon univoque une discipline mathématique, une géométrie appliquée aux rayons visuels et lumineux, et parce que l'arc-en-ciel est un phénomène complexe, qui comporte des aspects irréductiblement qualitatifs, dont l'optique est incapable de rendre compte. Il faut donc corriger l'énoncé initial, et dire que le pourquoi de l'arc-en-ciel ne relève de l'optique que κατὰ τὸ μάθημα, i.e., pour autant qu'il comporte des aspects géométriques. Dans cette perspective, ce n'est pas l'optique qui se trouve dédoublée: c'est la science explicative de l'arc-en-ciel. Quelle est maintenant la discipline qui prend en charge l'explication des aspects non géométriques du phénomène, sur lesquels l'optique n'a pas compétence? Point n'est besoin d'imaginer ici, pour les besoins de la cause, une "optique qualitative," dont le concept n'est nulle part mentionné par Aristote. La réponse le plus satisfaisante est à portée de la main. Il a été dit que le physicien connaît le ὅτι de l'arc-en-ciel; il n'a pas été dit (et il ne serait pas plausible qu'il eût été dit) qu'il ne connaissait que le ὅτι de l'arc-en-ciel. Rien ne s'oppose, dès lors, à ce qu'on lui attribue, en toute légitimité, la compétence nécessaire pour déterminer le διότι des aspects irréductiblement qualitatifs de l'arc-en-ciel, dont l'optique est par principe incapable de rendre compte. Le statut épistémologique de la théorie de l'arc-en-ciel est donc complexe, mais clair et cohérent: pour une partie, elle se rattache au cas où la connaissance du ὅτι et celle du διότι appartiennent à la même science (ici la physique); pour une autre partie, elle illustre le cas où la connaissance du ὅτι et celle du διότι relèvent de deux sciences distinctes, subordonnées l'une à l'autre (ici la physique et l'optique).

Il apparaît donc que l'adoption de la variante de l'Aldine éliminerait d'un seul coup toutes les difficultés sur lesquelles venait buter la lecture traditionnelle de notre passage: le changement du sens du terme "optique" à deux lignes d'intervalle; l'impossibilité d'assigner un modèle épistémologique stable et précis à la relation entre l'optique géométrique et une hypothétique "optique qualitative"; l'impossibilité de décrire de façon claire et cohérente l'intervention du physicien dans la théorie de l'arc-en-ciel, intervention qui devrait être à la fois limitée à la seule observation des faits, et cependant assez largement conçue pour englober la détermination de leur cause principale; les difficultés de superposition entre la remarque des *Analytiques* et l'exposé des *Météorologiques*.

IV

Voilà donc une variante bien intéressante sur le plan doctrinal. L'ennui est qu'on ne peut lui attribuer à peu près aucune valeur sur le plan paléo-graphique. Telle est la conclusion d'une petite enquête à laquelle je me suis livré, enquête nécessairement superficielle et incomplète, mais dont les résultats, en tout état de cause, ne sont pas encourageants. Voici ces résultats en résumé:

(1) L'omission de l'article τοῦ, en 79a12, se retrouve dans un grand nombre d'éditions anciennes: outre l'Aldine (Venise, 1495), celles de Casaubon (Lyon, 1590; Genève, 1605), de Du Val (Paris, 1619), de Buhle (Strasbourg, 1791), de Bekker (Berlin, 1831), de Weise (Leipzig, 1843), de Didot (Paris, 1848). Celles de ces éditions qui sont critiques (notamment celle de Bekker, dont l'apparat est ici muet) ne donnent aucune référence manuscrite pour appuyer cette leçon; il est donc vraisemblable qu'elles l'ont simplement empruntée, directement ou indirectement, à l'Aldine, et que ce *consensus* ne témoigne que de l'inertie des choses philologiques. L'omission est cependant "corrigée" dans l'édition d'Érasme (Bâle, 1539), et dans l'Aldine mineure, revue par Camotius (Venise, 1551); les deux leçons figurent côte à côte dans l'édition de l'*Organon* par Pacius (1584), où la variante avec l'article est indiquée dans la marge, et dans l'édition de Sylburg (Francfort, 1585), qui imprime l'article entre crochets droits, et qui indique dans son apparat son omission chez Pacius. À partir de l'*Organon* éditée par Waitz (Leipzig, 1846), les éditions modernes portent toutes l'article; Mure (Oxford Translation, 1928) en attribue à tort l'omission à une "obvious misprint" de Bekker; seul Ross (Oxford, 1949 et 1964) en reconduit correctement l'origine à l'Aldine.

(2) Il n'est pas tout à fait impossible que l'Aldine ait tiré cette variante de son modèle manuscrit, ou de l'un de ses modèles manuscrits; mais je ne suis pas en mesure de prouver que tel est le cas. On le sait, les modèles que l'éditeur vénitien a utilisés ont pour la plupart disparu; il signale lui-même, dans la Préface du second volume de son édition d'Aristote, que ces modèles, mis en pièces par les imprimeurs, ont péri "comme la vipère qui

met bas."[45] Cela n'empêche pas que les efforts de l'érudition moderne ont
permis de retrouver un certain nombre de ces modèles parmi les
manuscrits conservés dans nos bibliothèques;[46] mais malheureusement il
n'en a pas été ainsi pour le modèle de l'*Organon*.[47] On pourrait être tenté
de penser que si cette variante avait figuré dans le modèle manuscrit de
l'Aldine, la probabilité serait assez grande qu'on la retrouve dans l'un ou
l'autre des manuscrits conservés; dans cette perspective, j'ai consulté, non
pas la totalité des manuscrits conservés des *Seconds Analytiques* (il y en a
environ quatre-vingts),[48] mais l'échantillon assez représentatif (quinze
manuscrits) que l'on peut en trouver à la Bibliothèque Nationale de
Paris.[49] Le résultat de ce sondage a été négatif: tous les Parisini portent
l'article, à la seule exception du *Suppl. gr.* 141, qui date du XVIe siècle au
moins, et qui peut donc devoir sa leçon à l'Aldine. Ce résultat négatif ne
permet cependant pas d'exclure la possibilité que la variante de l'Aldine
provienne d'un manuscrit; en effet, les modèles de l'éditeur vénitien
étaient généralement des manuscrits peu anciens,[50] et il est fort possible
qu'ils aient porté des leçons propres qui n'ont pas eu le temps de se
disséminer dans d'autres manuscrits conservés. C'est là, je crois, tout ce
que l'on peut dire.

(3) La tradition indirecte n'est pas plus favorable. Le seul commentateur ancien qui cite l'expression qui nous intéresse est Philopon (182.2
Wallies), et il la cite avec l'article.

(4) Bien que l'Aldine ait bénéficié, directement ou indirectement, du
concours érudit de plusieurs humanistes,[51] je ne crois pas que l'on puisse
considérer l'omission de l'article comme une "conjecture intelligente"

---

[45] Cf. B. Botfield, *Praefationes et epistolae editionibus principibus auctorum veterum
praepositae* (Cambridge, 1861), p. 199; A. Dain, *Les manuscrits*, 2e éd. (Paris, 1964),
p. 161.

[46] Cf. Martin Sicherl, *Handschriftliche Vorlagen der Editio princeps des Aristoteles*,
Akademie der Wissenschaften und der Literatur (Mayence, 1976). Je remercie Guillaume
Rocca-Serra de m'avoir signalé cet ouvrage.

[47] M. Sicherl a retrouvé entre autres les modèles de l'*Historia animalium*, de la
Métaphysique, de l'*Éthique à Nicomaque*; il ne parle pratiquement pas de l'*Organon*.

[48] Cf. A. Wartelle, *Inventaire des manuscrits grecs d'Aristote et de ses commentateurs*
(Paris, 1963); et maintenant P. Moraux, *Aristoteles graecus*, vol. 1 (seul paru) (Berlin,
1976).

[49] Je remercie M. Charles Astruc, Conservateur au Département des Manuscrits, de
m'en avoir très aimablement facilité l'accès et la consultation.

[50] Les modèles retrouvés par M. Sicherl datent tous du XVe siècle.

[51] Cf. D. Harlfinger, "Die Überlieferungsgeschichte der Eudemischen Ethik," in
Untersuchungen zur Eudemischen Ethik, edd. P. Moraux et D. Harlfinger (Berlin, 1971),
pp. 18 sqq. (cité par M. Sicherl, p. 77). Plus généralement, M. Sicherl, pp. 11 sqq., et
passim.

introduite dans le texte sous l'influence de l'un d'entre eux. La leçon des manuscrits offre un sens satisfaisant à la lecture; et l'ensemble des raisons doctrinales que l'on pourrait avoir de préférer l'omission de l'article ne peut guère s'être présenté à l'esprit d'un réviseur qui ne disposait pas du loisir dont j'ai moi-même usé, et peut-être abusé.

(5) L'hypothèse d'une simple erreur de lecture ou d'impression dans l'Aldine ne peut être écartée. En collationnant son texte sur une étendue relativement grande (les treize premiers chapitres des *Seconds Analytiques*), j'ai pu m'apercevoir qu'il comporte un grand nombre d'écarts propres, au moins par rapport aux manuscrits dont les leçons sont indiquées dans les éditions modernes;[52] à côté des variantes qu'il partage (très éclectiquement, d'ailleurs) avec tel manuscrit ou groupe de manuscrits, il présente beaucoup de variantes non attestées ailleurs; et bon nombre d'entre elles ont toute apparence d'être des erreurs de lecture du modèle, ou bien de simples fautes d'impression. Dans son ensemble, le texte de cette vénérable édition est loin d'être assez soigné pour qu'une variante aussi minime que l'omission d'un article puisse être considérée comme appartenant à la tradition du texte.

Étrange situation, en définitive. La philologie offre à l'exégèse un cadeau empoisonné, sous les espèces de cette variante, si satisfaisante sur le plan du contenu, et si peu autorisée sur le plan de l'histoire du texte. Faut-il l'accepter, au mépris de la prudence scientifique? La refuser, au détriment de la compréhension philosophique? Le choix n'est pas facile.

V

J'aperçois, pour finir, deux solutions envisageables à notre problème.

(1) La première consiste à conserver le texte des manuscrits (τὸ δὲ διότι ὀπτικοῦ (sc. εἰδέναι), ἢ ἁπλῶς ἢ τοῦ κατὰ τὸ μάθημα), tout en l'interprétant dans le sens même sur la voie duquel la variante de l'Aldine nous a fortuitement mis: à savoir, la connaissance du pourquoi relève de l'opticien, soit qu'elle relève de l'opticien tout court, soit (plutôt) qu'elle relève *de ce même opticien* au niveau mathématique. Il n'est pas tout à fait impossible d'extraire ce sens de ce texte non modifié. En effet, le texte des manuscrits est *asymétrique*: l'article τοῦ est absent du premier membre de

---

[52] Beaucoup plus, en tout cas, qu'on ne pourrait le croire en lisant l'apparat critique de Ross, qui ne donne qu'une très petite sélection des variantes de l'Aldine: pour les treize premiers chapitres (plus de 16 colonnes Bekker), il en indique trois, alors qu'il y en a une bonne dizaine, en moyenne, par colonne.

la disjonction (ἢ ἁπλῶς), il est présent dans le second membre (ἢ τοῦ κατὰ τὸ μάθημα). Si cette disjonction avait pour fonction de séparer deux aspects du personnage de l'opticien, comme le suppose l'interprétation tradition-nelle, on s'attendrait à trouver l'article *de part et d'autre* (ἢ τοῦ ἁπλῶς ἢ τοῦ κατὰ τὸ μάθημα). Si elle portait, au contraire, sur deux aspects de l'explication scientifique de l'arc-en-ciel, comme je le suppose, on s'attendrait à ne trouver l'article *nulle part* (ἢ ἁπλῶς ἢ κατὰ τὸ μάθημα), comme dans l'Aldine. L'interprétation, quelle qu'elle soit, doit donc rectifier cette asymétrie. La lecture traditionnelle le fait en faisant refluer la construction du second membre sur le premier. Cette extrapolation n'est pas plus légitime, dans son principe, que celle qui, à l'inverse, lirait le second membre à la lumière et sous l'influence du premier. On y parvient en donnant à l'article τοῦ la valeur d'un démonstratif: la connaissance du pourquoi relève de l'opticien (le seul qui existe, l'opticien-mathématicien) tout court, ou plutôt elle relève de *ce même opticien* dans la mesure où le phénomène considéré comporte un aspect mathématique. Satisfaisante sur le plan doctrinal, cette solution présente cependant une difficulté gramma-ticale: l'article à valeur démonstrative ne paraît guère attesté dans la langue d'Aristote.

(2) Compte tenu de cette objection, une autre solution peut être pro-posée: celle qui consiste à remplacer franchement (par une conjecture qui semble paléographiquement défendable et grammaticalement acceptable) l'article τοῦ par le démonstratif τούτου. On lirait alors: τὸ δὲ διότι ὀπτικοῦ, ἢ ἁπλῶς ἢ τούτου κατὰ τὸ μάθημα, le sens restant, bien sûr, celui qui a été présenté ci-dessus. Tout bien pesé, c'est à cette suggestion que je m'arrêterai pour résoudre l'ensemble des problèmes de texte et de fond que soulève notre passage; et c'est elle que je me permets de soumettre aux aristotélisants, en commençant par celui en l'honneur duquel ces pages ont été rédigées.

7

Metaphysics and Psychology in Plotinus' Treatment of the Soul

John M. Rist

University of Aberdeen

The writings of Plotinus contain a number of problems which must always be faced by a man who tries to be intellectually honest and who is also a theist. Plotinus' view that the world as we know it is a direct result of the creative activity of the One or God might lead us to suppose that he also believed that everything is for the best in the world around us. But, like most other honest men, Plotinus has to admit that *prima facie* things are not like that. Like the Stoics, for example, Plotinus is aware that it looks as though good men suffer unjustly. Chrysippus had been worried by the same problem, and, at least according to Plutarch, had failed dismally to solve it.[1] In at least one place (4.3.[27].16) Plotinus admits that he cannot explain such sufferings: the explanations are unclear, and to the ignorant there appear grounds for censuring the maker of the cosmos. Of course, a number of traditional proposals are offered: such sufferings are accidents (ἐπόμενα) of the grand design – if you get in the way of the cavalry you are trampled down; or perhaps the individual's suffering is

---

A version of this paper was read at the Institute of Classical Studies of the University of London. I should like to thank Richard Sorabji for enabling me to try out a few ideas in a critical company.

[1] Plut., *Stoic. Rep.* 1051c (see svf 2: 1178). There have been recent discussions by H. Cherniss in his Loeb edition and by G. Kerferd, "The Origin of Evil in Stoic Thought," *Bull. of the John Rylands Library of the University of Manchester*, 60 (1978), 482-494.

Graceful Reason: Essays in Ancient and Medieval Philosophy Presented to Joseph Owens, CSSR, ed. Lloyd P. Gerson. Papers in Mediaeval Studies 4 (Toronto: Pontifical Institute of Mediaeval Studies, 1983), pp. 135-151. © P.I.M.S., 1983.

not evil because of its contribution to the good of the whole. But Plotinus does not like such solutions: he prefers to say that the innocent sufferer gains from his sufferings. It is wrong, he holds, to believe (as the Stoics believed) that some things are planned in the universe while others (presumably the so-called accidents) go as they will.

But the matter of the suffering of the just is only a part of the wider problem of theodicy. For beyond the suffering of the just man is the question why we are not all just men, why it is that there is injustice, and indeed vice in general, in the world. To such questions, I think, Plotinus has some sort of answer, and it is this which I chiefly want to discuss. In fact it seems that he wants to say that it is better that there be vices or sins in the world than that there not be a world. Now the vices and sins with which I wish to concern myself are obviously something to do with the soul. So what, it seems, Plotinus wants further to show, and what, I want to argue, he believes he is able to show – even though his argument may not be all set out in one place – is that it is in some important sense better for the soul to be capable of sinning than for it not to exist.

But first two preliminary points. What soul or souls are we talking about, and how do we know they sin anyway? These questions, for Plotinus, are not unimportant, and the answers to them, which are not too difficult to find, may give access to more difficult matters.

I

What soul then are we concerned with? In practice, in Plotinus' world, this question means, Is it the World Soul or the soul of the individual man? Let us re-organize the question and ask, in fact, two things: can the World Soul sin, and does the World Soul sin? In *Ennead* 2.9.[33], arguing against the Gnostics, Plotinus denies that it sins. Against a Gnostic view that the World Soul creates "after losing its wings" (2.9.4.1), Plotinus insists that the fact of creation itself indicates that the Soul has not lost sight of the One; such creation indicates not decline, but its opposite (not νεῦσις, but μὴ νεῦσις). It is mere blasphemy to argue that creation was the product of a lust for glory (ἵνα τιμῷτο). The creative force of the World Soul is an act of illumination (2.9.11); it does not involve the physical, spatial presence of the World Soul in the form of contact with material objects. The World Soul does not contact material objects τοπικῶς. The same idea occurs in less immediately polemical passages of the *Enneads*: at 3.9.3.5 the World Soul always remains "above"; in 4.8.4 the individual souls are free from sin so long as they remain above with the World Soul;

in 4.8.7 the World Soul, here specifically said to be inexperienced of evil
(ἀπαθεῖ κακῶν), *inspects* its inferiors, and the contact it has with them is
limited to the fact that it provides for them (χορηγούσῃ). What these
passages seem to show, of course, is not that the World Soul could not sin,
but that it does not sin. But it has been suggested that even that limited
claim is implicitly denied by at least one other text of Plotinus himself.

The crucial text is to be found at *Ennead* 3.7.11.15ff., a late treatise
(No. 45), and therefore, if divergent, of particular interest. The first point
to be made about it is that the context is cosmological. Plotinus is talking
not about the origin of evil, or of sin, but of the origin of the visible world.
The World Soul, he tells us, contains an unquiet faculty (δύναμις οὐχ
ἥσυχος), desirous of changing what it sees in the intelligible world into
something else. This means, I think, that the World Soul wants to create,
that its descent, in Plotinian terms used elsewhere, is voluntary:[2] οὐχ
ἥσυχος tells us that the World Soul is not still, that it moves away from the
intelligible world; it does not tell us that there is anything sinful about
such movement. But the same text contains difficult phrases. The nature
of the World Soul is πολυπράγμων – this need mean only that it is busy; "it
wishes to rule itself and belong to itself" (ἄρχειν αὐτῆς βουλομένης καὶ εἶναι
αὐτῆς). The latter language reminds us of 5.1.1, where, speaking of
individual souls in a much misunderstood passage, Plotinus lists a number
of conditions which form for them what he calls "the beginning of evil"
(ἀρχὴ κακοῦ). These conditions are audacity (τόλμα), coming-to-be (γένεσις),
primary otherness (ἡ πρώτη ἑτερότης), and "wishing to belong to themselves" – which last looks like our passage of 3.7.11. Indeed there is a
similarity, for although in 5.1.1 Plotinus is talking not about creation but
about the origin of sin, he seems in this part of the text to be discussing not
the specifiably sinful marks of particular souls, but the preconditions
which must occur if sin is to be possible for any soul at all. For the items
τόλμα, γένεσις and ἡ πρώτη ἑτερότης are not only present at the level of
individual souls; they exist in all that is other than the One. They cannot in
themselves, therefore, be marks of sin, but only preconditions of it. Even
τόλμα (as τολμήσας) can be applied to *Nous* at 6.9.5.29,[3] and "primary

---

[2] I accept what D. O'Brien says ("Le volontaire et la nécessité: réflexions sur la
descente de l'âme dans la philosophie de Plotin," *Rev. Phil.*, [1977], 401-422) on the
reconciliation of the notions of voluntary and necessary descent, including his support of
Theiler's important conjecture at *Enn.* 4.3.13.17-18. What Plotinus wants to deny is that
the choice of descending is deliberated.

[3] Cf. J. M. Rist, "Monism: Plotinus and some Predecessors," *HSCP*, 69 (1965), 341,
and see *Enn.* 3.8.8.32ff.

otherness" is above all the mark of what Plotinus calls intelligible matter,[4] the brute reality which is the common ground of all that is other than the One, but which significantly belongs in the intelligible world. Now in 5.1, after stating these preconditions of the sin of individual souls, Plotinus goes on, as we shall see, to the immediate *causes* of sin for the individuals: these are "delight in freedom" and what seems to be an excessive independence leading to the forgetfulness of their origin.

So the comparative evidence of 5.1.1, I would suggest, tells the exegete of 3.7.11 not that wishing to be on their own or to rule themselves is actually sinful, but that in certain circumstances these will provide some of the conditions in which sin can be committed. It seems then that if these circumstances arose for the World Soul, the *possibility* of sin would be present.[5] But can we discover what further conditions, if any, would be required for that possibility to be actualized, i.e., is the possibility a realizable possibility?

In trying to answer this, however, we need to digress. Sin, for Plotinus, involves change, with the associated possibilities of crime and repentance. If the World Soul sinned, that could entail, in the Plotinian world, one of two possibilities: either that Soul is always evil – which would run counter to Plotinus' whole thinking, for he would then have an eternal, but evil being such as he rejects out of hand for reasons we need not consider here; or if not an eternally sinful being, he would have a being who sins from time to time, and then repents of it, or is liable to repent of it. And of course it is such volatile, penitent divinities that he so detests in the systems of the Gnostics: we recall poor Miss Wisdom (*Sophia*) of the Gnostic myths[6] whose crime and repentance are mocked at *Ennead* 2.9.4.17ff. When will she destroy the world? For if she repents of it, what is she waiting for? If she hasn't repented yet, she never will; she's getting used to it and liking it better with the passage of time.[7]

If the World Soul is to be an eternal and unchanging reality, therefore, it cannot sin, even if many of the preconditions which allow individual souls to sin are present. Scholars who have put too much weight on

---

[4] On the topic generally see J. M. Rist, "The Problem of 'Otherness' in the *Enneads*," in *Le Néoplatonisme* (Paris, 1971), pp. 77-87. See 5.1.6.53, 6.4.24, 6.4.11.9 on the separation of *Nous* from the One by "otherness."

[5] Ibid., 83.

[6] 2.9.10.19.

[7] For further comment on "repentings" see 2.9.6.2. Note the variable meanings of *metanoia* in Gnostic texts (H.-C. Puech, *Entretiens Hardt*, 5 [Les Sources de Plotin], [Geneva, 1960], p. 189), but *alteration* seems basic to the word, and it is this alteration which is objectionable to Plotinus in a divine being.

Plotinus' language in 3.7.11 about the wishes of the World Soul can be content with the knowledge that the World Soul really does want to descend; its will to descend is identical with the necessity which makes it descend. The fact that it is like that makes it act as an inferior to the One, which does not and cannot descend. But in this respect *Nous* too is inferior – and we have noted that many of the same *conditions* for sinfulness exist at that level as well. But to wish to descend does not involve vice where such a wish is necessary, and to say that *x* is inferior to *y* does not entail saying that *y* is vicious. As Plotinus himself puts it, there is no need to say that "nature, the principle of growth, is evil because it is not perception, nor do we call the principle of perception evil because it is not reason. For if we did, we should be compelled to say that there are evils there (in the intelligible world) – for the soul is inferior to *Nous* and *Nous* is inferior to something else", i.e., the One (2.9.13.30ff.).

The World Soul is an eternal and unchanging reality, but unchanging does not mean inactive. Quite the contrary, for the One is the least inactive of all beings. But the activity of the World Soul must iself be constant and unvarying. For this to be the case, the Soul must always be identical with, in contact with, and bound to, what is in its turn constant and unvarying. That is an ontological demand which Plotinus fulfils by arguing that the World Soul is always in contact with *Nous*, and that, as we have seen, it always stands above the matter which it creates. It creates by illuminating and its contact, as it were, is always at arm's length. Thus we may dismiss a possible misunderstanding of the *Enneads*. It might be supposed that what causes sin in souls is contact with matter, but this is not always so. There is always contact with matter when there is sin, but some contacts with matter are not sinful. Nor must we assume, as D. O'Brien once falsely inferred that I had assumed, that where there is matter, there is always weakness (or vice) of the particular, associated soul.[8] In fact, as Plotinus himself says, the souls of the stars, and (apparently) of some men – all of whom are certainly in contact with matter in some way or another – do not sin.[9] In a famous text we read that the individual soul can descend to the material world and acquire knowledge of good and evil – a much more risky descent than that of the World Soul, and one to which we shall return; yet, if it escapes quickly, it will escape unscathed.[10]

---

[8] D. O'Brien, "Plotinus on Evil," in *Le Néoplatonisme* (Paris, 1971), p. 125.

[9] 1.8.5.30-34. This passage is well explained by O'Brien, "Plotinus on Evil," pp. 129-130. Cf. 4.8.2.41-42.

[10] 4.8.5.27ff.; cf. 4.8.7.11ff., but here the soul is only unscathed in so far as it avoids permanent damage.

Neither τόλμα nor the presence of matter then are causes of sin in the World Soul; it is clear that *in fact* the World Soul does not sin. It is also clear that a stronger claim can be made: that despite some of the important *preconditions* for sin being present to the World Soul, it does not even have the potentiality of sinning. There are no circumstances in which it could sin, for if it did, it could not be constantly and entirely in contact with the hypostasis of *Nous*. In other words we conclude both that the preconditions we have identified are not an adequate causal account of sin, and that the actual nature of the World Soul is such as to preclude it. As we have seen, what rules sin out for the World Soul is its position as third in the hierarchy of true being, its complete maintainance of contact with its priors even when engaged in the generation of the material world. It is therefore by focussing on this point that we shall find a clue to the different state of the majority of human souls at all times, and possibly of all human souls at some times.

II

In asking why an individual soul sins, and in acknowledging that individual souls do and have sinned, Plotinus is in a way facing a Platonic problem. It always seems to be difficult, when thinking about Plato, to understand where precisely the difference between gods and perfected or perfect souls is to be found. Yet there must be a difference, for the gods do not take on human bodies – they do not fall into the cycle of births and deaths – and souls do. There is something (morally) fragile about human souls, but exactly what it is Plato never makes clear. Certainly, at least according to the *Phaedrus*, it is not their tripartition, for the gods too are tripartite. So perhaps if we solve our problem for Plotinus we may help to solve it for Plato. Or perhaps we may not. At least the matter will not be pursued here.

The most relevant texts seem to be in the following treatises of the *Enneads*: 4.8; 5.1; 5.2; 3.9; 4.3. In chronological sequence that is numbers 6, 10, 11, 13 and 27. All these texts, therefore, were composed before the treatise against the Gnostics (2.9), which is number 33 on the chronological list, and we may assume that polemical considerations were not uppermost in Plotinus' mind when he composed them. I shall take them in chronological order merely for convenience. By proceeding in this way I shall be able to notice developments in the ideas if they appear, but I may as well state at the outset that in its general outline there seems little reason to posit such developments in Plotinus' thinking.

Ennead 4.8 begins with the famous "Many times wakening up to myself from the body," and proceeds with a bold survey of the opinions of the apparent authorities from Empedocles and Pythagoras to Plato, whose consistency on the question of the relation between the soul and the body, Plotinus tells us, is not easy to determine. The basic problem is how to reconcile the *Timaeus*, where the material world's excellence is insisted on, with more apparently pessimistic texts from the *Phaedo* and the *Republic* where falling into matter is a feature of the *guilty* soul (μεμψάμενος τὴν τῆς ψυχῆς ἄφιξιν, 4.8.1.40).

The enquiry begins in chapter 2 with a clear indication that it is the individual, not the World Soul, whose possible guilt is in question: it is appropriate, says Plotinus, to learn from him (Plato) about our soul; but such an enquiry naturally cannot be separated from the problems of the soul in general. And again, he asks immediately whether the maker (ποιητής) has acted well, or whether the World Soul is like our individual souls which need to plunge deeply (εἴσω πόλυ δῦναι, 1.8) into bodies if they are going to direct them. The World Soul, continues Plotinus, has no desires or sufferings (11.17-18), while the individual soul is in the grip of need (ἔνδεια) and is "scattered" (σκεδασθέντος).

Besides distinguishing the two kinds of souls, the chapter also distinguishes two kinds of caring-activity (1.27) of the soul. On the one hand, as we have already noticed, there is the general directive activity, the effortless regal overseeing (ἀπράγμονι ἐπιστασίᾳ βασιλικῇ, 1.28; cf. ὑπερέχουσα ἀπόνως, 4.8.8.24), which seems to deal in broad principles and large brush-strokes; and then there is the direct contact with individual physical objects which seems to accentuate the characterization of the agent by the object acted upon (τὸ πρᾶττον τοῦ πραττομένου τῆς φύσεως ἀναπιμπλᾶσα). It is this characterization by matter that causes the trouble for the individual soul, and which is again described as penetration (δύναμιν ... εἰς τὸ εἴσω πεμπούσης, 1.33). It is this plunging in (again repeated at 1.46, εἰς τὸ εἴσω ἔδυ, and 1.49) which generates the circumstances in which κοινωνία πρὸς σῶμα is harmful, for with penetration comes hindrance to νόησις and a filling (cf. 1.30) with pleasures, desires and pains (11.44-45), not to speak of a "lack of leisure" (ἀσχολία) and a real decline (as MacKenna puts it), a νεῦσις. Νεῦσις (contrary to what the Gnostics want to say in 2.9.4) is a word which applies to the *individual* soul, not to the World Soul.[11] And just as the

---

[11] Sometimes *neusis* is neutral (e.g., in 1.1.12); that is, it may or may not be a sin. But the criteria of sin are similar: *Neusis* is sinful when it goes with too close enslavement to an image.

activities of the World Soul and the individual soul are different in their descents, so the *causes* (αἰτιῶν, 4.8.3.5) of these activities are also divergent.

Chapter 4 of *Ennead* 4.8 formally introduces the three phases of the individual soul: the higher phase will remain ἐν τῷ νοητῷ and without trouble (ἀπήμονας, 1.5); then comes the World-Soul-like phase, which is the state in which the individual souls remain seated round the World Soul like subordinate powers round the Great King and do not leave their royal places – this is the overseeing we have considered already; finally there is the third and sinful phase, here described in detail by Plotinus for the first time, but in words which will recur: they become partial, they belong to themselves. This retreat to "their own" place results from a kind of weariness or even sickness (οἷον κάμνουσαι). This partial state is weak and "full of care" (as MacKenna well translates πολυπραγμονεῖ); the soul separates itself from the whole and, in an action the reverse of that recommended by Diotima in the *Symposium*, I suppose, settles on a particular. This is in Plotinian terms a false conversion – he uses the word στραφεῖσα which should be used for turning to the One and supplies a clue to Plotinus' thinking – and as a result of that conversion the individual soul "manages" the particular μετὰ περιστάσεως, "with close attendance," a rare but to my mind certain meaning in this text: contact between soul and its object of tendance is close now, but again in an "anti-Symposiac" vein, the soul tends externals (τὰ ἔξωθεν) and – again the phrase is repeated – "penetrates a lot inside" (πολὺ εἰς τὸ εἴσω). This, at the level of the individual soul, is the loss of wings of which Plato spoke in the *Phaedrus*. It is, Plotinus says, slavery.

Unlike the World Soul which remains above in effortless supervising of the cosmos as a whole, the individual soul sins twice (as 4.8.5.16 explains to us): it descends to bodies for the wrong reasons – that is the retreat to its own place, the voluntary and unnecessary self-isolation (later said to be φορᾷ οἰκείᾳ, 4.8.5.8-9), the sickness or weariness to which we have already alluded; and it acts badly when it has descended – this is the cosying-up to bodies, the particularization of concerns with its consequent pleasures, desires and pains. We can see in this duality of sin the two aspects of moral evil in the Plotinian world, one of which I can call metaphysical, where Plotinus talks about the isolation of the soul from its priors, the turning away from reality, and the other which I can roughly call psychological, in that it is characterized by pleasure and pain, love of particular bodies with the ensuing cares and anxieties which must come, as Diotima might have put it, from loving Alcibiades' body rather than his soul. There is no doubt that the individual soul, by nature, must descend;

no need to be indignant about that (4.8.7.4). The trouble, as Plotinus repeats yet again a few lines later, is that it has "plunged inside matter" (εἰς τὸ εἴσω δύοιτο). We can now see that this "plunge" is twofold. The Soul goes down for the wrong reasons and it behaves wrongly while it is there. But, of course, as Plotinus is to repeat elsewhere, we do not descend entire (4.8.8) – though we may be so dominated by our lower selves as to be ignorant of our higher. This ignorance is particularly engrained because of our pleasures: ἡδονὴ ἠπάτησε (4.8.8.22).

Let us summarize our findings on the individual soul from 4.8, so that we may conveniently add to them if new elements appear in other treatises; then we may proceed to explore what we have found in greater depth. We may assume, as O'Brien has well shown,[12] that the individual soul descends "of necessity," but that this necessity is for Plotinus compatible with the free and appropriate movement of the soul; there is no compulsion at either level, and so far no blame need be attached to what is "metaphysical necessity." We shall particularly notice these features in *Ennead* 4.3. But the descent of the individual soul is normally blameworthy and an act of sin in two distinct respects: there is in the individual soul corruption in the motive for descent in the first place, and this corruption presumably affects (or causes) the sinking into matter too deeply, with the corresponding emotional toll which occurs when the soul has once descended. These two sins can both be summarized as a false "conversion" of the soul. Two questions immediately arise: could the work of the individual soul have been performed without this corruption, and is the corruption a necessary precursor for some potential gain for the soul which could not have been otherwise attained? But before attempting these questions, let us see if any further data can be obtained about the nature of the twofold sin and the descent. Briefly then to *Ennead* 5.1.1, to which we adverted earlier. It was suggested that what Plotinus calls the ἀρχή of evil for individual souls (τόλμα, generation, primary otherness, wishing to belong to themselves) are preconditions which do not apply only to individual souls. But these souls are delighted with their freedom of choice – and we shall note in 4.3 that it is not this freedom of choice which produces their original descent – and the exercise of such delightful freedom leads them to very great separation, so that they lose the knowledge of their origin. Like children brought up for years away from home, they are ignorant of themselves and their fathers, and they get false ideas of what deserves honour and respect. The only remedy is

---

[12] See note 2.

144   J. M. RIST

twofold (1.22ff.). The soul must dishonour what it now honours, and
learn its "race" and birth, i.e., despise the goods of the body and recognize
its kinship with the divine – obviously Plotinus' version of the *Symposium*
again.

That is all we need to take from *Ennead* 5.1, and it adds little new
except the emphasis on the abuse of one's faculty of freedom (αὐτεξούσιον).
But we can probably assume that this abuse is in some way connected
with the retiring to one's own place (of 4.8) which is the behaviour of the
soul which is κάμνουσα; and we should notice that Plotinus translates his
rather more abstract and metaphysical language of isolation (of 4.8) into
the concrete image of the identity-crisis of the orphan who with his
ignorance of his father and his race is also ignorant of himself. It is hard
not to see the image of king Oedipus lurking somewhere behind Plotinus'
language.

I once wrote that *Ennead* 5.2.[11].1 (1.19ff.) is more specific than it is.[13]
Plotinus tells us here that the soul is "filled" by looking to its sources and
takes on a contrary motion of a different order – thus generating its image,
animal and plant life, when it "goes forth." In this section, in fact, Plotinus
does not specify what soul or souls he is talking about, and although my
previous proposal that he is dealing with individual souls may be
right – for the World Soul seems to make no movement to matter but
rather looks down from above – it is neither stated nor is it demonstrable,
and it would certainly have been enough to have said that Plotinus is
talking of individual souls looking back to the World Soul. So we pass to
3.9.[13].3, where there is no doubt that Plotinus is dealing with the
individual soul (or partial soul – ἡ μερική – as he calls it here). When this
partial soul is carried down to what is "after it," it turns to *non-being* (we
have not met so clear a formulation yet), and it does this when it turns its
will on itself (πρὸς αὐτὴν βουλομένη). Note how Plotinus blends the
metaphysical and the psychological language – he means not merely that
the soul wishes, as it were, to stand on its own feet, but that the passage is
to be read in the stronger sense of 5.1, that in the case of the individual
soul the conscious will is exclusively self-directed. This, of course, would
lead to the forgetfulness of which 5.1 warns us. Plotinus then speaks at the
end of the chapter of the second part of the twofold sin: by a δευτέρα
προσβολῇ (i.e., orientation), it shapes its image, which is "quite dark," and
goes to it rejoicing (ἡσθεῖσα). The false-pleasure word is repeated, though
here Plotinus does not mention a choice.

---

[13] J. M. Rist, *Plotinus* (Cambridge, 1967), p. 122.

Finally we come to 4.3 [27], of which much could be said, but O'Brien has said most of it already, and I do not wish to linger greatly. In so far as concerns the individual soul, we find the now familiar themes: souls that remain above are safe; the rest have "gone forth" (4.3.6.25) and revolted to "the pits" (ἀπέστησαν – cf. 5.1.1 – εἰς βάθος). The perfect soul does not sink (οὐ δῦσα), but "rides above," as it were – in a mixture of Plato's *Timaeus* and the *De Bono* of Numenius (4.3.7.16ff.);[14] and we notice that ἐποχέω normally seems to refer to the superiority of the star instance of superiority, the One itself. Whereas the World Soul is the architect of a fine and elaborate house (οἶκος τις καλὸς καὶ ποικίλος) which she will not abandon but to which she refuses to be tied down (4.3.9.29-30),[15] the individual soul is like the beleaguered sea-captain who is so engrossed in his ship that he goes down with her – an important text to which we shall return later (4.3.17.21). In 4.3.12 Plotinus tells us that human souls see their images, as it were in Dionysus' mirror, and sink downwards, though the depth of their descent is unequal (4.3.12.35), depending, it seems, on their previous experiences. Their descent is not against their will (reading Theiler's ἄκουσα at 4.3.13.17),[16] nor is it a matter of deliberation. It is an instinctive act, a leap (πηδᾶν), and some instinctive acts are positively good, others merely neutral, as to marriage (4.3.13.17ff.). Note, of course, that Plotinus is not ruling out wrong (or right) deliberation and choice once we are "down there." Here he is concerned only to show that the descent itself is not deliberated; nothing in that to contradict what we have seen elsewhere in 4.8 and 5.1, for he is not now talking about how *deeply* one plunges into the mire. That question is explored more fully, with consideration of the varying fortunes of various individuals, in chapter 15.

Before leaving 4.3, we should look at chapter 18, where the matter of deliberation (λογισμός) is made explicit. The problem is: does λογισμός have anything to to with the descent itself? From earlier parts of the *Enneads* we should expect the answer to be No. For the descent itself is intuitive; it depends on necessity and on the "unsoundness" of the individual soul. Once descent has occurred, however, deliberation comes into play; it is the mark of the soul that is perplexed (ἐν ἀπορῷ), full of cares and "weaker than it was." The craftsman deliberates when he does not know what to do, where his art is not up to an immediate resolution of the problem. Thus if the motives for the descent indicate the corruption of the

---

[14] ἐποχούμενον (Num., fr. 2.16, Des Places); and of the One, *Enn.* 1.1.8.9.

[15] Treatise no. 27. In the anti-Gnostic treatise 2.9 the image of the house returns (2.9.18.4).

[16] O'Brien, "Le volontaire."

individual soul's intuition, its behaviour here below marks the corruption
of its deliberative process.

Ennead 4.3 is no. 27 in Porphyry's chronological list of the *Enneads*;
soon after that Plotinus wrote *Against the Gnostics* (2.9 = no. 33).
Problems of the kind we are dealing with are correspondingly rare in later
treatises, and we may assume that after dealing with wrong-headed
versions of the descent in 2.9, Plotinus was largely willing to let the matter
rest. We may note in conclusion that if we follow Harder in thinking that
treatises 30-33 are one single large-scale work, then 4.3 (no. 27) is
probably brought still closer in time, as well as in content, to 2.9. But I
must confess that I have never seen the force of Harder's arguments
which have appeared so convincing to others.

<h2 style="text-align:center">III</h2>

We have now surveyed the material on the state of the soul and can turn
to questions of intelligibility and consistency. The individual soul
normally sins in the motives for its descent and in its behaviour down
here. What in fact does it do wrong, and is this wrong in some sense a
felix culpa? What it does when it is here is, I think, easier to understand
than why it wrongly descends, and one may therefore consider it first.
The unsound soul, having descended to the body, plunges into it, and this
plunging brings with it pleasures, desires, pain and cares. It is too close an
identification with the object of its concern, or, as I suggested, some kind
of conversion, a false conversion, to the wrong kind of object, with a
consequent loss of identity. Yet we recall that it is a lack of awareness of
self which characterizes union with the One, for example in 6.9.11, when
a soul is οὐδ' ὅλως αὐτός.

In order to understand what Plotinus is saying about the "black"
conversion to matter, let us further consider his remarks about self-
consciousness, its advantages and disadvantages. There are at least two
immediately relevant texts: if Socrates is in the intelligible world, we learn
in 4.4.2, he does not think that he is Socrates; and of course the converse
applies. If a man is too aware of his individual circumstances, his local
interests, his memory of "higher things" will disappear; not that he will
altogether lose touch with higher things, but that he will forget them, as
he identifies his ego, his conscious self, with the lower. Such identification
will sometimes take a form which we may call "self-consciousness," and
this may itself be productive of a kind of mental inefficiency. In the late
treatise 1.4.[46].10, Plotinus points out that the brave man, when acting
bravely, is not aware of the rules of courage and of his conformity to

them; and being gripped and intent on what one reads does not entail that
we are aware that we are reading. Quite the reverse, in fact, for, Plotinus
continues, the higher the activity on which one is engaged, the less
awareness one has that one is so engaged. If I might make a bold
suggestion at this point, it would be that Plotinus also thinks that a man's
higher levels he may be said to enjoy his activities, whereas lower down
he may act *in order to* enjoy his actions. He will then do things for
pleasure, in a necessarily self-conscious and deliberate way.

In this undesirable form of self-awareness the soul says, "It is I who do
this; it is I who feel that." That, I would suggest, is what Plotinus means
when he suggests that belonging to oneself can (but need not) have a bad
sense. The evil comes in seeing oneself as the centre of the world; that is a
state he refers to as sleeping, and from which we need to be awakened. It
necessarily entails forgetting one's origin and being in ignorance. Hence
one of the first stages in the awakening process is that of getting to know
who one is, of self-knowledge. In fact, to treat oneself as the centre of the
world is to identify not with what is above one but with what is below.
For the soul in this state will in practice tend to achieve likeness to what
are its own inferiors, to be enslaved to its own chattels, its products in the
material world. But at this point we might well ask why is there a material
world at all? And at least to that we have Plotinus' answer. Soul, to be
good, must create, and what is created must be an image of what is above.
It cannot be intelligible form, but the image of intelligible forms. But given
the necessity to create, why must both the creative process and the
subsequent immersion involve not just the possibility of evil but the fact of
evil for many individual souls?

In the first place, in at least one passage, Plotinus implies that the world
could not have been created without such evil. If that were true, and if the
world's creation is to be both necessary and right, then the paradoxical
result would appear that it is a good thing that souls normally sin. We
know the form of sin, at least for the descended soul: it is a too close
association with the product and a deliberate enjoyment of that
relationship. But is that association necessary for the world to be created,
or could the world equally be created by an effortless overview like that of
the World Soul? 1.4.10 seems to suggest that action on particular
sensibles can only be achieved by the use of the sense faculty. If that is the
case, then the soul can only deal with (and indeed create) sensibles by
means of a faculty which is liable to error. Hence in its dealings with the
material world the soul must make mistakes – or at least most souls must.
When, we should therefore ask, will that liability to error involve an
actual error? The answer will have to be: when judgments are made

without reference to what is higher than the sense-faculty, in other words, as we have seen, when the "I" forgets where it comes from. And what makes it forget? The answer is: the pleasurable images which must necessarily arise if a faculty of sense is to operate.

Interestingly enough, the key to all this seems to be provided by two chapters of *Ennead* 4.4, no. 28 in Porphyry's list, a treatise immediately following 4.3 which we have just discussed, but prior to 2.9 against the Gnostics. Let us finally see what it can offer. Perhaps the necessary existence of a sense-faculty for the individual soul will point us to an understanding of why that soul normally sins both in its descent and in its behaviour down here.

The key chapters seem to be 4.4.4 and 4.4.17. If the soul gives itself to its inferiors, the first text tells us, it gets what it wants by memory and imagination. Memory involves a state or condition (ὅταν διακέηται) which corresponds to previous experiences and visions. It is particularly potent if this condition exists without awareness of its causes. When one has this kind of unconscious memory, one is liable to be what one has (κινδυνεύει εἶναι ὃ ἔχει); and when such an experience, occurs, the soul falls deeper (11.14-15).

This seems to be the text we want. The soul's possession and necessary use of sense-organs involves the production of memories and images. The resulting state of the soul is a near-identity with those images, for the soul loses its ability to stand apart from them – and this near-identity is a further fall which the World Soul does not and indeed cannot undergo. If this is right, then the necessary use of the sense-faculty to work on the individual products of soul is harmful because it can only be undertaken at the price of awakening the dangerous faculties of memory and imagining. The result of such awakening is further sin, for as the previous chapter (4.4.3) has already put it, and 4.4.4, as we have seen, repeats, remembering (τὸ μνημονεύειν) is either thinking (νοεῖν) or imagining (φαντάζεσθαι). And a φαντασία arises not by "holding" (ἔχειν) something, i.e., at arm's length; it is a seeing and a condition (διάκειται). Then if one uses one's senses, one becomes conditioned by the objects of one's senses, and such conditioning cannot but be sinful, if to sin is to look away from one's priors.

Chapter 4.4.17 gives us more detail. The condition which the images and memories produce is one in which the "desiring faculty" is active. Already, in 4.8.[6].8, Plotinus had spoken of unconscious desires, enclosed in the desiring faculty, of which we become aware only when we grasp them by using our perception, or our reason, or both. And individual souls (11.17-18), distracted by sensation, "take hold of" more that is "unnatural," painful and disturbing. They are thus full of desires and the pleasure in these desires deceives them (ἡδονὴ ἠπάτησε). Now again similar ideas are developed in 4.4.17. We already know that the individual soul, using its senses, becomes conditioned by sense objects. These objects it remembers or more generally recalls as images. Such images (4.4.17.11) arise whenever the desiring faculty is stirred, presumably by the soul's awareness of an external object which recalls the past. And the images are themselves like sensations (οἷον αἴσθησις); they announce and report a past experience (ἀπαγγελτικὴ καὶ μηνυτικὴ τοῦ πάθους), while inviting us to pursue and acquire for ourselves the object of desire. In less euphemistic language, the sort of thing Plotinus seems to be thinking of here is that if Jeremy sees Susan (or something which reminds him of Susan) whom he has previously enjoyed sexually, memory of past pleasures will be revived in his imagination, and such memory will invite him to seek repetition of the pleasurable acts. The result of this, Plotinus continues, is disturbing, whether Jeremy in fact tries to satisfy his desires or whether he restrains himself. The same sort of thing arises, I think Plotinus says, with the desire for revenge, and for food, drink and shelter. In the confusion "higher" things are lost sight of, just as in an assembly the best man speaks but his words are drowned by the bawling and shouting of his inferiors.

In brief, then, the problem is this. The use of the senses brings with it both identification with the concerns of one's products – and the captain goes down with his ship – and a necessary development of the capacity to desire – which capacity can be further actualized when the appropriate circumstances occur. Even if these unavoidable desires are resisted, they are still disturbing. So we see that the chances are that the use of the senses, necessary though it is for creation and the organizing of the world, has these necessarily undesirable results. It is, as it were, Catch 22 for the soul; it must act in the world and it is right to do so (and presumably therefore wrong not to do so), but if it does, it will almost certainly sink too far and be "converted" to its inferiors. This seems at least to offer some explanation of the second of the soul's sins, the one it commits when it is down; it seems to mean that a real possibility of corruption is part of the necessary order of things for the individual soul. Does it, however, tell us anything about the first sin, the motive for descent in the soul that is κάμνουσα ?

It seems that if Plotinus' view is to add up, he would have to say that the motive for the descent is sinful if and only if, mixed with the soul's legitimate desire to order and create, is the awareness and pleasant anticipation of the sin it may well commit when it has descended; that is, if its motives for wanting to descend, unlike those of the World Soul which admittedly need not descend so far – are mixed. I must admit that I cannot find any clear statement of this sort, but there is a certain amount of indirect evidence which may suggest that Plotinus either could, or perhaps did, argue in this way. First, and more generally, in the Stoic tradition which Plotinus knew well, it is precisely this doing the right thing from less than pure motives which is commonly the mark of the non-sage, that is, of most of sinful humanity. A second point in favour of an interpretation on these lines may be found in a text to which we have already adverted (4.8.[6].5.28).[17]

Here we observe Plotinus pointing out that if after descending, the soul flees quickly, it will acquire knowledge of evil and know the nature of sin, but will not be harmed. But which soul would *want* to fly quickly? Surely only the one whose motives for descent in the first place were pure, that is, akin to the thoughts of the World Soul about the organization of the visible cosmos.

We come to soul's knowledge of evil iself. In the passage above it is suggested that this is sometimes harmless for the soul, and that the soul may avoid contamination. Later in 4.8 (4.8.7.15ff.) the contaminated soul can even benefit from such experience, in that its knowledge of evil may make knowledge of the good clearer. Here perhaps is where Plotinus saw his ultimate reconciliation. Souls must descend; so far, so good. Most souls (though not all) have mixed motives in their descent and plunge too deeply into evil when they have descended. But all souls, contaminated or not, need to return, and acquisition of a certain knowledge of the nature of the good is a necessary step in their homeward journey. Such knowledge may be easier for them to obtain (by contrast) as a result of the experience of evil. Hence the experience of evil – which is necessary – may even profit both the contaminated and the uncontaminated soul. Would Plotinus go so far as to say that it is a *necessary* precondition of their return? I suspect he might for the contaminated, for perhaps knowledge of evil is the only possible first step towards disentangling oneself from it, from rejecting that "conversion" to evil, that lack of awareness of evil and evil's nature which is the mark of the soul which is hopelessly ensnared. For if the soul recognizes what evil is, and that evil is a threat to it, by so knowing, it also knows that as a soul it is not good in itself. And if it knows that, then in Plotinus' language, it sees that there is no happiness in belonging to itself in "black" varieties either of self-awareness or of loss of

---

[17] O'Brien, "Plotinus on Evil," p. 131.

awareness of self in an absorption in matter. Without such realization, of course, the soul cannot even see the World Soul, let alone *Nous* and the One. Nor can it avoid surrendering to immediate pleasures which, through the desires, are constantly at hand to delude it. But given experience of the nature of evil, the soul can at least use its natural powers of deliberation, for awareness of evil provides something of the raw material of moral deliberation. Moral options become visible.

Finally, if we say that it is in virtue of mixed motives for descending that most souls sin in their descent as well as after their descent, we may wonder why some souls have mixed motives while others do not. Plotinus' first answer would probably be in terms of stains on the soul left by misdeeds in earlier incarnations. But why was there a *first* sin to leave such a stain? It is Plato's problem all over again: what is the fundamental moral difference between the soul of a god and the soul of a man? If the question is answerable, the answer must be in terms of the metaphysics of the dependent soul, not of its psychology. As so often, Plotinus' difficulties seem to be caused by too high an ontological evaluation of the human soul compared with the highest living being, within a theistic system. Perhaps Augustine became aware of this.

8

I fondamenti della metafisica di Plotino
e la struttura della processione

Giovanni Reale
Università Cattolica di Milano

I. Breve stato della questione

Gli strumenti di ricerca e la letteratura critica ed ermeneutica concernenti Plotino sono rimasti per lungo tempo e restano tuttora ad un livello decisamente inferiore rispetto a quelli di cui disponiamo per Platone ed Aristotele e per altri pensatori antichi. Solo fra il 1951 e il 1973 è stata pubblicata una edizione critica del testo delle *Enneadi* veramente attendibile[1] e solo nel 1980 un lessico.[2] Le monografie di insieme sono scarse ed i tentativi di determinare in maniera essenziale la struttura teoretica del pensiero plotiniano sono scarsissimi.[3] In particolare, si nota di sovente uno stanco ripetersi di *clichés* e di formule ormai decisamente obsolete, e,

---

[1] P. Henry e H. R. Schwyzer, *Plotini Opera*, 3 voll. (Paris, Bruxelles, 1951-1973). (Una *editio minor* di quest'opera è in corso di pubblicazione nella "Bibliotheca Oxoniensis" [Oxford, 1964-1977]. Ci rifaremo, nelle citazioni, alla *editio maior*.)

[2] J. H. Sleeman e G. Pollet, *Lexicon Plotinianum* (Leiden, Leuven, 1980).

[3] Per la bibliografia si veda: B. Mariën, "Bibliografia critica degli studi plotiniani con rassegna delle loro recensioni," riveduta e curata da V. Cilento, in Plotino, *Enneadi*, prima versione integra e commentario critico di V. Cilento, vol. 3, parte 2 (Bari, 1949), pp. 389-651; W. Totok, *Handbuch der Geschichte der Philosophie*, 1: *Altertum* (Frankfurt-am-Main, 1964), pp. 335-343; V. Verra, "Il neoplatonismo," in *Questioni di storiografia filosofica* a cura di V. Mathieu (Brescia, 1975), pp. 399-444. Si veda anche l'ampia bibliografia di M. L. Gatti, nel volume che citiamo alla nota 5, alle pp. 181-187.

Graceful Reason: Essays in Ancient and Medieval Philosophy Presented to Joseph Owens, CSSR, ed. Lloyd P. Gerson. Papers in Mediaeval Studies 4 (Toronto: Pontifical Institute of Mediaeval Studies, 1983), pp. 153-175. © P.I.M.S., 1983.

soprattutto, si nota la pervicace insistenza nel parlare di "emanazione" e di "emanazionismo" plotiniano, per lo più senza definire con esattezza che cosa si intenda con tale termine, con tutta una serie di errori che ne conseguono.

In questo studio vogliamo riprendere alcune idee su questo tema già da noi esposte in altri lavori[4] e di recente verificate in maniera analitica anche in un libro di una nostra allieva, la quale vi ha apportato alcune precisazioni e una serie di completamenti.[5]

Riteniamo che sia giunta ormai l'ora di abbandonare definitivamente l'idea che la metafisica plotiniana sia una forma di "emanazionismo." Riteniamo, anzi, che, lette in modo adeguato, le *Enneadi* sembrino presentare una dottrina che è, per molti rispetti, la netta antitesi dell'emanazionismo, ossia una dottrina che fa perno su una "processione" che si struttura secondo un ritmo ternario (che anticipa chiaramente il processo triadico di μονή, πρόοδος, ἐπιστροφή di Proclo, anche se con elementi che la rendono più complessa) il quale risulta imperniato soprattutto sul motivo centrale della θεωρία, che costituisce il vero asse portante dell'intero pensiero plotiniano.

Un inizio di chiarificazione si era già avuto nella seconda metà dello scorso secolo con *La filosofia dei Greci* di E. Zeller,[6] che, però, per il motivo che subito vedremo, non è riuscito ad imporsi. Zeller nota che l'*emanazione* implica, in senso stretto, un passaggio dall'Assoluto al finito, di natura tale che "quello partecipa a questo *una parte della propria sostanza*," [7] il che significa che l'emanazione intesa in questo senso implicherebbe un fluire della *sostanza* dell'Assoluto, ossia dell'Uno. Ora, nota giustamente lo Zeller, una siffatta concezione è espressamente smentita da Plotino in molti passi delle *Enneadi*,[8] dove si afferma che l'Assoluto permane in se medesimo e non esce da sé, essendo per sua natura impartecipabile, e, inoltre, essa risulta incompatibile con i capisaldi del sistema. "Pertanto – scrive lo studioso tedesco – la teoria dell'emanazione è lungi da Plotino, anche se alcune delle similitudini prese in senso stretto sembrerebbero portare ad essa." [9] Per contro, prosegue lo Zeller,

[4] Un primo anticipo abbiamo dato in G. Reale, "Plotino e la rifondazione della Metafisica," in Autori Vari, *Metafisica e Ontologia* (Padova: Antenore, 1978), pp. 11-13; un'ampia esposizione abbiamo dato in G. Reale, *Storia della filosofia antica*, vol. 4: *Le Scuole dell'età imperiale* (Milano: Vita e Pensiero, 1978 [1981³]), 459-616.

[5] M. L. Gatti, *Plotino e la metafisica della contemplazione* (Milano: Cusl, 1982).

[6] E. Zeller, *Die Philosophie der Griechen in ihrer geschichtlichen Entwicklung*, Dritter Teil, zweite Abteilung, 5. Auflage (Leipzig, 1923).

[7] Ibid., p. 560.

[8] Zeller rimanda a Plot., *Enn.* 3.8.9, 5.1.3, 5.5.9, 6.5.3, 6.9.5.

[9] Zeller, *Die Philosophie der Griechen*, p. 560.

due peculiarità accomunano il plotinismo con l'emanazionismo: (*a*) il passaggio dall'Assoluto al finito non avviene mediante un atto volontario dell'Assoluto nè mediante una necessità logica, bensì "durch eine rein physische Wirkung";[10] (*b*) tale passaggio comporta un graduale accrescersi di imperfezione, ossia una crescente diminuzione ontologica. Solo che, in Plotino, ciò che diminuisce non è la *sostanza* dell'Assoluto, come s'è detto, bensì la sua azione, ossia la *potenza* che da lui scaturisce. Le conclusioni di Zeller sono allora le seguenti: "Se a motivo di quelle somiglianze si vuole applicare anche a Plotino la categoria assai ampia della emanazione, lo si può fare (!); ma per la corretta determinazione della cosa, tuttavia, si dovrebbero distinguere due classi di sistemi di emanazione, ossia quello che intende l'emanazione come partecipazione della sostanza (*scil.*: dell'Assoluto), e quello che intende l'emanazione solamente come partecipazione della potenza (*scil.*: dell'Assoluto); solo in quest'ultimo senso la dottrina di Plotino può essere detta emanazionistica." [11]

Ma si noti come il ragionamento vacilli. La prima analogia fra emanazionismo e plotinismo non esiste. Infatti la derivazione del finito dall'Assoluto non si può affatto dire che avvenga "durch eine rein physische Wirkung," [12] trattandosi di una azione necessaria, sì, *ma dipendente da una originaria libertà trascendente e assoluta*, come vedremo. La seconda analogia è puramente apparente, perché la tesi secondo cui nel passaggio dall'Assoluto al finito è la *sostanza stessa* dell'Assoluto che, fluendo, si depotenzia gradualmente, è *essenzialmente* diversa dalla tesi secondo cui nel passaggio dall'Assoluto al finito è l'azione o la *potenza* dell'Assoluto che, fluendo, gradualmente diminuisce. L'analogia fra le due posizioni è prevalentemente accidentale, tanto è vero che Zeller stesso è costretto, proprio per tale motivo, a parlare di *due* classi di emanazionismo.

Ma l'estremo imbarazzo dello Zeller emerge, addirittura a livello tematico, in queste sue precisazioni: "Forse sarebbe ancor più esatto denominare la dottrina plotiniana come un *panteismo dinamico* [*scil.*: invece che come un tipo di emanazionismo]." [13]

Ma gli inconvenienti contro cui questa formula urta sono non meno numerosi di quelli che lo Zeller voleva evitare introducendola. Infatti Zeller stesso conviene che non si tratta di un panteismo che implichi *identità di sostanza* fra Dio e mondo, ma solo che il mondo non ha un

---

[10] Ibid., p. 561.
[11] Ibid.
[12] Ibid.
[13] Ibid.

proprio essere autonomo e che il finito è solo accidente e manifestazione di Dio; tutto deriva dalla forza che proviene dal principio, e questa forza non può essere separata dal principio medesimo; Dio, inoltre, è presente in tutti. Ma, daccapo, non si tratta di una presenza *della sostanza*, ma solo *della azione e della potenza* di Dio.[14]

E' evidente la contraddizione in cui si dibatte lo Zeller ed è quindi chiara la ragione per cui la sua proposta non ebbe successo. Infatti, c'è una radicale differenza fra l'asserire "tutto è *sostanza* di Dio" e "tutto è *potenza* di Dio." La prima proposizione implica *identità ontologica* fra Dio e mondo; la seconda proposizione, invece, implica che il mondo è *effetto* e Dio *causa*, e mantiene la distinzione fra *sostanza* di Dio ed *effetto* che da essa deriva. Panteismo è quello espresso dalla prima, ma non quello espresso dalla seconda proposizione. "Panteismo dinamico" è una vera e propria contraddizione in termini, giacchè l'aggettivo, inteso come vuole lo Zeller, finisce per essere la negazione del sostantivo al quale è applicato. Zeller aveva usato questa formula per la prima volta per designare la teologia del *Trattato sul cosmo per Alessandro*, opera giuntaci sotto il nome di Aristotele, e che Zeller riteneva scritta da un Peripatetico stoicizzante.[15] Ma proprio quest'opera dice *expressis verbis* che la *sostanza* di Dio è trascendente e che è immanente solo la sua *potenza*; e tale precisazione, con tutto ciò che dice il capitolo sesto di questo *Trattato sul cosmo* è esattamente *la negazione del panteismo*.[16] L'estremo disagio dello Zeller è molto istruttivo. In realtà, la metafisica plotiniana non si lascia rinchiudere nè nella formula dell'"emanazionismo" *tout court*, nè in quella più raffinata dell'"emanazionismo dinamico," e nemmeno in quella fuorviante del "panteismo dinamico," perchè implica uno stato di cose assai più complesso, rispetto al quale queste formule si presentano come veri e propri letti di Procuste.

Un buon passo avanti ha fatto nel 1913 H. F. Müller, in un saggio pubblicato sulla rivista *Hermes*. Lo studioso tedesco rilevava, come già Zeller, che l'"emanazione" in Plotino si trova nelle similitudini, le quali

---

[14] Ibid., pp. 560-561.

[15] E. Zeller, *Die Philosophie der Griechen*, Dritter Teil, erste Abteilung, 5. Auflage (Leipzig, 1923), pp. 563-670.

[16] A p. 397b16 l'Autore dice che alcuni degli antichi filosofi si sono spinti ad affermare che tutte le cose che appaiono ai sensi sono *piene di Dei*, ma precisa subito che questo ragionamento conviene, sì, alla *potenza divina* (θεία **δυνάμει**), ma *non* certo alla essenza o sostanza divina (οὐ μὴν τῇ γε **οὐσίᾳ**). Per quanto riguarda la problematica di questo testo e del *Trattato* in generale si veda G. Reale, *Aristotele, Trattato sul cosmo per Alessandro*, traduzione con testo greco a fronte, introduzione commento e indici (Napoli: Loffredo Editore, 1974).

possono chiarire, però – come nel nostro caso – anche trarre in inganno; ma molto più chiaramente di Zeller mette in evidenza una serie di elementi che sono in netta antitesi con l'emanazione e con ciò che essa implica. Per esempio, i concetti di modello e di immagine usati per esprimere il rapporto fra le ipostasi sono, contro il concetto di emanazione. E soprattutto il concetto del "permanere," che viene considerato come condizione necessaria perchè non solo il primo principio ma anche le altre ipostasi producano ciò che viene dopo di loro, è antitetico al concetto dello scorrere implicato nell'emanazione.[17] Ma il Müller aveva già visto che la forza creatrice, in Plotino, sta nel *schauen*, nel θεωρεῖν e che nelle *Enneadi*: "Die Vermittlung, durch die das Eine das Viele aus sich heraussetzt, kann keine andere sein als Schauen."[18] Purtroppo, Müller non ha sviluppato questo punto e lo ha lasciato poco più che a livello intuitivo.

Il concetto di contemplazione creatrice doveva solo nel 1921 emergere nella sua vera portata in un contributo di R. Arnou.[19] Questo studioso ha infatti magistralmente dimostrato che "la contemplation en tant que telle, τῷ εἶναι θεωρίᾳ (3.8.2) est activité pure et féconde."[20] Tesi, questa che è stata portata alle sue estreme conseguenze da V. Cilento, che in un suo saggio, scriveva: "Plotino rileva dall'ombra la 'contemplazione' fino a ipostatizzarla: la θεωρία è l'unica vera Ipostasi, l'Ipostasi creante: nella 'Contemplazione' si sommerge il mitico demiurgo."[21]

Dunque, per Plotino, non si dovrebbe parlare di un emanazionismo, bensì di un *contemplativismo metafisico*, o, se si preferisce, di un *contemplativismo trascendentale*, ossia di un contemplativismo che è ragion d'essere di ogni cosa. Ma la meccanica ideale, i modi e i ritmi secondo cui, dispiegandosi, la θεωρία crea tutte le cose, non sono stati spiegati nè da Arnou, nè, tanto meno, da Cilento. Ebbene, noi riteniamo che, mettendo a frutto alcuni rilievi ermeneutici fatti per la prima volta da A. Covotti[22] e successivamente da J. M. Rist[23] circa la *doppia attività* che è propria di ogni ipostasi (ogni ipostasi ha una attività "immanente," che

---

[17] H. F. Müller, "Plotinische Studien. I. Ist die Metaphysik des Plotinus ein Emanationssystem ?" *Hermes*, 48 (1913), 408-425.

[18] Ibid., p. 420.

[19] R. Arnou, ΠΡΑΞΙΣ et ΘΕΩΡΙΑ. *Etude de détail sur le vocabulaire et la pensée des Ennéades de Plotin* (Paris, 1921; Roma, 1972²).

[20] Ibid., p. 84.

[21] V. Cilento, "Contemplazione," in *La parola del Passato*, 1-3 (1946), 197-221, ora in V. Cilento, *Saggi su Plotino* (Milano: Mursia, 1973), p. 9.

[22] A. Covotti, *Da Aristotele ai Bizantini* (Napoli, 1935).

[23] J. M. Rist, *Plotinus, The Road to Reality* (Cambridge, 1967).

coincide con la sua stessa natura, e una attività che "esce al di fuori," per
così dire), e, tenendo ben presente lo statuto privilegiato peculiare della
prima ipostasi che è libertà autoponentesi, si possa determinare la dottrina
della contemplazione creatrice nel suo preciso statuto ontologico in modo
molto più preciso di quanto non si sia fatto in passato, e si possa così
individuare la cifra e la struttura della mtafisica plotiniana, come subito
vedremo. In questo senso ci siamo mossi nei precedenti lavori su
Plotino,[24] e in questo senso ha sviluppato le sue analisi esaminando tutti i
testi a disposizione Maria Luisa Gatti.[25]

II. I DUE PROBLEMI DELLA METAFISICA PLOTINIANA

Non si intende la metafisica plotiniana se non si prende coscienza del fatto
che nelle *Enneadi* i problemi ultimativi sono due e non uno solo, come era
stato in tutta la speculazione greca precedente. Anzi, sta proprio in questa
mancata distinzione la causa principale del fatto che si sia continuato e si
continui tuttora a parlare di "emanazione" e si perseveri in una serie di
equivoci.

Il problema della metafisica greca nella sua forma classica è il seguente:
"come si spiegano i molti?" o, meglio ancora, dal momento che si giunge
facilmente alla conclusione che i molti si spiegano solo in base ad un
principio *uno* (o in funzione di *alcuni* principi, che hanno però *funzioni
unitarie* in senso analogico), il problema si pone in questo modo: "perchè
e come dall'Uno derivano i molti?" E' questo che, per la metafisica
classica, si offriva come motivo di massima meraviglia, come Platone
espressamente notava: "Che i molti siano uno e l'uno sia molti è cosa
mirabile a dirsi."[26] Plotino, naturalmente, conosce perfettamente tale
problema e lo reimposta e lo discute come quello "che fu già famoso
presso gli antichi."[27] Tuttavia, al di sopra di questo problema egli ne pone
uno ancora più radicale: "perchè l'Uno stesso è ed è quello che è?"[28]
Domandarsi questo significa, evidentemente *mettere a problema lo stesso
Assoluto*, e significa chiedersi perchè l'Assoluto è ed è quello che è.
Significa, insomma, in qualche modo, domandarsi il perchè del principio,
ossia il perchè del perchè ultimo. Questo problema risulta assurdo nel
contesto della metafisica classica platonica e aristotelica. Il principio primo

---

[24] Cf. sopra, nota 4.
[25] Cf. sopra, nota 5.
[26] Plato, *Phil.* 14c: ἓν γὰρ δὴ τὰ **πολλὰ** εἶναι καὶ τὸ **ἓν** **πολλὰ** θαυμαστὸν λεχθέν.
[27] Plot. *Enn.* 5.1.6.
[28] E' la domanda attorno a cui ruota l'intero trattato di *Enn.* 6.8.

è l'*incondizionato*, ossia ciò che per definizione non è più suscettibile di essere messo in alcun modo a problema, ossia che non è suscettibile di essere sottoposto alla domanda del perchè. Aristotele direbbe che tale problema è strutturalmente decettivo, perchè è tale da condurre fatalmente ad un processo all'infinito. Ma Plotino esclude espressamente che la sua domanda abbia tale senso.[29] Con Plotino, dunque, la metafisica raggiunge gli orizzonti ultimi della domanda metafisica, distinguendo il problema dell'eteroproduzione (fondazione delle altre cose da parte del principio) e quello della *autoproduzione* del principio stesso.

Riassumendo, potremmo dire che i problemi supremi della metafisica plotiniana sono i seguenti due:

(1) perchè l'Uno?
(2) perchè e come dall'Uno i molti?

(1) La soluzione del primo problema è condizione necessaria per la soluzione del secondo, e, perciò, occorre iniziare da esso. Il metodo che largamente predomina nelle *Enneadi*, infatti, è quello *progressivo-deduttivo* (dall'alto al basso), mentre quello *regressivo-inferenziale* svolge una funzione prevalentemente protrettico-introduttiva, oppure di complemento (invece il momento ascetico-estatico della risalita all'Uno si colloca su un piano differente, essendo una forma di esperienza e di fruizione dell'Uno di carattere metalogico e metarazionale, anche se non illogico e non irrazionale).

La posizione del problema della autofondazione del principio, come è noto, deriva in Plotino dalla necessità di rispondere ad alcune istanze fatte valere in questo senso dagli Gnostici, ma con un notevole salto di qualità, che eleva il problema e la sua trattazione ben al di sopra del livello degli avversari, ad altezze tali che solo nel moderno idealismo trovano l'eguale, e, in questo modo, la soluzione del problema presenta valenze che vanno molto al di là delle istanze storico-teoretiche che lo hanno generato.

Ecco la risposta di Plotino.

L'Uno è *libertà assoluta*. Tutte le cose, infatti, sono libere in quanto e nella misura in cui *vogliono il Bene* e *muovono verso il Bene*. E l'Uno, che è il Bene, è libertà assoluta perchè non deve muovere verso qualcosa di ulteriore, ma è e persevera in se stesso, senza avere bisogno di nulla. L'Uno come Bene è creatore di se medesimo, è attività che si autopone, è *autoctisi*, per dirla con espressione che useranno gli Idealisti ma

---

[29] Cf. Plot. *Enn.* 3.8.11.

perfettamente plotiniana nel suo significato.[30] L'Uno è libertà assoluta nel senso che è creatore di libertà, ἐλευθεροποιός.[31] E' attività che pone il suo proprio essere. E' attività in cui l'essere non è condizione dell'agire, ma in cui, viceversa, l'agire produce l'essere, o, meglio ancora, è una forma di attività in cui c'è coincidenza, per così dire, di agire e di essere.[32] L'ὑπόστασις dell'Uno è la stessa attività (autoproduttrice).[33] L'attività (autoproduttrice) coincide con l'Uno stesso.[34] Egli esplica il suo atto volendolo, e, quindi, si può anche dire che la sua volontà e la sua essenza coincidono.[35] Dell'Uno-Bene dice esattamente Plotino: ὡς ἄρα ἐβούλετο, οὕτω καὶ ἔστιν.[36] E ancora:

> Ἐν δὲ τῇ τοῦ ἀγαθοῦ ὑποστάσει ἀνάγκη **τὴν αἵρεσιν καὶ τὴν αὐτοῦ θέλησιν** ἐμπεριειλημμένην εἶναι.[37]

Insomma: l'Uno, in quanto è ciò che volle e desiderò di essere, è creatore di sè, è *causa sui*:

> Εἰ οὖν ὑφέστηκε τὸ ἀγαθὸν καὶ συνυφίστησιν αὐτὸ ἡ αἵρεσις καὶ ἡ βούλησις – ἄνευ γὰρ τούτων οὐκ ἔσται – δεῖ δὲ τοῦτο μὴ πολλὰ εἶναι, συνακτέον ὡς ἓν τὴν βούλησιν καὶ τὴν οὐσίαν καὶ τὸ θέλειν · τὸ δὲ θέλειν <εἰ> παρ' αὐτοῦ, ἀνάγκη παρ' αὐτοῦ καὶ τὸ εἶναι αὐτῷ εἶναι, **ὥστε αὐτὸν πεποιηκέναι αὐτὸν** ὁ λόγος ἀνεῦρεν.[38]

L'Uno è *amore*, è precisamente amore di sè, αὐτοῦ ἔρως,[39] ed è ciò stesso che egli ama, nel senso che è forza operante produttrice di sè, e, quindi, di sè come oggetto del proprio amore:

> ... ὁ δ' εἰς τὸ εἴσω οἷον φέρεται αὐτοῦ οἷον **ἑαυτὸν ἀγαπήσας, αὐγὴν καθαράν, αὐτὸς ὢν τοῦτο, ὅπερ ἠγάπησε** · τοῦτο δ' ἐστὶν ὑποστήσας αὐτόν, εἴπερ ἐνέργεια μένουσα καὶ τὸ ἀγαπητότατον οἷον νοῦς. Νοῦς δὲ ἐνέργεμα · ὥστε ἐνέργημα αὐτός.[40]

L'Uno è, inoltre, *autovisione* o *autocontemplazione*; e quello che si potrebbe chiamare il suo "essere" è appunto *radicato in questa autovisione*:

---

[30] *Enn.* 6.8.7
[31] *Enn.* 6.8.12 (19).
[32] *Enn.* 6.8.7 (46-54).
[33] Ibid.
[34] *Enn.* 6.8.16 (25).
[35] *Enn.* 6.8.13 (7-8).
[36] *Enn.* 6.8.13 (8-9).
[37] *Enn.* 6.8.13 (43-45).
[38] *Enn.* 6.8.13 (50-55).
[39] *Enn.* 6.8.15 (1).
[40] *Enn.* 6.8.16 (12-16).

῎Ετι τοίνυν, εἰ ἔστι μάλιστα, ὅτι πρὸς αὐτὸν οἷον στηρίζει καὶ **οἷον πρὸς αὐτὸν βλέπει καὶ τὸ οἷον εἶναι τοῦτο αὐτῷ τὸ πρὸς αὐτὸν βλέπειν, οἷον ποιοῖ ἂν αὐτόν.**[41]

Plotino parla anche dell'Uno come "causa della causa" (**αἴτιον** δὲ ἐκεῖνο **τοῦ αἰτίου**).[42]

L'ipostasi dell'Uno, in conclusione, non sta nella sostanza, bensì sta nell'attività pura che pone, in un certo senso, la sua stessa sostanza:

Οὐδὲ γὰρ φοβητέον **ἐνέργειαν τὴν πρώτην τίθεσθαι ἄνευ οὐσίας, ἀλλ'** αὐτὸ τοῦτο τὴν οἷον ὑπόστασιν θετέον.[43]

Forse il passo seguente riassume meglio di ogni altro il pensiero di Plotino al riguardo:

᾿Ενέργεια δὴ οὐ δουλεύσασα οὐσίᾳ καθαρῶς ἐστιν ἐλευθέρα, καὶ οὕτως αὐτὸς παρ᾿ αὐτοῦ αὐτός. Καὶ γὰρ εἰ μὲν ἐσῴζετο εἰς τὸ εἶναι ὑπ᾿ ἄλλου, οὐ πρῶτος αὐτὸς ἐξ αὐτοῦ · εἰ δ᾿ αὐτὸς αὐτὸν ὀρθῶς λέγεται συνέχειν, **αὐτός ἐστι καὶ ὁ παράγων ἑαυτόν,** εἴπερ, ὅπερ συνέχει κατὰ φύσιν, τοῦτο καὶ ἐξ ἀρχῆς πεποίηκεν εἶναι. Εἰ μὲν οὖν χρόνος ἦν, ὅθεν ἤρξατο εἶναι, τὸ πεποιηκέναι κυριώτατον ἂν ἐλέχθη · νῦν δέ, εἰ καὶ πρὶν αἰῶνα εἶναι ὅπερ ἐστὶν ἦν, **τὸ πεποιηκέναι ἑαυτὸν τοῦτο νοείτω τὸ σύνδρομον εἶναι τὸ πεποιηκέναι καὶ αὐτό · ἓν γὰρ τῇ ποιήσει καὶ οἷον γεννήσει ἀιδίῳ τὸ εἶναι.**[44]

(2) Affrontiamo, ora, il secondo dei problemi, la cui soluzione è stata a lungo fraintesa a motivo delle pesanti ipoteche poste appunto dalle esegesi in chiave "emanazionistica," e che riserva una quantità di sorprese.

Il passo fondamentale, su cui ha richiamato per la prima volta l'attenzione A. Covotti, è contenuto nel quarto trattato della quinta *Enneade*:

᾿Επεὶ οὖν ἐκεῖνο μένει νοητόν, τὸ γινόμενον γίνεται νόησις · νόησις δὲ οὖσα καὶ νοοῦσα ἀφ᾿ οὗ ἐγένετο – ἄλλο γὰρ οὐκ ἔχει – νοῦς γίγνεται, ἄλλο οἷον νοητὸν καὶ οἷον ἐκεῖνο καὶ μίμημα καὶ εἴδωλον ἐκείνου. ᾿Αλλὰ πῶς μένοντος ἐκείνου γίνεται ; ᾿Ενέργεια ἡ μέν ἐστι **τῆς οὐσίας,** ἡ δ᾿ **ἐκ τῆς οὐσίας** ἑκάστου · καὶ **ἡ μὲν τῆς οὐσίας** αὐτό ἐστιν ἐνέργεια ἕκαστον, **ἡ δὲ ἀπ᾿ ἐκείνης,** ἣν δεῖ παντὶ ἕπεσθαι **ἐξ ἀνάγκης** ἑτέραν οὖσαν αὐτοῦ · οἷον καὶ ἐπὶ τοῦ πυρὸς ἡ μέν τίς ἐστι συμπληροῦσα τὴν οὐσίαν θερμότης, ἡ δὲ ἀπ᾿ ἐκείνης ἤδη γινομένη ἐνεργοῦντος ἐκείνου τὴν σύμφυτον τῇ οὐσίᾳ ἐν

---

[41] *Enn.* 6.8.16 (18-21).
[42] *Enn.* 6.8.18 (38).
[43] *Enn.* 6.8.20 (9-11).
[44] *Enn.* 6.8.20 (17-27).

162 G. REALE

τῷ μένειν πῦρ. Οὕτω δὴ κἀκεῖ · καὶ πολὺ πρότερον ἐκεῖ **μένοντος αὐτοῦ
ἐν τῷ οἰκείῳ ἤθει ἐκ τῆς ἐν αὐτῷ τελειότητος καὶ συνούσης
ἐνεργείας ἡ γεννηθεῖσα ἐνέργεια ὑπόστασιν λαβοῦσα, ἅτε ἐκ μεγάλης
δυνάμεως, μεγίστης μὲν οὖν ἁπασῶν, εἰς τὸ εἶναι καὶ οὐσίαν ἦλθεν ·**
ἐκεῖνο γὰρ ἐπέκεινα οὐσίας ἦν.[45]

Plotino distingue, dunque, (a) una ἐνέργεια **τῆς οὐσίας**, ossia una attività
di un essere, e (b) una ἐνέργεια **ἐκ τῆς οὐσίας**, ossia una attività che
scaturisce da un essere. Orbene, (a) l'attività che è propria di una cosa
coincide con l'atto stesso della cosa (fa tutt'uno con quello che la cosa è).
Invece (b) l'attività che scaturisce da una cosa deve necessariamente (ἐξ
ἀνάγκης) seguire a ciascuna cosa ed è distinta e differente dalla cosa
medesima. L'esempio che Plotino adduce è chiarissimo. Nel fuoco si
devono distinguere due attività: (a) quella per cui esso è intrinsecamente e
per sua essenza calore, e che, quindi, coincide con la sua stessa natura o
sostanza, ed è, precisamente, l'attività del permanere (μένειν) fuoco; (b)
quella che scaturisce dal permanere esso fuoco, ossia quell'attività che
deriva di conseguenza e vien fuori da esso. Ritornando al caso dell'Uno, si
ha quanto segue. (a) Vi è una attività propria dell'Uno, che è quella attività
per cui l'Uno è e permane quello che è, è potenza assoluta, ossia attività
autocreatrice, assoluta libertà, e questa attività è un μένειν; (b) vi è, poi,
l'attività che da quella scaturisce e che è potenza grandissima perchè è
potenza che scaturisce dalla massima potenza, e che, di conseguenza,
produce tutte le cose. La attività (a) è, dunque, essenzialmente la *libertà*
autocreatrice; l'attività (b) è attività che consegue ἐξ ἀνάγκης dalla prima.

Il Rist ha visto molto bene, a questo riguardo, che, se l'attività dell'Uno
consiste nel voler essere quello che è, nella libertà, appunto, di essere ciò
che è, allora si deve concludere che la *necessità* della attività dall'Uno è
una *necessità in un certo senso voluta*, conseguenza di una attività di
libertà, e che, pertanto, in un certo senso, "la creazione è libera, non più e
non meno di quanto non lo sia l'Uno stesso."[46] Forse l'affermazione del
Rist è un po' troppo audace. Meglio sarebbe dire che la creazione, ossia la
processione di tutte le cose dall'Uno, è un tipo di "necessità" *sui generis*,
ossia un tipo di necessità conseguente ad una "libertà," ossia una sorta di
necessità voluta.

E già questo basterebbe a distruggere l'esegesi emanazionistica. La
derivazione delle cose dall'Uno è un 'processo" che scaturisce da un μένειν
e, inoltre, è sotto il segno di una necessità che scaturisce da una attività di

[45] *Enn.* 5.4.2 (22-38).
[46] Rist, *Plotinus, The Road*, p. 83.

libertà. Questo è, anzi, addirittura l'opposto di quello che lo schema emanazionistico richiederebbe.[47]

III. Struttura della processione

Ma non è tutto.

La generazione delle ipostasi intelligibili (così come anche la generazione del cosmo fisico) implica, oltre alle due attività sopra illustrate, una ulteriore attività, che è altrettanto essenziale di quelle. Senza tale attività nulla potrebbe nascere e sussistere. Si tratta dell'attività del "rivolgersi" (ἐπιστρέφειν) per "guardare" e "contemplare" (θεωρεῖν) il principio. Se si fosse posto mente a questa attività, di certo il termine "emanazione" sarebbe stato quello da evitare nella maniera più categorica, perchè esso vieta proprio la comprensione di questo "ritorno contemplativo" che, come vedremo, ha luogo per ogni ipostasi.

In particolare, per quanto concerne la seconda ipostasi, di cui per prima cosa dobbiamo occuparci, è da rilevare come l'attività o potenza che scaturisce *dall'*Uno non generi senz'altro il *Nous*, bensì una sorta di "alterità" ossia una sorta di "indeterminato" e di "informe," che si "determina" e diviene "mondo di forme" *solo rivolgendosi all'Uno*, vale a dire *ritornando all'Uno*. E l'alterità indeterminata si determina precisamente nella *visione contemplativa* dell'Uno.

Ma la dinamica della deduzione della seconda ipostasi è particolarmente complessa. Lasciamo da parte la spiegazione che Plotino cerca di dare ricorrendo a concetti desunti dalle "dottrine non scritte" e dalla tradizione indiretta di Platone, perchè, anche se molto interessante, costituisce una spiegazione di rincalzo, parallela a quella fondamentale.[48] Questa spiegazione fondamentale può essere riassunta come segue. L'attività o potenza derivante dall'Uno, come abbiamo visto, deve *rivolgersi all'Uno e contemplarlo*. Tuttavia, tale rivolgersi contemplativo non è ancora il *Nous*, ma, piuttosto, la *condizione* che lo fa essere; Plotino distingue, infatti, due momenti. (*a*) Prima viene il momento del rivolgersi contemplativo della potenza verso l'Uno; in questo momento la potenza viene fecondata, riempita e colmata, tramite la contemplazione, dall'Uno. (*b*) Segue il momento della riflessione di questa potenza su se medesima in quanto fecondata dalla visione dell'Uno. I due momenti danno ragione, per così

---

[47] Per gli opportuni approfondimenti circa la problematica dell'Uno rimandiamo a Gatti, *Plotino*, pp. 13-28 e alle ulteriori indicazioni che si troveranno ivi nelle note.

[48] Cf. Gatti, *Plotino*, pp. 37-42 e Th. A. Szlezák, *Platon und Aristoteles in der Nuslehre Plotins* (Basel, Stuttgart, 1979), pp. 52-119.

164 G. REALE

dire, delle due facce del *Nous*, che è appunto *e* essere *e* pensare. (*a*) Nel primo momento, nasce l'*ousia*, ossia la sostanza, l'essenza e l'essere (che è il contenuto del pensiero); (*b*) nel secondo momento nasce il pensiero vero e proprio che riflette sull'essere. Nel secondo trattato della quinta *Enneade* si legge il testo fondamentale al riguardo:

> ὂν γὰρ τέλειον τῷ μηδὲν ζητεῖν μηδὲ ἔχειν μηδὲ δεῖσθαι οἷον ὑπερερρύη καὶ τὸ ὑπερπλῆρες αὐτοῦ πεποίηκεν ἄλλο · τὸ δὲ γενόμενον εἰς αὐτὸ **ἐπεστράφη** καὶ ἐπληρώθη καὶ ἐγένετο **πρὸς αὐτὸ βλέπον καὶ νοῦς οὗτος.** Καὶ ἡ μὲν **πρὸς ἐκεῖνο στάσις αὐτοῦ τὸ ὂν ἐποίησεν, ἡ δὲ πρὸς αὐτὸ θέα τὸν νοῦν.** Ἐπεὶ οὖν ἔστη πρὸς αὐτό, ἵνα ἴδῃ, ὁμοῦ νοῦς γίγνεται καὶ ὄν. [49]

La molteplicità rimane così dedotta. Il *Nous* è *e* essere *e* pensiero. Non solo, ma nel *Nous* l'*uni-totalità* della prima ipostasi diventa la *totalità dei molti*, la totalità di tutte le cose (tutte le Idee). Poichè, come abbiamo veduto, il *Nous* contempla l'Uno, ma anche se medesimo fecondato dall'Uno, non è che il *Nous* veda *immediatamente* l'Uno come molteplice, ma piuttosto, *mediatamente*, ossia vede se medesimo (gravido d'Uno) come molteplice, come il passo centrale di *Enneadi* 6.7.16 precisa.[50]

Maria Luisa Gatti ha raccolto ed esaminato tutti i testi concernenti il *Nous* nel suo duplice contemplare l'Uno e se medesimo, e alle pagine del suo libro rimandiamo il lettore per gli opportuni approfondimenti.[51] Le conclusioni sono che il *Nous nasce da* contemplazione ed *è esso stesso* per eccellenza contemplazione. Plotino parla, addirittura, di "vivente contemplazione," e di "contemplazione in persona."[52]

---

[49] *Enn.* 5.2.1 (7-14).
[50] *Enn.* 6.7.16 (9-22): Πρὸς δὴ τὴν τοιαύτην σκέψιν τάχ᾿ ἂν εἴη προὔργου ἄρξασθαι ἐντεῦθεν. Ἆρα, ὅτε ἑώρα πρὸς τὸ ἀγαθόν, ἐνόει ὡς πολλὰ τὸ ἓν ἐκεῖνο καὶ ἓν ὂν αὐτὸς ἐνόει αὐτὸν πολλά, μερίζων αὐτὸν παρ᾿ αὐτῷ τῷ νοεῖν μὴ ὅλον ὁμοῦ δύνασθαι ; Ἀλλ᾿ οὔπω νοῦς ἦν ἐκεῖνο βλέπων, ἀλλ᾿ ἔβλεπεν ἀνοήτως. Ἢ φατέον ὡς οὐδὲ ἑώρα πώποτε, ἀλλ᾿ ἔζη μὲν πρὸς αὐτὸ καὶ ἀνήρτητο αὐτοῦ καὶ ἐπέστραπτο πρὸς αὐτό, ἡ δὴ κίνησις αὕτη πληρωθεῖσα τῷ ἐκεῖ κινεῖσθαι καὶ περὶ ἐκεῖνο ἐπλήρωσεν αὐτὸ καὶ οὐκέτι κίνησις ἦν μόνον, ἀλλὰ κίνησις διακορὴς καὶ πλήρης · **ἑξῆς δὲ πάντα ἐγένετο καὶ ἔγνω τοῦτο ἐν συναισθήσει αὐτοῦ καὶ νοῦς ἤδη ἦν,** πληρωθεὶς μέν, ἵν᾿ ἔχῃ, ὃ ὄψεται, βλέπων δὲ αὐτὰ μετὰ φωτὸς παρὰ τοῦ δόντος ἐκεῖνα καὶ τοῦτο κομιζόμενος.
[51] Gatti, *Plotino*, pp. 42-59.
[52] *Enn.* 3.8.8 (1-30): Τῆς δὲ θεωρίας ἀναβαινούσης ἐκ τῆς φύσεως ἐπὶ ψυχὴν καὶ ἀπὸ ταύτης εἰς νοῦν καὶ ἀεὶ οἰκειοτέρων τῶν θεωριῶν γιγνομένων καὶ ἑνουμένων τοῖς θεωροῦσι καὶ ἐπὶ τῆς σπουδαίας ψυχῆς πρὸς τὸ αὐτὸ τῷ ὑποκειμένῳ ἰόντων τῶν ἐγνωσμένων ἅτε εἰς νοῦν σπευδόντων, ἐπὶ τούτου δηλονότι ἤδη ἐν ἄμφω οὐκ οἰκειώσει, ὥσπερ ἐπὶ τῆς ψυχῆς τῆς ἀρίστης, ἀλλ᾿ οὐσίᾳ καὶ τῷ ταὐτὸν τὸ εἶναι καὶ τὸ νοεῖν εἶναι. Οὐ γὰρ ἔτι ἄλλο, τὸ δ᾿ ἄλλο · πάλιν γὰρ αὖ ἄλλο ἔσται, ὃ οὐκέτι ἄλλο καὶ ἄλλο. **Δεῖ οὖν τοῦτο εἶναι ἐν ὄντως ἄμφω · τοῦτο δέ ἐστι θεωρία ζῶσα,** οὐ θεώρημα, οἷον τὸ ἐν ἄλλῳ. Τὸ γὰρ ἐν ἄλλῳ ζῶν τι ἐκεῖνο, οὐκ αὐτοζῶν. Εἰ οὖν ζήσεταί τι θεώρημα καὶ νόημα, δεῖ αὐτοζωὴν εἶναι οὐ φυτικὴν οὐδὲ αἰσθητικὴν οὐδὲ ψυχικὴν τὴν ἄλλην. Νοήσεις μὲν γάρ πως καὶ ἄλλαι · ἀλλ᾿ ἡ μὲν φυτικὴ νόησις, ἡ δὲ αἰσθητική, ἡ δὲ ψυχική. Πῶς οὖν νοήσεις ; Ὅτι λόγοι. **Καὶ πᾶσα ζωὴ νόησίς τις,** ἀλλὰ ἄλλη ἄλλης ἀμυδροτέρα, ὥσπερ καὶ ζωή. Ἡ δὲ

E come avviene la processione nella terza ipostasi, ossia dell'anima dal *Nous*?

Plotino, per dedurre la terza ipostasi, si rifà agli stessi moduli dei quali si è avvalso per dedurre la seconda ipostasi dalla prima.

Come abbiamo visto a proposito dell'Uno, infatti, Plotino distingue (*a*) una attività *del Nous*, ossia una attività che il *Nous* rivolge a se medesimo e che coincide con l'essenza stessa del *Nous* e (*b*) una attività derivante *dal Nous*, una attività che scaturisce dalla sua natura di *Nous* e che "esce fuori" da lui. La seconda attività, dunque, non solo deriva dalla prima, ma è *conseguenza della prima* in quanto il *Nous* produce qualcosa altro da sè proprio a motivo del proprio rivolgersi su se medesimo (gravido di Uno).

Ecco uno dei testi più significativi a questo riguardo:

> *Τὸ εἶναι ἐνέργεια, οὖν καὶ οὐδέν, πρὸς ὅ ἡ ἐνέργεια · πρὸς αὐτῷ ἄρα.* **Ἑαυτὸν ἄρα νοῶν οὕτω πρὸς αὐτῷ καὶ εἰς ἑαυτὸν τὴν ἐνέργειαν ἴσχει. Καὶ γὰρ εἴ τι ἐξ αὐτοῦ, τῷ εἰς αὐτὸν ἐν ἑαυτῷ.** *Ἔδει γὰρ πρῶτον ἑαυτῷ, εἶτα καὶ εἰς ἄλλο, ἢ ἄλλο τι ἥκειν ἀπ' αὐτοῦ ὁμοιούμενον αὐτῷ, οἷον καὶ πυρὶ ἐν αὐτῷ πρότερον ὄντι πυρὶ καὶ τὴν ἐνέργειαν ἔχοντι πυρὸς οὕτω τοι καὶ ἴχνος αὐτοῦ δυνηθῆναι ποιῆσαι ἐν ἄλλῳ.*[53]

Ma, daccapo, non basta l'attività o potenza che deriva dal *Nous* per generare l'anima. Occorre, infatti, che analogamente a quanto abbiamo visto a proposito del *Nous* nei confronti dell'Uno, anche ciò che deriva dal *Nous* si rivolga, a sua volta, a guardare e a contemplare il *Nous* medesimo. In effetti l'Anima, considerata come potenza derivante dal *Nous*, è, nei confronti del *Nous*, come l'indeterminato rispetto al determinato, come la materia rispetto alla forma. L'Anima diventa tale, secondo Plotino, nel momento in cui si rivolge a contemplare il *Nous*.

Ecco due dei testi più eloquenti.[54] Nel nono trattato della terza *Enneade* leggiamo:

> *Τὴν ψυχὴν αὐτὴν δεῖ ὥσπερ ὄψιν εἶναι, ὁρατὸν δὲ αὐτῇ τὸν νοῦν εἶναι, ἀόριστον πρὶν ἰδεῖν, πεφυκυῖαν δὲ νοεῖν · ὕλην οὖν πρὸς νοῦν.*[55]

ἐναργεστέρα αὕτη καὶ πρώτη ζωὴ καὶ πρῶτος νοῦς εἷς. Νόησις οὖν ἡ πρώτη ζωὴ καὶ ζωὴ δευτέρα νόησις δευτέρα καὶ ἡ ἐσχάτη ζωὴ ἐσχάτη νόησις. Πᾶσα οὖν ζωὴ τοῦ γένους τούτου καὶ νόησις. Ἀλλὰ ζωῆς μὲν ἴσως διαφορὰς τάχ' ἂν λέγοιεν ἄνθρωποι, νοήσεως δὲ οὐ λέγουσιν, ἀλλὰ τὰς μέν, τὰς δ' ὅλως οὐ νοήσεις, ὅτι ὅλως τὴν ζωὴν ὅ τι ποτέ ἐστιν οὐ ζητοῦσιν. Ἀλλ' ἐκεῖνό γε ἐπισημαντέον, ὅτι πάλιν αὖ ὁ λόγος πάρεργον ἐνδείκνυται θεωρίας τὰ πάντα ὄντα. Εἰ τοίνυν ἡ ζωὴ ἡ ἀληθεστάτη νοήσει ζωή ἐστιν, αὕτη δὲ ταὐτὸν τῇ ἀληθεστάτῃ νοήσει, ἡ ἀληθεστάτη νόησις ζῇ καὶ ἡ θεωρία καὶ τὸ θεώρημα τὸ τοιοῦτο ζῶν καὶ ζωὴ καὶ ἐν ὁμοῦ τὰ δύο.
[53] *Enn.* 5.3.7 (18-25).
[54] Tutti i passi concernenti il problema si vedano in Gatti, *Plotino*, pp. 64-65.
[55] *Enn.* 3.9.5 (1-3).

E nel primo trattato della quinta *Enneade* si afferma sull'Anima:

> ... εἰκών τίς ἐστι νοῦ · οἷον λόγος ὁ ἐν προφορᾷ λόγου τοῦ ἐν ψυχῇ, οὕτω
> τοι **καὶ αὐτὴ λόγος νοῦ** καὶ ἡ πᾶσα ἐνέργεια καὶ ἣν προΐεται ζωὴν εἰς
> ἄλλου ὑπόστασιν · οἷον πυρὸς τὸ μὲν ἡ συνοῦσα θερμότης, ἡ δὲ ἣν παρέχει.
> Δεῖ δὲ λαβεῖν ἐκεῖ οὐκ ἐκρέουσαν, ἀλλὰ μένουσαν μὲν τὴν ἐν αὐτῷ, τὴν δὲ
> ἄλλην ὑφισταμένην. Οὖσα οὖν ἀπὸ νοῦ νοερά ἐστι, καὶ ἐν λογισμοῖς ὁ νοῦς
> αὐτῆς καὶ ἡ τελείωσις ἀπ' αὐτοῦ πάλιν οἷον πατρὸς ἐκθρέψαντος, ὃν οὐ
> τέλειον ὡς πρὸς αὐτὸν ἐγέννησεν. **Ἥ τε οὖν ὑπόστασις αὐτῇ ἀπὸ νοῦ ὅ**
> **τε ἐνεργείᾳ λόγος νοῦ αὐτῇ ὁρωμένου. Ὅταν γὰρ ἐνίδῃ εἰς νοῦν,**
> **ἔνδοθεν ἔχει καὶ οἰκεῖα ἃ νοεῖ καὶ ἐνεργεῖ.** Καὶ ταύτας μόνας δεῖ
> λέγειν ἐνεργείας ψυχῆς, ὅσα νοερῶς καὶ ὅσα οἴκοθεν · τὰ δὲ χείρω ἄλλοθεν
> καὶ πάθη ψυχῆς τῆς τοιαύτης. Νοῦς οὖν ἐπὶ μᾶλλον θειοτέραν ποιεῖ καὶ
> τῷ πατὴρ εἶναι καὶ τῷ παρεῖναι · οὐδὲν γὰρ μεταξὺ ἢ τὸ ἑτέροις εἶναι, ὡς
> ἐφεξῆς μέντοι καὶ ὡς τὸ δεχόμενον, τὸ δὲ ὡς εἶδος.[56]

L'asse attorno a cui tutto ruota, resta, anche nel caso dell'Anima, *la contemplazione*, come risulta da queste affermazioni di Plotino:

> Εἰ οὖν πανταχοῦ δεῖ γίνεσθαι καὶ μὴ εἶναι ὅπου μὴ τὴν ἐνέργειαν τὴν
> αὐτὴν ἀεί τε τὸ πρότερον ἕτερον τοῦ ὑστέρου, ἥκει δὲ ἡ ἐνέργεια ἐκ θεωρίας
> ἢ πράξεως, πρᾶξις δὲ οὔπω ἦν – οὐ γὰρ οἷόν τε πρὸ θεωρίας – ἀνάγκη
> ἀσθενεστέραν μὲν ἑτέραν ἑτέρας εἶναι, **πᾶσαν δὲ θεωρίαν · ὥστε τὴν**
> **κατὰ τὴν θεωρίαν πρᾶξιν δοκοῦσαν εἶναι τὴν ἀσθενεστάτην θεωρίαν**
> **εἶναι ·** ὁμογενὲς γὰρ ἀεὶ δεῖ τὸ γεννώμενον εἶναι, ἀσθενέστερον μὴν τῷ
> ἐξίτηλον καταβαῖνον γίγνεσθαι. Ἀψοφητὶ μὲν δὴ πάντα, ὅτι μηδὲν
> ἐμφανοῦς καὶ τῆς ἔξωθεν θεωρίας ἢ πράξεως δεῖται, καὶ ψυχὴ δὲ **ἡ**
> **θεωροῦσα καὶ τὸ οὕτω θεωρῆσαν ἅτε ἐξωτέρω καὶ οὐχ ὡσαύτως τῷ**
> **πρὸ αὐτῆς τὸ μετ' αὐτὴν ποιεῖ καὶ θεωρία τὴν θεωρίαν ποιεῖ. Καὶ**
> **γὰρ οὐκ ἔχει πέρας ἡ θεωρία οὐδὲ τὸ θεώρημα.**[57]

Per ragioni di spazio dobbiamo limitarci alla processione quale è
presentata da Plotino a livello delle realtà intelligibili. Tuttavia, sarebbe
facile dimostrare – e in parte l'abbiamo già fatto altrove[58] – che anche la
processione del mondo sensibile da quello intelligibile avviene secondo
l'identico schema, senza alcune eccezione, giù giù fino alla materia, la
quale altro non è se non prodotto di quell'estrema attività dell'Anima che è
contemplazione indebolita ed illanguidita, e che, come tale, non ha più il

---

[56] *Enn.* 5.1.3 (7-24).
[57] *Enn.* 3.8.5 (27-30).
[58] Si veda a tale riguardo Reale, *Storia della filosofia antica*, 4: 555-573 e Gatti, *Plotino*,
pp. 78-92.

vigore sufficiente per rivolgersi verso chi l'ha generata, e che quindi non ha più la forza di contemplare a sua volta, e, proprio per questo, svanisce, diventa non-essere.

IV. Conclusioni

Il ritmo triadico nella processione è dunque evidente. E la qualifica di "emanazionismo," pertanto, non regge in alcun modo, in quanto risulta determinante, in questo processo, più che il momento del fluire, quello del rifluire, ossia più che quello dell'uscita, quello della *conversione*.
Molto interessante sarebbe studiare la terminologia con cui vengono indicati i tre momenti. Si avrebbe la sorpresa di trovare in Plotino, come già sopra accennavamo, largamente anticipato Proclo: μένειν – μονή, προ-ϊέναι – πρόοδος (e affini), ἐπιστρέφειν – ἐπιστροφή sono termini usati da Plotino per indicare i momenti della processione. (Sul termine πρόοδος usato per indicare l'insieme della processione, ritorneremo più avanti).

Ma non è sullo studio delle determinazioni lessicali che, qui, vogliamo soffermarci, ma, piuttosto, sullo studio delle determinazioni concettuali.

Chiamiamo, per semplificazione, *manenza* l'attività immanente e il μένειν di ogni singola ipostasi, *progressione* l'attività che deriva *da* ciascuna ipostasi e *volgimento* o *ritorno* il momento della conversione alla precedente ipostasi. Abbiamo visto che la chiave di questo movimento triadico è la contemplazione. Ebbene, nella prima ipostasi, che è il principio assoluto, i tre momenti non possono essere distinti. Tuttavia, è interessante notare come la μονή ἐν αὐτῷ dell'Uno sia detta essere una sorta di inclinazione dell'Uno verso se medesimo (νεῦσις αὐτοῦ πρὸς αὐτόν) e in un certo senso ἐνέργεια αὐτοῦ.[59] E questa, poco prima, è presentata come una sorta di "guardare verso se stesso" (οἷον πρὸς αὐτὸν βλέπει), e nel medesimo contesto, questa fa tutt'uno con l'autovolersi e con l'auto-crearsi.[60] L'Uno può essere detto meta-autocontemplazione, in cui i tre momenti *coincidono contratti*.

Nella seconda ipostasi, di primo acchito, sembrerebbe che il momento della contemplazione coincida *semplicemente con il momento del volgimento*, con l'ἐπιστρέφειν (verso l'Uno e verso sè in quanto potenza fecondata dall'Uno). Invece la cosa risulta più complessa e più interessante. M. L. Gatti ha dimostrato che già il momento della progressione dall'Uno, ossia l'attività che scaturisce *dall'*Uno è definita da

---

[59] *Enn.* 6.8.16 (24-26).
[60] *Enn.* 6.8.16 (18-24).

Plotino con termini che implicano strutturale riferimento alla contemplazione,[61] ossia come "forza visiva che non vede ancora," [62] ma che tuttavia "possiede impresso il tipo della visione," [63] e che, per questo appunto, può vedere l'Uno e diventare "visione veggente." [64] Ecco il passo fondamentale del terzo trattato della quinta *Enneade*:

> Διὸ καὶ ὁ νοῦς οὗτος ὁ πολύς, ὅταν τὸ ἐπέκεινα ἐθέλῃ νοεῖν. Εἰ μὲν οὖν αὐτὸ ἐκεῖνο, ἀλλ' ἐπιβάλλειν θέλων ὡς ἁπλῷ ἔξεισιν ἄλλο ἀεὶ λαμβάνων ἐν αὐτῷ πληθυόμενον · ὥστε ὥρμησε μὲν ἐπ' αὐτὸ οὐχ ὡς νοῦς, ἀλλ' ὡς **ὄψις οὔπω ἰδοῦσα**, ἐξῆλθε δὲ ἔχουσα ὅπερ αὐτὴ ἐπλήθυνεν · ὥστε ἄλλου μὲν ἐπεθύμησεν ἀορίστως ἔχουσα ἐπ' αὐτῇ φάντασμά τι, ἐξῆλθε δὲ ἄλλο λαβοῦσα ἐν αὐτῇ αὐτὸ πολὺ ποιήσασα. **Καὶ γὰρ αὖ ἔχει τύπον τοῦ ὀράματος · ἢ οὐ παρεδέξατο ἐν αὐτῇ γενέσθαι.** Οὗτος δὲ πολὺς ἐξ ἑνὸς ἐγένετο, καὶ οὗτος ὡς γνοὺς εἶδεν αὐτό, **καὶ τότε ἐγένετο ἰδοῦσα ὄψις.** Τοῦτο δὲ ἤδη νοῦς, ὅτε ἔχει, καὶ ὡς νοῦς ἔχει · πρὸ δὲ **τούτου ἔφεσις μόνον καὶ ἀτύπωτος ὄψις.** Οὗτος οὖν ὁ νοῦς ἐπέβαλε μὲν ἐκείνῳ, λαβὼν δὲ ἐγένετο νοῦς, ἀεὶ δὲ ἐνδιάμενος καὶ γενόμενος καὶ νοῦς καὶ οὐσία καὶ νόησις, ὅτε ἐνόησε · πρὸ γὰρ τούτου οὐ νόησις ἦν τὸ νοητὸν οὐκ ἔχων οὐδὲ νοῦς οὔπω νοήσας. Τὸ δὲ πρὸ τούτων ἡ ἀρχὴ τούτων, οὐχ ὡς ἐνυπάρχουσα · τὸ γὰρ ἀφ' οὗ οὐκ ἐνυπάρχει, ἀλλ' ἐξ ὧν · ἀφ' οὗ δὲ ἕκαστον, οὐχ ἕκαστον, ἀλλ' ἕτερον ἁπάντων.[65]

Ma se, poi, ci domandiamo in che cosa consista la *manenza* del *Nous* in quanto tale, noi troviamo una ulteriore sorpresa. La natura del *Nous* consiste nell'essere *coincidenza di visione e cosa vista*,[66] coincidenza di *contemplazione* e *contemplato*,[67] "contemplazione vivente," [68] come abbiamo già visto.[69]

Se così è, allora, si deve dire che la contemplazione non costituisce uno dei tre momenti della processione, ma che, viceversa, *i tre momenti della processione sono tre momenti strutturali della contemplazione*.

Analoghe conclusioni si debbono trarre anche per ciò che concerne l'Anima, che, come immagine del *Nous*, altre non è, in fondo, se non il *Nous* che si dispiega come ragione, e come ragione che, contemplando, crea tutto il resto del cosmo. Infatti, l'Anima nasce dal *Nous* che è la

---

[61] Gatti, *Plotino*, pp. 38-42.
[62] *Enn.* 5.3.11 (5): **ὄψις οὔπω ἰδοῦσα**.
[63] *Enn.* 5.3.11 (8): **ἔχει τύπον τοῦ ὀράματος**.
[64] *Enn.* 3.8.11 (2): ὄψις ὁρῶσα.
[65] *Enn.* 5.3.11 (1-18).
[66] *Enn.* 5.3.10 (14-16).
[67] *Enn.* 5.3.5 (21-23).
[68] *Enn.* 3.8.8 (11).
[69] Per ulteriori approfondimenti, cf. Gatti, *Plotino*, pp. 42-59.

"contemplazione vivente." E ciò che procede dalla "contemplazione vivente," anche già nel suo momento progressivo e derivativo, non può essere per sua stessa natura se non capacità di pensare. Insomma: ciò che deriva dal *Nous* è *capacità potenziale di pensare e capacità di ulteriormente contemplare*, e, in quanto *capacità* che deve attuarsi, è come un *indeterminato* (pensiero) e come una sorta di materia, ossia è possibilità e aspirazione ad essere pensiero. Ecco un passo splendido:

> *Τὴν ψυχὴν αὐτὴν δεῖ **ὥσπερ ὄψιν εἶναι, ὁρατὸν** δὲ αὐτῇ τὸν νοῦν εἶναι, **ἀόριστον πρὶν ἰδεῖν, πεφυκυῖαν δὲ νοεῖν · ὕλην οὖν πρὸς νοῦν**.*[70]

Il momento del *rivolgimento* o *ritorno* consiste nell'attuarsi di questa capacità, ossia nella fattiva contemplazione che ha come oggetto il *Nous* (e l'Uno medesimo, tramite il *Nous*).

E la manenza dell'Anima, che è l'ipostasi, ossia la realtà stessa dell'Anima, è *l'atto stesso nella sua perfezione ontologica della visione contemplante il Nous*. Ecco uno dei passi più interessanti:

> *Οὖσα οὖν ἀπὸ νοῦ νοερά ἐστι, καὶ ἐν λογισμοῖς ὁ νοῦς αὐτῆς καὶ ἡ τελείωσις ἀπ᾽ αὐτοῦ πάλιν οἷον πατρὸς ἐκθρέψαντος, ὃν οὐ τέλειον ὡς πρὸς αὐτὸν ἐγέννησεν. Ἥ τε οὖν **ὑπόστασις αὐτῇ ἀπὸ νοῦ ὅ τε ἐνεργείᾳ λόγος νοῦ αὐτῇ ὁρωμένου**. Ὅταν γὰρ ἐνίδῃ εἰς νοῦν, ἔνδοθεν ἔχει **καὶ οἰκεῖα ἃ νοεῖ καὶ ἐνεργεῖ**. Καὶ ταύτας μόνας δεῖ λέγειν ἐνεργείας ψυχῆς, ὅσα νοερῶς καὶ ὅσα οἴκοθεν · τὰ δὲ χείρω ἄλλοθεν καὶ πάθη ψυχῆς τῆς τοιαύτης.*[71]

Rivelativa, in questo passo, è soprattutto l'affermazione:

> *Ἥ τε οὖν ὑπόστασις αὐτῇ ἀπὸ νοῦ ὅ τε ἐνεργείᾳ λόγος νοῦ αὐτῇ ὁρωμένου.*[72]

Non abbiamo spazio per mostrare come i vari gradi all'interno dell'Anima (le diverse anime) e l'essere uno-e-molti della medesima dipendano da un *differente livello* di contemplazione e come tutto ciò che l'Anima produce concretamente si inserisca in questo complesso gioco del θεωρεῖν; tuttavia una conclusione già sopra letta ma che ora è necessario rileggere, sancisce, in maniera inequivoca, il pensiero di Plotino: "... nulla occorre all'Anima se non di essere *Anima* e, perciò, 'la Contemplante'; ed ecco che un tale atto di contemplazione, essendo, nei confronti di quello anteriore, più dal di fuori e perciò non identico, crea quell'oggetto che le è

---

[70] *Enn.* 3.9.5 (1-3).
[71] *Enn.* 5.1.3 (12-20).
[72] *Enn.* 5.1.3 (15-16).

posteriore: ma si tratta sempre di 'contemplazione che crea un'altra contemplazione.' E non ha limite, infatti, la contemplazione e neppure l'oggetto contemplato. Per questa ragione, ella è dappertutto." [73]

Per quanto concerne, poi, il significato dell'equazione contemplazione = produzione (θεωρεῖν = ποιεῖν), dopo quanto si è detto, non dovrebbero più sussistere dubbi. La meta-(auto)contemplazione della prima ipostasi è autocreazione, autoproduzione; la contemplazione del *Nous* è produzione delle Idee, visione che crea il cosmo noetico, visione totale e totalizzante; la contemplazione dell'Anima è ragione che produce la totalità delle forme (che derivano dalla visione delle Idee) e le squaderna e distende in tutte le possibili dimensioni e livelli (la *physis* non è se non l'orlo estremo dell'Anima del Tutto, momento ultimo del contemplare dell'Anima, ultima tappa della contemplazione creatrice).[74]

E questa equazione risulta essere più chiara proprio là dove parrebbe, di primo acchito, più paradossale. Lo stesso cosmo sensibile è tale, perchè è *mondo di forme* e la stessa materia è, in certo senso, una sorta di *forma infima*.[75] Ora, *creare è produrre forme*, ma produrre forme è, appunto, non altro che contemplare. Ecco l'affermazione di Plotino che nel modo più icastico sigilla questo concetto:

τὸ γὰρ ποιεῖν εἶναί τι εἶδός ἐστι ποιεῖν, τοῦτο δέ ἐστι πάντα πληρῶσαι θεωρίας.[76]

Dunque: la prima ipostasi è *meta-(auto)contemplazione*, il *Nous* è la *Contemplazione vivente*, l'Anima è la *Contemplante* per eccellenza e *tutto è contemplazione*.

Persisteremo, allora, nel parlare di "emanazione"? Come abbiamo detto, "emanazione" è una immagine, e, come tale, a motivo dell'inevitabile nesso di associazione, evoca altre immagini, che fanno surrettiziamente irruzione e, di conseguenza, pongono pesanti limiti alla comprensione delle *Enneadi*. Ma Plotino, in contesti puramente concettuali,

---

[73] *Enn.* 3.8.5 (27-31): ... καὶ ψυχὴ δὲ ἡ θεωροῦσα καὶ τὸ οὕτω **θεωρῆσαν** ἅτε ἐξωτέρω καὶ οὐχ ὡσαύτως τῷ πρὸ αὐτῆς τὸ μετ' αὐτὴν ποιεῖ **καὶ θεωρία τὴν θεωρίαν ποιεῖ**. Καὶ γὰρ **οὐκ ἔχει πέρας ἡ θεωρία οὐδὲ τὸ θεώρημα**. Διὰ τοῦτο δὲ · ἢ καὶ διὰ τοῦτο πανταχοῦ. Cf. Gatti, *Plotino*, pp. 71-78.
[74] Sulla *physis* plotiniana cf. Rist, *Plotinus, The Road*, pp. 86-102; M. I. Santa Cruz De Prunes, *La génèse du monde sensible dans la philosophie de Plotin* (Paris, 1979), pp. 77-88 e Gatti, *Plotino*, pp. 78-92.
[75] *Enn.* 5.8.7 (18-25): Ἀλλ' οὖν εἴδεσι κατέσχηται ἐξ ἀρχῆς εἰς τέλος, πρῶτον μὲν ἡ ὕλη τοῖς τῶν στοιχείων εἴδεσιν, εἶτ' ἐπὶ εἴδεσιν εἴδη ἄλλα, εἶτα πάλιν ἕτερα · ὅθεν καὶ **χαλεπὸν εὑρεῖν τὴν ὕλην** ὑπὸ πολλοῖς εἴδεσι κρυφθεῖσαν. Ἐπεὶ δὲ **καὶ αὕτη εἶδός τι ἔσχατον, πᾶν εἶδος** · τὸ δὲ καὶ πάντα εἴδη · τὸ γὰρ παράδειγμα εἶδος ἦν.
[76] *Enn.* 3.8.7 (21-22).

ha usato il termine esatto πρόοδος, ossia processione, per designare la generale derivazione di tutte le realtà dall'Uno e tale termine va rigorosamente mantenuto.[77] Ecco il passo, paradigmatico, che troppo spesso viene sottaciuto e dimenticato dagli studiosi:

Εἴπερ οὖν δεῖ μὴ ἓν μόνον εἶναι – ἐκέκρυπτο γὰρ ἂν πάντα μορφὴν ἐν ἐκείνῳ οὐκ ἔχοντα, οὐδ' ἂν ὑπῆρχέ τι τῶν ὄντων στάντος ἐν αὐτῷ ἐκείνου, οὐδ' ἂν τὸ πλῆθος ἦν ἂν τῶν ὄντων τούτων τῶν ἀπὸ τοῦ ἑνὸς γεννηθέντων μὴ τῶν μετ' αὐτὰ **τὴν πρόοδον** λαβόντων, ἃ ψυχῶν εἴληχε τάξιν – τὸν αὐτὸν τρόπον οὐδὲ ψυχὰς ἔδει μόνον εἶναι μὴ τῶν δι' αὐτὰς γενομένων φανέντων, εἴπερ ἑκάστῃ φύσει τοῦτο ἔνεστι τὸ μετ' αὐτὴν ποιεῖν καὶ ἐξελίττεσθαι οἷον σπέρματος ἔκ τινος ἀμεροῦς ἀρχῆς εἰς τέλος τὸ αἰσθητὸν ἰούσης, μένοντος μὲν ἀεὶ τοῦ προτέρου ἐν τῇ οἰκείᾳ ἕδρᾳ, τοῦ δὲ μετ' αὐτὸ οἷον γεννωμένου ἐκ δυνάμεως ἀφάτου, ὅση ἐν ἐκείνοις, ἣν οὐκ ἔδει στῆσαι οἷον περιγράψαντα φθόνῳ, χωρεῖν δὲ ἀεί, ἕως εἰς ἔσχατον μέχρι τοῦ δυνατοῦ τὰ πάντα ἥκῃ αἰτίᾳ δυνάμεως ἀπλέτου ἐπὶ πάντα παρ' αὐτῆς πεμπούσης καὶ οὐδὲν περιιδεῖν ἄμοιρον αὐτῆς δυναμένης. Οὐ γὰρ δὴ ἦν ὃ ἐκώλυεν ὁτιοῦν ἄμοιρον εἶναι φύσεως ἀγαθοῦ, καθόσον ἕκαστον οἷόν τ' ἦν μεταλαμβάνειν.[78]

E se mai ce ne fosse ancora bisogno, ricordiamo che tale πρόοδος è processione *cronologicamente aprocessuale*, ossia processione che si scandisce non secondo un ritmo di prima e di poi, ma secondo le categorie metafisiche della "condizione" e del "condizionato," come lo stesso Plotino avverte. Del resto, su questo punto, le riflessioni del Platone delle dottrine non scritte e della Antica Accademia restano paradigmatiche. Come gli Accademici antichi, Plotino dice chiaramente di usare un dato modo di esprimersi a *scopi puramenti didattici* (διδάσκων,[79] dice Plotino, così come gli Accademici antichi parlavano di διδασκαλίας χάριν).[80]

Infatti l'uomo è costretto a rappresentarsi una *dopo* l'altra le ipostasi, e così anche uno *dopo* l'altro i momenti delle medesime, perchè il suo pensiero è raziocinante, il che significa che, per scandire concettualmente i contenuti di pensiero, deve far uso del prima e poi cronologico. Ma in ciò che questo pensiero, raziocinando, coglie (ossia nel mondo dell'intelli-

---

[77] J. Trouillard, *La procession plotinienne* (Paris, 1955) ha già richiamato opportunamente l'attenzione su questo termine. Purtroppo le sue esegesi restano nel vago e lungi dal giungere alle questioni di fondo (come invece lo stesso autore riesce bene a fare per Proclo nei suoi noti saggi).

[78] *Enn.* 4.8.6 (1-18). Si vedano anche *Enn.* 5.2.1 (25-27) e 4.2.1 (44-45).

[79] *Enn.* 6.7.35 (29).

[80] Cf. Arist., *De caelo*, A 10, 280a1.

gibile), il "prima" e "poi" sono *organizzazione ontologica e struttura usiologica*, scevra di temporalità. Si tratta, come dicevamo, di scansione metafisica. Ecco uno dei passi che meglio esprimono questo ordine di concetti. Si legge nel quarto trattato della seconda *Enneade* che la materia (l'intelligibile) e le Idee "sono generate, in quanto hanno un principio; ingenerate, in quanto il loro principio è fuori del tempo; ma esse sono eternamente condizionate da un principio diverso da loro, non già in un perenne divenire, come in questo mondo, ma in un eterno essere, come nel mondo superno." [81]

Siamo ben lontani, dunque, da uno *scorrimento emanativo*.

In conclusione, il sostantivo più pertinente ad indicare la derivazione delle cose dall'Uno è quello di *processione*. E l'aggettivo che meglio lo qualifica è *contemplativa* (processione contemplativo-contemplante, se si preferisce), dove l'aggettivo non si limita ad esprimere una qualità estrinseca, ma è rivelativo dell'essenza stessa del sostantivo, perchè, per Plotino, il contemplare e la contemplazione sono veramente senza confini (*οὐκ ἔχει πέρας ἡ θεωρία οὐδὲ τὸ θεώρημα*),[82] e perchè tutto *è* contemplazione e tutto deriva *da* contemplazione (*πάντα τά τε ὡς ἀληθῶς ὄντα ἐκ θεωρίας καὶ θεωρία*).[83]

Le difficoltà e le aporie che sono implicite in questa metafisica non sono, dunque, quelle proprie dell'emanazionismo, ma stanno ad un livello assai più profondo. In primo luogo, nelle *Enneadi*, non si dà ragione del perchè, di necessità, la processione dia origine a ipostasi di grado via via *inferiore*. Se l'Uno è infinito, e la potenza che ne scaturisce è infinita, non si vede come e perchè l'altro dall'Uno che deriva (il *Nous*), che è a sua volta infinito, se ne distingua. L'*alterità* che si inserisce, distinguendo l'una dall'altra le ipostasi, resta un *presupposto* dato come necessario, ma inspiegato e inspiegabile. E così, analogamente, il salto di *qualità* fra intelligibile e sensibile resta difficilmente spiegabile con una semplice *variazione di quantità nella contemplazione* (la variazione dell'Intelligibile dipende da contemplazione nel suo *pieno vigore*, il sensibile da una contemplazione *illanguidita*).

La verità è che, qui, ci troviamo di fronte al problema della metafisica in assoluto più difficile. Parmenide e soprattutto l'eleatismo zenoniano e melissiano hanno tentato di risolverlo negando i molti e riducendo tutto

---

[81] *Enn.* 2.4.5 (24-28): Πότερα δὲ ἀίδιος ἡ νοητὴ ὁμοίως ζητητέον, ὡς ἄν τις καὶ τὰς ἰδέας ζητοῖ · **γενητὰ μὲν γὰρ τῷ ἀρχὴν ἔχειν, ἀγένητα δέ, ὅτι μὴ χρόνῳ τὴν ἀρχὴν ἔχει, ἀλλ' ἀεὶ παρ' ἄλλου**, οὐχ ὡς γινόμενα ἀεί, ὥσπερ ὁ κόσμος, ἀλλὰ ὄντα ἀεί, ὥσπερ ὁ ἐκεῖ κόσμος.

[82] *Enn.* 3.8.5 (30) e 3.8.7 (21).

[83] *Enn.* 3.8.7 (1-2).

all'Uno ("Se i molti fossero – diceva Melisso sfidando audacemente i sostenitori dell'esistenza dei molti – dovrebbero essere tutti quali io dico che è l'Uno").[84] Ma la posizione eleatica era stata già superata dai Fisici pluralisti e poi definitivamente da Platone e Aristotele al punto che, almeno nel contesto del pensiero greco, risultò per sempre non più riproponibile. Restava, quindi, come dato acquisito la esistenza di una molteplicità, non solo nel mondo fisico, ma altresì in quello intelligibile. Anzi, su questo punto la tradizione platonica e medioplatonica avevano vieppiù ingenerato la convinzione che la sfera dell'intelligibile sia strutturata *gerarchicamente*. E la gerarchia, al cui vertice già Platone aveva posto l'Uno,[85] nel medioplatonismo si era configurata come gerarchia di intelletto e di anima.[86] La grande novità di Plotino consiste nell'aver tentato di determinare i nessi che legano queste entità gerarchicamente ordinate e, quindi, di aver cercato di dedurle l'una dall'altra con il massimo rigore. Ma è proprio questo tentativo di rigorizzazione che meglio evidenzia quelle aporie di cui abbiamo detto e che solo il creazionismo sembra eliminare.

Si potrebbe obiettare che, dal momento che la processione necessaria dipende da un atto di libera autoctisi dell'Uno, come abbiamo veduto, la necessità stessa è voluta. Ne conseguirebbe che è l'Uno assoluto e infinito che, autovolendosi, vuole anche il necessario procedere di ipostasi via via *digradanti*, che derivano una dall'altra nel modo esaminato. Un passo nelle *Enneadi* sembrerebbe addirittura suonare a conferma: "è Lui (l'Uno) stesso, la necessità e la legge delle altre cose." [87] Allora, tutto l'universo, in tutte le sue dimensioni, risulterebbe una grandiosa teofania graduata, voluta *indirecte*. Ma, per quanto molte pagine delle *Enneadi* risultino leggibili in questa ottica, ve ne sono altre che mostrano come, in realtà, le cose siano più complesse. Plotino giunge addirittura a parlare di "audacia" ($\tau\delta\lambda\mu\alpha$),[88] e affaccia l'idea di "caduta," [89] vittima, in questi passi, di quegli

---

[84] Melisso, fr. 8 DK.

[85] Sulla strutturazione gerarchica della metafisica di Platone hanno insistito soprattutto gli studiosi della Scuola di Tubinga. Si veda in particolare H. J. Krämer, *Platone e i fondamenti della Metafisica* (Milano: Vita e Pensiero, 1982), parte 2, cap. 1, passim, e ivi le ulteriori indicazioni.

[86] Cf. Reale, *Storia della filosofia antica*, 4: 341-345.

[87] *Enn.* 6.8.10 (32-35): Καὶ τὸ μὴ ἥκειν πρὸς μηδὲν ἄλλο τὴν ὑπερβολὴν τῆς δυνάμεως ἐν αὐτῷ ἔχει, οὐκ ἀνάγκη κατειλημμένου, **ἀλλ' αὐτοῦ ἀνάγκης τῶν ἄλλων οὔσης καὶ νόμου.**

[88] Cf. V. Cilento, *Paideia antignostica, Ricostruzione d'un unico scritto da Enneadi, 3.8, 5.8, 5.5, 2.9* (Firenze: Le Monnier, 1971), pp. 253-254.

[89] *Enn.* 1.8.14.

avversari (gli Gnostici), che pure, nel complesso, egli riesce a respingere, anche se con qualche cedimento. Ma non vogliamo insistere sulle aporie del plotinismo, che ci porterebbero molto lontano, e vogliamo concludere, invece, con una notazione che non ci sembra sia stata mai fatta.

La civiltà greca, come è noto, è una civiltà della visione e della forma. Come pura visione e contemplazione è nata la filosofia, culto e celebrazione della forma è tutta la grande arte ellenica. Forme (geometriche) sono gli atomi di Leucippo, di Democrito e di Epicuro, e visione di queste forme è la vera conoscenza. Forme sono le Idee platoniche, e la *noesis* di queste forme è la vera conoscenza. La forma è il principio che *è* e *dà* essere in Aristotele, e astrazione di forme è la conoscenza. Siamo qui, per intenderci, in una situazione spirituale antitetica a quella che emerge dagli scritti biblici e dalla civiltà ebraica, che è, invece, contrassegnata dalla "parola" e dall'ascolto della parola (e Dio disse ... e la voce fu udita, etc.).

Ebbene, se così è, possiamo fare questa ulteriore riflessione. Platone nella *Repubblica* dice che il suo Stato è un ingrandimento dell'anima e che questo ingrandimento rende assai meglio comprensibile ciò di cui è ingrandimento. Ora, a noi sembra che la metafisica di Plotino sia esattamente un ingrandimento, una gigantografia, di quella caratteristica peculiare del mondo greco. Tutto, in essa, è visione, contemplazione, dispiegarsi di Idee e di forme e, anzi, *tutto si risolve senza residuo nella forma*, così come abbiamo visto esserlo nella contemplazione. Ecco il passo più significativo: "... L'universo è stretto dai legami della forma da cima a fondo: anzitutto, la materia dalle forme degli elementi; poi, sulle forme, altre forme, e poi altre ancora, novellamente; onde riesce finanche difficile, trovare la materia celata sotto tante forme. Ma poichè anch'essa è una certa forma – infima – questo nostro mondo è completamente forma e forme sono le cose universe; poichè il modello era già forma." [90]

Ma, proprio perchè portata ai limiti delle sue possibilità, questa caratteristica della Grecità, in Plotino, mentre celebra il suo supremo "inveramento," si "supera": infatti la forma viene audacemente dichiarata *orma dell'informe*.[91] La forma diventa, in tal modo, non più termine ultimativo, ma termine di rimando ad alcunchè di ulteriore: l'informe di

---

[90] *Enn.* 5.8.7 (18-24): Ἀλλ' οὖν **εἴδεσι κατέσχηται ἐξ ἀρχῆς εἰς τέλος**, πρῶτον μὲν ἡ ὕλη τοῖς τῶν στοιχείων εἴδεσιν, εἶτ' ἐπὶ εἴδεσιν εἴδη ἄλλα, εἶτα πάλιν ἕτερα · ὅθεν καὶ χαλεπὸν εὑρεῖν τὴν ὕλην ὑπὸ πολλοῖς εἴδεσι κρυφθεῖσαν. Ἐπεὶ δὲ **καὶ αὕτη εἶδός τι ἔσχατον, πᾶν εἶδος · τὸ δὲ καὶ πάντα εἴδη · τὸ γὰρ παράδειγμα εἶδος ἦν.**

[91] *Enn.* 6.7.33 (30-31): Τὸ γὰρ **ἴχνος τοῦ ἀμόρφου μορφή** · τοῦτο γοῦν γεννᾷ τὴν μορφήν, οὐχ ἡ μορφὴ τοῦτο.

cui la forma è orma è l'*infinito positivo*.[92] E in questo suo essere spiraglio sull'infinito, la forma realizza il suo massimo trionfo, ma, ad un tempo, chiude tutto un passato e dischiude orizzonti completamente nuovi, che portano ormai al di là dello spirito greco; appunto gli orizzonti dell'infinito e la contemplazione diventa visione d'infinito.

---

[92] L'Uno plotiniano è ἄμορφον e ἀνείδεον: cf. *Enn.* 6.7.17 (18, 40); 5.5.6 (4-5), appunto in quanto infinito. Sull'infinitudine dell'Uno, cf. quanto dicemmo in *Storia della filosofia antica*, 4: 507-511.

9

Are Plotinus and Albertus Magnus Neoplatonists?

Leo Sweeney, sj
Loyola University of Chicago

Plotinus (204/5-270) has been receiving considerable attention in the past three decades. Paul Henry and Hans-Rudolf Schwyzer published three volumes of their critical edition of his Greek text in 1951, 1959, and 1973.[1] In 1955 Richard Harder initiated the publication of the Greek text of the *Enneads* in chronological order, as well as of a German translation and commentary, in a series of volumes which Rudolf Beutler and Willy Theiler completed by 1971.[2] Harvard University Press got out the first three *Enneads* in the "Loeb Classical Library" in 1966-1967.[3] Finally, the

---

[1] *Plotini Opera* (Paris: Desclée de Brouwer, 1951-1973), Tomes 1-3. Tome 2 contains *Plotiniana Arabica*, which is the English translation by G. Lewis of Plotinus' text found in Arabic. Henry and Schwyzer's edition also is appearing in the Oxford Classical Texts (Oxford: Clarendon Press, 1964 sqq.), which furnishes textual revisions as suggested by scholars in reviews and critical studies.

[2] *Plotins Schriften* (Hamburg: Felix Meiner, 1956-1971), Bands 1-6, "Philosophische Bibliothek."

[3] In these three Loeb volumes A. Hilary Armstrong furnishes a revised Henry-Schwyzer Greek text, as well as a serviceable English translation and introduction to individual treatises. Harvard University Press as yet has not published the last three *Enneads*. Help in translating Plotinus's difficult Greek can be obtained also from V. Cilento, *Plotino Enneadi* (Bari: Laterza, 1947-1949), 3 volumes; E. Bréhier, *Plotin Ennéades* (Paris: Les Belles Lettres, 1924-1938; frequently reprinted); Marsilius Ficinus' literal Latin translation in F. Creuzer and G. H. Moser, *Plotini Opera Omnia* (Oxford: Typographicum Academicum, 1835). Stephen MacKenna's nineteenth-century translation is, even in its fourth and revised edition (1969), constantly misleading and of no value.

Graceful Reason: Essays in Ancient and Medieval Philosophy Presented to Joseph Owens, CSSR, ed. Lloyd P. Gerson. Papers in Mediaeval Studies 4 (Toronto: Pontifical Institute of Mediaeval Studies, 1983), pp. 177-202. © P.I.M.S., 1983.

Lexicon Plotinianum of J. N. Sleeman and Gilbert Pollet appeared in 1980.[4]

Besides those publications abundant secondary literature has dealt with Plotinus during the same years, as one can judge by consulting any volume of the *L'Année Philologique* from 1951 onwards. For example, Volume 22, which covers the year 1951, lists nineteen books and articles; Volume 25 lists twenty-three publications for 1954; Volume 30 seventeen for 1959; Volume 34 seventeen for 1963; Volume 39 sixteen for 1968; Volume 45 thirty-eight for 1974;[5] Volume 50 twenty-seven for 1979.[6]

What is noteworthy in that literature is not only its abundance but also the frequency with which scholars point out the differences between Plotinus and subsequent Greek Neoplatonists and express doubts as to whether his is the primary influence upon them. For instance, in *Porphyry's Place in the Neoplatonic Tradition: A Study of Post-Plotinian Neoplatonism* (The Hague: Martinus Nijhoff, 1974) Andrew Smith finds Plotinus and Porphyry differing on points in their conceptions of soul – e.g., its relationship to Intellect and to body, its descent from and ascent to higher levels, its fate after death, its transmigration.[7] As A. Hilary Armstrong observes, Porphyry virtually abandoned "the real distinction between Intellect and Soul, on which Plotinus sometimes insists very strongly." The latter always seems "to have considered it

---

[4] Leiden: E. J. Brill; Leuven: University Press, 1980. This first dictionary of the *Enneads* was worked on by Sleeman (University of London) from 1946 to 1957 and by Pollet (University of Louvain) from 1959 onwards. The latter revised the first draft of the dictionary in the light of Henry-Schwyzer's critical edition (see above, n. 1) and utilized the almost complete but unpublished "Index Verborum" compiled by Ludwig Früchtel (d. 1963).

[5] The increase in the number of studies in Volume 45 arises from the publication in 1974 of the acts of the Convegno Internazionale held at Rome, Oct. 1970, and published under the title, *Plotino e il Neoplatonismo in Oriente e in Occidente* (Roma: Accademia Nazionale dei Lincei, 1974): it contains twenty-nine studies on Plotinus, on which those by P. Hadot, W. Theiler, H. J. Blumenthal, H.-R. Schwyzer, J. Danielou, J. Rist and J. Pépin are most relevant for the purpose of this paper. A similar increase in Volume 42 issued from the publication in 1971 of the acts of the Colloques Internationaux du Centre National de la Recherche Scientifique: Sciences Humaines, held at Royaumont, June, 1969, and published as *Le Néoplatonisme* (Paris: Éditions du Centre National de la Recherche Scientifique, 1971), in which at least ten papers are devoted to Plotinus.

[6] A source of significant articles on Plotinus (and, more generally, on Neoplatonism) is the volumes published by the International Society for Neoplatonic Studies: R. Baine Harris, ed., *The Significance of Neoplatonism* (1976); idem, *Neoplatonism and Indian Thought* (1981); Dominic J. O'Meara, ed., *Neoplatonism and Christian Thought* (1981); R. Baine Harris, *The Structure of Being: A Neoplatonic Approach* (1981).

[7] See Smith, Chs. 1-5, the last of which ("An Evaluation of Eschatology in Porphyry and Plotinus," pp. 69-80) is especially informative. For a general summary see pp. 143-147.

important, from some points of view at least, to assert a certain transcendence of Intellect over Soul. ... It seems unlikely that he would have approved of Porphyry's tendency to monism here." [8] According to A. C. Lloyd, Porphyry emphasized monism here "because he was prepared to pay the price, a certain belief in the reality of the individual person, which Plotinus ... was not. ... [Together with Plotinus Porphyry denied] that the soul 'in itself', or essentially, was divided into parts. But Porphyry went quite beyond Plotinus as well as Plato in preventing any real distinction between the two [Intellect and Soul] by claiming that the soul could not be affected by anything. Quite consistently, he recognized only one kind of soul, the rational, which was possessed by men and brutes alike" (ibid., p. 288). In general, Porphyry seems "often to present a simpler doctrine than Plotinus; partly it is ... a matter of going back to second-century writers" (ibid., p. 292).[9]

In fact, Porphyry separates himself from his master also in epistemology and logic to the extent that R. Baine Harris believes Porphyry "set the stage for the formation of another kind of Neoplatonism, namely, a type that focuses upon the logic and categories of Aristotle. A case could be made ... that there really have been two forms of Neoplatonism operative in the history of Western philosophy, namely, the Neoplatonism ... of Plotinus and the Neoplatonism of Porphyry and, by and large, the latter has been far more influential than the former" (*Structure of Being*, pp. vii-viii). How, then, are we to characterize the two Neoplatonisms? Plotinus' brand entails a mysticism plus "a way of philosophizing [and of dialectics] that points to a form of knowing that is beyond dialectics" (ibid., p. vii) and that rejects "Aristotle's categories and a portion of his logic" (ibid., p. viii). Porphyry's sort sets aside "Plotinus' categories and logic as inadequate" and relies "heavily on both Aristotle's categories and logic in his own thought, especially in dealing with the physical or sensible world. If the case can be made that there is sufficient difference in the logic of Plato and Plotinus to justify the term 'Neoplatonism,' it can also be said ... that there is sufficient difference in the logic of Plotinus and Porphyry to serve as the basis for

---

[8] *Cambridge History of Later Greek and Medieval Philosophy* (Cambridge: University Press, 1967), pp. 266-267. Also see ibid., pp. 267-268: "The doctrine of Intellect was both the weak point and the growing point of Plotinian Neoplatonism; and this seems to be confirmed by what happened in the next few centuries." His account of Intellect "was not acceptable as it stood to any of his successors," although they "still show the influence of this majestic centre-piece of his speculation."

[9] See ibid., p. 276: "For the theory of the active and passive intellect in Aristotle's psychology and the theory of logic they [the Neoplatonists after Plotinus] went, as it were, behind Plotinus and were drawing much more on second-century material."

defining and delineating the various historical types of Neoplatonism"
(ibid., p. viii).[10]

But what of Plotinus and (say) Iamblichus? Recently John Whittaker
inquired whether "the influences upon Iamblichus which do not derive
from Plotinus – the influence of the Aristotelian tradition, of Middle
Platonism, of the milieu of the *Chaldean Oracles* and the Hermetic writings – " might not be so strong that the career of Iamblichus is
"explicable simply as a phenomenon of the third and fourth centuries
without Plotinus as a necessary presupposition?" Hence, Plotinus'
"historical importance may have been exaggerated. ... If the role of
Plotinus was not as great as has been supposed, then perhaps we should
be satisfied to regard Neoplatonism simply as a mode of philosophizing
characteristic of the third and following centuries of our era." [11]

In a paper occasioned (at least in part) by Whittaker's challenging the
traditional view of Plotinus as the founder of Neoplatonism, H. J.
Blumenthal states that Whittaker's interpretation is perhaps helpful ("it
stresses that later Neoplatonists were more liable than Plotinus to accept
non-philosophical explanations and procedures") but it is also misleading
("it can easily tend to exaggerate the importance of such elements [the
irrational material absorbed from the *Hermetica* and the *Chaldean
Oracles*] in later Neoplatonism," which was not so thoroughly corrupted
by irrationalism as once was commonly thought).[12] Yet Blumenthal
himself isolates four areas of disagreement between Plotinus and other
Neoplatonists: the relationship of soul and intellect (part of our mind
remains permanently active in the Intellect *versus* our soul descends as a
whole into the physical world; ibid., pp. 214-216), the interpretation of
Aristotle's categories (they pertain only to the sensible world *versus* they
apply also to intelligible being; pp. 216-219), the nature of time (time is

---

[10] According to Mary Clark, "Marius Victorinus Afer, Porphyry, and the History of
Philosophy," in *Significance of Neoplatonism*, pp. 265-273, Porphyry had great influence
upon Victorinus, as well as upon Chalcidius, Boethius and Macrobius, and "it was
Porphyry rather than Plotinus who was the point of contact between Latin philosophers
and Neoplatonism" (p. 268). His metaphysics of being rather than of unity (as was
Plotinus') issued into a triad of Being, Life and Thought, which Victorinus interpreted as
the Christian trinity of consubstantial persons. Had Victorinus used the Plotinian triad of
the One, Intellect and Soul, his trinitarian doctrine would have been a subordinationism
(ibid., pp. 265-266 and 270-271).

[11] *De Jamblique à Proclus*, Entretiens sur l'Antiquité Classique 21 (Genève: Fondation
Hardt, 1975), pp. 65-66.

[12] "Plotinus in Later Platonism," in *Neoplatonism and Early Christian Thought: Essays
in Honour of A. H. Armstrong* (London: Variorum Publications, 1981), p. 214.
Blumenthal's main aim is to discuss what Plotinus' Neoplatonic successors thought of him
(p. 212).

attached to Soul and eternity to Intellect *versus* Time and Eternity are hypostases in the intelligible hierarchy; p. 219), and the nature of evil (evil is matter or the negativity of matter incidentally causes evil in conjunction with soul *versus* evil is not matter, which is directly related to the One, but is a kind of teleological inadequacy; p. 220). Blumenthal's final conclusion: in some areas later Neoplatonists introduced Plotinus' views to corroborate their own but in others they differ substantially with him (p. 220).

The preceding sampling of secondary literature makes clear that subsequent Neoplatonists do diverge from Plotinus in their conceptions of soul and intellect, in their eschatologies and in their epistemology and logic; and, secondly, that such divergence is a legitimate basis for wondering how influential Plotinus actually was in those areas. But what the literature does not document is disagreement between Plotinus and them in basic metaphysics. This perhaps will prove to be the common ground that makes them all be authentic "Neoplatonists" and compensate for their differences in other and less crucial areas.

In what follows, then, I shall try to isolate what appears to be the main features of Plotinian metaphysics so as eventually to evaluate better the fundamental metaphysics of Porphyry, Iamblicus, Proclus, and others, who may thereby reveal themselves to be at one with Plotinus in this area and thus to be Plotinian Neoplatonists. But postponing such evaluation to another time and place, I shall in the second portion of this paper turn instead to Albert the Great (ca. 1200-1280), who is sometimes considered to be a medieval exponent of Neoplatonism. The question guiding my research will be: is his metaphysics sufficiently like Plotinus' that he deserves to be called "Neoplatonist"? Coupling Plotinus and Albert has the added advantage of allowing me to honor Joseph Owens all the more appropriately since he has tirelessly and brilliantly labored in both ancient Greek and medieval thought.

I. PLOTINUS' METAPHYSICS

My aim in reading Plotinus' *Enneads* is, then, to understand his metaphysics[13] by searching out his replies to these three questions: what does

---

[13] Metaphysics is contrasted with ethics, philosophy of man, cosmology and religion, all of which are to be found in the *Enneads* but will receive little or no direct attention. We shall attend rather to Plotinus' position on the real precisely as real and, thus, on unity wherever found. Plotinian metaphysics is then the knowledge of the real as real and not (as Aristotle expresses it) of beings as being, since reality is not being but unity. Were Aristotle's formula taken literally, metaphysics would be restricted to reflection on νοῦς, Soul and the physical world since the One transcends being.

"to be real" mean? what sort of causality does God exercise in producing existents which are, to some degree, other and lower than himself? upon what fundamental principles does his metaphysical position rest? During that search I shall not only attend to the chronological ordering of the *Enneads*[14] but I shall try to discern *what Plotinus himself had in mind* when he was writing this or that treatise – that is, my intent will be to study Plotinus on his own terms, within his own era and *Denkenswelt*.

Reality Is Unity

What, then, does he mean by "to be real"? In 6.9(9).1, his answer is inductive since it issues from reflections upon concrete cases. But it is difficult to understand because of the ambiguity of the Greek word εἶναι and its derivatives. In English we can express different dimensions of Plotinus' thought in three distinct ways.

(a) "The One exists" (= the One actually is = He is not merely a figment of the mind but does actually exists);

(b) "The One is real" (= the One is of value, significance, worth – in fact, He is supremely valuable and solely real);

(c) "The Intellect is but the One is not" (= the Intellect is one-many and, thus, is being [see 6.2(43).21.45-48]; the One is not because He transcends multiplicity and, thus, transcends being).

All those three distinct meanings Plotinus must express by the single verb εἶναι so that τὸ ἓν ἔστιν can signify (depending upon the context) either (a) that God exists or (b) that God is real or, when the negative οὐκ is added, (c) that God is not being. Such ambiguity is one reason why reading Plotinus is difficult and problematical.

But forewarned and thereby forearmed, let us now consider 6.9(9).1.1-8, where Plotinus sets down the concrete cases which furnish the evidence that reality is unity. All beings (he begins) are beings

> by the One, both those which are primarily so [= the νοῦς and the Soul] and those which are in some way classed among beings [= sensible things]. For

[14] Fortunately Porphyry lists Plotinus' treatises as he received them and, thus, provides us with their chronological order (see Porphyry, "The Life of Plotinus" in A. H. Armstrong [transl.], *Plotinus*, Loeb Classical Library [Cambridge, Mass.: Harvard University Press, 1966], pp. 12-25). Unfortunately, he did not respect that chronological order but edited them according to topics: see R. T. Wallis, *Neoplatonism* (New York: Charles Scribner's Sons, 1972), pp. 44-47.

I shall indicate the chronological place of each treatise cited below by a number in parenthesis – for example "6.9(9).1.1-8" means "Sixth *Ennead*, Treatise nine, ninth treatise chronologically, Ch. One, lines one to eight." The Greek text used is that of P. Henry and H.-R. Schwyzer, *Plotini Opera*, Vols. 1-3 (Paris: Desclée de Brouwer, 1951, 1959 and 1973). Unless otherwise indicated, translations are my own.

what could *be* if it were not one? If beings are deprived of what we call unity, they *are not*. For instance, an army or a choir or a flock no longer *is* if it is not one. In fact, neither a house nor ship *is* if it has not unity, for a house is one and a ship is one and if it loses its unity, a house is no longer a house or a ship a ship.[15]

Comment: What is meant by saying that if something no longer is one it no longer *is*? Possibly and probably, "is" has all three levels of meanings: "exists," "is a being" and "is real," the last of which nonetheless seemingly predominates. After a tornado hits an area (to restrict ourselves to one of Plotinus' examples), what exists is not a house but a pile of rubble; the house no longer is the being that it was; it no longer is real because it is valueless and worthless by losing its unity through the violent storm. This third meaning is especially relevant for our purposes since it stresses that to be real is to be one and a fall from unity is a fall also from reality. In fact, the unity which constitutes the reality of houses, ships, armies and the like, as well as of Intellect and of Soul, points to the One, which makes all of them be one (each in its own way) and thereby be real: "all beings are beings [= are real] by the One" (line 1).

A similar alignment of the One with the onenesses of other existents is also found in a later text. In 3.8(30).10.14ff., Plotinus expresses amazement that the many should come from the One. Yet such is the fact: the multiplicity of life does come from what is not multiplicity since the origin [= the One] is not divided up into the All [= the νοῦς and, eventually, the Soul] lest the All too be destroyed and, since the origin must remain by itself and be different from all else, lest the All not even come into being (lines 14-19). Accordingly, we must (Plotinus advises)

> go back everywhere to the one [in each existent]: in each there is some one to which you reduce it and this in every case to the one before it, which [however] is not simply one, until we come to the simply one, which cannot be reduced back to something else. [For example,] if we take the one of the plant – this is its source remaining within it[16] – and the one of the

---

[15] Lines 1-8: Πάντα τὰ ὄντα τῷ ἑνί ἐστιν ὄντα, ὅσα τε πρώτως ἐστὶν ὄντα, καὶ ὅσα ὁπωσοῦν λέγεται ἐν τοῖς οὖσιν εἶναι. Τί γὰρ ἂν καὶ εἴη, εἰ μὴ ἓν εἴη ; Ἐπείπερ ἀφαιρεθέντα τοῦ ἓν ὃ λέγεται οὐκ ἔστιν ἐκεῖνα. Οὔτε γὰρ στρατὸς ἔστιν, εἰ μὴ ἓν ἔσται, οὔτε χορὸς οὔτε ἀγέλη μὴ ἓν ὄντα. Ἀλλ᾽ οὐδὲ οἰκία ἢ ναῦς τὸ ἓν οὐκ ἔχοντα, ἐπείπερ ἡ οἰκία ἓν καὶ ἡ ναῦς, ὃ εἰ ἀποβάλοι ἂν ἡ οἰκία ἔτι οἰκία οὔτε ἡ ναῦς.

[16] This source would be the individual plant's share of what Plotinus had earlier in the same chapter spoken of as "the life of a huge plant, which goes through the whole of it while its origin remains and is not dispersed over the whole, since it is, as it were, firmly settled in the root. So this origin gives to the plant its whole life in its multiplicity, but remains itself not multiple but the origin of the multiple life" (lines 10-14; Armstrong's translation).

animal and the one of the soul and the one of the physical All, we are taking in each case that which is most powerful and valuable in it. But if we take the one of the beings which truly are – that one which is their origin and spring and power – shall we lose faith and think of it as nothing? [By no means; the One is truly real even though] it is certainly none of the things of which it is the origin: it is such, though nothing can be predicated of it – neither being nor entity nor life – as to be above all such existents.[17]

Comments: As was the case in 6.9.1.1ff. (see above), here Plotinus also proceeds inductively: he moves from the oneness we perceive in plants, animals, our souls and the physical universe to truly real beings (Soul and Intellect) and then to the One, who is fully real because of His sheer unity and transcendence of being. Secondly, the One gives them oneness and, thereby, also reality because their being one is what makes each of them worthy of esteem. And the oneness which the One furnishes also is that which is most powerful in them (see lines 25-26: τὸ δυνατώτατον καὶ τὸ τίμιον) and which constitutes their power to contemplate and thereby to make themselves and subsequent existents.[18] In fact, the power in them *is* the One – He is power[19] – just as the oneness in them *is* the One (see lines 26-27): each of them *is* the One-on-a-lower-level, each is a λόγος of the One.[20] This basic identity of each lower existent with the One balances Plotinus' other paradoxical statements that the One is other than all else (see ch. 9, lines 39-54; ch. 10, line 10): yes, God is other than all His

---

[17] Lines 20-31: Καὶ ἐφ' ἑκάστου μὲν τι ἕν, εἰς ὃ ἀνάξεις, καὶ τόδε τὸ πᾶν εἰς ἓν τὸ πρὸ αὐτοῦ, οὐχ ἁπλῶς ἕν, ἕως τις ἐπὶ τὸ ἁπλῶς ἓν ἔλθῃ · τοῦτο δὲ οὐκέτι ἐπ' ἄλλο. Ἀλλ' εἰ μὲν τὸ τοῦ φυτοῦ ἕν – τοῦτο δὲ καὶ ἡ ἀρχὴ ἡ μένουσα – καὶ τὸ ζῴου ἓν καὶ τὸ ψυχῆς ἓν καὶ τὸ τοῦ παντὸς ἓν λαμβάνοι, λαμβάνει ἑκασταχοῦ τὸ δυνατώτατον καὶ τὸ τίμιον · εἰ δὲ τὸ τῶν κατ' ἀλήθειαν ὄντων ἕν, τὴν ἀρχὴν καὶ πηγὴν καὶ δύναμιν, λαμβάνοι, ἀπιστήσομεν καὶ τὸ μηδὲν ὑπονοήσομεν ; Ἢ ἐστι μὲν τὸ μηδὲν τούτων ὧν ἐστιν ἀρχή, τοιοῦτο μέντοι, οἷον, μηδενὸς αὐτοῦ κατηγορεῖσθαι δυναμένου, μὴ ὄντος, μὴ οὐσίας, μὴ ζωῆς, τὸ ὑπὲρ πάντα αὐτῶν εἶναι.

[18] See chs. 3 sqq., where Plotinus sets forth his position on contemplation. Θεωρία is found on all levels of reality except the highest (the One transcends contemplation) and the single word expresses both (say) the Intellect's operative state of contemplating and its content (i.e., what is contemplated, what is caused by the contemplating). This content itself is in turn an operative state producing its own content, until one comes to the λόγος of plants, which are the content of Nature's operative state of contemplation but do not themselves contemplate. One may with profit consult John N. Deck, *Nature, Contemplation and the One: A Study in the Philosophy of Plotinus* (Toronto: University Press, 1967).

[19] After concluding the previous Chapter by observing that the One is other than all things and is before all of them, Plotinus initiates Chapter 10 with the statement that the One is "the power of all" (δύναμις τῶν πάντων): not only *can* the One produce all of them but He is in all as their δύναμις.

[20] On λόγος meaning "a higher existent as on a lower level," see Donald L. Gelpi, "Logos as a Cosmological Principle in Plotinus," (M.A. Thesis; St. Louis University, 1958); idem, "The Plotinian *Logos* Doctrine," *Modern Schoolman*, 37 (1960), 301-315.

products inasmuch as God Himself is not totally identical with God-on-a-lower-level, but this otherness does not eliminate the fact that whatever reality (oneness, δύναμις) is found on any subsequent level *is* God and, consistently, Plotinus' position is a monism. After all, to be real is to be one.[21]

The One as Cause

Now we can take up the question of what kind of causality the One exercises in producing lower existents. We already find an answer in 3.8.10.3ff.: His products flow out from Him as do rivers from a spring which is itself without origin, which gives itself wholly to them and yet is not depleted by them but remains itself at rest and unchanged.[22] A similar but more detailed reply is offered by an earlier treatise. In 5.2(11).1.3, Plotinus discusses how all existents come from the One, which is simple and has no diversity or doubleness. It is precisely

> because there is nothing in It that all things come from It: in order that
> being may exist, the One is not being but That Which generates being,

[21] Do Plotinus's texts themselves underwrite this conclusion? Yes, provided one realizes that although they disclose existents to be both distinct from and yet one with one another, the unity there disclosed overshadows their distinctness. (For a listing and discussion of texts see L. Sweeney, "Basic Principles in Plotinus' Philosophy," *Gregorianum*, 32 (1961), 507-510, n. 13.) The most apt comparison of this relationship between the One, Intellect, Soul and all other existents is that of a man and his integral parts. "Every man is both other than his hands or feet and the like and yet is physically joined to them all, each of which is really different from any other part and is less than the man in his entirety. In such a living being one finds a sort of real distinction but immersed in genuine unity, which overshadows it. The parts are really but, let us say, inadequately and only virtually distinct from one another and from the whole, but they are vitalized by a single soul and thus coalesce into an essential unity or *unum per se*. The distinction is, so to speak, accidental, the unity is essential. ... Something like that sort of inadequate real distinction seems to exist" between the One and all other existents without eliminating their radical unity and the basic monism which marks his metaphysics (ibid., p. 508). Also see A. H. Armstrong, "The Apprehension of Divinity in the Self and Cosmos in Plotinus," in *The Significance of Neoplatonism*, ed. Harris, pp. 187-198; Plato Mamo, "Is Plotinian Mysticism Monistic?" in ibid., pp. 199-215 (vs. Zaehner, Arnou, Rist); for references to studies by Trouillard, Carbonara, Bréhier and de Gandillac, see L. Sweeney, "Basic Principles of Plotinus' Philosophy," pp. 509-510.

[22] A fuller translation/paraphrase of the initial lines of the Greek is as follows: "That which is above life is the cause of life for the act which is the life of the Intellect is not first but itself flows out, so to speak, as if from a spring...." The Greek for lines 2-10: Τὸ δὲ ὑπὲρ τὴν ζωὴν αἴτιον ζωῆς · οὐ γὰρ ἡ τῆς ζωῆς ἐνέργεια τὰ πάντα οὖσα πρώτη, ἀλλ' ὥσπερ προχυθεῖσα αὐτὴ οἷον ἐκ πηγῆς. Νόησον γὰρ πηγὴν ἀρχὴν ἄλλην οὐκ ἔχουσαν, δοῦσαν δὲ ποταμοῖς πᾶσιν αὐτήν, οὐκ ἀναλωθεῖσαν τοῖς ποταμοῖς, ἀλλὰ μένουσαν αὐτὴν ἡσύχως, τοὺς δὲ ἐξ αὐτῆς προεληλυθότας πρὶν ἄλλον ἄλλη ῥεῖν ὁμοῦ συνόντας ἔτι, ἤδη δὲ οἷον ἑκάστους εἰδότας οἷ ἀφήσουσιν αὐτῶν τὰ ῥεύματα. In lines 10-14 Plotinus compares the source of reality to the life of a huge plant – see note 16 above. In 3.8.9.26 he likens the One to a voice filling empty space.

which is (so to speak) its first-born. Perfect because It seeks nothing has nothing and needs nothing, the One (as it were) overflows and Its superabundance makes something other than Itself. What has thus come about turns back to the One and is filled and thus becomes Its contemplator and so is Intellect.[23]

The Intellect, because it thus resembles the One, produces in the same way – that is, by pouring forth a multiple power which is a product resembling its maker: just as That Which was before it did, Intellect poured forth a likeness of itself. This act originating from entity [or Intellect] is Soul, which comes about while Intellect remains at rest, for Intellect too came about while That Which is prior to it remains unchanged.[24]

But Soul does not remain unchanged when it produces: it is moved and thereby brings forth an image. It looks There whence it came and is filled and thereupon goes forth to another opposed movement and thus generates its own image [= the sentient and vegetal levels of the physical universe].[25]

Comments: The similarity which this earlier passage has with 3.8.10.3-10, consists in the fact that each portrays the causality exercised by the One as literally "emanative." In the later text life "flows out" from the One as if from a spring (3.8.10.4: προχυθεῖσα ... οἷον ἐκ πηγῆς) – a spring which gives itself wholly to the rivers going forth from it (line 7: ἐξ αὐτῆς προελη-λυθότας), which in turn tarry for a while all together before flowing forth (line 8: ῥεῖν), although each knows even then the direction its streams will flow (line 9: τὰ ῥεύματα).[26] Also in 5.2.1.8, the One, as it were, overflows (οἷον ὑπερερρύη) and thereby It has made (line 9: πεποίηκεν) something which is, to a degree, other than itself[27] – that δύναμις which Plotinus will elsewhere call "intelligible matter" (see 2.4[12], chs. 1, 3-5) and which becomes the Intellect/Being by turning and contemplating the One and

---

[23] Lines 5-11: "Ἦ ὅτι οὐδὲν ἐν αὐτῷ, διὰ τοῦτο ἐξ αὐτοῦ πάντα, καὶ ἵνα τὸ ὂν ᾖ, διὰ τοῦτο αὐτὸς οὐκ ὄν, γεννητὴς δὲ αὐτοῦ · καὶ πρώτη οἷον γέννησις αὕτη · ὂν γὰρ τέλειον τῷ μηδὲν ζητεῖν μηδὲ ἔχειν μηδὲ δεῖσθαι οἷον ὑπερερρύη καὶ τὸ ὑπερπλῆρες αὐτοῦ πεποίηκεν ἄλλο · τὸ δὲ γενόμενον εἰς αὐτὸ ἐπεστράφη καὶ ἐπληρώθη καὶ ἐγένετο πρὸς αὐτὸ βλέπον καὶ νοῦς οὗτος. Lines 11-13 are not reproduced here since they relate why νοῦς is also τὸ ὄν and hence, are not crucial for my present purposes.

[24] Lines 13-18: Οὗτος οὖν ὢν οἷον ἐκεῖνος τὰ ὅμοια ποιεῖ δύναμιν προχέας πολλήν – εἶδος δὲ καὶ τοῦτο αὐτοῦ – ὥσπερ αὖ τὸ αὐτοῦ πρότερον προέχεε · καὶ αὕτη ἐκ τῆς οὐσίας ἐνέργεια ψυχῆς τοῦτο μένοντος ἐκείνου γενομένη · καὶ γὰρ ὁ νοῦς μένοντος τοῦ πρὸ αὐτοῦ ἐγένετο.

[25] Lines 18-21: Ἡ δὲ οὐ μένουσα ποιεῖ, ἀλλὰ κινηθεῖσα ἐγέννα εἴδωλον. Ἐκεῖ μὲν οὖν βλέπουσα, ὅθεν ἐγένετο, πληροῦται, προελθοῦσα δὲ εἰς κίνησιν ἄλλην καὶ ἐναντίαν γεννᾷ εἴδωλον αὐτῆς αἴσθησιν καὶ φύσιν τὴν ἐν τοῖς φυτοῖς. The reference to φύσις in line 21 may foreshadow its appearance in 3.8, chs. 3 and 4, as the Soul in its lowest descent towards matter and as the source of all λόγοι in plants.

[26] For the Greek text of 3.8.10.3-10 see note 22 above.

[27] Other only "to a degree" because it is God-on-a-lower-level: see above pp. 184-185 paragraph corresponding to notes 19-21.

thereby filling and actuating itself. In turn Intellect produces by similarly pouring forth (lines 14 and 16: προχέας ... προέχεε) intelligible matter and δύναμις, which, however, is now prone to plurality and motion and which becomes Soul by contemplating whence it came and thereby filling and actuating itself.[28]

Accordingly, both 3.8.10 and 5.2.1 depict the One as causing through emanation, which has in Plotinus' eyes several advantages over efficient causality. The One in causing remains perfect: His effects do not deplete or change Him. Emanative causality occurs spontaneously, automatically, necessarily: products arise thereby because God is totally perfect and not because He freely choses to produce them. Such causality safeguards Plotinus' monism: what overflows from the One – the intelligible otherness, matter, operative power[29] – is the One-on-a-lower-level. That is, the effects of emanation are not adequately distinct from their cause[30] and thereby differ from what results from efficient causality. For example, Plato's Craftsman in the *Timaeus*[31] is really other than both the Forms serving as exemplary and final causes of the visible world and their participants.[32] The father of whom Aristotle speaks in *Physics* 2.3, 194b29-32,

---

[28] The second moment of causality on the levels of both Intellect and Soul is exercised by intelligible matter, which fills and actuates itself by contemplating its source (the One and νοῦς, respectively). The difference between 5.2.1 and 3.8.10, is that the latter develops and elucidates the twofold notion of contemplation as operative state and content (see above, n. 18).

On "emanation," see A. H. Armstrong, "'Emanation' in Plotinus," *Mind*, 46 (1937), 61-66: Plotinus almost invariably uses the metaphors of development and growth from a seed or of the radiation of light from a luminous source – this latter he derives from the Stoic author Posidonius; John H. Fielder, "*Chorismos* and Emanation in the Philosophy of Plotinus," in *Significance of Neoplatonism*, ed. Harris, pp. 101-120; idem, "Concepts of Matter and Emanation in the Philosophy of Plotinus" (Ph.D. Dissertation; The University of Texas at Austin), pp. 138-207.

[29] Δύναμις here does not resemble Aristotle's prime matter but operative power (see *Metaphysics*, Δ, ch. 12, 1019a15-21). But Plotinus' δύναμις is not merely a faculty of an individual soul (as with Aristotle) but is the massive overflow from the higher source which helps constitute all lower existents by its actuating and filling itself through contemplation (see above, notes 18 and 28 [first prgr.]) and by "receiving" such actuations.

[30] See above, n. 21.

[31] That the *Timaeus* is to be taken literally, see Gregory Vlastos, "Disorderly Motion in the *Timaeus*" in *Studies in Plato's Metaphysics*, ed. R. E. Allen (New York: Humanities Press, 1965), pp. 379-399; idem, "Creation in the *Timaeus*: Is It a Fiction?" in ibid., pp. 401-419 (each article gives many references to scholars holding the dialogue to be mythical).

[32] On the Forms as models and goals, see *Timaeus*, 29D-31A. For a commentary see L. Sweeney, SJ, "Infinity in Plato's 'Philebus': A Bibliographical and Philosophical Study" (typescript), pp. 89-140 plus notes 175-280.

The fact that the Craftsman makes things be images of the Forms indicates that things participate in Forms. Accordingly, participation in Plato requires that both is really distinct from the child begotten or the sculptor from the statue carved.[33] Such adequately real otherness between effect and agent does not result from the causality which Plotinus ascribes to his God: Intellect, as well as Soul, *is* the One deploying on a lower level. The One is not an agent or craftsman. He transcends reasoning, judging, desiring, executing a task.[34] Because perfect, He overflows spontaneously and necessarily and this overflow, which is not really distinct from Him, becomes through contemplation the existents of the noetic, psychic and physical universe.[35]

Fundamental Principles

Let us now take up the third and final question concerning Plotinus: what basic principles are operative in his metaphysics? The first issues from reflection upon the primacy which he gives to unity (as we have already noted) and which can be expressed as follows: "Whatever is real is one" because to be real is to be one.[36] Any item is real because of its unity, with the result that the more unified something is, the more real it is. Consequently, that which is totally simple is also the Primal Reality – namely the One, which is the absolutely first and highest hypostasis.[37] On the other hand, an existent's lapse into multiplicity is

exemplary causes (Forms) and efficient causes (Craftsman) be operative and that participants be really distinct from both causes – see L. Sweeney, sj, "Participation in Plato's Dialogues: A Coincidence of Opposites," in *Order and Disorder: Coincidence of Opposites in the History of Thought*, ed. Paul and Marion Kuntz (in press). These requirements contrast participation in Plato with participation in Plotinus, for whom the One is emanative and not efficient cause and lower existents are not really distinct in an adequate fashion from Him (see n. 21 above). Accordingly, "participation" is to be taken much more literally in the *Enneads* than in Plato (or, for that matter, Aquinas): each lower existent is a "part" of the One since it *is* the One-on-a-lower-level because of Plotinus' monism.

[33] Also see *Meta.*, Δ, Ch. 2, 1013a29 sqq.

[34] Such functions Plato attributes to the Craftsman in the *Timaeus*, as is clear even from his initial explanation (29D-30A) of why the Craftsman ordered this world as he did. But Plotinus, when describing the causality of the One, replaces such verbs with "flowing," "overflowing," "pouring fourth," as seen above.

One should note, though, that on occasion he ascribes to God a mysterious sort of self-awareness. For listing and exegesis of texts, see J. M. Rist, *Plotinus: The Road to Reality* (Cambridge: University Press, 1967), pp. 38-52; W. T. Wallis, *Neoplatonism*, pp. 58-59.

[35] That Plotinus sets a low value on πρᾶξις and, hence, on efficient causality can be gathered from these texts in 3.8: ch. 1, 14 sq.; ch. 4, 30 sqq.; ch. 6, 1 sqq.; ch. 7, 1 sqq. For a good commentary see John N. Deck, *Nature, Contemplation and the One*, Ch. 9: "Making and 'Efficient Causality'," pp. 93-109.

[36] On this and subsequent principles see my "Basic Principles of Plotinus' Philosophy," pp. 511-512 (where texts are provided).

[37] See John P. Anton, "Some Logical Aspects of the Concept of *Hypostasis* in Plotinus," *Review of Metaphysics*, 31 (1978), 258-271 (with references to studies by

equated with a lapse into unreality – an equation which is equivalent to saying that the emanation of Intellect, Soul and Nature from the One is a movement of what is increasingly less perfect from what is more perfect. To go forth from a cause is to proceed from the perfect to the imperfect.[38] Once this is realized we can formulate a second fundamental principle: "The 'movement' from the One to subsequent existents is a 'movement' from a more perfect to a less perfect state."

This causal situation is, pradoxically enough, linked with a third metaphysical principle. Even though an effect is always less perfect than its cause, still whatever is genuinely real must by that very fact cause subsequent realities, which turn back to their source because of dependency upon it and desire for it. This principle, which issues into Plotinus' doctrines of procession and of reversion (πρόοδος and ἐπιστροφή), can be formulated thus: "Whatever is one, also is good." Obviously, it is an immediate sequel of his principle concerning unity, for that which is one is not only real but also is perfect and powerful. Now whatever is perfect and powerful automatically overflows and thereby produces another (but lesser) reality, which depends upon and tends back to its cause in love. Such is the twofold status which "good" signifies when predicated of an item – a reality and unity insofar as it is both the source of subsequents and the term of their love and tendency.[39] And the more

---

Armstrong, Rist, Deck, Wallis); Heinrich Dörrie, "Hypostasis: Wort- und Bedeutungsgeschichte," *Nachrichten der Akademie der Wissenschaften in Göttingen* (1955), pp. 35-92 (on Plotinus: pp. 68-74).

[38] By this process lower existents become increasingly determined and, thereby, less real. For example, 6.9(9).11.36 sqq.: "When [the human soul] goes down, it comes to evil and so to nonbeing." 6.5(23).12.16 sqq.: [In ascending back to God] you have come to the All and not stayed in a part of it, and have not said even about yourself, 'I am just so much'. By rejecting the so much you have become all – yet you were all before. But because something else other than the All added itself to you, you became less by the addition, for the addition did not come from real being (you cannot add anything to that) but from that which is not. When you have become a particular person by the addition of non-being, you are not all till you reject the non-being. You will increase yourself then by rejecting the rest, and by that rejection the All is with you." Determination so conceived helps preserve Plotinus' monism because what alone is real in any existent is the oneness it has from and with the One and not the apparent additions and individuation it has put on.

If the movement from the One downward is one of decreasing perfection and is an essential mark of Neoplatonism, Spinoza's position (where the divine substance progressively manifests itself first through attributes and then through modes, both general and particular, and thus moves from the more to the less perfect) is closer to Plotinus' than is Hegel's, whose Absolute Spirit moves from the less to the more perfect: from Categories (Being, Essence, Notion) through Nature to Spirit (Art, Religion, Philosophy).

[39] Plotinus frequently makes the following two points both in one and the same text and yet also separately – what is perfect gives rise to products inevitably, spontaneously,

unified something is, the more perfect and the more powerful it is, and the more aptly it can be designated as good. The result is that what is totally simple is also the Supreme Good — as the ultimate source of absolutely all else and the universal goal of all appetition, the One is also the Good. Whatever is one, then, is also good — good *to* others by producing them automatically and necessarily, good *for* others as the object of their seeking.

What is Neoplatonism ?

To conclude the first part of this paper and before considering Albert the Great, let us try to discern what the essence of Neoplatonism is when viewed in its fundamental metaphysics. From the data Plotinus has furnished, one may say that Neoplatonism is a monism (this mark seems absolutely crucial) and is the sort of monism which has at least these three essential traits.

(1) It posits as the primal reality an Existent
   (a) who is the One/Good because to be real is to be one — this equation means that reality is neither becoming (no matter how that word is taken — e.g., any sort of motion or change or activity or operation, whether temporal or eternal)[40] nor being (no matter how that word is taken — e.g., one-many, immutability, eternity, intelligibility, meaningfulness, actuality, etc.);
      (b) who consequently transcends all becoming, being, knowledge, description;
   (c) who nonetheless actually exists.
(2) It grants that there are existents (e.g., Intellect and intellects, Soul and souls, the physical world) other than that primal reality but in such a way that whatever reality they have *is* the One and, thus, they are at bottom identical with the One and are not adequately distinct from Him.[41]

---

automatically by reason of its very perfection and power and, secondly, each product turns back to its source because of desire and love. The following list includes examples of both kinds of texts: 5.4.1.20 sqq.; 5.1.6.15 sqq.; 5.1.7.5 sqq.; 5.2.1.1 sqq.; 2.9.8.10 sqq.; 5.3.11.1 sqq. Also see 5.5.12.1 sqq.: Desire for beauty is always conscious, but everything desires and aspires to The Good by a natural tendency and innate desire. Hence, The Good is prior to beauty. Also: 6.7.20.16 sqq. and ibid., 21.1 sqq.: The Good is prior to Intelligence because everything seeks the former and the latter is desirable only because of the former.

[40] Consequently, the One transcends the operations also of intellection and contemplation; see above, n. 18. But see n. 34 on the "self-awareness" ascribed to the One. On the One's totally transcending all attributes applicable to His effects, see 6.9.3.39 sqq. and 49 sqq.

[41] Because of this radical identity in reality of the One with all else, "real" cannot, it

(3) It finds two sorts of causality operative, the first of which is the spontaneous and inevitable going forth (πρόοδος) of effects from the One and is a movement from the perfect to the imperfect;[42] the second is the return (ἐπιστροφή) of effects to the One and, hence, is a movement of the imperfect to the perfect, which begins with contemplation but terminates with a soul's transcending contemplation and then becoming fully identified with the One.[43]

II. ALBERT THE GREAT

Ten centuries later than Plotinus there lived a Dominican friar who taught theology and philosophy at Cologne and Paris, who was a capable administrator and a prolific author, who described himself as a "Peripatetic" but who currently is rather often reckoned as a Neoplatonist: Albert the Great (ca. 1200-1280).[44] In order to test that current inter-

---

seems, be analogously predicated of Him and His effects because analogy rests on similarity (not identity) and genuine diversity. In fact, in any monism would not predication be univocal, not analogous?

[42] Acordingly, the flow of effects from the One is not creation, which requires causality to be free and efficient and an adequately real distinction to hold between effects and cause. See John N. Deck, *Nature, Contemplation and the One*, pp. 96-97. On the three factors which creation, strictly interpreted, entails, see L. Sweeney, sj, "Doctrine of Creation in the *Liber de Causis*," in *An Étienne Gilson Tribute* (Milwaukee: Marquette University Press, 1959), p. 288.

[43] On this ultimate identification see Plato Mamo, "Is Plotinian Mysticism Monistic?" pp. 199-215; A. H. Armstrong, "The Apprehension of Divinity," esp. pp. 192 sqq.; idem, "Form, Individual and Person in Plotinus," *Dionysius*, 1 (1977), 58-59; John Rist, *Plotinus: Road to Reality*, Ch. 16: "Mysticism," pp. 213-230.

[44] On Albert as Peripatetic see R. Kaiser, "Zur Frage der eigenen Anschauung Alberts d. Gr. in seinen philosophischen Kommentaren," *Freiburger Zeitschrift für Philosophie und Theologie*, 9 (1962), 53 sqq.; L. A. Kennedy, "The Nature of the Human Intellect According to St. Albert the Great," *Modern Schoolman*, 37 (1960), 121-123; James A. Weisheipl, "Albertus Magnus and the Oxford Platonists," *Proceedings of the American Catholic Philosophical Association*, 32 (1958), 124-139 (includes data on Albert's life and writings); idem, "Life and Works of St. Albert the Great," in *Albertus Magnus and the Sciences: Commemorative Essays* (Toronto: Pontifical Institute of Mediaeval Studies, 1980). On Albert as Neoplatonist see Vernon J. Bourke, *Aquinas' Search for Wisdom* (Milwaukee: Bruce, 1965), pp. 50-51; idem, *Augustine's Quest of Wisdom* (Milwaukee: Bruce, 1944), p. 300; Étienne Gilson, *History of Christian Philosophy in the Middle Ages* (New York: Random House, 1955), p. 431 (re the human soul Albert retained elements of "philosophical Augustianism"); F. Copleston, *History of Philosophy* (London: Burns Oates and Washbourne, 1950), 2: 297; Francis J. Catania, "'Knowable' and 'Namable' in Albert the Great's Commentary on the *Divine Names*" in *Albert the Great: Commemorative Essays*, ed. F. J. Kovach and R. W. Shahan (Norman: University of Oklahoma Press, 1980), p. 115.

On Albert's life and writings see F. J. Kovach, "Introduction," in *Albert the Great: Commemorative Essays*, pp. vii-xix.

pretation let us turn to his treatise, *Liber de causis et processu universitatis*, the first fourth of which is an investigation of the perfections attributable to the First Cause (knowledge, will, freedom, omnipotence, causality) and the last three-fourths is a commentary on the *Liber de causis*.[45] This last he thinks should be read as the final book of Aristotle's *Metaphysics* and was composed by a certain David the Jew, who culled statements from Aristotle, Avicenna, Algazel and Alfarabi and then added his own comments (*PU*, 2.1.1, p. 433D).[46] Albert's own treatise, probably written no earlier than 1265 and no later than 1272,[47] discloses (in my judgment) his own mature position on God and reality and this not only in its first 70 pages but also in its last 187 pages, where one finds rather frequent cross references to the earlier portion.[48]

[45] This influential but anonymous treatise, which was also called *Liber de expositione bonitatis purae*, was translated into Latin from Arabic by Gerard of Cremona (d. 1187). On its authorship see Richard C. Taylor, "St. Thomas and the *Liber de Causis* on the Hylomorphic Composition of Separate Substances," *Mediaeval Studies*, 41 (1979), 506, n. 3 (with references to other secondary literature); idem, "The *Liber de Causis*: A Study of Medieval Neoplatonism" (Ph.D. Dissertation; University of Toronto, 1981), pp. 54-70 (the anonymous author was probably a Muslim or Christian philosophical thinker living in the Middle East between 833 and 922 AD); Denis J. Brand, *The Book of Causes* (Niagara, N.Y.: Niagara University Press, 1981), pp. 1-7.

However uncertain the identity of the author may be, this is clear: he joins data from Proclus' *Elements of Theology* and Plotinus' *Enneads* with a doctrine of creation. See also Leo Sweeney, sj, "Doctrine of Creation in *Liber de Causis*," pp. 274-289 and idem, "Research Difficulties in the *Liber de Causis*," *Modern Schoolman*, 36 (1959), 109-116; A. Badawi, *La transmission de la philosophie grecque au monde arabe* (Paris: J. Vrin, 1968), pp. 60-72.

[46] Whenever necessary, I shall refer to Albert's treatise as *PU* (to avoid confusing it with the abbreviated title [*LC*] of the anonymous *Liber de Causis*). The Cologne critical edition (*Alberti Magni Opera Omnia*, Tomus 17, Pars 2) of Albert's *PU* has not yet appeared and, hence, I shall use the Borgnet edition (10: 361-628) in consultation with the Jammy edition (5: 528-655). Albert divided *PU* into books, tractates and chapters, which I shall cite in that order. Hence, this reference – *PU*, 2.1.1, p. 433D – means: *Liber de causis et processu universitatis*, Book 2, Tractate 1, Ch. 1, p. 433 of vol. 10 of the Borgnet edition, lower half of the second column on that page. Since Albert's *PU* does not extend beyond vol. 10 of the Borgnet edition, references will generally omit that volume number.

[47] On the dating of Albert's *PU* see R. Kaiser, "Versuch einer Datierung der Schrift Alberts des Grossen De Causis et Processu Universitatis," *Archiv für Geschichte der Philosophie*, 45 (1965), 129. For other information drawn from Kaiser's publications, see L. Sweeney, sj, "*Esse Primum Creatum* in Albert the Great's *Liber de Causis et Processu Universitatis*," *Thomist*, 44 (1980), 603, n. 13.

[48] For indications that Albert is taking a personal stand and is expressing his own thought in *PU*, see 1.4.3, p. 414D (the opinion of Hermes Trismegistus and others "pessimus error est et destruit omnes gradus entium"); ibid., p. 414D-415B (Avicebron's statement "valde debiliter est probatum ... [et] valde imperfectum ... valde inconveniens ... valde perverse dictum est"); 1.4.5, p. 419C (the theory proposed by *quidam* that "omne esse unum et quod diffusio primi in omnibus est esse eorum" is "pessimus error"); 1.4.8, p. 431C: the view of Isaac, Moyses Maimonides and other Jewish philosophers that the

How shall we approach Albert's book? We shall isolate his meta-physical position by observing how he answers three questions, the first of which is not (as with Plotinus) what "real" means (Albert does not explicitly address that question in *PU*) but concerns what knowledge someone can have of God. The second is what attribute best describes God (here his answer will imply that reality is light and thus unity – see below, n. 54). The third is in what sense effects "flow from" Him. In each case we shall be intent first on discerning (as with Plotinus) what Albert himself had in mind when replying to such an inquiry and, thereafter, on evaluating the possible Neoplatonic aspects of his reply.

Our Knowledge of God

What, then, can one know of God? Can we say He is "substance" or "being" or "wise" or "good" or "one"? No, if such terms are taken precisely as they arise within our human way of knowing (1.3.6, p. 409B: "secundum modum quo cadunt in nostrum intellectum, non dicantur de ipso"), for thereby they express substance, being, wisdom and so on [precisely *as caused, as limited*]. But if one concentrates solely on the perfection itself and neglects the way in which it has arisen in our mind, one is aware of substance only as substance, being as being, wisdom as wisdom. Accordingly, such perfections are found in and affirmed of God in a prior and more perfect fashion than in and of His effects (ibid.; "talia praedicantur de primo principio...: secundum naturam ipsius rei prius sunt in ipso quam in creatis et perfectus incomparabiliter majori perfectione"). Why so? Because they are present in Him as exemplary cause and, thus, the cause of substance, wisdom and goodness can only be Substance, Wisdom and Goodness (ibid.: "Oportet tamen quod ista dicantur de seipso et praedicentur per affirmationem eo quod ista per causam et exemplum primo sunt in ipso; et causa substantiae non potest esse nisi substantia; nec causa exemplaris sapientiae potest esse nisi sapientia; nec causa exemplaris bonitatis nisi bonitas"). Because creatures are images of divine substance, wisdom and goodness, such perfections also are predicable of them too but in a less perfect way. They are, then, attributed to God and creatures not univocally but analogously (ibid.: "Et hoc ideo quia causatum imitatur causam sed non consequitur perfectio-

---

celestial intelligences are angels we do not believe to be true: "sed nos hoc verum esse non credimus"; also see 1.4.7, p. 426D.

    For cross references to earlier sections of the *PU*, see 2.1.17, p. 461C; 2.1.20, p. 467B; 2.1.24, p. 474B; 2.4.11, p. 581D.

nem ejus; propter quod non est univoca praedicatio quando haec de primo et de secundis praedicatis praedicantur").[49]

To this account let us join a later explanation. When establishing in 2.4.7 that God transcends every name assigned Him because our nomenclature follows upon our human way of knowing Him, which arises from His effects (p. 578D), Albert infers that our naming Him entails negation (e.g., He is not substance as we are) and eminence (His substance exceeds ours infinitely: He is an infinite sea of substance whose limits completely escape us; p. 579A-B). Yet he immediately adds that one can attend to the perfection itself expressed by a "complete" name rather than to the name as such.[50] Thus, "substance" is "that which is self-subsistent and makes all else subsist," "intelligence" is "subsistent light which is the source of all intelligible light." In that case such perfections belong to the First Cause in a prior manner and to His effects only through Him (p. 579B-C).

Comments: Both 1.3.6 and 2.4.7 make two points clearly. Our knowing and naming the First Cause do entail negation: His reality exceeds all our attempts. But, secondly, we can and do affirm all "complete" perfections of Him: He *is* Being, Substance, Goodness, Unity, Wisdom, Intelligence and so on. Such affirmations are not merely through extrinsic denomination, as Plotinus would have it: the One is said to be being only inasmuch as He is the cause of being in others.[51] Not so for Albert: God causes being or substance or wisdom only because He *is* Being or

---

[49] For an intelligent but controversial interpretation of how Albert intends perfections to be analogously predicated of God and creatures, see Francis J. Catania, "'Knowable' and 'Namable' in Albert," pp. 97-128. Since he considers Albert to be comparatively "agnostic" *re* knowledge of God (*vs.* F. Ruello) because of his interpretation of *res significata/modus significandi,* Catania's exegesis of *PU* on this point would differ from mine. The basis of his interpretation apparently is that the *res significata* is intrinsically permeated by and inseparably linked with the *modus significandi* and cannot be considered without it – a situation which obtains even with reference to creatures.

In my exegesis of *PU* I find Albert coming close to echoing Aquinas' acceptance of the theory of absolute natures. See ST, 1.14, articles 1-12, esp. a. 3; *In 1 Sent.,* 2.1.3 solution; for my exegesis see "Metaphysics and God: Plotinus and Aquinas," *Miscellanea Mediaevalia* (Berlin: W. de Gruyter, 1963), 2: 237-238.

[50] A "complete" name is one which indicates a perfection which all existents are better off having than not having (*PU,* 2.4.7, p. 580A: "quod omnibus rebus melius esse quam non esse") and is contrasted with "diminutive" names – namely, those whose meaning entails also imperfection, as is the case with "motion" ("actus existentis in potentia"), "time" ("fluxus ab eo quod abiit in non esse incipit et terminatur in id quod nondum est"; ibid., p. 579D) and "matter."

[51] In "extrinsic denomination" a predicate is applied to a subject not because what is signified by the predicate is intrinsically in the subject but because the subject is related to something which does have that *significatum.*

Substance or Wisdom, as he explicitly says: "Causa substantiae non potest esse nisi substantia, nec causa exemplaris sapientiae potest esse nisi sapientia" (1.3.6, p. 409A). If such positive statements are alien to Plotinian Neoplatonism, as they seem to be, Albert is not Neoplatonic in this area.

"Intellectus Universaliter Agens"

But what of his position on the attribute which best describes the First Cause? What is the heart of God's reality from which all His other perfections flow? Albert replies clearly when discussing how we know God if He cannot be defined. His answer: we know Him from His effects, the first of which discloses Him better than the second or the third. That first effect is Intelligence and, thus, God is best described as "The Universally Agent Intellect" (2.1.24, p. 475B).[52]

But what is "intellectus universaliter agens"? Albert had explained the phrase almost one-hundred pages earlier. The First Existent, since He efficiently produces all other existents as the divine artist,[53] must be Intellect (1.2.1, p. 386D) – namely, the Universally Agent Intellect: He who makes things solely of and through Himself, He in whom *esse* and *id quod est* are identical, He who receives or undergoes nothing from anything, He who has no contrary or equal (p. 387B-C). Such an Intellect is like the sun, provided this latter is taken as the very essence of light making all things be visible, the very visibility of which consists in that light ("Omne visibile consistit in lumine sol") and is reduced to and grounded in it (p. 388A). Again, such an Intellect is like an art which would be identical with the light producing the artefacts, which would consist in nothing but that very illumination (p. 378B: "Omne artificiatum consistit in lumine artis sicut in effectivo producente") and are reduced to and based on it (p. 388A).[54] Accordingly, the Universally Agent Intellect is

---

[52] The passage terminates with Albert's granting that the description of God as "Universally Agent Intellect," even though the best we have, does not reveal *quid Deus sit*. (On why the question, *an Deus sit*, should not be raised, see 1.1.8, p. 377B-C.)

"Intelligentia" has a twofold signification in Albert, the first of which refers (as in the Latin quoted) to the initial created hypostasis ("intelligentia, cuius substantia intellectus est"). The second refers to *esse primum creatum*, which is the initial "flow" from God and which is also called "intelligentia," "simplex conceptus mentis," "lumen," etc. – see 2.1.19, p. 465B; 2.1.21, p. 468B; L. Sweeney, SJ, *"Esse primum creatum* in Albert," p. 612, n. 27 and p. 629, n. 56; also n. 64 below. In order to distinguish the two meanings I capitalize the English word to express the intellectual substance (thus: Intelligence) and use lower case to express the initial flow from the First Cause (thus: intelligence).

[53] See 1.1.11, p. 385A and C: the First Principle is efficient cause primarily and, thereafter, is formal or exemplary cause.

[54] The radical unity of all creatures with God as Universally Agent Intellect can be inferred from the Latin text. Just as light is the very essence of the sun and of things

in essence subsistent Light,[55] which produces all other existents, either immediately (other intelligences) or mediately on several levels (e.g., souls; natural forms which illumine matter and, thus, constitute our physical universe).[56] They all consist in that light and are resolved back into it and are grounded in it. They all emanate from it and thereby each receives its *id quod est* and *esse*: that Intellect illumines them all, without itself being illumined by anything prior (p. 387c). It thereby differs from all other agent intellects, each of which illumines what is subsequent to them only in dependence upon the divine illumination and not in virtue of its own *id quod est*. Hence, "agent intellect" is not applied to the First Principle univocally [but analogously] (p. 388c).

Comment: Albert's statement that "God is Agent Intellect" has, in the light of 1.3.6 and 2.4.7 (analyzed above) and the currently studied text, several characteristics. It entails negation insofar as the divine intellect is not identical with a human or, for that matter, any created intellect. It also entails eminence since the divine intellect infinitely exceeds all other intellects: it *is* His very substance and *id quod est*, by and through which He acts. But it is also an affirmation that analogously God is Intellect through intrinsic denomination. He produces all other intellects because He Himself *is* Intellect. This affirmation separates him from Plotinian Neoplatonism.

That separation is also suggested by the fact that all creatures not only consist in the divine illumination which constitutes them, to which they

---

visible and just as light is identical with art and with the artefact, so too light (as will be clear in the immediately subsequent lines of the text) is the very essence of the divine intellect and of all created things, which differ among themselves to the degree they entail darkness (see n. 56 below).

[55] See 2.4.7, p. 579c: "Erit enim intelligentia omnis intellectibilis luminis fons per seipsam."

[56] The various grades of existents result from their progressively falling away from light and encountering darkness. See 1.4.5, p. 418D and p. 419A: "Sicut dicit Isaac, semper posterius oritur in umbra praecedentis. Umbram autem vocamus differentiam per quam coarctatur et obumbratur amplitudo luminis a priori procedentis. ... Primum autem lumen occumbit in ipso per hoc quod aliud est in ipso esse et quod est; et hoc quidem intelligentia est.... Et sic de omnibus, quod semper aliquem occasum et obumbrationem prioris constituitur sequens differentia entis, sicut sensibile in umbra intellectualis et vegetabile in umbra sensibilis; corpus autem contrarietate determinatum in umbra coeli, quod sola corporeitate determinatum est; commixta vero corpora consequenter consequuntur in obumbratione et remissione qualitatum elementalium. ... Per quod patet quod ordinem in gradibus entium non facit nisi casus et occubitus a lumine primi entis." Also see ibid., c. 8, p. 428 sqq.; 1.4.2, p. 412D, *re* the four ways in which the "flow" from God is linked with recipients – *distans, cadens, occumbens, oppressum tenebris* – and thus comes to constitute diverse levels of creatures (intelligences, souls, heavenly bodies, terrestial things).

are reducible and which grounds them, but they also are present in the
subsistent Light Which is God Himself. The First Principle is (Albert
writes in 2.1.20, p. 467B) absolutely perfect: all perfections and
excellences are in Him, although they are completely one and cause no
multiplicity in Him at all. ("Primum enim principium in omnibus
nobilibus bonitatibus est perfectum, licet sint unitae, nullam penitus multi-
plicitatem inducentes"), for privations, motions and compositions are in
Him immaterially, nondeficiently, immutably and simply – the manner in
which lower existents are always present through their *rationes* in what is
higher. These *rationes* or ideal forms, as Plato would express them, are
not only found in the light proceeding from the universally Agent
Intellect, where they are incorruptible and more perfect in every way than
they are in things (p. 467C). But they are also in the First Principle itself
and, thus considered, are all one with one another and with that Intellect
(p. 467D).[57] That presence of all perfections in God again contrasts Albert
with Plotinus, for whom the One is without any of the perfections He
causes: none of them are present in Him.[58]

The "Flow" of Effects From Cause

The third area in which Albert discloses his metaphysics concerns
divine causality and, more precisely, the "flow" of effects from God, a
topic to which he devotes an entire tractate of twenty-one pages. What are
the salient points made there?

In our everyday world water *flows* from a spring and feeds a brook.
The spring causes the brook: one and the same water which flows from
the spring constitutes the brook. A philosopher observing that situation
would call the spring an "univocal" cause of the stream since one and the
same perfection (water) is in both cause (spring) and effect (brook). Such
univocal causality is one example of "flow": the same identical form is in
both the source and the recipient of the "flow" (1.4.1, p. 410D: "Non enim
fluit nisi id quod unius formae est in fluente et in eo in quo fit fluxus, sicut
rivus ejusdem formae est cum fonte a quo fit fluxus et aqua in utroque est
ejusdem speciei et formae. ... Similiter enim idem est fluere quod univoce
causare).[59]

[57] For exegesis of 2.1.20, see L. Sweeney, "*Esse Primum Creatum* in Albert," pp. 634-
641. Also see 1.3.6, p. 409C-D.

[58] On Plotinus see the portion of this paper corresponding to notes 23 and 25 above;
also n. 40.

[59] Another example of a univocal "flow" would be a ray of light emitted by the
sun – see ibid., p. 411D.

But God is not a univocal cause since He is not in the same genus as any of His effects. And yet (as seen above) their perfections are all in Him; creatures are like Him, "being" and "intelligence" and "wisdom" and so on can be analogously predicated of Him and of them. He is, then, their analogous cause: one and the same perfection ("being" or "substance" or "light") is intrinsically in Him and in them but differently: e.g., He *is* Being, they have being through participation.[60] Consequently, the perfections they have in common "flow" (literally) from Him to them, in much the same way as the perfection of art "flows" from the mind of the artist eventually and mediately into the artefact (1.4.6, p. 420D: "[Fluxus iste] erit ergo inter ea quae per analogiam dicuntur, in quibus secundum quasi instrumentale est ad primum. Et forma qua fluit primum, magis ac magis coarctatur et determinatur secundum quod fluit in secundo vel in terito, et sic deinceps, sicut in exemplo diximus de arte quae a mente artificis fluit in spiritum, de spiritu in organa membrorum, de organis in instrumenta, et de instrumentis in materiam: in omnibus enim his idem est quod fluit, licet secundum aliud esse sit in primo et secundum aliud in secundo et sic deinceps").[61]

But how does one account for the fact that such perfections "flow" from God at all? What (so to speak) causes Him to pour them out upon creatures? In answering Albert says nothing of the divine will and freedom[62] but bases God's pouring out perfections on creatures on the fact that He is all perfect and supremely generous (1.4.1, p. 411c). And the "flowing forth" of perfections from Him to creatures is an incessantly on-

---

[60] On causes as analogous, univocal and equivocal, see L. Sweeney, SJ, *A Metaphysics of Authentic Existentialism* (Englewood Cliffs, N.J.: Prentice-Hall, 1965; Ann Arbor, Michigan: Books On Demand, 1977), pp. 232-234.

On why *esse* is not predicated of God and creatures univocally but analogously, see 2.1.17, p. 462c-D.

[61] Albert uses the example of art frequently to illustrate the divine "flow" – for instance, 1.4.2, p. 413A; ibid., c. 6, p. 420D sq.; ibid., c. 8, p. 429A; for more references see my *"Esse Primum Creatum* in Albert," p. 640, n. 74.

[62] In fact, he rejects the divine will as an explanation of the diversity of creatures originating from God: since "ab uno non est nisi unum, nec potest intelligi quod ab omnimode uno per se diversa sint aequali processione. Si enim dicatur quod hoc est verum in agentibus per essentiam et non in his quae agunt per voluntatem, hoc absurdum est. In primo enim est voluntas quod essentia; et sicut primum invariabile est secundum essentiam, ita invariabile est secundum voluntatem" (2.4.14, p. 587D sq.). For Albert's long treatment of divine will and freedom, see 1.3, chs. 1-2 and 4.

Perhaps one source of his rejection of the will to explain the origin of creatures may be his hostility to Avicebron, who gave prominence to the will in the First Cause. For indications of Albert's refusal of Avicebron's philosophy see 1.1, chs. 5 and 6; also 1.4.3, pp. 414D sq.; 1.4.8, p. 428B. Also see James Weisheipl, OP, "Albertus Magnus and Universal Hylomorphism: Avicebron," in *Albert the Great*, ed. Kovach and Shahan, pp. 239-260.

going process. As the universally Agent Intellect God knows Himself and, as subsistent Light, He is always sending forth forms, by which He constitutes everything which is (ibid., p. 411D: "Fluxus semper est in fieri. ... Inter omnia autem quae principiorum habent nomen et rationem, praecipue si fluit, est intellectus agens, qui lumine quod sibi est de se, sic semper formas emanat, quibus constituit ea quae agit").[63] The first of those forms or light is *esse primum creatum*,[64] which flows from God as act from Act,[65] which contains all other subsequent perfections (e.g., *vivere, sentire, intelligere*) as acts too and active powers.[66] As these flow forth and thus enable *esse* to disclose and develop its contents, God as extrinsic and efficient cause and "esse primum creatum" as primal intrinsic cause produce the substantial entities of Intelligences, Souls, the heavens and terrestrial things.[67] In all of these entities passive potency or receptivity is

[63] That God's knowing Himself produces creatures see 1.4.8, p. 428B and p. 429C.

[64] See 2.1.17, p. 462A: "Relinguitur ergo quod esse sit primum creatum et quod alia causata non creata sint, et quod nullum causatorum prius esse possit quam esse. Esse ... [ut] processus enim simplex prius a causa prima procedit ut actus in esse constituens omne quod est. Ex hoc autem quod primum est sequitur quod simplicius sit omnibus aliis: simplicissimum enim est quod in aliud resolvi non potest. Esse autem est in quo constat resolutio entium." Also see 2.1.15, p. 458D; 2.1.19, p. 456C; 2.1.20, p. 467B and D; 2.3.10, p. 539B. For exegesis of these passages (as well as those cited in notes 65-69 below) see L. Sweeney, "*Esse Primum Creatum* in Albert," pp. 610 sqq.

Esse primum creatum is also called "simplex intelligentia" and "simplex conceptus mentis" – see above n. 52, second prgr. On what *esse* itself means (e.g., entity, essence, act of essence, intelligibility of *ens*), see L. Sweeney, SJ, "*Esse* in Albert the Great's Texts on Creation in *Summa de Creaturis* and *Scriptum in Libros Sentiarum*," in *Albert the Great*, ed. Kovach and Shahan, pp. 65-95.

[65] See 1.4.1, p. 411B: "Dici potest quod [esse] fluat secundum quod est actus ab actu"; 2.1.20, p. 467B-C: God "producit esse ab esse suo increato...; et ideo dicit Aristoteles in VII *philosophiae primae* quod actus est ab actu: actus ejus quod fit [est] ab actu ejus quod facit." Also see 2.2.23, p. 513D; 2.5.15, p. 607B. On God as Act see 1.2.3, pp. 391D-392A; 1.4.1 and 2, pp. 411C and 413C; 2.2.4, pp. 484D-485A.

[66] See 2.1.17, p. 461D: "[Esse] non educitur ex aliquo in quo formalis inchoatio sit ipsius, sicut vivere educitur ex esse et sentire ex vivere et rationale ex sensibili. ... Et quia esse virtutem suam influit super omnia sequentia, propter hoc sicut esse actus est entium, ita vivere viventibus est esse, et sentire est esse sentientibus et ratiocinari est esse rationalibus...; et hanc virtutem, quod scilicet quodlibet istorum sit esse quorum est, sequentia non possunt habere nisi a primo quod est esse"; 2.1.19, p. 465B-C, ibid., p. 465D.

[67] For Albert "esse primum creatum is act. In fact, its contents (*vivere, intelligere, sentire*) are acts too. These, then, are related to *esse* as acts to act and not as acts to potency. Hence, their coming forth from *esse* is not an eduction of acts from potency but an unfolding of acts from act through the threefold extrinsic causality (efficiency, exemplarity, finality) of the Act who is *esse increatum* and *intellectus universaliter agens*. Together with *esse primum creatum*, they are simultaneously the *potentiae activae* within the procession or 'outflow' of light by which He causes all creatures to be and to be what they are in the cascade of reality reaching down to matter" (L. Sweeney, "*Esse Primum Creatum* in Albert," pp. 641-642; also see ibid., p. 623, n. 44).

On the origin and differentiation of Intelligences, Souls, etc., see ibid., p. 612 and n. 29 for multiple references; also n. 56 above.

not itself an intrinsic component but consists in an extrinsic factor: the distance at which each entity stands from its causes and, eventually, from God.[68]

Comments. In this area of his metaphysics Albert would seem to move closer to Plotinus than in those surveyed previously. His very choice of the word "fluere" to express how created existents arise from God, as well as His comparing their origin from Him to a stream fed by a spring, appears to parallel Plotinus' Greek (see paragraphs of this paper which correspond to notes 23-28). Secondly, the fact that the German Dominican is silent, when describing creation,[69] on God's free choice and speaks as though the production of creatures is automatic, spontaneous and, in that sense, necessary (created perfections result and flow out from Him because He is fully perfect and contemplates Himself) also makes him resemble the Greek author.

That resemblance, however, encounters obstacles, since Albert's position appears, at first sight, not to be a monism by his stressing the distinction between God and His effects in many texts. Let us take two samples. How is God (he asks in 1.1.11) the First Principle? As an efficient cause inasmuch as He is Artist. But an artist is distinct from all the artefacts he makes. Therefore, the divine Arist is distinct from all creatures and is a constitutive part of none of them (p. 385A: "Cum vero omnia secundum esse dependeant ad ipsum et emanent ex ipso, ... oportet quod primum principium sit efficiens sicut artifex, distinctus ab omnibus et nullo modo commixtus ipsis"). Approximately seventy-five pages later: the first creature ("esse primum creatum") presupposes nothing but the Creator, who nonetheless is other than it, for the First Principle does not become an essential part of anything. Thus, *esse* is not predicated univocally of that Principle and its effect (2.1.17, p. 462c).[70]

But does such textual emphasis on God's distinction from His effects clear him of the charge of monism? Plotinus also affirms the One to be

---

· [68] See 1.4.5, p. 419D: "[Procedens] secundum id quod est, in potentia est et non in actu antequam sit in potentia, ergo esse differentiam habet a primo esse. Tertium autem ejus quod a primo et secundo est, similiter in potentia ad secundum, et hoc magis in potentia est quam secundum, et sic deinceps"; 2.1.14, p. 458A; 1.4.8, p. 428c; 2.2.5, p. 486D; 2.2.14, p. 499c; 2.4.1, pp. 572A and B; for commentary on those texts see L. Sweeney, "*Esse Primum Creatum* in Albert," pp. 642-645.

[69] Albert has creation in mind, obviously, in the multiple places in which he speaks of *esse primum creatum* and in some of which he defines creation – see, for instance, 2.1.17, p. 461B: "Creare est ex nihilo producere. Quod autem causat non supposito quodam alio quo causet, sequitur quod causet ex nihilo; primum autem causat non supposito quodam alio quo causet; primum ergo causat ex nihilo. Causatio ergo ipsius creatio est."

[70] Other texts on distinction between God and creatures are: 1.4.3, p. 414B; 1.4.5, p. 419D sq.; 2.1.6, p. 442D; 2.4.2, p. 573c-D.

other than the Intellect and the other existents which emanate from Him, and yet he simultaneously maintains they are one with the One to the extent they are real: they are the One-on-a-lower-level (see paragraphs above corresponding to notes 14-21). Might Albert's position be similar? We would be more sure if he unequivocally equated reality with unity (as does Plotinus). Although such an equation seems lacking, he apparently does speak as though to be real is to be light,[71] which perhaps is equivalent to giving primacy to unity in reality.

As to Albert's conception that the passive potency which *esse primum creatum* encounters in substantial entities (see lines above which correspond to notes 64-68) is the extrinsic situation in which such an entity finds itself rather than an intrinsic component (see above, n. 68), one may at least infer that such a conception marks a departure from a strictly Aristotelian doctrine of potency and act.[72]

III. CONCLUSIONS

The immediately preceding section on Albert's theory of causality has disclosed it to be similar to Plotinus'. According to each author effects "flow from" God as a stream from an inexhaustible spring – a "flowing forth" which is spontaneous and necessary. But in the two previous sections Albert appeared to be unlike Plotinus. God for the former *is* Being, Substance, Wisdom and other "complete" perfections: the core of His reality is, in fact, His being "intellectus universaliter agens." The Plotinian God transcends those perfections: He is above being, substance, wisdom and intellect. Moreover, Albert's God is first and foremost an efficient cause and contains all the perfections of His effects: the *rationes* of all creatures are present in the subsistent Light which is God. Plotinus' God is not an agent but an "emanative" cause, Who is Himself without any of the perfections He causes: none of them is present in Him.

---

[71] See 1.2.1, p. 388A: "Omnis res ab illo est in quod resolvitur sicut in suae constitutionis principium. Ex quo ergo omne quod est, sive sit per se sive per accidens, sive sit per naturam sive per animam, sive corporeum sive sit incorporeum, resolvitur in tale lumen intellectus agentis et id ad aliud resolvi non potest"; 1.4.8, p. 428B. In fact, God *is* pure light (2.1.25, p. 475D). In and through that light He pre-possesses the forms of all things and, then, establishes and distinguishes all of them (1.3.6, p. 409D). Because the divine light extends everywhere, God is omnipresent (1.2.5, p. 394B). As already argued (see n. 54 above), one can infer from 1.2.1, pp. 386D sqq. the radical unity of all things with God as Universally Agent Intellect: light is the essence of sun and of visible things, light is the essence of art and artefact, light also is the essence of the divine intellect and of all creatures.

[72] See L. Sweeney, SJ, *"Esse Primum Creatum* in Albert," pp. 642-646.

Clearly, determining the extent to which the Latin author is or is not Neoplatonic has been made possible by our tracing the basic lines of Plotinus' metaphysics (see above, "What Is Neoplatonism ?"). Because for Plotinus to be real is to be one, his God is sheer unity and, thereby, must be above being, intellect and all the other perfections of His effects. The fact that Albert's God *is* Being, Substance, Wisdom and Intellect and contains all perfections suggests that reality for him is not simply unity but is, in some sense of the word, "being" (under the influence of Exodus 3:14 ?), despite his implying that unity and reality are coterminous,[73] and despite the fact of his conceiving of causality as the "flowing forth" of effects from cause.

Accordingly, taking Albert as a test case in which Plotinus' metaphysics is taken as a criterion of authentic Neoplatonism encourages us when we turn to Iamblichus, Proclus, Pseudo-Dionysius and other Greek philosophers. If reality for them is unity, if their primal God is the One-Good, if He transcends being, intellect and all other such attributes, if his mode of causing lower existents is by necessary overflow or procession, then their positions are authentically Plotinian Neoplatonisms. This is true no matter how far they may differ from Plotinus in their conceptions of soul and intellect, in their eschatologies, in their epistemology and logic. This is also true no matter how much they may have added to Plotinus' "pure position" [74] such apparently alien elements as theurgy from the *Chaldean Oracles* (as happens in Iamblicus and Proclus)[75] or the Trinity and Incarnation from Christianity (as in Pseudo-Dionysius)[76] or a doctrine of creation from the Koran or Old and New Testaments (as in the *Liber de causis*).[77] But deciding in this fashion whether or not such authors are Plotinian in their Neoplatonism must be reserved for another occasion.

---

[73] This implication is based on his apparent identifying reality with light (see above, n. 71). This identification becomes less surprising if "being" is for him equivalent to "oneness." If this equivalence proves true, Albert's metaphysical position fits more readily into a Plotinian Neoplatonism.

[74] A "pure position" is in contrast to what Gilson (*History*, p. 238) calls a "complex": "A doctrinal complex is a more or less organic whole, made up of interrelated theses which are frequently found united despite the diversity of their respective origins. ... It is a syncretic combination of elements united together by their common neoplatonist inspiration."

[75] On Proclus see L. Sweeney, sj, "Participation and the Structure of Being in Proclus' *Elements of Theology*," in *Structure of Being*, ed. Harris, pp. 140-155 and 177-181.

[76] See William J. Carroll; "Participation in Selected Texts of Pseudo-Dionysius the Areopagite's *The Divine Names*," Ph.D. Dissertation; Washington, D.C.: The Catholic University of America, 1981.

[77] See above, notes 42 and 45.

10

Deus Creator Omnium
Plato and Aristotle in Aquinas' Doctrine of God

Cornelia J. de Vogel
Rijksuniversiteit, Utrecht

Since the days of Antiochus of Ascalon ancient philosophers have tried to come to a certain synthesis of what major thinkers had achieved. Carneades, no doubt, was a great thinker too. His criticism was essentially directed against Stoic arguments and theories which on important points proved not solid enough to stand his critical analysis. Yet confidence in constructive philosophical thought was not lost. It must be possible, after all, for human thinking to reach truth. Scepticism could not have the last word. And was there no solidity in the thoughts of the ancients? Antiochus did not think them beaten. Behind the New Academy he went back to the *veteres*. He did not find an essential conflict between their positions, neither in metaphysics nor in the theory of knowledge. So we find in Cicero's *Academica* a fresh attempt at building up a theory of knowledge which claimed to be able to attain truth and in doing so did not abandon the basic conviction that a meta-physic is essentially possible and ontologically justified.

Now the remarkable thing is that the terms in which Varro expounded Antiochus' theory of knowledge in Cicero's *Academica posteriora* (8.30f.) do recall Plato's doctrine of Ideas "that are always one and the same, identical with themselves and only accessible to the intellect" as the true objects of knowledge, and could indeed by modern interpreters be understood in such a sense that Antiochus would appear to have reintro-

Graceful Reason: Essays in Ancient and Medieval Philosophy Presented to Joseph Owens, CSSR, ed. Lloyd P. Gerson. Papers in Mediaeval Studies 4 (Toronto: Pontifical Institute of Mediaeval Studies, 1983), pp. 203-227. © P.I.M.S., 1983.

duced the Platonic Ideas in their transcendent sense.[1] On the other hand, the same text could be interpreted the other way round, by taking the *ideas* or *species* in the Aristotelian sense as indicating the "forms" that are "in" concrete things. Now since Antiochus regarded the philosophy of Academics and Peripatetics as in essential agreement and differing only in words – *rebus congruentes nominibus differebant*[2] – this first and highly professional attempt at a philosophical synthesis must appear to us just as unsatisfactory as it is interesting. Hence, we shall leave the discussion on Antiochus of Ascalon aside[3] and proceed to give our own analysis of the chief points of difference between the two thinkers, considering first the contrast in their view of reality, next the background of their theory of knowledge, then how transcendent Being was conceived by Aristotle, and finally what problems were involved in this conception. Next we shall see in which sense Plato's metaphysics of transcendent Being was integrated into St. Thomas Aquinas' concept of God.

I. THE METAPHYSICAL CONTRAST

For Plato, Reality in the full sense of the term is not the phenomenal world we see with our eyes but an invisible, unchangeable order to be grasped by the intellect only.[4] Closely related to it by ontological kinship is

---

[1] W. Theiler, *Die Vorbereitung des Neuplatonismus* (Berlin, 1930), pp. 40ff., defended this view which was later supported by G. Luck, *Der Akademiker Antiochos*, Noctes Romanas 7 (Bern, 1953). R. E. Witt, *Albinus and the History of Middle Platonism* (Cambridge, 1937), argued against Theiler that, according to Cicero, *Academica priora* 2.30, Antiochus was essentially a Stoic in his theory of knowledge and not a transcendentalist. Witt's view was shared and well defended by A. M. Lueder, "Die philosophische Persönlichkeit des Antiochos von Askalon," doctoral thesis (Göttingen, 1940). Witt focussed on Albinus as the first to go back to Plato's metaphysics which, no doubt, he did although he was not the first or only philosopher of the second century to do so. Not only was there Philo of Alexandria before him, but also in the Christian Justin's *Dialogus cum Tryphone* 4 we find the noetic reality of Plato's metaphysics fully recognized; and certainly no less in Plutarch's explanation of the ε on the wall of the Delphic temple (*De E apud Delphos* 17-20, 391F-393B).
   In Albinus' *Didaskalikos* there was, no doubt, an important part of Aristotelian logic. I think it would be arguing a bit too rashly, however, to declare Albinus' theology to be a mixture of Aristotelian and Platonic metaphysics as has been done not infrequently.
[2] Cicero, *Academica posteriora* 1.4.17.
[3] The essential texts with notes are found in my *Greek Philosophy* 3rd ed., vol. 3 (Leiden, 1973), nos. 1199-1200.
[4] *Phaedo* 61c-69e: the philosopher does not seek things here but that which we can grasp by the intellect only (here called soul-by-itself); *Republic* 5, 475d-480a and 6, 484a: philosophers are those who seek Truth, which is true Being, the object of knowledge and always identical with itself; *Cratylus* 439c-440b; *Philebus* 59a-c.

our soul, which by its thinking power is able to get hold of it.[5] The changing world of visible things is not just an unreal appearance; it has its *part* of reality,[6] realized in it by a mixture with that indefinite element which by itself lacks all form and substance. So it may be called a mixture of Being and Non-being.[7]

Reality itself is "archetypal" or "exemplary" by providing a limit. It is also exemplary in a moral sense by its ontic perfection. It is unity, order, beauty, goodness. The principle of Number is in it. On it depend all goodness and order in man and in the visible world. That too has its part of Beauty and of Order. But it is never primary; it has no substance of itself.

Such is Plato's doctrine of reality. Aristotle's is very different indeed. He starts from this our visible, moving and changing world. He accepts it as a "given" reality which we have to explain as such. Motion is a reality. We cannot deny it by declaring it to be "unreal," as Parmenides did. The question we have to ask is, how do things come into being? How do we get hold of them as a "this" or "that"? The problem of physical being has to be solved in a more satisfactory way than Plato's. And next there is the problem of knowledge: knowledge of this changing world with its ever shifting appearance. Can we know physical objects?

These are Aristotle's problems starting from Plato and Parmenides. He develops a theory of physical being, a theory of coming-to-be and passing away, and a theory of knowledge in which the intellect proves able to grasp the unchanging essence of physical things. Things here are real and they can be known. We can explain the physical process of coming-to-be and passing away by a set of rational principles, and we can know these changing things because they have an intelligible essence within themselves by which they are what they are.[8]

---

[5] *Phaedo* 79b-d; cf. *Phaedrus* 245c-246a: the soul is a self-moving principle. *Laws* 726c-727a, 892a-d, 895e-896b: priority of Soul to body.

[6] *Republic* 5, 478a-479b.

[7] *Philebus* 26d. Cf. *Timaeus* 52a: the "second kind" is that which bears the same name as full noetic Reality and is ὅμοιον to it. "Resemblance" or similarity is a way of expressing "participation." See also *Timaeus* 37c6-d2.

[8] The starting point is clearly expounded in *Physica* 1.1-3; chapter 7 gives the main lines of Aristotle's own theory which in chapters 8 and 9 is declared to be the true solution of the problems that were left open by the Presocratics and by Plato. *Physica* 2 expounds Aristotle's theory of the process of nature more explicitly. The theory applies to the whole of the visible world. A special treatise deals with "coming-to-be and passing-away" in this our "sublunar" world which is of primary reality to us, while not being "primary reality" in the absolute sense. How closely this theory of nature is linked up with Aristotle's theory of knowledge we shall see in our next section.

206   C. J. DE VOGEL

Is then this our physical world the whole of reality? Far from that. *Τὸ ὂν λέγεται πολλαχῶς*: "Being" is a term that is used in many senses. May we say on different levels? Surely we must say so, for Aristotle says that there are three kinds of *ὄντα*, three different sorts of being,[9] which are the objects of three theoretical sciences. The objects of these sciences are described as (1) things that exist separately but are not immovable, (2) things that are immovable but presumably do not exist separately but are embodied in matter,[10] (3) things that exist separately and are immovable. The last are the object of the first science or "theology," the second fall under "some" of the mathematical sciences.[11] The predominance of the "first science" is emphasized: it is universal while being first (*Metaphysica* E.1, the end).

In *Metaphysica* Λ.1 the three *οὐσίαι* (kinds of being) are depicted by the description that two of them are sensible – of which one part is eternal and the other perishable – and the third is immovable.[12] This third kind then is described *Ἀκαδημικῶς*, according to the views of Plato, Xenocrates and Speusippus – a description which, together with the account of the physical process given in the following chapters, might give support to the conclusion that this book of the *Metaphysica* was of a comparatively early date rather than of a late one.[13] However, we shall leave aside these questions of dating. What is of interest in our present search is the fact that for Aristotle reality is essentially expressed in concrete things, understood as composites of form and matter, of which "form" is the intelligible essence that is fully realized in that potential being which for Aristotle is "*ὕλη*." The term was not used by Plato, and certainly his "receiving" principle in the *Timaeus*, though formless and undetermined, was very different from Aristotle's *ὕλη*, which as "potential being" had a marked predisposition to become this or that concrete thing. And what is still more important, the form realized in its *ὕλη* becomes an object which is recognized as a real being without any restrictions. It is real and it is

[9] *Metaphysica* E.1, 1025b18-21, starts by saying, "Since science of nature is about a *γένος τοῦ ὄντος*," and then immediately goes on to explain, "for it is about a kind of *οὐσία* which has the principle of its movement and rest within itself." Here *ὄν* and *οὐσία* are interchangeable terms. In the same way Λ.1, 1069a30, reads *Οὐσίαι δὲ τρεῖς* – "There are three kinds of being."
[10] This is not said of *all objects* of mathematics, but of the objects of *some* mathematical sciences.
[11] Aristotle regarded numbers as not existing separately. However, the heavenly bodies did exist separately, but were certainly not without some kind of matter.
[12] *Metaphysics*, Λ, 1069a30-31, 33-36.
[13] L. Elders, *Aristotle's Theology* (Assen, 1972), p. 54, notes, "The chapter seems to be very early."

knowable. To man it is even primary reality in so far as this sensible world of ours is actually "our" reality. Although the *phenomenal* world is the one in which we have to live, a Platonist will always be aware of the fact that a more perfect and more "true reality" is beyond it. In Aristotle, however, that idea has disappeared completely. Whatever may be found to exist as "moving causes" in an order transcending ours, our visible world is "reality" in the full sense. This implies indeed a very great and profound difference between Plato's and Aristotle's outlooks on life and human affairs.

Let us now first see on the one hand how this tremendous difference works out in the theory of knowledge and, on the other, what are the consequences with regard to natural things. After that inquiry we shall try to find our way in the higher regions of the ἀκίνητος οὐσία.

II. THEORY OF KNOWLEDGE

For Aristotle, knowledge takes its origin in sense perception, without being reached by it. The essential point is that after repeated perception the intellect is able to grasp the universal from the sense data. It must be noticed that in *Analytica posteriora* 2.19 the knowledge of the universal seems to be reached, as it were, automatically by a natural process: the flow of repeated sense impressions leads to memory; next by repeated memories it constitutes experience; next, when a stand is reached, the universal is so to speak automatically singled out as one and the same in its entirety (100a6-9).

How can such a thing happen? Aristotle simply replies, "The soul is so constituted as to be capable of this process" (a12-13). Up to this point the word νοῦς does not occur. But it does occur a bit further on in section b5-15. In this passage νοῦς and ἐπιστήμη are coupled and they are coupled in the kind of thinking by which we unfailingly reach truth. So here νοῦς actually appears as the faculty by which truth is "grasped" without the possibility of error. An intuitive faculty, we might say. And is not this something like an *a priori*? Such then is the function of the "active νοῦς" which we hear of in *De anima* 3.5, 430a10-25.

In this kind of subject matter it is almost traditional to oppose Plato's intuitionism of transcendent "Forms," which we have known in a previous existence and may "recall" by introspection, to Aristotle's theory which so obviously is dominated by sense perception. Yet on closer inspection the antithesis appears by no means as radical as it is usually supposed to be, not even if we think of the *Phaedo* and *Republic*, let alone if we take the *Theaetetus* into account. Certainly in the *Phaedo* philosophers are advised to turn away from the senses as soon and as radically as possible. Yet it is with sense perception that they have to begin. Moreover, it is granted that *seeing* a certain person (e.g., Simmias) or a certain object (e.g., his lyre) may lead us to remember something we cannot see. In the *Theaetetus* the function of the senses in the process of knowledge is analyzed with more precision. The conclusion, reached in 186d, is "knowledge is not in the impressions made by the senses but in the reflexion upon them."

In the theory of knowledge, then, both for Plato and for Aristotle the object to be known is an *ideal content*. Moreover, for both of them this "truth" must be "grasped" directly by the mind, by some intuitive faculty of "seeing" the essential.

However, there is a metaphysical difference between the one and the other. For Plato the object of knowledge is not the concrete thing. It is not *in* concrete things either, although they *do* point to "true Reality" by an undeniable resemblance. The real object of knowledge is of a clearly transcendent order. For Aristotle, on the other hand, "truth" is actually *in* the concrete things, not immediately visible, but to be grasped by the intellect, and this in the full sense: it is really the concrete thing that is known by knowing its intelligible essence.

A later generation could construct a synthesis here: a certain mystical way of "grasping" the real essence of things by an intuitive vision might arise. We find traces of this in Arabic versions, in which the vision of "Forms" in the invisible world "yonder" is ascribed either to Aristotle or to some Aristotelian philosopher. Al-Kindī[14] cites Aristotle as telling of "the Greek king whose soul was caught up in ecstasy, and who for many days remained neither alive nor dead. When he came to himself he told the bystander of *various things in the invisible world* and related what he had seen – *souls, forms, and angels.*" This is indeed a lovely platonized (or rather late-neoplatonized) version of a Syrian or Arabic heir of late Greek wisdom. A similar vision is ascribed by the twelfth-century Arabic philosopher Ibn Ṭufayl to his hero Ḥayy ibn Yaqẓān, who was the object of lively interest in England and in the Netherlands in the second half of the seventeenth and in the eighteenth centuries.[15] The underlying inter-

[14] Cited in *Aristotelis Fragmenta Selecta*, ed. W. D. Ross (Oxford, 1955), p. 23: Eudemus, frag. 11; English translation in *Aristotle, Selected Fragments*, ed. W. D. Ross (Oxford, 1952), p. 23.

[15] The life of Ḥayy ibn Yaqẓān was translated into Latin by Edward Pocock (Oxford, 1671) and into English by George Ashwell (London, 1686). This was almost immediately followed by a Dutch translation by Adriaan Reland (Rotterdam, 1701 and Utrecht, 1721). In the 18th century the story of Ibn Yaqẓān became a true literary success in the Netherlands. I dealt with it in a conference paper, "Plato, Aristotle and the Ideal of the

pretations of knowledge as a kind of mystic vision, taught both by Plato and Aristotle, is expressed with a striking precision by Plutarch, *De Iside et Osiride*, c. 77, 382D-E.[16]

III. The Akinetos Ousia

Plato's metaphysics was one of purely spiritual being which he refers to as τὰ νοητά. Aristotle, too, held a metaphysics of pure spiritual beings. There cannot be any doubt that he intended to conceive his noetic beings in such a way as to correct Plato's conception which he rejected as a total failure. A failure because in Aristotle's view it could not do what was needed. Metaphysically speaking, what was needed was a Principle or Being which could account for the existence of this our sensible world in the absolute sense of being its total cause. Aristotle could not find such a Principle in Plato's conception of a noetic Reality which, nonetheless, was clearly conceived as a "hypothesis," in the Greek sense of a logically and ontologically necessary *ground*, to explain both the "being" – comprehending both the "existence" and the qualitative nature of "all things" – and our knowledge of them. It cannot serve that purpose, Aristotle declares, for while being conceived as perfect and therefore exemplary Being, it does not account for the existence of a sensible world at all, since an efficient cause is lacking. Now since Aristotle thought this way – a view which at this stage of our argument we simply take as a starting point without checking its content with regard to its metaphysical correctness – it is clear what he was aiming at by his own conception of purely spiritual Being.

Aristotle starts from the *factum* of a moving world. Motion does not spring from itself; it is always caused by something external to the moving object. Within this visible world an infinite series of moving causes can be detected to explain one single motion. The very process of generation cannot be explained by pointing to one physical efficient cause: "A man begets a man." A meta-physical man-in-himself is not needed. But is the physical efficient cause sufficient in itself? Aristotle supplies his account

---

Contemplative Life," given in Italian at Genoa and published in the *Giornale di Metafisica* (Genoa, 1961), pp. 450-466. It was printed in English (unfortunately with a large number of misprints) in *Philippiniana Sacra*, 2 (1967), 672-692 – the theological review of the oldest university in the Far East, the University Santo Tomás in Manila. The Dutch text can be found in my volume entitled *Theoria* (Assen, 1967), pp. 154-171; the Ibn Ṭufayl story is found on pp. 161-166.

[16] *Aristotelis Fragmenta Selecta*, p. 22: Eudemus, frag. 9.

with the sober addition, "and the sun." [17] That is to say, though organic beings generate themselves, the heavenly bodies, especially the sun, have an important part in the physical process of generation.

The quotation is found in the final passage of *Physica* 2.2. It is a passage in which the author wishes to indicate where precisely the border line between physics and metaphysics has to be drawn. The physicist is concerned with an εἶδος, but with an εἶδος that is realized in matter, not with any separately existing *eidos*. Such a separately existing εἶδος would not have any function at all with regard to physical things, and Aristotle therefore rejects it completely. However, he does see that the physical process of generation points to a higher kind of reality which transcends the physical order. In that superior order new questions have to be asked such as, what is the cause of the planetary motions, and how are we to explain the external motion of the outer οὐρανός? It is here that for Aristotle physics lead the way to metaphysics, for external motion must have an eternal cause and an eternal cause cannot be found in the order of nature.

In *Physica* 8 Aristotle argues purely from physics: the fact of an eternal process of motion necessarily requires the existence of an eternal first Movent which, while being First, must be itself unmovable and, while being eternal, must be always active. Aristotle expresses its perfection in terms of quantity: it can have no parts nor magitude because in a finite magnitude resides a finite force which could not be the cause of eternal motion. Hence it must be incorporeal, having nothing potential within itself. And it will be exempt from any change, for the motion caused by it is both continuous and perfectly unitary. Lastly, Aristotle localizes the First Movent with regard to the universe: the outer οὐρανός moves with the highest speed; it must depend immediately on the First Movent; therefore, the First Movent is situated nearest the οὐρανός, outside of it. [18]

It is clear from Aristotle's argument that he conceives the First Movent as the ultimate cause of *all* motion, not only of that of the outer heavens but also of the eternal process of physical generation. Somehow there seems to be a continuity. The argument is carried on in *Metaphysica* Λ.7, 1072b4-11. It has been argued that there is something which moves unceasingly without being moved: the unmoved Movent of the outer heavens. This Movent must be eternal and substantial, and full of reality (1072a25: ἀίδιον καὶ οὐσία καὶ ἐνέργεια). Now that which is moved, even by the first and best kind of motion, can also be otherwise. That is to say, it is

---

[17] *Physica* 2.2, 194b13.
[18] The argument of *Physica* 8 is summed up and concluded in ch. 10, 267a27-b9.

not necessarily such as it is. Its Mover, however, which eternally moves it without being moved, is by necessity that which it is; it could not be otherwise while being full reality, and in so far it is in a good state – καλῶς ἔχει, Aristotle's way of expressing "it is perfect Being" – "and in this sense [i.e., 'therefore,' or 'as such'] it is First Principle."

Certainly the predicate καλῶς ἔχει sounds very different from a modern theist's words, and even from Plato's "God is good." Aristotle is making an ontological statement. He is reflecting on a Being which he recognizes to be *per se* and *a se* while being "immovable," i.e., not liable to any change or influence whatsoever – it proves to be completely independent. This is a high status. Such a being is a "Principle," and even in the strictest sense both the heavens and Nature depend on it (1072b13-14).

These words are immediately followed by the description of the διαγωγή of this highest Being (b14-30). It is described in terms of life and thinking, and its thinking is from the outset qualified as "thinking-in-itself" which is about "that which is best in itself." Next, as if such a qualification needed to be protected against any form of detraction from its intended absoluteness, the author adds, "and Thinking in the fullest sense is about that which is best in the highest degree" (b18-19). The word "God" is not yet mentioned, but it is used thrice toward the end of the passage, in lines 25-30.

The actual function of the intellect (νοῦς) is "something divine," Aristotle thinks; it occurs in man by actually "grasping" the intelligible object, by "touching" it, so that the intellect and its object become united to the point of identification. If, therefore, such is the actual thinking process which happens in the human mind now and then but is always realized in God, this compels our wonder. Once more Aristotle marks the difference between human thinking and the Thinking Mind of God. Just as he made a double distinction between the "thinking-in-itself" about "that which is best in itself" and human thought, so here again he draws a double distinction: God is *always* in that blessed state in which we *sometimes* are; this is wonderful – but it is not enough to say so. It has to be reinforced: "And if He is in a better state, this compels our wonder yet more. And He *is* in a better state indeed."

It would hardly be possible to "separate" God more radically than Aristotle did when describing his First Movent's thinking in its absoluteness: it is a self-contemplation which categorically excludes everything of a lower level than the Highest-Himself. His is the undisturbed joy – Aristotle says pleasure – of that contemplation. If a moving force goes out of Him, it is clear that this happens not by purpose or deliberate will but as a consequence of His perfection. Πᾶν τέλειον γεννᾷ, said Plotinus. And so it is with Aristotle's God. He is Cause, even a universal cause: "On such a Principle the heavens and Nature depend."

The philosopher also tells us *how* this happens: a kind of attraction to Him goes out of Him to that which immediately depends on Him, the outer heavens. Should we really ascribe a soul to the οὐρανός who would be "loving" God in His perfection?

It is quite understandable that ancient commentators took it that way, and that Arabic philosophers followed them. Plato certainly regarded the stars as ensouled living beings, and from a number of quotations from the Περὶ φιλοσοφίας Aristotle appears to have held the same or a similar view,[19] probably a few years earlier than *Metaphysica Λ*. Ascribing a soul to the outer οὐρανός and to other heavenly spheres as well must have been a rather familiar idea to the philosophers of late antiquity who could easily imagine that Aristotle's unmoved Movers were divine Minds corresponding to the Souls of the celestial spheres they had to move. Whether Aristotle himself conceived it that way is another question. I am rather inclined to demythologize the heavenly spheres of Aristotle and understand the moving forces going out from the First Movent as an "attraction" in the physical sense.

IV. PROBLEMS INVOLVED IN ARISTOTLE'S CONCEPTION

That was one problem which Aristotle left to us. There are more, but this one is quite fundamental since it concerns the very character of Aristotle's explanation of the universe: did he look at it as a living being, ruled by a universal psychic force of upward striving love, from the lowest stage of being, ὕλη "longing" for its Form, through the whole order of the cosmic spheres, all ensouled beings, loving their unmoved Movent, up to the outer οὐρανός which "loves" the First Movent because of its ontic perfection? It is curious that this beautiful and poetic dream of a living universe has been so generally ascribed to Aristotle who, as a matter of fact, did not do much to evoke it but rather gave manifold indications against that pious dream. In the vi[th] Symposium Aristotelicum (1972) J. B. Skemp,[20] treating the theme "The Activity of Immobility," made a sober remark, saying, "It may perhaps be remarked that in spite of the words κινεῖ ὡς ἐρώμενον Aristotle says little about ἔρως – far less, in fact, than Plato. Both in *De generatione et corruptione* 2.10 and in the biological

---

[19] *Aristotelis Fragmenta Selecta*, pp. 90-94: Περὶ φιλοσοφίας, frag. 21-27.
[20] *Études sur la Métaphysique d'Aristote*, Actes du vi[e] Symposium Aristotelicum (Paris: Vrin, 1979), p. 237.

account in *De generatione animalium* the whole emphasis is on the heat which promotes generation (due to the ὑπέκκαυμα created by the sun's movement in his sphere in the one case and the internal θερμόν in the other)." He was right. J. M. Rist, quoted by Skemp in the same paper,[21] was certainly not the first in making *Physica* 1, 192a16-25, in which Aristotle speaks of a "desire" of ὕλη for its εἶδος, the basis of that lovely view of an upward striving love pervading the universe, from the most humble kind of being up to the transcendent Movers, all "longing for" the perfection of the First.

The assumption of such a universal upward striving makes it possible to come to a fine coherent whole of "all things created" longing for Him who is their ultimate Cause and End.[22] However, there are serious objections to that theory. First, in *Physica* 1.9 Aristotle opposes his theory on coming-to-be to Plato's, arguing that, whereas three principles are needed to explain the genesis of a physical object, Plato assumed only two. While two opposites must be assumed that exclude each other, a third principle is needed as a recipient for the positive of the two. So "matter" is a πρός τι: it does not exist in and for itself but is an element predisposed to receive its form with which it will unite into a concrete natural being. In fact, this account is somewhat one-sided, for Aristotle views the form not as a being that exists independently either; we might say the form too is a πρός τι in so far as it needs a ὕλη in order to be realized as a natural thing. But of the two components, matter and form, it is the form that makes the concrete being that which it is. And so Aristotle can say that matter "longs for" its form, in view of becoming "something." This is rather a natural way of speaking, but it is clearly a metaphorical one.

Further, when in natural objects the form is realized in its matter, then the "end" of a process is reached: the thing is that which it is. To be sure, within the realm of Nature further processes of "becoming something" are possible; new forms may be accepted in the thing which in that case becomes again "matter" relative to its new form. Such is the process of physical change. But it is confined to the order of Nature. Where is the "longing" for a form which in its absoluteness belongs to a higher order, not needing matter at all? Is it not rather the case that natural things having reached their end within themselves are not disposed to have any

---

[21] Ibid., p. 236.

[22] This interpretation is rather widespread among scholastics, but this view is also shared by Karl Barth, *Die kirchliche Dogmatik*, 4.2 (Zollikon-Zurich, 1955), p. 838. See also L. B. Geiger, *Aristote et Saint Thomas d'Aquin* (Louvain, 1957), esp. p. 202.

further desire? The physical order of Aristotle is, so it appears, rather a
closed order. Only νοῦς transcends it; the active intellect of man, which by
its nature is not of the natural order but has come to man "from without,"
will return to those higher regions as soon as the human composite dies.

"Yonder" a whole series of purely spiritual Beings are supposed to
exist: they are the unmoved Movers of the heavenly spheres, divine
beings, "gods," as Aristotle declares in the final passage of *Metaphysica*
Λ.8.[23] Of course, he is not identifying them with the First Movent; nobody
will suppose that. But apparently there is a whole series of divine beings
goign down from the heavenly spheres nearest the outer οὐρανός to those
which are nearest the earth. It is rational to believe that the divine νοῦς of
man will find its place in the spheres nearest the earth.

Now the ἀκίνητα that move the heavenly spheres are all purely spiritual
beings, pure "forms," having their "end" in themselves. How then to
attribute a "desire" for the First Movent to them as for their supreme and
ultimate Good? Such an idea does not fit into Aristotle's conception of
purely spiritual Being. Each of them is conceived as a Substance *in se*,
working on its celestial sphere by its perfection. By that very perfection,
however, it cannot be supposed to have any "love" or desire for any
supposedly higher Being beyond it. It is an "object of love" to its heavenly
sphere, which may be either explained by supposing those spheres to be
ensouled or simply as a matter of physical attraction. Anyhow, it is not the
ἀκίνητα themselves that may be supposed to "desire" any Being beyond
them.

This line of argument, I think, follows Aristotelian conceptions. They
really do not give us reasons for accepting that beautiful dream of upward
striving love throughout the universe, directed toward the highest
Good – God – in his supreme perfection.

That was one problem. When going back to the basic chapter 6 of Book
Λ, I find there another one. First it is argued (1071b19ff.) that eternal
motion can only be caused by a principle whose very essence is act. Of
such a principle, then, Aristotle speaks, as he often does, in the plural;
"these substances must be without matter; for they must be eternal if
anything is eternal. Therefore they must be act."

It is to the ἀκίνητα, the unmoved Movers of the heavenly spheres, that
he is thus referring in the plural. Their number will be fixed and their role
explained in another chapter (8).

[23] *Metaphysica* Λ.8, 1074a38-b20.

Further on in chapter 6 (1072a9-17) he speaks of the two kinds of movement which rule the cosmic order: there is a constant cycle (that of the first οὐρανός), always remaining the same and the cause of the permanence in the world, and there is also another movement (the sun's) which works in different ways (ἄλλως καὶ ἄλλως) – in one way "in virtue of itself" (καθ' αὐτό) but also in another way (κατ' ἄλλο). What is this ἄλλο? Is it the first, or is it something else? Aristotle replies that it is better to say the first. For that was the cause of permanence or uniformity, and something else is the cause of variety (of generation and death), and both together of eternal variety.

> This then is the character of the cosmic motions. What need then is there to seek for other principles? (1072a17-18)

In this passage it is suggested in a way that "the heavens and nature" depend on the First Movent in so far as the sun is said to have its own movement, although it moves in virtue of "the first." It has also been said at the end of chapter 4 (1070b34-35) and it is said again in chapter 7 (1072b13-14) that there is a ubiquitous causality of the First Movent. It even seems at the end of chapter 6 that no other principles are needed. Yet a whole system of heavenly spheres is introduced, each of which is moved by its own unmoved Mover, to account for the movements of the planets. This is, to put it mildly, somewhat unexpected after the end of chapter 6. And I am really not so sure that we can solve the inherent problem by the lovely dream of upward striving love.

If it be asked after all, is there one ultimate total cause or are there many causes, I think that we might reply for Aristotle that there is one ultimate cause and there are many causes. Is there one God or many? – One and many. That at least is what Aristotle holds, and apparently with satisfaction.

Lastly there is the vexing problem of Providence. In the first unmoved Mover, thinking of itself in its absoluteness, there seems to be no place for the thought of anything of a lower level, say of our world and human things. Some readers of Aristotle, both ancient and modern, have felt reminded of Epicurus' blessed gods who, undisturbed by suchlike troubles, lead an august life of eternal bliss in lofty isolation. Others followed the way of a more Platonic and rather Augustinian interpretation, declaring that in Aristotle's view "intelligible Being" as such is "the best": as the object of divine Thinking it *is* the divine Mind itself. From this perspective the forms of visible things can certainly not be excluded from the divine Thinking: qua νοητά they are "in" the Mind of God, in a different way from our mind, but certainly they are his. By such

an interpretation divine Providence would no doubt be saved, and a
wonderful theology of a "theistic" God would be the upshot. Texts of
Aristotle pleading in favour of divine Providence are not lacking. So this
interpretation would meet a real need.

No doubt one can construct such a theology on reasonable grounds. St.
Thomas did, and from his point of view with the greatest right. However,
if it be asked what *Aristotle* said and had in mind, we cannot declare that
this is what he said or even that the logical sequence of his argument
would necessarily lead this way. No, it does not. Keeping within the
framework of his argument we must state the following.

(1) Aristotle offers a coherent account of the physical world, physical
objects having their "end" in themselves which is realized by efficient
causes.

(2) It is not altogether a closed account: the efficient causes transcend
the physical order. "A man produces a man – *and the sun*." No "ideal
man" is needed for the process of generation, *but moving causes* are not
limited to the physical world. They depend on further causes, going up to
the heavenly bodies and – so it appears sometimes – to the First Moving
Power that moves everything (*Metaphysica* Λ.4, the end, and 5,
1071a35f.).

(3) However, when the Prime Mover is described in his essence, we
cannot say that in Aristotle's view Divine Thinking by thinking of Itself
implicitly thinks the intelligible forms of all things existing.[24] That is not
Aristotle but a Platonized Aristotle as he has been understood from late
Antiquity onward by Alexandrian commentators of the Neoplatonist
school and by the Syrian and Arabic philosophers who were the heirs of
late Greek philosophy. This is also the Platonized Aristotle who, interpreted by such important Arabic commentators as Avicenna and
Averroes, found his way to the Christian philosophers and theologians of
the high Middle Ages in the twelfth and thirteenth centuries.

V. PLATO AND ARISTOTLE IN ST. THOMAS AQUINAS

St. Thomas studied Aristotle in the then recent Latin translations and he
did so using the commentaries of Averroes. From Aristotle he took his
information on the Platonic Ideas – *ideae separatae* – existing by
themselves, independently, outside of the Mind of God. That is what he

---

[24] On this I agree substantially with J. Owens in *Études sur la Métaphysique d'Aristote*,
Actes du viᵉ Symposium Aristotelicum, pp. 219f.

supposed Platonic doctrine to be; this he rejected as going against the Christian doctrine of creation. On the other hand he absorbed Plato's metaphysics of transcendent Being, understanding it in the spirit of true Platonism in the same way as it had been understood before him by St. Augustine.[25] Augustine acknowledged Plato's νοητά to be the Word or Wisdom of God. God, the cause of all things, knows all things in Himself not as *alia a se* but as *causatum* which has its origin in Him. In *Summa contra gentiles* 49 Thomas quotes Dionysius the Areopagite, *De divinis nominibus* 5.7: not by seeing concrete things, but by their noetic presence in Him as Cause He knows all things.

Here we have come to another important source of Platonism in St. Thomas, the Areopagitica and their background, Proclus. There is no reason to consider Proclus, the *Liber de causis* and Dionysius to be the only or even the essential source. Klaus Kremer[26] was well aware of the danger of making a one-sided approach, and of course if one is conscious of the limits of one's work, one is justified in doing so in some special study. I think, however, that Kremer might at least have mentioned Augustine with some emphasis as another Platonic influence on St. Thomas, be it only to prevent the misunderstanding that "Platonism" came to St. Thomas solely, or at least essentially, by the Proclus lineage. As a matter of fact, that misunderstanding has regrettably been promoted by Kremer's work.[27]

---

[25] In *De veritate*, q. 3 "De ideis," Thomas refers to Augustine; also in sт 1.14.5 and 1.15.1 and 2. God knows all things in Himself, for the Cause of all things knows the causatum. Cf. sᴄɢ 1.54.

[26] Klaus Kremer, *Die neuplatonische Seinsphilosophie und ihre Wirkung auf Thomas von Aquin* (Leiden, 1966).

[27] E.g., p. 187, Kremer mentions as a correction made by Thomas on "the Platonists" that he totally abandoned the distinction between God as the *bonum* or *unum* and the idea of Being. "God *is* Being." Was not this the place to prevent the error that Thomas would have been the first to correct in the Platonists? Augustine made it with the greatest emphasis (*De libro arbitrio*, 2.15.39). Was it not worth while to remember that?

Another serious misunderstanding is not only not prevented, but is directly advocated by Kremer, pp. 190f., where he profoundly misinterprets Plato, *Republic* 509b. Following an older German tradition which separated Plato as much as possible from Plotinus, he rather naively denies that Plato held what he calls "a principle, which represents the fulness of being, or say the *ipsum esse subsistens*, which is surpassed by the Good as the actual top of Being." Now for the readers of books 5 to 7 of the *Republic* this is hardly credible talk. How can one deny that in those books Plato is concerned with *intelligible Being as the* ὄντως ὄν ? (See, e.g., 476b-480a; at the beginning of book 6, 484b, the definition of the φιλόσοφος; 509d-11e. What does Kremer think the νοητόν to be?) Next, after reading 508e-509b, how can anyone deny that "above knowledge and truth" – which according to the whole preceding argument is "reality-itself" (= *ipsum esse subsistens*) – there is said to be "something else, which is still more beautiful than

Moreover, it must be remembered that Thomas, when studying Aristotle's *Metaphysica*, found in Averroes the information that Aristotle called the forms, immanent in things, θεῖα, which is correct. Hence God knows the "forms" of things, i.e., God knows the intelligible essence of things. Both Avicenna and Averroes remained Aristotelians in holding that God knows things only in general. Thomas replied that that would make a very imperfect kind of knowledge; God must know things in their individuality.[28]

It is remarkable that those modern interpreters of Aristotle who explain the divine Thinking-of-Himself as thinking intelligible objects – since the intelligible object is identified with the divine Mind itself who is thinking it – argue in principle along the lines of Avicenna's and Averroes' argument but use it to pass from the immanent εἶδος to Plato's transcendant νοητόν. That is, for example, what Brentano did and what in our generation happened in the minds of H. J. Krämer and J. N. Findlay.[29]

---

these"; next, that these two, knowledge and truth, are referred to as ἀγαθοειδῆ (similar to the Good), but not to be considered as the Good-itself which is *the Cause* of both of them and therefore to be ranked higher: "It is *not Being*, but *ranks still higher than Being, surpassing it in dignity and power.*" That is clear language. And how can Kremer, after reading the following pages with the basic opposition of νοητόν to αἰσθητόν – which any reader of the *Republic* will understand as "true Being" ("Reality itself" = *ipsum esse subsistens*) to that which, as an εἰκών of Reality, does not have any "substance" in itself – tell us that this means only that the Good is better than "all *created* being" ("dass sie alles *geschaffene* Sein übertrifft")? Plato in the *Republic* does not speak of "created being," only of "real Being" – which is the νοητόν, directly caused by the ἀγαθόν, which as a Cause is ranked "beyond" true Being – and of "visible things" which are never called "being" without restriction; not in the *Timaeos* either, where a "created world" is described as a beautiful "image" of that which is true Reality. Kremer is seriously in error here in the most elementary understanding of Plato's text.

[28] ST 1.14.6; SCG 1.50.

[29] H. J. Krämer in his first great work, *Arete bei Platon und Aristoteles* (Heidelberg, 1959), started with a realistic-historical account of Aristotle's concept of God in *Metaphysica* Λ. He stated that there was no place there for divine Providence – the Thinking of God being strictly confined to Himself – and came to the rather unsatisfactory conclusion that Aristotle's explanation of the universe suffered heavily from that "episodicity" which he condemned in others. However, in his next work, *Der Ursprung der Geistphilosophie* (Amsterdam, 1964), Krämer appears to have taken the way of a highly speculative interpretation: thinking, so he says, is always of a νοητόν and implies the identification of the thinking mind with its object. The Divine Mind, therefore, always thinks the νοητόν, and in thinking it the νοητόν is God-Himself (p. 404). Krämer remarkably explains divine Thinking as an impersonal process, a "Selbstbewegung der Begriffe" (pp. 410-412). He even declares this to be a question of mathematical order: "Was denkt, ist zunächst die Ordnung selbst, in ihr und durch sie aber die Zahl." Here Number is supposed to be the essential principle of the cosmic order. Moreover, Number is in particular the principle that makes relations possible. As such it is at the same time

We found St. Thomas when reflecting on the Divine knowledge referring also to Dionysius, *De divinis nominibus* 5.7. In this remarkable chapter 5 we find the Good identified with pure Being and referred to as "Him who gives being to everything that exists" (par. 4). With a reference to Exodus 3:14 Dionysius says, "*He who is* (ὁ ὤν) is in power and ὑπερουτιώδως the substantial cause of all existence, of all essence, of all being in time, duration and becoming." Again, referring to 1 Timothy 1:17 he says, "Therefore, they call him 'King of the ages', King eternal, because everything exists in Him and is related to Him. He himself is not in time, He is the Being of beings, which comes forth from Being which precedes all ages."

He explains (ch. 5): He precedes as Principle and Cause. All beings participate in Him and He is present to every being. The first in which all things participate is existence. After that comes life, wisdom and divine resemblance. And (ch. 6-7): on this all other things depend – unity, number and order, harmony and power, intellection, reason and sense-perception, motion and rest, friendship, concordance and distinctions, all come forth from Being.

---

the model of intelligible living and of thinking ("die Ur- und Grundform des intelligibilen Lebens- und Denkvollzug").

This may seem to us a rather strange and artificial theory. Can one really declare the order of number to be something like a thinking mind?

Up to a certain degree Krämer has noticed something which is actually present in Plato's thought. In a well-known and important passage of the *Sophistes*, when reflecting on perfect Being, he comes to the statement that it is not possible that perfect Being should be without life and motion, soul and intelligence (248e-249a). Here we see, indeed, something like *impersonal thinking*: perfect Being appears to be living, ensouled and "wise." I think that we have to acknowledge that it is seen here as a ζῷον, and because perfect, an ensouled and thinking one. We find this confirmed in *Timaeus* 37d where the visible world, which has been made after its eternal example, is welcomed by the divine Craftsman as a perfect living being.

Of Plato's "perfect Being" we can say, in fact, that "it thinks," that is to say, it is involved in an impersonal thinking process. However, declaring "the order of Number" to be an impersonal thinking process is a different thing. The *Sophist* passage is not concerned with number, and applying the notion of ζῷον to a numerical Order can only be done by starting from later developments, which can hardly be said to be either representative of or originally identical with the Greek conception of thinking.

Krämer once more deals explicitly with Aristotle's conception of divine Thinking in "Grundfragen der aristotelischen Theologie," *Theol. und Philos.*, 44 (1969), 363-382, 481-505. Cf. J. N. Findlay, *Plato, The Written and Unwritten Doctrines* (London, 1974), p. 364. On the other hand P. Aubenque, *Le problème de l'être chez Aristote* (Paris, 1962), pp. 487 and 499 n. 5, keeps more strictly to Aristotle's text and finds good sense in it. For him "la Pensée qui se pense elle-même" remains "la pensée qui se pense elle-même." So does O. Gigon in his article, "Aristotle," in *Th.R.E.*, 3: 748.

Of this remarkable account, which, by the way, bears a few unmistakable Pythagorean features, the essential element is found again in St. Thomas, SCG 1. He refutes that wrong interpretation of the Areopagitica which declared God to be the "formal being," that is, the essence of all things. A few generations earlier this had been taught at Paris by Amalric of Bena and was also held by David of Dinant. Thomas replies (ch. 26): God is not the formal being of things. Things have different natures, God has one essence, and He *is* his essence. In it all different qualities, and first of all existence iself, are comprehended as a unity. They are rooted in Him and stem from Him. But He himself is not directly "in us." There is a certain resemblance but not the direct presence of God. *In a sense* He is in all things, namely as their cause; but not as their form or essence.

Again in chapter 29: there is in things a certain likeness to God. There is a likeness and there is not. Thomas refers here again to Dionysius, *De divinis nominibus*, ch. 9 in which both the likeness and the unlikeness are explicitly dealt with. That which in God is perfect is very imperfect in created things. They *receive* their likeness from Him. Hence it can never be said that "God is like his creatures."

Again in SCG 1.54 Thomas refers to Dionysius, *De divinis nominibus* 5.5. St. Thomas' chapter is about the question, "How the Divine Essence, which is one and simple, yet is the particular likeness of all things intelligible." The "forms" or essences of things can only be in the Divine Mind. Hence Dionysius speaks of *exemplaria* (παραδείγματα καὶ προορισμοί). Thomas once more refers to Augustine's *De diversis quaestionibus lxxxiii*, qu. 46: "et *rationes rerum* pluraliter in Mente divina esse dicit."

In chapter 65 and following, Thomas argues that God also knows things which are particular, non-eternal, temporal, non-necessary; that He knows that which is infinite and knows even things futile and vile: "Quantum enim aliqua virtus activa est fortior, tanto in remotiora suam actionem extendit" (SCG 1.70). Here we are literally in Proclus, *Elementatio theologica*, who expounded his view of Divine knowledge and power as follows:

> Every god has an undivided knowledge of things divided, and a timeless knowledge of things temporal; he knows the contingent without contingency, the mutable immutably, and in general all things in a higher mode than belongs to their station. (Prop. 124)
>
> All the powers of the gods, taking their origin above and proceeding through the appropriate intermediates, descend even to the last existents and the terrestrial regions. (Prop. 140)

> All that is generative in the gods proceeds in virtue of the infinitude of divine potency, multiplying itself and penetrating all things. (Prop. 152).[30]

St. Thomas read and meditated on the *Liber de causis* which is not a pure rendering of Proclus' *Elementatio* but a theistic version of it.[31] However, its contents, the Proclean origin of which was clear to him, interested him so much that he requested William of Moerbeke to provide him with a Latin translation of that work of Proclus. About 1270 we find Thomas working on that Latin text. Important elements of the doctrine of the Areopagite were found in it: that there is one First Cause of all things existing, and that this Cause is identified with the Good; that Being or Essence is the first that comes forth from it and that from Being "all the principles which participate the divine character" come forth (prop. 11, 12 and 138); that the divine knowledge, by virtue of its own infinite potency, extends to everything being. Proclus enlarges on this in a way which we recognize in the long series of Thomas' arguments in scg book 1, from chapter 64 onwards; we found similar views of Divine thinking in earlier mentioned chapters. However, there are striking differences. We found Dionysius identifying the Good with Being-itself, and next speaking of "Him who is" as imparting "being" to all things. Neither the first-mentioned identification nor the following development is found in Proclus. With him all things "proceed" from the first Cause, but this coming-forth is described as an impersonal process which in its very outset happens as by an inner necessity. There is no "He who is" who by His divine Will imparts being to other things.

In Proclus, though he says most emphatically that "all that exists proceeds from a single first cause" (propr. 11), the remarkable thing is that in treating "the operation of primary Causes on later things" he always speaks in the plural and sometimes, in particular in the beginning, in the rather vague terms of a neutral collective – such as τὰ πρότερα καὶ αἰτιώτερα (prop. 56) or πᾶν τὸ ὁλικώτερον ἐν τοῖς ἀρχηγικοῖς (prop. 70) – but later on, in the long section on Divine Henads, he speaks of "the gods." We find Proclus particularly interested in the *immediate* operation of the First Cause on all "later" things, down to the most humble and unworthy kinds of being. After Plotinus – and Plato! – this concern for the directness of the working of the First Cause even on matter is something new and more or less surprising.

---

[30] Translation of E. R. Dodds in his *Proclus, The Elements of Theology* (Oxford, 1933); see his commentary on this proposition, p. 266.

[31] I gave my view in "Reflexions on the Liber de Causis," *Vivarium*, 4 (1966), 67-82.

That the First Principle in virtue of its infinite potency in fact "imparts" something of its unity to sensible things, and thus extends even to matter, was also true for Plotinus as it had been for Plato. However, those earlier thinkers viewed that working of the First and highest as mediated by at least two classes of secondary and tertiary causes, those of the νοῦς level and those of the soul level. For Plato, the Good is not immediately the cause of cosmic order and, say, of the unity and beauty of sensible things. This world of ours has, so he thought, its heavenly example in the intelligible Order which alone is the ὄντως ὄν; and the direct cause of its order is that divine Soul which, created by a God who is a divine Intellect himself, pervades our world and by its presence bestows harmonious proportions, unity, beauty and permanence on it. Likewise, Plotinus believed that even Matter partakes of Goodness. But he did not at all imagine that the One directly illuminated Matter because νοῦς and Soul were supposed not to penetrate that far. His thought took the way of progressing intermediate causes: Matter partakes of the good because, and in so far as, it is illuminated by Soul; and that is what actually happens if, and only if, the Soul continues looking at that which is "before her," i.e., νοῦς.[32] Proclus basically accepts the same ontological order. He too speaks of "secondary principles" and of his gods as "proceeding through the appropriate intermediaries." Yet the secondary beings are all headed by a first and sovereign cause (prop. 97) from which they derive their productive power. The primary cause is a more determinative principle (prop. 56); it is both prior and more efficacious; it remains present in its participants and does not withdraw when the secondary causes have ceased to work (prop. 70).

Thus Proclus can say that things are brought into being "by the Gods immediately" and that the Divine is present even in that which seems most remote from it. He does not mean, however, that *the One* would act directly on all things. For him the One is beyond participation. "The gods" which he introduces as primary causes of all things are the Henads which he places at the head of each ontological level of being. There are also ἐγκόσμιοι ἑνάδες which represent the One immediately. To their immediate operation Proclus attributes the order of lifeless material things.

Dodds[33] remarked that this is a post-Plotinian development but that Proclus was not the first to apply it; it is found in principle in the *Metaphysics* of his predecessor Syrianus. In an earlier paper[34] I raised the

---

[32] *Enneads* 3.9.3.7-16; 4.8.6.16-28; 2.3.18.8-22. These passages are quoted in the same context in my article, "Reflexions...," pp. 75f.

[33] In his comments on proposition 57 – *Proclus, The Elements of Theology*, p. 231.

[34] "Reflexions on the Liber de Causis."

question of how these fifth-century Platonists came to emphasize so strongly the universality and immediate operation of the First Cause(s) in every part of the universe. I suggested that this development might be due to Christian influence: it might be a reaction to the Christian belief in an almighty Creator. Since that belief spread so widely in their age, those late Greek Platonists may have felt the need of constructing some counterpart to Christian theism by formulating more clearly the actual influence of the First Cause on everything derived from it. I think indeed that this need may be behind Proclus' theory of divine Henads.

Another question concerns the rank given to Being in Proclus' system. It is not so surprising to find "Being" mentioned first after the One. Plato himself spoke of the Good as the Cause of intelligible Being and emphatically placed the Good beyond it. For Plotinus τὰ νοητά, which are identical with Divine νοῦς, are first of all τὰ ὄντα. These are on no account "being" because they are thought of. They are not a product or "Setzung des Denkens." They are "Being" primarily, the ὄντως ὄν. So it is in Proclus too. However, that the First Cause itself should be identified with Being, as was done by the Areopagite and by the author of the *Liber de causis*, was not in Proclus. With the Areopagite the memory of Exodus 3:14 is alive just as it was in Augustine, and the author of the *De causis*, who from the outset of his work followed Proclus on the greater intensity and further reaching influence of the First Cause, separated himself from Proclus in speaking of the First Cause as "being." No doubt he followed his own religious tradition in this.

This is not the place to deal more explicitly with the particulars of Proclus' metaphysical system. However, it must be noticed that the form he gave to Neoplatonism was rather different from Plotinus' conception as expounded in, e.g., *Enneads* 5.1, the treatise on the three basic hypostases. Plotinus' rendering of Plato's thought was of a strict soberness in its structure. His doctrine of the three hypostases was very consciously and emphatically kept within these limits. Though Neoplatonism was handed down to later generations in the East Greek world from the beginning of the sixth century onward in the form which Proclus gave to it, and through the Areopagitica and the *Liber de causis* it had a considerable influence on Western Christian thought in the Middle Ages, it should not be overlooked that Neoplatonism in its earlier and more sober form had shown such a great thinker as St. Augustine the way to integrate Plato's metaphysics of transcendent Being into his Christian thought. In this Augustine took up the line of Platonism which existed among the thinking members of Christian churches from the second century onward, from Justin Martyr who had defined God as the eternal Being of

Plato's Ideas and their Cause, and from Origin who had found the "Forms" of all things as living in the Word of God according to John 1:4.

We must remember that Augustine's Platonism entered the Western Christian World before the Areopagitica and lived on in such a leading thinker as Anselm of Canterbury and in the School of Chartres. It was present to St. Thomas' mind before he came into contact with the Areopagitica and the *Liber de causis*. Proclus' *Elementatio theologica*, in the Latin form which William of Moerbeke gave it about 1268/1270, was "new material" for theologians in those days. As such the work asked for a commentary. When coming across the doctrine of the Divine Henads, Thomas, who had received his information about Plato's Ideas from Aristotle's *Metaphysica*, took those Proclean Henads to be the supposed "substantiae separatae" of Plato and dismissed them duly as a kind of pseudo-gods. A strange error, so it might seem to us; yet an understandable one. In fact Thomas was not far from understanding that which the Platonic Ideas really meant.[35] That he actually accepted them when reflecting on Divine Thinking and thus gave them their place in his doctrine of God appears clearly both in *Summa theologiae*, I, question 14 and following and in *Summa contra Gentiles* 1. What we find there is simply that Thomas introduced Plato's metaphysics of transcendent Being into Aristotle's conception of the Divine thinking Mind, restoring the bond of the Creator God with his creation through that reception. We found that in doing so, Thomas referred both to St. Augustine and to Dionysius' book, *On Divine Names*.

No doubt it was perfectly clear to St. Thomas that the Neoplatonism of Proclus could give rise to a few misinterpretations that would involve rather serious doctrinal errors. He refuted at least one of them, namely the theory that God is the "form" or essence of all things, and he prevented, in principle at least, a few others that could spring from the idea of "coincidence of opposites." In this matter a chapter in Dionysius' book, *On Divine Names*, became the basis for a few very unfortunate developments.

Here we come to a rather interesting problem. Those later developments which are generally referred to as forms of Neoplatonism will be found, in fact, to be running against the most elementary principles of Platonic philosophy. The following two doctrines are involved:

(1) From the thesis that opposites are one in God the inference is made that God is beyond moral good and evil ("jenseits von Gut und Böse").

(2) God-Absolute Being is identical with the nothing.

[35] This was excellently expounded by J. N. Findlay in his *Plato*, pp. 389ff.

Both these inferences are completely alien to the mind of Plato and to Plotinus as well. For Plato nothing was as important for man as the conviction that God is good and cannot be the cause of any evil, and nothing was as far from him as connecting the Cause of Being with non-being. Such a thought would have been to him the utmost of ἀσέβεια. And so it was for Plotinus too. How far he was from the idea of an amoral God may be seen from his violent reaction to those gnostics – they may have been Christians (!) – who pretended that there is a direct access to God for anyone. To those people Plotinus replies almost fiercely: how will they "look at Him" while being in the grip of passions and making no attempt to purify their souls? "God, if you talk about Him without true virtue, is nothing but a word." [36] As for non-being, for Plotinus that meant a complete lack of Good, which means that for him it was separated from the First as radically as possible.

I do not think that in this matter Proclus actually differed very much from earlier Platonism. With him there is certainly not a trace of mixing up the First and Absolute with the οὐδέν. On the contrary, such a thought is almost immediately discarded in the opening section of the *Elementatio*, proposition 5, toward the end. Did he give rise to misunderstanding concerning the coincidence of opposites? When reading the Areopagite's *De divinis nominibus*, chapter 9, it does not seem so. This chapter does not say anything either unreasonable or incorrect. However, problems might arise with the final paragraph of Dionysius' chapter 5. The text reads: "He who pre-exists is the beginning and end of all things, their beginning since He is their Cause and their end because all is done for His sake. He is also the limit of all things and their infinity, while being exalted above all infinity and limit, principles that stand, as it were, the one against the other." [37]

God is the πέρας and ἀπειρία of all things, while at the same time He is exalted above πέρας and ἀπειρία – the basic opposite principles in the universe. They were held to be so from the early Pythagoreans onward to Plato and the Academy, and in the Pythagorico-Platonism of later centuries. Proclus taught, according to this tradition, that Being is composed of those two elements, thus placing the infinite Principle "after" the First. "Prior to all that is composed of limit and infinitude there exist substantially and independently the first Limit and the first Infinity," he says (prop. 90).

[36] *Enneads* 2.9.15.39f.
[37] Ὁ προὼν ... πέρας πάντων καὶ ἀπειρία, πάσης ἀπειρίας καὶ πέρατος ὑπεροχικῶς ἐξῃρημένος τῶν ὡς ἀντικειμένων.

It is typical of Proclus that he could not identify the πέρας with the One, as was done by Plato himself and by earlier Pythagoreans. We find the ἀπειρόν placed under the μονάς as early as the second century BC,[38] but in that treatise the μονάς was the First Principle itself. Further, we find in Proclus a systematic method of hypostatizing abstracts so that he could, for instance, place "Being" as a wider concept "before" Eternity (prop. 87), and Infinity before Being. We find the Areopagite following Proclus in not taking the basic opposite Principles into the First. That was, however, done by the author of the *Liber de causis* who wrote (prop. 15), "Primum creans est infinitum purum." Dionysius did not go that far. Yet he *did* say that ὁ πρόων, "He who exists before all things," was the πέρας and ἀπειρόν of all things. And in chapter 9 we find him saying that God's greatness is without limits and His smallness without quantity; upon which he declares that God "as a unifying and transcendent Cause comprehends opposites within Himself under the mode of identity." This is true, no doubt, but it could give rise to misinterpretation and to such fatal consequences as in fact were drawn from it in later centuries.

As for St. Thomas, he simply integrated the notion of infinity into his concept of God. For the almighty Creator of all things of course had infinite power and dignity and in that sense could rightly be called infinite. No confusion with the nothing was possible in that perspective. When in later so-called Neoplatonism that thought came in, we must make the statement that this kind of perversion of Platonism did not follow at all from the essence of Platonic thought, as little as pantheism could be said to be a necessary consequence of Platonism.

There are some modern scholars who, in reply to the Tübingen theory of Platonism as a system of derivation from two ultimate principles, have expressed the opinion that Platonism had to end in immanentism, and that Christianity, in fact, had to turn to Aristotle in order to "save" its theological thought from that fatal tendency and to find the way to a concept of a really transcendent God.[39] Now this is a view which is curiously blind to the essence of Platonism which is, in fact, a theory of transcendent Being and was so strongly dominated by that vision that we must duly acknowledge it to be a profound intuition of what the Divine Mind actually is. This is how St. Augustine understood it through the mediation of the Neoplatonism of Plotinus and Porphyry. It is worth

---

[38] Supposing that the "Pythagorean books" referred to by Alexander Polyhistor went back to that age.

[39] This was E. Berti's reaction to K. Gaiser's book, *Platons ungeschriebene Lehre* (Stuttgart, 1963), as presented in *Giornale di Metafisica*, 19 (1964), 546-557.

noticing that Proclus' Neoplatonism also does not show any tendency to immanentism; on the contrary, it is a clear and outspoken philosophy based on the idea of a transcendent ultimate cause and on transcendent being.

Platonism, including the Neoplatonism of Proclus, had a whole series of true and false developments. By "true" or legitimate developments we have to understand those that keep the essential character of Platonism, that is, the character of a philosophy of transcendent Being. Wherever that character is abandoned, we no longer have Platonism at all; a pseudo-Platonism has arisen.

From the point of view of theology we must say that both Plato and Aristotle made important contributions to theology in its proper sense; moreover, that both of them showed deficiencies in their theological thinking – Plato by not coming to a metaphysical synthesis at all and Aristotle by separating his transcendent God from the world. What Christian theology had to do, and actually did, was to integrate Plato's metaphysics of transcendent Being into its own idea of a transcendent God. Aristotle's theory of the Prime Mover was used in Christian theology only at a much later date. It is St. Thomas Aquinas who by making a thorough use of Aristotle came to that integration of Platonic metaphysics in the framework of Aristotle's thought which might almost be called a synthesis. I used that term myself when in my inaugural discourse at the University of Utrecht in 1947 I spoke on the problems of continuity and difference between Plato and Aristotle, and considering their metaphysical thought in a historical perspective, ended with St. Thomas as a kind of synthesis.[40] After so many years I find in J. N. Findlay's work on Plato an elegant and striking expression of the character of that synthesis in the formula, "the hands are Aristotle's but the voice is that of Proclus or Plato." [41]

By this expression the accent is put on the Platonic character of St. Thomas' doctrine of God. I think that this is correct. For it is by introducing Plato's metaphysics of transcendent Being into the formal void of Aristotle's Prime Mover's Mind that the relation of the transcendent God to the world that depends on Him is rationally established and Divine Providence assured.

---

[40] *Een groot Probleem in de Antieke Wijsbegeerte, gezien in zijn historisch Perspectief* (Utrecht, 1947).

[41] Findlay, *Plato*, p. 394.

11

Intorno al fondamento dell'essere

Cornelio Fabro, css
Università di Perugia

L'essere nel titolo ha significato soggettivo, non oggettivo ossia l'essere non è inteso come il fondato ma come il fondante: esso è il primo atto e il primo Principio. Secondo Aristotele la filosofia è ἐπιστήμη τῶν πρώτων ἀρχῶν καὶ αἰτιῶν θεωρητικήν[1] e questo nel testo nel quale si dice che la meraviglia (τὸ θαυμάζειν) è il primo stimolo del filosofare. I primi principi e la prima causa stanno insieme alla base ed al vertice del filosofare: a scopo didattico diciamo che i primi principi stanno alla base, cioè all'inizio del cammino che è la filosofia, mentre la prima causa e per Aristotele le cause fondamentali sono quattro, subito elencate nel nostro contesto al capitolo seguente: τὰ αἴτια λέγεται τετραχῶς e la chiama τὴν οὐσίαν καὶ τὸ τί ἦν εἶναι ... ἐτέραν δὲ τὴν ὕλην καὶ τὸ ὑποκείμενον, τρίτην δὲ ὅθεν ἡ ἀρχὴ τῆς κινήσεως, τετάρτην ... τὸ οὗ ἕνεκα καὶ τἀγαθόν.[2]

Aristotele è legato al problema originario nel pensiero greco della φύσις, come realtà di movimento, i cui principi sono indicati come il termine di "causa" la cui esigenza cioè il significato "principale" è assolto in modo diverso nelle quattro cause ora indicate. Nel libro (7) sulla "Sostanza," dopo aver dato l'elenco delle categorie, il Filosofo fa la dichiarazione programmatica che ha fermato anche l'attenzione di Heidegger:[3] καὶ δὲ καὶ τὸ πάλαι τε καὶ νῦν καὶ ἀεὶ ζητούμενον καὶ ἀεὶ ἀπουρούμονον, τί τὸ ὄν, τοῦτό ἐστι τίς ἡ οὐσία.[4]

---

[1] *Metaphysica* A, 2, 982b9.
[2] *Metaph.* A, 3, 983a26-32. – L'origine storica è indicata più sotto: I, 5, 1010a1 ss.
[3] Cfr. M. Heidegger, *Was ist das – die Philosophie?* (Pfullingen, 1956), p. 24.
[4] *Metaph.* Z, 1, 1028b2-4. Riferendo questo testo, prima di Heidegger, J. Owens, osservava con ragione: "Knowledge of any type of *Being* whatsoever must be reduced to Knowledge of Entity." (*The Doctrine of Being in the Aristotelian Metaphysics*, Toronto, 1951, p. 183).

Graceful Reason: Essays in Ancient and Medieval Philosophy Presented to Joseph Owens, CSSR, ed. Lloyd P. Gerson. Papers in Mediaeval Studies 4 (Toronto: Pontifical Institute of Mediaeval Studies, 1983), pp. 229-237. © P.I.M.S., 1983.

Per Aristotele, com'è noto, il τὸ ὄν è un plesso polisemantico ossia è un termine (semantema) suscettibile di più significati in quanto conviene diversamente – secondo la tradizione aristotelica è detto "analogicamente" [5] – alla οὐσία ch'è l'ente principale, ed in dipendenza dalla sostanza alle altre categorie che sono le sue modificazioni: è così che τὸ ὄν λέγεται πολλαχῶς[6] ossia che l'ente si presenta in molti modi ai quali deve attendere il discorso di fondo sul significato della realtà che è ciò che deve fare la filosofia. Ed Aristotele, come già Platone ma in altro modo, sembra fermarsi qui: a sviscerare il significato dei "modi" (di apparire) dell'ente come sostanza, quantità, qualità, relazione..., secondo la gerarchia che vede la sostanza al primo posto. E l'essere della sostanza cioè la sua sostanzialità? Nelle realtà materiali si tratta della composizione di ὕλη (πρώτη) e μορφή (εἶδος ἐν τῷ συνθετῷ), nelle spirituali lo εἶδος e il νοῦς soltanto cioè l'intelligenza.

Sembra chiaro quindi che per Aristotele – e su questo punto il pensiero antico non è andato aldilà – lo εἶναι è riferito al contenuto del reale (all'essenza e ai suoi principi) ed alla sua struttura. E l'essere come tale? Aristotele, che afferma l'eternità del mondo non arriva a dire con Hegel che "l'essere e il nulla sono la stessa cosa (*dasselbe*)": però l'essere, a suo avviso (e questo è il punto), come verbo cede al nome la principalità semantica; "essere" – possiamo dire – resta in Aristotele il 'verbo ausiliare', anzi possiamo dirlo l'ausiliare universale, la funzione di connessione universale. La conclusione sembra ovvia: come ogni attribuzione, sia nominale sia verbale, si esprime mediante l'*esse*, così l'*esse* a sua volta si esprime (ed esprime) mediante [l'esse del] l'attribuzione. Un'emergenza propria dell'*esse*, come atto primo in sé e positività fondante κατ' ἐξοχήν, è per l'Aristotelismo inconcepibile. Con ciò non si vuol dire che l'*esse* si risolva in quest'attribuzione: Aristotele non è Kant e la φύσις, come presentarsi in atto dell'essere, non si discute (essa è ἀρχή come totalità sia si ὕλη come di ἕξις, εἶδος, ἐντελέχεια).[7] L'*esse* come atto perciò non si realizza anzitutto e perciò non si risolve nella funzione copulativa; infatti per Aristotele (come per ogni posizione di realismo) lo *esse* della proposizione, come atto unificante S e P, ossia la copula non è primario e fondante ma secondario e fondato.

---

[5] Aristotele nella *Metafisica* non usa il termine ἀναλογία ma l'aggettivo ἀνάλογον. Cfr. spec. Θ, 6, 1048a37 e b7.

[6] *Metaph.* Γ, 1, 1003a33.

[7] *Metaph.* Δ, 4 (φύσις), 1014b32 ss.; Z, 17, 1032a24; Λ, 3, 1070a11 ecc. – Lo riconosce anche un filosofo moderno vicino ad Heidegger: "He [Aristotele] expressly stated that he wanted to treat the question, what is being? as if it were the same as the question, what is substance?" (W. Marx, *The Meaning of Aristotle's Ontology* [The Hague, 1954], p. 29).

Il τὸ ὄν ὡς ἀληθές si fonda sullo *ens reale* categoriale[8] la cui figura (σχῆμα) prima e principale è la "sostanza" (οὐσία): tutta la "filosofia prima" di Aristotele si articola come una θεωρία dello *ens* come sostanza. Sembra quindi che nell'aristotelismo la priorità spetti al nome sul verbo, perché il verbo è aggiunto al nome per esprimere l'azione e la passione della sostanza, le forme e i modi del divenire.

Questo è confermato dall'affermazione capitale, che sta a fondamento del compendio della filosofia del linguaggio, che Aristotele espone nel *De interpretatione* ove, a confesma che il verbo ("parlare, scrivere, correre...") da solo non significa nulla, aggiunge come argomento che lo stesso *esse — est* come tale non è (da solo), non significa da solo nulla e quindi che lo *esse*, come tale e propriamente, non è. Sembra quasi di leggere Heidegger il quale anche afferma che l'essere non è ma "si dà" (*es gibt*), ossia si presenta e si giustifica come *Sein des Seienden* ch'è l'evento e quindi si trova soltanto nell'accadere dell'evento. Ma non è facile seguire le tappe del cammino dal τὸ εἶναι del Filosofo fino al *Sein* di Heidegger. Questo non è direttamente neppure il tema della presente ricerca che intende limitarsi alla indicazione della originalità dello *esse* tomistico.

Comunque in questa indicazione il riferimento, un riferimento di fondo e non discorsivo o sistematico, sembra indispensabile per poter in qualche modo avvicinarci a ciò che costituisce la "essenza" del pensare cioè la realtà del pensare e quindi il fondamento della verità del pensiero.

Impostato il problema dell'essere come atto, nella metafisica aristotelica, nel suo significato fondamentale — fondato sulla φύσις-οὐσία come realtà in atto, sia essa composta oppure semplice, passiamo adesso al confronto cioè all'indicazione della riduzione dell'essere in Heidegger che ci suggerisce poi il ritorno alla risposta tomistica. Heidegger si richiama alla posizione più consistente e più coerente che egli chiama *Kehre* cioè la "svolta."

Fra le ricerche più notevoli della *Kehre* di Heidegger è il testo del suo semestre invernale 1951-1952 ed estivo 1952 con titolo: "Che significa pensare?" (*Was heisst Denken?*).[9] Il tema ovvero la tesi o dichiarazione ch'egli presenta subito, in apertura di discorso, è chiara ed esplicita (il testo è messo distaccato e tutto in corsivo); la formula nell'originale è molto densa e può essere tradotta, mi sembra come segue:

---

[8] *Metaph.* Θ, 10, 1051b1 ss.
[9] Tübingen, 1954. Nel 1952 con lo stesso titolo H. ha tenuto una conferenza alla Radio bavarese, pubblicata poi sul "Mercur" (1962), p. 601 ss., e riprodotta nel vol. *Vorträge und Aufsätze*, p. 129 ss. Essa presenta la tematica centrale del corso riprodotto dal volume.

> La cosa che fa più pensare nel nostro tempo pericoloso è che noi ancora non pensiamo.[10]

Heidegger prende come guida delle sue riflessioni (che sono molto pertinenti quando pensiamo all'attuale situazione della filosofia e all'avanzare, anzi all'imporsi, delle umane scienze) prima il poeta Hölderlin e poi Nietzsche poeta, saggista, filosofo ecc., passanda attraverso Schopenhauer, ossia la segnalazione del primato del volere sul pensare e con ciò – con la riduzione del pensare al fare – rileva l'abisso dell'oblio radicale dell'essere. Di qui la reazione radicale di Heidegger di "lasciare essere" l'ente e risolversi a pensare l'essere nell'ente, di rivolgersi all'essere e di risolversi a far parlare l'essere dell'ente. La filosofia non deve essere una riflessione astratta su contenuti formali astratti, ma deve riportarsi dai contenuti del reale alla realtà del reale, a ciò che in noi alimenta la meraviglia del sempre nuovo, del sempre originale, del ciò che zampilla sempre dalla totalità e pienezza profonda della natura.

Heidegger spiega i termini della sua tesi: "la cosa che fa più pensare" è ciò che ci dà da pensare. C'è una certa cosa la quale da se stessa, a partire da essa (*her*) come dalla sua casa, ci dà da pensare (Heidegger usa spesso queste metafore). C'è una cosa che ci richiama a questo, che noi dobbiamo riflettare ad essa, quella cioè che noi pensando ci volgiamo ad essa: il pensare. Ciò che ci fa di più pensare, che ci dà più da pensare, non è pertanto stabilito da noi,[11] non è sorto da (*durch*) noi, non è rappresentato ossia "posto innanzi" (*vor-gestellt*) da noi. Ciò che appunto ci si propone da pensare, ciò che fa più pensare – nel linguaggio ordinario ha il senso di "la cosa più preoccupante, la più urgente, la più strana e stravagante... – è questo che noi ancora non pensiamo. E questo, secondo Heidegger, perché l'essere è rimasto finora "non-pensato" (*ungedacht*). Una constatazione invero strana, almeno come prima impressione, dopo due millenni e mezzo di pensiero metafisico.

Heidegger spiega che l'essere (*Sein*) per tutta la metafisica fin dall'inizio del pensiero occidentale, come di solito esso è inteso, significa il "puro presentarsi," il presentarsi della presenza (*das reine Anwesen, die anwesende Anwesenheit*) come il presente permanente, come l'"ora" (*jetzt*) che continuamente sta. Ma questo per Heidegger è possibile unicamente

---

[10] "Das Bedenklichste in unserer bedenklichen Zeit ist, dass wir noch nicht denken" (p. 3).

[11] Questo è importante ed è la reazione di Heidegger al principio moderno della coscienza; quindi tutti quegli heideggeriani che legano fortemente Heidegger al principio d'immanenza non fanno questa distinzione di Heidegger che è l'essere che deve parlare, perché è l'essere che si presenta nell'essente.

nel pensiero moderno che identifica non solo essere e pensare ma di *conseguenza* – si badi bene, perché quest'identificazione è un atto di volontà e di libertà – pensare e fare cioè pensare e volere.[12] Heidegger perciò cita non compiacenza ed approvazione, qui ed altrove, l'espressione potente di Schelling: "Volere è l'essere originario." [13]

E "*Wollen*" qui, commenta subito Heidegger, significa "l'essere dell'essente nel Tutto" (p. 35); tutto fa capo al "volere" e questo è stato visto già da Leibniz con l'attività della monade, ma si continua in Jacobi, Kant, Fichte, Schelling, Schopenhauer, Nietzsche ... et si può aggiungere come precursore lo stesso Hume con la scoperta del *belief* nel senso di *kind of force* e primo motore della coscienza.

Concepito come "volere" l'essere s'incunea nel tempo, nel tempo esistenziale di cui *Sein und Zeit* ha esposto la struttura. Tutto ciò ch'è rimasto "non-pensato" in ogni metafisica è questo "μετά" ossia il platonismo, l'aver ipotizzato un altro mondo al di sopra della physis: di qui la perdita dell'essere in quanto il presente – ch'è l'essente in essere – passa e rimane passato nel passato e diventa un "fu" (*es war*).[14] Invece la volontà, il volere – ecco l'emergenza dominante del fare nel pensiero moderno – sfugge a questo risucchio del presente nel passato; essa si libera dal contrario ch'è il "fu," quando vuole il ritorno continuo di ciò ch'è stato. E questo è espresso da Nietzsche con la teoria dello "eterno ritorno del simile." E conclude: "La volontà è salvata dalla contro-volontà" (*Widerwille*) se essa vuole il continuo ritorno del simile. Così la volontà vuole l'eternità di ciò che ha voluto. La volontà vuole l'eternità di se stessa. La volontà è l'essere originario. L'essere originario dell'essente è la volontà come il volere dell'eterno ritorno del simile che ritorna eternamente.

L'eterno ritorno del simile è il supremo trionfo della metafisica del volere, che vuole eternamente il proprio volere. È la redenzione dalla

---

[12] M. Heidegger, *Schellings Abhandlung über das Wesen der menschlichen Freiheit* (1809), (Tübingen, 1971), p. 12. – Nel nostro insegnamento non si insiste abbastanza su questo che forse è più importante: l'identificazione di pensare e volere che sta alla radice dell'identità di essere e pensare, perché in tanto c'è l'identità di essere e pensare in quanto il pensare si appropria dell'essere mediante la volontà. E' questa, secondo Heidegger, l'essenza del pensiero moderno.

[13] H. cita *Schellings Abhandlung* ..., p. 35, le "Ricerche sulla essenza della libertà umana" di Schelling: "Es gibt in der letzten und höchsten Instanz gar kein anderes sein als Wollen. *Wollen ist Ursein* [corsivo nostro], und auf dieses allein passen alle Prädikate desselben; Grundlosigkeit, Ewigkeit, Unabhängigkeit von der Zeit, Selbstbejahung. Die ganze Philosophie strebt nur dahin diesen höchsten Ausdruck zu finden" (Schelling, *Untersuchungen*...; W W. Abt. 1, Bd. 7, p. 350).

[14] L'essere dal futuro entra nel presente e poi, finito il presente della presenza, diventa passato, diventato passato ecco che l'essere muore e noi perdiamo l'essere.

"vendetta" (*Rache*) di cui parla Nietzsche che attua il "passaggio" (*Übergang*) all'essere fondamentale di ogni essente: questo è infatti, secondo Nietzsche, il compito e il significato del Superuomo. È importante rilevare che Heidegger qui – come farà più propriamente nel posteriore monumentale *Nietzsche* del 1961 – unifica i due momenti della concezione nietzschiana: a) *la volontà di potenza* e b) *l'eterno ritorno del simile* – ma anche Nietzsche resta nella scia della *Vergessenheit des Seins* – l'essere come volere è l'ultime tappa della perdita dell'essere.

Per Heidegger allora il vero cominciamento non è l'ente – *das Seiende* – ma l'essere: *das Sein*, l'essere dell'essente ed il suo rapporto all'uomo. Ma questo, osserva subito, cioè il rapporto dell'essere all'essenza dell'uomo come rapporto di quest'essenza e del suo sorgere come essenza, non è stato dall'Occidente ancora pensato. Perciò noi non possiamo tutto questo ancora pensarlo e nominarlo in modo sufficiente (*zureichend*). Ma poichè la relazione dell'essere e dell'essenza dell'uomo porta a conclusioni circa l'apparire dell'essere e l'essere dell'uomo, perciò questa relazione è nominata all'inizio della metafisica occidentale. Heidegger indica soprattutto le proposizioni fondamentali di Parmenide e di Eraclito che ricorrono di continuo soprattutto negli Scritti della *Kehre* ed osserva: "Ciò che essi dicono non sta soltanto all'inizio, ma è l'inizio stesso del pensiero occidentale che noi ancora ci rappresentiamo in un modo soltanto storico, troppo ingenuo, troppo ristretto" (p. 45). Ed il pensiero dell'essere sta diventando sempre più difficile come già Aristotele diceva, che noi di fronte alle cose più manifeste della natura, siamo come la civetta davanti alla luce del sole ed egli però parla "dell'intelletto della nostra anima" ($τῆς$ $ἡμετέρας$ $ψυχῆς$ $ὁ$ $νοῦς$),[15] quindi come una condizione inevitabile della nostra natura e non di un effetto storico-speculativo, di un falso passo nel cammino della riflessione. Possiamo invece dire – e questo ci permette di rilevare ancora l'originalità del cominciamento tomistico con lo *ens* dell'essere – ch'è Heidegger prigioniero di una concezione inautentica dell'essere che ha i suoi poli nel plesso scolastico di *essentia-existentia* nella *Einstellung* o impostazione fenomenologica dell'essere come puro apparire ossia come presenza del presente.

Giustamente Heidegger rileva che "la distinzione dell'essenza e dell'esistenza (*Was-sein* = contenuto – *Dass-Sein* = fatto) non contiene soltanto una tesi del pensiero metafisico. Essa mostra un evento nella storia dell'essere." [16] E parimenti Heidegger mette in guardia dal riportare

---

[15] *Metaph.* B, 1, 993b9-11.
[16] M. Heidegger, *Nietzsche* (Pfullingen, 1961), 2: 329 ss. Giustamente Heidegger qualifica la metafisica scolastica di essentia-existentia come la caduta irreparabile

l'origine della distinzione scolastica di essentia ed existentia al pensiero greco.

Nell'inizio della sua storia infatti l'essere è inteso come il "sorgere" (φύσις) e il disvelarsi (ἀλήθεια). Sotto questo aspetto prende rilievo il carattere di presenza e consistenza nel senso di trattenersi (οὐσία che qui Heidegger rende con Verweilen).

Per Aristotele quindi il presente che appare nel presentarsi è ciò ch'è uscito dal nascondimento e sta nella sua consistenza in stato di riposo (Ruhe) ma è un riposo ch'è il risultato di tutto il processo del farsi della cosa in atto ossia come "opus" (ἔργον = Werk). Si potrebbe dire, sempre pensando alla φύσις, che la οὐσία è l'essere fatto in quanto riferito al farsi che lo fa essere in cui appunto consiste la φύσις. Essa indica e abbraccia il divenire o farsi di tutti gli enti secondo una totalità illimitata: spazio e tempo esprimono il limite (πέρας) ch'è proprio del particolare, ma il Tutto è illimitato (ἄπειρον). L'eternità del mondo nel pensiero classico coincide col fondamento della sua realtà: sta quindi agli antipodi, come Heidegger ha ben visto, alla existentia della Scolastica.

Il merito di Heidegger è la rivendicazione dell'essere originario, ch'è stata travisata dall'antropologia sia di tipo kantiano che pone l'essere nella copula dell'atto di giudicare (Maréchal, Rahner, Coreth, Lotz ...), sia di tipo psicanalitico che pone inaccessibile l'origine del comportamento della coscienza perché nascosta nell'inconscio.

Giustamente Heidegger denunzia come all'origine di siffatta deviazione, decisiva per tutta la storia dell'occidente, la coppia di Was-sein e di Dass-sein, ossia di essentia e di existentia che ha preteso di spiegare l'essere dell'ente mediante la distinzione di "possibilità" (Möglichkeit) e "realtà" (Wirklichkeit) lasciando perciò sempre l'essere in ombra cioè nell'oblio. In questo la sua denunzia perciò ha colto il segno.

Ma essa colpisce lo stesso Heidegger e questo perchè egli pretende di ridurre il Sein al "fenomeno" neutro della "presenza pura" cioè al presentarsi senz'alcuna profondità nell'incalzare degli eventi e nel destino delle nazioni e degli individui: un divenire puro denso d'incognite e di problemi, nella traiettoria del Dasein dalla nascita alla morte. L'estrinsecismo scolastico della existentia, come fatto del darsi e presentarsi ch'è concepito come "causale" nel senso verticale della dipendenza, diventa "casuale" nell'ontologia fenomenologica di Heidegger nel senso orizzon-

dell'essere. Ma di questo non è responsabile la dotttrina biblica della Creazione di cui proprio quella concezione della Scolastica, in antitesi con l'esse tomistico, è il travisamento.

tale di un "essere-nel-mondo" dove la dominante è il "mondo" (*Welt*) ma di cui non sappiamo né donde venga né dove vada.[17]

Perciò – ed è il punto cruciale – alla distinzione puramente di ragione della scolastica fra *essentia* ed *existentia* (*cum fundamento in re*, perché – d'accordo col cristianesimo – si ammette che il finito è stato creato e quindi non è uscito da sé dalla possibilità alla realtà) ed alla "separazione" che Heidegger rivendica al *Sein* rispetto al *Seiende* con l'illuminazione (*Lichtung*) da ciò ch'è illuminato ed entra nell'illuminazione, S. Tommaso oppone la composizione reale di *essentia* e di *esse* rispettivamente come atto e potenza, (principi reali tutti e due, non soltanto come possibilità e realtà) in funzione del rapporto di partecipante e partecipato dove l'*esse* è il trascendentale attuale ch'è partecipato da ogni essenza e da tutte le perfezioni le quali sono quelle che sono ed hanno quel che hanno – la propria essenza fino all'ultimo destino, in virtù dell'*actus essendi*.

Così il *Sein selbst* che Heidegger pone a *Grund* del *Seiende* ha il suo riscontro nell'*Ipsum esse*:[18] ma l'*ipsum esse per essentiam* è costitutivo solo in Dio, ogni creatura va detta *ens per participationem*. Così Heidegger forse sfugge all'identità di *Sein-Wesen* nel *Seiende*, ma solo liquefacendosi in un lucore vago e indeterminato ch'è la presenza pura. Eppure per strano che pssa sembrare, ma non è poi tanto strano, anche per S. Tommaso l'intelligenza si illumina mediante la presenza dell'*esse* nell'*ens* e solo così (così almeno ci sembra) è possibile fare il cominciamento assoluto con lo *ens* ch'è identico tanto nella riflessione vitale spontanea dello spirito quanto in quella rigorosa speculativa.[19]

Infatti "... Ens dicitur id quod *finite* participat esse et hoc est proportionatum intellectui nostro cuius objectum est quod quid est, ut dicitur in III De anima; unde illud solum est capabile ab intellectu humano quod habet quidditatem participantem esse."[20]

Aristotele aveva presentato l'intelletto agente οἶον τὸ φῶς, ma dopo aver detto ch'esso è αἴτιον e ποιητικὸν τῷ ποῖεν πάντα:[21] di qui la possibilità ossia

---

[17] Per questo Heidegger non è in grado di rispondere all'interrogativo di Leibniz, che forma la tematica di fondo della *Einführung in die Metaphysik* (1953): "Perché c'è piuttosto l'esente e non il nulla?" – interrogazione capitale alla quale l'immanentismo non potrà mai rispondere se non riportando l'apparire dell'essere al nulla della possibilità di coscienza.

[18] Riscontro proporzionale, richiamo d'istanze speculative.

[19] Questo è decisivo nella riduzione al fondamento e si trova solo in S. Tommaso, in tutta la storia della filosofia.

[20] *In libro De causis*, lect. 6; ed. Saffrey, p. 47, 13-17; Pera nr. 175, p. 47 a.

[21] *De anima*, 3.5, 430a11-13.

il pericolo dell'unico principio spirituale per tutto il genere umano. Così fece l'averroismo nell'evo medio cristiano insidiando la consistenza e molteplicità delle persone e negando perciò la libertà di scelta. Ed è ciò che ha portato a termine il pensiero moderno interpretando l'essere come l'attuarsi sempre in sviluppo della ragione identificando quindi l'essere con la volontà, interpretando la libertà come la spontaneità creativa della ragione e con Heidegger – in questo anch'egli epigono del *cogito* come l'essenza della verità. Al circolo di verità-libertà egli non ha fatto che sostituire il circolo di libertà-verità. In cosa convergono Heidegger e S. Tommaso? In tutto e in niente.

Convergono in tutto in quanto S. Tommaso ha rivoluzionato il concetto di *esse*, ha rivoluzionato l'interpretazione dell'*ens* e della libertà, quindi ha operato nel suo tempo un capovolgimento completo. (E questo l'avvertirono i contemporanei e anche i suoi confratelli gli davano addosso; lui invece tutto tollerava con pazienza.)

Vanno d'accordo? Nella istanza teoretica fondamentale cioè che la verità s'illumina nell'essere e la verità illumina l'essere, ma differiscono nel concetto di *esse* e di *ens*. L'essere per Heidegger è il puro presentarsi fenomenologico, è l'avvertirsi esistente nel mondo, nella *Welt*. Di difficile in quello che dice Heidegger, c'è solo la terminologia.

La *Welt* è per Heidegger fondante, mentre per S. Tommaso il mondo è fondato non ab estrinseco come un artifice che da un legno tira fuori una statua, ma ab intrinseco è dall'intrinseco: che fa uscire l'ente dal nulla.

Infine, Heidegger dice che il destino del pensiero-occidentale è una caduta continua, questo è esatto e in questo son d'accordo con Heidegger; solo si spera che lo sforzo nella aspirazione al vero aiuti l'uomo a non cadere nell'abisso.

Fa eccezione S. Tommaso ch'é partito con l'*ens* (*cuius actus est esse*), mentre la filosofia classica fa leva sulle essenze o nature di un mondo eterno e increato a sé stante e per sé operante nel gioco complesso degli atomi o degli elementi. La filosofia (o teologia) sia agostinista come aristotelica, compressa quella tomistica, giocano col binomio *essenti – existentia* fondato sull'evento della creazione. Mentre per S. Tommaso l'evidenza dello creazione non è fondante, ma fondata precisamente a partire dallo *esse* ch'é l'atto dello *ens* come di ogni forma ed essenza.

Allora é stato grave errore, ma inevitabile conseguenza dell'impostazione essenzialistica del pensiero occidentale, identificare *esse* con *existentia* e sono ambigue le formule di *esse in actu* e di *esse actu* le quali competono alla *essentia* in quanto é passata dalla possibilità alla realtà, si tratti dell'attività immanente della φύσις o della causalità estrinseca trascendente della creazione.

12

The Date and Context of Aquinas'
De aeternitate mundi

James A. Weisheipl, OP
Pontifical Institute of Mediaeval Studies

Virtually everyone who has written on the short life and many works of St. Thomas Aquinas has had something to say, however brief, about his much-studied treatise *De aeternitate mundi*, consisting of 313 lines, usually published among the *Opuscula Philosophica*.[1] Not, however, until the critical work of Pierre Mandonnet (1858-1936) did scholars give much serious attention to the dating of his various works in an attempt to understand the context, sources, and purpose of each work written by him. In the eighty some years since Mandonnet's first major work, innumerable Thomists and medievalists have come to see the importance of such historical studies in making ever more clear the intent and meaning of the author. Concerning this treatise alone dozens of scholars

---

[1] In the Piana edition of the *Opera omnia* (Rome 1570-1571), this *opusculum* is numbered 27; in the Parma edition of 1852-1873, it is numbered 23. Often in the past scholars would refer simply to Op. 27 or Op. 23 without giving the usual title of this work, which sometimes has the added phrase *contra murmurantes* found in some late MSS of *De aeternitate mundi*. Actually this phrase occurs in Boethius of Dacia's *De aeternitate mundi*: "Nulla est contradictio inter fidem et Philosophum. Quare murmuras contra Philosophum, cum idem secundum eum concedis?" (ed. Sajó, 1964 [repr. *Corpus Philosophorum Danicorum Medii Aevi* 6/2, 1976], lines 826-827). In the Leonine edition (Rome, 1974), the *De aeternitate mundi* is printed among the *Opuscula* in vol. 43, pp. 85-89, preceded by a long critical preface, pp. 53-81.

Graceful Reason: Essays in Ancient and Medieval Philosophy Presented to Joseph Owens, CSSR, ed. Lloyd P. Gerson. Papers in Mediaeval Studies 4 (Toronto: Pontifical Institute of Mediaeval Studies, 1983), pp. 239-271. © P.I.M.S., 1983.

have tried to put it into context.[2] In the early decades of this century when Mandonnet and Grabmann were virtually the only authorities on the chronology of St. Thomas' writings, *De aeternitate mundi* was taken to stem from his second Parisian regency, and it was commonly dated sometime in 1270. Reasonable as this date seemed, there was always somes uneasiness about the *adversarii* noted in the text. Even apart from this, as early as 1923 Franz Pelster proposed an early dating for the treatise, putting it before the First Part of the *Summa theologiae*. The immediate response of Mandonnet to this suggestion did not satisfy Pelster, who held to his opinion to the end of his days. But soon others saw difficulties both about the date and about the *adversarii*, so that today one cannot hope to settle the question unless all of those views are taken into consideration and evaluated. In my own book *Friar Thomas d'Aquino* I too assumed the reasonableness of 1270 as the date of *De aeternitate mundi*, and I accepted the arguments of Fr. Ignatius Brady that John Pecham was the specific target, and indeed one particular *determinatio* of Pecham at his inception in the early months of 1270.[3] Since certain doubts have arisen in my own mind, I decided to reconsider the entire question of dating and circumstances of its composition as a tribute to Fr. Joseph Owens, who has done so much to further an understanding and love of our Common Doctor.

Consequently this study will be divided into three parts. First, the views of leading scholars will be examined. Second, a brief analysis of *De aeternitate mundi* itself will be given. Third, some further precisions will be suggested concerning the date and context of this work in its historical and ideological setting.

I. EARLIER VIEWS OF SCHOLARS

For his doctoral dissertation at Louvain Pierre Mandonnet, a Dominican from the Province of France, presented a pioneering masterpiece, *Siger de Brabant et l'Averroïsme latin au XIIIᵉ siècle* (1st ed. Fribourg, 1899; 2nd

---

[2] An extensive bibliography, not pretending to be complete, can be found in John F. Wippel, "Did Thomas Aquinas Defend the Possibility of an Eternaly Created World? (The *De aeternitate mundi* Revisited)," *Journal of the History of Philosophy*, 19 (1981), 21-37.

[3] James A. Weisheipl, *Friar Thomas d'Aquino* (New York: Doubleday, 1974), pp. 286-288; 385, where I also said "no English translation" exists. On the contrary, there is an excellent translation by Cyril Vollert in St. Thomas Aquinas, Siger of Brabant, St. Bonaventure, *On the Eternity of the World* (*De aeternitate mundi*), trans. from the Latin with an Introd. by Cyril Vollert, sj, Lottie H. Kendzierski, and Paul M. Byrne (Milwaukee: Marquette University Press, 1964).

ed., 2 vols., Louvain, 1911). Naturally as a Dominican, Mandonnet was brought up in the teachings of St. Thomas, and many of Thomas' works were discussed in the original dissertation. From 1909 onward, he published a series of studies in *Revue Thomiste* called "Des écrits authentiques de saint Thomas d'Aquin," which were revised and corrected in his now famous edition with this title of 1910. From then on Mandonnet's fame as an authority on the authenticity and chronology of Thomas' writings was secure, but he never ceased writing, studying, teaching, and revising his earlier views until his death in 1936 at the age of almost 78.[4] Not surprisingly Mandonnet's early concentration on Siger of Brabant predisposed him to see almost everything in the high Middle Ages in terms of "Latin Averroism" and Aristotelian philosophy. Perhaps for this reason he always considered *De aeternitate mundi* to be a philosophical work, Thomas' final answer to the Latin Averroists in the Faculty of Arts at Paris around 1270: "To me this little disquisition is clearly connected with the Parisian Averroist polemics, and I have dated its composition to 1270; but it could be one or two years later."[5] Mandonnet never had any doubts about this. In his mind *De unitate intellectus contra Averroistas* and *De aeternitate mundi contra murmurantes* both belong to the same context, both to be dated 1270, and both published among the *Opuscula Philosophica*, as in his own edition of 1927.

Mandonnet's view of *De aeternitate mundi* seem to have been taken generally by all the leading authorities, apparently without further study or question. All the work had been done by Mandonnet in his *Siger de Brabant*. Msgr. Martin Grabmann, who examined a great many manuscripts throughout his lifetime (1875-1949) and who was himself an eminent authority in these matters, merely wrote in the final edition of his *Die Werke des hl. Thomas von Aquin*: "Mandonnet puts the writing in 1270, Glorieux at the beginning of 1271, Walz in 1270."[6] Apart from listing the various titles this *opusculum* has in the manuscripts, Grabmann merely discussed Pelster's novel position only to reject it. Fr. Angelo Walz, a German Dominican who dedicated his best years to teaching and

    [4] See the bibliography by R.P. Mandonnet in *Mélanges Mandonnet*, 1 (Paris: Vrin, 1930), pp. 7-17.

    [5] P. Mandonnet, *Bulletin tomiste*, 1924 (1), p. [71]; idem, "Chronologie sommaire de la vie et des écrits de saint Thomas," *Revue des Sciences Philosophiques et Théologiques*, 9 (1920), 151.

    [6] M. Grabmann, *Die Werke des hl. Thomas von Aquin*, 3rd ed. (Münster i. West.: Aschendorf, 1949), p. 341.

writing at the Angelicum in Rome, likewise placed the treatise in the Latin Averroist controversies at Paris, and gave 1270 as the date without comment or further study.[7]

Canon Fernand Van Steenberghen built his reputation at Louvain on the bones of Mandonnet, particularly in his two volume masterpiece *Siger de Brabant d'après ses œuvres inédites* (Louvain, 1931-1942). Although he himself always rejected the cogency of Thomas' position about the indemonstrability of the temporal beginning of the world, he also dates *De aeternitate mundi* as "probably around 1270."[8] But he made a tantalizing suggestion that this short, compact answer to a single question might possibly be the original *determinatio* for *Quodlibet* 12, a.7, since all we have of this *Quodlibet* is a highly abbreviated *reportatio*. The question here, sometimes listed as q.6, a.1, asks: "Utrum caelum vel mundus sit aeternus." The highly abbreviated *responsio* is a reply in the negative summed up in nine lines that actually say more than is contained in *De aeternitate mundi*. In any case, this *Quodlibet* is generally dated during Advent of 1270, which would be satisfactory to Van Steenberghen, but which would coincide with the condemnation of this thesis on December 10, of which there is no mention in either work.

Ignatius T. Eschmann, the German Dominican who taught for many years at the Institute of Mediaeval Studies, likewise made no special study of the context of this work, but he did note that Thomas' *opusculum* was one of the texts of current interest to Godfrey of Fontaines (Paris, Bibl. Nat., MS lat. 16297), "gathered during the years 1270/72." From this observation Eschmann cautiously concluded, "The chronology may, with sufficient probability, be determined accordingly."[9]

Without any hint of an explanation, Msgr. Palemon Glorieux, who was studying this "recueil scolaire" of Godfrey in 1931, boldly declared,

[7] A. Walz, "Chronotaxis vitae et operum S. Thomae de Aquino," *Angelicum*, 16 (1939), 466; idem, *Saint Thomas d'Aquin*, adaptation française par Paul Novarina, Philosophes Médiévaux, 5 (Louvain, 1962), p. 159.

[8] F. Van Steenberghen, *Siger de Brabant d'après ses œuvres inédites*, 2 (Louvain, 1942), pp. 549-550. For a clear summary of his reasons for rejecting Thomas' position, see his *Thomas Aquinas and Radical Aristotelianism* (Washington, DC: Catholic University of America Press, 1980), pp. 1-27. Finding all of Thomas' arguments for the existence of God inconclusive and ineffective, Van Steenberghen seems to argue that the only valid proof today must begin with the factual creation of the universe in time, and from there argue to an eternal Creator; see his *Le problème de l'existence de Dieu dans les écrits de s. Thomas d'Aquin*, Philosophes Médiévaux, 23 (Louvain-la-Neuve, 1980), pp. 338-358. This is the very position of the Mutakallimūn, rejected so fervently by Moses Maimonides in *The Guide of the Perplexed*; see esp. 1.71.

[9] I. T. Eschmann, "A Catalogue of St. Thomas's Works," in E. Gilson, *The Christian Philosophy of St. Thomas Aquinas* (New York: Random House, 1956), pp. 409-410.

"[Thomas'] *De aeternitate mundi* dates from the beginning of 1271, *sans doute*."[10] In a footnote to this sentence, Glorieux noted that he cannot justify here all the dates given above, "but the work is completed, and will appear elsewhere *sans doute*." As far as I known, this justification has never appeared, but many others have used the authority of Glorieux for giving 1271 as the date of composition of Thomas' work. Vernon Bourke likewise gives 1271 without particular reason, but, like all the above, places it in the Latin Averroist context.[11] Perhaps Fr. J. Perrier summarized this common view best when he said, "It is very probable that [*De aeternitate mundi*] belongs to the disputations against the Parisian Averroists, and was written either at the same time or a little after the treatise *De unitate intellectus*, that is, in the years 1270-71."[12]

Fr. M.-D. Chenu apparently was well aware on reading *De aeternitate mundi* that it really is a theological work, directed to the so-called Augustinian theologians of the Faculty of Theology rather than to the better known Averroists of the Faculty of Arts. So he described the treatise in the Parisian context of 1270, but saw it as part of St. Thomas' confrontation with both extremes: Augustinian theologians claiming traditional orthodoxy and Averroist philosophers claiming the rights of reason in the name of Aristotle (and Averroes).[13]

There can be little doubt today that tenets, such as the eternity of the world, unicity of the human intellect, and denial of divine concern for singulars and human affairs, were fundamental to a certain view among philosophers at Paris in the 1260s and 1270s. This tendency or movement in the Faculty of Arts, at least, can be called "Latin Averroism" (as Mandonnet proposed) or "Radical Aristotelianism" (as Van Steenberghen insists) or anything else ("secular," "integral," and "heterodox" Aristotelianism are also fashionable), provided one explains the meaning intended (*Quid de nominibus?*). Concretely the individuals were certainly Siger of Brabant and Boethius of Dacia, and probably others we know not of. Thirteen brief propositions, commonly called "Averroist," were solemnly condemned at Paris by Bishop Stephen Tempier on 10 December 1270.[14] The first and most characteristic thesis for this kind of

[10] P. Glorieux, "Un recueil scolaire de Godefroid de Fontaines," *Recherches de Théologie ancienne et médiévale*, 3 (1931), 46.

[11] V. Bourke, *Aquinas's Search for Wisdom* (Milwaukee: Bruce, 1965), p. 162.

[12] J. Perrier, *Opuscula omnia S. Thomae Aquinatis* (Paris: Lethielleux, 1949), p. 52.

[13] M.-D. Chenu, *Introduction à l'étude de s. Thomas d'Aquin* (Paris: Vrin, 1950), pp. 289-290.

[14] Denifle-Chatelain, *Chartularium Universitatis Parisiensis* 1: 486-487, n. 432. See John F. Wippel, "The Condemnations of 1270 and 1277 at Paris," *The Journal of Medieval and Renaissance Studies*, 7 (1977), 169-201.

"Averroism" was the first one singled out by the bishop's theologians: "Quod intellectus omnium hominum est unus et idem numero." The fifth proposition is the one we are concerned about: "Quod mundus est aeternus." The tenth was not peculiar to Averroes: "Quod Deus non cognoscit singularia." The other ten propositions follow logically from one or another of these. The thirteen propositions condemned by Tempier in December 1270 are basically contained in the list of fifteen propositions that the Dominican Giles of Lessines sent to Albert the Great for comment prior to the condemnation on December 10. Albert at that time was about seventy years of age and living in the Dominican priory of Heilige Kreuz in Cologne. In the covering letter Giles of Lessines asked Albert's opinion about the "articles, which Parisian masters who are considered the more eminent are proposing in the schools (*quos proponunt in scholis magistri Parisienses, qui in philosophia maiores reputantur*)." [15]

Replying to the fifth article, Albert says the question of the eternity of the world is indeed a very old question, but one cannot deduce an affirmative answer from Aristotle's arguments. Aristotle merely proves that the first motion cannot be produced by a physical generator, nor can it be corrupted by any physical source. [16] The burden of Albert's subsequent explanation is to show that the entire universe with all its variety and motions "must be reduced to a single source, which is the substantial cause of that multiplicity." Such a drive of all things to a First is possible only because of some *similitudo essentialis* among the multitude, which *similitudo* is produced by the First by some flow (*fluxus*). Then Albert asks: "Does it make any sense to say that the First produces this *similitudo* in things that are already existing *in natura et esse*?" Since this makes no sense, it must be that the First "causes this likeness in all things, producing all of them *secundum essentiam et in esse naturali et substantiali*." Therefore, says Albert, all things are *factum secundum substantiale esse et naturale*. It follows necessarily, then, that none of these things can possibly be "eternal" in the sense of not having a *principium essendi secundum substantiam et naturam*. [17] In other words, what Albert says here is that no creature, being by definition a reality

---

[15] Albertus Magnus, *Opera Omnia*, ed. Colon., 17/1: 31.5-7. The background of *De quindecim problematibus* is clearly presented by Bernhard Geyer in the *Prolegomena* to the Cologne edition, pp. xix-xxi.

[16] Albertus Magnus, *De quindecim problematibus*, 5: "Quod autem mundus sit aeternus, sicut quinto inducunt, antiqua valde quaestio est, quamvis ex probatione Aristotelis haberi non possit, sed quod a nullo generante motus primus factus sit et a nullo physice corrumpente possit desinere. Hoc autem optime improbat Moyses Aegyptius in libro, qui *Dux neutrorum* vocatur." *Opera Omnia*, 17/1: 37.14-20.

[17] Ibid., 38.5-28.

dependent *in esse* on another, can be "eternal" in the sense of not being dependent. That is, no creature, being by its very nature dependent *in esse*, can ever be independent. If, then, to be eternal means to be independent *in esse*, then no creature can be "eternal." No doubt by 1270 Albert would further hold (with Thomas) that there is no reason why a creature with total dependence *in esse* on the First could not be "eternal" in the sense of not having a beginning, as he had always held in his Aristotelian paraphrases. Clearly what Albert was doing in this reply to Giles of Lessines in 1270 was providing an argument showing the sense in which no creature can be "eternal" without saying that in another sense a creature could have been eternal, as Aristotle thought, if God had willed it.

Others writing at Paris around this period show how much alive the issue was. Giles of Rome's compendium entitled *Errores philosophorum* is commonly dated around 1270-1271, wherein the eternity of the world as an error is ascribed to Aristotle, Averroes, Avicenna, and Algazel.[18] The *De aeternitate mundi* of Siger of Brabant is usually dated around 1271,[19] since it is in the "recueil scolaire" of Godfrey of Fontaines.[20] Similarly the *De aeternitate mundi* of Boethius of Dacia cannot be dated better than "the environs of 1270."[21] Therefore 1270 is not an unreasonable date for the *De aeternitate mundi* of St. Thomas.

The earliest modern voice dissenting from the usual dating seems to have been Franz Pelster, SJ (1880-1956), who as early as 1923 argued that St. Thomas' *De aeternitate mundi* must be dated prior to the First Part of his *Summa theologiae*.[22] Moved first by a statement[23] in the *Concordantia*

---

[18] Giles of Rome, *Errores philosophorum*, ed. J. Koch, trans. John O. Riedl (Milwaukee: Marquette University Press, 1944), *per totum*. Msgr. Koch dates this work after 1268 and before 1273, preferring "around 1270" (ibid., pp. lv-lix). But since book lambda of Aristotle's *Metaphysics* is always cited as book 12 in Giles' *De generatione*, and sometimes as book 12 in the *Errores philosophorum*, the latter work must have been written after January 1271; see Weisheipl, *Friar Thomas d'Aquino*, p. 361.

[19] For the variety of opinions see the introduction of L. H. Kendzierski to her translation of Siger's treatise (note 3), pp. 76-78; see also B. Bazán, the critical edition of *De aeternitate mundi*, Philosophes Médiévaux, 13 (Louvain, 1972), pp. 62*-66*, 77*-78*. Judging from all the evidence known of this work from scholars who have edited his text of *De aeternitate mundi*, it would seem that this work was written sometime in 1271 or 1272.

[20] See Glorieux, "Un recueil scolaire"; John F. Wippel, *The Metaphysical Thought of Godfrey of Fontaines* (Washington, DC: Catholic University of America Press, 1981), pp. xvii-xviii *et passim*.

[21] *Boethii Daci Opera*, Corpus Philosophorum Danicorum Medii Aevi, ed. N. G. Green-Pedersen, 6/2 (Copenhagen, 1976), pp. xix-xxiii.

[22] F. Pelster, "De concordantia dictorum Thomae: Ein echtes Werk aus des letzten Lebesjahren des hl. Thomas von Aquin," *Gregorianum*, 4 (1923), 72-105, esp. pp. 91-94.

[23] In c. 31, the longest chapter in the *Concordantia "Pertransibunt plurimi,"* devoted

dictorum Thomae sometimes attributed to Thomas, which Pelster considered authentic,[24] he noted Thomas' statement about the infinite number of souls that would have to exist *in actu* if the world were eternal. In the *opusculum* Thomas explicitly says God could have created an eternal world without creating man from all eternity; moreover "it has not yet been demonstrated that God cannot make an infinity of things in act" (lines 306-308). This uncertainty, Pelster argued, must antedate the certainty Thomas shows in *Summa theologiae* 1, q.7, a.4 (dated 1266-1268 for the entire First Part) and even *Quodlibet* 9 (dated Lent 1258). In these passages Thomas notes that Avicenna and Algazel deny the possibility of an actual infinity of things ordered *per se*, but allow for an actual infinity of things ordered *per accidens*, such as the use of an infinite number of hammers one after the other, given an eternal being able to use them, or an infinite number of human souls separate from the body. In the *Summa* article Thomas explicitly concludes: "Impossibile est ergo esse multitudinem infinitam in actu, etiam per accidens." On this statement Pelster rested his case, although other scholars reacted negatively.[25]

The difficulties of such a case are many. The first rests with the category of an actual infinity *per accidens*. As used by Avicenna and taken up in Algazel's paraphrase, it included both an infinite succession (*ut sit non totum simul, sed successive*) – which Thomas always allowed – and the simultaneous existence of an infinite number of souls separated from the body, supposing that mankind existed from all

---

exclusively to the problem of the eternity of the world, the author described the order of argumentation: "Sed utrum possint esse actu, diximus differendum usque alias; et idem diximus in praedicto tractatu [*De aeternitate mundi*], quod nondum erat ostensum infinita actu esse non posse, nec adversarii nobis hoc ostenderunt, quod tamen nos postea in prima parte *Summae* ostendimus recitata opinione Algazelis, et certum habuimus quod infinita esse [non] possunt etiam per accidens, ut ibi ostensum est." *De concordantiis*, c. 31, in S. Thomae Aquinatis, *Opera Omnia* (Paris: Vives, 1875), 28: 572a.

[24] This concordance, usually called "Pertransibunt plurimi" from its incipit, was first published by Antonio Pizamano at Venice in 1490 as an authentic work of Thomas, designated as *opusculum* 72. Thereafter it was published in every *Opera Omnia* from the Piana edition (1570-1571) to the Paris Vives edition (1871-1872) among the *opuscula*, either as Op. 72 or Op. 65. Its authenticity has been heatedly disputed in recent times, but it was considered authentic by Ptolemy of Lucca in his list: "[35.] Item dicitur fecisse tractatum de concordantia dictorum suorum." Critical text in Antoine Dondaine, "Les 'Opuscula fratris Thomae' chez Ptolémée de Lucques," *Archivum Fratrum Praedicatorum*, 31 (1961), 154.

[25] Pelster replied to his critics in his last publication, "Zur Echtheit der Concordantia dictorum Thomae und zur Datierung von De aeternitate mundi," *Gregorianum*, 37 (1956), 610-621.

eternity.[26] This latter case provided a difficulty for many reasons. As early as 1253 Thomas noted (*In 2 Sententiarum*, d.1, q.1, a.5 ad 6) that this objection to the impossibility of an actual infinity of things "is stronger (*fortior*) than all the others," just as he noted in the later *opusculum*, among the arguments put forward by the adversaries, and originally suggested and resolved by the philosophers, "the more difficult (*difficilior*) concerns the infinity of souls" (lines 297-299).

A more serious weakness in Pelster's case, however, is the fact that no one, not even St. Thomas, has ever in fact demonstrated the impossibility of such an actual infinity – as Thomas explicitly says in the *De aeternitate mundi*. The Mutakallimūm, as Moses Maimonides explained at length,[27] used the impossibility of an actual infinity of souls to prove that the world could not have existed from all eternity. Noting this source, St. Thomas says that Rabbi Moses referred to this argument, "ostendens praedictam rationem non esse demonstrationem."[28] Apparently Avicenna himself devised this extended category since he held for both an eternal world and the immortality of human souls separated from the body. Therefore he allowed for such a *per accidens* infinity, whereas the Mutakallimūm, wanting to be more philosophical than the philosophers, claimed that such was impossible; and therefore the worlds could not have been eternal.

Further it must be admitted that not even St. Thomas demonstrated the impossibility of such an infinity in the *Summa* passage under discussion. From revelation (Genesis, 1.26-28) Thomas knew that God made a first man; consequently there will be no infinity of souls, even if one granted

---

[26] Clearly Avicenna, who held for an eternal world and the immortality of the human soul, introduced the new kind of *per accidens* infinite to allow for an actual infinity of immaterial substances, as St. Thomas indicates (ST 1, q. 46, a. 2 ad 8). This was clearly paraphrased by Algazel (*Metaphysics* 1, tr.1, divisio 6, ed. Muckle [Toronto, 1933], pp. 40-41). Algazel's objection to this was refuted by Averroes (*Tahafut al-Tahafut* 1.1), who noted that Avicenna alone among all the philosophers allowed for the possibility of an actual infinity of separated substances. See *Averroes' Tahafut al-Tahafut (The Incoherence of the Incoherence)*, trans. from the Arabic with intro. and notes by Simon van den Bergh (Oxford: University Press, 1954), 2: 13 (for p. 14.6) to 2: 15 (for p. 15.1). St. Thomas' reply to this objection in the *Summa* (since there cannot be an actual infinity of souls, the world cannot be eternal) is simply that this is not a demonstration, i.e., there are various ways this objection has been answered (1, q. 46, a. 2 ad 8). On this being the more difficult (*difficilior*) objection, see Leonine ed., p. 89.299 note.

[27] Moses Maimonides, *Guide of the Perplexed* 1, c.71, trans. with introd. and notes (Chicago: University of Chicago Press, 1963), pp. 180-184; also 1, c.73, eleventh premise, ibid., pp. 212-213, *et passim*.

[28] St. Thomas, *In 2 Sent.*, dist. 1, q. 1, a. 5 ad 6, referring to Moses Maimonides, *Guide* 1, c.73, and Algazel's *Metaphysics* 1, tr. 1, div. 6.

Avicenna's view of the body's dimished hold on the separated soul – which is clearly contrary to the revealed doctrine of the final resurrection of the body. But this is altogether different from providing a real demonstration in philosophy. At no time did Thomas himself provide a solid demonstration that God cannot create an actual infinity of souls separated from the body. Therefore Thomas could write, even as late as 1270: "Praeterea non est adhuc demonstratum quod Deus non possit facere ut sint infinita actu."

Finally, if more proof were desired, one could point to *Quodlibet* 12 and *De unitate intellectus*, both indubitably dated in 1270 to show: (1) that Thomas admitted that God could, strictly speaking, produce an infinite number of things *in actu*, since "non repugnat potentiae Dei absolutae, quia non implicat contradictionem";[29] and (2) that Thomas used this same passage in Algazel to resolve the Aristotelian difficulty of an infinity of souls in an eternal universe: "Similiter et animas humanas, quae sunt separabiles a corporibus per mortem, concedimus esse infinitas numero, quamvis habeant esse simul, quoniam non est inter eas ordinatio naturalis, qua remota desinant esse animae."[30]

Consequently the internal argument Pelster used to date *De aeternitate mundi* before the First Part of the *Summa* (1266) and *Quodlibet* 9 (Lent 1258) does not hold force. The possible authenticity of *Concordantia dictorum Thomae* (commonly known as "Pertransibunt plurimi" from its opening words) is another matter.

Fr. Ignatius Brady, OFM, of Grottaferrata, had settled on 1274 as the date and occasion of the work, when he claimed to have shown that Aquinas's *De aeternitate mundi* was written against John Pecham's *determinatio* at his inception as Master in Theology early in 1270, on which occasion Pecham denied the possibility of an eternal world.[31] According to Fr. Brady, "Thomas may courteously have spared Pecham on the more formal occasion of the vesperiae and aulica, and then have reacted publicly at the *resumptio*."[32] That is, the second of the four questions circulated beforehand to the Masters was disputed by Pecham at his vesperies: "Utrum aliquid factum sit vel fieri potuit de nihilo ordinaliter."

[29] St. Thomas, *Quodl.* 12, q. 2, ad 2. *Quodl.* 12 was not discovered until the fourteenth century in the form of a *reportatio*; it belongs, with *Quodl.* 1-6, to Thomas' second Parisian regency. See Weisheipl, *Friar Thomas*, pp. 367-368.

[30] St. Thomas, *De unitate intellectus*, c. 5 (ed. Leon. 43: 313.322-326).

[31] I. Brady, "John Pecham and the Background of Aquinas's *De aeternitate mundi*," in *St. Thomas Aquinas, 1274-1974, Commemorative Studies*, ed. A. A. Maurer (Toronto: Pontifical Institute of Mediaeval Studies, 1974), 2: 141-178.

[32] Ibid., p. 154.

The third of these questions was disputed *in aula* on the following day: "Utrum mundus potuit fieri ab aeterno." These two questions edited by Fr. Brady are thought to be Pecham's *resumptio* of these (because of the frequent use of *respondebatur*) "at the first available opportunity." These two difficult texts were carefully edited by Fr. Brady with the help of Dr. Girard Etzkorn.[33]

Supposedly on this occasion of Pecham's inception Friar Thomas, prompted by the rebuke of his students for remaining silent on the previous evening, took Pecham to task: "This opinion of yours cannot be held because it is against such and such a Council."[34] The Council in question, of course, would have been the Fourth Lateran in 1215, which declared the universality of God's creation of everything *ex nihilo*.[35] William of Tocco, who narrates the incident, may not have been a university man at Paris, but he notes that this dispute on the "following day" (*die crastino*) was *in aula Domini Episcopi*, not the *resumptio* "at the first available opportunity" – which might have been some days later and before his own students, not the senior *magistri* of the University. In any case, Fr. Brady would have Thomas' *De aeternitate mundi* written immediately after the confrontation. In that case, one would expect the two questions edited by Fr. Brady or at least the second and more substantive question to substantiate the claim. As we will see, much remains to be desired of such a proof.

In a final footnote added to the proofs, Fr. Brady noted that the article in question "quite unintentionally is an answer to that of Thomas Bukowski," who had argued persuasively that St. Thomas in *De aeternitate mundi* is "almost certainly arguing against St. Bonaventure."[36] If Fr. Brady had demonstrated his thesis, namely that John Pecham's

---

[33] Ibid., pp. 156-178.

[34] This famous incident is narrated by William of Tocco, *Hystoria beati Thomae de Aquino*, c. 27 (ed. A. Ferrua [Alba: Edizioni Domenicane, 1968], pp. 68-70).

[35] In the decree "Firmiter" (11-30 Nov. 1215): "... qui sua omnipotenti virtute simul ab initio temporis utramque de nihilo condidit creaturam, spiritualem et corporalem, angelicam videlicet et mundanam." Denizger-Schönmetzer, 800; see Thomas, *Super primam decretalem*, ed. Leon. 40в: 29-39, esp. lines 410-443. On the background of this Council, see P. M. Quay, "Angels and Demons: The Teaching of iv Lateran," *Theological Studies*, 42 (1981), 20-45.

[36] Brady, "John Pecham," p. 154, note 41, referring to Thomas Bukowski, "An Early Dating for Aquinas, *De aeternitate mundi*," *Gregorianum*, 51 (1970), 277-304. Bukowski replied to Fr. Brady in "J. Pecham, T. Aquinas, et al., on the Eternity of the World," *Recherches de Théologie ancienne et médiévale*, 46 (1979), 216-221. Bukowski argues that Brady has not "proved" that Thomas' *opusculum* is a reply to Pecham's *Quaestiones*. Rather, he argues, Pecham's late *quaestio* seems directed more to the Averroists, while Thomas' treatise could still be an early attack on Bonaventure.

resumptio early in 1270 was the real target of Thomas' *opusculum*, then his article would have been, unintentionally and indirectly, an answer to that of Bukowski. A brief consideration will show that the question is still open.

First, Fr. Brady is convinced that Thomas' *opusculum* betrays a "sense of immediacy and urgency ... directed against a specific person and a specific disputation," which "took place around or shortly before the syllabus of 10 December 1270." He acknowledges, however, that

> we can hardly say that the opuscule of Saint Thomas goes on to attack point for point the demonstration of Pecham. Such a facile proof of identity would be almost too much to expect. Nonetheless, since these five arguments labour under the deficiencies Thomas had previously warned against in the *Summa* I, 46, 1-2, and now repeats in *De aeternitate*, nn. 4-7, especially the failure to see that there is no repugnance between the concept of something created and that of always existing, we have something of a case.[37]

Similarly Fr. Brady argues that the three "authorities" used by the *adversarii* of the opuscule, namely John Damascene (in lines 258-260), Hugh of Saint-Victor (in lines 262-264), and Augustine in *De civitate Dei* 12.15 (in lines 282-292), are used also by the Franciscan John Pecham, although not always to the same purpose or in the same context. Nevertheless,

> the cumulative effect of the rather consistent parallels between the Question(s) of Pecham and the *De aeternitate mundi* leads, it seems to me, to only one conclusion: that the opuscule of Aquinas was indeed provoked by the disputation of the Franciscan.[38]

The first question by Fr. Brady ("Utrum aliquid factum sit vel fieri potuit de nihilo ordinaliter") has nothing to do with Thomas' *De aeternitate mundi*. Its burden is to show that "Creation is an article of faith, and never has any infidel ever fully understood it" (ed. Brady, p. 159). Thus Plato held for an uncreated matter and exemplar (as well as God), while Aristotle does not have a clear opinion, although he does say that there is no power (*virtus*) except from God.[39] While Thomas may not

---

[37] Brady, ibid., p. 151.
[38] Ibid., p. 152.
[39] "De rerum vero principio primo non habet Aristoteles manifestam sententiam, quamvis dicat quod non est virtus nisi a Deo" (Pecham, q. 1, ed. Brady, p. 161). Brady gives as the source for this view of Aristotle, *Ethic. Nic.* 1, c.9 (1099b10) and 2, c.1 (1103a25).

have agreed with Pecham's conclusion, none of the twenty-eight arguments "quod non" or the five "contra" enter Thomas' *De aeternitate mundi* or any other recognized work.

The second question edited by Fr. Brady ("Utrum mundus potuit fieri ab aeterno") pertains directly to our discussion. Among the thirty-one arguments proving that the world "could have been from eternity," only three conclude with any necessity; among the fourteen arguments against the view, four, as Fr. Brady pointed out, are refutations of arguments found in the *Summa* of Thomas, and could be of interest, but none prove that Thomas' opuscule was written specifically against this question.

In his *responsio* to the question Pecham begins by acknowledging that creation of the world in time is an article of faith, but insists that a rational investigation of the question is not prejudicial to faith, as long as one does not assent to faith *propter rationem*, but arrives at its understanding with the merit of faith. Hence those who have discussed creation without faith have all erred either by default in not attributing it [creation] to him, or by excess in attributing creation to others rather than to God. (ed. Brady, p. 173)

Then Pecham gives five arguments to show that "the world was not eternal, but rather created in time."

The first is based on the true meaning of "past" in the world's becoming *(fieri)*: everything past was at one time present, and not past; but nothing of this sort can be eternal, since only God is eternal and he made time together with creatures, as Augustine says (*Super Genesim contra Manichaeos* 1.2.4, not quoted by Thomas). Therefore God made time, which passes into the past, which is the beginning of time.

The second is based on participated being: whatever is participated is limited and contracted in being; but eternity is unlimited time, which is contrary to being participated. – If one objects that time is not an infinite magnitude *in actu*, since its parts are not simultaneous, I answer that time is a kind of being *(tempus est aliquod ens)*. Therefore infinite time is infinite being equal to the eternity of God, at least *a parte ante*. But Augustine says no creature can equal God (*De civitate Dei* 11.5, but not same sentence quoted by Thomas; *Super Genesim contra Manichaeos* 1.2.4, not quoted by Thomas, but similar passages are). Therefore.

The third is based on the world's origin in non-being "because it is *ex nihilo*, and so at some time was not." – If it is objected (Thomas, ST 1.45.2 ad 2) that this *de nihilo* should be understood negatively as *de non-aliquo* [sic] so that *non-esse* did not precede the world by any duration, I answer: just as annihilation *(versio in non-esse)* cannot coexist with future eternity, so past eternity cannot coexist with its coming from non-being *(eductio de non-esse*). And as John Damascene says, "Creation by the will of God is not coeternal with God, because it is not fitting (*non aptum natum est*) that something drawn from non-being should be coeternal with him who is eternal and without beginning" (*De fide orthodoxa* 1.8, quoted by Thomas, lines 258-260).

The fourth is based on the measure of the world's coming-to-be, namely the 'nunc': the 'now' of creation is the terminus of its being *a parte ante*; but what has an initial terminus, does not have an infinity of being (*essendi*). If therefore the world was produced in time, it was produced at the beginning of time. Hugh of Saint-Victor speaks about the moment of production (*De sacramentis* 1.5, not quoted by St. Thomas).

The last is based on the course of time, since one revolution [of the spheres] is later than another, as tomorrow is later than today. In an infinite time there would be infinite lateness, so that today's revolution or tomorrow's would never come. Thus, as Augustine says, the mutability of time can never be coeternal with the immutability of eternity (*De civitate Dei* 12.15, quoted more fully by Thomas, lines 282-292).

Pecham concludes his *determinatio* with the universal statement that the world in no way is capable of being "eternal" or "of interminable duration": *mundus nullo modo capax fuit aeterne vel interminabilis durationis*. He then adds that those who claim that the world is coeternal with God are motivated by a false notion (*fundamento*): either they believe that a God existing before the world existed would be idle (*otiosum*), or they imagine that otherwise a "space of time" would precede the world, or they do not believe that God can make something new without changing his will or himself. All of which false notions (*fundamenta*) Augustine refutes (*De civitate Dei* 11.4, not quoted by St. Thomas).

From all of this it is hard to see how Thomas was responding to "a specific person and a specific disputation" (Brady, p. 146), namely to John Pecham's *resumptio* as edited by Fr. Brady. Even granting that Thomas was quoting Pecham's authorities from memory and not altogether too accurately (p. 151), which I doubt in this case, it is hard to see Thomas' treatise as specifically directed to this unique question of Friar John Pecham. Rather it would seem more likely, as I hope to show, that Thomas' *De aeternitate mundi* was directed neither at John Pecham specifically, nor at Bonaventure specifically, but at a universal stance of many *adversarii*, both old and new, who always used the same arguments and the same authorities, to prove the logical incompatibility of an "eternal" world with its having been "created." But before we consider the evidence, we should consider briefly the explicit content of Thomas' opuscule.

II. THE CONTENT OF *DE AETERNITATE MUNDI*

Acknowledging the truth of revelation that the world had a beginning of its duration, one raises the question of whether it could have always existed, that is, have been without such a beginning. In seeking the true solution to this problem, points of agreement with our adversaries should be distinguished from points of disagreement.

If one maintained that besides God something could have always existed that was not made by him, this would be an abominable error contrary to faith and to the philosophers, who profess and demonstrate that nothing at all exists except what is caused by him who uniquely and most truly has existence (*esse*). If, however, one understands that something always existed that was caused by God in the totality of its being, then one might legitimately ask whether such could be the case. If one says this is impossible, this would be either because God cannot make something to have existed always (*quod semper fuerit*), or because such a thing could not be done (*non potuit fieri*), even though God had the power. Considering God's infinite power, all agree that God could make something to exist always; so it remains to be seen whether such a thing could be produced.

If then one says this cannot be done, this would be for one of two reasons: either there is no "passive potentiality" for such a situation or there is an intrinsic contradiction (*propter repugnantiam intellectuum*) between "being created" and "being eternal." The first need not detain us, since it would be heretical to say that any passive potentiality is pre-supposed to creation, for then this potentiality itself would not be created. But even from this it would not follow that God could not make a creature to exist always.

In the second way something cannot be done because of a logical contradiction (*propter repugnantiam intellectuum*), just as one cannot make an affirmation and negation to be true simultaneously, although some say he can do this and some say he cannot since this is a non-being, a non-entity. But it is clear that he cannot do this, because the doing destroys the non-doing. But if one claims that God can do this, it would not be heretical to say so, although, as I believe, it would be false, just as that the past not be past includes a contradiction. There have been indeed some reputedly great men (Peter Damiani, supposedly Gilbert of Poitiers, and others) who said that God can undo the past.[40] Although they said

---

[40] Peter Damiani, *De divina omnipotentia*, c. 4 (PL 145: 601c). For the impact of this opinion on later discussions, see William J. Courtenay, "John of Mirecourt and Gregory

that God could make the past not be the past, they were not considered heretics.

We must investigate, therefore, whether these two concepts are logically incompatible (*repugnantia sit intellectuum*), namely that something be created by God (*aliquid sit creatum a Deo*) and have always existed (*semper fuerit*). Whatever may be the truth of the matter, it would not be heretical to say that something made by God always existed. "Although I believe that if there is an intrinsic contradiction, it would be false; if, however, there is no contradiction, then not only is it not false, it is even [not] impossible; otherwise to say anything else would be erroneous."[41] For since God's omnipotence exceeds all understanding, it would be derogatory to deny him the power to produce whatever is perfectly intelligible to our understanding – the question of "sin" is not to the point here, since of itself sin is non-being.

"The whole question, therefore, comes to this: whether to be created by God according to a thing's entire substance (*esse creatum a Deo secundum totam substantiam*) and not having a beginning of its duration (*non habere durationis principium*) are mutually repugnant or not" (lines 77-80).

The purpose of this work, then, is to show that there is no intrinsic contradiction or mutual repugnance between these two concepts. If there is such a repugnance, it would have to arise from one of two sources or both: either because every cause must precede the creature in duration or because non-being or *nihil* must precede the creature in duration inasmuch as it is created *ex nihilo*. The first case is discussed in lines 88-157, and the second in lines 158-210.

A. "First," Thomas says in a rare use of the first person singular, "I will show (*ostendam*) that an agent cause, namely God, need not precede his effect in duraction, if he had so willed:"

(1) No agent cause producing its effect *subito* need precede it by any duration. But God produces creatures not by motion of any sort, but *subito* by creation. Therefore God need not precede creation by any

---

of Rimini on Whether God Can Undo the Past," *Recherches de Théologie ancienne et médiévale*, 40 (1973), 224-256; 41 (1974), 147-174.

[41] "Tamen credo, quod si esset repugnantia intellectuum, esset falsum; si autem non est repugnantia intellectuum, non solum non est falsum sed etiam < non est > impossibile: aliter esset erroneum, si aliter dicatur" (ed. Leon. lines 67-71 with note supplying words in angle brackets); see Preface § 24 explaining variant readings and explaining sense intended by St. Thomas and the editors. For a comparison of certain printed editions (Perrier, n. 3; Marietti, 297) and Godfrey's ms, Paris, Bibl. Nat., ms lat. 16.297, fol. 68rb, see Wippel, "Did Thomas Aquinas Defend," pp. 30-36.

duration. The major can be proved inductively by every case of instantaneous change, as illumination by light. But this can also be proved by reason, as follows:

In the very moment anything exists, its activity has also begun to be, as when fire begins to be, its heating activity has also begun to be. But in instantaneous (*subita*) actions, the beginning and the end of an action are simultaneous, or rather are identical, as in all indivisibles. Therefore in the instant a cause that produces its effect *subito* exists, the term of its action can also be realized, and this is precisely what is meant by its effect. Therefore no intellectual absurdity is involved in saying that an agent cause need not precede its effect in duration. Such an absurdity, however, does exist in agents that produce their effect through motion, since the beginning of motion must come before the end. And since people are accustomed to think of making things (*productiones*) by motion, they do not readily understand that an agent cause need not precede its effect in duration. This is why many inexperienced minds, concentrating on a few cases, easily pontificate on this question. Nor can one object that God is a voluntary, not an inanimate agent, because the will also need not precede the effect in duration, exception where a process of deliberation is involved – which Heaven forbid we attribute to God.

(2) A cause that produces the whole substance of a thing is no slower than one that produces only the form from the potentiality of matter. But the latter can produce its effect the very instant the cause itself exists, as in illumination by the sun. With far greater reason, then, can God cause his effect to be whenever he himself exists.

(3) The only reason an effect cannot exist the same instant as the cause is that some element is wanting. But there is nothing wanting in God's causality. Therefore an effect of his can exist *semper*, since he does; so God need not precede the effect in duration.

(4) No agent lacks ability (*virtus*) by the mere fact of being a voluntary agent, least of all God. But those who attack the arguments of Aristotle in which things are shown to come from God *semper* (from eternity) say that the argument would follow if God were not a voluntary agent. Therefore, even though he is a voluntary agent, it still follows that he could cause the effect never to have been without existence.

So it is clear that no logical contradiction is involved in asserting that an agent need not precede its effect in duration, since whatever involves a logical contradiction cannot be brought about by God that it exist.

B. Second, Thomas considers the logical implications of creatures having come from nothing (*factum ex nihilo*). Does this exclude them from always having been, that is, *nunquam non fuisse*? Or is it possible that "something made from nothing" could also have always existed from God?

(1) That there is no contradiction between *factum ex nihilo* and always to have been from God is proved by Anselm's statement in his *Monologium*, c.8,[42] where a prior duration of *nihil* to creation is denied, as when a person is sad "for no reason at all," and the constitution of creatures is affirmed: "With the exception of the supreme essence, all things that exist were made out of nothing (*ex nihilo*), that is, not out of somehing (*non ex aliquo*)."

(2) Even assuming that *ex nihilo* meant an order of priority in the sense of *post nihil*, one must distinguish between a priority of time or duration and a priority of nature. One cannot argue from a more universal priority of nature, which all must concede, to a more particular priority of duration, so that first there would be "nothing," then later a "something." Left to itself in the order of nature a creature is nothing (*sibi relicta in se considerata nihil est*); the only *esse* a creature has is *ab alio*. *Unde prius naturaliter est sibi nichilum quam esse* (lines 194-195). Therefore the being of a creature does not consist in first being nothing and afterward "something," but rather "its nature is such that it would be nothing, if left to itself" (lines 199-200). Just as air left to itself is dark, since its only illumination comes from the Sun, so if it were always (*semper*) illumined, its illumination would always be from the Sun. This in no way means that first there had to be darkness before light, as is evident from the stars and orbs that are always illumined by the Sun.

Therefore it is evident that "being made by God" and "never without existence" do not involve any contradiction. If there were some contradiction, it is surprising that St. Augustine did not see it, since this is the best way to deny the eternity of the world, which he did in *De civitate Dei* 11 and 12. In fact he seems to suggest the absence of any contradiction in the same work (10, c.31) when speaking of the Platonists, who say that even if there is no priority of time, the universe would always be but a vestige of its maker, just as an eternal footprint would always indicate an eternal foot, and so forth.[43] It is also surprising that none of the greatest philosophers ever saw a contradiction between eternity and creation.

---

[42] Anselm, *Monologium*, c. 8, *Opera Omnia*, ed. F. S. Schmitt (Edinburgh, 1946-1961), 1: 23.

[43] Augustine, *De civitate Dei* 10, c. 31 (PL 41: 311; CCL 48: 309); also 11, c. 4 (PL 41: 319; CCL 48: 324).

Even those, like Aristotle, who held that the world is eternal "nevertheless taught that it was made by God" (*nihilominus ponunt eum a Deo factum*). They perceived no logical contradiction. So it must be that those who so subtly perceive it alone are intellectuals, from whom comes wisdom (cf. Job 12:2)!

Finally Thomas considers certain stock objections against his position, two being from authority and one from reason. (1) St. John Damascene says: "What is brought into existence from non-existence is not apt (*aptum natum*) to be co-eternal with him who is without beginning and is eternal." [44] (2) Hugh of St. Victor says: "The ineffable power of omnipotence would not have anything co-eternal with it, so as to have help in creating." [45]

To these and similar statements that attribute "eternity" to God alone Thomas utilized the distinction made by Boethius between two kinds of eternity.[46] One is the interminable succession, such as Plato attributed to the world, as did Aristotle himself. The other is an interminable presence of life *totum simul*, which is proper to the divine mind alone. In this latter sense no creature can be "eternal"; nor is it the sense of the discussion, although it was fear of putting creatures on a par with God in duration that aroused the *adversarii*. The reason no creature can be like God in the proper sense of "eternity" (*interminabilis vitae possessio*) is that he alone is immutable, as Augustine explains.[47]

(3) The final objection is the standard philosophical difficulty based on the impossibility of an actual infinity. If the world existed from eternity and man's soul is immortal, there must now be an infinite number of souls. Although the ways of answering this objection are many, Thomas here gives only three: (i) God could have made the world without men and souls; (ii) God could have made the world eternal and created man at a certain point in time, as he did *de facto*; (iii) "It has not yet been demonstrated that God cannot make an infinity of things actually to exist."

All other objections are dismissed here "either because they have been answered in other works, or because some are so feeble that they lend probability to their opposite by their very fragility."

---

[44] John Damascene, *De fide orthodoxa* 1, c. 8 trans. Burgundio of Pisa, ed. E. M. Buytaert (Saint Bonaventure, NY: Franciscan Institute, 1955), p. 32.

[45] Hugh of St-Victor, *De sacramentis* 1, c. 1 (PL 176: 187B).

[46] Boethius, *De consolatione philosophiae* 5, prosa 6 (PL 63: 859; CCL 94: 101): "Aeternitas igitur est interminabilis vitae tota simul et perfecta possessio."

[47] Augustine, *De civitate Dei* 12, c. 16 (PL 41: 364-365; CCL 48: 372); also *De Gen. ad lit.* 8, c. 23 (PL 34: 389); *Conf.* 11, c. 30 (PL 32: 826).

III. Some Further Considerations

A careful reading of St. Thomas' text, which we have tried to give, ought to convince the reader that this opuscule is not a philosophical work. It is not directed against Aristotle or radical Aristotelians, such as Siger of Brabant, Boethius of Dacia, or any of their followers; nor is it a defense of Aristotle or Aristotle's arguments against his opponents. It is not a close analysis of Aristotle's text, such as one finds in *De unitate intellectus contra Averroistas*, clearly dated 1270. There seems, however, to be a close connection between the opuscule and Thomas' commentary (*Sententia*) on Aristotle's *Physics*, where the arguments are examined in context. It would seem that this commentary was written at least in part after the beginning of 1271, since Book Lambda of the *Metaphysics* is twice referred to as Book 12, and Book Kappa itself implied when Thomas says, "ut in *Metaphysica* probatum est" (*In 3 Physica*, lect. 7, n. 11). The view that will be suggested is that *De aeternitate mundi* is a theological work, directed at an almost universal stance (and not against any one theologian or work), connected with a better understanding of Aristotle's arguments in *Physics* 8.

The precise question formulated in *De aeternitate mundi*, however, belongs entirely to the theologian. Questions concerning the power of God and the limits of human reason are the domain of theology, as well as the Church. The Fourth Lateran Council had declared on 11 November 1215 that there is only one true and eternal God (*unus solus verus Deus, aeternus...*) and that he alone created all things, spiritual and corporeal, at the beginning of time out of nothing (*qui sua omnipotenti virtute simul ab initio temporis utramque de nihilo condidit creaturam, spiritualem et corporalem*). It belongs to the theologian to determine whether unaided human reason can demonstrate the existence of one God, creation of the universe out of nothing, and the eternity of the world, although he needs logic to do so. Mindful of this prerogative of theology, the Faculty of Arts at Paris issued the statute "Noverint universi" on 1 April 1272.[48] It strictly forbade masters and bachelors in arts to discuss purely theological questions or, in matters touching both philosophy and theology, to determine a disputed question contrary to the faith. This statute was issued fifteen months after the condemnation of thirteen Averroist theses in December 1270. St. Thomas himself was fully aware of the role of the theologian in determining the limits of human reason. For him it was just as important to present sound arguments in defense of the faith as not to

---

[48] *Chartularium Universitatis Parisiensis*, ed. Denifle-Chatelain 1: 499-500, n. 441.

prejudice the faith by bad arguments, "lest perhaps someone, presuming to demonstrate what is of faith, induce non-demonstrative arguments, which offer occasion for laughter to infidels who think it is for these reasons that we believe what is of faith." [49] Similarly the Church has always declared it her prerogative to determine what the human mind can know with certainty regarding God and what it can in no way demonstrate or comprehend, as she did in the First Vatican Council.[50]

The question Thomas formulated in *De aeternitate mundi* is very precise: is it possible that a created world exist without a beginning? Or more positively: could the world have been created by God from all eternity so that it always existed (*semper*) and was never without existence?

The background or "common opinion" against which Thomas argued his novel position went back more than seventy years; some would claim perpetuity to the view that no creature, by its very nature, could be or could have been eternal, since "eternity" is an attribute unique to God. Even apart from the decree "Firmiter" of the Fourth Lateran Council, there were many theologians who brought the charge of "heresy" against any view that would attribute "eternity" of any sort to creatures.

Centuries of Christian speculation on the first verse of Genesis had yielded, even before the thirteenth century, at least four tenets in the Christian doctrine of creation: that God alone created the world; that he created the world out of nothing (*ex nihilo*); that he created the world immediately without secondary causes; and that he created the world with a temporal beginning, that is, at the beginning of time, and not from eternity. All of these questions were heatedly debated throughout the thirteenth century. The question of creation *ex nihilo* and "with a beginning" are of concern here.[51]

Even before Aristotle's *Physics* and *Metaphysics* were translated and known in Paris, the Latins seem to have known that Aristotle taught the eternity of the world. Calcidius (mid-fourth century) in his obscure way noted that Aristotle *sine genitura et sine interitu dicit mundum esse divina providentia perpetuitati propagatum.*[52] From Peter Lombard (ca. 1100-

---

[49] Thomas, st 1, q. 46, a. 2; also *In 2 Sent.*, dist. 1, q. I, a. 5; *De pot.* q. 3, a. 14; *Quodl.* 3, q. 14, a. 2.

[50] Denzinger-Schönmetzer, *Enchiridion Symbolorum*, ed. 36, nn. 3000-3045.

[51] For an excellent survey of these problems in the thirteenth century, see Steven E. Baldner, "Four Hitherto Unedited 'Quaestiones' on Creation Attributed to St. Bonaventure," Ph.D. thesis (Toronto, 1981).

[52] Calcidius, *Timaeus* N. 283, ed. J. H. Waszink (London-Leiden: Brill, 1962), p. 286.5-6. In a note to these lines, the editor, referring to Zeller, claims that Aristotle nowhere says the world was *sine genitura*, but frequently says it was *sine interitu*. If by the former is meant "without a cause," Zeller and Waszink are correct.

1160) the early schoolmen learned that Plato taught there were three
initia, namely God, the exemplar, and matter: *ipsa increata, sine principio,
et Deum quasi artificem, non creatorem*. They also learned from him that
Aristotle said there were two *principia*, namely matter and species, and a
third called *"operatorium"*; *mundum quoque semper esse et fuisse*.[53] This
information Peter Lombard indicated came from Walafrid Strabo![54]

When the Latin translations of Aristotle's *Physics* became known in
Paris at the end of the twelfth century, scholastic masters could see for
themselves that in Book 8 of the *Physics* Aristotle did indeed teach that the
world, time, and motion are eternal; this could easily have been taken as a
denial of creation. Roger Bacon, writing in 1292, claimed that Aristotle's
natural philosophy and metaphysics were condemned and "excommuni-
cated at Paris before the year 1237 because of the eternity of the world
and of time, and because of the book *De divinatione somniorum*, which is
the third book of *De somno et vigilia*."[55] Certainly Robert Grosseteste,
glossing Aristotle's *Physics* between 1228 and 1232, was particularly
incensed at the false and heretical position of Aristotle.[56] Indeed he
thought that his position made creatures equal to God.[57] But Albert the
Great, commenting on the *Sentences* in the mid-1240s, was frankly
embarassed by Peter Lombard's claim, and admits that "what is said here
is not found in the books of Aristotle that have come down to us." He
notes that at the end of *Physics* 1 Aristotle says there are three principles of

---

[53] Peter Lombard, *Sententiae in 4 Libris Distinctae*, ed. 3a, ed. I. Brady et al.
(Grottaferrata, 1972), 2, dist. 1, c. 1, n. 2 & c. 3, n. 4.

[54] Ibid., notes to these numbers, pp. 330-331, *Prothemata Glossae ordinariae* to
Genesis 1. For the sources, see editor's note at the beginning of dist. 1 (ibid., p. 329) and J.
de Blic, "L'œuvre exégétique de Walafrid Strabon et la Glossa ordinaria," *Recherches de
Théologie ancienne et médiévale*, 16 (1949), 5-28, esp. 20-25.

[55] Roger Bacon: "et Parisius excommunicabantur ante annum Domini 1237 propter
eternitatem mundi et temporis, et propter librum de divinacione sompniorum, qui est
tertius de sompno et vigilia et propter multa alia erronee translata." *Compendium studii
theologiae*, ed. H. Rashdall (Aberdeen: Academic, 1911), p. 33. This undoubtedly refers to
1231 when Gregory ix renewed the prohibition of Aristotle's books in natural philosophy
decreed by the Provincial Council of Paris in 1210 *ex certa causa prohibiti* (*Chart. Univ.
Par*. 1: 138, n. 89). There seems to be no contemporary evidence indicating that "eternity
of the world" was one of those reasons. The year 1237 was a particularly significant year
for Bacon, probably his first year in Paris teaching arts; everything before 1237 was
probably hearsay.

[56] Roberti Grosseteste, *Commentarius in VIII libros Physicorum Aristotelis*, ed. Richard
C. Dales (Boulder: University of Colorado Press, 1963), pp. 144-147. For date, sources,
and influence, see pp. ix-xxi. On the separate circulation of this section, see R. C. Dales,
"Robert Grosseteste's treatise *De finitate motus et temporis*," *Traditio*, 19 (1963), 245-266.

[57] "Et hec falsa ymaginacio infinitatis temporis ex parte ante inducit necessario falsam
ymaginacionem perpetuitatis motus et mundi et creature coequeve deo." *Commentarius*,
lib. 8, ed. Dales, p. 147.

nature, namely matter, form, and privation, "but this is neither false nor heretical ... while the third [principle] attributed to him, is not found there." [58] It is difficult to know what the early scholastic theologians thought of Aristotle.

Paris theologians of the early thirteenth century, for the most part, seem to have been blinded by the revealed fact that God did in fact create the universe with a beginning in time (Genesis 1.1). Somehow they seem to have made "having a beginning" (*incipit*), or "coming after nothing" (*post nihil*) essential to the notion of being a creature, rather than total dependence on God. William of Auvergne, one of the most influential even before he became bishop of Paris (1228-1249), defined creation as the *novitas existendi* of a being *ex nihilo* by the immediate will of the Creator.[59] For him, the world at first did not exist (*prius non esse fuit mundus*), then suddenly it existed; and since there cannot be an infinity of past time, the world began to be *in tempore et ex tempore*.[60] William apparently thought an "eternal world" was a necessary world that emanated necessarily and naturally from God, such as Avicenna taught – a clearly heretical view.

One of the stock objections from philosophy that was mentioned by all scholastic theologians, one that Thomas used to his advantage, was simply stated in the *Summa fratris Alexandri*: "cum causa posita ponatur causatum, ab aeterno fuit mundus." [61] Since God is the cause of the world and he is eternal, the world too should be eternal. Scholastic theologians were firmly attached to God's immutability and free choice. They were unanimous in seeing that God's will is free and that things come about "when" it has been determined for them from eternity without any change in God. But the standard view, taken by Franciscans and seculars alike (and some Dominicans), was that God had to precede creation, and *nihil* had to precede created being.[62] St. Bonaventure, of course, never

[58]   Albert, *In 2 Sent.*, dist. 1, a. 11, ed. Borgnet 27: 30b.
[59]   William of Auvergne, *De universo* 1, c. 23 in *Opera Omnia* (Paris, 1674), 1: 618ϝ; see also 1, c.11, and *De trinitate*, c. 10, ed. B. Switalski (Toronto: PIMS, 1976), pp. 66-73. Steven E. Baldner, "Four ... 'Quaestiones'," pp. 12-24.
[60]   William of Auvergne, *De trinitate* c. 10, ed. Switalski, pp. 67-68.
[61]   *Summa fr. Alexandri* P. 1, lib. 2, q. 2, tit. 4, c. 1, a. 1, obj. 8, ed. Quaracchi (1928), vol. 2, n. 67, p. 85a.
[62]   "Mundum esse ab aeterno sive sine principio est impossibile" (*Sum. fr. Alexandri* 1, n. 64, ed. Quaracchi (1924), p. 95). "Credo impossibile simpliciter, quia implicat contradictionem" (Bonaventure, *Super Sent.* 1, dist. 44, a. 1, a. 4, ed. minor, Quaracchi (1934), 1: 626b). "Dico quod Deus non potuit creare mundum vel creaturam aliquam sibi coeternam" (Richard Fishacre, *Super Sent.* 2, d. 12). "Bene concedo quod de ratione creati est non esse ab aeterno, nec fieri posse" (Albert, *In 1 Sent.* d. 44, a. 1, ed. Borgnet, 26: 390a).

forgave the philosophers (*nimis ratiocinantes*) for thinking that the world was eternal and consequently, uncreated.[63] But for him, this was the natural and pitiful state of human reason without faith.[64] In his first *Collatio in Hexaemeron* in 1270, he referred to the difficulties of pagan philosophers regarding an eternal world, "despite the truth extorted from Aristotle [*Topics* 1.11.104b15-17] that eternity of the world cannot easily be proved."[65] "Nor," he said, "has any philosopher maintained that something is both *de nihilo* and 'eternal',"[66] although this is precisely Thomas' view of Aristotle, and it is the view proposed in the opuscule as not impossible.

Surprisingly even St. Albert seems to have had a blind spot regarding this problem, at least in his lectures on the *Sentences* and in his Parisian questions. On the one hand, Albert recognized that a cause need not precede the effect in duration. He quoted the example given by St. Augustine concerning an eternal footprint being a vestige of an eternal foot, and the illumination of the hemisphere being simultaneous with the sunrise. The very words Albert uses to describe the philosophers might have been Thomas' own: "Therefore even though the Philosophers concede that God is the cause of the whole world – *sicut omnes concedunt* – they need not for this reason maintain that the world began."[67] On the other hand, Albert insisted in those same works that the *nunc temporis* of creation had to be preceded by the *nunc aeternitatis* of God.[68] Albert

---

[63] "Sed in omnibus iis novem ratio luxuriata est et excessit. Nam quantum ad rerum quidditatem, quidam nimis ratiocinantes mundum possuerunt aeternum, cum eius causa sit aeterna." Bonaventure, *Collationes in Hexaemeron*, visio 1, Collatio 2, n. 21, ed. Delorme (Quaracchi, 1934), p. 84; see also ibid., n. 13, p. 55; *Super Sent.* 2, dist. 1, p. 1, a. 1, q. 2, editio minor, Quaracchi (1934), pp. 15-16.

[64] For notes and exposition of this, see A. A. Maurer, *Medieval Philosophy*, rev. ed. (Toronto: PIMS, 1982), pp. 140-141.

[65] "... quod mundus sit aeternus, quod non habent pro inconvenienti, cum tamen hoc non probari possit de facili, ut innuit Aristoteles, principio *Topicorum*.... Istud ergo dictum de corde hominis veritatem extirpat." *Collationes in Hexaemeron*, ed. Delorme, p. 55.

[66] "Nec quisquam philosophorum posuit hoc, quod aliquid sit de nihilo et sit aeternum." Ibid. Also *Super Sent.* 2, d. 1, p. 1, a. 1, q. 2 (ed. minor, Quaracchi [1934], 2: 15a): "Dicendum quod ponere mundum aeternum esse sive aeternaliter productum, ponendo res omnes ex nihilo productas, omnino est contra veritatem et rationem, sicut ultima ratio probat [i.e., supra f.]; et adeo contra rationem, ut nullum philosophorum quantumcumque parvi intellectus rediderim hoc posuisse."

[67] "Ergo etiamsi concedunt philosophi quod Deus est principium totius mundi, sicut omnes concedunt, non est necesse ponere propter hoc mundum incipisse." Albert, *In 2 Sent.* dist. 1, a. 10, ed. Borgnet 27: 27a. Also *Summa de creaturis* P. 2, q. 80, a. 1, ed. Borgnet 35: 651.

[68] Albert, *In 2 Sent.* dist. 1, a. 10, ed. Borgnet 27: 29-30; *Summa de creaturis* P. 2, q. 80, a. 1, ed. Borgnet 35: 651-654.

had no doubt that the "world began, as Moses said," and that this was more probable even according to unaided reason. What was demonstratively impossible was that the world came to be by motion and generation, or that it will cease to be in this manner; "and this alone is what the arguments of Aristotle prove; hence they conclude nothing contrary to the faith." [69] While Aristotle is exonerated, certain Greek and Arabic commentators on Aristotle, like Alexander, Themistius, and Averroes, "undoubtedly lead to heresy." [70]

The Franciscan master William of Baglione consciously opposed the view of Thomas, expressed in the *Summa*, on the possibility of eternal creation. In his disputation on the question, held during the scholastic year 1266-1267 before Thomas returned to Paris, he contended that one can demonstrate both that the world *is not* and *cannot be* eternal.[71] As we have already seen, the Franciscan John Pecham disputed this question early in 1270, determining against Thomas that the world *is not* and *could not have been eternal*.[72] The five arguments Pecham used were discussed above. We need only note here that Pecham's inspiration is clearly that of Bonaventure: "All those who have spoken of creation without faith (*sine fide*) have erred either by default in not attributing it to God, or by excess in attributing it to others than God." But Pecham seems to go further than Bonaventure in considering his arguments for creation in time to be demonstrative, rather than probable and persuasive.[73]

Recently Fr. John F. Wippel of Catholic University of America has made a very careful study of the development of Thomas' approach to this question in seven distinct works besides *De aeternitate mundi*.[74] After

---

[69] "Et hoc solum probant illae rationes, quae sunt Aristotelis. Unde illae nihil contra fidem concludunt." Albert, *In 2 Sent.* dist. 1, a. 10, ed. Borgnet 27: 29a.

[70] "Et per haec patet solutio ad omnia illa quae sunt adducta usque ad quartam viam, quae non est Aristotelis, sed commentatorum qui absque dubio haereses induxerunt." Ibid.

[71] See Ignatius Brady, "The Questions of Master William of Baglione o.f.m., *De aeternitate mundi* (Paris 1266-67)," *Antonianum*, 42 (1972), 368, 370.

[72] Brady, see above n. 31.

[73] Rather than explain precisely what truths of faith are demonstrable by philosophical reasoning, as Thomas had done, Bonaventure was more concerned to show how little philosophers have *de facto* understood of (i) creation *ex nihilo*, and (ii) the beginning of the world in time, despite their reasonableness. There is no evidence that he would allow either to be demonstrable by reason, whereas Pecham presented both as equally demonstrable and demonstrated. See Baldner, "Four ... 'Quaestiones'," pp. 108-149.

[74] Wippel, "Did Thomas Aquinas Defend." The relevant passages considered are: *In 2 Sent.* dist. 1, q. 1, a. 5 (ca. 1253); scg 2, cc. 31-38 (ca. 1260); *De pot.* q. 3, a. 17 (1256-1266); *Quodl.* 3, q. 14, a. 2 (1270); st 1, q. 46 (ca. 1266); *Quodl.* 12, q. 6, a. 1 (Advent 1270); *Comp. theol.* cc. 98-99 (1269-1973).

serious consideration of the arguments in each of these seven works, Fr.
Wippel concludes that "in none of these texts ... does he maintain
positively and without qualification that an eternal world is indeed
possible." [75] In his earliest discussion, *In 2 Sententiarum*, Thomas
maintained that *no one has demonstrated* either the eternity or beginning
of the world: it is a contingent fact, depending solely on the free choice of
God, and history itself is contingent. In his disputed questions *De potentia*
q.3, a.14, Thomas even shows that there is *no intrinsic contradiction*
between "being created" and "always existing"; here he had "all the
necessary ammunition at hand in order to take the final step and to assert
positively that an eternally created effect is indeed possible; yet he
hesitates to do so." [76] But in *De aeternitate mundi* "Thomas does indeed
defend the possibility of an eternally created world." [77] He even disarms
his opponents in the Faculty of Theology by suggesting in advance that,
whether it be true or false, such a view would not be heretical; and that
such a view is not only not false, but to hold its contrary would be
erroneous in the faith.

The main point of Fr. Wippel's study can be stated briefly: "In my
opinion Thomas Aquinas did not clearly defend the possibility of eternal
creation or of an eternally created world prior to his *De aeternitate
mundi*." [78] In *De potentia*, q.3, a.14, "he seems to come very close to
asserting that an eternally created world" is possible. But only in *De aeternitate mundi* does Thomas argue that since these two notes – to be created
and always to exist – are not mutually exclusive, "it is possible for an
effect (and for the world) to be produced from eternity by God." [79]

In view of this major contribution to Thomistic scholarhip, Fr. Wippel
raised two relevant questions: (1) Why did Thomas hesitate to defend this
stronger position prior to his *De aeternitate mundi*? (2) Why did he go
farther in this work than in all the others and maintain that an eternally
created world is possible? Realizing that we may never know the right
answers, I should like to make a suggestion that might be helpful.

Everyone knows that in this question of reason and revelation St.
Thomas followed the lead of Rabbi Moses ben Maimon or Maimonides,
as he is better known. His *Guide of the Perplexed* was translated into

---

[75] Wippel, pp. 29-30.

[76] Ibid., p. 28.

[77] Ibid., p. 31. "Sic ergo patet quod in hoc quod dicitur aliquid esse factum a Deo et
nunquam non fuisse, non est intellectus aliqua repugnantia." Thomas, *De aeternitate
mundi*, ed. Leon. p. 88.211-213.

[78] Wippel, p. 36.

[79] Ibid.

Latin, apparently between 1230 and 1236,[80] and was of tremendous help to Albert the Great, Thomas Aquinas, and to many others. The three views (*triplex positio*) concerning this problem, given by Thomas in his *Scriptum super Sententias* are taken from Moses Maimonides (*Guide* 2, c.13). Thomas explicitly refers the reader of the *Scriptum* to Rabbi Moses, *Dux neutrorum* 1, c.73, where Maimonides resolved the difficulty of an infinite number of souls used by Algazel to show that the world must have had a beginning in time.

More important for our purpose here is the claim of Maimonides in *The Guide* 2, c.15, "to make it clear that Aristotle possesses no demonstration for the world being eternal, as he understands [demonstration]." That is, according to Maimonides, Aristotle himself "knows that he possesses no demonstration with regard to this point." The entire chapter is devoted to proving that "Aristotle cannot be supposed to have believed that these statements [in his writings] were demonstrations, for it was Aristotle who taught mankind the methods, the rules, and the conditions of demonstration." [81] He even gave the clinching evidence commonly used by Thomas and others, namely Aristotle's *Topics* 1.11, 104b15-17, where Aristotle lists "Whether the world is eternal?" as a difficult problem suitable for dialectical reasoning. When Thomas presented his view of the question for the first time, he said:

> I therefore say that there are no demonstrations for either side of the question, but [only] probable or sophistical arguments for both sides. And the words of the Philosopher indicate this when he says in I *Topics*, c.11, that there are certain problems for which we do not have a [real] answer (*ratio*), such as whether the world is eternal. Hence he himself never intended to demonstrate this problem. This is evident from his manner of proceeding, because wherever he discussed this question, he always added some persuasive measure either from the opinion of the majority or from

[80] The careful work of Prof. Wolfgang Kluxen of the University of Bonn suggests that the Latin version of the *Guide*, called *Dux neutrorum*, was made between 1230 and 1235. For the medieval Latin translations of this work, see W. Kluxen, "Literargeschichtliches zum lateinischen Moses Maimonides," *Recherches de Théologie ancienne et médiévale*, 21 (1954), 23-50; idem, "Die Geschichte des Maimonides im lateinischen Abendland als Beispiel einer christlich-jüdischen Begegnung," *Miscellanea Mediaevalia*, Bd. 4 (Berlin: de Gruyter, 1966), pp. 146-182. A humanist revision of one Latin translation, a less fortunate choice, was made by the Dominican bishop of Nebbio in Corsica, Augustinus Justinianus (Giustiniani), and published at Paris in 1520. A better version was published by the Hebraist Johannes Buxtorf at Basel in 1629.

[81] Moses Maimonides, *Guide of the Perplexed*, trans. by Shlomo Pines (Chicago: University of Chicago, 1963), pp. 289-293.

the suitability of the reasons, none of which are in any way proper to one who intends to demonstrate.[82]

All of this depends entirely on Moses Maimonides in its Latin translation *Dux neutrorum*.

In the *Summa theologiae* 1, q.46, a.1, Thomas again insists that Aristotle's arguments are not demonstrative *simpliciter*, but only *secundum quid*, namely to contradict the opposition among the ancients. This, Thomas thinks, is evident from (i) the fact that these arguments in *Physics* 8 and *De caelo* 1 are against definite opinions, such as Anaxagoras, Empedocles, and Plato; (ii) the testimony of antiquity alleged by Aristotle are only persuasive arguments; and (iii) Aristotle explicitly said in *Topics* 1 [11, 104b15-17] that there are certain dialectical problems for which we do not have a reason, such as "whether the world is eternal."

Again, in his disputed questions *De potentia*, which are contemporary with the above *Summa*, Thomas used the reasoning of Maimonides, claiming that Aristotle's arguments at the beginning of *Physics* 8 are "rationes disputantis contra positionem," since they are against the opinions of Anaxagoras and Empedocles "contra quas disputare intendit."[83] While in *De potentia* q.3, a.17, Thomas did not refer to the passage in *Topics* 1.11, he did note the intrinsic weakness of Aristotle's arguments involving motion before motion, and time before time.

These same points had been made by Albert the Great, particularly in his paraphrase of Aristotle's *Physics* around 1250. He not only pointed out the non-demonstrative character of Aristotle's arguments and insisted that neither eternity nor beginning in time could be demonstrated by human reason, but he also argued that Aristotle knew he had no demonstration. The influence of Moses Maimonides is clear:

> One might very well ask, if everything we have said is true, then why did Aristotle, who understood far more subtle things, not say them? I say positively, it seems to me that Aristotle knew perfectly well that there was no necessity in his arguments to prove the eternity of the world. He shows this in many books of *De caelo et mundo*, where he says he is looking for answers out of sheer curiosity as a philosopher, and holds views that can be more easily contradicted than some others. This was an indication that he knew he did not have a demonstration, because a demonstration cannot

[82] Thomas, *In 2 Sent.* dist. 1, q. 1, a. 5, ed. Mandonnet (Paris, 1929), 2: 33-34; see Maimonides, *Guide* 2, c. 15, trans. Pines (Chicago, 1963), p. 290.

[83] Thomas, *De pot.* q. 3, a. 17; also ad 15.

be contradicted in any way, and even if it were contradicted by everyone, it would not on that account be any less necessary than if it were contradicted by no one. In the *Physics* Aristotle is accustomed to give only physical conclusions that can be proved by physical arguments. But the beginning of the world by creation (*per creationem*) is neither a physical statement, nor can it be proved by arguments of physics (*physice*). And so it is thought that Aristotle was silent about this [other] way in physics, and did not touch upon it expressly except in the book *De natura deorum*, which he edited.[84]

What Albert understood by the book *De natura deorum*, "which he edited," remains mysterious, but Albert's point here, inspired by Moses Maimonides, is that Aristotle himself realized that this arguments for an eternal world were not conclusive.[85]

When, however, Thomas came to write his own literal commentaries (*Sententiae*) on Aristotle's text, he saw more clearly the significance of an eternal world for the integrity of Aristotle's argument leading to a First Mover who is the cause of the total being of the world (*causa essendi totius mundi*). That is to say, Thomas rejected his own earlier interpretation, that Aristotle considered his arguments to be only probable. Before taking up the many weaknesses in Aristotle's arguments for an eternal world in *Physics* 8.1, Thomas notes explicitly:

> But some, vainly trying to show that Aristotle is not speaking contrary to the faith, have said that Aristotle here did not intend to prove as true (*quod Aristoteles non intendit hic probare quasi verum*), that motion is perpetual, but to give a reason for both sides as for a doubtful matter (*inducere rationem ad utramque partem, quasi ad rem dubiam*). This seems frivolous (*frivolum*) from the very procedure employed. Besides, he uses perpetuity of time and motion as a starting point (*quasi principio*) to prove that a First Principle exists, both here in Book VIII and in *Metaphysics* XII. Hence it is plain that he takes this [premise of an eternal world] as proven.[86]

---

[84] Albert, *Physica* 8, tr. 1, c. 14, ed. Borgnet 3: 555a-b; see Moses Maimonides, *Guide* 2, c. 15, trans. Pines, p. 290. Bonaventure in his commentary on the *Sentences* (ca. 1255) remarked: "Quidam tamen moderni dicunt Philosophum nequaquam illud sensisse nec intendisse probare, quod mundus omnino non coeperit, sed quod non coeperit naturali motu." *Super Sent.* 2, dist. 1, a. 1, q. 2 (editio minor, 2: 15b).

[85] See J. A. Weisheipl, "Albert's Disclaimers in the Aristotelian Paraphrases," *Proceedings of the Patristic, Mediaeval and Renaissance Conference* (Villanova), 5 (1980) in press.

[86] "Quidam vero frustra conantes Aristotelem ostendere non contra fidem locutum esse, dixerunt quod Aristoteles non intendit hic probare quasi verum, quod motus sit perpetuus; sed inducere rationem ad utramque partem, quasi ad rem dubiam: quod ex ipso modo procedendi *frivolum* apparet. Et praeterea, perpetuitate temporis et motus *quasi principio utitur* ad probandum primum principium esse, et hic in octavo [c. 6] et in XII

In the long, tightly reasoned debate that follows, showing that Aristotle's arguments do not necessarily hold, Thomas introduces no new insights, that is, none that had not been employed before.

But when the eternity of motion, taken as proved, is used to show the existence and nature (*qualis sit*) of the First Unmoved Mover, the significance of this premise becomes clear:

> Just as some things are always true (*semper vera*) but have a cause of their veracity (*causam suae veritatis*), so Aristotle understood that some things are always being (*semper entia*), such as celestial bodies and separated substances, which nevertheless would have a cause of their being (*causam sui esse*). From this it is evident that although Aristotle held for an eternal world, he did not [thereby] believe that God is not a cause of its very being (*causa essendi ipsi mundo*), but a cause only of its motion, as some have said.[87]

This becomes of crucial importance when Thomas comes to show that for Aristotle the First Mover is a *causa essendi* of the world. In the middle of a long digression against Averroes' rejection of Alexander's interpretation of Aristotle, Thomas says:

> Everything that is not its own *esse*, shares *esse* from the First Cause, which is its own *esse*. Hence even Averroes himself admits in *De substantia orbis* that God is the cause of the heavens (*causa celi*) and not only of their motion. This cannot be unless it is because they [the heavens] have *esse* from him. But the only being (*esse*) they have from him is perpetual. Therefore they have perpetuity from another (*ab alio*).
>
> Indeed Aristotle's statements are also consistent with this, when he said in *Metaphysics* v and above at the beginning of this Eighth Book, that some things are necessary which have a cause for their necessity. This being supposed, the solution is plain according to the mind of Alexander, that just as a celestial body has "being moved" from another, so also it has "being" (*sicut corpus caeleste habet moveri ab alio, ita et esse*). Hence just as perpetuity of motion demonstrates the infinite power of the mover, not the

---

Metaphys. [c. 6]; unde manifestum est, quod *supponit hoc tanquam probatum.*" Thomas, *In 8 Phys.*, lect. 2, n. 16.

[87] "Est autem valde notandum quod hic dicitur; quia ut in II *Metaph.* [c. 1, 993b23-32] habetur, eadem est dispositio rerum in esse et in veritate. Sicut igitur aliqua sunt semper vera et tamen habent causam suae veritatis, ita Aristoteles intellexit quod essent aliqua semper entia, scilicet corpora caelestia et substantiae separatae, *et tamen haberent causam sui esse*. Ex quo patet quod quamvis Aristoteles poneret mundum aeternum, non tamen credidit quod Deus non *sit causa essendi ipsi mundo*, sed causa motus eius tantum, ut quidam dixerunt." Thomas, *In 8 Phys.*, lect. 3, n. 6.

body moved, so too the perpetuity of its duration demonstrates the infinite power of the cause from which it has being (*esse*).[88]

Numerous passages could be cited to show that at least during St. Thomas' second regency in Paris, he saw most clearly that Aristotle argued from the eternity of the world (proven) to a mover who was the *causa essendi* of the world, but two must suffice. In *De articulis fidei* (between 1261 and 1270) Thomas first listed the error of Plato, "who held that the world was made by God but from preexistent matter," and then the error of Aristotle, "qui posuit mundum a Deo factum sed ab aeterno." [89] In *De substantiis separatis*, c.9 (clearly after the beginning of 1271) Thomas is most explicit:

> One should not think that just because Plato and Aristotle held that immaterial substances and even celestial bodies always existed, that they

---

[88] "Omne enim quod non est suum esse, participat esse a causa prima, quae est suum esse. Unde et ipsemet confitetur in libro *De substantia orbis*, quod Deus est causa caeli non solum quantum ad motum eius, sed *etiam quantum ad substantiam ipsius: quod non est nisi quia ab eo habet esse*. Non autem habet ab eo esse nisi perpetuum: habet ergo perpetuitatem ab alio. Et in hoc etiam consonant dicta Aristotelis qui dicit in V Metaphys. [c. 5] et supra in principio huius octavi [c. 1] quod quaedam sunt necessaria quae habent causam suae necessitatis. Hoc ergo supposito, plana est solutio secundum intentionem Alexandri, quod *sicut corpus caeleste habet moveri ab alio, ita et esse*. Unde sicut motus perpetuus demonstrat infinitam virtutem motoris, non autem ipsius mobilis; ita et perpetua eius duratio *demonstrat infinitam virtutem causae a qua habet esse*." Thomas, *In 8 Phys.*, lect. 21, n. 14.

[89] "Secundus error est Platonis et Anaxagore, qui *posuerunt mundum factum a Deo sed ex materia preiacenti*; contra quos dicitur in Psalmo 'Mandavit et creata sunt,' id est ex nihilo facta. Tertius est error Aristotelis, qui *posuit mundum a Deo factum sed ab eterno*; contra quem dicitur Gen. 1:1 'In principio creavit Deus celum et terram'." Thomas, *De articulis fidei*, ed. Leon. 42: 246.112-119. In trying to show that St. Thomas did not impute the doctrine of creation to Aristotle, Anton C. Pegis had considerable difficulty with certain texts of Thomas. But in the last analysis he rested his case on a "decisive text" in the Mandonnet edition of this work (*Opuscula* [Paris, 1927], 3: 3), which reads, "Tertius est error Aristotelis, qui posuit mundum a Deo factum non [*sic*] esse, sed ab aeterno fuisse." A. C. Pegis, *St. Thomas and the Greeks* (Milwaukee: Marquette University Press, 1939), fn. 64, pp. 101-102. The Leonine edition does not even list "non" as a variant reading — besides, the structure of the sentence cannot take it. Similarly, by a peculiar interpretation of ST 1, q. 44, a. 2 "Utrique igitur (*sc.* Plato and Aristotle)," this becomes a "decisive passage" contradicting all other passages, including *De pot.*, q. 3, a. 5. See E. Gilson, *The Spirit of Mediaeval Philosophy* (New York: Scribner, 1940), fn. 4, pp. 438-441, esp. p. 440; A. C. Pegis, "A Note on St. Thomas, *Summa Theologica*, I, 44, 1-2," *Mediaeval Studies*, 8 (1946), 159-168. We must remember that the essential meaning of creation is nothing more or less than "total dependence in being on a *causa essendi*," and this is what Thomas applied totally to Aristotle, and partially to Plato, i.e., Plato *exempted matter*, while Aristotle's entire error concerning creation was that is was *eternal*. See n. 90.

thereby dismissed a cause of their being (*eius causam essendi*). They deviate from the faith not for saying that they are uncreated (*increata*), but for saying that they always existed (*semper fuisse*); the opposite of this is maintained by the Catholic faith.[90]

The commentary on the *Metaphysics* and on *De caelo*, where Thomas makes the same claim, presupposes the solution worked out in the *Physics* and are known to be late from extrinsic evidence.[91]

It would seem, then, that Thomas hesitated to defend the stronger position prior to his *De aeternitate mundi* because he thought that Aristotle himself did not take the position of the eternity of the world seriously, as Moses Maimonides, Albert the Great, and Thomas himself had believed. But once he was convinced, while commenting on the *Physics* early in his second Parisian regency, that Aristotle really thought he had demonstrated the eternity of the world, Thomas saw with unmistaken clarity the compatibility of "being created" and "being always," since Aristotle himself had seen it. While Thomas himself had seen the compatibility when disputing *De potentia* in Rome (between 1265 and 1268), he did not realize that Aristotle likewise saw no incompatibility.

If this is true, then Thomas' *De aeternitate mundi* must be dated with or shortly after his commentary on the *Physics*. Since two out of the five references to *Metaphysics* Lambda are given as "in Book 12," and Book Kappa itself is referred to once implicitly, the commentary on the *Physics* must be dated around 1270-1271, or at least after early 1271. But why Thomas took it upon himself to write the opuscule *De aeternitate mundi* is not so clear. It is, as we have said, a theological work, and it is against the common view of contemporary theologians that "being created" and "always existing" involve an intrinsic contradiction, and therefore are impossible. This work does not seem to be against any one theologian in

---

[90] "Non ergo aestimandum est quod Plato et Aristoteles, propter hoc quod posuerunt substantias immateriales seu etiam caelestia corpora semper fuisse, *eis subtraxerunt causam essendi*; non enim in hoc a sententia catholicae fidei deviarunt quod *huiusmodi posuerunt increata, sed quia posuerunt ea semper fuisse*: cuius contrarium fides catholica tenet." Thomas, *De substantiis separatis*, c. 9, ed. Leon. 40: D 58.215-221.

[91] For similar passages in other works, see Thomas, *In 2 Metaph*. lect. 2, n. 7 (Marietti, p. 295); *In 6 Metaph*. lect. 1, n. 21 (1104); *In 1 De caelo*, lect. 8, n. 14; *Expositio super primam decretalem*, ed. Leon. 40: E 35.432-434; *De quattuor opositis*, c. 4, n. 595; cf. *In 5 Metaph.*, lect. 6 (esp. nn. 839-841). Here it is not a question of what Aristotle personally thought (or Plato, for that matter) — on this the scholars are divided, but on what St. Thomas thought they meant — on this there cannot be any doubt, certainly not after Thomas returned to Paris for a second regency in 1269.

particular, neither Bonaventure, nor Pecham, as such; nor does it seem to be against any one particular composition or dispute. Thomas' arguments are too general for that and the authorities quoted are too commonplace. The opuscule seems rather to be against the opinion that prevailed among Parisian theologians, at least from the time of William of Auvergne, and would continue long after Thomas' death, as can be seen from later theologians.[92] The *adversarii* are one and all those who see a contradiction between "being created" and "always existing." The rare use of the first person singular, "I will show" (*ostendam*), indicates to me a personal involvement and responsibility in resolving a particular problem. The caustic use of Job 12.2 indicates a demand to be shown the contradiction that neither Aristotle nor Augustine were able to see. It is, in short, a work that demands a reply or capitulation by the theologians.

---

[92] See the discussion in John F. Wippel, *The Metaphysical Thought of Godfrey of Fontaines* (Washington, DC: Catholic University of America, 1981), pp. 152-169, 373, and bibliography.

13

Quidditative Knowledge of God
According to Thomas Aquinas

John F. Wippel

The Catholic University of America

In a well-known statement in his *Summa contra gentiles* Thomas Aquinas observes: "Concerning God, we cannot grasp what he is, but what he is not, and how other things are related to him." [1] This statement, echoed as it is in many other passages in his writings, comes from a Thomas Aquinas who is equally well-known, if not more so, for having developed a theory of analogical predication of divine names. This is the same Thomas who had also criticized others, especially Moses Maimonides, for having unduly restricted our knowledge of God. [2] Without intending here to discuss Thomas' theory of analogy of being (that would be subject matter for another study), I would like to stress the following point. [3] Not only does Aquinas maintain that we can reason from knowledge of the existence of effects to knowledge of God as their cause; he also holds that we can predicate certain names of God in more than metaphorical fashion. Of course, one may reply, but only negatively, by removing from any such name all that implies limitation or imperfection or any creaturely

---

[1] "Non enim de Deo capere possumus quid est, sed quid non est, et qualiter alia se habeant ad ipsum, ut ex supra dictis patet." scg 1, c. 30 (Rome, 1934), p. 32.

[2] Reference will be made below to Thomas' critique of Maimonides in *De potentia*, qu. 7, art. 5, and st 1, qu. 13, art. 2.

[3] For what is perhaps the finest single treatment of Thomas' doctrine of analogy see Bernard Montagnes, *La doctrine de l'analogie de l'être d'après saint Thomas d'Aquin* (Louvain-Paris, 1963).

Graceful Reason: Essays in Ancient and Medieval Philosophy Presented to Joseph Owens, CSSR, ed. Lloyd P. Gerson. Papers in Mediaeval Studies 4 (Toronto: Pontifical Institute of Mediaeval Studies, 1983), pp. 273-299. © P.I.M.S., 1983.

mode of being. To say, for instance, that God is eternal is really to make
the point that he is not temporal. To say that God is simple is to deny any
kind of composition to him. To say that he is immutable is to deny all
change of God. In short, in each of these cases the perfections signified by
such names are negative, not positive and cannot, therefore, tell us what
God is in himself.[4]

Granted all of this, however, there are other names. When we say that
God is good, we do not simply mean that he causes goodness in creatures.
According to Aquinas, it is rather because God is good that he can
produce goodness in creatures.[5] Here, then, one may ask, are we not
dealing with a positive name and thereby saying something positive about
God? And if so, are we not also thereby implying that we have some
knowledge concerning what God is? Or to take the name frequently
singled out by Aquinas as most appropriate for God, what do we mean
when we describe God as "He Who is" (*Qui est*)? Does not this name,
which expresses a most sublime truth, as Thomas himself has phrased it,
tell us something about the divine nature?[6] Does it not signify something
more than what God is not and the mere fact that he is? Against any such
conclusion, however, there still stands the Thomistic stricture: when it
comes to our knowledge of God we can know that he is; we cannot know
what he is.

My purpose in this paper will be to examine somewhat more fully
Thomas' reasons for defending this seemingly restrictive view concerning
our knowledge of God, as well as what he understands by it. The first
section of this study will concentrate on some representative texts taken
from Thomas' earlier discussions of this issue, that is, from his *Expositio
super Librum Boethii De trinitate* and his somewhat later *Summa contra
gentiles*. The second part will be devoted to discussions taken from later
works, especially from the Disputed Questions *De potentia Dei* and from
the First Part of the *Summa theologiae*.

---

[4] For forceful statements of the negative side of our knowledge of God according to
Thomas see Antonin D. Sertillanges, *Les grandes thèses de la Philosophie Thomiste* (Paris,
1928), pp. 67-80; Etienne Gilson, *The Christian Philosophy of St. Thomas Aquinas* (New
York, 1956), pp. 108-110; Anton C. Pegis, "Penitus Manet Ignotum," *Mediaeval Studies*,
27 (1965), 212-226.

[5] See, for instance, *De potentia*, qu. 7, art. 6; st 1, qu. 13, art. 2.

[6] "Hanc autem sublimem veritatem Moyses a Domino est edoctus ... ostendens suum
proprium nomen esse Qui Est." scg 1, c. 22, p. 24. Cf. st 1, qu. 13, art. 11. Also see
Gilson, *The Christian Philosophy*, pp. 92-95.

I

Thomas' reasons for defending this position are complex. At the risk of some oversimplification, one may suggest that they follow both from his theory of knowledge and from his great appreciation for the transcendence of God, for the sublime otherness of the divine reality. While both of these considerations enter into Thomas' various discussions of this issue, I shall begin by focusing on his theory of knowledge insofar as this controls his thinking about man's knowledge, especially man's philosophical knowledge, of God. Perhaps nowhere else has Thomas so carefully spelled out his thoughts on this point as in one of his early writings, his Commentary on the De trinitate of Boethius (ca. 1258-1259).[7] There, in question 1, article 2, Thomas asks whether the human mind can arrive at knowledge of God.[8] In beginning his reply Thomas notes that a given thing may be known in one of two different ways. On the one hand, it may be that it is known by its proper form, as when the eye sees a stone by means of the form (species) of that stone. On the other hand, something may be known by means of a form which belongs to something else, but which bears some likeness to the thing that is known. For instance, a cause may be known through its likeness insofar as this likeness is found in its effect; or a man may be known by means of the form that is present in an image of that same man, such as a statue or a picture. Even when something is known in the first way – by means of its proper form – this can happen in one of two ways: either (1) by means of a form which is identical with that thing itself (as God knows himself through his essence); or (2) by means of a form which is in some way derived from the object that is known (as when a form is abstracted from the thing that is known; or when a form is impressed on the intellect of the knower by the object known, as in knowledge by means of infused species).[9]

Thomas immediately examines each of these possibilities with respect to his immediate concern – man's knowledge of God. According to Aquinas' theory of knowledge, in this life the human intellect is necessarily directed to forms which are abstracted from sense experience. Given this, in this life we cannot know God by means of that form which

---

[7] For this date and for those of other works by Aquinas cited here see James A. Weisheipl, *Friar Thomas d'Aquino. His Life, Thought, and Work* (Garden City, NY, 1974). For this work see p. 381.

[8] *Expositio super librum Boethii De trinitate*, ed. Bruno Decker (Leiden, 1959), p. 63. "Utrum mens humana possit ad dei notitiam pervenire."

[9] Ibid., p. 64, l. 21 – p. 65, l. 9.

is identical with the divine essence. (Thomas does comment in passing that it is in this way that God will be known by the *beati* in the life to come.)[10] Appeal to a form or species which might be impressed by God on our intellect – some kind of infused species – will not resolve our problem, continues Thomas. No such likeness will enable us to know the divine essence because God infinitely surpasses every created form. Moreover, God cannot be known by us in this life by means of purely intelligible (and infused) forms, since our intellect is naturally ordered to forms derived from phantasms and hence from sense experience.[11]

Having eliminated the possibility that in this life we might know God in any of these ways, Thomas is forced to fall back on the one that remains – God may be known by means of a form that is proper to something else but which bears some likeness to him. As Thomas puts it, in this life God can be known by us only by means of forms found in his effects. But, continues Thomas, effects are of two kinds. One kind is equal to the power of its cause. Knowledge of such an effect can lead fully to knowledge of the power of its cause, and, therefore to knowledge of that cause's quiddity. Here Thomas has in mind what in other contexts he describes as univocal causes.[12] There is another kind of effect which falls short of the power of its cause. Knowledge of this kind of effect will enable us to know that its cause exists. In other contexts Thomas describes such causes as equivocal.[13] It is in this second way that every creature stands with respect to God. Because of this, in the present life we are unable to arrive at any knowledge of God beyond our awareness that he is (*quia est*). Nonetheless, Thomas does allow for some gradation in our knowledge that God is. One knower may reach more perfect knowledge that God is than another; for a cause is known more perfectly from its effect insofar as through that effect the relationship between the two is more fully grasped.[14]

With this last point in mind, Thomas now introduces some further precisions into his analysis of the kind of knowledge "that God is" which

---

[10] Ibid., p. 65, ll. 9-13. For more on this see H.-F. Dondaine, "Cognoscere de Deo 'quid est'," *Recherches de Théologie ancienne et médiévale*, 22 (1955), 72-78.

[11] *Expositio super librum Boethii*, p. 65, ll. 14-20.

[12] Ibid., p. 65, ll. 20-23. For more on Thomas' distinction between univocal and equivocal causes see Montagnes, *La doctrine de l'analogie*, pp. 47-49 and especially n. 62.

[13] *Expositio super librum Boethii*, p. 65, ll. 23-26. For other passages in Thomas see the references cited by Montagnes, as indicated in the preceding note.

[14] Ibid., p. 65, l. 26 – p. 66, l. 5. Note in particular: "Et tamen unus cognoscentium quia est alio perfectius cognoscit, quia causa tanto ex effectu perfectius cognoscitur, quanto per effectum magis apprehenditur habitudo causae ad effectum."

is available to man in this life. Always bearing in mind that no creature can ever be equal to the power of its divine cause, Thomas singles out three elements which enter into our examination of the relationship which obtains between creatures, viewed as effects, and God, their cause. First of all, any such effect comes forth from God. Secondly, in some way any such effect is like its cause. Thirdly, any such effect falls short of its cause.[15]

Corresponding to these, Thomas distinguishes three ways in which the human intellect can advance in its knowledge that God is, even though, he hastens to add, it will not reach knowledge what God is. Such knowledge that God is will be more perfect, first of all, insofar as God's power in producing is more perfectly known through his effects; secondly, insofar as God is known as the cause of nobler effects, which bear a greater likeness to him; and thirdly, insofar as we come to realize more and more clearly how far removed God is from everything that is found in his effects. This corresponds to the threefold approach to knowledge of divine things which Thomas here, as on so many other occasions, traces back to Dionysius: the way of causality, the way of eminence, and the way of negation.[16] What must be stressed here, of course, is Thomas' unyielding warning that none of these ways will ever deliver *quid est* or quidditative knowledge of God to man in this life. In fact, in replying to the first objection, Thomas comments that in this life we reach the peak of our knowledge of God when we come to realize that we know him as unknown (*tamquam ignotum*), in other words, when we come to recognize that his essence surpasses anything we can apprehend in this life, and, therefore, that what God is remains unknown to us.[17]

---

[15] Ibid., p. 66, ll. 6-10.

[16] Ibid., p. 66, ll. 10-16. For discussion of these texts also see Siegfried Neumann, *Gegenstand und Methode der theoretischen Wissenschaften nach Thomas von Aquin aufgrund der Expositio super librum Boethii de Trinitate* (*Beiträge zur Geschichte der Philosophie und Theologie des Mittelalters* 41/2) (Münster, 1965), pp. 152-153; Leo Elders, *Faith and Science. An Introduction to St. Thomas's Expositio in Boethii De Trinitate* (Rome, 1974), pp. 31-33; Ruedi Imbach, *Deus est intelligere. Das Verhältnis von Sein und Denken in seiner Bedeutung für das Gottesverständnis bei Thomas von Aquin und in den Pariser Quaestionen Meister Eckharts* (*Studia Friburgensia*, 53 [Freiburg, 1976]), pp. 121-124. For Dionysius see *De divinis nominibus* 7.3 (PG 3.872).

[17] *Expositio super librum Boethii*, p. 67, ll. 2-6: "Ad primum ergo dicendum quod secundum hoc dicimur in fine nostrae cognitionis deum tamquam ignotum cognoscere, quia tunc maxime mens in cognitione profecisse invenitur, quando cognoscit eius essentiam esse supra omne quod apprehendere potest in statu viae, et sic quamvis maneat ignotum quid est, scitur tamen quia est." Also see his reply to objection 2 (ll. 7-9). For another text dating from roughly the same period (1256-1259), see *De veritate*, qu. 2, art. 1, ad 9: "Ad nonum dicendum, quod tunc intellectus dicitur scire de aliquo quid est, quando definit ipsum, id est quando concipit aliquam formam de ipsa re quae per omnia

Interestingly, in concluding the corpus of his reply in this same article, Thomas notes that the human intellect can be aided in its effort to arrive at greater knowledge of God by a new illumination, given through the light of faith and the gifts of wisdom and understanding. Nonetheless, even when elevated by such supernatural gifts, the human intellect remains incapable of achieving knowledge of the divine essence.[18] In other words, neither faith nor the infused gifts of the Holy Spirit will give us knowledge of the divine essence or quiddity in this life. Hence we cannot overcome this difficulty simply by falling back on religious faith, or by taking refuge in a theology which presupposes faith.

In other discussions within this same Commentary on the *De trinitate* Thomas continues to develop this thinking. For instance, in question 6, article 3 he asks whether our intellect can view the divine form itself.[19] In his reply he again distinguishes between knowing that something is and knowing what it is. For us to arrive at *quid est* knowledge of a thing we must have access to the essence or quiddity of that thing either immediately or else by means of other things which do manifest its quiddity. Once more Thomas appeals to his theory of knowledge in order to remind the reader that in this life the human intellect cannot immediately grasp the essence of God or, for that matter, of other separate substances. Man's intellect is immediately directed only to concepts that are drawn from phantasms and hence ultimately based on sense experience. At best, therefore, we can *immediately* grasp the quiddities of sensible things, but not of things that are purely intelligible.[20]

Thomas does concede that we can arrive at *mediate* quidditative knowledge of some intelligibles, that is, of those whose quiddity or nature is perfectly expressed by the quiddities of sensible things. Here he has in mind our capacity to know the quiddity of a genus or species by beginning with *quid est* knowledge of man and animal and then by noting the relationship between them. But sensible natures cannot express or

---

ipsi rei respondet. Iam autem ex dictis patet quod quidquid intellectus noster de Deo concipit, est deficiens a repraesentatione eius; et ideo quid est ipsius Dei semper nobis occultum remanet; et haec est summa cognitio quam de ipso in statu viae habere possumus [Leonine ed: possimus], ut cognoscamus Deum esse supra omne id quod cogitamus de eo; ut patet per Dionysium in 1 cap. *de Mystica Theologia.*" See *S. Thomae Aquinatis Quaestiones Disputatae.* Vol. 1: *De Veritate*, ed. R. Spiazzi (Turin-Rome, 1953), p. 26. For the same in the Leonine edition see *Sancti Thomae de Aquino opera omnia*, 22.1 (Rome, 1975), p. 42.

   [18] *Expositio super librum Boethii*, p. 66, l. 18 - p. 67, l. 1.
   [19] "Utrum intellectus noster possit ipsam formam divinam inspicere" (ibid., p. 218).
   [20] Ibid., p. 220, ll. 5-14.

reflect the divine essence or, for that matter, the essences of created separate substances, in sufficient fashion for us to attain to quidditative knowledge of either. Neither God nor created separate substances belong to the same genus as corporeal entities, at least when genus is taken in the natural or physical sense. Moreover, as Thomas explicitly states farther on in this discussion, God himself falls under no genus. Wherefore, concludes Thomas, names which are extended to separate substances apply to them and to sensible creatures almost equivocally. He cites with approval Dionysius' description of such names as "unlike likenesses." [21] And if the way of similitude is not sufficient of itself to make known to us the essences or quiddities of separate substances, neither is the way of causality. The effects produced by separate substances in our world are not equal to the power of their causes, and hence cannot enable us to reach quidditative knowledge of those causes.[22]

In developing a point to which he had already referred in question 1, article 2, Thomas reiterates his contention that in this life we cannot reach quidditative knowledge of separate substances even by means of revelation. Revelation itself is expressed in human language. Language presupposes concepts. Concepts are derived from sense experience. But, as we have already seen, according to Aquinas no path that begins from sense experience can deliver *quid est* knowledge of immaterial entities.[23]

Having stated this point so forcefully, Thomas must now come to terms with the Aristotelian view that we cannot know that something is unless in some way we also know what it is – either by perfect knowledge, or at least by some kind of confused knowledge.[24] For instance, if someone knows that man exists and wishes to determine what man is by defining him, he must already understand the meaning of the term "man." Presumably, in this case he will already have some prior knowledge of man in terms of his proximate or remote genus and by means of certain accidents. In other words, just as in demonstration so too in definition some kind of foreknowledge is presupposed.[25]

How, then, can one know that God and other separate entities exist unless one also knows what they are in some way? Direct knowledge of

---

[21] Ibid., p. 220, l. 16 - p. 221, l. 3. For Dionysius see *Cael. hier.* 2.4 (PG 3, 141).

[22] *Expositio super librum Boethii*, p. 221, ll. 2-6.

[23] Ibid., p. 221, ll. 7-20. Note in particular: "Et sic restat quod formae immateriales non sunt nobis notae cognitione quid est, sed solummodo cognitione an est, sive naturali ratione ex effectibus creaturarum sive etiam revelatione quae est per similitudines a sensibilibus sumptas."

[24] Ibid., p. 221, ll. 21-24. Here Thomas refers to the beginning of Aristotle's *Physics*, for which see *Phys.* 1.1 (184a23-b12).

[25] *Expositio super librum Boethii*, p. 221, l. 24 - p. 222, l. 2.

them by reason of any proximate or remote genus has been ruled out. Nor
can one appeal to knowledge of them by reason of their accidents. God
has no accidents. If created separate substances do have accidents, their
accidents remain unknown to us.[26]

At this point Thomas seems to have reached an impasse. All is not lost,
however, since it is here that he introduces knowledge by way of
negation. Instead of knowing separate substances in terms of any genus,
we may substitute negative knowledge. For instance, when we know that
such entities are incorporeal, we are really negating configuration and
other corporeal qualities of them. The more negations we know of them,
the less confused is our resulting knowledge. Thus by successive
negations, prior negations are contracted and determined just as is a
remote genus by its appropriate differences. Hence, as regards separate
substances and especially as regards God, Thomas concludes that we can
know that they are by reasoning from effect to cause. Instead of knowing
what they are we must substitute knowledge of them by negation, by
causality, and by transcendence (*per excessum*).[27] Thomas reaffirms this
same conclusion in question 6, article 4.[28]

It is interesting to turn from the Commentary on the *De trinitate* to the
somewhat later *Summa contra gentiles* (1259-1264). We began this study
by citing a text from Book 1, c. 30 of that work to this effect: we cannot
understand what God is, but only what he is not, and how other things
are related to him.[29] Already in chapter 14 of Book 1 Thomas had set
the stage for this dictum. There, after his lengthy presentation of
argumentation for God's existence in chapter 13, Thomas comments that
when it comes to our knowledge of God's properties, we must make
special use of the way of negation (*via remotionis*). Perfectly consistent

---

[26] Ibid., p. 222, ll. 5-21. See l. 4: "... eo quod deus in nullo genere est, cum non habeat
quod quid est aliud a suo esse ...."

[27] Ibid., p. 222, l. 22 - p. 223, l. 17. For an even earlier statement on our knowledge of
God by way of negation see *in 1 Sent.*, d. 8, q. 1, a. 1, ad 4 (Mandonnet 1: 196-197). For
helpful commentary see Joseph Owens, "Aquinas – 'Darkness of Ignorance' in The Most
Refined Notion of God," in *Bonaventure and Aquinas. Enduring Philosophers*, ed. Robert
W. Shahan and Francis J. Kovach (Norman, Oklahoma, 1976), pp. 69-86.

[28] Article 4 is directed to this question: "Utrum hoc possit fieri per viam alicuius
scientiae speculativae" (*Expositio super librum Boethii*, p. 223), that is, whether we can
behold the divine form through any speculative science. From his reply note in particular:
"Et ideo per nullam scientiam speculativam potest sciri de aliqua substantia separata quid
est, quamvis per scientias speculativas possimus scire ipsas esse et aliquas earum
condiciones, utpote quod sunt intellectuales, incorruptibiles et huiusmodi" (p. 227, ll. 25-
28). Also see his reply to objection 2: "... quamvis quiditas causae sit semper ignota, et ita
accidit in substantiis separatis" (p. 228, ll. 18-19).

[29] See above, n. 1.

with the reasoning we have seen in his Commentary on the *De trinitate*, he again writes that the divine substance completely surpasses any form our intellect can reach. Hence we are unable to grasp the divine substance by knowing what it is. Still, he adds, we can have some knowledge of it by knowing what it is not. Insofar as we negate more and more things of God, we come closer to knowledge of him. One negative difference will be contracted by another, and that by still others, thereby leading us to more precise knowledge of God. By continuing this procedure in ordered fashion, we will be able to distinguish God from all that He is not. Still, even though we may thereby reach a proper consideration (*propria consideratio*) of God's substance by knowing that he is distinct from everything else, our knowledge will not be perfect. We will still not know what God is in himself.[30]

In the succeeding chapters of Book 1 Thomas proceeds to do just this.[31] He applies the *via negationis* in ordered fashion in order to show, for instance, that God is eternal (ch. 15); that there is no passive potency in him (ch. 16); that there is no matter in him (ch. 17); that there is no composition in God (ch. 18); that he is not subject to violence (ch. 19); that he is not a body (ch. 20); that he is his essence (ch. 21); that in him *esse* and essence are identical, i.e., not distinct (ch. 22); that he is without accidents (ch. 23); that no substantial difference can be added to God (ch. 24); that he is not in any genus (ch. 25); that he himself is not the formal *esse* of other things (ch. 26);[32] and that he is not the form of any body (ch. 27). Even in chapter 28, in attempting to establish the divine perfection, Thomas continues to use the way of negation – by showing that any absence or limitation of perfection is to be denied of God.[33]

[30] SCG 1, c. 14, p. 15. Note in particular: "et sic ipsam apprehendere non possumus cognoscendo quid est. Sed aliqualem eius habemus notitiam cognoscendo quid non est ... et sic per ordinem ab omni eo quod est praeter ipsum, per negationes huiusmodi distinguetur; et tunc de substantia eius erit propria consideratio cum cognoscetur ut ab omnibus distinctus. Non tamen erit perfecta: quia non cognoscetur quid in se sit."

[31] Note that he uses as a point of departure and as a working principle in this procedure the conclusion from his argumentation for God's existence in ch. 13 – that God is completely free from being moved in any way ("Ad procedendum igitur circa Dei cognitionem per viam remotionis, accipiamus principium id quod ex superioribus iam manifestum est, scilicet quod Deus sit omnino immobilis"). SCG 1, c. 14, p. 15.

[32] Thomas also uses this discussion to make the point explicitly that God is not in any way to be identified with *esse commune* (ibid., p. 27).

[33] One of Thomas' arguments rests upon the identity of essence and *esse* in God. Because that being which is its own *esse* must possess *esse* according to the total capacity (*virtus*) of being itself, it can lack nothing of the perfection which may pertain to being. As we have mentioned in passing, in ch. 22 Thomas establishes identity of essence and *esse* in God by following the negative way, that is, by showing that in God essence and *esse* are not distinct. For the argument in ch. 28 see pp. 29-30.

In chapter 29 Thomas offers some precisions concerning the likeness that does and does not obtain between God and creatures. Granted that no created effect can be equal to its divine cause either in name or in definition, still there must be some likeness between them. This follows because it is of the very nature of action for an agent to produce something that is like itself. And this in turn follows from the fact that something can act or function as an agent only insofar as it is in act. Since God is an equivocal cause and therefore surpasses in perfection any and all of his effects, any form present in an effect will be realized in God only in higher and more eminent fashion. In other words, there will be likeness and unlikeness between God and creatures at one and the same time – likeness because as a cause he produces things that are in some way like himself; unlikeness because whatever is found in God can be present in other things only in deficient fashion and by participation.[34] (If only in passing, it should be noted that defense of some kind of likeness between creatures and God will be absolutely crucial for Thomas' rejection of purely equivocal predication of names of God in chapter 33, and for his defense of analogical predication of divine names in chapter 34.)

In chapter 30 Thomas distinguishes between two kinds of names that one might wish to apply to God. Some names signify perfection without including any limitation or imperfection in their formal meaning. Names such as these, here illustrated by goodness, wisdom, and *esse*, and often referred to as pure perfections in the scholastic tradition – can be said of God in some nonmetaphorical way. This is not true of another kind of name which necessarily implies some creaturely and imperfect mode of being in its very definition. No such name can be applied to God except metaphorically.[35]

At this point one might wonder whether Thomas is not now preparing to go beyond the way of negation and to allow for some kind of affirmative naming of God, perhaps even for some kind of quidditative knowledge of the divine. Almost as if in anticipation of our query, Thomas immediately introduces a crucial distinction. Granted that certain names such as those he has just mentioned do not include any imperfection in that which they signify (*quantum ad illud ad quod*

---

[34] Ibid., p. 31. Note in particular: "Ita etiam et Deus omnes perfectiones rebus tribuit, ac per hoc cum omnibus similitudinem habet et dissimilitudinem simul. ... Quia igitur id quod in Deo perfecte est, in rebus aliis per quandam deficientem participationem invenitur ...."

[35] Thomas adds that names which express (pure) perfections together with the mode of supereminence whereby they pertain to God can be said of God alone. What he has in mind are complex names such as "supreme good," "first being," etc. ("... sicut summum bonum, primum ens, et alia huiusmodi"), p. 31.

significandum nomen fuit impositum), they do involve some deficiency in the way in which they signify, in their *modus significandi*. This follows because we express perfections by names in accord with the ways in which we conceive these perfections. Since our intellect derives its knowledge from sense experience, in conceiving such perfections it does not surpass the mode in which it finds them realized in sensible things. Because of the matter-form composition of sensible things, in conceiving them we distinguish between a form and that which has the form. Hence, when we signify any perfection concretely, we also signify it as involving distinction between itself and the subject in which it is realized. If we signify the perfection in abstract fashion, we cannot then signify it as something which subsists but only as that by means of which something else subsists. According to either mode of signification imperfection is implied.[36]

For instance, we might apply the name "good" to God in concrete fashion by saying that God is good. In this case the way in which "good" signifies – concretely, implies some kind of composition and distinction between the perfection, on the one hand, and the subsisting subject on the other. Or we might apply this same name to God in abstract fashion, by describing God as goodness. The abstract way of signifying will imply that divine goodness is not itself subsistent. In either event, even when we are dealing with pure perfections, some kind of deficiency is implied by the *modus significandi* of any such name. Thomas now cites Dionysius to

---

[36] See in particular: "Dico autem aliqua praedictorum nominum perfectionem absque defectu importare, quantum ad illud ad quod significandum nomen fuit impositum: quantum enim ad modum significandi, omne nomen cum defectu est. ... Forma vero in his rebus invenitur quidem simplex, sed imperfecta, utpote non subsistens: habens autem formam invenitur quidem subsistens, sed non simplex, immo concretionem habens. Unde intellectus noster, quidquid significat ut subsistens, significat in concretione: quod vero ut simplex, significat non ut quod est, sed ut quo est. Et sic in omni nomine a nobis dicto, quantum ad modum significandi, imperfectio invenitur, quae Deo non competit, quamvis res significata aliquo eminenti modo Deo conveniat ..." (ibid., pp. 31-32). For earlier appeal to this distinction when discussing the divine names see Thomas, *In I Sent.*, d. 22, q. 1, a. 2 (Mandonnet 1: 535). Note in particular: "... omnia illa nomina quae imponuntur ad significandum perfectionem aliquam absolute, proprie dicuntur de Deo, et per prius sunt in ipso quantum ad rem significatam, licet non quantum ad modum significandi, ut sapientia, bonitas, essentia, et omnia hujusmodi ...." For further discussion of this distinction see Hampus Lyttkens, *The Analogy between God and the World* (Uppsala, 1952), pp. 375-382; idem, "Die Bedeutung der Gottesprädikate bei Thomas von Aquin," in *Philosophical Essays Dedicated to Gunnar Aspelin on the Occasion of his Sixty-fifth Birthday*, ed. Helge Bratt et al. (Lund, 1963), pp. 80-84. For more on Thomas' usage of this distinction in his Commentary on the *Sentences* see Battista Mondin, *St. Thomas Aquinas' Philosophy in the Commentary to the Sentences* (The Hague, 1975), pp. 92-93, 100-101 (note the additional references given in n. 29). Also see Luis Clavell, *El nombre propio de Dios segun santo Tomas de Aquino* (Pamplona, 1980), pp. 143-146.

this effect, that such names (those signifying pure perfections) are both affirmed and denied of God – affirmed because of the meaning of the name; denied because of their *modus significandi*, the way in which they signify. Shortly thereafter, Thomas makes the remark with which our study began: "Concerning God we cannot grasp what he is, but what he is not, and how other things are related to him." [37]

Two important points should be kept in mind from Thomas' discussion in chapter 30. First of all, his application of the distinction between the *res significata* and the *modus significandi* appears to be all embracing. No matter what name we may apply to God, its creaturely *modus significandi* must be denied of him. Secondly, in the final part of this chapter Thomas seems to distinguish between names which are negative in their formal meaning (*res significata*), such as eternal or infinite, and others which are not, such as goodness, wisdom, etc.[38] But even when names of the second type are applied to God, one must deny of them the creaturely *modus significandi*. In other words, the *via negativa* seems to apply in three different ways. First of all, the perfections assigned to God until the discussion in chapter 30 all seem to have been discovered by the process of successive negations. Secondly, they also seem to include the negation of something in their formal meaning, as, for instance, infinity is the negation of finiteness. Thirdly, while names such as goodness and wisdom do not include anything negative in their formal meaning, even they carry with them a creaturely *modus significandi* when they are applied to God. This too must in turn be denied of him.

In chapter 37 Thomas explicitly attempts to show that God is good. If one would expect him to admit of some kind of knowledge of God that is positive rather than negative, and perhaps even quidditative, it would be here. In arguing for God's goodness Thomas recalls that he has already shown that God is perfect. God's goodness follows from this. In establishing God's perfection in chapter 28 Thomas had in fact used the *via negativa* (taken in the first of the three senses I have just distinguished, as the process of successive negations). He continues to do so here, at least by implication. For instance, he recalls that in chapter 13 he had shown that God is the first unmoved mover. But God moves insofar as he is an object of desire, as the *primum desideratum*. This implies that he is truly

[37] scG 1, c. 30, p. 32. For the reference to Dionysius the editors cite *Cael. hier.*, c. 2, § 3, and also refer to *De div. nom*, c. 1, 5.

[38] "Modus autem supereminentiae quo in Deo dictae perfectiones inveniuntur, per nomina a nobis imposita significari non potest nisi vel per negationem, sicut cum dicimus Deum aeternum vel infinitum; vel etiam per relationem ipsius ad alia, ut cum dicitur prima causa, vel summum bonum" (scG 1, c. 30, p. 32).

good. Thomas assumes that we will recall that he has shown that God is the first unmoved mover by proving that he is not a moved mover. Another argument reasons that because God is pure actuality, and because all things desire to be in actuality according to their proper mode – which is for them to be good – God himself is good. But, one may ask, why does Thomas describe God as pure actuality? His answer is that he has already shown (see ch. 16) that God is not in potency.[39]

In succeeding chapters Thomas shows that God is goodness itself, that there is no evil in God, and that God is the good for every other good.[40] Since many of the particular arguments introduced in these chapters also follow the negative way, since all of them presuppose that God is good, and since Thomas has used the way of negation to show that God is good, one may conclude that even in establishing God's goodness Thomas has continued to use the process of successive negations. This is not to say, of course, that the name "goodness" itself is negative in its formal meaning (negative in the second sense distinguished above).[41]

For confirmation one may turn to Thomas' own assessment of his procedure in SCG 1, cc. 14-42 as he refers back to this in Book 3 of the same work. In Book 3, chapter 39 he is attempting to show that no demonstrative knowledge of God can ever suffice to give perfect happiness to man. Thomas comments that by the path of demonstration one does come closer to a proper knowledge of God. By this procedure

---

[39] Even the final argument in this chapter, based upon the axiom that the good tends to diffuse itself, presupposes the way of negation. Thomas interprets this Neoplatonic axiom in the sense of final rather than efficient causality. He notes that the good of any given thing is its act and its perfection. But everything acts insofar as it is in act. By acting it passes on being and goodness to other things. Hence a sign of a thing's perfection is that it can produce its like. But the essence of the good consists in the fact that it is desirable. This is to identify the good with the end, the final cause. It is this that moves an agent to act, and justifies the Neoplatonic axiom just mentioned – *bonum est diffusivum sui et esse*. But such diffusion of goodness and being pertains to God. For it has been shown above (see ch. 13) that God is the cause of being for all other things. Therefore he is truly good. Presupposed, therefore, for application of goodness to God is one's previous demonstration that he is the first cause, that is, that he is not a caused cause.

[40] See cc. 38 ("Quod Deus est ipsa bonitas"), 39 ("Quod in Deo non potest esse malum"), 40 ("Quod Deus est omnis boni bonum"). As regards ch. 38, Thomas argues, for instance, that actual *esse* for a given thing is its good. But God is not only being in act, but *ipsum suum esse*. Therefore he is not only good but goodness itself. In ch. 22 Thomas had used the way of negation to show that God is *ipsum suum esse*, by showing that there is no distinction in him between essence and *esse*. In two other arguments in ch. 38 Thomas shows that God is not good by participation. Therefore he is goodness itself.

[41] For Thomas' procedure in arriving at knowledge that God is good see the remarks in the preceding note. As I interpret him, however, even though he continues to use the way of succeeding negations to establish the conclusion that God is good or goodness, he acknowledges that the name "goodness" is not negative but positive in content.

one removes from God many things and thereby understands more clearly how different he is from all else. Thomas recalls that he had used this approach in Book 1 in demonstrating that God is immobile, eternal, perfectly simple, one, and other things of this kind. In reviewing the path he had followed there, Thomas remarks that one can arrive at proper knowledge of something not only by affirmations but by negations. Thomas stresses this important difference between these two kinds of proper knowledge. Proper knowledge gained by succeeding affirmations may yield *quid est* knowledge of a thing as well as knowledge concerning its difference from all else. If one reaches proper knowledge of a thing by succeeding negations, granted that one will know how that thing differs from others, the quiddity of that same thing will remain unknown to him. Only this second kind of proper knowledge of God is available to man in this life.[42]

In chapter 49 Thomas argues that neither created separate substances nor men can arrive at *quid est* knowledge of God by reasoning from effect to cause. By following this path at best we can know that God is, that he is the cause of all else, and that he supereminently surpasses all else. At this highest point in our knowledge of God, we are conjoined to a God who remains, as it were, unknown. This happens when we know of God what he is not. What he is remains completely unknown to us (*penitus ignotum*).[43]

II

In order to determine whether Thomas ever softened his views concerning this final point, we shall now turn to two somewhat later sets of texts: (1) a series of articles in qu. 7 of the *De potentia* (disputed at

---

[42] scG 3, c. 39, p. 263. Note in particular: "... per negationes autem habita propria cognitione de re, scitur quod est ab aliis discreta, tamen quid sit remanet ignotum. Talis autem est propria cognitio quae de Deo habetur per demonstrationes." Compare this with Thomas' remark in scG 1, c. 14 about the *propria consideratio* concerning God's substance which is available to us by following the path of successive negations.

[43] scG 3, c. 49, pp. 279-281. Note in particular: "Et hoc est ultimum et perfectissimum nostrae cognitionis in hac vita, ut Dionysius dicit, in Libro *De Mystica Theologia* [capp. I, II], *cum Deo quasi ignoto* coniungimur: quod quidem contingit dum de eo quid non sit cognoscimus, quid vero sit penitus manet ignotum. Unde et ad huius sublimissimae cognitionis ignorantiam demonstrandam, de Moyse dicitur, *Exodi xx*, quod *accessit ad caliginem in qua est Deus*" (p. 280). For Dionysius see especially 1.3 (PG 3.1000). For more on this see Pegis, "Penitus Manet Ignotum," pp. 217-218. Opinions vary concerning the precise dating of Bk III of the *Summa contra gentiles*. For discussion see Weisheipl, *Friar Thomas d'Aquino*, pp. 359-360. But whether one places this as early as 1259 or as late as 1264 (the latest likely date for Bk 4), it clearly antedates both qu. 7 of the *De potentia* and the first part of the *Summa theologiae*, which are to be examined below.

Rome, 1265-1266); and (2) the slightly later discussion of the divine names in the First Part of the *Summa theologiae* (ca. 1266-1268).[44]

To begin with the *De potentia*, in question 7 Thomas examines in considerable detail the issue of divine simplicity.[45] In article 1 he follows the path of negation to establish the fact that God is simple.[46] In article 2 Thomas denies to God any kind of distinction between substance (or essence) and existence (*esse*). While this is evidently phrased in negative fashion, one might wonder whether Thomas has not in some way here gone beyond the way of negation. Such a suspicion is envisioned by the first objection. According to John Damascene: "That God is is manifest to us, but what he is in his substance is completely incomprehensible and unknown (to us)." But what is known to us cannot be unknown at the same time. Therefore, God's *esse* is not identical with his substance or essence.[47]

In replying Thomas distinguishes two ways in which *ens* or *esse* may be understood. They may signify the essence of a thing or its act of existing, on the one hand; but on other occasions they simply signify the truth of a proposition. Given this distinction, continues Thomas, when Damascene says that God's *esse* is manifest to us he is taking *esse* only in the second way – as signifying the truth of the proposition "God is." But it is only when *esse* is taken according to the first usage that we can say God's *esse* is identical with his essence or substance. When *esse* is taken in this first way, God's *esse* remains unknown to us, just as does his essence.[48]

---

[44] For these datings see Weisheipl, pp. 363, 361.

[45] See *S. Thomae Aquinatis Quaestiones Disputatae*. Vol. 2: *De Potentia*, ed. Paulus M. Pession (Turin-Rome, 1953), pp. 188-190.

[46] Ibid., pp. 188-189.

[47] For objection 1 see p. 190: "Dicit enim Damascenus, in I lib. *Orth. Fidei* [cap. I et III]: *Quoniam quidem Deus est, manifestum est nobis; quid vero sit secundum substantiam et naturam, incomprehensibile est omnino et ignotum.* Non autem potest esse idem notum et ignotum. Ergo non est idem esse Dei et substantia vel essentia eius." For the text from John Damascene see *Saint John Damascene. De Fide Orthodoxa* (Burgundio translation), ed. Eligius M. Buytaert (St. Bonaventure, NY, 1955), Bk. 1, ch. 4, p. 19, ll. 3-5.

[48] *De potentia*, qu. 7, a. 2, ad 1 (pp. 191-192): "Ad primum ergo dicendum, quod ens et esse dicitur dupliciter, ut patet v *Metaph.* ... Quandoque enim significat essentiam rei, sive actum essendi; quandoque vero significat veritatem propositionis, etiam in his quae esse non habent: sicut dicimus quod caecitas est, quia verum est hominem esse caecum. Cum ergo dicat Damascenus, quod esse Dei est nobis manifestum, accipitur esse Dei secundo modo, et non primo. Primo enim modo est idem esse Dei quod est substantia: et sicut eius substantia est ignota, ita et esse. Secundo autem modo scimus quoniam Deus est, quoniam hanc propositionem in intellectu nostro concipimus ex effectibus ipsius." Cf. ST 1, qu. 3, art. 4, ad 2. For Gilson's usage of these passages to support his interpretation of Thomas' views concerning quidditative knowledge of God see *Elements of Christian Philosophy* (Garden City, NY, 1960), pp. 143-145.

In article 4 Thomas uses the way of negation to show that divine names such as "good" or "wise" or "just" do not predicate anything accidental of God. At the same time, at least some such names do not appear to be negative in the second of the three ways we have distinguished above – in their definition. Hence, introduction of names such as "good" and "wise" naturally gives rise to the important discussion in article 5.[49] There Thomas asks whether such names signify the divine substance. First of all, he presents what he regards as extreme versions of the negative view. Some, most particularly Moses Maimonides, hold that such names do not signify the divine substance. As applied to God, they may be understood in two different ways. On the one hand, they may be taken to point to some similarity between God's effects and the effects of other things which are known to us. For instance, to say that God is wise is not to imply that wisdom is really anything in God, but rather that he acts after the manner of one who is wise in ordering his effects to their proper ends. To say that he is living is only to indicate that he acts in the fashion of one who is living, that is, that he acts of himself. On the other hand, such names may be applied to God negatively. In this sense, to say that God is living is not to imply that life is anything really present in God. It is rather to negate of him any inanimate mode of being. To say that God is intelligent is not to signify that intellect is present in the divine being, but rather to deny of God the mode of being enjoyed by brutes.[50]

Thomas criticizes each of these ways of applying divine names as insufficient and even as unfitting (*inconveniens*). Against the first he objects that there would then be no difference between saying that God is wise and that God is angry or that he is fire. God would be called angry simply because he acts like someone who is angry when he punishes. He would be called fire because in purging he acts as does fire. So too, according to the theory, he would be named wise only because he acts in the manner of one who is wise in ordering his effects. This, counters Thomas, stands in opposition to the practise of saints and prophets. They permit us to apply some names to God, but not others. According to the

---

[49] "Quinto quaeritur utrum praedicta nomina significent divinam substantiam" (*De potentia*, qu. 7, art. 5, p. 196).

[50] Ibid., p. 198. For this in Maimonides see *The Guide of the Perplexed. Moses Maimonides*, tr. Shlomo Pines (Chicago, 1963), 1, cc. 52-59 (pp. 114-143). Note in particular ch. 58 (pp. 134-137). For a noncritical edition of the medieval Latin version see *Rabi Moysi Aegyptii Qui dicitur Dux Neutrorum seu dubiorum* (Paris, 1520; repr. Frankfurt/Main, 1964), 1, cc. 51-58 (ff. 18v-23v). For the all important ch. 57 (according to the numbering in the Latin version) see ff. 22r-22v. For an earlier reference to Maimonides (and to Avicenna) see Thomas, *In 1 Sent.*, d. 2, q. 1, a .3 (Mandonnet 1: 67-68).

present position, all such names could with equal justification be affirmed or denied of God. As a second argument against Maimonides, Thomas recalls that Christians hold that creation has not always existed – a point, he adds, that is conceded by Maimonides. Before creation God did not in fact operate in any of his effects. According to this way of understanding divine names it would therefore follow that before creation God could not have been described as good or as wise, something Thomas rejects as contrary to faith. He does soften this criticism by allowing that Maimonides might counter that before creation God could have been called wise, not because he then acted as one who is wise, but because he could so act. But, counters Thomas, this would be to concede that the term "wise" does signify something which is really present in God, and hence that this name does signify the divine substance; for whatever is in God is identical with his substance.[51]

Thomas next turns to the second way in which such names might be understood, that is, as pure negations. Against this he comments that there is no name of any species by which something could not be denied of God as unfitting for him. The name of any species includes a difference by which other species are excluded. For instance, the name "lion" includes this difference – that it is fourfooted. By means of this lion differs from bird, since it excludes a bird's mode of being. If names were applied to God only in order to deny things of him, not only might we say that God is living in order to deny of him the mode of inanimate things; we might also say that he is a lion in order to deny of him a bird's mode of being. Thomas' point again seems to be that according to this approach, any name could be applied to God. Thomas follows this up with an interesting reflection. Our understanding of any negation is based on some prior affirmation, just as any negative proposition is proved by means of one that is affirmative. Therefore, unless the human intellect could affirm something of God, it would be unable to deny anything of him. But it will know nothing of God in affirmative fashion unless something that it knows is positively realized in God.[52]

Thomas now cites Dionysius for support in developing his own position. Names of this kind, he counters, do signify the divine substance, but in deficient and imperfect fashion. Immediately the reader wonders, is

---

[51] *De potentia*, qu. 7, a. 5, p. 198. Note in particular the concluding part of Thomas' second counterargument: "Et sic sequeretur quod aliquid existens in Deo per hoc significetur, et sit per consequens substantia, cum quidquid est in Deo sit sua substantia."

[52] Ibid. Note in particular: "... unde nisi intellectus humanus aliquid de Deo affirmative cognosceret, nihil de Deo posset negare. Non autem cognosceret, si nihil quod de Deo dicit, de eo verificaretur affirmative."

this not to say something more about God than what he is not? Thomas justifies his claim that such names do in some albeit imperfect way signify the divine substance by recalling that every agent acts insofar as it is in act and, therefore, produces something that is like itself. Hence the form found in an effect must in some way also be present in its cause although, as we have seen, this may happen in different ways. When an effect is equal to the power of its agent, the form of that effect will be of the same kind as that of its cause (*secundum eamdem rationem*). When the effect is not equal to the power of its cause, the form of the effect will be present in the cause in more eminent fashion; for the agent must have the power to produce that effect. Such is true of equivocal agents, as when the sun generates fire. Since no effect is equal to the power of God, the form of no effect will be present in God in the same way it is present in that effect, but in more eminent fashion. Hence forms which are realized in divided and distinct fashion in different effects are united in God as in one single though common power.[53]

In developing this point Thomas notes that the various perfections realized in creatures are likened to God by reason of his unique and simple essence. Since the human intellect derives its knowledge from created things, it is informed by the likenesses of perfections it discovers in creatures, such as wisdom, power, goodness, etc. If creatures are in some though deficient way like God because of the presence of such perfections in them, our intellect can be informed by intelligible species of these same perfections. When the human intellect is assimilated to a given thing through an appropriate intelligible form or species, that which it conceives and formulates by means of such a species must be verified in that thing itself. This follows from Thomas' conviction that knowledge involves an assimilation of the intellect to that which is known. If this is so, those things which the intellect thinks or says about God insofar as it is informed by such intelligible species must in fact be truly present in him.[54]

Thomas immediately cautions, however, that such intelligible species which are present in the human intellect cannot be adequate likenesses of the divine essence. Otherwise, our intellects would comprehend the divine

---

[53] Ibid. Note Thomas' opening remark in this discussion: "Et ideo, secundum sententiam Dionysii (capit. xii *de divinis Nominibus*), dicendum est, quod huiusmodi nomina significant divinam substantiam, quamvis deficienter et imperfecte." This seems to be an interpretation rather than an exact quotation on Thomas' part. I have been unable to find any precise statement in cap. 12 of *The Divine Names* indicating that such names signify the divine substance. J. Durantel rather sees in Thomas' text a general reference to ch. 13, § 3. See his *Saint Thomas et le Pseudo-Denis* (Paris, 1919), p. 197.

[54] *De potentia*, qu. 7, art. 5, pp. 198-199.

essence and our conception of God would perfectly capture his essence (*esset perfecta Dei ratio*).⁵⁵ Given all of this, Thomas concludes that while names of this kind do signify "that which is the divine substance," they do not perfectly signify it (the divine substance) as it is in itself but only as it is known by us.⁵⁶ Presumably by "names of this kind" Thomas still has in mind those which signify pure perfections – names such as "good," "wise," "just," etc. In concluding the corpus of this article, he comments that while such names do signify the divine substance, they do so only in imperfect fashion, and not so as to comprehend it. Because of this the name "He who is" (*Qui est*) is most fittingly applied to God; for it does not determine any form for God, but signifies *esse* without determination.⁵⁷

Additional clarifications appear in some of Thomas' replies to objections in this same article 5. Objection 1 counters that according to Damascene names such as those here under discussion do not tell us what God is in his substance. Hence they are not predicated substantially of God.⁵⁸ In replying Thomas comments that Damascene's point is to show that such names do not signify what God is, if this be taken to mean that

---

⁵⁵ "Si autem huiusmodi intelligibilis species nostri intellectus divinam essentiam adaequaret in assimilando, ipsam comprehenderet, et ipsa conceptio intellectus esset perfecta Dei ratio, sicut animal gressibile bipes est perfecta ratio hominis" (ibid.).

⁵⁶ "... et ideo licet huiusmodi nomina, quae intellectus ex talibus conceptionibus Deo attribuit, significent id quod est divina substantia, non tamen perfecte ipsam significant secundum quod est, sed secundum quod a nobis intelligitur" (ibid.). Note how differently this crucial passage is interpreted by Maritain and by Gilson. For Maritain see his *Distinguish to Unite or The Degrees of Knowledge*, tr. Gerald B. Phelan (New York, 1959), p. 425: "Names signifying, although only ananoetically, '*id quod est divina substantia*' do indeed tell us in some manner what God is," although only in a "more-or-less imperfect, but always true fashion." Here Maritain is rejecting Sertillanges' general interpretation of this issue. For Gilson see his *The Christian Philosophy of St. Thomas Aquinas*, pp. 109 and especially p. 458, n. 47. There, in criticizing Maritain's reading, Gilson comments: "In using this text ... we must keep in mind the exact thesis which St. Thomas is developing, namely, that the divine names signify the substance of God, that is, they designate it as actually being what the names signify. It does not follow from this that these designations give us a positive conception of what the divine substance is."

⁵⁷ *De potentia*, qu. 7, art. 5, p. 199. "Sic ergo dicendum est, quod quodlibet istorum nominum significat divinam substantiam, non tamen quasi comprehendens ipsam, sed imperfecte: et propter hoc, nomen *Qui est*, maxime Deo competit, quia non determinat aliquam formam Deo, sed significat esse indeterminate." In support of the last point in his text Thomas cites John Damascene, *De fide orthodoxa* 1, ch. 9, pp. 48-49, ll. 13-17. He finds his general solution confirmed by Dionysius' remark in ch. 1 of the *Divine Names*: "quia Divinitas omnia simpliciter et incircumfinite in seipsa existentia praeaccipit, ex diversis convenienter laudatur et nominatur." For this see ch. 1, § 7, transl. John the Saracen (*Dionysiaca*, 1 [1937] 50).

⁵⁸ *De potentia*, qu. 7, art. 5, pp. 196-197. For the citation from Damascene see his *De fide orthodoxa* 1, ch. 9 (p. 48, ll. 8-12).

they define and comprehend his essence. This is why Damascene has
added that the name *Qui est* is most properly attributed to God, since it
signifies God's substance without determining it (*indefinite*).[59] Here, then,
we seem to find Thomas distinguishing between some kind of imperfect
knowledge of God's substance, on the one hand, and comprehensive and
defining knowledge, on the other. Apparently it is only the latter that is
denied when Thomas says that we cannot know what God is. The former,
which does not seem to be purely negative in content, is here defended by
Aquinas.

In replying to the second objection, Thomas reminds us that he has not
forgotten the restriction which follows from the way in which we signify
divine names. According to this objection, no name which signifies the
substance of a thing can truly be denied of it. But according to Dionysius,
in the case of God negations are true while affirmations are inexact
(*incompactae*). Hence such names do not signify the divine substance.[60]
Thomas counters that as regards the *res significata* – the perfection
signified by such names – these names are truly applied to God because
that which they signify is really present in him in some way. But as
regards their *modus significandi*, such names can be denied of him. Every
such name signifies a definite form, and cannot be realized in God in that
fashion. Hence these names can also be denied of him insofar as they do
not belong to him in the way in which they are signified. Dionysius has
this restriction in mind – their *modus significandi* – when he describes
such names as *incompactae*. Thomas concludes by again appealing to the
threefold way according to which Dionysius states that such names are
predicated of God. First, there is the way of affirmation, as when we say
that God is wise. This we must affirm of God because there must be in
him a likeness of that wisdom we discover in his effects. Secondly,
because wisdom is not realized in God in the way we understand and
name it, we introduce the way of negation and say that God is not wise. In
other words, we deny of God the creaturely *modus significandi* which is
always conjoined with our speech about God. Thirdly, since wisdom is

[59] "Ad primum ergo dicendum, quod Damascenus intelligit, quod huiusmodi nomina
non significant quid est Deus, quasi eius substantiam definiendo et comprehendendo;
unde et subiungit quod hoc nomen *Qui est*, quod indefinite significat Dei substantiam,
propriissime Deo attribuitur" (*De potentia*, qu. 7, a. 5, ad 1, p. 199).
[60] Ibid., p. 197. For the citation from Dionysius' *De caelesti hierarchia*, ch. 2 ("in
divinis negationes sunt verae, affirmationes vero incompactae") Thomas seems to have
combined the translations by John Scotus Eriugena and by John the Saracen. See
Durantel, *Saint Thomas et le Pseudo-Denis*, p. 73. For confirmation see sт 1, qu. 13, a. 12,
ad 1.

not denied of God because he falls short of it but rather because it is present in him in supereminent fashion, we can say that God is superwise (*supersapiens*) – the way of eminence.[61] Presumably, what we do in this third case is negate all imperfection and limitation of wisdom as we apply this to God.

As Thomas points out in replying to objection 4, he does not intend to say that God is wise only in this sense that he causes wisdom in us. On the contrary, it is because God is wise that he can cause wisdom (cf. qu. 7, art. 6).[62] On the other hand, in replying to objection 6, Thomas again reminds us that his claim that such names signify the divine substance does not imply that we can therefore either define or comprehend God's quiddity. It is this defining or comprehensive knowledge that Damascene has in mind when he denies that we can know what God is.[63]

As we turn to the slightly later first part of the *Summa theologiae*, we find Thomas again defending essentially the same position as in the *De potentia*. In question 2, article 3 he presents his famed "five ways" to establish God's existence. In introducing question 3 he remarks that once we have recognized that something is, it remains for us to investigate how it is in order to arrive at *quid est* knowledge of it. In the case of God, however, we cannot know what he is, but what he is not. Thomas then lays down a program for his subsequent discussion. He will proceed by examining (1) how God is not; (2) how God is known by us; and (3) how God is named by us.[64]

In questions 3 to 11 Thomas concentrates on the first phase – determining how God is not. It is only in question 12 that he asks how God is known by us, and in question 13 that he takes up the issue how God is named by us. Accordingly, we have it on Thomas' own word that

[61] *De potentia*, qu. 7, a. 5, ad 2, p. 199.

[62] Ibid. For qu. 7, art. 6 see pp. 201-202: "quia cum effectus a causa secundum similitudinem procedat, prius oportet intelligere causam aliqualem quam effectus tales. Non ergo sapiens dicitur Deus quoniam sapientiam causet, sed quia est sapiens, ideo sapientiam causat."

[63] Ibid., pp. 199-200. "Ad sextum dicendum, quod ratio illa probat quod Deus non potest nominari nomine substantiam ipsius definiente, vel comprehendente vel adaequante: sic enim de Deo ignoramus quid est." Cf. also his reply to objection 14: "... illud est ultimum cognitionis humanae de Deo quod sciat se Deum nescire, in quantum cognoscit illud quod Deus est, omne ipsum quod de eo intelligimus, excedere" (p. 200).

[64] *Summa theologiae*, Leonine manual edition (Marietti: Turin-Rome, 1950), p. 13. "Sed quia de Deo scire non possumus quid sit, sed quid non sit, non possumus considerare de Deo quomodo sit, sed potius quomodo non sit. Primo ergo considerandum est quomodo non sit; secundo, quomodo a nobis cognoscatur; tertio, quomodo nominetur."

294	J. F. WIPPEL

in examining God's simplicity, perfection, infinity, immutability, and unity, he is determining how God is not. We should also note that after discussing God's perfection in question 4, Thomas devotes question 5 to a study of goodness taken generally, and question 6 to God's goodness. In other words, even Thomas' defense of divine goodness continues to fall under the *via negativa*, or his effort to determine how God is not. As we shall find confirmed below, this is not to say that goodness itself is negative in meaning, but that we apply it to God by following the path of negation (see the first sense of the way of negation). Even in question 12 ("How God is known by us") Thomas continues to stress the *via negativa* and to deny that human reason can arrive at *quid est* knowledge of God.[65]

In question 13, article 2, Thomas again asks whether any name can be said of God substantially. He comments that neither those names which are said of God negatively (that is, which are negative in content) nor those which signify God's relationship to creatures can signify his substance in any way. But concerning names which are said absolutely and affirmatively of God – names such as "good," "wise," etc., Thomas once more presents the two extreme versions of the negative position we have already seen from the *De potentia*. According to some, even though such names are said affirmatively of God, they really deny something of him. To say that God is living is really to make the point that God is not in the way inanimate things are. Thomas continues to assign this position to Maimonides. He notes that according to another view (which he does not here attribute to Maimonides) such names signify nothing but God's relationship to creatures. To say that God is good is merely to make the point that he causes goodness in creatures.[66]

Thomas rejects both of these positions, and for three reasons. First of all, neither position can explain why certain names can be said of God with greater justification than others. Secondly, it would follow that all names are said of God *per posterius* rather than *per prius* (as medicine is said to be healthy only because it causes health in an animal). Thirdly, such theories run counter to the intention and practice of those who speak of God. When they say that God is living, they intend to signify something more than that he causes life in us, or that he differs from the inanimate.

After rejecting these positions as too restrictive, Thomas concludes that names of this type do signify the divine substance. They are predicated of

---

[65] See in particular qu. 12, art. 12. Note his reply to objection 1: "Ad primum ergo dicendum quod ratio ad formam simplicem pertingere non potest, ut sciat de ea quid est: potest tamen de ea cognoscere ut sciat an est" (p. 62).

[66] Ibid., p. 64.

God substantially, but fall short of any adequate representation of him.[67] As Thomas recalls, such names can signify God only insofar as our intellect can know him. But the human intellect derives its knowledge of God by reasoning from creatures. Hence it can know God only insofar as creatures represent him. God contains in himself in simple and undivided fashion all perfections found in creatures. Wherefore, any creature can represent God and be like him only insofar as it possesses some perfection. Since God belongs to no genus or species, no creature can represent him by belonging to the same genus or species. Hence, creatures can represent God only as the supreme principle from whose likeness all effects fall short, but each of which achieves some degree of likeness to him. This is enough for Thomas to continue to insist here, as he had in the *De potentia*, that such names (affirmative ones) do signify the divine substance, but imperfectly, just as creatures imperfectly represent God.[68] Thomas reinforces his point by noting that when we say God is good we do not merely mean that he is the cause of goodness (Theory II), or that he is not evil (Theory I). Rather, what we call goodness in creatures preexists in God according to a higher mode. Wherefore, it does not follow that God is good because he causes goodness; rather, because he is good, he produces goodness in creatures.[69]

In replying to objection 1, Thomas once more must contend with John Damascene's statement that those things which we say of God do not signify what he is in his substance, but what he is not. Thomas again interprets this to mean that no such name perfectly expresses what God is; but every such name does imperfectly signify him, just as creatures imperfectly represent him.[70] As in the *De potentia*, therefore, we find Thomas distinguishing between a perfectly comprehensive and quidditative knowledge of God, which he continues to deny to man, and an

---

[67] "Et ideo aliter dicendum est, quod huiusmodi quidem nomina significant substantiam divinam, et praedicantur de Deo substantialiter, sed deficiunt a repraesentatione ipsius" (p. 65).

[68] Ibid. Note in particular: "Sic igitur praedicta nomina divinam substantiam significant: imperfecte tamen, sicut et creaturae imperfecte eam repraesentant."

[69] Ibid. "Cum igitur dicitur *Deus est bonus*, non est sensus, *Deus est causa bonitatis*, vel *Deus non est malus*: sed est sensus, *id quod bonitatem dicimus in creaturis, praeexistit in Deo*, et hoc quidem secundum modum altiorem. Unde ex hoc non sequitur quod Deo competat esse bonum inquantum causat bonitatem: sed potius e converso, quia est bonus, bonitatem rebus diffundit...."

[70] Ibid., pp. 64, 65. For the citation from Damascene see n. 58 above. Note Thomas' reply: "Ad primum ergo dicendum quod Damascenus ideo dicit quod haec nomina non significant quid est Deus, quia a nullo istorum nominum exprimitur quid est Deus perfecte: sed unumquodque imperfecte eum significat, sicut et creaturae imperfecte eum repraesentant."

imperfect knowledge of the divine substance or essence, which he now defends.

In question 13, article 3, Thomas asks whether any names can be said of God properly (*proprie*). In replying Thomas once more reminds us that we know God from perfections which we find in creatures, and that such perfections are realized in God in more eminent fashion. Since our intellect understands these perfections as they are present in creatures, it can only signify them as it understands them. This leads Thomas to recall the distinction between that which such names signify when they are applied to God and the way in which they signify. Some names – names that signify pure perfections – are properly said of God as regards that which they signify. This is not true, however, of their *modus significandi*, since the way in which these names signify is still that which is appropriate to creatures.[71] In replying to objection 2, Thomas appeals to this same distinction to account for Dionysius' statement that such names are more truly denied of God. What Dionysius really has in mind is that the creaturely *modus significandi* of such names is to be denied of God.[72]

In subsequent articles of this same question 13 Thomas draws out the implications from these conclusions.[73] Because different divine names signify different concepts which are themselves drawn from different perfections as realized in creatures, these divine names are not mere synonyms (art. 4). In article 5 Thomas offers his well-known critique of univocal and equivocal predication of such names of God, and again falls back on predication of such divine names only by analogy or proportion. Here, as in the *Summa contra gentiles* and in the *De potentia*, he rejects the analogy of many to one and accepts only the analogy of one to another.[74]

---

[71] Ibid., pp. 65-66. Also see his reply to objection 1.

[72] Ibid., p. 66.

[73] For some interesting reflections on Thomas' procedure in qu. 13 see Klaus Riesenhuber, "Partizipation als Strukturprinzip der Namen Gottes bei Thomas von Aquin," in *Sprache und Erkenntnis im Mittelalter, Miscellanea Mediaevalia*, 13/2 (Berlin-New York, 1981), 969-982. For another interesting but more widely ranging study see Ludwig Hödl, "Die philosophische Gotteslehre des Thomas von Aquin O.P. in der Diskussion der Schulen um die Wende des 13. zum 14. Jahrhundert," *Rivista di filosofia neo-scolastica*, 70 (1978), 113-134, especially 114-120.

[74] ST 1, qu. 13, art. 5 (pp. 67-68). Cf. *De potentia*, qu. 7, art. 7 (p. 204); SCG 1, c. 34 (p. 34). It is interesting to observe that as in the *Summa theologiae*, so too in the *De potentia* Thomas explicitly takes up the question of analogical predication of divine names only after he has already defended the possibility of substantial predication of some names of God (see *De pot.*, qu. 7, art. 5). This would suggest that when discussing Thomas' doctrine of analogical predication of divine names in these two works (ST, *De pot.*), one would be well advised to do so only after having addressed oneself to the issue of substantial (or essential) predication of divine names.

Although Thomas' doctrine of analogy has not been my primary concern in this study, perhaps I should here stress the point that if Thomas has admitted that as regards their *res significata* some names can be predicated of God substantially and properly, such can happen only by analogy. Not only must one deny of God the creaturely *modus significandi* which such names carry with them when we apply them to God; even as regards that which they signify (their *res significata*), such names cannot be applied to God univocally. For one to say anything else would be to reduce Thomas' doctrine of analogy to veiled univocity.

In question 13, article 6 Thomas writes that certain names such as "good" are said of God not merely metaphorically and not merely because God causes goodness in creatures, but essentially (*essentialiter*). Hence, as regards that which such names signify, they are said of God *per prius*. But as regards the order of discovery, such names are first applied by us to creatures. Because of this they retain their creaturely *modus significandi*.[75] According to article 11 the name "He who is" is supremely proper or appropriate to God. As Thomas clarifies in replying to objection 1, this is true if one concentrates on that by reason of which this name is assigned, that is *esse*, and if one has in mind its *modus significandi*. But if one rather thinks of that which the divine name is intended to signify – the *res significata* – the name "God" is more appropriate. And even more appropriate than this is the name "Tetragrammaton," which is intended to signify the singular and incommunicable substance of God.[76] Finally, according to article 12, affirmative statementq can be made about God.[77]

III

In concluding this study I would like to recall that from the beginning of his career until its end Thomas consistently denies to man in this life

[75] "Utrum nomina per prius dicantur de creaturis quam de Deo" (pp. 68-69). Note in particular from Thomas' reply: "Sed supra ostensum est quod huiusmodi nomina non solum dicuntur de Deo causaliter, sed etiam essentialiter. Cum enim dicitur *Deus est bonus*, vel *sapiens*, non solum significatur quod ipse sit causa sapientiae vel bonitatis, sed quod haec in eo eminentius praeexistunt."

[76] Ibid., p. 74. For fuller discussion of this see Armand Maurer, "St. Thomas on the Sacred Name 'Tetragrammaton'," *Mediaeval Studies*, 34 (1972), 275-286. Maurer finds this view that the name "Tetragrammaton" is in one sense more proper to God than the name "He Who is" unique to Thomas' *Summa theologiae* in contrast with his earlier works (p. 278), and also identifies Maimonides as Thomas' source for this later precision (pp. 282-285). This is another indication that Thomas was taking Maimonides very seriously at this point in his career. For more on Thomas' discussion of these names see Clavell, *El nombre propio de Dios*, pp. 146-156.

[77] ST 1, qu. 13, art. 12 (pp. 74-75).

quidditative knowledge of God. He has frequently made this point by stating that we can know that God is and what God is not, but not what God is. On the other hand, even in earlier discussions such as those in the *Summa contra gentiles* or, for that matter, in his Commentary on the *Sentences* he has defended the validity of some kind of nonmetaphorical predication of divine names.[78] What I have not found in these earlier discussions, however, is explicit defense of man's ability to apply some names to God substantially or, according to the language of sт 1, q. 13, a. 6, essentially. Nonetheless, joined with this admission in these later works is Thomas' continuing refusal to admit that we can arrive at quidditative knowledge of God in this life. How, then, is one to fit all of this together?

First, I would suggest, one should define quidditative knowledge or knowledge of what God is very strictly, even as Thomas himself has done. He has made it clear, for instance, in the *De potentia* and in the First Part of the *Summa theologiae*, that when he agrees with John Damascene that we cannot know what God is, what he is thereby excluding is comprehensive and defining knowledge of God. This kind of knowledge of God Thomas had always denied to man in this life. In fact, as he had explained in another early work, the *De veritate*, our intellect is said to know of something what it is when it defines it, that is, when it conceives some form concerning that thing which corresponds to it in every respect.[79]

Secondly, as we have seen, in the *De potentia* and in the *Summa theologiae*, Thomas has explicitly stated that we can apply some names to God substantially or essentially. This type of divine naming is restricted, of course, to names which are positive in content and which imply no limitation or imperfection in their formal meaning – in other words, to names signifying pure perfections. On this point there seems to have been

---

[78] For an interesting examination of key texts taken from *In 1 Sent.*, *De ver.*, sсg, *Comp. theol.*, *De potentia*, and sт 1, see Montagnes, *La doctrine de l'analogie de l'ètre*, pp. 65-93.

[79] See *De veritate*, qu. 2, art. 1, ad 9, as cited above in n. 17. For much the same point that I am making here see Jean-Hervé Nicolas, "Affirmation de Dieu et connaissance," *Revue thomiste*, 44 (1964), 221, n. 2. Texts such as these, argues Nicolas, exclude "seulement une connaissance des attributs divins *à partir de son essence*, autrement dit ils excluent une connaissance quidditative de Dieu, non la connaissance de son essence." On the other hand, allowance for some chronological development on Thomas' part between the sсg and the *De potentia* such as I am here proposing might have made Nicolas' task of reconciling Thomas with himself less difficult. See, for instance, the remarks on p. 200 and n. 2 of his article.

some development in Thomas' thinking between the time of the *Summa contra gentiles* and the *De potentia*.

Thirdly, if one wonders why such development has occurred, I would suggest that it is because Thomas came to take Moses Maimonides' restrictive position concerning the divine names very seriously. It is within the context of his refutation of Maimonides both in the *De potentia* and then in the *Summa theologiae* that Thomas counters by defending the possibility of substantial predication of certain divine names.

Fourthly, even in these later discussions Thomas continues to insist that one should distinguish between the perfection (*res*) that is signified by such names, and the way in which the perfection is signified. If these names can be affirmed of God as regards that which they signify, one must always deny of them their creaturely *modus significandi*. This is why Thomas can continue to say that such names are both to be affirmed and denied of God.

Finally, if one wonders why in the *Summa theologiae* and even thereafter, for instance, in his commentary on the *Liber de causis*, Thomas continues to say that we cannot know what God is, or even that what God is remains completely unknown to us, this is for the reasons already indicated.[80] In such contexts he is taking the expression *quid est* knowledge strictly, as equivalent to comprehensive and defining knowledge. This he will never grant to man in this life. Moreover, he is also reminding us that no matter what name we may apply to God, its creaturely *modus significandi* must be denied of him.

---

[80] See *Sancti Thomae de Aquino super Librum de causis expositio*, ed. Henri D. Saffrey (Fribourg-Louvain, 1954), p. 43. There, in commenting on proposition 6, Thomas writes: "... ille enim perfectissime Deum cognoscit qui hoc de ipso tenet quod, quidquid cogitari vel dici de eo potest, minus est eo quod Deus est." After citing Dionysius' *Mystical Theology* (ch. 1) to this effect that man "*secundum melius* suae cognitionis *unitur* Deo sicut *omnino ignoto*," Thomas comments on this remark from prop. 6 of the *Liber de causis*: "Causa prima superior est narratione." Thomas explains that the term *narratio* is to be taken as meaning "affirmation" because: "quidquid de Deo affirmamus non convenit ei secundum quod a nobis significatur; nomina enim a nobis imposita significant per modum quo nos intelligimus, quem quidem modum esse divinum transcendit." In other words, the creaturely *modus significandi* is to be denied of any positive statement we may make about God. See Thomas' concluding remark from his commentary on this same proposition: "Sic ergo patet quod *causa prima superior est narratione*, quia neque per causam, neque per seipsam, neque per effectum sufficienter cognosci aut dici potest" (p. 48). Thomas' Commentary seems to date from 1271-1272 (Weisheipl, *Friar Thomas d'Aquino*, p. 383). For Dionysius see *De mystica theologia* 1.3 (PG 3.1001), and *Dionysiaca* 1, p. 578. For fuller discussion see Pegis, "Penitus Manet Ignotum," pp. 212-216.

14

The Metaphysics of Religious Art
Reflections on a Text of St. Thomas Aquinas

W. Norris Clarke, SJ

Fordham University

The purpose of this essay is to draw out the implications hidden in a single brief text of St. Thomas (*Summa theologiae* 1, q. 84, a. 7) for understanding the metaphysical and epistemological structures latent in religious art. I came rather suddenly to the realization of these implications one day when I was travelling in India and was studying a splendid bronze sculpture of Shiva, the dancing God, with eight arms – somewhat of a challenge, at first, to our ordinary Western artistic sensibilities. I would like to share with my readers my reflections on that day, as a sample of what seems to me the ever-fresh fecundity of the philosophical thought of St. Thomas as applied to areas outside of philosophy itself. This is my humble way of joining in this tribute to Father Joseph Owens, whose life-work has also been dedicated so long and fruitfully to the unfolding of the riches hidden within the texts of St. Thomas.

A brief preliminary clarification as to what I mean by "religious art." I am taking the position – controversial, perhaps – that there is a distinctively religious character to certain works of art that is somehow intrinsic to them, and not merely due to the extrinsic accident that they are inserted in a religious setting or even illustrating some religious subject matter. Thus the mere fact that a painting – let us grant a good one in itself – depicts a mother lovingly holding a child and carries the title

Graceful Reason: Essays in Ancient and Medieval Philosophy Presented to Joseph Owens, CSSR, ed. Lloyd P. Gerson. Papers in Mediaeval Studies 4 (Toronto: Pontifical Institute of Mediaeval Studies, 1983), pp. 301-314. © P.I.M.S., 1983.

"Madonna" does not make it automatically a piece of religious art. There
must be something within the painting itself which gives expression to the
religious dimension. Perhaps the simplest way to define or identify this
characteristic, so as to apply to all the religious traditions of mankind,
whether they use the name "God" or not for the Ultimate Reality they are
in quest of, is to describe it as *a thrust toward Transcendence*, a reaching
beyond the ordinary, all too painfully limited level of our human lives
toward a higher, more ultimate dimension of reality freed from these
limitations. In a word, it is the reaching out of the finite toward the
Infinite, expressed through finite sensible symbols. I take it that the
symbol, in this rich context of psychology, art, and religion, may be aptly
described as man's ever unfinished effort to express in form what is
beyond all form and expression.[1] The challenge – and the genius – of
authentic religious art is therefore to succeed somehow in giving effective
symbolic expression to this thrust toward Transcendence. I am not going
to argue here that such authentic and distinctively recognizable religious
art exists. The striking examples of it in many religious cultures seem to
me sufficient evidence for the fact. My effort here will be focused toward
uncovering the hidden metaphysical and epistemological structure behind
such art.

The text of St. Thomas which I wish to unpack is the famous one on the
dependence of all our human thinking on the imagination as a springboard; this dependence in turn is the expression in the cognitive life of the
deeper metaphysical union of soul and body to form a single *per se* unity,
the unified being that is man. This text is from the *Summa theologiae*, Part
1, Question 84, Article 7, first the body of the article, which lays out the
foundational doctrine, and then more specifically the *Reply to Objection 3*,
which applies this general doctrine to how we know higher, purely
spiritual beings, in particular God. Let me first quote the text of the article:

> I answer that, in the state of the present life, in which the soul is united to a
> corruptible body, it is impossible for our intellect to understand anything
> actually, except by turning to phantasms. And of this there are two
> indications. *First* of all because the intellect, being a power that does not
> make use of a corporeal organ, would in no way be hindered by the lesion
> of a corporeal organ, if there were not required for its act the act of some
> power that does make use of a corporeal organ. Now sense, imagination
> and the other powers belonging to the sensitive part make use of a

---

[1] For a good explanation of the meaning of symbol and its role in religious experience
and worship, see Thomas Fawcett, *The Symbolic Language of Religion* (Minneapolis:
Augsburg Publishing House, 1971).

corporeal organ. Therefore it is clear that for the intellect to understand actually, not only when it acquires new knowledge but also when it uses knowledge already acquired, there is need for the act of the imagination and of the other powers. For when the act of the imagination is hindered by a lesion of the corporeal organ, for instance, in the case of frenzy, or when the act of the memory is hindered, as in the case of lethargy, we see that a man is hindered from understanding actually even those things of which he had a previous knowledge. *Secondly*, anyone can experience this of himself, that when he tries to understand something, he forms phantasms to serve him by way of examples, in which as it were he examines what he is desirous of understanding. For this reason it is that when we wish to help someone to understand something, we lay examples before him from which he can form phantasms for the purpose of understanding.

Now the reason for this is that the power of knowledge is proportioned to the thing known. Therefore the proper object of the angelic intellect, which is entirely separate from a body, is an intelligible substance separate from a body. Whereas the proper object of the human intellect, which is united to a body, is the quiddity or nature existing in corporeal matter; and it is through these natures of visible things that it rises to a certan knowledge of things invisible. Now it belongs to such a nature to exist in some individual, and this cannot be apart from corporeal matter; for instance, it belongs to the nature of a stone to be in an individual stone, and to the nature of a horse to be in an individual horse, and so forth. Therefore the nature of a stone or any material thing cannot be known completely and truly, except inasmuch as it is known as existing in the individual. Now we apprehend the individual through the sense and the imagination. And therefore, for the intellect to understand actually its proper object, it must of necessity turn to the phantasms in order to perceive the universal nature existing in the individual. But if the proper object of our intellect were a separate form, or if, as the Platonists say, the natures of sensible things subsisted apart from the individual, there would be no need for the intellect to turn to the phantasms whenever it understands.

Objection 3: There are no phantasms of incorporeal things, for the imagination does not transcend space and time. If therefore our intellect cannot actually understand anything actually without turning to the phantasms, it follows that it cannot understand anything incorporeal. Which is clearly false, for we understand truth, and God, and the angels.

Reply to Objection 3: Incorporeal beings, of which there are no phantasms, are known to us by comparison with sensible bodies of which there are phantasms. Thus we understand truth by considering a thing in which we see the truth; and God, as Dionysius says, we know as cause, by way of excess, and by way of remotion. Other incorporeal substances we know, in the state of the present life, only by way of remotion or by some comparison to corporeal things. Hence, when we understand something about these beings, we need to turn to the phantasms of bodies, although there are no phantasms of these beings themselves.[2]

The body of the article expresses the classic teaching of St. Thomas on the necessary collaboration between intellect and sense knowledge (either the external senses or the imagination) for all *natural* acts of *understanding* in a human subject. I stress "natural" in order to leave open the possibility of various modes of supernatural infused knowledge which could bypass the senses. I also stress "understanding" in order to leave open the possibility of some directly intuitive acts of knowledge (whether natural or supernatural), such as the intuition of one's own self as conscious active presence. Any conceptual *understanding* of the nature of this self would involve the cooperation of sense and abstractive intellect. The cognitional theory itself is grounded, as St. Thomas clearly points out, in the metaphysical *per se* unity of soul and body to form a single being. All this is too well known to need any further commentary here by me.[3]

Our special interest in this article is twofold: first, the way in which such a mode of knowing tied to imagination can come to know purely spiritual beings, in particular God, of which there can be no sense image. This is by way of introduction. Our second and primary focus of interest is in how this way of knowing is reflected in religious art. The *Reply to Objection 3* contains in very condensed form the essence of St. Thomas' teaching on how a human knower can come to know God, a purely spiritual and infinite being, through the collaboration of sense and intellect. This doctrine is also well known, but let me summarize it briefly.[4]

I. THE MIND'S ASCENT TO GOD

St. Thomas insists that we have no direct intellectual understanding of God's being as it is in itself. We must always begin with the knowledge of the sensible world, and then allow ourselves to be "led by the hand," as

---

[2] Translation by Anton Pegis: *Basic Writings of St. Thomas Aquinas* (New York: Random House, 1944), 1: 808-810.

[3] The entire book by Karl Rahner – *Spirit in the World*, trans. William Dych (New York: Herder and Herder, 1968) – is an extended commentary on this one article of St. Thomas. Although we do not agree with all the details of the author's interpretation of St. Thomas, his exposition of the main point of the text – the dependence of all man's knowing on the senses as a starting point – is very rich and illuminating.

[4] For a convenient reference, see my *The Philosophical Approach to God* (Winston-Salem: Wake Forest University Publications, 1980), chapter 2: The Metaphysical Ascent to God.

he puts it elsewhere,[5] by material things, in a dialectical process of "comparison with sensible things," as he says in our present text, all the way up to an indirect knowledge of God as ultimate cause, with all the attributes appropriate for such a cause.

It is hard for us to appreciate today what a revolutionary stand that was in St. Thomas' own time. The common doctrine of the dominant Augustinian school before him and in his own time (e.g., St. Bonaventure) had by the mid-thirteenth century assimilated the new Aristotelian technical theory of knowledge by abstraction from the senses with respect to the material world around us, since St. Augustine's illumination theory was focused more on necessary and eternal truths or judgments and had little to say about the formation of *concepts* about the material world. This Aristotelian "face of the soul," as they put it, looked down, as it were, on the material world around it and abstracted the forms of sensible things from matter. But there was also a second, definitely higher and more noble, face of the soul, more directly illumined by God, which looked directly up to know spiritual things, such as one's own soul, angels, God, eternal turths, etc.[6]

St. Thomas resolutely rejected this doctrine of two natural faces of the soul, one looking down into the world of matter, the other looking directly up into the world of spirit.[7] The structure of our natural human knowledge is far more humble, he believed. There is only the one face of the soul, which is turned directly only toward the material cosmos around it as presented through the senses. Then, by the application of the basic inner dynamism of the mind, its radical and unrestricted exigency for intelligibility − which can be expressed as the first dynamic principle of knowledge: the principle of the intelligibility of being, "omne ens est verum"[8] − we can step by step trace back the intelligibility of this material

---

[5] Cf. st 1, q. 12, art. 12; 1, q. 43, art. 7: "Now the nature of man requires that he be led by the hand to the invisible by visible things (ut per visibilia ad invisibilia manuducatur)."

[6] For the medieval Franciscan doctrine of the two faces of the soul as proposed by St. Bonaventure, see E. Gilson, *History of Christian Philosophy in the Middle Ages* (New York: Random House, 1955), p. 336.

[7] Cf. *Quaestiones disputatae de anima*, art. 17, my translation: "For it is manifest that the human soul united to the body has, because of its union with the body, its face turned toward what is beneath it; hence it is not brought to fulfillment except by what it receives from these lower things, namely by forms (*species*) abstracted from phantasms. Hence it cannot arrive at the knowledge either of itself or of other things except insofar as it is led by the hand by these abstracted forms."

[8] This notion of the radical unrestricted dynamism of the human spirit toward the unlimited horizon of being and ultimately to the Infinite itself as the fullness and source of all being is clearly in St. Thomas, in his doctrine of the natural desire for the beatific vision, but it has been highlighted as the foundation for all metaphysics and natural

world to its only ultimate sufficient reason, a single infinite spiritual Cause that is God. Man is the lowest and humblest of the spirits, whose destiny it is to make his way in a spiritual journey through the material world back to is ultimate Source and his own ultimate home.

What is the general structure of this ascent of the mind to God from the sensible world? It passes along the classic "Triple Way" first outlined by Pseudo-Dionysius the Areopagite and adapted to his own use by St. Thomas[9] – as well as by many other thirteenth-century Christian thinkers. St. Thomas refers to it very tersely in our present text when he says that we know God "as cause, and by way of excess, and by way of remotion." We first discover God as ultimate cause of all material and finite beings, since no material being in particular, and no finite being in general, can be the sufficient reason for its own existence. What more can we say about this First Cause? Here the Triple Way of Pseudo-Dionysius enters in more explicitly: (1) the way of *positive affirmation* of divine perfections grounded in the causal relation; (2) the way of *negation* or "remotion," when we remove from what we have affirmed any limit or imperfection; and then (3) the way of *reaffirmation* of the perfection in question by expanding it to an *infinite degree*. This final stage St. Thomas calls the ways of "excess," a somewhat pale translation of the Latin *excessus*, which means a "going out of itself" by the mind in a movement beyond all finites toward the Transcendent.

The *first step* of affirmation based on causality rests on the principle that every effect must in some way, at least analogously, resemble its cause, since all that is in the effect – as effect – must come from its cause, and a cause cannot give what it does not possess in any way, at least in some equivalent higher mode of perfection. Hence we can affirm that whatever positive perfection we find in creatures must have its counterpart, either in an equal or in some higher analogous equivalent mode, in the cause.

The *second step*, that of negation or remotion, purifies what can be affirmed of God in a proper and literal mode of speech (opposed to a metaphorical mode). Since God is pure spirit and infinite in perfection, we cannot affirm literally and properly of Him any perfection which contains within its very *meaning* some note of imperfection or limitation. This eliminates at once a whole class of attributes or predicates which can be

---

theology by the Transcendental Thomist School, e.g., Maréchal, Rahner, Lonergan, etc. For a convenient exposition see my *Philosophical Approach to God*, chapter 1: The Turn to the Inner Way in Contemporary Neo-Thomism.

[9] Cf. sт 1, q. 12, art. 12, and elsewhere.

applied literally to material beings or finite creatures but not to infinite pure spirit. Thus we cannot argue that because God is the Cause of the perfection of eyesight in creatures, therefore He has finitely good eyesight; for eyesight implies the built in limitation of matter and finitude. A rather small number of basic attributes remains which describe perfections which we first find exemplified in creatures in a limited way, but which contain no imperfection or limitation in their meaning. That is, they are purely positive unqualified perfections, values which we must judge to deserve our unqualified approval, to be unqualifiedly better to have than not to have. Such are, for example, existence, unity, goodness, beauty, activity, power, intelligence, will, love, etc. These alone can be affirmed positively and properly of God, not metaphorically. But they too must first be purified of any imperfection or limitation we find attached to them in creatures.

Once we have thus purified them by "removing" all traces of imperfection and limitation, we can then, in the *third step*, reaffirm them of God, adding the index of infinity. Here the mind leaps beyond what it can directly represent or conceive in a clear concept, and, borne aloft by what Plato called "the wings" or "*eros*" of the soul, i.e., the radical drive of the spirit toward the total intelligibility and goodness of being, projects out the positive content of the perfection it is affirming, along an ascending scale of analogy, to assert that this perfection must be found in infinite fullness in God, though the mind cannot directly see or clearly conceive just what this fullness is like in itself. This movement of the mind beyond all finite beings, and hence all clear concepts, is called in our text "the way of excess," that is, the mind's going out of itself (*ex-cedere*) beyond all finite concepts.

II. Application to Religious Art

Now let us apply this basic movement or ascent of the mind toward God to the domain of religious art. How does the work of art succeed in its own way in leading us through sensible symbols to make this leap beyond all sensible symbols toward the Infinite which they symbolize, that is itself beyond all form and symbol? Let us first note that the general structure of the two movements is strikingly similar. Both must start from sense images. And both must make a final leap beyond images and concepts toward a Transcendent Infinite beyond all images and concepts. The way of passing from the first step to the last differs in each. The philosophical ascent follows a purely interior path of intellectual analysis, insight, argument, etc. The work of religious art, on the other hand, must somehow stimulate, through the very medium of sensible symbols themselves, the leap of the mind and heart to what is beyond them. How can the work of religious art pull off this remarkable feat of leading its viewer (or hearer) beyond itself, beyond even the entire world of symbols and matter? It seems to me that the process follows very closely the triple path outlined in our present text, in the *Reply to Objection 3*: (1) comparison, (2) remotion, (3) élan toward the Transcendent.

The first step corresponds to St. Thomas' "comparison with sensible things." It selects some sensible symbolic structure which suggests some positive similitude, however distant, to the Transcendent reality the artist is trying to express. Thus he can lay out symbols of power, majesty, wisdom, love, etc. as found in our world.

The second step corresponds to the "remotion" or purification stage in St. Thomas' Triple Way. Here the artist must suggest the radical difference between his sensible symbol, taken literally, and the Beyond he is trying to express through it. This is equivalent to the removal of limitation and finitude from our concepts in the philosophical ascent. The artist expresses it by introducing a note of strangeness or dissimilitude of some kind into the primary similitude he has first laid down, in order to indicate that what he is pointing to is far different from, and higher than, the original sensible springboard from which he started.

There are many ways an artist of genius can do this, some crude and simple and obvious, such as the lifting of a human figure above the earth, encircling it with a halo of light, etc. Or it can be in some striking creative way that breaks the mold of the ordinary, jolting the viewer into the awareness that the work of art is pointing beyond this dimension of ordinary experience. Such, for example, are the Hindu statues of Shiva, Creator and Destroyer of worlds, portrayed as a dancer with six, eight, ten arms. Since the upraised hand and arm is a sign of power, a human figure with six arms breaks through our accustomed images and evokes a power beyond that of ordinary humans. It is a similitude shot through with dissimilitude, at once a comparison with sensible things of our experience and a negation of them in their present limited state. Or, to turn to Byzantine Christian art, consider the great icons, which sometimes seem so strange to us in the West, in part because we do not understand what the artist is trying to accomplish. An icon of Mary, the Mother of God, for example, will first exhibit a positive similitude with the human figure of a woman. But if we examine the face we notice a strange unearthly, fixed, and apparently empty stare in the eyes, unlike any ordinary human look. This is the negative moment, the affirmation of dissimilitude, which stimulates us to recognize that she is looking with the eyes of the soul beyond our material world directly into timeless eternity, into the world of the spirit and the divine, beyond change and motion.

There are an inexhaustible number of other, sometimes infinitely subtle and sophisticated, ways in which an artist of genius can suggest this negative moment of breaking the similitude with our world: e.g., the elongated figures of the saints in El Greco, the monumental, often frightening masks of African ritual art, the cone emerging from the top of the head in statues of the Buddha, etc. If this dimension of negativity, of purification from the limitations of our world is not present in some way in a work of art, it may indeed be good art, but cannot, it seems to me, qualify as properly religious art. It remains too stuck in the world of our ordinary human reality to help us spread the wings of the soul and soar toward the Transcendent. This criterion can lead us, I think, to disqualify as religious art many famous paintings and sculptures labelled "Madonnas," both in our own and in earlier times – including not a few by renowned Renaissance artists, such as Raphael himself. The absorption of these Renaissance artists in particular in exploiting to the full the new realism of the human form effectively stifles, all too often, any élan toward the Transcendent. We remain absorbed in the natural beauty of womanhood and childhood in themselves.

The *third step*, the élan toward the Transcendent beyond the merely human and the finite, is really only the other side of the previous stage and so closely woven into it as to allow only conceptual abstraction from it. This is the most mysterious aspect of a work of religious art, where the individual genius of the artist comes most to the fore – a genius often eluding explicit analysis. Somehow, by the dialectical opposition and complementarity of the two preceding positive and negative steps the artist must stimulate our minds, hearts, and feelings, set them resonating in depth, so that they will be spontaneously inspired to take off from the natural, the thisworldly, the material, and the finite to reach out on the wings of the spirit toward the transcendent Mystery of the Infinite, the divine. Great religious art has an uncanny power to draw us thus out of ourselves, to help us to take off and leave behind both ourselves and the work of art. Thus it is the express aim of Hindu religious music, for example, to draw the listener slowly, through the quality of the music, into a meditative state, which gradually deepens so that the listener is drawn beyond himself into communion with the Transcendent and forgets all about the music. All the examples we gave previously as illustrations of the negative moment are also examples, through the very dynamism inherent in the expression of this negative moment, of how religious art can stimulate the élan of the spirit toward the Infinite: the statue of the dancing Shiva, the great Byzantine icons, the paintings of El Greco, the African ceremonial masks, etc. So too the reverent contemplation of certain statues of the Buddha, if one follows carefully the continuous rippling folds of his garments, can have a quasi-psychedelic effect and draw one deep into contemplation. So too the great Tibetan Buddhist paintings, which are carefully designed as meditation guides. So too the Pietà of Michelangelo, by its deeply moving expression of the meditative silence of Our Lady, draws us into her own contemplation of her son, as God-man and Savior of the world through His Passion.

One of the most obvious and striking examples, one deeply familiar to St. Thomas himself, is the medieval Gothic cathedral, Chartres, for instance, whose soaring élan of incredibly attenuated, almost demateria-lized, stone columns and arches, suffused with light from the sun beyond the structure iself, admirably symbolizes the soaring of the human spirit in adoration and prayer toward the transcendent God, the Light of all finite minds, who "dwells in light inaccessible." [10]

What is happening in all these instances is that the artist has found a way through his symbolism to tap into and trigger off the great underlying, ever present, but ordinarily latent dynamism of the human spirit toward the Infinite. Thus stimulated, the simmering coals of this immense underground longing of the spirit suddenly flame up into consciousness and, using the symbol as a springboard, leap out toward the hidden Magnet that draws them. Just how the artist succeeds in doing this is his own secret, and often the secret of a whole tradition, once the initial geniuses have found the way. But it seems that the individual artist must himself experience this soaring of the spirit in order to charge his symbols with the power to do this for others. The work of a lesser artist, who either has not had the personal experience of this élan of the spirit, or who has not found the way to incarnate it effectively in sensible symbols, just will not stimulate the viewer (or hearer) to take off on the wings of his own spirit, but will leave him earthbound, stuck in the finite, the thisworldly. His artwork may be good art in itself, but not good religious art. Too much so-called religious art is of this earthbound quality.

It should be noted that the sensible symbols themselves are not capable of directly imaging or representing the Transcendent in the fullness of its own reality, any more than our philosophical concepts, and in fact less so. Their power comes from their ability to set resonating the underlying

---

[10] Cf. O. von Simpson, *The Gothic Cathedral* (Princeton: Princeton University Press, 1956), chapters 3-4.

dynamism of the human spirit toward the Infinite and offer it a channel (perhaps, to change the metaphor, we might say a lightning rod) through which it can flash into consciousness, and thus allow our integral human consciousness, mind, heart, and will, to soar for a moment toward the Transcendent Magnet that draws it secretly all the time, the Good in which all finite goods participate, the Ultimate Final Cause that draws us implicitly through all limited particular final causes. This radical dynamism of the human spirit toward the Infinite is the *dynamic* a priori of the human spirit, constitutive of the very nature of finite spirit. But the *human* spirit, in order to pass from the state of latent active potency, just under the level of consciousness, to actuality on the conscious level, needs to be triggered by some initial reference to the world of sense and imagination, since the human act of knowledge is the act of the whole human being, soul and body together.

Once triggered off by the sensible image, this dynamism of the spirit can use the latter as a springboard to reach out toward the Transcendent in two main ways: (1) in a purely intellectual way by the use of abstract analogous philosophical concepts, or (2) in a more total existential way, by the use of sense images as symbols which set resonating the integral psychic structure of man, mind, will, imagination, emotion – or, if you will, to use the synthetic term preferred by the oriental tradition, the entire "heart" of man. The intellectual path of concepts points more accurately and explicitly toward the Infinite as infinite. But because these concepts are so abstract and imprecise, they move only the mind. The path of the sensible symbol, on the other hand, is much vaguer and less explicit on the intellectual level, but by its much richer evocative power it sets resonating the whole psyche (including the body in which it is so deeply rooted), and thus tends to draw the whole person into existential communion with the symbolized that it points to. The aim of the abstract concept (or, more accurately, on the judgment in which the concept is imbedded) is to lead us toward deeper intellectual comprehension of the Transcendent Mystery; the aim of the artistic symbol is to lead us into deeper existential communion with this same Mystery. Both ways are needed, and complement each other; neither can supplant the other.

The last point to note in our discussion of the text of St. Thomas is his interesting addition about our mode of knowing purely spiritual beings, which are higher than ourselves but still finite. St. Thomas says that because they are not the efficient cause of our material cosmos or ourselves we cannot use the path of causal similitude, the first of the Three Ways by which we come to know God. Hence we can know them, he says, only "by comparison or remotion." He does not even mention here the *excessus* or élan of the mind. This seems to suggest that it is in fact easier to come to know God and something about his nature than to know angels. This is certainly true with respect to our first coming to know of the *existence* of angels compared to knowing the existence of God. Since they are not the cause of our universe, it is not possible to make a firm argument that they must exist under pain of rendering our universe unintelligible, as one can do for the existence of God, in the Thomistic perspective. One has to learn of the existence of angels (both good and bad) either through some Revelation, which we accept on faith, or by some merely suasive argument (such as that they are needed to complete the harmony of the universe as expression of God).

Does this inferiority of our knowledge of the existence of angels compared to our knowledge of the existence of God hold also for an understanding of their nature? St. Thomas does not tell us here. But one might make the case that this position could be defended, since our knowledge of God contains one added note of precision that cannot be applied to any finite spirit, namely that God is the infinite fullness of all perfection and situated very precisely at the apex of all reality and value for us. Thus it is easier for our concepts about God, joined with the pointing index of infinity, to tap into the underlying dynamism of the human spirit toward the Infinite and stimulate the inner leap of the spirit (*excessus*) toward its ultimate Source and Goal. It would then follow, if we transfer this argument to the sphere of religious art, that it would be in principle easier to create a work of art symbolizing God (or at least our relation to God) than one symbolizing angels. Interesting thesis! and one that contains not a little truth.

However, we do find in fact that the symbolic representation of higher spiritual beings (e.g., angels, both good and evil) is common in religious art, not only in the Christian but in other traditions as well. And the experience of the viewer, including the leap of the mind beyond the sensible symbol, seems to be very similar to the experience of religious art referring directly to God himself. So I would prefer to fit it in to the same basic structure outlined above, using not the causal similitude between God and creature but the doctrine of participation of all finite beings in the unitary perfection of God. Since all finite beings, both material and spiritual, proceed from the same ultimate Source, and every effect must to some degree resemble its cause, it follows that all of them must participate in some analogous way in the basic transcendental perfections of God, such as existence, unity, activity, power, goodness, beauty, etc. This immediately posits a bond of analogical similitude between all creatures, reaching in an ascending hierarchy of being from the lowest material being all the way up to Infinite Spirit. Furthermore all intellectual beings share a bond of analogous similitude in the order of spirit, both with God and each other. It follows that in a work of art, through the dialectical interplay of comparison and remotion, similitude and dissimilitude, the dynamism of our spirit can be stimulated to leap beyond the sensible symbol toward something higher and better than ourselves, *along the way of God*, along the ascending ladder of being towards its infinite apex, hence worthy of our profound reverence. The attractive power of the higher, precisely because it leads along the path of participated goodness towards the infinite goodness of the Source, can trigger the élan of the spirit to soar beyond our present level of incarnate spirit towards the realm of pure finite spirit, even though this be only a finite participation in Infinite Spirit, which alone is the ultimate Magnet activating the entire life of our minds and wills and enabling them to transcend their own level.

III. Conclusion

Our aim has been to follow the lead of St. Thomas in uncovering the underlying metaphysical and epistemological structures supporting the ability of authentic religious art to give symbolic expression to the Transcendent and our relation to it. The epistemological structure is based on St. Thomas' distinctive theory of human understanding as a synthesis of sense and intellect, according to which any act of the intellect must first find footing in some image of the senses or the imagination and then use it as a springboard to go beyond the sense world, either to the formal essence of the sensible thing itself or to its cause. The ascent of the mind to know God takes place through a triple process of (1) causal similitude, (2) negation of all imperfections and limits, i.e., negation of exact or univocal similitude, and (3) reaffirmation of the purified perfection together with a projection of it toward infinite fullness, accomplished by a burst into consciousness of the radical unrestricted drive of the human spirit toward the Infinite – a drive that is constitutive of the very nature of finite spirit as such. This élan or *excessus* of spirit enables it to leap beyond its own level and all finite beings to point obscurely through the very awareness of its own dynamism (the *pondus animae meae* of St. Augustine) toward the Infinite. The metaphysical underpinnings of this theory of knowledge are (1) the integral union of body and soul to form a single being with a single unified field of consciousness; (2) the radical drive of the spirit (intellect and will) toward the Infinite as ultimate Final Cause; and (3) the doctrine of creation, explained in terms of participation and causal similitude, which grounds a bond of analogical similitude not only of all creatures with God but also of all creatures with each other.

The inner dynamism of the authentically religious work of art follows the same path of ascent. It must first put forth a positive symbolic expression of some similitude with the Transcendent; then partially negate this similitude, by introducing some element of strangeness or dissimilitude with our ordinary experience on a finite material level. The dialectical interplay of similitude and dissimilitude must then be artfully contrived so that by its very structure it taps into and awakens the ever present but latent dynamism toward the Infinite that lies at the very root of all finite spirit, so that our spirit takes wings and soars in an élan or *excessus* (a going out of itself) reaching beyond the sensible symbol toward lived communion of the integral human being with the Transcendent Reality it is trying to express. The genius of the artist consists in his ability to give symbolic expression to dissimilitude within similitude in such a way as to set resonating the deep innate longing within us all for the Transcendent, so that the work of art finally leads us beyond itself in a self-transcending movement, "dying that we might live" more deeply – an analogue of the loss of self in order to find the true self characteristic of all authentic religious living. To sum it up in St. Thomas' own extraordinarily terse but pregnant terms: *comparatio, remotio, excessus*.

15

Analysis by Principles and Analysis by Elements

Kenneth L. Schmitz
Trinity College, Toronto

In the sixteenth and seventeenth centuries widespread distrust of analysis by *principles* contributed to the acceptance of analysis by *elements*. More precisely, the challenge to the validity and significance of analysis by *ontological*[1] principles resulted in the rise of analysis by *quantitative* elements. The latter was not unknown hitherto, of course, but under new conditions of thought and life it assumed new forms and unprecedented power, leading in modern physics to the search for basic particles and in chemistry to the search for simple elements. The pervasive collapse of ontological analysis took place largely outside of the universities and north of the Alps and Pyrenees.[2] What was distinctive about the change was

---

[1] In the discussion that followed upon my first professional paper ("Natural Wisdom in the Manuals," *Proceedings*, ACPA [1956], pp. 160-181) I was asked by Fr. Owens (rhetorically, I suspect) whether the term "ontological" ought to be used nowadays by someone in the Aristotelian or Thomistic metaphysical tradition. I replied that it ought not to be used, and I think that my answer then was prudent, given the context in Catholic intellectual circles. The meaning associated with Leibniz and Wolff, viz., that ontology was the study of *ens possibile*, was being communicated indirectly through some of the scholastic manuals then in wide use. Moreover, the Heideggerian stress on ecstatic possibility (*existentialia*) was beginning to command quite general attention in North American. Since then, however, the preferred term "metaphysical" has also fallen upon ambiguity in the uses to which positivists and some linguistic analysts have put it; so that it seems to me to be desirable to retrieve a neutral meaning of the term ontological, viz., "analysis in terms of being," and to develop the further and more determinate meaning in the exposition itself.

[2] The quite different situation that prevailed in Italy has often been remarked upon; for there the universities played a more important part in the change of thought. In Spain, of course, the older ontological analysis remained somewhat more secure.

Graceful Reason: Essays in Ancient and Medieval Philosophy Presented to Joseph Owens, CSSR, ed. Lloyd P. Gerson. Papers in Mediaeval Studies 4 (Toronto: Pontifical Institute of Mediaeval Studies, 1983), pp. 315-330. © P.I.M.S., 1983.

that analysis by quantitative elements broke loose from the subordinate role it had played within an ontological context. Moreover, it came to be associated with a quite general redefinition of the interests and limits of knowledge underway in European culture, and even came to be its definitive factor. This did not mean, however, that ontological analysis was entirely eliminated; nor could it be. Fragments survived for a while and the language persisted long after its previous meaning had departed. There was still *talk* about matter and form, of essence and existence, of cause and end, but the whole status of ontological analysis itself was displaced into a kind of intellectual limbo. The underpinnings of scientific discourse were taken to be either obviously given (and so not in need of further clarification), or posited hypothetically (in the service of analysis undertaken with laudable motives), or matters of deeply rooted human belief (and so both inevitable and ineradicable). In any event, it was widely accepted that conceptions which lay beyond the reach of quantitative analysis neither needed nor could admit of rational articulation; nor could they receive rational justification. A curtain of primitive positivism descended upon a region of intellectual life that had hitherto been appreciated as the domain of first philosophy and of philosophical wisdom.

This redirection of philosophical effort – indeed, its reversal – is patent in the writings of the most influential early modern philosophers whose thoughts set down the framework surrounding the intellectual labours of the scientists. At the beginning of the seventeenth century Francis Bacon expressed a quite general hope for "the new philosophy or active science":

> I have made a beginning of the work – a beginning, as I hope, not un-important: – the fortune of the human race will give the issue; – such an issue, it may be, as in the present condition of things and men's minds cannot easily be conceived or imagined. For the matter in hand is no mere felicity of speculation, but the real business and fortunes of the human race, and all power of operation.[3]

His sometimes express contempt for Plato and Aristotle, his excoriation of the schoolmen as spinners of insubstantial spider's webs, his depiction of the idols to which the human mind is prey, his appeal for light-bearing and fruit-bearing experiments, and his search for middle axioms, neither too general nor too particular – these forged a strategy for the invention of a new logic, a new mode of discourse which placed human felicity at the

---

[3] From the Preface to *The Great Instauration*, the argument to the sixth part (*The English Philosophers from Bacon to Mill*, ed. E. A. Burtt [New York: Modern Library, 1939], pp. 22-23).

forefront and centre of human enquiry, but understood it primarily as mastery over nature. Bacon's sometime secretary, Thomas Hobbes, wrote that the language of first philosophy was threadbare, and that

> the first grounds of all science are not only not beautiful, but poor, arid, and, in appearance, deformed.[4]

Nevertheless, he urged that philosophy pursue these grounds, isolating them as corporeal elements, which could serve in the orderly construction of a body of knowledge; that body of knowledge would then serve to determine men in the performance of actions and the production of goods "for the commodity of human life." Descartes made the same point with more subtlety and learning. In a well-known passage from a letter to Abbé Picot, he had written:

> Thus all philosophy is like a tree, of which metaphysics is the root, physics the trunk, and all the other sciences the branches that grow off this trunk, which reduce to three principal ones: namely, medicine, mechanics and morals ... But just as it is not from the roots or the trunks of trees that we gather the fruit, but only from the extremities of their branches, so the chief use of philosophy depends on those of its parts which we can learn only last of all.[5]

With many of his contemporaries he shared the opinion that Aristotle and his followers had invented dubious "potencies," "forms," and "final causes," that obscured the plain and evident starting points of knowledge, the "seeds," "*principia*," or "*initia*."[6]

Now, it is in a writing of one of the leading spokesmen of the older ontological analysis that we read the following:

> All sciences and arts are directed in an orderly way toward one thing, that is, to the perfection of man, which is his happiness.[7]

So that what is at issue is not the desirability of human happiness, nor the need that knowledge contribute to that happiness. What is at issue is how

---

[4] *De corpore* 1.1.1 and 6 (*Body, Man, and Citizen*, trans. R. S. Peters [London: Collier-Macmillan, 1962], pp. 24 and 27).

[5] From the Preface to the French translation of the *Principles of Philosophy* (in the English translation by John Veitch; cited from *A Discourse on Method* ... [London: Dent, 1946], pp. 156-157, and slightly emended by N. Kemp Smith, *New Studies in the Philosophy of Descartes* [New York: Russell and Russell, 1953], p. 31).

[6] From a letter to Father Dinet: *Œuvres de Descartes*, ed. C. Adam and P. Tannery [Paris: Cerf, 1904], 7: 580; in English: *The Philosophical Works of Descartes*, ed. E. S. Haldane and G. R. T. Ross [Cambridge, 1911, rpt. 1970], 2: 359.

[7] *Proemium* to St. Thomas Aquinas' *Commentary on Aristotle's Metaphysics*, trans. V. J. Bourke in *The Pocket Aquinas* (New York: Washington Square, 1960), p. 145.

man ought to enquire in order to acquire that knowledge which can
contribute to his happiness. At the deepest level of enquiry, is the
philosopher to draw the highest wisdom from consideration of the source
upon which all good depends – as Plato sought participation in the
archetypal Forms, as Aristotle sought contemplation in self-thinking
Thought, or as St. Thomas sought to prepare himself for union with
Ipsum Esse Subsistens? Or, was he to proceed from isolated elements – the simple natures of Bacon, the corpuscles of Hobbes, the seeds
or clear and distinct ideas of Descartes – to composite knowledge,
methodical production and commodious results? The disjunction seems
forced: why not both? After all, the ancients sought results (in the arts)
and not only principles; and the moderns sought basics (the elements) and
not only results. But the disjunction is severe because the question is about
fundamental enquiry; it is a question of emphasis and primacy. It asks: in
which direction is thought to flow when it is engaged at its deepest level?
Does thought seek out foundations only in order to leave them for
something better, or does it seek them out in order to unite itself with that
which is highest and best? At least until rather recently in our culture,
there have been two prevalent modes of discourse about foundations:
discourse in terms of ontological principles and discourse in terms of
quantitative elements.[8] With their contending claims in mind, it is
instructive to read and reflect upon an early work of St. Thomas,[9] in
which he takes stock of his Aristotelian heritage, not without enriching it
with his own understandings.[10] The struggle in the sixteenth and
seventeenth centuries between the two contending modes of discursive
analysis stands between us and St. Thomas, so that every attempt to
understand his meaning becomes an effort to recover the ontological
mode of discourse, and offers an opportunity for further self-knowledge.

---

[8] "... recently ... prevalent": a third mode of discourse, the historical, is as ancient as
the other two, but it has come to prominence as a candidate for foundational thinking only
in the past century or so.

[9] *De principiis naturae*, ed. J. J. Pauson (Fribourg: Société Philosophique, 1950).

[10] Pauson, ibid., p. 72, remarks: "In *De Principiis*, influences of Avicenna, Averroes,
Boethius, and the translations of Aristotle from the Arabic are visible, but the synthesis
belongs strictly to St. Thomas. No general integration of the works of these authors could
possibly bring about this end product, even though the phraseology of almost every part
of it can be duplicated from their works." For a general consideration of the nature and
sources of St. Thomas' own positions regarding the distinction of the sciences, the nature
of actuality and the role of sacred doctrine insofar as they add to or diverge from Aristotle,
see Joseph Owens, "Aquinas as Aristotelian Commentator," in *St. Thomas Aquinas 1274-
1974; Commemorative Studies* (Toronto: Pontifical Institute of Mediaeval Studies, 1974),
1: 213-238.

In *On the Principles of Nature* St. Thomas distinguishes the term "principle" from the term "element" by the intermediary term "cause":

> Principle is as it were a more extensive term than cause, and cause more extensive than element.[11]

This lapidary statement bears scrutiny, since it might be misunderstood and taken as saying no more than that "principle" is the genus of "cause" and "element," and that the latter two are to be included in "principle" as two species of a common genus, "cause" being a superior species, and "element" an inferior one. Or, because we tend today to restrict the term "cause" to productive force, we might mistake "principle" as the broad genus that includes "cause" as a species along with other constitutive factors, such as "end," "form" and "matter," taken as other species; and then take "matter" as a more inclusive species that contains "element" as a subordinate and less inclusive species. Much more is meant, however; or rather, what is meant is not a classification into genera and species at all. This is borne out by what follows. For St. Thomas immediately takes up the divers senses of the term "cause."[12] A little further on[13] he makes explicit the analogous character of being and its principles; and he concludes the brief work with an insistence upon the radical diversity among the various principles of natural being. Even the matter, form, and privation considered in one category differ irreducibly from the same principles considered in another category. We may well ask: Do the terms, "matter," "form," and "privation," retain a unity that survives the radical diversity of the categories? We may put St. Thomas' reply in other words: each term expresses a similarity of role played out by one item in a category in respect to other items in that category. Thus, "privation" indicates a certain non-being in the category of quantity, and again in the category of quality; but what it is to lack quantity is irreducibly other than what it is to lack quality. In his own words translated:

> Yet, the matter of substance and of quantity, and similarly their form and privation, differ generically [*differunt genere*] but agree only by way of proportion [*conveniunt solum secundum proportionem*] – in the sense that just as the matter of substance is related to the substance according to the

---

[11] Translation by V. J. Bourke in *The Pocket Aquinas*, p. 70. The Latin (ed. Pauson, p. 93) reads: "... principium aliquomodo est in plus quam causa, et causa in plus quam elementum."

[12] Ibid., ed. Pauson, pp. 93-94; trans. Bourke, pp. 70-71.

[13] Ibid., ed. Pauson, pp. 102-104: "... diximus quod substantia et quantitas differunt genere, sed sunt idem secundum analogiam"; trans. Bourke, pp. 75-76.

characteristic meaning of matter [*in ratione materiae*], so, too, is the matter of quantity related to quantity.[14]

The distinction between "principle," "cause," and "element," then, is not meant to set forth the decreasing extension of genera and species, but to exhibit the network of analogously related features of being. The tension is created by the univocal tendency of human speech and the analogous diversity inherent in real being.

St. Thomas concedes that we may sometimes use the term "principle" interchangeably with that of "cause"; but he insists that there is an important distinction between causal and non-causal principles. We may call something a "principle" simply because it is first in its own order, whether any real consequences (*esse posterioris*) follow from it or not. For

everything from which [*a quo*] a change takes its start is called a principle.[15]

Whereas a cause, strictly speaking, is

that sort of first item from which [*de illo primo, ex quo*] the existence of the consequent [*esse posterioris*] follows.[16]

And again, a cause is

that from whose being another being follows [*id ex cuius esse sequitur aliud*].[17]

And so, we must distinguish what is a principle in the weak, non-causal sense from what is a principle in the strong, causal sense. Thus, in the analysis of a change, we must distinguish between what is at the beginning as starting-point only and what is at the beginning as source. It follows, too, that we must distinguish between what is "consequent upon" something and what is "consequent from" something.[18] In the alteration of a surface from black to white, therefore, the old paint is found at the beginning of the change as a starting-point but not as its source; and the fresh paint is consequent upon [*a quo*] the old, but not at all a consequent of [*ex quo*] the old paint. The fresh paint is, rather, along with the painter a cause of the change.[19]

---

[14] Ibid., ed. Pauson, p. 104; trans. Bourke, p. 77.

[15] Ibid., ed. Pauson, p. 91; trans. Bourke, p. 68.

[16] Ibid.

[17] Ibid., ed. Pauson, p. 91; trans. Bourke, p. 69.

[18] Ibid., ed. Pauson, p. 91; trans; Bourke, pp. 69-70.

[19] Ibid., ed. Pauson, p. 91: "sed quando aliquid movetur de nigredine ad albedinem, dicitur quod nigredo est principium illius motus, et universaliter omne id a quo incipit esse motus dicitur principium, tamen nigredo non est id ex quo consequitur *esse* albedinis. ... Et propter hoc, privatio ponitur inter principia et non inter causas, qui privatio est id a quo

We may, then, legitimately use the term "principle" to designate an item as first in any given order without expecting real consequences [esse posterioris] to follow from it. Nevertheless, there will be at least implicit reference to other items in the order, including subordinate principles. An order is a unified totality, i.e., a plurality of items brought into unity in some fashion. That which is the ground of the unity is the primary principle of the order and endows it with its distinctive character. The other items are its principiates; we might even say, its "consequences," though not necessarily *real* consequences. That is, the relationship of principle and principiates need not consist in the communication and reception of real being: the black is a principle of the change but not its source. Today we might be tempted to call the black – that is, the black as the not-white in the order of colour – a necessary "condition" for the change. But to the extent that the term "condition" suggests "circumstance" it is too external to satisfy the requirements of ontological analysis. For privation is no mere circumstance, since it is "constitutive" of the very subject at the starting-point of its change, in the way that lack of health "belongs to" and is "part of" the very being of the patient undergoing cure. Privation, then, is "constitutive" of the order of changing beings.

Nevertheless, privation is not a *primary* principle. St. Thomas writes that it is not a principle *per se*, but only a principle *per accidens*;[20] and he distinguishes this principle in the weak sense from the four causes which are principles in the strong sense, i.e., causes *per se*. Elsewhere[21] he remarks that each of the categories includes its own version of the incomplete (*imperfectus*) and the complete (*perfectus*). Radically taken, these are privation and possession (*habitus*), and the two form the primary contrariety within each categorial order. Finally, they reduce to non-being and being respectively. Now the order within which privation plays out its role is that of alteration, and the principiates are the consequences that both follow upon and follow from the principles operative in that

---

incipit generatio." [Italics added.] Earlier (ed. Pauson, pp. 82-83), in setting forth the three principles of nature – matter, form and privation – St. Thomas seems to speak of privation as a principle *ex quo*: "forma est id ad quod est generatio, alia duo [scil., materia et privatio] sunt ex parte eius ex quo est generatio." But here privation is assimilated to matter which is a cause, and since it coincides with it, it is the same in subject and differs from it only in its meaning and function; that is, it is the matter *qua* lack, rather than *qua* passive potency: "Unde materia et privatio sunt idem sujecto, sed differunt ratione." Trans. Burke, p. 63.

[20] Ibid., ed. Pauson, p. 90; trans. Bourke, p. 68; also ed. Pauson, pp. 83-84; trans. Bourke, p. 65.

[21] In his *Commentary on the Physics of Aristotle*, 3.1, par. 8. Cf. *De principiis naturae*, ed. Pauson, pp. 95-96; trans. Bourke, p. 71.

alteration. The privation is a subordinate principle because the alteration is directed towards the possession of the new form and the new being. No institution of real consequences arises from it, whereas they do from form and the other causes.

These causes cooperate to produce a complex result in and through the change. St. Thomas remarks that the same thing (*idem*) may have several causes. Moreover, the same thing may be the cause of contrary effects. Even more, what is a source in one order or along one line of causality may be a consequent in another:

> idem sit causa et causatum respectu eiusdem, sed diversimode: one thing [may] be both cause and effect with regard to another item, but in a different fashion.[22]

Thus, in the line of agency, the activity of walking may be a source of health (*principium*); and health can be its consequence (*principiatum*).[23] But conversely, in the line of finality, that same walking, the very same activity at the same time, may be a consequence; for, inasmuch as health is that for the sake of which the walking is done, health will be in a different way the source or principle of the activity, and walking will be its derivative or principiate. In sum, health will be principle in an order other than that within which walking is principle. The four causes, then – agency, end, form and matter – are each first in their own order, and each contributes in its distinctive way to the complex resultant being. It need only be added[24] that, over-all, i.e., in the interplay among the orders, the end is rightfully called "the cause of causes," since for its sake alone does the causality of the other causes come into play. The *interplay of orders* is not a random affair, but rather gives expression to the inherent unity-in-diversity that characterizes the analogical order appropriate to being and its beings.

It is important, moreover, to recognize that the analogical character of being does not result from the gathering of its divers principles into itself. On the contrary, being is the principle of principles; and so, their analogical character expresses the original diversity that characterizes being itself. The diversity, then, is not merely *between* principles; nor even between the embodiments of each principle within the various categorial orders. The analogical diversity is rooted *within* each principle itself. A thorough-going ontological analysis of change will show that each

---

[22] Ibid., ed. Pauson, p. 93; trans. Bourke, p. 70.
[23] The terms are not in the *De principiis*, but they express the general concept of order.
[24] Ibid., ed. Pauson, pp. 93-94; trans. Bourke, pp. 70-71.

principle discharges quite opposite functions. At the first level of such an analysis it may be said that matter is the principle of continuity (as substrate or subject) and that form is the principle of difference (as definitive of the kind or qualification). But when the analysis is carried deeper, the analogous diversity inherent within each principle discloses itself.[25] Thus, matter cannot be identified simply with the substrate as the principle of continuity; for it is also the potential source of diversity. The coming into being of a child as the term of a change is its coming to be diverse from and other than its parents. Now matter plays a role in that diversification, since it is the root capacity for just such diversification even while it also provides both the link with the parents in the process and a real basis for the continuing relation between parents and child. Matter is, then, principle of both continuity and discontinuity in the order of potency. Or again, the form of something specifies it and sets it off from others unlike it. Form is, then, a principle of difference or definition. But in defining the thing, form establishes an agreement of that thing with others of its kind. In the coming to be of something the form is communicated by the causes: *omne agens agit sibi simili*. Form is, then, at once a principle of likeness and unlikeness, of continuity and discontinuity, of identity and non-identity.

It is this coincidence of being and non-being in ontological principles which Hegel sought to incorporate from Aristotle, but which he dispersed into a dialectical movement of negative and positive moments.[26] There is no such fundamental dialectic in Aristotle or St. Thomas, but rather a sort of "simultaneity" according to which a principle is the determinant and source of quite divers consequences *in its own order*. So that matter is not to be identified simply with and exhausted in its contribution to continuity within change; nor is form to be identified without qualification with and exhausted in its contribution to the differentiation that comes about in and

[25] This point has been made in regard to the subject of becoming and the act of becoming by one of the most profound metaphysicians of the Thomistic revival, Gerard Smith, in *The Philosophy of Being: Metaphysics I* (New York: Macmillan, 1961), pp. 29-30.

[26] Indeed, the Hegelian *moments* are neither ontological principles in the sense developed here, nor are they quantitative elements. But the articulation of their difference would carry us too far from our present theme. Suffice it to note here that the Hegelian moments have the nominalist units of late medieval and early modern thought as their remote ancestors − units of analysis that paved the way for the quantitative elements of particle analysis. Hegel attempted to break down their independence by implicating the units in a self-determining process of mutual constitution, i.e., of co-constitution within the system. Whereas ontological principles are co-determinant within their source, and whereas elements come together to constitute results, dialectical moments constitute each other within the system.

through the change. As principles, they are the source at once of identity and non-identity, each within its own order: matter within the order of passive potency, form within the order of formal actuality, and other basic principles within their own orders. It is this inherent diversity that shows that they are principles (i.e., original) and not merely components (i.e., elementary). It seems to me that this more deeply embedded diversity within each principle is the basis for the diversity St. Thomas points out in regard to the four causes.[27]

In his brief consideration of the term "element" in the *Principles*[28] St. Thomas takes the term to stand for those items that contribute to the composition of some real thing by entering into it and becoming part of its matter. These components belong, therefore, in an order of causality, and precisely that of material causality; and so, they may be called "material causes." He writes of them in the plural, showing that he had in mind what may be called "secondary matters," items that are qualitatively formed in some way, rather than the pure indeterminacy of primary matter. But, although they are secondary matters, they are primary components. That is, first of all, in the order of material composition, the elements are *components* out of which some material composite comes to be formed (*ex quibus est compositio rei*).[29] And secondly, they are *primary* components, and not those parts (*membra*) of a body which are themselves made up of qualitatively different components, as the hand is made of flesh and bones, and they of still other qualitatively distinct components. Since elements enter into the composite itself, they are intrinsic principles. They continue to reside (*remanere, in ea*) in the composite, unlike bread which passes away into blood. And finally, although an element may be divided into quantitative parts, it is indivisible into qualitatively different parts, i.e., into parts which differ in kind (*quae differunt secundum speciem*). Along with his contemporaries, St. Thomas thought that such bodies as water and earth were quantitatively divisible (into drops and pieces) but qualitatively simple; and so he took them to be elements. Analysis by quantitative elements was to show him wrong as to the fact: water is divisible into qualitatively distinct components. But that same mode of analysis was to agree that elements in their simplest form were those particles that would not yield – or at least had not yet yielded – to further analysis.

---

[27] *De principiis naturae*, ed. Pauson, pp. 93-96; trans. Bourke, pp. 70-72.

[28] Ibid., ed. Pauson, pp. 91-93; trans. Bourke, pp. 69-70.

[29] Ibid., ed. Pauson, p. 91; trans. Bourke, p. 69.

According to St. Thomas, then, the term "element" designates those items which enter as qualitatively simple components into any primary process of material composition. The term "principle" designates any item which, being first in its order, has consequences (principiates), at least implicitly, though not necessarily real consequences (*esse posterioris*). The thrust of ontological analysis, then, is carried forward by those principles which are causes, and analysis by element-principles remains subordinate to material causality and the other causes. It is quite other with analysis by quantitatively determined elements. For in this mode of analysis, they focus the primary thrust of the mind as it probes nature and challenges the apparent indivisibility of the most recently discovered particle.

Analysis by quantitatively determined elements has had astounding success from the sixteenth century on to our own day. Francis Bacon can be seen as an interim thinker, slighting the use of mathematics in determining the nature of elements, and searching for qualitative elements that had an ill-defined material basis. These elements (*minima*)[30] had in his own thought almost broken away from the earlier ontological context. The nature of distinctness had already begun to harden as early as the late thirteenth century, in part perhaps through a tendency in Platonism to make formal difference primary. In William of Ockham a radical nominalism implied in principle the impossibility of the Aristotelian metaphysical analysis as it was developed by St. Thomas. For mandatory for such an analysis is the possibility of an analogical diversity among the ontological principles, and even within them (as was indicated above). That is to say, the character of unity must be such that it can tolerate a diversity whose principles exist together in a real composite, so that one can speak of a "real composition," of a complexity belonging to the thing and not merely constructed by the mind. Later it became usual for Schoolmen to speak in terms of a "real distinction" among the principles that constitute a being. Although used occasionally earlier, this less suitable, negative locution may have become prominent as a concession to pressure exerted upon scientific and philosophical discourse by nominalism and by analysis into quantitative elements. In any event, the

---

[30] *Novum Organum*, 2: vi (ed. T. Fowler, 2nd ed. [Oxford: Clarendon, 1889], p. 354; Burtt, *The English Philosophers*, p. 92). These "real particles (2: viii: Burtt, p. 94; Fowler, p. 357) are not atoms since they do not exist in a void. Their relation to the "simple natures" (2: v: Burtt, p. 90; Fowler, p. 351), which might almost be thought of as formal elements, remains unclarified. For all that, each time one rereads Bacon there arises an expectation that his own road of enquiry retains a latent power of physical analysis that has been prematurely thrust aside by quantitative analysis. Regarding mathematics, see ibid., 1: xcvi (Burtt, p. 67; Fowler, p. 300).

distinguishing mark of the older metaphysics stemming from Aristotle was that its ontological principles could be really distinct without being really separate. To paraphrase the poet: *There* is being, two in one, *there* is number slain; *there* is really only one, yet two remain. Such a diversity of ontological principles is a diversity *in* being: it is not simply a division made for the convenience of the enquiring human mind. And yet, it need not be a diversity *of* beings; that is, it need not be a physical separation into numerically distinct, really existent entities. In a word,the diversity is not a distinction *in mente*, but rather a distinction *in re*, an otherness prior to the intervention of the human mind.[31]

During the seventeenth and eighteenth centuries any distinction that was not a distinction of reason (*in mente*) – and thereby grounded in the formal structure of the human mind – was being forced to take shape as a separation. If it failed to do that – as the faculties or powers of the soul, for example, had been held to be really distinct from it without being separate from it – then that distinction risked and eventually would receive the charge of being unimportant, irrelevant and unfruitful for scientific and even for philosophical purposes. The best known kinds of separation among the philosophers are perhaps the Cartesian dualism of body and soul, the separation of theology from philosophy, and the precise lines that guarded the clarity of one idea from another; but also the self-isolation of each Humean impression. Nevertheless, the units of seventeenth-century mechanics and eighteenth-century chemistry were undoubtedly even more influential. Physical things were analyzed in order to isolate their component parts. The convergence of mathematical learning and physical analyis-by-separation-into-numerically-determined-material-components led to a general quantification of rational discourse, so that other modes of rational discourse which had earlier been considered to be scientific in the broad sense and philosophical tended to be dismissed from the field of serious enquiry. To use the older language, form and matter were fused by quantification to become the primary units of explanation in the light of which reality itself was to be understood. New meaning was undoubtedly gained, but the horizon of intelligibility was reduced, for better

---

[31] St. Thomas discusses how causes can coincide or differ in number and in kind, both with respect to the process of generation and to the thing that results from the generation (*De principiis naturae*, ed. Pauson, pp. 97-98): "... tres causae possunt incidere in unum, scilicet forma, finis et efficiens, ... finis incidit cum forma in idem numero, quia illud idem numero quod est forma generati, est finis generationis. Sed cum efficiente non incidit in idem numero, sed in idem specie. ... Materia autem non coincidit cum aliis, quia materia ex eo quod est ens in potentia, habet rationem imperfecti; sed aliae causae, cum sint actu, habent rationem perfecti; perfectum autem et imperfectum non coincidunt in idem." (Cf. trans. Bourke, pp. 72-73.)

and for worse. A simplification of discourse was under way, and with it the redefinition of the possibilities of human understanding.

A keen observer might have expected the fate that awaited the web of causes and other principles associated with ontological analysis. As the mode of quantitative analysis took control of the scientific reason, formal causality (*forma*) tended to dissolve into relations in the real order and ideas in the rational order. With Hobbes, forms were reduced to shapes brought about by the geometrical distances between points. With Descartes, they were mathematical-like relationships between the clear and distinct products of analysis. With Leibniz, they were internal relations of exemplarity; and his attempt to re-employ the principle of *entelechy* in order to ground *phenomena bene fundata* in the monads served a continuum of incorporeal monads ranging from the unconscious and obscure to the self-conscious and clear, rather than the gradation of specifically different, real substances formed by Aristotle's principle. With Locke, the metaphysical status of real essences was precarious, to say the least.[32] What quite generally disappeared from the main stream of scientific and philosophical thought, in any event, was the pre-quantitative and pre-qualitative ontological character of form as substantial form. Form was no longer *natura*: "that by which a thing has existence," that which "makes something to be actually." [33] There are no such natures in the work of Galileo, Hobbes, Descartes or Spinoza, nor in Locke, Hume and Kant; nor would they be welcome. The terms "form" and "formal" come to stand in the new thought-world for patterns, structures, designs and interrelationships, i.e., for something formed, a result; they cease to stand for a principle. More precisely, form was no longer taken as the first item in a certain order of being from which real consequences follow. In a word, form ceased to be a cause.

So, too, with the final cause or end (*finis*). The struggle against final causes neither began with Galileo nor ended with Molière and Voltaire, not even with Darwin and Thomas Huxley. Nevertheless, in the seventeenth century it was reduced to a feature of human agency, i.e., to

---

[32] In confirmation of the foregoing see: Hobbes, *De corpore*, 1.1.5 (Peters, *Body*, pp. 26-27); Descartes, *Discourse*, part 2, rule 3 (Haldane and Ross, *Works*, 1: 92; Adam and Tannery, *Œuvres*, 6: 18-19); Leibniz, *Monadology*, no. 18 (*The Monadology and Other Philosophical Writings*, ed. R. Latta [Oxford, 1898, rpt. 1948], p. 229 and fn. 32; *Opera philosophica quae exstant Latina* ..., ed. J. E. Erdmann [1840], augmented by R. Vollbrecht [Aalen, 1959], 2: 706b); Locke, *Essay Concerning Human Understanding* 3.9, no. 12 (ed. J. W. Yolton, 2nd ed. [London: Dent, 1964, rpt. 1972], 2: 82).

[33] *De principiis naturae*, ed. Pauson, pp. 80-81: "omne a quo aliquid habet esse, sive substantiale sive accidentale, potest dici forma; ... Et quia forma facit esse in actu, ideo forma dicitur esse actus. Quod autem facit actu esse substantiale, dicitur forma substantialis." (Cf. trans. Bourke, p. 62.)

purpose, the self-conscious motive for certain kinds of action. It was declared inappropriate as a principle of reality over-all. Here again, Francis Bacon's ambiguity is telling.[34] With few exceptions (and those vague) he tends to relegate finality to theology and the divine purpose, on the one hand, and to morality and human activity, on the other. Of course, Bacon was not a mechanist, but in the matter of final causes his influence joined with that of mechanism to drive final causality into its merely subjective anthropological corner or to let it out of the world through a theological chimney flue.

Nor did agency or efficient causality (*causa efficiens*) escape the reduction, for the very understanding of agency itself was transformed. In the earlier ontological context, "to produce" meant "to communicate being" (*dare esse, influxus entis*): "A cause is that from whose being another being follows."[35] In the analysis in terms of quantitatively determined elements, however, productive causality came to mean an active force or impulse that initiated change by transference of energy to another, resulting in displacement of particles in a new configuration and with an accelerated or decelerated rate of motion among the particles.

The particles themselves came to be understood as the primary and rudimentary material components. This sense of "element" seems, at first glance, to be exactly equivalent to St. Thomas', but it is not in at least three very important respects. The elements according to St. Thomas were material, of course, and they were formed, so that they exhibited distinctive qualitative properties: "an element is not divisible into parts that differ in kind."[36] The first difference, then, between the old and the

[34] The whole aphorism (*Novum Organum*, 2: ii: Burtt, p. 88; Fowler, pp. 345-346) is worth noting: "In what an ill condition human knowledge is at the present time, is apparent even from the commonly received maxims. It is a correct position that 'true knowledge is knowledge by causes.' And causes again are not improperly distributed into four kinds: the material, the formal, the efficient, and the final. But of these the final cause rather corrupts than advances the sciences, except such as have to do with human action. The discovery of the formal is despaired of. The efficient and the material (as they are investigated and received, that is, as remote causes, without reference to the latent process leading to the form) are but slight and superficial, and contribute little, if anything, to true and active science. Nor have I forgotten that in a former passage I noted and corrected as an error of the human mind the opinion that forms give existence. For though in nature nothing really exists beside individual bodies, performing pure individual acts according to a fixed law, yet in philosophy this very law, and the investigation, discovery, and explanation of it, is the foundation as well of knowledge as of operation. And it is this law, with its clauses, that I mean when I speak of *forms*; a name which I the rather adopt because it has grown into use and become familiar." Cited from *The English Philosophers from Bacon to Mill*, ed. E. A. Burtt (New York: Modern Library, 1939), pp. 88-89. The last sentence makes clear his understanding of form as law.
[35] See notes 16 and 17 above.
[36] See note 28 above.

new sense of "element" is that the qualitative character of an element may
be an important prelude to determining its difference from other elements,
but it is not to be permitted to enter into the strict scientific account which
sets forth its true and genuine constitution. That constitution must be
determined by a set of numerically determinable values, such as mass,
density, etc. In the older sense of element, on the contrary, the sensible
qualities were constitutive of the physical nature of the element itself. It
was this empirical dependence that led Kant to scold the older physicists,
for keeping human reason in the "leading-strings" of nature.[37] Another
way of expressing this first difference regarding the character of elements
is to see the new mode of analysis as moving away from the previous
primacy of the physical body towards the primacy of the mathematical
body. Following in the wake of this shift, the earlier distinction between
common sensibles and proper sensibles was transformed into the
separation of primary qualities (the mathematically determinable and
so-called "objective" properties) and the secondary qualities (which became "subjective"). In this way rational discourse withdrew from the
immediacy of lived perceptual and sensible experience, to return to it only
insofar as it was susceptible of numerically determinate values.

More fundamental yet, the first difference points beyond itself to a
deeper difference. For the concept of "physical body" does not only stand
for qualitatively formed material. It stands more deeply for a "natured"
body, i.e., for a body possessed of active potency (powers) and passive
potency (matter). At its base lies that pure indeterminacy and utterly
determinable capacity known as "prime matter." And so the very
conception of material causality (*materia*) gives way, and a move of the
scientific and philosophical intelligence towards the surface, towards
phenomena is underway. It will reach a certain high-point in Kant, but it
is significant that even Hobbes makes much of "effects or appearances." [38]

The third and more general difference rests upon the absence of the
act/potency relationship from the new mode of analysis. In the older
analysis, an ontological composite unit existed as the composition of the
incomplete (*imperfectus*) and the complete (*perfectus*). Now, that
ontological unit can be *really one* being (*ens per se et unum*) – and not two
or more beings, not simply an organization or system of particles – only if
the imperfect in the physical order must be traced back to and grounded in
the radically passive and thoroughly determinable principle called "prime
matter." For only such a radically determinable principle – a principle

[37] *Critique of Pure Reason*, second Preface, B xiii (trans. N. Kemp Smith, *Immanuel Kant's Critique of Pure Reason* [London: Macmillan, 1950], p. 20).
[38] *De corpore*, 1.1.2 (Peters, *Body*, p. 24).

which has nothing in itself but the capacity to receive such a determination – can receive that determination from the other causes. Such a radically determinable principle can receive from them the determination to be *a* being, to be *radically* one; so that the ontological unit that results (*ens per se et unum*) is not merely a collection of relatively self-subsistent particles. In such an analysis of physical being, then, complexity and simplicity are not exclusive alternatives at war with one another; but rather, to be composite and to be one are reconciled and integrated in a really composite ontological unit. This comes about in the physical order only insofar as a principle of utter determinability (prime matter) receives the determinations of the other causes (of the agent and the end) by way of the determinative causality of the form. In other words, or rather, in the language of Aristotle and St. Thomas, this utterly indigent principle – for it would be too much to speak the language of Plato here and call it the "lover" of being and the forms – this utter capacity is indispensable for the analysis of physical nature in terms of ontological principles.

Nevertheless, at the centre of the ontological analysis of physical nature in terms of the four causes, as set out in St. Thomas' *Principles*, there lies the properly *metaphysical* consideration of physical nature. For metaphysics alone can make explicit the ground and distinctive character of analysis in terms of ontological units.[39] Now, for such a task we need the recognition of *esse*, that principle which St. Thomas has shown in many of his works to be the most proper and explicit character of being. It seems to me unlikely that a general ontological analysis in terms of the four causes can make much headway in the face of the brilliant success of the quantitative analysis of physical nature, unless such an ontological analysis deepens its discourse by turning to the leading principle of being understood as actuality, viz. existence (*esse*). The primacy of such actuality rests – not upon its being the cause of all causal activity, though it is that as the principle of finality – but upon this: that *esse*, as the most determinative and actual of everything that is, is the supreme ontological principle, the principle of all the principles of being. It seems to me further that such a metaphysical analysis can situate and even enhance the unmistakeable gains of analysis by elements, placing that analysis in a deeper and broader context. In his own philosophical work, as well as in his interpretation of St. Thomas, Aristotle and others, Joseph Owens has lighted a path towards such a metaphysics and its future.[40]

[39] See Kenneth L. Schmitz, *The Gift: Creation*, The Aquinas Lecture (Milwaukee: Marquette University, 1982), pp. 111-118.

[40] See Joseph Owens, *St. Thomas and the Future of Metaphysics*, The Aquinas Lecture (Milwaukee: Marquette University, 1957).

16

The Nature of Book Delta of the *Metaphysics*
According to the Commentary of Saint Thomas Aquinas

Ralph McInerny

University of Notre Dame

There are two general problems associated with Thomas' commentaries on Aristotelian works, perhaps particularly his commentary on the *Metaphysics*. The first affects the whole tradition of commentaries from Hellenistic times and stems from the bombshell Werner Jaeger threw into Aristotelian studies during the first quarter of the century.[1] All the great commentaries on the *Metaphysics*, Greek, Arabic, Latin, presuppose that the work is a literary whole; indeed, a significant aspect of the commentator's task consists of showing the interrelation of the parts of the work, in short its order. If Jaeger is right about the literary disunity of the *Metaphysics*, the commentary tradition is called severely into question. The second great problem has to do with the value of Thomas' commentaries on Aristotle for determining what he, Thomas, thinks about this or that.

Discussions of the second point are many and various. From Chenu and Gilson to the 1974 essay by Father Joseph Owens, there has been a significant development of assessment.[2] It seems fairly clear that there are

[1] Werner Jaeger, *Aristotle: Fundamentals of the History of His Development* (Oxford, 1948).

[2] M. D. Chenu, OP, *Introduction à l'étude de Saint Thomas d'Aquin* (Montreal, 1954), pp. 173-198; E. Gilson, *A History of Christian Philosophy in the Middle Ages* (New York, 1955), p. 367: "There is no philosophical writing of Thomas Aquinas to which we could apply for an exposition of the truths concerning God and man which he considered knowable in the natural light of reason. His commentaries on Aristotle are so many

Graceful Reason: Essays in Ancient and Medieval Philosophy Presented to Joseph Owens, CSSR, ed. Lloyd P. Gerson. Papers in Mediaeval Studies 4 (Toronto: Pontifical Institute of Mediaeval Studies, 1983), pp. 331-343. © P.I.M.S., 1983.

no apriori literary and/or historical considerations which can settle the status of the commentaries. Finally, one must simply read them carefully and develop a theory of their nature against the background of that reading.

As for the first question, much post-Jaegerian study of the *Metaphysics* has devoted itself to finding larger or smaller ordered units within the fourteen books, clustering series of books in various ways, while conceding the main point that the fourteen books simply do not make up an ordered whole. Elsewhere, I have expressed my own views on the status of Jaeger's major claim about the *Metaphysics* as this is grounded on a reading of E.1.[3] In the present paper, I propose to consider the fate of Book Delta of the *Metaphysics* and then draw attention to Thomas' remarkable commentary on it.

I

Jaeger's remarks about Delta in his second work on the composition of Aristotle's work is succinct. In the course of providing an overview of the *Metaphysics*, he writes, "The postscript to the introductory book, the so-called little Alpha, comes after big A simply because they did not know where else to put it. It is a remnant of notes taken at a lecture by Pasicles, a nephew of Aristotle's disciple Eudemus of Rhodes; Alpha, Beta and Gamma belong together. Delta, on the other hand, was still known as an independent work in Alexandrian times, as a sound bibliographical tradition informs us. Epsilon is a short transitional passage leading to Zeta, Eta, Theta. These three form a whole, but their connection with the

---

expositions of the doctrine of Aristotle, not of what might be called his own philosophy. As a commentator, Thomas could add to the text something of his own, but this was not his principal intention. We may find fragmentary expositions of his own philosophical conceptions in some particular treatises, for instance in the *De ente et essentia*. Generally speaking, however, we must resort to the theological writings in order to find them fully developed, but following a theological order. This is the only mode of historical existence they have, and whatever order of exposition he might have chosen to follow in philosophy, the theology of Thomas Aquinas remains for us the only place where his own rational view of the world is to be found." On this, see James Collins, "Toward a Philosophically Ordered Thomism," *The New Scholasticism*, 32 (1958): 301-326. Joseph Owens, "Aquinas as Aristotelian Commentator," *St. Thomas Aquinas 1274-1974, Commemorative Studies* (Toronto: PIMS, 1974), 1: 213-238.

[3] Ralph McInerny, "Ontology and Theology in Aristotle's Metaphysics," in *Mélanges à la Mémoire de Charles de Koninck* (Quebec: Les Presses de l'Université Laval, 1968), pp. 233-240. See now Pierre Aubenque, "La pensée du simple dans la *Métaphysique* Zeta 17 and Theta 10," *Études sur la Métaphysique d'Aristote*, Actes du VIe Symposium Aristotelicum (Paris: Vrin, 1979), pp. 69-80, with discussion pp. 81-88.

previous books seems to be problematical...." [4] That isolation and dismissal of Delta from consideration sets the tone for the approach of later scholars.

> Delta is evidently out of place where it is, and as evidently it is a genuinely Aristotelian work. It is referred to in Epsilon, Zeta, Theta and Iota, as well as in the *Physics* and the *De Generatione et Corruptione* – either by the vague phrase ἐν ἄλλοις or as τὰ περὶ τοῦ ποσαχῶς or by some variant of this title; and under this title it occurs in Diogenes Laertius' list, in which the *Metaphysics* does not occur. It is a useful preliminary to the *Metaphysics*, but it is not a preliminary to it in particular. Some of the notions discussed in it (κολοβόν, ψεῦδος) are not appropriate to the *Metaphysics*, and it is apparently earlier than the physical works while the rest of the *Metaphysics*, in its present form, is later. [5]

Ross takes it that Delta was inserted in its present place because Gamma 1004a28 was taken to promise an examination of varieties in the meanings of terms, perhaps because E.1026a34 is the first backward reference to Delta. [6]

Joseph Owens, in his magisterial *The Doctrine of Being in the Aristotelian* Metaphysics, [7] having reviewed the chronologies of others (who find no integral place for Book Delta) goes on to his own lengthy and illuminating effort to read *Aristoteles ex Aristotele* but, despite the crucial role he assigns *pros hen* equivocals, clearly accepts the view that Delta is an independent treatise which casts no light on whatever unified development there is in the fourteen books. This is not, of course, to say that Owens does not make extended use of Delta in his study.

Not all Aristotelian commentators have been willing to take the genetic and/or chronological approach as obligatory. Indeed, recent introductory works, after mentioning the incredible diversity of scholarly opinions on the structure and order of the *Metaphysics*, simply set the controversy aside and say, in effect, let's read Aristotle. [8] While this might seem slightly obscurantist, the same cannot be said of the remarks of Stephen Barker, who may be called a repentant evolutionist. [9] The judicious remarks of W.

---

[4] *Aristotle*, pp. 169-170.

[5] W. D. Ross, *Aristotle's Metaphysics: A Revised Text With Introduction and Commentary* (Oxford, 1958), 1: xxv.

[6] Ibid., p. xxxi.

[7] Third edition (Toronto: PIMS, 1978).

[8] D. J. Allen, *The Philosophy of Aristotle* (London: Hutchinson, 1952); Marjorie Grene, *A Portrait of Aristotle* (Chicago, 1963); G. E. R. Lloyd, *Aristotle The Growth and Structure of His Thought* (Cambridge, 1968).

[9] Stephen Barker, *Aristotle's Politics* (Oxford, 1946).

K. C. Guthrie in Volume 6 of his *A History of Greek Philosophy*[10] serve to introduce a needed sympathetic distance from the excesses of Jaeger and his more enthusiastic imitators.

But it should not be thought that doubts about the function of Book Delta within the *Metaphysics*, or indeed of its claim to a place among the other books, is a consequence of a genetic approach to Aristotle. The Everyman edition of the *Metaphysics* shifts Delta to the beginning of the work, thereby taking its cue, one might suppose, from the faintly dismissive title the Oxford translation gave the book: A Philosophical Lexicon – a vocabulary list, as it were, useful for finding one's way around the Aristotelian terrain.

If it is the case that in recent years, for whatever reason or reasons, Book Delta has been considered more or less out of place among the fourteen books of the *Metaphysics*, a notable exception to the trend is found in Giovanni Reale's *The Concept of First Philosophy and the Unity of the Metaphysics of Aristotle.*[11] Chapter 8 of his study is devoted entirely to Book Delta and Reale is quite aware that he is bucking a trend. But then Reale's general argument is that there is nothing to prevent a unitary reading of the *Metaphysics* as it has come down to us. For all that, his treatment of Delta comes at the end of his study, after his treatment of all the other books, and he concedes at the outset that Delta seems less amenable to the kind of reading he has been recommending.

> The majority of modern interpreters consider Book Delta as a treatment originally conceived as a work standing by iself, only later inserted into the *Metaphysics* and not by Aristotle. It seems to us – and we will shortly prove it – that we possess good reasons for reading it precisely in the place and position in which the tradition has transmitted it.[12]

There are thirty chapters in Book Delta which is devoted to the analysis of that many terms. Contrary to scholars like Bonitz who could find no criterion or criteria for inclusion in the list, and no order among the terms on it, Reale holds that criteria are indeed discernible. Not only is there a repeated technique observed in the laying out of many meanings of a term and a subsequent attempt to reduce the plurality of meanings to unity, there is a plan, Reale feels, in the selection of the terms for consideration.

[10] W. K. C. Guthrie, *A History of Greek Philosophy*, 6: *Aristotle, An Encounter* (Cambridge, 1981).

[11] Giovanni Reale, *The Conception of First Philosophy and the Unity of the Metaphysics of Aristotle*, translated by John R. Catan (Albany: State University of New York Press, 1980).

[12] Ibid., p. 338.

First of all, negatively, terms which fall to the practical or productive sciences are not included. Second, most positively, Reale maintains that the book limits itself to theoretical concepts which specifically pertain to the object of first philosophy or which are in some way related to that object. We would be surprised, he remarks, to find such a discussion in the *Physics*, for example. It seems inescapable then that the terms "have been selected with the purpose of clarifying the metaphysical inquiry and thus not by chance." [13]

Reale then locates the view of Carlini midway between "the excessively schematic distinctions of Saint Thomas" and the overly empirical one of Ross. [14] In developing his view that there is a logical connection among the discussions of Delta, he argues for its fitting placement where traditionally it has been placed and confronts some consequences of the genetic interpretation of Delta.

Reale's study of the *Metaphysics* is ample indication that the turning away from the host of problems raised by Jaeger need not be due to obscurantism or indifference to the historical vagaries involved in the transmission of texts. Without endorsing every aspect of Reale's argument, we can cite his book as counterevidence to the claim or suggestion that there is something amusingly naive in the way in which Hellenistic, Arabic, and Latin commentators, Thomas Aquinas among them, approached the works of Aristotle. There is thus no apriori scholarly impediment to taking Thomas' commentary as a guide in seeking to understand the *Metaphysics* of Aristotle.

For purposes of this article, we need not concern ourselves thematically with the second major issue mentioned at the outset, namely, the value of the commentaries for revealing Thomas' own thoughts on the matters under discussion in the book being commented on. Rather, I shall say some things about the way in which Thomas understands Book Delta. Reale summarized Thomas' view in the following way:

> Saint Thomas discovered an order even in the internal divisions of the material of Book Delta. For him, the book would be divided into three parts: the first part concerns the clarification of terms concerning the first cause (chapters 1-5); the second is dedicated to the terms indicating the object of first philosophy and the parts thereof (chapters 6-15); the third is concerned, finally, with terms indicating the various determinations of being (chapters 16-30). [15]

[13] Ibid., p. 340.
[14] Ibid., p. 341.
[15] Ibid., p. 340.

This is the interpretation that Reale regards as "excessively schematic" but he does not enlighten his reader as to the precise nature of the excess. His own understanding of the plan of the book[16] bears a strong family resemblance to that of Saint Thomas. But let us turn now to Thomas' commentary on Book Delta of the *Metaphysics*.

II

Whatever else can be said of Book Delta, it must be stressed that the terms it discusses are all instances of what Aristotle calls *pros hen* equivocals and Thomas calls – though he does not emphasize this in his commentary on Book Five – analogous terms. Thus it is that Thomas says that Aristotle, having determined what this science considers, now in Book Five begins his examination of those objects. "And because the things considered in this science are common to all things, and are not said univocally of them, but rather of some primarily and others secondarily, he first distinguishes the meanings of the words which fall to the consideration of this science." [17] The backward reference is to the preceding book and it is there Thomas makes clear that, in his usage, the adverb *analogice* and the adverbial phrase *secundum analogiam*, translate such Aristotelian phrases as *pollakos legetai*.[18] The Greek counterparts of *analogia* and *analogice* do not occur here in the Aristotelian text, despite the fact that the Latin words are loan words from the Greek. It seems to be the case that Aristotle nowhere uses *analogia* or *kat'analogian* in the way Thomas uses *analogice* and *secundum analogiam*, namely to speak of the relations among many meanings of the same term.[19] In any case, Thomas accepts Aristotle's argument that the way to get sufficient unity for a science of being as being is to see that "being" is an analogous term and that one sense of it takes priority over the others. The same will be true of other terms used in metaphysics and Book Five is devoted to spelling this out.

---

[16] Ibid., pp. 339-340.

[17] *In V Metaphysica*, lect. 1, n. 749: "Et quia ea quae in hac scientia considerantur, sunt omnibus communia, nec dicuntur univoce, sed secundum prius et posterius de diversis, ut in quarto libro est habitum, ideo prius distinguit intentiones nominum, quae in huius scientiae consideratione cadunt."

[18] "Quaecumque communiter unius recipiunt praedicationem, licet non univoce, sed analogice de his praedicetur, pertinent ad unius scientiae considerationem: sed ens hoc modo praedicatur de omnibus entibus: ergo omnia entia pertinent ad considerationem unius scientiae, quae considerat ens inquantum ens, scilicet tam substantias quam accidentia." (*In IV Metaphysica*, lect. 1, n. 534).

[19] *Pace* G. L. Muskens, *De vocis* ANALOGIAS *significatione ac usu apud Aristotelem* (Groningen, 1943).

Given this role of the book in the development of the science of being as being, we are prepared for the structure of the book. "Any science is concerned with a subject, properties and causes; that is why Book Five is divided into three parts. First, it clarifies the meanings of terms which signify causes; second, the meanings of terms which signify the subject of the science, or parts of that subject.... Third, of those which signify the properties of being as being." [20]

Perhaps it would be well to recall the way in which the Aristotelian conception of science guides discussions in books prior to Delta. The great protreptic opening of the *Metaphysics* moves gracefully into the conception of science, the role of causes, and anchors the notion of wisdom to it. "... all men suppose what is called Wisdom to deal with the first causes and the principles of things; so that, as has been said before, the man of experience is thought to be wiser than the possessors of any sense-experience whatever, the artist wiser than the man of experience, the master-worker than the mechanic, and the theoretical kinds of knowledge to be more of the nature of Wisdom than the productive. Clearly then Wisdom is knowledge about certain principles and causes" (981b28-982a1). The first three aporiae in Book Beta are unintelligible without reference to Aristotelian scientific methodology: whether the investigation of the causes belongs to one or to more sciences; whether such a science should survey only the first principles of substance, whether one science deals with all substances. Consider the following passages.

> If there is a demonstrative science which deals with them, there will have to be an underlying kind, and some of them must be demonstrable attributes and others must be axioms (for it is impossible that there should be demonstration of all of them); for the demonstrations must start from certain premisses and be about a certain subject and prove certain attributes. (B.2 997a5-10)
>
> For every demonstrative science investigates with regard to some subject its essential attributes, starting from the common beliefs. (997a20)

Passages like these could be multiplied. In Book Beta, the demands of Aristotle's concept of science generate difficulties for the proposed inquiry, and it is quite clear that unless these difficulties can be resolved,

---

[20] *In V Metaphysica*, lect. 1, n. 749: "Cuiuslibet autem scientiae est considerare subjectum, et passiones, et causas; et ideo hic quintus liber dividitur in tres partes. Primo determinat distinctiones nominum quae significant causas; secundo, illorum nominum quae significant subjectum huius scientiae vel partes eius, ibi, 'Unum dicitur aliud secundum accidens.' Tertio nominum quae significant passiones entis inquantum est ens, ibi 'Perfectum vero dicitur' ...."

the great project laid out at the outset of Alpha, as well as the Platonic version of that aspiration toward Wisdom, will be incoherent. That Aristotle holds that they can be resolved is clear from the crisp opening of Gamma: "There is a science which investigates being as being and the attributes which belong to it in virtue of its own nature." How can this be if the *genus subjectum* is also a predicable genus, univocally common to the more specific expressions of that subject matter? The theory of words said in many ways is, again, the answer to that difficulty. Being is not a genus, but the principal meaning of "being," *ousia* provides the subject matter of the science we are seeking.

An attentive reader of the preceding books will look to Delta to continue this appeal to the structure of Aristotelian science. St. Thomas finds that that is precisely what Aristotle does in Delta. Some words of multiple meaning discussed in the book bear on causes, others on the subject, yet others on attributes of the subject of the science. Let us have before us the outline Thomas makes of Delta:

Words of Interest to Metaphysics having several meanings

I.   Those which signify causes
    a. generally
              "principle" (lesson 1)
              "cause" (lessons 2-3)
              "element" (lesson 4)
    b. specially
              "nature" (lesson 5)
    c. modally
              "necessity" (lesson 6)
II. Those which signify the subject of the science
    a. as such
      i.   "one" and "many" (lessons 7 & 8)
      ii. "being" (lesson 9)
      iii. "substance" (lesson 10)
    b. parts of the subject
      i.   and first of "one"
          aa. first parts of "one" and "many"
              "same"
              "diverse"
              "different"
              "similar and dissimilar" (lesson 11)
          bb. secondary parts of plurality
              "opposites"
              "contraries"

                        "diverse in kind" (lesson 12)
            cc. "prior and posterior" (lesson 13)
        ii. of "being"
            aa. as divided by act and potency
                "potency" (lesson 14)
                "impotency"
                a metaphorical sense of "potency"
            bb. as divided into categories
                "quantity" (lesson 15)
                "quality" (lesson 16)
                "relation" (lesson 17)
III. Words signifying properties of the subject
    a. those signifying perfection of being
        i. pertaining to perfection itself
                "perfect" (lesson 18)
            aa. signifying modes of the perfect
                "term" (lesson 19)
                "per se"
                "dispositive" (lesson 20)
                "habitus"
        ii. those pertaining to totality
                "part"
                "whole" (lesson 21)
                "genus"
    b. those signifying imperfection
                "false"
                "accident" (lesson 22)

This is the schema that can be gleaned from the taxonomic remarks
Thomas makes at the beginning of the various lessons of the commentary
and which is laid out for the reader in the Marietti edition of Cathala
(1925). Reale found this structure excessively schematic despite the
kinship, already noted, between his views and those of Thomas. One
might say that Reale endorses the general schema while finding some
difficulties with it, and that seems a reasonable reaction.

At the very outset it is clear that Thomas sees far more than the general
order of the schema just given. For example, he suggests the reason why
"principle" is discussed before "cause" and "cause" before "element."
"Procedit autem hoc ordine, quia hoc nomen Principium communius est
quam causa: aliquid enim est principium quod non est causa; sicut
principium motus dicitur terminus a quo. Et iterum causa est in plus
quam elementum."[21] This leads the reader to want to test the details of the

---

[21] Ibid., n. 750.

ordering and to wish that Thomas had given a reason, as he does not, for the treatment of "one" preceding that of "being." What we are given at the outset of Thomas' discussion of the second main part of Delta, is this:

> Postquam Philosophus distinxit nomina quae significant causas, hic distinguit nomina quae significant id quod est subjectum aliquo modo in ista scientia. Et dividitur in duas partes. Primo ponit sive distinguit nomina quae significant subjectum huius scientiae. Secundo ea quae significant partes subjecti. .... Subjectum autem hujus scientiae considerandum, cujusmodi est ens et unum: vel sicut id de quo est principalius intentio, ut substantia. Et ideo primo distinguit hoc nomen unum ... secundo hoc nomen ens ... tertio hoc nomen substantiae...."[22]

We are given the reason for regarding "being" and "one" and "substance" as standing for the subject rather than for a part of the subject of metaphysics, but none for the priority of the treatment of "one." Elsewhere[23] Thomas says things which suggest that any discussion of the meaning of "one" is going to presuppose the meaning of "being." "Unum enim addit indivisionem supra ens. Dicitur enim unum ens indivisibile vel indivisum." Indeed, this point is made at the outset of the book of the *Metaphysics* devoted to the discussion of unity.[24]

When Thomas goes on to the second part of the second part, that is, to the words which signify parts of the subject of metaphysics, he subdivides it into two: the words which signify parts of one and those which signify parts of being. Why is there no third division, words signifying parts of substance? "Substantia enim quae etiam posita est subjectum huius scientiae, est unum solum praedicamentum non divisum in multa praedicamenta."[25] This reason might seem to militate against "substance" being listed along with "one" and "being" as signifying the subject of the science. Thomas has said that "substance" is not as common as "being" and "one" but it is what the science chiefly aims to discuss. In order to understand that, we must understand the way Thomas explains the opening of Gamma.

"There is a science which considers being as being and that which belongs to it *per se*."[26] None of the particular sciences considers being as being as its subject. How can something so general provide sufficient focus for a science? The whole point of the introduction of the discussion of analogous names at that point is to show that the primary analogate of

---

[22] Ibid., lect. 7, n. 842.
[23] Cf. *In X Metaphysica*, lect. 3, n. 1974.
[24] Ibid., lect. 1, n. 1920.
[25] *In V Metaphysica*, lect. 11, n. 906.
[26] *Metaphysics*, 4.1, 1003a17.

such a word gives us the focus we need for a science. But substance is the primary analogate of "being." Ergo, etc. Here is Thomas' statement of the argument.

> Hic ponit quod haec scientia principaliter considerat de substantiis, etsi de omnibus entibus consideret, tali ratione. Omnis scientia quae est de pluribus quae dicuntur ad unum primum, est proprie et principaliter illius primi, ex quo alia dependent secundum esse, et propter quod dicuntur secundum nomen; et hoc ubique est verum. Sed substantia est hoc primum inter omnia entia. Ergo philosophus qui considerat omnia entia, primo et principaliter debet habere in sua consideratione principia et causas substantiarum; ergo per consequens ejus consideratio primo et principaliter de substantiis est.[27]

Thus, in Delta, words which signify parts of the subject of the science as designated by "being" are based on the division of being by act and potency and by the categories, but substance is not listed among the latter. Indeed, the terms which are listed are "quantity," "quality" and "relation." Why don't the names of the other categories occur here? "Alia vero praedicamenta praetermittit, quia sunt determinata ad aliquod genus rerum naturalium; ut patet praecipue de agere et pati, et de ubi et quando."[28] If we think Thomas has forgotten the last remark when "passio" comes up in the discussion of "habitus," he makes it clear that he has not.[29]

These few soundings indicate why one tends to agree with Reale to the degree that his position is that, while in the main the schema Thomas finds in Delta expresses what is in the book, there are occasional puzzles that Thomas does not dispel. A further example of the latter would be the bewildering way in which "accident" keeps showing up in Delta. In discussing "one," Thomas distinguishes what is one per se and one per accidens.[30] The same distinction is made when the modes of "being" are discussed. In Lesson 22, we find "accidens" coming up for discussion again. Given Thomas' search for order in the book, we are likely to think he should have said something about that.

It is important to stress that such expectations are aroused by Thomas' illuminating remarks about the detailed interrelations of the parts of Delta. The fact that he does not explicitly spell everything out does not, of course, mean that he would be unable to reply to such requests. However

---

[27] *In IV Metaphysica*, lect. 1, n. 546.
[28] *In V Metaphysica*, lect. 15, n. 977.
[29] Ibid., lect. 20, n. 1069.
[30] Ibid., lect. 7, nn. 843-847.

that may be, Thomas commentary enables us to see the link of Delta with Gamma.

Gamma has brought to the fore, and not for the first time, the role that Aristotle's conception of science, developed in the *Posterior Analytics*, plays in his efforts to find a science beyond physics and mathematics. It is as if the formal conception of science is already had and one is asking how it is instantiated in the case of a putative science of being. Aristotle's recognition that "being" is not common to the things that are, or to the kinds of thing there are, as a univocal term is common to its subjects, enabled him to find sufficient focus for a science of being. Such common terms as "being" and "one" range over kinds, again not univocally but, as Thomas will put it, analogically. This means that one meaning of such terms takes precedence over the others. The privileged position of the discussion of substance in metaphysics is thereby established.

Now, in Delta, as Thomas reads it, we are confronted with something a good deal more organized than a random list of words. This is not a philosophical lexicon, *sans phrase*. The words under discussion are chosen because of their significance for the science we are seeking. If "being" and "one" are analogous, it will be necessary to distinguish their several meanings and to look for an order among them. The same turns out to be true of words signifying parts of the subject, properties of the subject and causes of the subject. No one can fail to see that Delta is a collection of words "said in many ways," of analogous terms. Gamma has prepared us to expect such a discussion of analogous terms and has given us an inkling of the criteria for inclusion in or exclusion from a list which would be useful to a metaphysician. There are all kinds of analogous terms which are of little interest to the metaphysician.

III

The student of Thomas' commentary on Aristotle's *Metaphysics* cannot fail to be impressed by its relentless search for, and discovery of, the order of the twelve books which made up Thomas' version. This is something which must be judged as such, by comparing the text and Thomas' remarks upon it, not by appeals to "the nature of commentaries" or allegedly established characteristics of them. Many students of Thomas are in the grips of the idea that he somehow, genially, read into texts his own agenda, making them say things they do not mean, for purposes of his own. It may be that some version of that claim can be established in the case of one or another Thomistic commentary. That would enable us to conclude nothing about the commentary on the *Metaphysics*.

Thomas' reader will, at the very least, dismiss as unserious the view that Delta is simply a list of words, a lexicon which functions as an introduction to Aristotelian vocabulary. The pattern that Thomas sees among the words discussed, appealing to the Aristotelian concept of science, of subject, cause and attribute, is securely grounded in the text itself, thus linking it to the preceding books in terms of something formal and fundamental to what is going on. It would be a task of Quixotic dimensions to argue that Thomas is *reading into* the text what is not there. Clearly what he is doing is *reading out* of the text what is plainly before the reader.

One who agrees that Delta, in its main lines, is structured as Thomas sees it, can nonetheless, as the foregoing indicated, question some of the more detailed claims for order. He may also notice difficulties for the claim to order that Thomas does not deal with. But the appeal to the structure of Aristotelian science in reading Delta, far from being the importation of thirteenth-century predilections into a mid fourth-century BC text, is indeed the key to the book.

17

The Background of Aquinas' Synderesis Principle

Vernon J. Bourke

St. Louis University

What is under consideration here is the first practical principle enunciated by St. Thomas in his much discussed article on the precepts of natural law.[1] In this version it is formulated as: *"Hoc est ergo primum praeceptum legis, quod bonum est faciendum et prosequendum, et malum vitandum."* This formula, "that what is good is to be done and sought after and what is evil is to be avoided," is by no means the only way in which Thomas expressed the principle, as we shall see. Although some interpreters appear to think that it is original with St. Thomas, scholars have known for a long time that various versions of this principle are found in many patristic and medieval writers.[2] The present study will try to show that the principle goes back to many similar formulae in the Old and New Testaments. Moreover this biblical background may cast some light on the character of this principle and on its relevance to present-day ethics.

I. Various Formulae of the Principle in Aquinas

It is necessary, first of all, to consider some of the passages where St. Thomas dealt with this principle in works other than the familiar text of

---

[1] *Summa theologiae*, 1-2, q. 94, art. 2, c. Some of the historical research for the present study was utilized in an article published as: "El principio de la sinteresis; fuentes y función en la etica de Tomas de Aquino," *Sapientia*, 35 (1980), 615-626. This study has a quite different emphasis.

[2] Much of the immediate background (12th and early 13th century) has been well covered by Dom Odon Lottin in "Syndérèse et conscience aux xiie et xiiie siècles," in *Psychologie et Morale* (Gembloux: Duculot, 1949), 2: 103-235.

Graceful Reason: Essays in Ancient and Medieval Philosophy Presented to Joseph Owens, CSSR, ed. Lloyd P. Gerson. Papers in Mediaeval Studies 4 (Toronto: Pontifical Institute of Mediaeval Studies, 1983), pp. 345-360. © P.I.M.S., 1983.

Summa theologiae 1-2, 94.2. This textual survey will indicate how the principle appears in different formulations and grammatical expressions, how it is related to the habitus called synderesis (which is not even mentioned in the legal treatment of 1-2, 94.2), how it is involved with cognition and appetition, and how it is associated with the virtue of justice. It has often been said that St. Thomas is his own best interpreter and certainly in the case of this principle that observation is well founded. A person who reads only 1-2, 94.2 is ill equipped to understand what Aquinas thought of the starting-point for practical reasoning.

At several points in his commentary on the second book of Peter Lombard's *Sentences* St. Thomas related the habitus of synderesis to the knowing of natural law principles and particularly to the first principle. Thus, in answer to an objection which said, "but the act of synderesis is to recoil from evil (*remurmurare malo*) and such an act is good," he explained that, "the universal principles of what is naturally right (*juris naturalis*) come under synderesis, whence arises the necessity of recoiling from everything that is done against the naturally right (*contra jus naturale*)." [3] This occurs in a discussion of how demons act from bad will, and so only the rejection of evil-doing is mentioned. But in many of the versions of the synderesis principle in both St. Thomas and his predecessors the injunction against doing evil is stated before the requirement to do good. The same emphasis on the negative injunction is found in a passage where Aquinas is commenting on Distinction 24 of Book 2:

> It is requisite that practical reasoning proceed (*deducatur*) from certain self-evident principles, such as, that what is evil is not to be done, that the precepts of God are to be obeyed, and so on: and the habitus for these is synderesis.[4]

From the beginning of his teaching career Aquinas connected the first principle of practical reasoning with the habitus of synderesis, whose function is to intuit certain self-evident principles of behavior.

A few years later, toward the end of the 1250s, Aquinas devoted Question 16 of his disputations *On Truth* to a thorough explanation of

---

[3] *In 2 Sent.* 7.1.2, ad 3 (Parma ed., 6: 447): "In synderesi autem sunt universalia principia juris naturalis, unde oportet quod remurmuret omni ei quod contra jus naturale fit." Obj. 3 had said: "sed actus synderesis est remurmurare malo, hoc autem bonum est."

[4] *In 2 Sent.* 24.2.3 c: "Oportet quod ratio practica ab aliquibus principiis per se notis deducatur, ut quod est malum non esse faciendum, praeceptis Dei obediendum fore, et sic de aliis: et horum quidem habitus est synderesis." (Note that *deducatur* in this and similar texts does not have the logical meaning that "deduced" has in English.)

synderesis and its working. Here we find him using the standard synderesis principle formula found in his immediate predecessors in theology:
"the task of synderesis is to recoil from evil and incline toward good." [5]
Whether the prohibition of evil action precedes the injunction to do good
is discussed by Thomas in *On Truth*, Question 18. Here the main problem
is whether the remission of fault (*culpae remissio*) precedes the infusion of
grace, and one objection asserted that turning away from evil is naturally
prior to doing good. To this Aquinas replied that this priority applies in
the order of actions (*operationes*) but does not mean that the habitus of
avoiding evil is infused prior to that of inclining to do good.[6] In this case
we have a formula that speaks of the "avoidance" of evil (*vitatio operis
mali*) and the "performance" of a good deed (*operatio operis boni*). Oddly,
an argument *Sed contra* in *On Truth*, Question 24, states that there are
two opposed "powers" (*potentiae*) in man: one is synderesis which always
tends toward the good; and a second is sensuality which always inclines
toward evil. According to this argument man requires a third power, free
choice (*liberum arbitrium*), whereby he may tend either way.[7] Thomas
offers no formal rejection to this argument, except to conclude the body of
his article by saying that *liberum arbitrium* is indeed one power. Clearly
he knew at this early period that some people thought that the main work
of synderesis is to incline one toward good deeds.

In the *Questions on Evil* (some eight years later) Thomas included an
objection which stated that synderesis is never lost in a person (*numquam
extinguitur*), for it always recoils from evil. Here his reply is that the
universal principles of natural right pertain to synderesis and no one is
mistaken about such principles – but the process of practical reasoning
from such principles can be mistaken because of the influence of passions
or sinful habits.[8] So, in the period 1266-1267, Thomas alternated between
giving priority to the negative or the positive injunction in the synderesis
principle.

At about this same time Aquinas was beginning his *Summa theologiae*.
In its first part we find another explanation of synderesis. Here its action is
described in the traditional formula: "to prompt one toward the good and
to recoil from evil" (*instigare ad bonum et murmurare de malo*).[9] It will be

---

[5] *De veritate*, 16.2, c: "et hoc est synderesis, cujus officium est remurmurare malo et
inclinare ad bonum." Cf. q. 16.1, ad 12: "Actus autem hujus habitus naturalis, quam synderesis nominat, est remurmurare malo et inclinare ad bonum."

[6] *De verit.* 28.7, obj. 6 and ad 6 and ad primum.

[7] *De verit.* 24.5, sed contra et c.

[8] *De malo*, 3.12, obj. 13 and ad 13.

[9] ST 1.79.12, c.

noted that the good is mentioned first and that infinitives are used, not necessarily implying moral necessity or obligation but simply stating the function of synderesis.

Of course the key text on the synderesis principle is the well known passage in the treatise *De legibus* in the *Summa theologiae*.[10] Here the formula for the first principle of natural law (*lex naturale*) is stated in terms that imply some sort of obligation: "*Hoc est ergo primum prae-ceptum legis, quod bonum est faciendum et prosequendum, et malum vitandum.*" These gerundives now express what is called a command (*praeceptum*) that one ought to do and promote what is good concretely, and conversely one ought to avoid what is evil. The stress on oughtness, here, may be explained by the legal context, of course. Earlier in the *Summa theologiae* (actually starting with Part 1, Question 75) Thomas had provided detailed studies of the human soul and its functions, the character of moral good and evil, the role of man's various powers, the *habitus* of virtue and vice – all considered as interior sources (*principia*) of moral activity. When he came to 1-2, question 90 (beginning the treatise on laws), he offered a brief but important prologue to explain that he is now turning to the two great *exterior* influences (*principia*) on human acts. These are, he says, law (*lex*) and grace (*gratia*): "God is the external principle that moves toward the good (*movens ad bonum*) and God instructs us through law and assists us through grace." [11] In this context Thomas is giving the positive precept the first place.

When we look at Question 100 in the *Prima Secundae* we find one explanation of why St. Thomas and most of his predecessors gave priority to the avoidance of evil. Discussing the order in which the precepts of the Decalogue occur, he says that in the carrying out of an operation (*in executione operis*) vices must first be eradicated before virtues are cultivated – and this is why the thirty-third Psalm says, "Turn away from evil and do good," and the first chapter of Isaiah reads, "Cease to do evil, learn to do good." However, Thomas adds, in the order of knowing (*in cognitione*) virtue precedes wrongdoing.[12] So, he argues, there is good

---

[10] st 1-2.94.2, c. For an exposition of the meaning of this text see Germain G. Grisez, "The First Principle of Practical Reason: A Commentary on *S.T.* 1-2, 94, 2," *Natural Law Forum*, 10 (1965), 168-201. Eric D'Arcy, *Conscience and Its Right to Freedom* (New York: Sheed & Ward, 1961) offers a quick survey of Lottin's historical studies on syn-deresis, and in Chap. 3 has some excellent remarks on the synderesis principle as a purely formal rule. Much the same approach is taken in Guido Fasso, *Storia della filosofia del diritto*, vol. 1: *Antichità e medioevo* (Bologna: il Mulino, 1966), pp. 260ff.

[11] st 1-2.90, prologo.

[12] st 1-2.100.6, ad 2: "Etsi enim in executione operis prius extirpanda sint vitia quam

reason for putting the positive precepts (which indicate various good things to be done) before the negative commands in the Decalogue. Of significance here is the influence of the biblical use of imperatives in these versions of the synderesis principle. Also, St. Thomas is now stressing the cognitive character of the synderesis principle, in contrast to the affective role assigned to it by many of his immediate predecessors. We shall see later that Aquinas commented, in the last years of his life, on several of these Old Testament formulations of the synderesis principle.

Since law is concerned with what is just, one might expect to find some version of the first principle of natural law in St. Thomas' treatise on Justice, later in the *Summa theologiae*. There, in treating the integral parts (component factors) of justice, he does teach that to turn away from evil and do good are the distinctive features of the just person. Here too, the influence of the Psalms is evident. An objection cites Psalm 33.15 (*diverte a malo et fac bonum*) and Peter Lombard's comment to the effect that simply *not* to do evil is without merit, for only doing good is meritorious.[13] Thomas' answer is that to turn away from evildoing, considered as a constituent of justice (*pars justitiae*) does not mean a pure absence of activity but rather a movement of will repudiating the evil, as the Latin word *declinatio* indicates.[14] This action of turning down some evil action is indeed meritorious, Aquinas concludes. Among other things significant in this treatment under justice are two points. First, the synderesis principle (whatever its formula) is a two-part rule: to do good is not identical with the avoidance of evil. So any thorough analysis of the meaning of the synderesis principle should investigate both the negative and the positive injunctions. Second, the precepts to do good and avoid evil apply to human activity under all types of virtue, because in its broad sense justice (and natural law) applies not only to one's relations to others but also to one's self-perfection.[15] Since law is an expression of justice, this suggests that the synderesis principle is not merely the first rule of

---

inserendae virtutes, secundum illud Psalmi xxxiii, 13: 'Declina a malo, et fac bonum'; et Isaiae i, 16: 'Quiescite agere perverse, discite benefacere'; tamen in cognitione prior est virtus quam peccatum."

[13] sᴛ 2-2.79.1, obj. 2.

[14] Ibid., ad 2: "declinare a malo, secundum quod ponitur pars iustitiae, non importat negationem puram, quod est non facere malum.... Importat autem motum voluntatis repudiantis malum, ut ipsum nomen declinationis ostendit. Et hoc est meritorium, praecipue quando aliquis impugnatur ut malum faciat, et resistit."

[15] Ibid., c: "Dicendum quod si loquamur de bono et malo in communi, facere bonum et vitare malum pertinet ad omnem virtutem.... Sed iustitia secundum quod est specialis virtus, respicit bonum sub ratione debiti ad proximum."

altruistic actions but is the starting-point for all virtuous considerations, feelings and interior actions.

At the end of his life St. Thomas commented orally on the first fifty-four Psalms.[16] References to the synderesis principle occur in three Psalms. The thirty-third we have seen cited in the treatise on justice (as we noted at footnote 13). Now, in the year 1273, Thomas gives the synderesis principle in a slightly different reading of the Psalm: "*diverte a malo, et fac bonum.*"[17] (As we saw above, at note 12, his reading was, "*declina a malo.*") As usual in the Old Testament formulations, the synderesis principle is in the imperative form. Aquinas' explanation mentions the two integral parts of justice but is mainly concerned with whether what is commanded by the negative injunction is meritorious. Here, in commenting on the Psalm, he suggests that the verb *divertere* may mean a pure negation of action – and in that case the failure to do anything is not meritorious.[18]

In the text used by St. Thomas, Psalm 36.19 had the formula, "declina a malo, et fac bonum." His comments on it are important to our study, as may be seen in my literal translation:

> And so he [the Psalmist] says, "Turn away from evil and do good." Now these two parts of justice correspond to the precepts of law, for justice is ruled by law. In the law there are certain affirmative precepts that are fulfilled by doing what is good; and there are some that are negative, fulfilled by turning away from evil. Moreover, by these two [kinds of precepts] the natural inclination of appetite is brought to perfection, for it has two objects: good and evil, since appetite naturally tends toward the good and flees from false evil.[19]

Besides again relating this imperative form of the synderesis principle to justice and law, this text brings out the connection of the affirmative and negative injunctions to the two objects of appetite in man. While the legal

---

[16] J. A. Weisheipl, *Friar Thomas d'Aquino* (Garden City, NY: Doubleday, 1974), pp. 368-369, dates this commentary on the Psalms in late 1273.

[17] *In Psalmos Davidis Expositio*, 33.13 (Parma ed., 14: 267).

[18] Ibid. "Divertere a malo non est quid meritorium, si divertere dicat solum negationem...."

[19] *In Ps.*, 36.19 (Parma ed., 14: 287): "Et ideo dicit, *Declina a malo, et fac bonum*. Hae autem duae partes justitiae correspondent praeceptis legis: justitia enim regulatur lege. In lege sunt quaedam paecepta affirmativa, quae implentur faciendo bonum; et quaedam sunt negativa, quae implentur declinando a malo. Item per haec duo perficitur naturalis inclinatio appetitus, cujus sunt duo objecta: scilicet bonum et malum, quia appetitus naturaliter tendet in bonum, et refugit malum falsum." (In modern versions this and other numberings of the Psalms will vary: the present text in the *Jerusalem Bible* [Garden City, NY, 1968], p. 707, is at Psalm 37.27, "Never yield to evil, practice good.")

text in 1-2, 94.2 speaks as if man's natural inclinations were only toward "goods," this passage in the *Commentary on the Psalms* makes it clear that man is naturally inclined to flee from what he sees as evil.[20] In this same portion of the comment on Psalm 36, Thomas mentions several other places in the Old Testament where we are told to reject evil and practice what is good. One is to Psalm 44.5, where Thomas' text has, "*Dilexisti justitiam, et odisti iniquitatem.*" This is a formula in which universal terms (justice and iniquity) are used rather than the concrete *bonum* and *malum*. However, Aquinas' comment on this verse returns to the concrete words, saying that this instruction means that man should abandon (*deserat*) the evil and adhere (*adhaereat*) to the good.[21]

II. Origins of These Formulae of the Synderesis Principle

From this survey of various formulations of the synderesis principle in Aquinas' writings it becomes evident that the compound rule in regard to good and evil is sometimes expressed by nouns (performance and avoidance), sometimes by infinitives (to recoil from/to incline toward), sometimes by gerundives implying oughtness (in discussions of law and justice), and frequently in quotations from the Bible by blunt imperatives. The Book of Psalms had an important influence on the way that Thomas (and many of his predecessors) expressed the first principle of practical reasoning. Besides Aquinas' use of the imperative formulae from three passages in the Psalms, there are two texts from Isaiah that he cited in commenting on Psalm 36. The first (Isaiah 1.17) uses imperatives: "Cease to do evil, learn to do good" (*quiescite agere perverse, discite benefacere,* in Thomas' Latin).[22] He also mentions a second text (Isaiah 7.15): "On curds and honey will he feed until he knows how to refuse evil and choose good." Here Thomas has the infinitives *reprobare* and *eligere.*[23]

---

[20] In ST 1-2.94.2, c, after enunciating the synderesis principle Thomas says: "omnia illa ad quae homo habet naturalem inclinationem, ratio naturaliter apprehendit ut bona, et per consequens ut opere persequenda, et contraria eorum ut mala et vitanda." (This establishes a direct relation between the rightness of natural appetition and natural cognition in the practical order.)

[21] *In Ps.*, 44.5 (Parma ed., 14: 322). Thomas says in part: "Sed haec directio consistit ut homo deserat malum et adhaereat bono.... *Dilexisti justitiam.* Item debet odire iniquitatem, quia si non diligat justitiam, non ducit ad bonum."

[22] Besides mentioning Isaiah 1.17 in his remarks on Psalm 34, Thomas comments on it in his *Postilla super Isaiam* (Parma ed., 14: 435b) but his explanation adds nothing to what we have seen previously.

[23] In Thomas' discussion *In Isa.*, 7.15 (Parma ed., 14: 461b) his text reads: "Butyrum et mel comedet, ut sciat reprobare malum, et eligere bonum." The commentary gets involved in the grammatical problem of the usage of "*ut.*"

The New Testament has two passages in which a version of the synderesis principle occurs. One is at 1 Peter 3.11, where it is said that
"anyone who wants to have a happy life ... must never yield to evil but
must practice good." [24] I have not found a reference to this text in St.
Thomas. However, Romans 12.9-10, "Hate what is evil, hold to what is
good," is treated in Aquinas' *Commentary on St. Paul*. His text reads,
"*Odientes malum, adhaerentes bono.*" [25] Relating this injunction ("Be ye
detesters of evil and adherents of the good") to the preceding discussion by
St. Paul of "love without pretense," St. Thomas says that Paul teaches that
love (*dilectio*) ought to be pure (*debet esse pura*) and that it ought to be for
the sake of the virtuous good.[26] He leaves no doubt that he takes the
Pauline text to imply obligation.

It would seem, then, that the New Testament is not as rich a source of
synderesis principle formulations as the Psalms and Isaiah. Still it is clear
that the Bible must have had some considerable influence on the
formulation of the synderesis principle, since (as we shall see) it does not
seem to occur in the ethical writings of thinkers unfamiliar with the
Judaeo-Christian Scriptures.

Classical Greek and Roman ethics, to my knowledge, does not contain
anything like the principle, "Do good and avoid evil." Of course it is
impossible to establish a historical negative of this sort – but in several
years of research for my *History of Ethics*, nothing really like the synderesis principle was found. One might expect some version of the
principle in Aristotle's treatment of the concretely just thing (*to dikaion*) in
the fifth book of the *Nicomachean Ethics*. But there is no mention of it
there. Thomas does (1-2, 94.2, c.) preface his statement of the synderesis
principle by quoting the Aristotelian dictum that "good is what all desire,"
but that is so broad a meaning that it would cover even morally evil
objects of perverted desire.[27] While there is no doubt that the general
tendency of all things toward what is good for them is the germ of the

---

[24] The English of 1 Peter 3.11 is from the *Jerusalem Bible*, p. 302 of the New
Testament.

[25] *Expositio in omnes S. Pauli Epistolas*, cap. 12, lect. 2 (Parma ed., 13: 124).

[26] Ibid. (p. 124, col. A): "docet quod dilectio debet esse pura, cum dicit, *Odientes
malum*. ... tertio docet quod dilectio debet esse honesta, cum dicit, *Adhaerens bono*: ut
scilicet aliquis adhaereat alteri propter bonum virtutis."

[27] Aristotle's *Nicomachean Ethics* (in the version used by Thomas) said right at the start
(1.1, 1094a3) that "they" (Thomas takes this to mean the *Philosophi*) state that "*bonum* [*est*]
quod omnia appetunt." The dictum occurs in several places in Aristotle: *Topics*, 116a19-
20; *Rhetoric*, 1362a23; and *Eth. Nic.*, 1172b10-15. R. A. Gauthier, *L'Éthique à
Nicomaque* (Louvain-Paris: Nauwelaerts, 1970), 2: 4, attributes the dictum to Eudoxus.

synderesis principle, yet this broad description of "good" is not the same as any formula of the synderesis principle.

On the other hand, from the time of St. Augustine onward, Christian thinkers in every century discuss the several texts from the Old and New Testaments that enjoin the avoidance of moral evil and the performance of good deeds. The rule, "Avoid evil and do good," is not usually associated with synderesis in the patristic period, even though the term *synderesis* is known in Latin from St. Jerome onward.[28]

St. Augustine is the first major Christian thinker to discuss the formula, "Declina a malo et fac bonum," from the Psalms.[29] At no point does he suggest that this principle of action is intuited. For Augustine it is a well-known text from Scripture. He does not use the term synderesis. In the next (sixth) century Cassiodorus offers similar comments on Psalm 33.15. His remarks are incorporated in the later standard *Glosses* on the Bible.[30] After a little more than a century Alcuin provides a text that is much used in the following centuries:

> Prudence is the knowledge of things divine and human, insofar as it is given to man; whereby one should understand what man ought to be on his guard against, and what he ought to do; and this is what is read in the Psalm, "turn away from evil and do good."[31]

Noteworthy is Alcuin's use of the gerundives (*quid cavendum sit homini, vel quid faciendum*) to explain the obligation expressed in the biblical imperatives.

Probably the first known formulation of the synderesis principle in English may be dependent on Alcuin's much read work. A tenth-century sermon by an unknown preacher in early English quotes "some Psalm" that says, "Gecyr fram yfele & [and] dó gód" (refrain from evil and do good).[32] In these centuries immediately preceding the thirteenth

---

[28] See my *History of Ethics* (New York: Doubleday, 1968), p. 91.

[29] For a fuller treatment of Augustine's usage, see my *Joy in Augustine's Ethics* (Villanova: Villanova University Press, 1979), Appendix v: "Augustine and the Origins of the Synderesis Rule." In Augustine consult: *Enarrationes in Psalmos*, xxxiii, n. 19: "Sed quid est, *Declina a malo*? ... Non solum *declina a malo* sed et *fac bonum*." Also see *De civitate Dei*, 19.4.4.

[30] Cassiodori, *In Psalterium Expositio*, super Ps 33.15 (PL 70: 237).

[31] Alcuini, *De virtutibus et vitiis*, cap. 35 (PL 101: 637). In the Ciceronic *De inventione rhetorica*, 2.160, *prudentia* was defined as "rerum bonarum et malarum neutrarumque scientia."

[32] The Old English text is edited in full in P. E. Szarmach, "Vercelli Homily xx," *Mediaeval Studies*, 35 (1973), 1-26; for the synderesis principle formula, see p. 15, lines 25-26.

occurrences of the synderesis principle become quite frequent. An eleventh-century *Book of Proverbs* compiled by the German Othlo of St. Emeran indicates that even the common people were acquainted with the injunction from the Latin Bible: "Declina a malo et fac bonum."[33] From the twelfth century on, the development of canon law and theological syntheses provided writings in the *Summa* form which discussed versions of the synderesis principle in greater detail. An example from ecclesiastical law is provided by Uguccione da Pisa who spoke of "natural reason, that power of the soul whereby man distinguishes good from evil, by choosing the good and spurning evil."[34] While this formulation stressed the natural knowing of the principle, Peter Lombard's comment on Psalm 33.15 relates it directly to the biblical source. Peter says that the Psalmist's injunction implies the avoidance of fault (*culpa*) plus the meriting of eternal life and reward (*vitam et palmam*) by actually doing what is good.[35] From this point on theologians (including St. Thomas) debate this question of merit for the avoidance of evil (frequently at great length).

A curious development in early thirteenth-century treatises is the use of a negative version of the golden rule to illustrate the first principles of practical reasoning. Thus John of La Rochelle says: "Just as in the case of speculative matters there are certain ones that are self-evident (*per se nota*) ... so also in practical matters there are self-evident principles of action, such as: what you do not wish done unto you, don't do to others.[36] Another Franciscan contemporary of St. Thomas, Matthew of Aquasparta says almost the same thing in his *Disputed Questions*.[37] The golden rule (in any of its versions) is, of course, not equivalent to the synderesis principle, for this widely accepted golden principle is applicable only to altruistic actions, while the synderesis principle covers both good and evil for self as well as for others.

---

[33] Othloni, *Libellus Proverbiorum*, ed. W. C. Korfmacher (Chicago: Loyola University Press, 1936), p. 16, n. 12.

[34] "Ratio scilicet naturalis, vis animi ex quo homo discernit bonum et malum, eligendo bonum et detestando malum." This text from Uguccione's *Summa super decretum* (post AD 1188) is quoted from Guido Fasso, *La legge della ragione* (Bologna: il Mulino, 1964), p. 56, citing Biblioteca Palatina di Parma, MS 1222, fol. 1r.

[35] Petri Lombardi, *Glossa*, Ps 33.15 (PL 191: 343).

[36] Johannis de Rupella, *Summa de vitiis*, in the portion of the Bruges and Troyes MSS edited by O. Lottin in *Psychologie et Morale*, 2: 170.

[37] For the Matthew of Aquasparta text in his *Quaestiones Disputatae* (based on the Assisi MS) see: A.-H. Chroust, "The Philosophy of Law of St. Thomas Aquinas: His Fundamental Ideas and Some of His Historical Precursors," *American Journal of Jurisprudence*, 19 (1974), 19.

Interesting, too, is the fact that Thomas' teacher, St. Albert, held that there is no single practical principle that is the first rule of synderesis.[38] His reason for this lies in Albert's contention that there are many first principles of speculative and practical reasoning.

From this survey of the centuries from Augustine to Aquinas it is evident that the real origin of the formula, "Do good and avoid evil," is in the Bible. The rule is not a new discovery made by Thomas Aquinas when writing his *Prima Secundae* but is actually a commonplace among Christian writers of the preceding eight centuries. This conclusion does not necessarily contravene Aquinas' claim that the synderesis principle is known by some sort of intellectual insight: what we have found is that the expressions in which the synderesis principle is stated depend very largely on Scripture and its commentaries.

III. AQUINAS ON HOW THE SYNDERESIS PRINCIPLE IS KNOWN

Among his many excellent studies of the metaphysics of Thomas Aquinas, Joseph Owens has devoted one to what is usually called the "principle" of causality.[39] In it he shows that the causal proposition is a far more complex item of human knowledge than is suggested in many recent Thomistic works on epistemology and metaphysics. It is all very well to say with charming simplicity that speculative and practical first principles are self-evident – but it has been known since the time of Boethius that at least some of these principles are immediately known only to the learned.[40] St. Thomas recognized the complexity of our cognition of first practical principles, as the following text from his *Commentary on Book Four of the Sentences* indicates. The English is intentionally literal in my version because there is no complete translation of this work. Strangely the passage occurs in an article that asks whether it is contrary to the "law of nature" for a man to have plural wives.

---

[38] Albert's emphasis on the plurality of first practical principles is found in an unprinted section of the *Summa de Creaturis* (from the Cologne MS GB f. 79, fol. 176r), for which see Chroust, p. 22. Chroust is dependent on M. Grabmann, *Drei ungedruckte Teile der Summa de Creaturis Alberts des Grossen* (Quellen und Forschungen zur Geschichte des Dominikanerordens in Deutschland, Heft 13, 1919), pp. 65ff.

[39] See Joseph Owens, "The Causal Proposition – Principle or Conclusion?" *The Modern Schoolman*, 32 (1955), 159-171, 257-270, and 323-339.

[40] Boethii, *De hebdomadibus*, 1 (PL 64: 1311) pointed out that some *communes conceptiones* are evident to all (such as the equality axiom) while others (such as that incorporeals cannot occupy space) are evident only to educated people. St. Thomas refers to this distinction many times: see the beginning of his *Expositio in librum Boethii de Hebdomadibus*, and his *De veritate*, 10.12, c.

My answer is that there are certain principles naturally present in all things whereby they are not only able to perform their appropriate actions (*operationes*) but also by means of which they render these suitable (*convenientes*) to an end – whether they be actions that are appropriate to anything by virtue of the nature of its genus, or that are appropriate from the specific nature, as it is suited to a magnet understood generically that it fall downward, but from the nature of its species [as magnetized] that it attract iron. Just as forms are principles of actions in things that act as a result of natural necessity, by which they perform appropriate actions that are suited to their end, so also in the case of beings that are able to know the principles of acting are knowledge (*cognitio*) and appetite (*appetitus*). Hence there must be a natural conception in the cognitive power and a natural inclination in the appetitive power, whereby an act suited to the genus or species is rendered fitting to the end. But since among other animals man knows the rational meaning (*rationem*) of his end, and the orderly relation (*proportionem*) of his deed to the end, therefore the natural conception impressed on him (*ei indita*) by which he is directed to act suitably is called the natural law (*lex naturalis*) or natural right (*jus naturale*). In other beings it is called natural instinct (*aestimatio*)....[41]

Several points need to be stressed in analyzing this first half of Aquinas' early explanation of the principles of natural law or rightness. Throughout the article he insists that human actions are good when they are judged to be suited to man's end. This judgment involves an appraisal of any proposed kind of action in relation to the nature of man considered generically (as a living substance) or specifically (as a rational animal). Both knowledge and appetite play a part in such an appraisal of the appropriateness of a given sort of action. (Recall that he is dealing with the general question: is the plurality of wives living with one man contrary to what is naturally right?)

Here he does not develop the role of human appetition in practical thinking and action – but he does point out that there is in man a tendency, within the generic or specific nature, to approve and do actions that are suited to the end of that nature. Notice that Thomas is not talking here about the activities and problems of an individual person in his concrete circumstances: rather he is explaining how man (considered universally) arrives at some universal judgments and tendencies that will help him to live well. More important to Thomas in this article is the exploration of how natural law (either *jus* or *lex*) is grasped. This brings

---

[41] *In 4 Sent.* d. 33.1.1 (Parma ed., 7.2: 967). The identical (except for punctuation) text may also be read in sᴛ 3 *Supplementum*, q. 65, 1 (Ottawa ed. [1945], 5: 272*b-275*a) but it does not belong in sᴛ.

him to stress the *cognitive* approach to rightness in human activity. Under the influence of Boethius (and of Euclid's teaching on axiomatic knowledge) Aquinas argues that human beings (as rational) are endowed with the inborn ability to know immediately certain initial and obvious propositions (such as the Euclidean and Boethian principle that equals subtracted from equals leave equals). These *communes conceptiones* (e.g., what "equality" means) are found in both the theoretical and practical orders of knowledge. The broad but non-detailed knowledge of what "good" means (the *ratio* of *bonum*) is one of these universally known conceptions. Notice that *ratio* designates a relation (as when we speak of a mathematical ratio) between a proposed kind of action and the nature of man and his end. In this portion of this key text we are left with the conclusion that one way of grasping what is naturally right (the *jus naturale*) is through knowing certain universal judgments about deeds that are generically or specifically appropriate to the kind of being that man is. Expressed in general rules, these judgments are principles or precepts of natural law (*lex naturalis*).

At the end of this lengthy article Thomas will conclude that having several wives is not opposed to human nature, considered generically, but the more specific one's consideration becomes the more does it seem clear that such plurality of wives causes trouble and is opposed to the law of nature, viewed specifically.[42] It is to the explanation of this more specific way of thinking that Thomas turns next in this article.

> The natural law, therefore, is nothing other than a knowledge (*conceptio*) naturally implanted in man, whereby he is directed in a fitting manner (*convenienter*) in his own deeds; this suitability may stem from either his generic nature, as in generating offspring, or eating, or other such actions, or it may arise from his specific nature, as in reasoning or like actions. Everything that makes an action unsuitable to an end that nature tends toward, as a result of any given action, may be said to be against the law of nature. Now an action can be unsuitable either to the primary end (*fini principali*) or to the secondary one; and whether this be so may occur in two ways. One way depends on something that completely impedes the end, as when too much or too little eating obstructs bodily health (the primary end of eating) and it also interferes with success (*bonam habitudinem*) in carrying out business activities (a secondary end). A second

---

[42] *In 4 Sent.* d. 33.1.1, *ad finem solutionis* (Parma ed., 7.2: 967b): "Pluralitas ergo uxorum neque totaliter tolit neque aliqualiter impedit primum finem [matrimonii], cum unus vir sufficiat pluribus uxoribus fecundandis, et educandis filiis ex eis natis; sed secundum finem etsi non totaliter tollat, tamen multum impedit, eo quod non facile potest esse pax in familia."

way depends on something that renders the suitable attainment of either the primary or secondary end difficult, as in the case where eating is improper (*inordinata*) because of impropriety in time. So, if an action is unsuitable to its end, in the sense of completely obstructing the primary end, then directly through the law of nature it is prohibited by the primary precepts of the law of nature, which play the same role in regard to actions (*in operabilibus*) that axiomatic items of knowledge (*communes conceptiones*) play in regard to speculative problems. But if it be unsuitable to either the primary or secondary end in some more limited way (*quocumque modo*), in the sense that it makes attainment of the end difficult or less fitting (*minus congruam*), then it is prohibited not by the primary precepts of the law of nature but by the secondary ones that are derived from the primary principles – just as the conclusions to speculative problems get their validity (*fidem habent*) from the self-evident principles. This is how an action under consideration is said to be against the law of nature.[43]

This part of the article introduces the distinction between the primary end and the secondary end of a human action. The example of taking food to sustain one's health (the primary reason for such an action), or for a social or business purpose (a secondary end), is still meaningful today. Thomas maintains that it is a more serious matter to eat in such a way as to ruin one's health than to eat (or drink) in a way that would upset one's relations with one's fellow men. In so distinguishing the primary and secondary ends of a given human institution (such as matrimony, which is the problem in this article), St. Thomas is not talking about the same thing as the difference between man's end considered generically or specifically. The ultimate end of man may be viewed in relation to either his animal or his rational nature. Some kinds of actions, such as self-destruction, are not appropriate to any kind of animal. But other types of action that are peculiar to rational beings, such as speaking truthfully, are viewed in relation to man's specifically natural end. The primary precepts of the law of human nature are, of course, dependent on an awareness of their propriety in relation to man's ultimate end.

There is still another distinction that Thomas makes between two kinds of practical knowledge. This involves the difference between *prudentia* and *scientia practica*. Both involve "practical reasonableness" but not in the same way. It is unfortunate that some recent interpreters of St. Thomas are using the expression "practical reasonableness" to cover both *prudentia* and *scientia practica*.[44] One of the clearest explanations of

---

[43] Ibid., at the sentence: "Lex ergo naturalis..." (Parma ed., 7.2: 967a).

[44] For this confused use of "practical reasonableness" for both *prudentia* and *scientia practica* see G. Grisez and Russell Shaw, *Beyond the New Morality* (Notre Dame:

the difference between practical knowledge (such as ethics) and prudence is found in Aquinas' *Questions on the Virtues in General*. There, in answer to an objection citing Aristotle's statement that his purpose in ethics is not *to know* virtue but rather to show how to acquire it, and indeed to instill it,[45] Thomas says this:

> The Philosopher is speaking here about practical science (*scientia practica*) but prudence (*prudentia*) means more (*plus importat*) than practical science. For it is universal judgment (*universale judicium*) about things to be done that come under practical science: for example, that fornication is evil, that theft is not to be done, and the like. Now even while a person has this kind of science, it may happen that rational judgment concerning a particular act is interfered with, so that one may make a false judgment. For this reason it [science] is said to have little value for virtue, since while it is present a man may sin against virtue. However, to prudence belongs the making of a right judgment concerning individual actions (*recte judicare de singulis agibilibus*), insofar as they are to be done now. This sort of judgment is corrupted by sin of any kind: so, as long as prudence remains in charge, a man does not sin. Hence it has a great influence on virtue; even more, it is the cause of virtue.[46]

The principle of synderesis is important for both kinds of practical reasoning. It is the starting-point for the kind of thinking about the universal rules of morality that is typical of the work of the moral scientist, whether theologian or ethicist. Just as a logician continually employs the principle of non-contradiction in his theoretical science, so the ethicist is governed by the synderesis principle in all his correct reasoning about practical matters. He is not thinking about what he must do in a particular personal situation but the ethicist is trying, as expertly as he can, to reason to general conclusions about the kinds of things that are generally good to do and the types of bad acts that are to be avoided.

Also practical, but quite personal, is the other kind of moral reasoning that may be governed by the habit of prudent thinking and acting. This too involves the use of the synderesis principle – not to reach universal conclusions about types of activity but rather to conclude that a particular proposed action, here and now, is good and to be done, or evil and not to be done. The average person need never formulate the principle of syn-

---

University of Notre Dame Press, 1974), p. 72; and John Finnis, *Natural Law and Natural Rights* (Oxford: Clarendon Press, 1980), Chap. V: "The Basic Requirements of Practical Reasonableness."

[45] Cf. *Nic. Ethics*, 2.2, 1103b26-28.
[46] *De virtutibus in communi*, art. 6, ad primum.

deresis; he uses it quite naturally in his practical thinking, just as he avoids self-contradiction without knowing the terms of the theoretical principle of non-contradiction. It is unfortunate that in modern times the term "prudence" has acquired the pejorative meaning of astuteness. Perhaps greater insistence on its original significance may help to restore its proper usage, as designating right reasoning concerning concrete problems of moral activity.

IV. Five Points in Conclusion

From this survey of the background of St. Thomas' teaching on the synderesis principle, the following points may be made.

First, in the mind of St. Thomas the synderesis principle has imperative force; this is implied in his use of gerundives to express it and in his broad awareness of the biblical formulae that are imperative in form.

Second, the synderesis principle is intuited, in the sense that as soon as men begin to perform acts of practical reasoning they make implicit use of this principle. In the case of at least some ethical experts some rule similar to the synderesis principle is explicitly formulated.[47]

Third, the good/evil in various formulations of the synderesis principle are not abstract goodness or badness; the good is not identical with transcendental *bonitas*, for it has no contrary.

Fourth, the synderesis principle is a formal principle: it does not tell us what is good or what is evil; these must be known by reasoning and not by simple intuition.

Finally, the synderesis principle functions differently in moral science and in personal reasoning about one's own moral problems.

---

[47] For an interesting argument for the principle, "that we ought to do good and to prevent or avoid doing harm," see William Frankena, *Ethics* (Englewood Cliffs: Prentice-Hall, 1963), p. 37.

18

Maimonides and Aquinas on Creation
A Critique of their Historians

William Dunphy

St. Michael's College, Toronto

During the past century, as intellectual historians of the western world
began to focus on its medieval period, it was inevitable that some of them,
familiar with the same chronological era in Jewish thought, would trace
its influence on some of the major Christian thinkers of the thirteenth
century. To the extent that Rabbi Moses ben Maimon, known as
Maimonides, and Thomas Aquinas were recognized as outstanding
representatives of their respective eras, and because Aquinas explicitly
refers to Maimonides' *The Guide of the Perplexed* more than eighty times
in his own writings, it was inevitable that some of these historians would
turn their attention to the question of the influence of the famous Jewish
thinker on the thought of the Christian theologian.

A helpful survey of the work of many of these historians by Jacob
I. Dienstag appeared in *The Monist*, entitled "St. Thomas Aquinas in
Maimonidian Scholarship."[1] One of the points of comparison and
influence dealt with by many of these scholars concerned the question of
the so-called "eternity of the world." All seemed to agree that Aquinas
made great use of Maimonides' view that Aristotle and his followers could
not demonstrate that the world is eternal, any more than the religious men

---

[1] Jacob I. Dienstag, "St. Thomas Aquinas in Maimonidian Scholarship," *The Monist*,
58 (1974), 104-118. In addition, he edited a collection of many of these articles reproduced
from the journals in which they originally appeared: *Studies in Maimonides and
St. Thomas Aquinas* (KTAV, 1975).

Graceful Reason: Essays in Ancient and Medieval Philosophy Presented to Joseph Owens, CSSR, ed.
Lloyd P. Gerson. Papers in Mediaeval Studies 4 (Toronto: Pontifical Institute of Mediaeval Studies,
1983), pp. 361-379. © P.I.M.S., 1983.

of *Kalam* could demonstrate its beginning in time. These same historians also seemed to agree that while Aquinas concurred with Maimonides in that view, he parted company with his illustrious Jewish predecessor by claiming to be able to demonstrate by reason alone that the world is created. Maimonides, they said, claimed that this could be held only on the basis of a divine revelation.

I propose to examine the views of several of these scholars and then, following a presentation and analysis of Maimonides own position, I will attempt to show all of these historians to have been mistaken on this supposed point of difference between Aquinas and Maimonides.

One of the studies mentioned by Dienstag was Anselm Rohner's 1913 treatment of *"Das Schöpfungsproblem bei Moses Maimonides, Albertus Magnus und Thomas von Aquin."*[2] In its conclusion, Rohner first compared Maimonides with Albert, and asserted that both are in agreement that it is only through divine revelation that we know that the world is created. In a footnote to his statement, that according to Maimonides human reason cannot answer the question whether the world is eternal or created, Rohner explained that Maimonides does not clearly distinguish the "fact" of creation from the "when" of creation (das Dass von dem Wann der Schöpfung) when he uses the word "created."[3] Then in comparing Maimonides and Aquinas, Rohner stated: "that the world is created can be demonstrated by reason, according to Thomas Aquinas; we can know this only through revelation, asserts Maimonides."[4] He saw both thinkers in agreement that it is only through faith (*durch den Glauben*) that we can know that the world has a beginning in time, and that there is no demonstration of this. But he saw a difference of degree between them on the theological and philosophical untenability of the Aristotelian doctrine of the eternity of the world. For Rohner, whereas Aquinas holds that mere reason can demonstrate that the world is not eternal, Maimonides will assert only that the world, in all of its tremendous variety, can be better explained, and with fewer doubtful points, through revelation's account of creation than through the Aristotelian position.[5]

Along with the work of Rohner, Dienstag cited a more recent treatment of this problem of creation and an eternal world, stemming from a 1945

    [2] It appeared in *Beiträge zur Geschichte der Philosophie des Mittelalters* 11.5 (Münster-i.-W., 1913).
    [3] Ibid., p. 135.
    [4] Ibid., p. 136.
    [5] Ibid., pp. 136-137.

doctoral thesis of Lottie H. Kendzierski. Her article appeared in 1956 and was entitled "Maimonides' Interpretation of the 8th Book of Aristotle's *Physics*." [6] The 1520 Latin version of *The Guide* prepared by Giustiniani[7] served as the basis for her analysis of Maimonides' doctrine. Her conclusion was that while both Maimonides and Aquinas would agree that the eternity of the world could not be demonstrated, "St. Thomas deviates from Maimonides in insisting that creation can be demonstrated."[8] Her explanation of the basic reason for this major difference between the two thinkers was that: "Maimonides' difficulty in proving creation can be resolved in his confusion of creation and creation in time, since for him creation always carries with it the added notion of a first instant of duration."[9]

A third study mentioned by Dienstag is the 1953 article "The 'Antinomy' of the Eternity of the World in Averroes, Maimonides and Aquinas" by the historian of Islamic philosophy, Majid Fakhry.[10] For our present purposes, we will leave aside his interesting setting of the question against the backdrop of the famous antinomy in Kant's *Critique of Pure Reason*, as well as his, I think, erroneous contention that Maimonides was influenced by Averroes in this matter.[11]

As Fakhry saw it, Maimonides "makes no pretenses to prove the thesis of the creation of the universe *ex nihilo*." He could, however, show the possibility of such a demonstration "by showing that the pretenses of his opponents to prove the contrary are groundless." He could turn as well to "Faith," wherein "the doctrine of creation *ex nihilo* acquires added credibility." At this point, Fakhry quoted Maimonides: "Only demonstra-

---

[6] It appeared in *The New Scholasticism*, 30 (1956), 37-48.

[7] *The Guide of the Perplexed* was written by Maimonides in Arabic. It was first translated into Hebrew by Samuel ibn Tibbon in 1204. A second Hebrew translation by Judah al'Harizi followed shortly thereafter. It was from this second Hebrew translation that the first Latin translation was made sometime during the 1230s. (See W. Kluxen, "Literaturgeschichtliches zum lateinischen Moses Maimonides," *Récherches de Théologie Ancienne et Médiévale*, 21 [1954] 23-50.) Agostino Giustiniani prepared an edition of this translation from several manuscripts in 1520. It was published in Paris with the title, *Rabi Mossei Aegyptii Dux seu Director dubitantium aut perplexorum*. Medieval Latin writers often referred to it as the *Dux neutrorum*. This edition is now available in a facsimile edition by Minerva (Frankfurt a.M., 1964).

[8] Kendzierski, p. 47, n. 40.

[9] Ibid., p. 48.

[10] It appeared in *Le Museon*, 66 (1953), 139-155, and is reprinted in the Dienstag collection, *Studies ...*, pp. 107-123.

[11] For a discussion of the possible influence of Averroes on the thought of Maimonides at the time he was writing *The Guide*, see H. A. Wolfson, *Repercussions of the Kalam in Jewish Philosophy* (Cambridge, Mass.: Harvard University Press, 1979), pp. 187-188, n. 57.

tive proof should make you abandon the theory of creation, but such proof does not exist in nature."[12]

After noting that Aquinas "owes [his] ingenious method of settling the antinomial problem of eternity to Maimonides," Fakhry claimed a superiority of Aquinas over Maimonides on two points: "There is, in the first place, the lucid and trenchant manner in which the problem is discussed, which is proper to the Angelic Docter alone ...; there is, in the second place, the distinction which Aquinas draws between the two problems of creation and the beginning of creation and which, as we have suggested, eluded Maimonides."[13] For Aquinas, "the beginning of the universe is indemonstrable and must on that account be received as an article of faith ... yet creation *ex nihilo* can be demonstrated successfully ...." As Fakhry concluded "in this way he avoids following in the fallacy of Maimonides, who undertakes to establish the thesis of creation *ex nihilo* by repudiating a completely unrelated thesis (that of eternity) – and therefore launches his most vehement attack against an illusory foe."[14]

Our final example drawn from Dienstag is "the great historian of Christian philosophy, Etienne Gilson ... who continuously demonstrated, in many of his books and articles, the role of Maimonides in the thought of St. Thomas."[15] One of Gilson's articles cited by him is the famous "Pourquoi Saint Thomas a critiqué Saint Augustin" which led off the very first volume of the periodical, *Archives d'Histoire Doctrinale et Littéraire du Moyen Âge*. In the section of that article, "*La critique Thomiste des Motecallemin*," Gilson showed the textual dependence of Aquinas' knowledge of these "motecallemin," as presented in his *Summa contra gentiles*, on Maimonides' *Guide of the Perplexed*.[16]

In a long excerpt from *The Christian Philosophy of St. Thomas Aquinas*, in which Gilson had noted the use made by Aquinas of Albert the Great and Moses Maimonides in resolving the problem of creation, Dienstag quoted him as follows: "Maimonides will only admit creation on the ground of faith. But St. Thomas bases it on demonstrative reason. The two agree on two points: that it is impossible to demonstrate the world's beginning in time, and that it is always possible to deny the eternal existence of the universe. Albert the Great, on the other hand, admits with Maimonides that creation *ex nihilo* can only be known by faith. ...

---

[12] Fakhry, p. 147.
[13] Ibid., pp. 152-153.
[14] Ibid., p. 154.
[15] Dienstag, "St. Thomas ...," p. 111.
[16] Gilson, "Pourquoi ...," *Archives*, 1 (1926), 8-25.

Against both these philosophers, St. Thomas maintains the possibility of demonstrating the creation of the universe *ex nihilo*. ... But, in conceding, with Maimonides, the logical possibility of a universe created from all eternity, he refuses to confuse truths of faith with those that are objects of proof." [17]

In a work not cited by Dienstag, his *History of Christian Philosophy in the Middle Ages*, Gilson continued to show the Maimonidean influence on Aquinas. With respect to Maimonides' preferred way to prove the existence of God, i.e., in the supposition that the world is eternal, Gilson noted: "that is exactly the attitude Saint Thomas was to adopt with regard to the same problem." [18] Again, with respect to the criticism Maimonides directed against the *mutakallimūn*, he "has been both an inspiration and a model to Thomas Aquinas." [19] However, in a footnote, Gilson stated that in "Maimonides' mind, [the doctrine of *creatio ex nihilo*] is identical with that of creation in time." [20]

One point, therefore, on which all of the above historians seemed to be in agreement is that Maimonides identified creation, or creation *ex nihilo*, with creation *de novo*, and, to the extent that the latter cannot be demonstrated but only known through divine revelation, Maimonides, unlike Aquinas, will hold that creation cannot be demonstrated.

In an effort to challenge this judgment and to show the close harmony of Aquinas and Maimonides on this important matter, I will set forth the views of Maimonides, using the excellent English translation of S. Pines,[21] along with the Latin translation made from the second Hebrew translation of Maimonides' Arabic original, and which circulated in Europe from the early 1230s.[22] For the texts regarding Maimonides' proofs for the existence of God (*Guide* 2, Introduction and Chapter 1) we are fortunate to have, in addition to the 1520 Giustiniani version, Kluxen's 1963 edition from manuscripts of that same portion of the *Guide* which circulated during the thirteenth century as a separate treatise under the title *De uno deo benedicto*.[23]

As is well known, Maimonides dedicates his *Guide of the Perplexed* to a former pupil, Rabbi Joseph, son of Rabbi Judah, and to those like him

---

[17] Dienstag, pp. 111-112; in Gilson's work, the quotation is from pages 151-152.

[18] Gilson, *History* ..., (New York, 1955), p. 230.

[19] Ibid., p. 231.

[20] Ibid., p. 650, n. 41.

[21] Maimonides, *The Guide of the Perplexed*, translated with an Introduction and Notes by Shlomo Pines (Chicago, University of Chicago Press, 1963).

[22] See above, n. 7.

[23] W. Kluxen, "Rabbi Moyses (Maimonides): *Liber de uno deo benedicto*," *Miscellanea Mediaevalia*, 4 (1966), 167-182.

who, "being perfect in religion and character, and having studied the
sciences of the philosophers and come to know what they signify," are
plunged into a state of perplexity and confusion by literalist explanations
of the Law which seem to contradict what they know to be true by
reason.[24] Maimonides structures his work according to his own
pedagogical logic of misdirection, obscurity and deliberate contradiction,
but promises, to those few individuals who are both attentive and
properly prepared for the task, to remove most of their perplexities and to
provide intimations of the mysteries and secrets of the Torah.

Towards the end of Part One of *The Guide*, and in preparation for what
he will claim to be the strongest possible demonstrations of the
foundations of the Law, namely the existence, unity and non-corporeality
of God, Maimonides presents a history of a certain kind of theology, i.e.,
the *kalam*, found first within Christianity, then within Islam and, to a
lesser extent, within Judaism. Its essential character, according to him,
was basically apologetic, that is, seeing that many of the opinions of the
philosophers were contrary to fundamental tenets of their religion, "they
started to establish premises that would be useful to them with regard to
their belief and to refute those opinions that ruined the foundations of
their Law." [25]

In this way, they first sought to demonstrate "that the world is created
in time" (*quod mundus est novus*). That being the case, they could then
demonstrate "that it has a maker who has created it in time" (*quia
factorem habet qui fecit ipsum de novo*), that he is one, and that he is not a
body.[26]

Maimonides then states his absolute aversion to this approach because
"every argument deemed to be a demonstration of the temporal creation
of the world (*quae dicunt esse probationes innovitate mundi*) is
accompanied by doubts and is not a cogent demonstratione except among
those who do not know the difference between demonstration, dialectics,
and sophistic argument." [27] And further, everyone who engages in
speculation, who is perceptive, and who has acquired true knowledge of
reality and does not deceive himself, "knows that with regard to this
question – namely the eternity of the world or its temporal creation – no
cogent demonstration can be reached (*scit quod ad scientiam hujus
quaestionis de novitate vel antiquitate mundi non pervenit homo per*

---

[24] *The Guide*, ed. Pines, Introduction to the First Part, pp. 5-6.
[25] *The Guide*, 1.71, p. 177.
[26] Ibid., p. 179; Giustiniani, fol. 29ᵛ.
[27] Ibid., p. 180, fol. 29ᵛ.

demonstrationem certam) and that it is a point before which the intellect stops." [28] Therefore, to base one's proof for the existence of God on such an indemonstrable foundation is the height of folly for Maimonides. The correct method is rather to follow the philosophers, even though their methods "are founded upon the doctrine of the eternity of the world" (*per vias philosophorum, quae sunt viae fundatae super antiquitatem mundi*). It is not because he believes in that eternity nor concedes the point to the philosophers, but rather that such demonstrations of the existence, unity and incorporeality of God can be achieved "without making a judgment upon the world's being eternal or created in time" (*absque eo quod judicemus praecise an est mundus antiquus an novus*), and thus "will be perfect, both if the world is eternal and if it is created in time" (*sive mundus sit antiquus sive novus*).[29] A further benefit of this approach will be that "we shall not cause the true [read biblical] opinion ... to be supported by a foundation that everyone can shake and wish to destroy, while other men think that it has never been constructed." [30] Maimonides will, of course, argue strenuously that the philosophers' position of the world's being eternal entails more doubts and difficulties than the biblical position of its having a beginning in time. But this will take place only after having established the demonstrations, already achieved by the philosophers with their eternal world, of the existence, unity and in-corporeality of God. Besides, these demonstrations, unlike those of the Mutakallimūn, do not abolish the very natures of things, nor call into question the validity of our experience of the sensible world.[31]

The next step for Maimonides is to set forth in chapter 72 a summary statement of what for him is demonstrably true concerning the universe as a whole and in its parts, since this is the only valid starting point for proving that God exists (*non est demonstratio super ipso, nisi a natura entis in suo universo et in partibus ejus*).[32] The remaining four chapters of Part One of *The Guide* Maimonides devotes to the Mutakallimūn. In chapter 73 he sets forth twelve premises which, he claims, are absolutely fundamental to all of the Mutakallimūn attempts to demonstrate that the world had a beginning in time, that God exists, is one and incorporeal. Chapter 74 presents the seven "principal methods of the Mutakallimūn in establishing the coming-into-being of the world in time" (*Istae sunt*

---

[28] Ibid.
[29] Ibid., p. 181; fol. 30ʳ.
[30] Ibid.
[31] Ibid., p. 182.
[32] Ibid., p. 183; fol. 30ᵛ.

credulitates de viis Loquentium in assertione novitatis mundi). Once this is granted, "it followed of necessity that it has an artificer who has produced it in time with a purpose and by the use of will and freedom of choice." [33] Chapter 75 presents five of their methods to demonstrate the oneness of God, while the concluding chapter gives three of their "proofs" refuting God's corporeality, which he characterizes as "even feebler than their proofs in favor of belief in unity." [34] His final judgement on all men of *Kalam* is that "they have abolished the nature of being and have altered the original disposition of the heavens and the earth by thinking that by means of those premises, it would be demonstrated that the world was created in time *(probaretur novitas mundi).* In consequence whereof, they have not demonstrated the creation of the world in time *(super novitate mundi)* and have destroyed for us the demonstrations of the existence and oneness of the deity and of the negation of His corporeality. For the demonstrations, by means of which all this can be made clear, can only be taken from the permanent nature of what exists, a nature that can be seen and apprehended by the senses and the intellect." [35]

Part Two of *The Guide* opens with Maimonides' promised presentation of the premises on which the philosophers base their demonstrations concerning God's existence, oneness and incorporeality. The list of twenty-six premises, which seems to be original with Maimonides, contains twenty-five that he considers well and truly demonstrated, and a twenty-sixth that Maimonides does not concede but will grant by way of an hypothesis. This is the premise regarding the eternity of the world *(antiquitas mundi).* The actual premise is that "time and movement are eternal, perpetual, existing *in actu*" *(tempus et motus sunt sempiterni et semper in actu* [G]; *tempus et motus sunt aeterna, continua, semper reperta in actu* [K]).[36]

Maimonides sees a difference between Aristotle and his commentators on this premise, the latter claiming the premise as both necessary and demonstrated, while Aristotle holds it to be true but does not claim that it has been demonstrated. The Mutakallimūn on the other hand seek to demonstrate its impossibility. "But to me," says Maimonides, "it seems that the premise in question is possible – that is, neither necessary,as is affirmed by the commentators of the writings of Aristotle, nor impossible, as is claimed by the Mutakallimūn." [37] He promises to deal with all of this

---

[33] Ibid., c. 74, p. 222; fol. 37ᵛ.
[34] Ibid., c. 76, p. 227.
[35] Ibid., p. 231; fol. 38ᵛ.
[36] Ibid., Part 2, Introduction, p. 240; fol. 39ᵛ; Kluxen, p. 176.
[37] Ibid., p. 241.

after setting forth the demonstrations concerning God's existence, oneness and incorporeality.

The first way of demonstrating these matters, which Maimonides ascribes to "the most excellent among the philosophers" (boni philosophi [G]; philosophorum famosi [K]),[38] starts from the existence of a mover for whatever is generated or corrupted and concludes ultimately to the necessity of admitting that there exists a mover of the first sphere, whose motion had been demonstrated to be eternal and perpetual, which mover could not be a body or a force in a body, nor be itself in motion either per se or per accidens, nor be subject to division or change.

At this point Maimonides identifies this first, unmoved mover with the biblical God. "Now this is the deity, may His name be sublime; I am referring to the first cause moving the sphere" (Hic autem motor est Creator benedictus, scilicet causa prima motus caeli [G]; Et iste est essentia scilicet prima causa, movens caelum [K]).[39]

Following a brief second way, which Pines thinks may belong to Alexander of Aphrodisias, Maimonides introduces a third way as follows: "a third philosophic speculation about this subject is taken over from Aristotle's argumentation, even though he sets it forth with a view to another purpose." [40] Readers of Aquinas' tertia via will easily recognize the stages of this demonstration. Beginning with the sensibly evident fact that there are existents, one of three possible alternatives must be true: none of these existents is subject to generation and corruption; all of them are generable and corruptible; some are and some are not generable and corruptible. The first two are shown to be incompatible with our own experience, leaving the third alternative as true, which entails that there is something that exists that is not generable or corruptible, whose existence therefore is necessary and not possible (necessarium esse non possibile esse [G]; est necesse esse non possibile esse [K]). That necessity must be due to itself or to another. In the latter instance, its esse would only be possible with respect to itself, while its necessity would be due to that other as to its cause. Ultimately one must conclude to the existence of a necesse esse whose necessity is due to itself alone, that is uncaused and, indeed, the cause of every other existent.

Maimonides notes at this point that this is a demonstration "concerning which there can be no doubt, no refutation, and no dispute, except on the part of one who is ignorant of the method of demonstration."

---

[38] Ibid., c. 1, p. 246; fol. 40ᵛ; Kluxen, p. 179.
[39] Ibid.
[40] Ibid., p. 247.

After drawing several inferences based on premises twenty, twenty-one and twenty-two, Maimonides concludes: "It thus has been demonstrated in this speculation that there is an existent that is necessary of existence (*quod est ens quod est necesse esse omnibus modis* [G]; *quod unum est quod necesse est esse in seipso* [K]) and is so necessarily with respect to its own essence, and that this existent has no cause for its existence and has no composition in itself, and for this reason is neither a body nor a force in a body." And, as an attentive reader of Aquinas' *tertia via* might expect, Maimonides explains "It is He who is the deity, may His name be sublime" (*qui est Creator benedictus* [G]; *et ille est deus benedictus* [K]).[41]

The fourth philosophic way, reported by Maimonides, is based on our experience of seeing things passing from a state of potentiality into actuality and concludes to the necessity that there exist a cause of that passage which is wholly actual, and thus without any potentiality whatsoever.

To this conclusion, Maimonides adds that this being, "separate from matter, in which there is no possibility whatsoever, but that exists in virtue of its essence, is the deity" (*abstractus vero in quo nulla est possibilitas omnino, sed est ens in substantia sua, ipse est Creator* [G]; *et abstractum in quo nulla est possibilitas ullo modo, sed est inventum esse in seipso, et est deus* [K]).[42]

The remainder of this chapter is taken up with two further proofs for the oneness of God plus another method of refuting the belief in His corporeality. The Kluxen text of the *De uno deo benedicto* ends with the first of the two added proofs that God is one. The Giustiniani rendition, however, has the following conclusion of the second proof: "et ita necesse est omnibus modis ut perveniatur finaliter ad unum qui esset causa esse hujus mundi qui est unus quolibet modo, sive in eo quod incepit esse postquam non fuit, sive ex parte necessitatis quod unum proveniat ex alio."[43]

The resemblances between this chapter of *The Guide* and the famous *quinque viae* of St. Thomas are obviously more than superficial. Granted that only in Aquinas' *tertia via* does there seem to be a direct textual dependence, yet the manner of proceeding and ultimate purpose seem to

---

[41] Ibid., pp. 247-248; fol. 40^v; Kluxen, p. 181. Note that earlier, in Part One, c. 60 Maimonides had referred to God as one "whose existence ... is necessary" (*necesse esse*), and in c. 61, speaking of that most sacred name of God, the Tetragrammaton, speculated that it might perhaps signify "necessary existence" (*necesse esse*). See Pines, pp. 146, 148; Giustiniani, fol. 24^{r-v}.

[42] Ibid., 249; fol. 41^r; Kluxen, p. 182.

[43] Ibid.

be the same for the two thinkers. Both are reporting ways that philosophers have demonstrated the existence of God, from which one can then make inferences regarding His oneness and incorporeality. Each add, for the benefit of their co-religionists, that the unmoved mover and the necessary being, and the wholly actual actualizer is, in fact, the biblical creator. Furthermore, both accept as an unproved hypothesis underlying their proofs, an eternal world, albeit Aquinas does so only implicitly.

In short, both Maimonides and Aquinas think that certain demonstrations of the philosophers are valid to prove that there exists a creating God, on whom everything else in existence depends for its existence, irrespective of whether that creation be "eternal" or have a commencement in time. Further, both Maimonides and Aquinas hold that there can be no valid demonstration resolving that issue; we know with absolute certainty that the world had a beginning in time only through the biblical revelation. Indeed, both thinkers attack the efforts of their own "Mutakallimūn" who seek to demonstrate that truth, because, in the eyes of unbelievers who are trained in what constitutes valid demonstration, the whole religious belief could be subject to ridicule.[44]

If my analysis of this section of *The Guide* is correct, then I do not see how the almost universal judgement of those scholars who have compared the thought of Maimonides and Aquinas on this point can stand, namely the view that Maimonides thinks that creation *ex nihilo* cannot be demonstrated but only believed through faith, while Aquinas maintains the opposite.

Any historian of philosophy reaching such a conclusion about his predecessors should feel a certain nervous apprehension – a bit like the mother watching a parade and judging everyone to be out of step except her son. The obvious question that arises, why did so many experienced scholars reach the opposite conclusion, deserves an attempt at an answer. Let us consider, in order, the sample of historians whose views were reported above.

Throughout his treatment of Maimonides on the problem of creation, A. Rohner consistently used the expression "the creation of the world" (*die Schöpfung der Welt*) where the Latin version of Maimonides has "*novitas mundi*" and the English version by Pines has "the temporal creation of the world." In similar fashion, Rohner spoke of "the Mutakallimūn proofs for the creation of the world" (*Beweise der Muta-*

---

[44] See, for example, *The Guide* 2.16, p. 293 and Aquinas, *Summa Theologiae* 1.46.2; *Summa contra gentiles* 2.38.

kallimūn für die Weltschöpfung),[45] whereas the same English and Latin versions of Maimonides usually refer to the Mutakallimūn proofs of "the temporal creation of the world" (*probationes innovitate mundi*) or to their "methods in establishing the coming-into-being of the world" (*credulitates de viis Loquentium in assertione novitatis mundi*).

One explanation for this practice of Rohner might lie in the translation of Maimonides he used, that of S. Munk.[46] It might be helpful to list together with passages from Munk's translation cited by Rohner, the corresponding English and Latin versions of Pines and Giustiniani.

Referring to Maimonides' assessment in *Guide* 1, 71 of the method of the Mutakallimūn (Rohner, p. 20, n. 4):

> Munk 1: 346: "... or dès qu'il est établi que le monde est créé, il est indubitablement établi qu'il y a un ouvrier qui l'a créé."
>
> Pines, p. 179: "and when it is thus established that the world is created in time, it is likewise undoubtedly established that it has a maker who has created it in time."
>
> Giustiniani, fol. 29ᵛ: "... quod mundus est novus, et cum hoc astruitur, astruitur etiam sine dubio quia factorem habet qui fecit ipsum de novo."

Further, in the same place (Rohner, p. 20, n. 5):

> Munk 1: 347: "En effet, tout penseur pénétrant qui cherche la vérité et ne s'abuse pas lui-même sait bien que cette question, je veux dire (celle de savoir) si le monde est éternel ou créé, ne saurait être résolue par une démonstration décisive...."
>
> Pines, p. 180: "and everyone who engages in speculation, who is perceptive, and who has acquired true knowledge of reality and does not deceive himself, knows that with regard to this question – namely the eternity of the world or its temporal creation – no cogent demonstration can be reached...."
>
> Giustiniani, fol. 29ᵛ: "Quilibet autem speculator mundus et verus qui non decipit animam suam, scit quod ad scientiam hujus quaestionis de novitate vel antiquitate mundi, non pervenit homo per demonstrationem certam."

One more example should suffice, that of the opening sentence of c. 13 of *The Guide*, Part 2, cited by Rohner on p. 24:

---

[45] See, for example, Rohner, p. 14.
[46] S. Munk, *Le Guide des Égarés. Traité de theologie et de Philosophie par Moïse ben Maimon dit Maïmonide*, 3 vols. (Paris, 1856-1866).

Munk 2: 104: "Sur la question de savoir si le monde est éternel ou créé, ceux qui admettent l'existence de Dieu ont professé trois opinions différentes."

Pines, p. 281: "There are three opinions of human beings, namely, of all those who believe that there is an existent deity, with regard to the eternity of the world or its production in time."

Giustiniani, fol. 46ᵛ: "Opiniones hominum de antiquitate vel novitate mundi apud omnes qui credunt quod Deus est, sunt tres."

It would seem then that Rohner had been misled by the Munk translations when he claimed, in a long explanatory footnote on that opening sentence of c. 13 of *The Guide*, Part 2, that Maimonides shares with the Mutakallimūn a certain confusion regarding creation for they do not distinguish "between the 'that' and the 'when' of creation" (*zwischen dem Dass und dem Wann der Schöpfung*) with the result that "to be created" and "to have a beginning" are for them synonymous, correlative concepts.[47]

However, Rohner came to his reading of Maimonides with Aquinas' clear distinction between the two expressions clearly in mind. He should, therefore have been more alert to a footnote in Munk's translation of that very same opening sentence of c. 13, in which Munk noted that the literal rendition of Maimonides' words was actually "*Les opinions des hommes sur l'éternité du monde ou sa nouveauté....*"[48] Indeed, Munk several times used the expression "*la nouveauté du monde*" instead of his usual "*la création du monde*," and in the context of the very quotations cited above as examples.

A final comment regarding Rohner's article concern his claim that whereas Aquinas holds that mere reason can demonstrate that the world is not eternal, Maimonides will only assert that the biblical view raises fewer difficulties than the Aristotelian position. On this point as well, Rohner's view cannot stand. Aquinas is in complete agreement with Maimonides who claim only that "all those arguments (for the eternity of the world) have a certain point through which they may be invalidated and the inference drawn from them against us shown to be incorrect."[49] Aquinas also never claims that he can demonstrate that the world is not eternal but rather that none of the arguments seeking to prove its eternity

---

[47] Rohner, p. 24 n. 1.
[48] Munk 2:104 n. 2.
[49] *The Guide* 2.16, p. 294.

do so with demonstrative force (*non de necessitate concludunt; nec demonstrative probari potest*).[50]

The Kendzierski article cited by Dienstag poses several additional problems, for her article contains several serious misinterpretations of the thought of Maimonides. One example should suffice: "Maimonides admits," she wrote, "that Aristotle is correct in saying that prime matter is eternal and could not possibly have been produced; but that he will believe that God created it from nothing." [51] If correct, Kendzierski has pinpointed the hitherto elusive source of the so-called doctrine of the "double truth," whereby something could be held to be true in philosophy while, at the same time, its contrary could be held to be true by faith! Actually, in the text cited by the author, Maimonides is listing a whole series of Aristotelian positions that he judges to be correct and which are not contrary to the biblical account of creation. Herewith Maimonides: "He [Aristotle] said that the first matter is subject to neither generation nor passing away and began ... to make clear that it was impossible that the first matter was generated. And this is correct. For we [i.e., following the biblical account] do not maintain that the first matter is generated as man is generated from the seed or that it passes away as man passes away into dust. But we maintain that God has brought it into existence from nothing and that after being brought into existence, it was as it is now [i.e., as Aristotle described it]." [52]

Let us, however, consider her explanation of the major difference she saw between Aquinas and Maimonides on the demonstrability of creation. Maimonides, she claimed, simply confused the two notions of "creation" and "creation in time." Incredibly, the textual reference she cited for her statement that, for Maimonides, "proofs for creation are not valid," would seem to make the opposite point – "... ad scientiam hujus quaestionis de novitate vel antiquitate mundi non pervenit homo per demonstrationem certam." She found it necessary to add parenthetically "(and here Maimonides implies creation and temporal beginning, thus opposing creation to eternity as if eternal creation were intrinsically impossible)." [53]

Not at all! As we have seen, a simpler and more direct textual analysis would recognize that, after having proven the existence of a First, Unmoved Mover, and of a *Necesse Esse* on whom the entire universe

---

[50] See, for example, st 1.46.1 and scg 2.32.
[51] Kendzierski, p. 41.
[52] *The Guide* 2.17, pp. 296-297.
[53] Kendzierski, p. 48.

depends for its existence, Maimonides is here concluding that demonstrative proofs for either the eternity of the world (*antiquitas mundi*) or for its beginning in time (*novitas mundi*) are not to be had.

Majid Fakhry also seemed to equate what Maimonides has to say about the biblical teaching of a creation that is both *ex nihilo* and *de novo*, with a doctrine of creation *ex nihilo*. Thus, Fakhry had said, "... the doctrine of creation *ex nihilo* acquires added credibility from the fact that 'it was held by our Father Abraham and by our Teacher Moses'." However, the Pines translation here has: "And this, in addition to the fact that the world's being produced in time is the opinion of *Abraham our Father* and our prophet *Moses*...." And Giustiniani: "Praesertim etiam cum novitas mundi sit fides Abrahae patris nostri, et Moysi prophetae nostri." [54]

Fakhry had also added that, according to Maimonides, "Only demonstrative proof should make you abandon the theory of creation; but such proof does not exist in nature." However in Pines we read: "Do not turn away from the opinion according to which the world is new, except because of a demonstration. Now such a demonstration does not exist in nature." Giustiniani has: "Non recedas ergo ab opinione novitatis mundi nisi propter demonstrationem; sed talis demonstratio non est in natura." [55]

One might wish to excuse Fakhry's confusion here by pointing the finger at the Friedländer translation of *The Guide* which he cited. Indeed, Friedländer routinely used the terms "creation" or "*creatio ex nihilo*" in those places where Pines and Giustiniani have respectively "temporal creation" or "*creatio de novo*." [56] However, Fakhry consistently missed the point of Maimonides' criticism of Aristotle and his followers on the question of the eternity of the world. For Maimonides, it was not the eternity, but rather the absolutely necessary character of the emanation of all things from a First Cause that destroys the foundations of biblical religion. As he put it in 2.25, "... the belief in eternity the way Aristotle sees it – that is, the belief according to which the world exists in virtue of necessity ... destroys the Law in its principle ...." [57] Indeed, in the next sentence, Maimonides asserted that, "if, however, one believed in eternity according to the ... opinion of Plato ... this opinion would not destroy the

---

[54] Fakhry, p. 147; Pines, p. 320; Giustiniani, fol. 54^r.

[55] Fakhry, p. 147; Pines, p. 322; Giustiniani, fol. 54^v.

[56] *The Guide for the Perplexed*, translated from the original Arabic text by M. Friedländer, 3 vols. (London, 1881-1885); revised and republished in one volume, minus the notes, in 1904. In this latter, see for example pages 133, 192, 194 and 195.

[57] *The Guide*, ed. Pines, p. 328.

foundations of the Law ...."[58] Thus, Fakhry's jibe about Maimonides "attacking an illusory foe" cannot stand.

The case of Etienne Gilson is somewhat different. He referred his readers, in the works cited above, to both the French translation of *The Guide* by Munk and to Friedländer's English translation. His joint comparisons of Aquinas on creation with both Maimonides and Albert the Great owed much to the conclusion of what was considered the classic treatment of that question, Rohner's "*Das Schöpfungsproblem bei Moses Maimonides, Albertus Magnus und Thomas von Aquin.*" In addition, Gilson specifically referred his readers to another classic, L. G. Levy's *Maimonide*, for the claim that "Maimonides will only admit creation on the ground of faith."[59]

However, in the pages cited by Gilson, Levy used the Munk translation to phrase the question about which there were three opinions, namely, "whether the world is eternal or created (éternel ou créé)." Levy also went on to characterize Maimonides' efforts in the immediately following chapters of *The Guide* as an attempt "to prove that creation is not impossible." And then, Levy continued, "being given that the question of knowing if the world is eternal or created remains undecided, our author will rally to the biblical solution."[60] It seems clear, then, that Levy also, as an historian of Maimonides, used the expression "creation" to mean "creation *de novo*."

Another standard work on Jewish thought to which Gilson regularly referred his readers was that of G. Vajda, *Introduction à la Pensée Juive du Moyen Âge*. He also seems regularly to equate "creation with "creation" *de novo*" for he spoke of the Mutakallimūm proofs for creation ("des preuves *kalâmiques* de la creation") as failing to establish decisively the created character of the world ("*ne conduit pas à établir d'une manière indiscutable le caractère créé du monde*").[61] To his credit, however, Vajda saw clearly the essential point of Maimonides criticism of the Aristotelian's eternal world, namely, its strictly necessitarian character.

Where does all of this leave us? If the foregoing analysis of Maimonides' doctrine is correct, namely that, like Aquinas after him, he judged that some of the philosophers had indeed proven the existence of a creating God on whom the entire universe is dependent for its very existence and further that, like Aquinas, he judged that the question

---

[58] Ibid.
[59] L. G. Levy, *Maïmonide* (Paris, 1911), p. 70.
[60] Ibid.
[61] G. Vajda, *Introduction à la Pensée Juive du Moyen Âge* (Paris, 1947), p. 138.

whether this created world was *ab aeterno* or *de novo* was not susceptible to demonstrative proof and could be known only through a divine revelation, then one is still left with the question why it was that Munk, Friedländer, Levy, Vajda, Gilson and the others did not grasp this point.

Perhaps a look at the way H. A. Wolfson treated this subject might provide us with an approach to answer this latter question. Wolfson wrote extensively and profoundly on the Jewish intellectual tradition, its roots in Hellenic, Patristic and Islamic thought, and its "repercussions" in medieval Christian thinkers. There follow some not untypical quotations from a sampling of his many articles. The first three are from "The Platonic, Aristotelian and Stoic Theories of Creation in Hallevi and Maimonides."[62]

> Though both Hallevi and Maimonides believe in creation *ex nihilo*, they admit that such a belief cannot be established by reason. Neither of them agrees with the Kalam, whether the Moslem or the Jewish Kalam, in believing that creation *ex nihilo* can be established by demonstrative reasoning.[63]
>
> ... Maimonides declares that the creation of the world *ex nihilo* can no more be established by a "decisive demonstration" than the eternity of the world, but, unlike Hallevi, he believes that the former, even on mere speculative grounds, is more probable than the latter. More fully, too, Maimonides goes into a detailed refutation of the Kalam stock arguments for creation *ex nihilo*.[64]
>
> Maimonides, however, tries to show the untenability of the Aristotelian theory of the eternity of the world, or at least its inferiority to the theory of creation, on purely rational grounds. He does not assume *a priori* that it is contradictory to Scripture. Quite the contrary, he openly declares: "We do not reject the eternity of the universe, merely on the ground that certain passages in Scripture confirm its creation" ....[65]

The next quotation is from his book on Kalam: Of all the works we have quoted as containing Kalam arguments for creation, only Maimonides' *Moreh Nebukim* and Averroes' Long Commentaries on Aristotle were translated into Latin. When, therefore, we find that some

---

[62] This article appeared originally in *Essays in Honour of the Very Rev. Dr. J. H. Hertz, Chief Rabbi of Great Britain* (London, 1942), pp. 427-442. It was reprinted together with other articles of Wolfson in the first volume of the two volume *Studies in the History of Philosophy and Religion*, edited by I. Twersky and G. H. Williams (Cambridge, Mass.: Harvard University Press, 1973), pp. 234-249. The following three page references will be to this collection.

[63] *Studies*, 1:235.

[64] Ibid., p. 236.

[65] Ibid., pp. 245-246.

of these arguments are included by Albertus Magnus, Thomas Aquinas, and Bonaventura among the arguments quoted by them as having been advanced in proof of creation, we have to examine the relation of these arguments to the corresponding arguments quoted by Averroes and Maimonides. Both Averroes and Maimonides, as we have seen, refuted these arguments, the former because he did not believe in creation as traditionally interpreted by those whom he describes as "the Loquentes [that is the Mutalallimun] of the three religions existing nowadays"; the latter simply because, as he says, these arguments "are subject to doubts and none of them constitutes a decisive demonstration, except for those who do not know the difference between demonstration, dialectic [that is, probable reasoning], and sophism," and are thus not valid enough to establish the belief in creation which is common, as he says, to "the three of us, namely Jews, Christians, and Muslims." [66]

It seems clear, therefore, that Wolfson did not hesitate to characterize the Mutakallimūn arguments opposed by Maimonides as arguments for "creation," or for "creation *ex nihilo*," taking these expressions as more or less equivalents for "creation *de novo*." Indeed, one can see this operative in the following text and explanatory footnote by Wolfson: "Averroes, who was a contemporary of Maimonides, maintains that the creation of the world, that is to say, creation *ex nihilo*, cannot be demonstrated by reason."[67] In the footnote to this, Wolfson cited a Latin translation of Averroes' *Tahafut al-Tahafut* as follows:

> "*Et rediit quaestio utrum sit possible, ut sit mundus antiquus, et aeternus, aut innovatus ... Et non numeratur haec quaestio inter intellectuales.*"
> Further, what the Asharites had to say, namely, "*quod natura possibilis sit innovata et creata a nihilo,*" is not demonstrative.[68]

One could not, surely, charge Wolfson with simply being confused on this point. In one, packed and informative article, "The Meaning of *Ex Nihilo* in the Church Fathers, Arabic and Hebrew Philosophy, and St. Thomas," he showed the close correspondence between Maimonides and Aquinas in delineating the different senses of "*ex nihilo*" in understanding creation. Wolfson also understood that "St. Thomas' *post non esse* is Maimonides' *post privationem* [in his Latin version], for *non esse* and *privatio* in these two statements mean the same thing and, in fact, the

---

[66] H. A. Wolfson, *The Philosophy of the Kalam* (Cambridge, Mass.: Harvard University Press, 1976), pp. 455-456.

[67] Wolfson, "*The Platonic, Aristotelian and Stoic Theories of Creation ...*" in *Studies*, 1: 236.

[68] Ibid.

underlying Arabic term *ma'dūm* in Maimonides' statement means both 'privation' and 'non-existence'." [69] However, according to Wolfson, the meaning of *post*, for both Aquinas and Maimonides, had "to be purged of any implication of time, inasmuch as time came into existence only with the creation of time."[70]

From all of this, we are left with the fact that Wolfson saw nothing unusual or incorrect in using "creation," even "creation *ex nihilo*," in a generic fashion, with "creation *de novo*" sometimes implied as a species. What this seems to mean then is that the many eminent Jewish historians of Maimonides did not have uppermost in their minds the clear distinction Aquinas had made between "creation" and its duration, whether *ab aeterno* or *de novo*, when they analysed *The Guide of the Perplexed*. And why should they have? However, when the historians of medieval Latin philosophical authors turned to study Maimonides' possible influence on Aquinas, they were certainly aware of that distinction by Aquinas. Apparently though, they simply relied on the historians and translators of Maimonides as authoritative guides to his doctrine. Thus when reading that Maimonides held that there was no clear demonstration to prove either the eternity of the world or its creation and that "he rallied to the biblical solution" to settle the issue, they then saw what they judged to be a major difference between Maimonides and Aquinas.[71]

If, however, the whole of this article is not without foundation, perhaps the time has come to resolve that alleged difference and to recognize in yet another, fundamental way, the fruitful "repercussion" of the thought of the Jewish rabbi on that of the Christian theologian.

---

[69] *Studies*, 1: 216-217. This article appeared originally in *Mediaeval Studies in Honor of J. D. M. Ford* (Cambridge, Mass., Harvard University Press, 1948), pp. 355-370.

[70] *Studies*, 1: 215.

[71] In an article that appeared after this was written, Richard Dales continues this tradition of misinterpretation. Relying on the Friedländer translation of *The Guide*, as well as on the 1520 Latin version published by Giustiniani, Dales claims that Maimonides considered invalid any proof of God's existence based on creation from nothing, and that, indeed, creation could not be proved. See Richard Dales, "Maimonides and Boethius (*sic*) of Dacia on the Eternity of the World," *The New Scholasticism*, 56 (1982), 306-319.

19

Thomas d'Aquin et Siger de Brabant
en quête d'arguments pour le monothéisme

Fernand Van Steenberghen
Université de Louvain

I. État de la question

On a souvent loué la lucidité avec laquelle Thomas d'Aquin a formulé le problème de l'existence de Dieu. Alors qu'il vivait dans un milieu culturel saturé de valeurs religieuses, il n'a jamais admis que l'affirmation de Dieu fût évidente: cette vérité doit être démontrée et cette démonstration n'est pas facile.[1] Cette thèse en implique une autre: l'athéisme, ou plutôt l'agnosticisme, ne trahit pas nécessairement la débilité mentale ou la mauvaise foi: si l'existence de Dieu doit être démontrée et si cette démonstration n'est pas un jeu d'enfant, celui qui ne saisit pas la rigueur des preuves qu'on lui propose n'est pas pour autant un esprit borné ou pervers. Beaucoup d'apologistes modernes auraient bien fait de s'inspirer de ces enseignements de S. Thomas, dont la position était partagée par de nombreux maîtres ès arts, entre autres par Siger de Brabant.

Bien entendu, S. Thomas n'en reste pas à cette position assez pessimiste: s'il met en relief tout ce qui fait obstacle à la connaissance rationnelle de Dieu, c'est pour souligner le secours inestimable que la révélation a

---

[1] Outre les pages bien connues où Thomas d'Aquin rejette l'évidence de l'existence de Dieu, on lira les chapitres de la *Summa contra gentiles* dans lesquels il montre combien la connaissance rationnelle de Dieu est laborieuse pour la plupart des hommes (1.4, 3.38 et 39). On trouvera des commentaires sur ces thèmes dans mon livre récent: *Le problème de l'existence de Dieu dans les écrits de S. Thomas d'Aquin*, Philosophes médiévaux 23 (Louvain-la-Neuve, 1980), en particulier pp. 326-327 et 348.

Graceful Reason: Essays in Ancient and Medieval Philosophy Presented to Joseph Owens, CSSR, ed. Lloyd P. Gerson. Papers in Mediaeval Studies 4 (Toronto: Pontifical Institute of Mediaeval Studies, 1983), pp. 381-400. © P.I.M.S., 1983.

apporté à la faiblesse de l'esprit humain: grâce aux prophètes, aux livres inspirés et surtout à Jésus-Christ, la connaissance de Dieu est aisément accessible à tous ceux qui sont touchés par ces messages divins; dès lors le refus de l'athée et même l'abstention de l'agnostique sont beaucoup moins excusables. Des considérations analogues peuvent être faites à propos d'un problème très voisin de celui de l'existence de Dieu: le problème de l'unicité divine ou du monothéisme. C'est ce que je voudrais montrer ici en évoquant les efforts réalisés par Thomas d'Aquin et, un peu plus tard, par Siger de Brabant, pour démontrer philosophiquement la thèse mono-théiste. Le lecteur comprendra aisément qu'il ne s'agira pas d'une étude approfondie: il y faudrait un volume. Il s'agira d'une exploration rapide, dans le but de mettre en relief les textes qui seront présentés et d'ouvrir ainsi un chantier qui pourrait attirer de jeunes chercheurs.

Avant d'aborder les textes, rappelons la situation historique dans laquelle Thomas et Siger ont travaillé. Il est clair que le climat monothéiste régnait partout au XIIIᵉ siècle: Chrétiens, Juifs et Musulmans professent tous l'existence du Dieu unique, créateur de l'univers. Cette adhésion unanime s'appuie évidemment sur l'enseignement très ferme des grandes religions monothéistes. Mais des maîtres comme Thomas d'Aquin et Siger de Brabant ont eu le mérite de poser clairement le problème au plan de la pensée philosophique. Ils ont compris qu'une preuve de l'existence de Dieu ne saurait être complète si elle n'implique pas la démonstration de l'unicité divine, sans quoi elle ne dépasserait pas le polythéisme.

En bonne méthode, il fallait interroger d'abord l'histoire de la pensée. Or celle-ci offrait aux médiévaux des pistes variées. Aristote, le maître par excellence, avait conclu à l'unicité du Premier Moteur comme clef de voûte de sa cosmographie: la première sphère, qui enveloppe l'univers matériel tout entier, est aussi le premier mobile, qui doit être mû par un Moteur unique, acte pur exempt de toute puissance. Au livre 12 de la *Métaphysique*, le Stagirite avait ajouté des considérations d'un autre ordre, au terme desquelles il avait conclu que les êtres répugnent à être mal gouvernés et qu'une pluralité de chefs n'est pas bonne; le Principe de l'univers doit donc être unique.[2] Il semble que la démonstration du Pre-mier Moteur en physique n'ait pas donné pleine satisfaction à Aristote, puisqu'il fait appel ici à un argument très différent, basé sur l'ordre de l'univers. Rappelons enfin que Thomas et Siger mettent tous deux au cré-dit du Stagirite la doctrine de la création: c'était une opinion assez répan-due au XIIIᵉ siècle.

---

[2] Aristote, *Métaphysique*, 12.10, 1076a3-4. Cf. Van Steenberghen *Le problème*, pp. 262 et 297-298.

Platon, Plotin et leurs disciples, grecs ou arabes, représentaient, pour les maîtres du moyen âge, une tradition fort différente de l'aristotélisme. Mettant en œuvre la dialectique des degrés de perfection et de la participation, le platonisme et le néoplatonisme étaient parvenus à l'affirmation de l'Être premier conçu comme plénitude d'être et de perfection: le Bien chez Platon, l'Un chez Plotin, la Cause première chez Avicenne. L'univers tout entier, esprits et corps, émane de cette plénitude primordiale. Cette fois nous sommes en présence d'un monothéisme rigoureux, mais la question sera de savoir comment l'esprit humain parvient à établir solidement l'existence de l'Être suprême.

En opposition à la thèse monothéiste, il faut rappeler d'abord le polythéisme des religions païennes de l'antiquité, en Orient, en Grèce et à Rome. Religions populaires sans doute, mais qui ont exercé une certaine influence sur les écoles de philosophie comme sur la vie sociale et politique.

Il faut rappeler aussi le courant dualiste, que le xiiie siècle a connu surtout sous la forme du manichéisme ancien et de ses survivances médiévales (Cathares, Albigeois). Les scolastiques ont connu les réfutations du manichéisme dans les écrits de S. Augustin.

Quant aux courants matérialistes et panthéistes qui traversent l'antiquité, ils concernent le problème de l'existence de Dieu et n'intéressent pas directement celui de l'unicité divine.

II. Thomas d'Aquin

Dès le *Scriptum super Sententiis* (1253-1256), le problème de l'unicité divine est abordé trois fois expressément. Analysons sommairement ces trois articles, de manière à bien situer la position de S. Thomas au début de sa carrière.

Utrum Deus sit tantum unus[3]

Les objections sont construites sur de jolis sophismes. (1) D'une cause unique et simple ne procède qu'un seul effet; or les perfections de l'univers sont multiples; il est donc logique de les attribuer à des divinités multiples, comme l'ont fait les polythéistes païens. (2) Un être parfait se reproduit. (3) Plus on s'éloigne de la matière indifférenciée, plus les formes se multiplient et se diversifient; la pluralité maximale doit donc se trouver en Dieu, qui est le plus éloigné de la matière.

---

[3] Thomas de Aquino, *Scriptum super libros Sententiarum*, 1, dist. 2, q. 1, a. 1; éd. P. Mandonnet (Paris, 1929), 1: 59-61.

Les arguments en faveur de l'unicité ne sont pas moins suggestifs. (1) Les degrés d'être impliquent l'existence de l'Être suprême unique, dont tous les autres participent. (2) S'il existait plusieurs dieux spécifiquement distincts, un seul pourrait être parfait, les autres différant nécessairement du premier par privation de quelque perfection. Si ces dieux étaient numériquement distincts, ils devraient comporter la matière (principe d'individuation) ou quelque autre puissance. (3) Un être dans lequel l'*esse* et l'*essentia* s'identifient ne peut être participé[4] et multiplié, car la participation implique que la même essence abstraite (*eadem secundum rationem*) soit reçue dans divers existants (*non secundum idem esse*); or en Dieu l'*esse* ne peut être distinct de l'*essentia*, sinon son *esse* serait reçu et dépendrait d'une cause.

Chose curieuse, la solution tient en cinq lignes. Comme le dit Denys, toute multitude procède de l'unité. Il faut donc que la multitude des êtres qui forment l'univers soit ramenée à un seul principe de tous les êtres, qui est Dieu. C'est, en effet, ce que la foi suppose et ce que la raison démontre.

Il semble que "ce que la raison démontre" doit être cherché dans les *Contra* présentés ci-dessus et dans les réponses aux objections, dont voici le résumé. (1) Les perfections créées forment un ordre de subordination et dépendent donc d'un principe unique. Même si ces perfections n'étaient pas subordonnées, l'unicité du Premier Principe ne serait pas exclue, car ce qui est un dans le principe peut être multiple dans ses effets: le principe précontient éminemment les perfections de ses effets. (2) La perfection de l'essence divine exclut la reproduction, car l'être produit serait dépendant de sa cause et comporterait, de ce fait, une certaine potentialité; il ne serait donc pas un second Dieu.[5] D'ailleurs ce qui est perfection dans la créature n'est pas nécessairement perfection pour le Créateur, comme l'agressivité furieuse (*esse furibundum*) est qualité pour le chien, mais serait indigne de l'homme. (3) L'unicité de la matière tient au fait qu'elle est pure puissance, tandis que l'unicité divine tient au fait que Dieu est acte pur.

Essayons de résumer l'apport de cet article. Le principe invoqué dans la brève solution s'appuie sur l'autorité de Denys; ce postulat devrait être démontré. Les considérations développées dans les *Contra* et dans les réponses aux objections ne sont pas sans valeur, mais elles restent assez sommaires. On peut y discerner l'esquisse de six preuves de l'unicité divine:

---

[4] Le terme "participé" est ici synonyme de "multiplié."
[5] On s'attendrait ici à une allusion à la génération du Fils dans la Trinité: c'est la plus parfaite génération concevable et elle ne compromet pas l'unicité de la nature divine.

– Les degrés d'être dans les créatures révèlent l'existence de l'Être le plus parfait et unique (c'est déjà le thème de la *Quarta via*).

– Dieu étant être par essence, il n'est pas multipliable.

– L'ordre de l'univers révèle l'unicité de sa Cause première.

– Dieu est unique parce qu'il est acte pur.

À ces arguments positifs s'ajoutent des arguments *ab absurdo*:

– S'il existait plusieurs dieux, un seul serait parfait.

– Dieu ne saurait créer un effet semblable à lui, car cet effet serait nécessairement moins parfait que sa cause.

Utrum Deus possit dici unus[6]

Il s'agit, dans cette *Distinctio*, de la valeur des mots dont nous nous servons pour parler de Dieu. Le mot *unus* désigne ici l'unité et non l'unicité. Cet article ne concerne donc pas directement notre problème, mais on notera que l'unicité refait surface dans le premier *Contra*, car c'est bien de cela qu'il s'agit dans le texte du *Deutéronome*: "Écoute, Israël, le Seigneur ton Dieu est le Dieu unique." La réponse *Ad primum* nous intéresse également, car S. Thomas y distingue l'unité métaphysique (l'indivision, qui convient à Dieu comme à tout être et lui convient même éminemment) et l'unité numérique ou quantitative; celle-ci ne peut être attribuée proprement à Dieu en tant qu'elle relève du genre quantité; toutefois certains caractères de l'unité numérique appartiennent à Dieu, comme l'indivisibilité et le fait d'être fondement de toute mensuration: absolument simple, Dieu est absolument indivisible; comme Créateur, il est la cause exemplaire et la mesure suprême de toute chose, y compris les nombres.[7] S. Thomas ajoute: *vel aliquid huiusmodi*; on pourrait observer ici qu'il existe un trait commun à l'unité numérique et à l'unicité: c'est l'opposition à "plusieurs": comme le nombre *un* s'oppose à tous les autres, qui sont tous "plusieurs," l'être unique exclut tout autre être de même nature.[8] L'opposition à "plusieurs" est donc un troisième caractère de l'unité numérique qui est attribuable à Dieu.

---

[6] Thomas de Aquino, *Scriptum super libros Sententiarum*, 1, dist. 24, q. 1, a. 1; éd. Mandonnet, 1: 574-577.

[7] Le genre "quantité" est évidemment étranger à Dieu. Mais la différence spécifique qui définit l'"unité" *ad perfectionem pertinet*; elle possède des caractères qui sont attribuables à Dieu.

[8] On voit qu'il faut distinguer avec soin l'*unité métaphysique* (indivision), l'*unité numérique* ou *quantitative* (principe du nombre) et l'*unicité* (exclusion de la pluralité). S. Thomas ne distingue pas toujours clairement unité et unicité. Cf. Van Steenberghen *Le problème*, p. 300.

Utrum sint plura prima principia[9]

Cette fois nous retrouvons expressément le thème de l'unicité divine et c'est l'objection dualiste qui s'affirme d'abord: puisqu'il existe un *Summum bonum*, il semble qu'il doit exister aussi un *Summum malum*, en vertu du principe d'Aristote: si un contraire existe dans la nature, l'autre existe aussi. L'objection dualiste revient sous des formes légèrement différentes dans les *Videtur* 2 et 3. Les *Videtur* 4 et 5 s'appuient sur l'existence, dans le monde, de multiples contraires et d'une extrême variété, ces faits paraissant exclure l'existence d'une Cause unique.

Le premier *Sed contra* reprend le principe-postulat énoncé dans la brève solution du premier article analysé plus haut: l'unité précède toute multitude, car la pluralité naît de l'unité. Le deuxième déclare que, s'il existait plusieurs premiers principes, il devraient être composés, or aucun composé n'est premier. Le troisième est plus compliqué: par une série de disjonctions, S. Thomas tend à prouver qu'une dualité de premiers principes est impossible.

Dans le corps de l'article, il propose trois arguments pour démontrer que le Principe absolument premier doit être unique. Le premier est basé sur l'ordre de l'univers: cet ordre suppose l'existence d'un Bien suprême vers lequel tendent tous les êtres. Le deuxième s'appuie sur la nature des êtres: les natures diffèrent en perfection, mais aucune ne s'identifie à son *esse*, car toutes peuvent être pensées sans qu'on sache si elles existent; leur *esse* est donc reçu et il faut remonter finalement à un Être dont la nature s'identifie à son *esse* (*cuius natura sit ipsum suum esse*) et qui est la cause unique de tous les autres; car l'être (*natura entitatis*) est commun à tous les êtres d'une manière analogique et cette unité des êtres causés requiert l'unicité de la cause. Tel est l'argument d'Avicenne. La troisième preuve est fondée sur l'immatérialité divine: Aristote démontre que la cause motrice du ciel doit être immatérielle; or la diversité des êtres immatériels ne peut provenir que d'une différence de perfection ou d'actualité et au sommet de cette hiérarchie il ne peut exister qu'un seul Acte pur, duquel procède tout ce qui est mêlé de puissance.

Le corps de l'article s'achève en un aperçu historique assez suggestif, dans lequel S. Thomas dénonce trois erreurs contraires à l'unicité du Premier Principe. Celle des *primi naturales* (les présocratiques), qui ont professé le matérialisme et ont affirmé l'existence de plusieurs premiers principes matériels. Celle des dualistes: Empédocle (l'Amitié et la Haine),

---

[9] Thomas de Aquino, *Scriptum super libros Sententiarum*, 2, dist. 1, q. 1, a. 1; éd. Mandonnet, 2: 10-16.

Pythagore (le Bien et le Mal), qui est à l'origine de l'hérésie des Mani-
chéens. Enfin celle d'Anaxagore et de Platon, qui distinguent deux absolus: la Matière (incausée) et l'Agent (l'Intelligence) qui ordonne le chaos.
Platon ajoute toutefois un troisième principe absolu: les Formes séparées,
exemplaires des choses corporelles.

La réponse aux objections dualistes est importante. Sans pouvoir ana-
lyser dans le détail ce long exposé, j'en relève les idées principales. Le mal
absolu est impossible car tout être est bon au moins en tant qu'être. Rien
ne s'oppose directement au Bien absolu. Aucun agent ne poursuit le mal
directement (*per se*) car le mal est une privation et celle-ci ne peut être le
terme d'une tendance. Il n'est pas vrai que le mal est plus répandu que le
bien: s'il s'agit du mal physique (*malum naturae*), il n'atteint qu'une
infime partie de l'univers, puisque le ciel en est exempt et est de loin la
partie la plus vaste du monde corporel; s'il s'agit du mal moral (*malum
culpae*), la majorité des anges est demeurée fidèle; quant aux hommes, des
distinctions s'imposent et finalement, si un homme est vraiment homme,
c'est-à-dire s'il décide d'agir selon les jugements de sa raison, il agira le
plus souvent bien et ses défaillances seront exceptionnelles; mais il est vrai
que beaucoup d'hommes s'attachent surtout à leur nature inférieure et se
laissent attirer par les jouissances sensibles; l'homme qui accepte cette
déchéance subit une véritable aliénation (*efficitur quasi alius*) et se met au
niveau des animaux.

Aux deux dernières objections S. Thomas répond que les "contrariétés"
et la diversité sont dues aux causes prochaines. Mais si l'on considère
l'ensemble de l'univers, on aperçoit une harmonie essentielle entre les
êtres et leur ordination à une fin ultime unique. Ainsi Dieu est à la fois
l'Agent premier, l'Exemplaire et la Fin dernière du monde créé.

Il était nécessaire de s'arrêter assez longuement au premier ouvrage de
S. Thomas. Nous pourrons être plus brefs dans la suite, nous bornant à
relever les idées nouvelles qui apparaîtront dans ses écrits ultérieurs.

Pour le *De ente et essentia* (vers 1254), il faut rappeler l'essai de démonstration de l'existence de Dieu qui se lit au chapitre 4, car il conclut à
l'existence de l'*Esse subsistens*, évidemment unique puisqu'il exclut toute
essentia limitatrice et est donc l'Être non-fini ou infini, qui ne s'oppose à
rien et qui est la plénitude de la perfection ontologique.

Le thème de l'unicité est abondamment traité au chapitre 1.42 de la
Summa contra gentiles (1259-1264). On n'y trouve pas moins de seize
arguments en faveur de l'unicité, presque tous présentés assez sommairement. Je dois me borner à une simple énumération, qui sera suivie de
quelques réflexions.

1. Il ne peut exister deux Biens suprêmes.

2. Il ne peut exister plusieurs êtres absolument parfaits, car ils ne sauraient se distinguer.

3. L'ordre de l'univers se réalise suffisamment par un seul Principe premier; or une seule cause vaut mieux que plusieurs.

4. Le Premier Moteur doit être unique pour que le premier mouvement (celui du premier ciel) soit un, continu et régulier.

5. Tous les mouvements des êtres corporels dépendent du premier mouvement, qui a pour fin le Premier Moteur, substance spirituelle. Donc les autres substances spirituelles doivent aussi dépendre du Premier Moteur.

6. L'ordre qui existe entre les êtres de la nature implique que ces êtres soient ordonnés à une fin unique. Notre monde est donc gouverné par un seul Principe d'ordre. Mais il n'existe pas d'autre monde que le nôtre (ceci est affirmé sans aucun essai de preuve). Il n'existe donc qu'un Ordonnateur de l'univers, que nous appelons Dieu.

7. Il est impossible que plusieurs êtres nécessaires existent, car ils devraient se distinguer par autre chose que la nécessité d'exister.

8. Autre développement, cette fois très étendu, du même argument.

9. S'il existait deux dieux, ils ne pourraient se distinguer sans être composés de *natura* et d'*esse*, ce qui est exclu de l'Être divin.

10. La nécessité d'exister convient à l'Être nécessaire en raison de son individualité. Elle ne saurait donc convenir à un autre individu.

11. La nature divine est de soi individualisée, sinon il y aurait composition en Dieu. Dès lors cette nature n'est pas communicable à un autre.

12. S'il existait plusieurs dieux, la nature divine ne saurait être numériquement une en chacun. Il faudrait donc un principe d'individuation distinct de cette nature, ce qui est exclu par la simplicité divine.

13. L'*esse* propre de chaque chose est unique. Or Dieu s'identifie avec son *esse*. Il est donc impossible qu'il existe plusieurs dieux.

14. L'unité d'une chose est mesurée par son être. Or la nature divine est souverainement être. Elle est donc souverainement une.

15. En chaque genre on trouve un premier qui est la mesure de tous les êtres contenus dans le genre. Or tous les êtres ont en commun l'être. Il faut donc qu'il existe un Être premier, principe unique de tous les êtres.

16. En tout gouvernement, celui qui commande désire l'unité: aussi la monarchie est-elle la meilleure forme de gouvernement, comme nous avons une tête unique pour tous les membres du corps. Cela montre à l'évidence que l'unité est due à celui qui gouverne. C'est pourquoi Dieu, qui est la cause de tous les autres êtres, doit être reconnu comme absolument unique.

Au terme de cette longue énumération de preuves, S. Thomas en appelle à l'autorité des livres saints, puis il rejette sommairement les erreurs du paganisme et surtout le dualisme manichéen. Il attribue aussi un certain dualisme aux Ariens, qui, forcés par l'Écriture de reconnaître la divinité du Fils, ont vu en lui un Dieu subordonné au Père, Dieu suprême.

La lecture de ce long chapitre est assez décevante: on a l'impression d'une rédaction hâtive, au cours de laquelle l'auteur accumule pêle-mêle une longue série d'arguments de valeur très inégale. Quelques-uns sont groupés sur la base de leur affinité (1-2, 4-5, 7-8, 10-12), mais on n'aperçoit aucun principe d'ordre pour l'ensemble du chapitre.

Une preuve de l'existence de Dieu basée sur l'ordre de l'univers est esquissée à la fin du chapitre 1.13: *Ad hoc etiam*. Cette preuve conclut à l'existence d'un Ordonnateur unique.

Au chapitre 2.15, S. Thomas montre que Dieu est cause d'être pour tous les êtres limités. Le premier argument (*Omne enim ...*) fournit les éléments d'une preuve rigoureuse de l'existence de Dieu et de son unicité.[10] Nous la retrouverons dans le *De potentia* (1265-1267).

Dans ces importantes questions disputées, l'unicité divine est déjà traitée implicitement en 3.5: *Utrum possit esse aliquid quod non sit a Deo creatum*. La réponse est négative et trois preuves sont proposées. La première, qui est la meilleure, conclut à l'existence de la Cause infinie et unique en partant de la similitude ontologique des êtres finis. La deuxième annonce la *Quarta via* de la *Summa theologiae* et conclut à l'existence de l'Être souverainement parfait. La troisième s'élève des êtres composés d'*esse* et d'*essentia* à l'Être unique qui est acte pur, sans essence limitatrice.[11]

Le très long article 6 reprend le thème déjà rencontré dans le *Scriptum super Sententiis* et dans la *Summa contra gentiles*: *Utrum sit unum tantum creationis principium*. On y trouve 26 *Videtur* et l'on constate avec surprise que les 21 premiers et le 23ᵉ s'appuient sur l'existence du mal et tendent à justifier le dualisme. Les quatre autres essaient d'établir que Dieu ne peut être la cause des réalités composées (22, *ab uno simplici non procedit nisi simplex*) ni des corps corruptibles (24-26). À ces 26 *Videtur* S. Thomas oppose 3 *Sed contra*: l'Écriture atteste que Dieu est l'unique créateur de tout; le mal est enraciné dans la nature du bien; Aristote prouve qu'un seul Premier Moteur meut tous les êtres sans exception.

---

[10] Cf. Van Steenberghen, *Le problème*, pp. 130-131.
[11] Ibid., pp. 139-143.

La *solutio* commence par un exposé historique. Trois déficiences y sont dénoncées, qui sont à l'origine du dualisme: conception étriquée des contraires, mise sur pied d'égalité des contraires, méconnaissance de l'ordre universel. Ensuite trois arguments sont proposés pour établir l'unicité du Premier Principe.[12] Le premier développe la preuve déjà formulée à l'article précédent. Lorsqu'une perfection commune se retrouve dans des êtres divers, il faut en rendre compte par une cause unique; or l'être est commun à tout ce qui existe; il existe donc un Être unique, cause de tous les autres; mais l'être est bon, car tous les êtres ont l'appétit de l'être. Deuxième argument: tout agent agit selon qu'il est en acte; or le mal n'est pas acte, mais privation; c'est pourquoi rien n'agit en tant qu'il est mauvais; le mal ne saurait donc être principe créateur des choses mauvaises. Troisième argument: l'ordre de l'univers implique l'unicité du Premier Principe; cet ordre ne peut résulter du hasard,[13] car ce qui a lieu par hasard ne se produit que rarement, alors que l'ordre de l'univers est réalisé toujours (dans le monde supérieur des sphères célestes) ou le plus souvent (dans le monde sublunaire).

Le chapitre 1.15 du *Compendium theologiae* (1265-1267) aborde le problème de l'unicité divine. Il est utile de s'arrêter à ce bref chapitre car, dans cet écrit qui résume la doctrine catholique, S. Thomas retient les arguments qui lui paraissent les meilleurs. Trois preuves sont sommairement développées. (1) S'il existait plusieurs dieux, ils devraient appartenir à un genre commun ou à une espèce commune; or il a été démontré que Dieu n'est ni un genre, ni une espèce. (2) L'essence divine est individualisée de soi et donc incommunicable. (3) Une forme n'est multipliable que par des différences spécifiques ou par des différences individuelles; or l'*Esse subsistens* exclut toute addition de différences.[14]

En ce qui concerne la *Summa theologiae* (*Prima pars*, 1266-1268), je me bornerai à quelques brèves remarques, car j'ai étudié ailleurs l'article consacré à l'unicité divine.[15] La *Prima via* ne conclut légitimement à l'existence d'un unique Premier Moteur que si l'on admet la cosmographie périmée d'Aristote.[16] La *Quarta via* conclut à l'existence du *Maxime ens*

---

[12] S. Thomas écrit: "tribus rationibus ostenditur *ad praesens*." Il paraît soucieux de noter que sa démonstration n'est pas exhaustive.

[13] L'édition Marietti (Turin, 1949) écrit deux fois *casualiter* au lieu de *causaliter* dans le texte de la *Tertia ratio* (p. 52).

[14] Sur ce chapitre du *Compendium theologiae*, cf. Van Steenberghen, *Le problème*, p. 316.

[15] Ibid., pp. 297-303.

[16] Ibid., p. 178.

unique, mais la démonstration n'est pas rigoureuse.[17] La *Quinta via* démontre l'existence d'une Intelligence à l'origine de la biosphère, mais ne prouve pas que cette Intelligence est la cause créatrice unique de l'ordre des êtres finis.[18] Le problème de l'unicité divine est traité ex professo en 11.3; on y lit trois arguments, qui s'appuient respectivement sur la simplicité divine, la perfection infinie de Dieu et l'unité du monde; le deuxième seul est rigoureux, mais il peut être simplifié.[19]

Notons enfin que, dans la dernière leçon du commentaire *In Metaphysicam* (1270-1272), on trouve des considérations sur l'ordre de l'univers qui rappellent les exposés antérieurs de S. Thomas sur ce thème.[20]

Essayons maintenant de formuler les conclusions qui se dégagent de cette enquête rapide. S. Thomas résume parfois sa pensée par l'axiome "Toute multitude procède de l'unité." Est-ce pour lui un premier principe évident? Il ne semble pas, puisqu'il propose de multiples preuves du monothéisme. Lorsqu'on tente de les classer, on peut discerner quelques lignes de pensée dominantes.

1. Le Premier Moteur est unique. Cette preuve est insuffisante à nos yeux, d'abord parce qu'elle suppose la cosmographie géocentrique d'Aristote, ensuite parce que le Premier Moteur n'est pas le Créateur.[21]

2. L'ordre de l'univers implique l'unicité de sa cause. Cette preuve n'est pas non plus rigoureuse. Comment prouver que l'univers matériel constitue un ordre unique? Comment savoir si rien n'existe en dehors de ce que nous connaissons? Comment montrer que l'ordre de l'univers (y compris éventuellement des êtres immatériels) requiert une cause créatrice?[22]

3. Plusieurs arguments s'appuient sur l'individualité et la simplicité divines et reviennent à ceci: ce qui constitue l'individualité d'un être est incommunicable; or Dieu étant simple, il n'y a rien en lui qui soit distinct de ce qui constitue son individualité. Si la simplicité divine est établie, ces arguments sont valables. Toutefois ils excluent seulement la possibilité de plusieurs dieux *de même espèce*; ils ne prouvent pas qu'il ne peut exister plusieurs Absolus totalement indépendants.

4. On trouve dans le *De potentia* (3.6) une preuve basée sur la critique du dualisme. S. Thomas montre fort bien qu'on ne peut mettre sur pied

---

[17] Ibid., pp. 212-228.
[18] Ibid., pp. 234-235.
[19] Ibid., pp. 297-303.
[20] Ibid., pp. 271-272.
[21] Ibid., pp. 177-180.
[22] Ibid., p. 302.

d'égalité le bien et le mal; mais la preuve suppose établi qu'il existe une Cause unique du bien; le monothéisme est donc déjà acquis pour ce qui concerne le bien.

5. Reste une longue série de preuves, assez variées dans leur formulation, mais qui ont en commun leur caractère strictement métaphysique. Tantôt on passe des degrés d'être au *Maxime ens*. Tantôt on oppose les être finis, composés d'*esse* et d'*essentia*, à l'Être infini, *Esse subsistens*. Tantôt on oppose la *natura entitatis*, commune à tous les êtres limités, aux essences multiples et diverses. Tantôt on oppose à l'Acte pur unique ou à l'Être parfait les êtres imparfaits, composés d'acte et de puissance. Toutes ces démonstrations ne sont pas rigoureuses dans leur forme. La meilleure est celle qui, partant de la similitude ontologique des êtres finis, opposés par leurs essences, conclut à l'existence de l'Être infini.

Bref, soumis à de multiples influences, Thomas d'Aquin ne semble pas avoir surmonté pleinement une certaine confusion. Il n'a pas mis en pleine lumière le seul argument rigoureux, qui consiste à déduire l'unicité divine de l'infinité: Être infini, Dieu est nécessairement unique, car, s'il existait plusieurs dieux, ils s'opposeraient et seraient donc finis.[23]

III. Siger de Brabant

Thomas d'Aquin venait de quitter Paris et allait bientôt terminer sa carrière lorsque maître Siger entreprit de commenter la *Métaphysique* (vers 1273). Il y aborde à plusieurs reprises la question du monothéisme et il est captivant de voir comment cet aristotélicien fervent, ouvert toutefois à d'autres influences, notamment à celle de Proclus et à celle de Thomas d'Aquin, traite ce problème, dont il saisit parfaitement l'importance. L'intérêt de ces textes se trouve accru du fait que nous possédons maintenant les deux reportations parallèles de Munich (M) et de Cambridge (C), entre lesquelles de notables différences peuvent être relevées.[24] Voici comment les choses se présentent.

Le problème est abordé une première fois en 2.8, dans les deux reportations. Le titre est différent dans la forme: *Utrum semper existentia possint habere principium* (M); *Utrum sempiterna habeant causam*

---

[23] Ibid., pp. 300-303.
[24] La reportation découverte à Munich, éditée par le P. Graiff en 1948, a été rééditée, après diligente révision, par M. W. Dunphy, *Siger de Brabant. Quaestiones in Metaphysicam*, Philosophes médiévaux 24 (Louvain-la-Neuve, 1981). La reportation de Cambridge, découverte par le P. A. Maurer, sera éditée par lui prochainement (Philosophes médiévaux 25).

efficientem (C). La structure des deux questions est tout à fait parallèle, mais les différences rédactionnelles sont assez considérables.

Le problème est repris au livre 3, mais ici les divergences entre M et C s'accentuent. En M, Siger revient jusqu'à trois fois au problème du monothéisme. D'abord en 3.7: *Utrum in intelligentiis possint esse duo prima*. Ensuite à la question 8, séparée de la précédente par un *Commentum* (commentaire littéral) et annoncée en ces termes par une note marginale: *Redit ad dubitationem prius motam*; titre de la question: *Utrum sit una causa effectiva omnium*. Enfin à la question 12: *Utrum omnium sit causa una*; cette fois Siger lui-même annonce la reprise: *Considerationem nostram posuimus ....* En C, une seule question (3.5) correspond aux trois questions de M et l'intitulé rappelle celui des questions 8 et 12 de M: *Utrum omnium effectuum sit una causa effectiva prima*.[25]

Ces données posent évidemment le problème plus général des relations entre M et C. Sont-ce deux reportations du même cours ou s'agit-il de deux cours différent14s? Lorsque j'ai publié *Maître Siger de Brabant* en 1977, je n'avais pas étudié personnellement la question des rapports entre les quatre textes retrouvés des leçons de Siger sur la *Métaphysique*. Je me suis borné à mentionner les opinions des érudits et c'est ce qui explique la divergence que M. Dunphy a relevée entre la p. 96 (où je reprends la thèse de M. Duin) et la p. 185 (où je cite l'opinion du P. Dondaine et du P. Bataillon, adoptée depuis par M. Dunphy lui-même). Nous serons bientôt en possession du texte intégral de C grâce à l'édition du P. Maurer et nous disposerons ainsi des quatre reportations en édition critique. Alors seulement la comparaison minutieuse des textes sera possible et je n'ai donc pas l'intention de traiter ici le problème dans son ensemble. Je voudrais seulement apporter une modeste contribution à ce travail à propos des questions relatives au monothéisme.

Voici mes conclusions actuelles après examen des textes.[26] En ce qui concerne la question 8 du livre 2, les différences rédactionnelles sont-elles dues aux deux reportateurs du même cours? Je n'oserais l'exclure, mais il me paraît plus vraisemblable que C reflète un autre cours, dans lequel Siger a lui-même modifié la présentation de ses idées. On notera que, même dans cette hypothèse, des divergences rédactionnelles peuvent

---

[25] La reportation de Godefroid de Fontaines (P) contient un résumé de la q. 2.8 (Graiff, pp. 48-50). Cette reportation sera rééditée dans le volume du P. Maurer qui est sous presse. Mais P ne donne rien qui corresponde aux questions du livre 3 (7, 8 et 12 pour M, 5 pour C).

[26] Je renvoie à l'édition de Dunphy pour M et à celle de Maurer pour C.

encore être le fait des reportateurs; dès lors, même si C paraît meilleur dans l'ensemble, certains passages peuvent être moins corrects en raison de défaillances du reportateur. Quant au livre 3, si M et C sont des reportations du même cours, il faut admettre (avec M. Duin) que l'étudiant reportateur de C a entrepris lui-même un travail de refonte des textes, groupant en une seule question de C les matériaux contenus en trois questions de M. Cela me paraît invraisemblable pour deux raisons. D'abord le regroupement des matériaux s'accompagne de nombreuses modifications rédactionnelles, qui impliquent parfois une évolution assez nette dans la pensée. Je n'en relève ici qu'un exemple particulièrement suggestif. En M, la question 7 s'achève sur une note plutôt sceptique.[27] Cette réserve a disparu dans le passage parallèle de C, où il est dit fermement que le *perfectissimum* est *ens per essentiam*, tous les autres l'étant *per participationem*.[28] Ensuite chacune des deux reportations possède des questions qui sont absentes dans l'autre. D'après une première enquête portant surtout sur les titres des questions, la situation est la suivante:

Questions propres à M	Questions propres à C
2.13	2.10, 12, 14 à 19, 26
3.1, 2, 3, 14, 26	3.10, 11, 13, 15, 17, 19, 23, 26
4.27	4.1, 2
5.11 et 16	5.10 à 13

M s'arrêtant brusquement au cours du *Commentum* qui suit la question 5.22, la comparaison est exclue à partir de 5.23 de C.

Peut-on imaginer que chacun des deux reportateurs ait laissé tomber une série de questions traitées par le maître, alors qu'il s'agit parfois de questions d'un vif intérêt, par exemple 3.1 en M et 4.1-2 en C? Il est beaucoup plus plausible d'attribuer à Siger lui-même le choix des questions qu'il voulait traiter, ce choix dépendant de contingences personnelles que nous ignorons.

Venons-en maintenant à l'examen des doctrines. Puisque j'ai déjà étudié les questions de M dans des travaux antérieurs, je donnerai ici un aperçu des positions défendues en C.[29]

---

[27] "Verum est quod dicit Averroes quod ad hanc conclusionem rationes Avicennae non excedunt probabiles rationes" (Dunphy, p. 99, lignes 75-76).

[28] Ed. Maurer, 3.5, p. 85, lignes 77-82.

[29] On trouvera une analyse des textes de M dans F. Van Steenberghen, *Maître Siger de Brabant*, Philosophes médiévaux 21 (Louvain-Paris, 1977), pp. 296-301. Ces pages reproduisent substantiellement une communication faite en 1961 au congrès de Cologne

2.8. Un passage de la *Métaphysique* suggère à son exégète la question de savoir si les êtres éternels (les sphères célestes et les substances séparées qui les meuvent) ont une cause efficiente. Il semble que non, car la cause efficiente est principe de mouvement et de transformation, or les êtres éternels ne sont pas sujets à transformation. De plus, ce qui a une cause efficiente peut être et ne pas être, or les êtres éternels sont nécessaires. Enfin ce qui a une cause efficiente peut disparaître si la cause disparaît, or les êtres éternels n'ont aucune puissance à ne pas être.

En admettant que certains être distincts du Premier Être sont éternels, leur éternité n'exclut pas qu'ils soient causés. Car il faut distinguer la cause efficiente qui transforme et celle qui donne l'être; la première seule a un effet nécessairement temporel. Il n'y a donc pas contradiction entre être éternel et être causé. Mais cela ne suffit pas à prouver qu'il existe des êtres éternels causés: Pythagore admettait l'existence de plusieurs principes éternels indépendants (*inconnexa*). Si toutefois on démontre que tous les êtres de l'univers procèdent d'une Cause première unique, il faut reconnaître que tous les autres êtres éternels sont causés. Proclus a tenté cette démonstration, mais il a prouvé seulement que tout effet dépend d'une cause première, il n'a pas prouvé que tous les effets dépendent de la même cause première. Cependant Aristote a démontré contre Pythagore qu'une pluralité de principes indépendants est impossible, car l'univers est naturellement ordonné de la meilleure manière, or la meilleure ordination d'une multitude requiert un principe unique.

On répondra aux objections que la cause des êtres éternels n'est pas une cause qui transforme; que les êtres éternels ne sont pas contingents, mais nécessaires de leur nature (*ex se formaliter*), bien qu'ils soient causés (*ex alio effective*); enfin que la cause des êtres nécessaires est elle-même nécessaire de soi et ne peut donc pas disparaître.

3.5. Siger rappelle d'abord qu'il a démontré au livre 2 la dépendance de tout effet vis-à-vis d'une cause première. Il s'agit maintenant d'établir que tous les effets dépendent d'une Cause première unique. Diverses voies ont été proposées, mais aucune ne permet de savoir si les substances séparées sont causées ou incausées: elles ne dépendent certes pas d'une *causa fieri*, mais elles pourraient dépendre d'une *causa esse*. Nous n'avons aucun moyen direct de trancher la question, car les effets de ces substances ne sont pas intermittents, elles n'ont en elles rien d'accidentel et nous ne connaissons pas l'essence de leur Cause éventuelle. Pourtant Aristote,

---

et publiée en 1963 dans les actes de ce congrès: *Le problème de l'unicité divine dans la métaphysique de Siger de Brabant*, Miscellanea mediaevalia 2 (Berlin, 1963), pp. 441-445.

Avicenne, Proclus et presque tous les Péripatéticiens professent qu'il existe une seule cause efficiente de l'univers. Bien entendu, l'autorité ne suffit pas à découvrir la vérité, mais ces philosophes ont été mus eux-mêmes par des raisons; pourquoi ne chercherions-nous pas à les trouver comme eux? Notons enfin que celui qui refuse d'adhérer aux principes évidents sous prétexte qu'ils ne sont pas aussi certains que les données des sens, se trompe et ne parviendra jamais à la connaissance d'une conclusion vraie. Toutes les voies proposées jusqu'ici étant insuffisantes, il faut en trouver de nouvelles.[30]

Siger en expose neuf.

1. La première part de la considération du Premier Moteur. On peut établir l'existence d'un Premier Moteur unique dans notre univers et Aristote a suffisamment réfuté l'hypothèse d'un monde distinct du nôtre. Mais cela ne prouve pas que ce Premier Moteur est la cause efficiente de tous les autres êtres, car on peut être premier en perfection sans l'être dans l'ordre de la causalité efficiente. Toutefois il y a lieu de distinguer "plus parfait" (*perfectius*) et "le plus parfait" (*perfectissimum*): ce qui est plus parfait et ce qui est moins parfait sont tous deux des êtres par participation, tandis que le plus parfait est être par essence; de ce qu'un être par participation n'est pas cause d'un autre être tel il ne suit pas que l'être par essence n'est pas cause des êtres par participation.

Comment montrer que l'être par essence est cause des autres? Supposons établi qu'il existe dans l'ordre total des êtres un Être premier, le plus parfait, qui est la fin de la quintessence (c'est-à-dire du ciel) et duquel dépendent le ciel et toute la nature, comme le prouve Aristote au livre 12 de la *Métaphysique*. Cet être est donc la fin de tout l'univers. Dès lors on peut raisonner comme suit:

M: Les êtres qui sont ordonnés à une même fin sont ordonnés entre eux.

m: Tous les êtres de l'univers sont ordonnés à la même fin.

C: Tous sont ordonnés entre eux.

Nouveau raisonnement:

M: Les êtres qui sont ordonnés entre eux et à la même fin dépendent nécessairement de la même cause efficiente.

m: Tous les êtres de l'univers sont tels.

C: Tous dépendent de la même cause efficiente.

[30] Cette longue introduction (Maurer, pp. 82-84, lignes 3-54) correspond à celle de M en 3.7, Dunphy, pp. 97-98, lignes 3-47, mais les différences rédactionnelles sont considérables.

La dernière majeure se prouve par la raison et par un exemple. Par la raison: la fin correspond à l'agent, car tout effet est dirigé vers sa fin par un agent; si tous les êtres de l'univers tendent vers la même fin, c'est qu'ils ont reçu leurs natures et leurs formes d'une cause unique. Par un exemple: si tous les soldats d'une armée sont ordonnés entre eux et vers la même fin, qui est le chef, c'est parce que la volonté du chef les a ordonnés de cette manière.

Siger confirme cet argument par un exposé d'Averroès (*Physique*, 2) et par celui d'Aristote à la fin du livre 12 de la *Métaphysique*.[31]

2. La deuxième voie est fondée sur l'analogie de la notion d'être. Tout ce qui se trouve dans les effets leur vient de leur cause. Mais tous les êtres possèdent une manière d'être qui les rapporte à un seul.[32] Donc cela leur vient de leur cause commune unique. En effet, les effets étant proportionnés à leur cause, il est nécessaire que l'unité de la manière d'être de tous les êtres leur vienne de l'unité de leur cause. On ne peut objecter que l'unité de la notion d'être résulte de l'unité de la substance, car il faut expliquer aussi l'analogie des substances entre elles et celle-ci est due à l'unité de leur cause. Il ne suffit pas de dire que toutes les substances imitent un Être suprême, car cette communauté dans l'imitation ne peut s'expliquer que par leur cause commune.[33]

3. La troisième voie exploite la notion d'acte pur.[34] Dans le réel, un seul être est le plus parfait de tous (c'est le Premier Moteur). Or on est parfait selon qu'on est en acte. Donc un seul être est acte pur et tous les autres comportent une certaine dose de puissance. Mais on agit selon qu'on est en acte. Si donc tous les êtres distincts du Premier sont déficients en actualité, ils le sont aussi en causalité. Ceci fonde deux caractères qui se révèlent dans les êtres: (1) Plus on s'éloigne de l'Acte pur, plus la puissance étend son empire: puissance à être et à penser dans les substances séparées (mais cette double puissance est toujours actuée et n'entraîne donc ni succession ni changement); puissance (à être et) *ad ubi* dans les corps célestes; puissance au changement substantiel dans les corps

---

[31] Pour la première voie, cf. Maurer, p. 84, ligne 55 – p. 86, ligne 20; Dunphy, 3.7, pp. 98-99, lignes 48-76 et 3.8, pp. 101-103, lignes 3-69. Mais les deux exposés diffèrent notablement.

[32] Je traduis *ratio essendi* par "manière d'être." C'est un des nombreux sens du terme *ratio* relevés par L. Schütz, *Thomas-Lexikon*, 2ᵉ éd. (Paderborn, 1895). Cf. p. 689 sub o. Ce sens paraît exigé par le contexte.

[33] Pour la deuxième voie, cf. Maurer, pp. 86-87, lignes 21-55; Dunphy, 3.8, p. 103, ligne 70 – p. 104, ligne 17.

[34] On notera que les voies 3 et 4 de M sont interverties en C.

inférieurs. (2) Plus on s'éloigne de l'Acte pur, moins la causalité est universelle: les substances séparées agissent sur tous les corps; les corps célestes agissent sur tous les corps inférieurs; ceux-ci ne causent d'autres êtres que dans les limites de leur espèce.[35]

4. Quatrième voie. Les effets s'opposent entre eux en vertu de leurs causes prochaines et particulières, mais ils sont unis entre eux en vertu de leurs causes plus éloignées et plus universelles: l'homme et le cheval ont des causes prochaines en raison desquelles ils s'opposent, mais ils dépendent l'un et l'autre du soleil. Dès lors, considérés par rapport à la cause la plus universelle et à l'absolument Premier, ils sont unis absolument par cette cause efficiente unique. Cet argument peut être confirmé comme suit: à l'ordre des effets correspond l'ordre des causes; donc des effets divers procèdent de causes diverses et des effets communs procèdent de la même cause; dès lors, puisque l'être est commun à tous les effets, il faut qu'il procède d'une cause unique.[36]

5. Cinquième voie. C'est la preuve d'Avicenne. Lorsque quelque chose est commun à deux êtres différents, ce caractère ne peut être essentiel à aucun des deux, car, s'il était essentiel à l'un, il serait exclu de l'autre. Il ne peut donc exister plusieurs êtres auxquels l'être appartiendrait en vertu de leur essence. Objecter à cela et à la preuve précédente que le terme *esse* est équivoque, c'est contredire ce qui a été démontré plus haut: la notion d'être est analogique et l'analogie des êtres est fondée sur l'unicité de leur cause.[37]

6. Sixième voie. Aucun être ayant un être déficient et diminué n'est par soi. Or c'est le cas pour tous les êtres sauf un. Donc un seul être existe par soi. Il résulte de cela que ce qui est tel suprêmement (*maxime tale*) est la cause de tout ce qui est tel à des degrés divers et inversement: ce qui est cause des autres est suprêmement tel.[38]

7. Septième voie. Celle-ci ne diffère des précédentes que par le vocabulaire. Ce qui est par essence est cause de tout ce qui est par participation.

[35] Pour la troisième voie, cf. Maurer, pp. 87-88, lignes 56-85; Dunphy, 3.8, p. 105, lignes 28-44 (*Quarta via*).

[36] Pour la quatrième voie, cf. Maurer, p. 88, lignes 86-99; Dunphy, 3.8, pp. 104-105, lignes 18-27. La confirmation des lignes 94-99 correspond à l'*Alia ratio* de M q. 3.12, p. 109, lignes 10-15. On a ici un nouvel exemple de remaniement qu'on ne peut attribuer à l'étudiant-reportateur.

[37] Pour la cinquième voie, cf. Maurer, p. 88, ligne 100 – p. 89, ligne 27; Dunphy, 3.12, pp. 109-110, lignes 16-40.

[38] Pour la sixième voie, cf. Maurer, pp. 89-90, lignes 28-42; Dunphy, 3.12, p. 110, lignes 41-56.

Or un seul être est par essence. Donc il n'existe qu'une Cause efficiente de tous les autres. Être par participation, c'est être particulièrement ou posséder une partie de l'être; c'est donc être d'une manière déficiente. Par contre, être par essence, c'est posséder totalement la perfection de l'être. L'être par essence est donc le plus parfait de tous et il est la cause de tous les êtres déficients.[39]

8. Huitième voie. Ce qui peut être et ne pas être n'est déterminé à être que par une cause et il faut remonter finalement à un nécessaire par soi. Or celui-ci est unique: en effet, s'il y en avait plusieurs, ils devraient se distinguer par autre chose que la nécessité d'être; il y aurait donc en eux composition et quelque chose d'accidentel, ce qui est exclu du nécessaire par soi.[40]

9. Neuvième voie. C'est l'argument de Proclus. S'il n'y a pas de causes, rien n'est connaissable. S'il y en a, ou bien elles remontent à l'infini et, de nouveau, rien n'est connaissable; ou bien elles forment cercle et alors la même chose est pour elle-même meilleure (comme cause) et moins bonne (comme effet); ou bien il faut s'arrêter à une cause première, et cela dans chaque genre de causes. Faut-il remonter à une cause unique? Proclus l'a prouvé plus haut comme suit. Si toute multitude n'est pas seconde par rapport à l'un, ou bien elle est antérieure par nature à l'un, ou bien elle lui est égale par nature. La première hypothèse est exclue, car le multiple participe de l'un et ne saurait donc lui être antérieur par nature. La seconde hypothèse est également exclue, car, dans ce cas, le multiple serait un sans participer à l'un, ce qui est impossible.[41]

La place me fait défaut pour procéder à la discussion de chacune de ces voies, pour comparer en détail les textes parallèles de M et de C, enfin pour essayer de déterminer dans quelle mesure Siger dépend de Thomas d'Aquin: il y a une parenté indéniable entre certains des arguments proposés ici et certaines pages de S. Thomas; et nous savons par ailleurs que Siger connaissait plusieurs écrits de son éminent collègue théologien et qu'il avait pour lui grande estime. Je dois me borner ici à quelques réflexions.

---

[39] Pour la septième voie, cf. Maurer, p. 90, lignes 43-55; Dunphy, 3.12, pp. 110-111, lignes 57-68.
[40] Pour la huitième voie, cf; Maurer, p. 90, ligne 56 – p. 91, ligne 5; Dunphy, 3.12, pp. 111-112, lignes 69-15.
[41] Pour la neuvième voie, cf. Maurer, pp. 91-92, lignes 6-28; Dunphy, 3.12, pp. 112-113, lignes 16-48.

Une première impression se dégage de l'examen des textes: Siger a bien profité de ses lectures des écrits de Thomas d'Aquin. Il a laissé tomber ce qui était moins solide et a repris ce qui était le meilleur. Le contraste est assez saisissant entre les seize "preuves" hétéroclites de la *Summa contra gentiles* (1.42) et les neuf voies que Siger propose en C. Toutes se situent au niveau de la réflexion métaphysique: même celle qui part du Premier Moteur dépasse manifestement les perspectives du Stagirite par une réflexion assez pénétrante sur la finalité.

On aura remarqué que la critique du dualisme manichéen, qui occupe presque tout un long article du *De potentia*, est tout à fait absente des exposés de Siger: il semble avoir aperçu que là n'était pas le problème fondamental de l'unicité divine.

Au delà de formulations encore imparfaites, on aperçoit, dans les textes de Siger, les éléments essentiels de l'authentique preuve métaphysique du monothéisme: à l'origine de tous les êtres finis, déficients, composés de puissance et d'acte, opposés entre eux mais aussi semblables en tant qu'êtres, êtres par participation, il faut reconnaître l'existence d'un Être non-fini ou infini, plénitude d'être, absolu (ou nécessaire par soi); cet être est évidemment unique puisque, plénitude d'être, il ne s'oppose à rien, il n'est limité par rien; on ne peut être distinct de lui qu'en participant à sa souveraine perfection.

On reconnaîtra volontiers que maître Siger a traité le problème du monothéisme en vrai métaphysicien. Chez lui comme chez Thomas d'Aquin, l'expression de la pensée est souvent défectueuse: ils parlent en scolastiques du xiiie siècle et ne dominent pas pleinement les sources variées qu'ils exploitent. Mais au delà du langage qui porte la marque du temps, on aperçoit en eux d'authentiques penseurs.

20

Francisco Araujo, OP, On the Eternal Truths

Norman Wells

Boston College

Among the many strains of pagan Greek wisdom absorbed by Christian wisdom, the tradition of uncreated, eternal essences, attended by necessary eternal truths, has proved to be most resistant to final assimilation.

As a case in point, one may note a persistent paradox within the Augustinian perspective, highlighted by contemporary scholars,[1] and explicitly cited as a difficulty by Matthew of Aquasparta:

> Item, quaero: cum video aliquod verum immutabile, ut "omne totus est maius sua parte" et "septem et tria decem sunt," quid video? Aut aliquid creatum aut aliquid increatum. Non creatum, quoniam nullum creatum immutabile vel aeternum. Non increatum, quia istud video perspicue; Deum videre perspicue est beatum esse. Sed hic non sumus beati, nec quicumque videt est beatus; ergo etc.[2]

---

[1] See A. Maurer, CSB, *Medieval Philosophy* (New York: Random House, 1962; 2nd ed.: Toronto: Pontifical Institute of Medieval Studies, 1982), p. 11: "It is a persistent difficulty for interpreters of St. Augustine to know precisely the nature of these immutable truths. They cannot be creatures, because creatures are mutable and truth is immutable. Neither can they be God himself or his Ideas. For we see the truth, but outside of extraordinary states, such as ecstasy, we cannot see God or his Ideas, which are identical with himself." G. Smith, SJ, *Natural Theology* (New York: Macmillan, 1951), p. 43: "Obviously, anything not God must, if it be at all, be a creature. Any Christian metaphysic must agree to that. Yet the truth of *seven and three are ten* is, according to St. Augustine, neither God nor creature. Just where, in the Christian dichotomy by which whatever is not God is a creature, and whatever is a creature is not God, does *seven and three are ten* fit?

[2] *Quaestiones disputatae De fide et De cognitione: De cognitione*, q. 2, obj. 28 (Quaracchi: Collegium S. Bonaventure, 1951), p. 228.

Graceful Reason: Essays in Ancient and Medieval Philosophy Presented to Joseph Owens, CSSR, ed. Lloyd P. Gerson. Papers in Mediaeval Studies 4 (Toronto: Pontifical Institute of Mediaeval Studies, 1983), pp. 401-417. © P.I.M.S., 1983.

The burden of this dilemma, then, inclines one to acknowledge the eternal truths as some *tertium quid*, other than God and other than creatures.

That just such an influence has been exerted is borne out by the Parisian condemnation of 1241:

> Septimus [error], quod multe veritates sunt ab eterno, que non sunt Deus. Hunc errorem reprobamus, firmiter enim credimus, quod una sola veritas sit ab eterno, que est Deus.[3]

The further fact that, in 1243 and 1256, general chapters of the Dominican Order prescribed these errors to be deleted from all copy books is a graphic witness that this condemned perspective on the eternal truths was still circulating.[4]

At the end of the thirteenth century, Richard of Middleton expressed his misgivings about Henry of Ghent's doctrine on eternal essences, their eternal *esse essentiae*, and the eternal truths attending them. He did so, not only because this position came all too close to Plato's position, but because it approximated the error condemned by William of Auvergne at Paris in 1241. Were the essence of an ass or a lion endowed with an eternal *esse essentiae*, accompanied by eternal essential truths, and were it acknowledged, as it must be, that these essences were not God, then these eternal essential truths are not God.[5] This very text of Richard of Middleton, along with its misgivings about Henry of Ghent's doctrine and the Parisian condemnation of 1241 would be repeated by Dionysius the Carthusian in the fifteenth century.[6]

A distant echo of this refrain will reverberate at Salamanca in the late sixteenth century as Michael de Palacios, confronted with this recalcitrant

[3] *Chartularium Universitatis Parisiensis*, ed. H. Denifle and E. Chatelain, 4 vols. (Paris, 1889-1897), 1:170-172, no. 128. Looking back in medieval thought, this is connected with the teaching of Scotus Erigena on the divine ideas. See P. Duhem, *Le système du monde*, 5 vols. (Paris: Hermann, 1913-1917), 5: 337-340; J. Paulus, *Henri de Gand* (Paris: J. Vrin, 1938), p. 108; E. Gilson, *History of Christian Philosophy in the Middle Ages* (New York: Random House, 1955), p. 773b. See also the comment of J.-D. Robert, OP, *Approche contemporaine d'une affirmation de Dieu* (Bruges: Desclée de Brouwer, 1962), p. 105: "L'histoire de la philosophie et de la théologie, surtout dans une certain tradition dite 'augustinienne' (bien qu'elle ne représente pas la doctrine authentique de saint Augustin), nous montre à l'œuvre une tendance assez persistante et qui consiste à faire du monde des 'vérités éternelles' (ou des 'possibles') un monde 'en soi' et, en quelque sorte, intermédiaire entre le réel contingent et Dieu, la doctrine des 'idées éternelles' de Scot Erigène est un exemple typique de cette tendance, qui peut revêtir milles formes particulières."

[4] See W. A. Hinnebusch, OP, *The History of the Dominican Order* (New York: Alba House, 1973), 2: 121.

[5] The text of Richard of Middleton is from his *Super 4 libros Sententiarum*, 1, d. 35, a. 1, q. 4 (Brixiae, 1591), p. 303 and is cited by J. Paulus, *Henri de Gand*, p. 129, n. 1.

[6] *Opera omnia: In 1 Sent.*, d. 35, q. 2 (Tournai, 1896-1913), 20: 389.

doctrine of eternal essences, will intone: "Scite igitur articulus Parisiensis hanc essentiarum damnavit aeternitatem." [7]

In the early seventeenth century, Martin Meurisse, OFM, will remark somewhat sarcastically on the revival of this doctrine of eternal essences "apud aliquos, alioquin doctos et subtiles, in Universitate Parisiensi...." [8] Finally, in exasperation at the treatment of the God of Abraham, Isaac and Jacob after the fashion of a Jupiter or Saturn, subject to the Styx and the Fates, René Descartes will denounce what he considered to be the blasphemous consequences of the doctrine of uncreated eternal essences and uncreated eternal truths.[9] Hereafter, these essences and their eternal truths will be creatures. In an ironic turnabout, Descartes had arrived at a conclusion which, on its face, reaffirmed the very error condemned at Paris in 1241 – many eternal truths other than God! Whether their status as genuine creatures would render them more acceptable, remains to be seen.

What also remains to be seen in these matters is something of the late Medieval-Renaissance struggles with a strain of positions, not unlike that cited in 1241 at Paris, and which have vigorously resisted the therapy of prior warnings, condemnations and solutions. A significant example of these struggles can be profitably addressed in the instance of a disciple of Thomas Aquinas, Francisco Araujo, OP (1580-1664) who, at one point, held the first chair in theology at the University of Salamanca before becoming bishop of Segovia in 1648.[10] The fact that his name and doctrine are absent from Marcial Solana's *Historia de la Filosofía Español, Época del Renacimiento, Siglo xvi*[11] is an obvious indication of our contemporary neglect of the man and his contributions to the issues mentioned above.

A modest attempt to correct this oversight can be made initially by seeing Araujo as the enlightened disciple of his master, and his master's

---

[7] *In Primum Librum Magistri Sententiarum Disputationes: In 1 Sent.*, d. 8, disp. 2 (Salmanticae, 1574), p. 81r.

[8] See *Rerum Metaphysicarum libri tres ad mentem Doctoris Subtilis*, q. 15 (Paris, 1623), 1: 173 where, after an almost verbatim rendering of Suarez' description of Scotus' criticism of Henry of Ghent (see nn. 14, 25 below) the author claims: "Haec sententia abhinc aliquot annis revixit apud aliquos, alioquin doctos et subtiles, in Universitate Parisiensi, qui existimantes realitatem essentiae non peti ab existentia; sed essentiam esse realem seclusa existentia; consequenter docuerunt essentias esse reales ab aeterno, licet tantum in tempore coeperint existere."

[9] See n. 89 below.

[10] H. Hurter, *Nomenclator Literarius Theologicae* (Oeniponte: Libraria Academica Wagneriana, 1910), 4: cols. 5-6; J. Quétif and J. Échard, *Scriptores Ordinis Praedicatorum* (Paris, 1719-1721), 2: 609-611. For further biographical data, see C. O'Brien, OP, "El enigma de Francisco de Araújo," *La ciencia tomista*, 89 (1962), 221-234.

[11] (Madrid, 1941).

doctrine, in critical confrontation with his contemporary, Gabriel
Vasquez, sj (ca. 1551-1604) over the issue of whether or not there is some
eternal and immutable truth *extra divinum intellectum*.[12] We shall then
see Araujo broaden this discussion by drawing up a catalogue of historical
positions on the eternal truths current in his day, accompanied by his
enlightening critical commentary. Finally, his own position will be
developed as a foundation for his prior critical comments.

I

Araujo's confrontation and discussion with Vasquez takes place in an
appendix to a broader question which he had previously considered at
some length: *Utrum omnia dicantur vera ab una prima veritate?*[13] The
appendix addresses itself to the more specific question noted above: *An
extra divinum intellectum veritas aeterna et immutabilis reperiatur?*[14] This
latter had arisen because of what Araujo had perceived to be a striking
disagreement between Gabriel Vasquez and Thomas Aquinas. Vasquez
had asserted that there is eternal truth "after a fashion" (*quodammodo*),
extra divinum intellectum. This was claimed to be the case in the sense
that anything of itself, by nature, is apt to measure or terminate a true

---

[12] See n. 14 below.

[13] *Commentaria in universam Aristotelis Metaphysicam*, Bk. 2, q. 2, a. 5 (Burgis et
Salmanticae, 1617), pp. 226-233. (Hereafter referred to as CAM.)

[14] CAM, pp. 233-240. The occasion for this *Dubium Appendix* is a difficulty raised in
regard to Araujo's third conclusion in the preceding discussion (CAM, p. 230: "Tertia pars
conclusionis [tertiae], quod omnes res denominentur ab intellectus divini veritate per se et
primario.") to the effect that: "Ultimo arguitur: Sequitur ex eadem conclusione, omnes res
dici veras veritate aeterna et immutabili. Consequentia est falsa, ergo et antecedens.
Sequela patet, quia ibi docemus dici veras divina veritate, quae est aeterna et immutabilis.
Minor vero probatur. Nam si res creatae essent verae veritate aeterna et immutabili,
daretur extra Deum aliquid aeternum et immutabile, quod est falsum. Ut hoc argu-
mentum plenius dissolvamus, sequens dubium appendix instituimus." Considerable
concern, positive and negative, seems to have been focused at this time on *aliquid
aeternum et immutabile extra Deum*. Suarez' rendering of Scotus' criticism of Henry of
Ghent will use the phrase to describe the position of the latter. See *Disputationes
metaphysicae*, 31.2.2 in *Opera omnia*, ed. Vives (Paris, 1856-1877), 26: 229. (See n. 25
below for Vasquez's vigorous criticism of such an attribution.) In the same context, Suarez
will go on to accuse the *Thomistae*, influenced by Capreolus and Henry of Ghent, of
granting an *entitas aeterna et increata extra Deum*, *Disp. metaphys.*, 31.2.5; 26: 230. On
the same score, Francis Albertinus, sj, while acknowledging his debt to Capreolus and
Henry of Ghent, had insisted upon the essence of a creature, endowed with its own *esse
essentiae* as *a parte rei extra intellectum divinum*. See *Corollaria seu Quaestiones
theologicae*, disp. 1, q. 1 (Lugduni, 1616), 2: 7: "Hoc esse essentiae, seu quidditativum
absolutum intrinsecum, quod, ut probatum est, habet creatura ante existentiam, est a parte
rei extra intellectum divinum...."

judgment of itself in any intellect whatsoever, and from eternity, if there were an eternal intellect.[15] This clearly flies in the face of Thomas Aquinas' prevailing position that no truth is eternal or immutable save in the divine intellect. For truth is properly in an intellect, and only the divine intellect is eternal.[16]

Araujo responds to this controversy by embracing and defending Aquinas' position. He establishes that eternal truth exists only in the divine intellect first from the authority of Augustine and Anselm.[17] He then argues that the divine intellect is measured by eternity, in keeping with the perspective of Thomas Aquinas.[18] In the third instance, his point is proved by an argument from unfittingness. For the contrary position would require that truth in the divine intellect would be affected with a temporal dimension and subject to change. This is clearly absurd as it diminishes divine simplicity and immutability.[19]

With this in hand, Araujo directly confronts Vasquez' position and proceeds to establish that no truths are eternal and immutable other than those which exist in the divine intellect, as has just been indicated.[20] If eternal truth were to be acknowledged outside the divine intellect, it could be understood in only two ways. First, if it were a matter of truth in a created intellect. Secondly, if it were a case of transcendental truth which is *in rebus ipsis*, and which Araujo insists ought to be designated as a relation to the *veritas intellectus* rather than that truth itself.[21] But neither of these can be immutable and properly eternal as far as Araujo is concerned. For no creature is eternal. Indeed, if there were no eternal intellect, there would be no eternal truth.[22]

Araujo opposes Vasquez' position on three counts. Contrary to Vasquez' perspective, he insists that there is no transcendental truth which

---

[15] CAM, p. 233a. See G. Vasquez, sj, *Commentaria ac Disputationes in primam partem Sancti Thomae: In 1 S. Th.*, q. 16, a. 8, disp. 78, cap. 2 (Lugduni, 1631), 1: 303b.

[16] CAM, p. 233a. The dossier of texts from Aquinas which are listed here by Araujo figures prominently in the research of A. Maurer, csb. See his "St. Thomas and Eternal Truths," *Mediaeval Studies*, 32 (1970), 91-107; "St. Thomas and Changing Truths," *Atti del Congresso Internationale, Tommaso d'Aquino nel suo Settimo Centenario* (Napoli: Edizione Domenicane Italiane, 1977), 6: 267-275; *St. Thomas and Historicity* (Milwaukee: Marquette University Press, 1979).

[17] CAM, p. 233b.

[18] Ibid.

[19] CAM, pp. 233-234.

[20] CAM, p. 234ab.

[21] CAM, p. 234a. For Araujo's discussion of transcendental truth in the section preceding the Appendix, see CAM, p. 227. For Araujo's recapitulation of Vasquez' argument in terms of transcendental truth, see CAM, pp. 238b-239.

[22] CAM, p. 234a.

is eternal. For, prior to divine knowledge, no sufficient connection (on the part of the *objecta enunciabilia*) or non-repugnance was given which could be conceived by an eternal intellect.[23] Such a connection or non-repugnance would be real or of reason.[24] It cannot be real because this would give us an eternal reality distinct from God. This is clearly false and contrary to faith.[25] Indeed, to protect himself from such an heretical shortcoming, Araujo reports that Vasquez denies that such a consequence follows from his perspective. For Vasquez does not claim this *esse aeternum* is a reality. Rather, the only point made is that there is a mere non-repugnance of eternal *adaequabilitas* with any eternal intellect, if there were one.[26] In response to this qualification by Vasquez, Araujo comments that this would seem to reduce the non-repugnance to an *ens rationis*.[27]

Indeed, nourished by the milk of the Peripatetic tradition and breathing its air, Araujo knows that, in addition to the range of *ens reale*, there is

[23] CAM, p. 234b. See n. 76 below.

[24] Ibid.

[25] Ibid. Vasquez would likely protest this rendering of his position. For, while criticizing Suarez's interpretation of Henry of Ghent's position, Vasquez notes his sympathy for Henry's perspective but not to the extent of *aliquid extra Deum*. See Vasquez, *In 3 S. Th.*, q. 17, a. 1, disp. 72, cap. 2 (Lugduni, 1631), 1: 483. For another sympathetic rendering of Henry's position by Vasquez, see n. 56 below. For the questionable interpretation of Henry by Suarez which qualifies him as one of the *Recentiores quidam* noted by Vasquez, see n. 14 above.

[26] CAM, p. 234b. See Vasquez, *In 1 S. Th.*, q. 16, a. 8, disp. 78, cap. 2; 1: 303b: "Ex eo vero, quod dicamus, omnem veritatem etiam rerum creatarum esse aeternam, non sequitur aliquid ab aeterno extra Deum subsistere; haec enim veritas solum dicitur esse aeterna quatenus res ex se non repugnant ut intelligantur ab aeterno, si ab aeterno intellectus sit." See n. 29 below. Though Vasquez would seem to want to take advantage of the negative considerations in the expression *non repugnantia* (as Suarez does, as noted in n. 56 below), he runs afoul of the double-negative cast, indicating a positive reality and a positive *esse*. This charge is made in telling fashion by B. Mastrius, *Disputationes in 12 Arist. Stag. libros Metaphysicorum*, disp. 8, q. 1, a. 3.32 (Venice, 1646), 2: 69: "Aliqui enim, ne videantur creaturis ab aeterno tribuere aliquod esse positivum, per eam non repugnantiam nolunt intelligi possibilitatem positivam ad existendum, sed meram negationem repugnantiae, et impossibilitatis, quam vocant realitatem privativam .... Hic modus dicendi non placet, quia conceptus objectivi rerum in mente divina sunt positivi, et important esse essentiale rerum, quod est esse positivum; tum quia negatio negationis est quid positivum, ut negatio tenebrae est lux, negatio caecitatis est visus, sed negatio repugnantiae est negatio negationis, quia est negatio impossibilitatis, ergo quid positivum importare debet ...." This text must be linked with another in Mastrius where he cites some names in lieu of the above *aliqui*. See ibid. 2: 77a where Suarez is cited by name but not Vasquez.

[27] CAM, p. 234b. See n. 76 below. Such a position on *non repugnantia* would seem to put it beyond the critical scope of Mastrius' point in the preceding note. Indeed, Araujo and Mastrius would appear to be the extremes on this question with Vasquez and Suarez attempting to take intermediate positions.

only *ens rationis*.[28] But this *non repugnantia* professed by Vasquez cannot be relegated to the level of an *ens rationis* in Araujo's view. For a *forma rationis* has no other *esse* than an *esse objectivum*, the-being-of-being-an-object, or the-being-of-being-known in an intellect exercising an act of knowing. Yet this *non repugnantia* proposed by Vasquez belongs to things *ab aeterno*, independent of any knowing on the part of the divine intellect. To be sure, Araujo notes that, even if there were no intellect *ab aeterno aut ex tempore*, this *non repugnantia* would still belong to things, as Vasquez himself had claimed. It is clearly no *ens rationis*.[29]

This same conclusion must be reached when it is realized that the range of *ens rationis* is exhausted by negation, privation and relation, in keeping with Thomas Aquinas.[30] *Non repugnantia* is not a pure negation, as a chimera, since it has some real foundation.[31] It is clearly no privation since it is not a lack of a form due to some subject.[32] Nor can it be a relation, unless it be claimed to have *esse objectivum* in an intellect.[33]

Drawing forth the consequences of Vasquez' position, Araujo concludes that all propositions and their *objecta enunciabilia* must be equally possessed of eternal truth since this *non repugnantia* belongs to all such objects so that they can be conceived.[34] It holds not only for essential propositions akin to *homo est animal*, but it holds also for the likes of *Antichristus erit* or *Petrus existit*. It is Araujo's claim that Vasquez must

---

[28] Ibid.

[29] Ibid. See Vasquez, *In 1 S. Th.*, q. 16, a. 8, disp. 78, cap. 2; 1: 303b: "Quare licet nullus intellectus esset ab aeterno, si tamen esset futurus in aliquo tempore et potuisset esse antea, et antea in infinitum, haec enuntiatio, *Antichristus erit*, vel, *Homo et animal*, diceretur aeternae veritatis quia ex se ab aeterno non repugnat vere intelligi, vel in tempore, non determinato principio." *In 1 S. Th.*, q. 10, a. 3, *Notationes* ...; 1: 125a: "Non enim ex eo quod possint produci, aut ex eo quod cognoscantur possibiles sunt; sed contra, ex eo quod in se non implicant contradictionem, intelliguntur a Deo, et produci possunt, ut disputatione illa ostendemus." Vasquez is referring to Disp. 104 where the same point is made. See n. 56 below. At this point, and in the light of Araujo's forthcoming criticisms of Suarez, a comparison of Vasquez' texts in this note with Suarez' position would not be out of order, especially *Disp. metaphys.*, 8.7.27; 25: 304: "... etiamsi intellectus apprehendat illam hypothesim impossibilem in re positam, nimirum quod omnis intellectus, etiam divinus, cessaret ab actuali rerum conceptione, nihilominus adhuc esset in rebus veritas, nam et compositum ex corpore et anima rationali esset verus homo, et aurum esset verum aurum, etc. vel secundum veritatem essentiae, si intelligamus non manere existentes ...." See the citation of this by Christian Wolff in n. 91 below.

[30] Ibid.

[31] CAM, p. 234b-235a.

[32] CAM, p. 235a.

[33] Ibid. See n. 76 below.

[34] Ibid.

admit the latter two propositions to be eternal truths as well.[35] This last point, however, Araujo considers to be untenable since the latter two propositions involve contingent considerations and the copula is not divorced from temporal dimensions.[36] Furthermore, it is a matter of faith that, *Revera Antichristus futurus est aliquando. Non repugnat Antichristum fore*, is not a matter of faith.[37]

II

With Vasquez dispatched, Araujo develops his own position further and relates it to an interesting catalogue of historical positions on the issue of the eternal truths. On his own behalf, Araujo contends that all created beings can be called true, in virtue of eternal truth, and true *ab aeterno*, by way of an extrinsic denomination. For he had previously taught, following Aquinas, and bolstered by Anselm, that all created beings are extrinsically denominated to be true from God's unique formal truth.[38] For all this, however, Araujo wishes to acknowledge that some propositions are said to have eternal truth in a special fashion (*specialiter*). This is because of the necessary connection of the predicate with the subject. Such a connection is eternal in a negative sense, however, because, of itself, it has no cause of its defectibility.[39]

Adverting to the history of this question of the eternal truths in his own day, Araujo notes that there have been many who have insisted that there are no propositions of eternal truth in a categorical sense. They will, however, grant that there are eternal truths in an ampliative or conditional sense.[40] But others maintain that there are surely eternal truths in the

[35] Ibid. The instance of *Petrus existit*, however, does not appear in Vasquez's text. See n. 29 above and n. 50 below.

[36] Ibid.

[37] Ibid.

[38] Ibid.

[39] CAM, p. 235b. See nn. 62, 66 below. For Aquinas on this, see Maurer, "St. Thomas and Eternal Truths," p. 101, nn. 37-39. Suarez is aware of this doctrine of negative eternity in Aquinas. Indeed, he even quotes a text of St. Thomas indicating that this explicit formula is derived from Aquinas. See *Disp. metaphys.*, 6.6.7; 25: 231a "... et ideo recte dixit S. Thomas, 1 part., quaest. 16, art. 7 ad 2, *universalia dici solere esse ubique et semper non positive, sed negative ....*" It is important, however, especially in the light of Araujo's criticism of Suarez' position, to note that this doctrine of negative eternity does not figure in Suarez' classical discussion of the eternal truths in *Disp. metaphys.*, 31.12.38-47; 26: 294-298. See my "Suarez on the Eternal Truths," *The Modern Schoolman*, 58 (1981), 73-104 and 159-174, especially the latter section.

[40] Ibid. Araujo here refers to "quidam Nominales quos referunt et rejiciunt Soto libro 2, Summular., cap. 10, sec. 3 et Fonseca 5 Metaphysic., cap. 5, qu. 1, sec. 4 & 5." These *Nominales* will be referred to in nn. 46, 62 below under the rubric of *primus*

instance of those propositions in which a predicate has a necessary connection with a subject and the copula is divested of a temporal consideration. This is certainly the case with essential propositions in the categorical sense.[41] The exponents of this latter tradition, however, are by no means unanimous in explaining the sense and significance of this second perspective on the eternal truths. They can be classified into three distinct perspectives.[42]

Some say that essential propositions are eternally true because they are eternally known in and by the divine intellect.[43] Others insist that the eternal truth of such propositions is not derived from the divine intellect but from the very identity (or diversity) which obtains between the terms of a proposition (*extrema enunciabiles*). That is, the truth of *homo est animal* is the identity of man with animal which, from eternity, is nothing in act. It is something, however, in objective potency in which the essence of man is said to have been *ab aeterno*. This, in turn, is understood to be hypothetical, in the sense that *homo est animal* is to be taken in the sense of *si homo est, est animal*.[44] The rest of those cited by Araujo maintain that propositions are true eternally because they express an intrinsic connection of predicate with subject, a connection which is eternal. This connection does not cease when the singular being or essence ceases, nor does it come to be, even though the essence comes to be.[45]

---

modus dicendi. P. Fonseca, *Commentaria in Metaphysicorum Aristotelis Stagiritae libros,* Bk. 5, cap. 5, q. 1, sect. 2 (Cologne, 1651), 2: cols. 317-318, lists Harvey Nédellec and Ockham for the position here described by Araujo.

[41] Ibid. Araujo here refers to Soto, Fonseca, Suarez, Sylvester of Ferrara, Cajetan, Harvey Nédellec, Capreolus, Soncinas and Albert the Great.

[42] Ibid. When these three *modi dicendi* are added to the position of the Nominales cited in n. 40 above, we have four *modi dicendi*. This explains the four rejoinders of Araujo. See nn. 46-53 below.

[43] CAM, p. 236a. Araujo indicates that Suarez attributes this position to Thomas Aquinas. See *Disp. metaphys.*, 31.12.40; 26: 294-295; 31.12.46; 26: 297-298; 31.2.8; 26: 231. (For Araujo's rejection of Suarez' attribution here, see n. 49 below.) Despite Araujo's later criticism, Suarez is also referring to the position of Capreolus and those who follow him, preparatory to raising a difficulty to such a contention. See n. 49 below and my article, "Capreolus on Essence and Existence," *The Modern Schoolman*, 38 (1960), 1-24.

[44] Ibid. Araujo cites Suarez and Fonseca here.

[45] Ibid. This tradition is opposed to the perspective of Capreolus as influenced by Henry of Ghent and is represented by Soncinas, *Quaestiones metaphysicales*, Bk. 4, q. 12 (Venice, 1498), B4v-B5v and *In 9 Metaphys.*, q. 4; T3r where he refers to "quidam thomistae qui dicunt quod rebus corruptis manet quidem esse essentiae licet non maneat esse existentiae propter quod propositiones necessariae verificari possunt etiam rebus destructis"; Sylvester of Ferrara, *Commentaria in Summam contra gentiles*, Bk. 2, cap.52, ed. Leonina (Rome, 1920-1930), 13: 389b. Both Soncinas and Sylvester deny the doctrine in Capreolus of the uncreated, actual, eternal essences on the part of creatures. They still insist, however, on uncreated, eternal, essential truths.

Araujo finds each of these four perspectives to be deficient. The first is found wanting for three reasons; because it flies in the face of some classical texts of Augustine; because *scientia* concerns itself with necessary and perpetual truths; because an eternal truth is one whose copula is divested of temporal considerations.[46]

The second perspective which acknowledges eternal truths because of the eternity they enjoy in the divine mind by being known therein and thereby is found equally deficient.[47] Araujo, somewhat paradoxically, finds fault with this because a proposition such as, *homo est animal*, is not only eternally true in God's intellect but also in one's own intellect, in the negative sense sanctioned by Thomas Aquinas.[48] It is for this reason that Araujo insists that Suarez's attribution of this second point of view to his master is uncalled for.[49] Moreover, this second perspective suffers an additional shortcoming. Given its outlook, it follows that all propositions, even those dealing with contingent objects, are equally eternal truths. For they too are in the divine intellect. Araujo notes, however, that he had shown this to be false in opposing Vasquez's position.[50]

The third approach, which insists upon the identity of subject and predicate in the objective potency of man, fails because objective potency was nothing prior to the production of things *extra Deum*. If it isn't God, nor anything produced by God, objective potency is accordingly not *ab aeterno*, nor are there *res aeternae* in objective potency *extra Deum*.[51]

---

[46] CAM, p. 236ab.

[47] Ibid.

[48] Ibid. This second perspective, then, is clearly deficient in Araujo's eyes for overlooking the notion of negative eternity which enables one to talk of eternal truths *in meo intellectu*. See nn. 62-73.

[49] Ibid. In addition to criticizing directly Suarez' attribution of this position to Aquinas (see n. 43 above), Araujo is also criticizing obliquely the interpretation of eternal, essential truths in Aquinas issuing from Capreolus, *Defensiones theologiae Divi Thomae Aquinatis: In I Sent.*, d. 8, q. 1, a. 1, ed. Paban-Pègues (Turin: Alfred Cattier, 1900), 1: 304. What here distresses Araujo is Capreolus' failure to honor Aquinas on negative eternity as well as his insensitivity to the eternal truth of contingent propositions *in intellectu divino*, even though Capreolus explicitly grants that God eternally knows existence as well as essence. See *In I Sent.*, d. 8, q. 1, a. 2, arg. 6 ad 1; 1. 330.

[50] Ibid. It is to be noted that Araujo is not opposed to contingent, existential truths being eternal, *in divino intellectu*, in the positive sense of eternal. He is opposed to them being acknowledged as *aequaliter verum et aeternum*, and on a par with the necessary, essential truths therein. For the difference, *in divino intellectu*, between necessary, essential truths and contingent, existential ones according to Araujo, see nn. 75-77 below.

[51] CAM, p. 237a. For the specter of equivocation which attends the use of *potentia objectiva* as either an extrinsic denomination or an intrinsic denomination. See F. Albertinus, *Corollaria*, disp. 1, q. 3; 2: 12a.

Finally, the fourth position is found wanting because the connection of predicate with subject is identified with the essence of the thing in question. So, just as no essence is eternal *extra Deum*, no such connection is either.[52] Moreover, just as an essence is produced and corrupted upon the production and corruption of singular things, so is such a connection produced and corrupted.[53] Any attempt, then, in this fourth approach to detach this subject-predicate connection from essence and to consider it in itself as the *potentia objectiva* of things (understood as *non repugnantia*, as Araujo will note shortly) is rejected by Araujo. In his view, this *potentia objectiva* of things is identical with their essence. Since the essences are not eternal, this *potentia objectiva* cannot be eternal, as was noted versus the third tradition.[54] In addition, Araujo makes the point that the *potentia objectiva* of something is the same as *non repugnantia ad esse talis rei*.[55] As such, it cannot be considered to be something positive existing *ab aeterno*, as Araujo indicated against Vasquez. Consequently, these same arguments indicate the shortcomings of Suarez's position on *potentia objectiva*.[56]

---

[52] Ibid. Araujo is not only disturbed at the severing of the essential truths from the essences in question, in this tradition, he is also distressed at the way this tradition has developed in someone like Soncinas, *Quaestiones metaphysicales*, Bk. 5, q. 10 (Venice, 1588), 65b: "Tertio. Si per impossibile Deus non esset et nulla causa agens, hominem esse animal esset verum, ergo hoc complexum non est a causa agente, patet consequentia. Antecedens probatur, quia Lynco. Primo posteriorum, dicit hujusmodi enunciabilia esse perpetuae veritatis." See also D. Soto: "Et probo quod essentia non habet causam quod sit essentia vel conveniat rei cuius est essentia. Nec Deus fecit illud quia non est factibile, quia, si per impossibile non esset Deus, esset verum dicere 'Homo est animal rationale'," cited in L. A. Kennedy, csb, "La doctrina de la existencia en la Universidad de Salamanca durante el siglo xvi," *Archivo Teológico Granadino*, 35 (1972), 26. Suarez reports this position, *Disp. metaphys.*, 31.12.45; 26: 297b. In turn, this tradition will be vigorously opposed by Descartes. See n. 89 below.

[53] Ibid.

[54] Ibid.

[55] Ibid.

[56] Ibid. Araujo is referring, in an admittedly inadequate fashion, to the tendency in Suarez, when discussing the essences of creatures prior to creation, to shift from the context of *potentia objectiva* or *possibile objectivum* as extrinsic denominations to that of *potentia logica, possibile logicum* and *non repugnantia*. This slippage from one potency to the other is further developed in my "Suarez and the Eternal Truths," 81-84 and 167-169. Though Suarez would wish to take advantage of the negative considerations in *non repugnantia*, the double-negative cast comes back to haunt him as equivalent to the position of Vasquez criticized by Araujo. See the text of Mastrius in n. 26 above. For Vasquez on *potentia logica* in relation to Henry of Ghent, see *In 1 S. Th.*, q. 25, a. 3, disp. 104, cap. 4; 2: 510b: "In hanc sententiam ex parte consentit Henricus quodlib. 6, q. 3 cuius doctrina accurate notanda est, mirifice namque illustrabit sententiam Doctoris Angelici. Advertit ergo dupliciter posse Deum considerari potentem, primum in se ipso, deinde relate ad aliud .... Eadem proportione posse passivum creaturarum bifariam

In a parting shot, Araujo opposes Suarez with an obvious *ad hominem* argument.[57] He refuses to grant Suarez's rendering of *homo est animal* as *si homo est, est animal*.[58] A conditional proposition is not a species of categorical proposition, as Araujo sees it. A categorical proposition, then, cannot be taken in the sense of a conditional one.[59] Such a lapse on Suarez's part evokes Araujo's *ad hominem* aside : "... nec miror Suarez in hoc deceptum fuisse; propterea quod res est ad Summulas pertinens, in quibus ipse parum versatus est."[60]

III

With his critical task completed, Araujo proposes what he considers to be the true way to express the position on the eternal truths. His statement is forthcoming in the form of three conclusions.[61] First, Araujo emphasizes that the eternal truths are to be understood in the special sense (*specialiter*) already noted. This consideration is also to be appreciated as the consequence of his negative critique of the perspective embraced by the *Nominales*.[62] His second consideration clarifies this "special sense." Eternally true propositions, in the negative sense, are to be acknowledged because the verbal copula lacks existential import as it expresses the essential, necessary connection of predicate with subject.[63] Moreover, his negative criticisms of Vasquez's and Suarez's positions are to be seen as reinforcing this conclusion.[64]

His third conclusive comment is of some significance. Araujo insists therein that this necessary connection is not said to be eternal because it has an *esse positivum extra Deum ab aeterno*.[65] Rather, the necessary connection is characterized as *eternal* only in a negative sense, in much

---

quoque cogitari potest, uno modo, ut in se ipso absolute absque ullo respectu quod nihil aliud est, quam rem aliquam non implicare contradictionem ut sit, et vocari potentia logica ..." For a recent discussion of this text in Henry of Ghent, see J. Wippel, "The Reality of Nonexisting Possibles According to Thomas Aquinas , Henry of Ghent, and Godfrey of Fontaines," *Review of Metaphysics*, 34 (1981), 748-749. Also see Vasquez in *In 3 S. Th.*, q. 17, a. 1, disp. 72, cap. 2; 1: 483a.

[57] Ibid.
[58] Ibid.
[59] CAM, p. 237b.
[60] Ibid.
[61] Ibid.
[62] Ibid.
[63] Ibid.
[64] Ibid.
[65] CAM, p. 238a.

the same fashion in which universals are described as incorruptible and eternal in a negative sense.[66] In no way does this indicate any real, positive *esse existentiae extra Deum* (nor any *esse essentiae*, for that matter), prior to the generation of singular things. Such a positive *esse existentiae extra Deum* is the unfortunate consequence of the positions of Vasquez and Suarez due to their failure to take advantage of Aquinas' doctrine of negative eternity in the matter of the eternal truths. For Araujo, this teaching on negative eternity entails only an *esse suae causae* and an *esse objectivum* or *esse cognitum* in the divine mind.[67]

This third, and most critical part of his conclusions, is established in three different ways, all inspired by Thomas Aquinas.[68] First, Araujo cites the texts of Aquinas wherein the claim was made on behalf of eternal truths taken, not in a positive, but in a negative sense, *ratione remotionis*. That is, it is to be understood to the extent that one removes from the essential truth in question whatever is conducive to a contrary disposition.[69]

In his second proof, where he strives to give proper linguistic expression to the notion of negative eternity, Araujo calls upon the established usage of the term *perpetua*. It signifies what always belongs to something unless otherwise prevented *per accidens*.[70] For example, we claim fire always (*perpetuo*) rises because the tendency to rise is acknowledged always (*perpetuo*) to belong to fire.[71] Another instance of this usage is found in the *Book of Wisdom* to the effect that: "Justice is perpetual and immortal!"[72]

The third proof derives from Araujo's conviction that this negative mode of eternity is adequate to establish the necessary, essential propositions, such as *homo est animal, homo est risibilis* etc., to be eternal truths and to distinguish them from contingent propositions. Nothing further needs be asked for as far as Araujo is concerned.[73] Since essential propositions express a connection which does not include actual

---

[66] Ibid.

[67] Ibid.

[68] Ibid.

[69] Ibid.

[70] Ibid. On Aquinas' use of the term *perpetua*, see Maurer, "St. Thomas and Eternal Truths," p. 101.

[71] CAM, p. 238ab.

[72] CAM, p. 238b.

[73] Ibid. Consistent with this, Araujo acknowledges eternal falsehoods as well. See CAM, p. 238b. For the same point in Aquinas, see Maurer, "St. Thomas and Eternal Truths," p. 102, n. 43.

existence, nor do they need it for their truth, they differ on three counts from existential, contingent propositions.[74] Essential propositions cannot be rendered false; they are necessarily conformed to the divine intellect independently of any free determination of the divine will; these necessary, eternal truths are necessarily conformable, and invariably so, to any other intellect whatsoever.[75] In keeping with this, Araujo does not shrink from insisting on the possibles as antecedent, by reason of omnipotence, to what purports to be God's speculative knowledge. It is this omnipotence which serves as the reason founding the relation of possibility or non-repugnance.[76]

Contingent, existential propositions, on the other hand, can be rendered false in the absence of the existents involved; they are known by God, but

[74] Ibid.

[75] Ibid., "... quod illae (*Homo est animal* etc.) nequeunt falsificari et sunt conformatae necessario divino intellectui independenter ab omni libera Dei determinatione, et quantum est de se, sunt necessario conformabiles et indefectibiliter cuilibet intellectui ...." It would appear from this and the following footnote that Araujo is denying that God freely constitutes creatures as possible. For a recent controversy on this issue, see L. Dewan, OP, "St. Thomas and the Possibles," *The New Scholasticism*, 53 (1979), 76-85; B. H. Zedler, "Why are the Possibles Possible?" *The New Scholasticism*, 55 (1981), 113-130; J. F. Wippel, "The Reality of Nonexisting Possibles," pp. 729-758.

[76] CAM, p. 239b: "... per hoc patet solutio primae confirmationis cuius antecedens debet similiter distingui: sunt possibiles possibilitate intrinseca et positiva, nego: denominatione quadam extrinseca, concedo. Sed hanc adhuc actu non habent, nisi ut divino intellectui erant objecta et ab illo cognita, ut possibilia: fundamentaliter vero erant possibilia antecedenter ad Dei cognitionem, ratione omnipotentiae, quae est veluti ratio fundandi illam relationem possibilitatis sive non repugnantiae." Also see Araujo's response to an argument of Vasquez on behalf of an intrinsic non-repugnance *extra divinum intellectum*, CAM, p. 239a: "... et illa non repugnantia tantum est denominatio rationis ex Dei omnipotentia proveniens, quae tantum habuit esse objectivum ab aeterno in divino intellectu: et sicut relatio scibilis est quaedam denominatio rationis in objecto scibili ex ordine ad scientiam possibilem haberi de illa, reperta: ita ratio possibilitatis, ac non repugnantiae est denominatio rationis ex Dei omnipotentia, in rebus, ante earum productionem." This is tantamount to claiming that creatures are possible because God can cause them! Although Araujo does not make use of it, there is textual warrant for this in Aquinas. See *I S. Th.*, q. 9, a. 2. (See B. Zedler, "Why are the Possibles Possible?", p. 125. See also L. Dewan, "St. Thomas and the Possibles," pp. 83-84: "I regard as a guiding light in the doctrine of the possibles, as proposed by St. Thomas, the point that absolute possibles are not so called by preference to a cause or power. If one says that God's vision of the possibles *follows* from his seeing his own causal power, this does not respect that doctrine.") What this says for Araujo's position on Aquinas' notion of the absolute possible is difficult to say. For Araujo's work, *In primam partem D. Th. commentariorum tomus primus* (Matriti, 1647), does not there address directly the questions pertinent to this issue. In denying any *possibilitas intrinseca et positiva*, at the outset of this note, Araujo is concerned explicitly with Vasquez and Suarez. It could very well be that their rendering of such a notion made Araujo wary of assimilating it lest he capitulate, at the same time, to an underived *esse essentiae* or *esse possibile*, in some fashion.

in terms of His practical knowledge, because God has freely determined
their objects; on the plane of the created intellect, such contingent
propositions are known to be true, but not necessarily nor invariably. For
no created intellect will judge such considerations to be perpetually so,
after the fashion of necessary connections.[77]

IV

In this brief consideration of Francisco Araujo we have encountered a
man who was inspired by the existential tradition on truth pioneered by
Thomas Aquinas, his master. True to this heritage, he was a perceptive
critic of the various representatives of the essentialist tradition on truth in
his age, just as Thomas Aquinas was in his. This is borne out in his
persistent refusal to acknowledge any real, positive, intrinsic existence on
the part of the eternal truths, the burden of the positions of Vasquez
and Suarez and others, as Araujo reads them.[78] The doctrines of *non
repugnantia* and *potentia logica* where they occur in both Vasquez and
Suarez, for all their attempts to forestall it, cannot help but restore and
reinstate an eternal essence, endowed with its own *esse essentiae*, in the
sense of an intrinsic *esse possibile*, to the center-stage of the discussion.[79]

Indeed, on this latter score, though in an admittedly muted fashion, to
be sure, Araujo manifests himself to be an equally perceptive critic of
essentialism within the Thomist tradition. This is represented by
Capreolus, *princeps Thomistarum*, who has been deeply influenced by
Henry of Ghent's position on essence and its *esse essentiae*,[80] and by
Soncinas, who, in rejecting the uncreated, eternal essences of Capreolus
and Henry of Ghent, insists upon uncreated, eternal truths apart from any
eternal essences and, at least hypothetically and *per impossibile*, apart
from God.[81] Both Capreolus and Soncinas would appear to have
understood the non-existential use of the copula, in the instance of the
eternal truths, in terms of an *esse veritatis propositionis*.[82] Since *entia*

---

[77] CAM, p. 238b, 239ab.

[78] See n. 65 above as well as nn. 29, 52.

[79] See n. 26 above.

[80] See nn. 43, 49 above.

[81] See nn. 45, 52 above.

[82] See Capreolus, *In 1 Sent.*, d. 8, q. 1, a. 1; 1: 305; Soncinas, *In 5 Metaphys.*, q. 5; 65.
Soncinas is taking issue with the position of Harvey Nédellec which claims that "ea quae
sunt necessaria necessitate connexionis habent causam effectivam." With neither
Capreolus nor Soncinas in mind, Harvey criticizes a precursor of their position in
Quaestiones quodlibetales 1, q. 10 (Venice, 1513; repr.: Ridgewood, NJ, 1966), fol. 23ra.

rationis equally involve an *esse veritatis propositionis* and entail no
efficient cause, then the eternal truths lack any efficient cause.[83] This tends
to sunder eternal truths from essence as well as existence and reduce
metaphysics to the formalism of a logic.

Araujo equally rejects the perspective of Capreolus for his blindness to
the positive eternity of the existential truths in the divine mind, while
insisting on the essential truths alone as eternal therein,[84] as he rejects the
perspective of Soncinas for detaching the eternal, essential truths from the
essences of existing entities and from the divine intellect.[85] Also, each,
in turn, has failed to take advantage of Aquinas' doctrine of negative
eternity.

It is Araujo's doctrine on positive eternity which enables him to
accomodate the existential truths as properly eternal in the divine mind;[86]
while it is his doctrine on negative eternity which makes it possible for
him to do justice to the necessary, essential truths without detaching them
from the essences in question and without restoring any vestige of the
positive, uncreated *esse essentiae* of Capreolus and Henry of Ghent, or
the positive *non repugnantia* of Vasquez and Suarez.[87] In such fashion,
Araujo is able to avoid the shortcomings of the positions he has criticized.
In all this, it is difficult to assess Araujo's original contribution to the
discussion of these issues and to the initial originality of his master,
Thomas Aquinas. Perhaps the most significant aspect of Araujo's position
is his refusal to compromise with the doctrine of an *esse essentiae* and
with any of the unacceptable consequences noted above.

Historically, however, rather than the existential tradition in Araujo, it
is the essentialist tradition abroad in Capreolus and Soncinas, as well as
Vasquez and Suarez, which has gone on to influence thinkers like
Mersenne, Arnauld, Caterus and the philosophers and theologians of the
Sorbonne.[88] Faced with the challenge of their perspective on the eternal

---

[83] See Capreolus and Soncinas in preceding note.

[84] See nn. 43, 49 above.

[85] See nn. 45, 52 above.

[86] See nn. 16-22 above.

[87] See nn. 39, 49, 56, 61-73 above.

[88] Mersenne's position is implicit in Descartes' correspondence of the early 1630s,
Œuvres de Descartes, ed. C. Adam and P. Tannery (Paris: J. Vrin, 1969), 1: 145-153;
Caterus' position is in the *First Objections* to Descartes' *Meditations*, ed. Adam and
Tannery, 7: 93 ll. 8-16, esp. l. 14; see the philosophers and theologians of the Sorbonne in
the *Sixth Objections*, 7: 417-418, (See the text of Martin Meurisse, ofm, in n. 8 above.) In
all this, the problem has to do with the uncreated essences of creatures, uncreated
inasmuch as they do not derive from God as a creative efficient cause. This is the position
clearly espoused by Arnauld in the *Fourth Objections*, 7: 212 l. 5 – 213 l. 4. Gassendi
erroneously takes this to be Descartes' position in *Fifth Objections*, 7: 312-321. See also

truths, embodied in his famous description: "... si Deus non esset, nihilominus istae veritates essent verae," Descartes will issue a resounding charge of blasphemy.[89] His only recourse, in order to sequester these renegade eternal truths, is to declare that, as forthcoming from God as a creative efficient cause, they are genuine creatures. The God of Descartes is the cause of what is really possible as well as of what is really actual.

Descartes' insistence upon this creation of the essences of creatures, along with their eternal truths, was difficult to sustain. For such a claim admits no more than the conditional necessity of the essential truths. Such a stand could only alarm those like Malebranche[90] and Leibniz[91] who were convinced that the status of *scientia* demanded more than merely conditionally necessary truths for its subject-matter. It is not surprising, then, to see both return to the tradition of the uncreated essences of creatures, Malebranche to the Augustinian strain and Leibniz to the Suarezian version. It will be the dissolution of these traditions, as vulnerable to the Kantian critique, that ushers in our contemporary predicament with the "historicity" of all truth.

---

the pointed query of Burman on this issue, *Conversation with Burman*, trans. J. Cottingham (Oxford: Clarendon Press, 1976), [36]; 24: "Is essence then prior to existence? And in creating things, did God merely give them existence?

[89] See *Correspondance*, 1: 149 l. 26.

[90] See *Recherche de la vérité. Éclaircissement 10, Œuvres complètes de Malebranche*, ed. G. Rodis-Lewis (Paris 1962-1964), 3: 127-143; B. K. Rome, *The Philosophy of Malebranche* (Chicago: Regnery, 1963), pp. 109-116.

[91] See *Letter to Fabri*, in *Sämtliche Schriften und Briefe* (Berlin: Akademie-Verlag, 1962). Series 2, 1: 299; *Monadology*, 46, in *Die philosophischen Schriften von G. W. Leibniz*, ed. C. J. erhardt (Hildesheim: G. Olms, 1961), 6: 614. For the persistence of the Suarezian perspective, see the reference of Christian Wolff to the text of Suarez cited in n. 29 above, *Philosophia prima sive Ontologia*, 1.3.6, # 502, ed. J. École (Hildesheim: G. Olms, 1962), pp. 387-388: "Franciscus Suarez Disput. Metaphys. 8, Sect. 7 f. 192 et seqq. ad veritatem transcendentalem requirit entitatem realem ipsius rei, quae nihil tamen ei intrinsecum superaddit: etsi autem veritatem istam independenter ab intellectu ei tribuit, ita ut ens verum sit, si vel maxime in nullo intellectu, ne quidem divino, dari per impossibile supponatur ejus idea; eam tamen rem aptam reddere agnoscit, ut ipsa in intellectu repraesentari possit, qualis est."

Joseph Owens, CSSR: A Bibliography

This bibliography[1] is divided into four parts: books (including dissertations), articles, book reviews by Father Owens, and critical writings about him. Reviews of Father Owens' books are listed with the title and edition reviewed. Longer review articles and critical discussions of these books are listed among the critical writings. The arrangement of listings is alphabetical by title within the first two categories, and alphabetical according to author title in the latter two categories. A chronological listing of works by Father Owens to 1981 can be found at the end of Catan's collection of papers by Owens on Aristotle (no. 2).

I. Books

1 *Aquinas on Being and Thing.* Niagara Falls, N.Y.: Niagara University Press, 1981. 33 p.

2 *Aristotle: The Collected Papers of Joseph Owens.* Edited by John R. Catan. Albany: State University of New York Press, 1981. 249 p. Chronological bibliography of Joseph Owens, pp. 229-239.

3 "The Common Nature. A Study in St. Thomas Aquinas and Duns Scotus." Licentiate Dissertation. Toronto: Pontifical Institute of Mediaeval Studies, May 1946. 119 leaves; bibliographical notes. Unpublished – available in PIMS Library, Toronto.

4 "The Doctrine of Being in the Aristotelian *Metaphysics.* A Study in the Greek Background of Mediaeval Thought." A thesis presented in partial fulfilment of the requirements for the Degree of Doctor of Mediaeval Studies in philosophy. Toronto: Pontifical Institute of Mediaeval Studies, Nov. 1948. 2 vols.; 713 leaves; bibliographical notes. MS available in PIMS Library, Toronto.

[1] The original version of this bibliography was prepared by Thomas Mathien. Special thanks for assistance are owed to Margaret McGrath, the reference librarian at St. Michael's College in Toronto, to Maggie Channon who first typed the manuscript, and to Father Owens who kindly provided a list of current writings. The original research was carried out under the auspices of the Bibliography of Philosophy in Canada, supported by a SSHRCC grant.

Graceful Reason: Essays in Ancient and Medieval Philosophy Presented to Joseph Owens, CSSR, ed. Lloyd P. Gerson. Papers in Mediaeval Studies 4 (Toronto: Pontifical Institute of Mediaeval Studies, 1983), pp. 419-433. © P.I.M.S., 1983.

5   *The Doctrine of Being in the Aristotelian* Metaphysics. *A Study in the Greek Background of Mediaeval Thought.* With a preface by Étienne Gilson. Toronto: Pontifical Institute of Mediaeval Studies, 1951. xi, 461 p. Bibliography, pp. 425-446. Publication of doctoral thesis (no. 4).

> *Bulletin Thomiste* 9 (1954-1956): 150 (L.-B. Geiger); *Classical Review* 67/n.s. 3 (1953): 22-24 (D. A. Rees); *Dominican Studies* 6 (1953): 234 (I. H.); *Franciscan Studies* 34 (1952): 425-428 (P. Borgmann); *Freiburger Zeitschrift für Philosophie und Theologie* 1 (1954) 334-335 (A. Hufnagel); *Giornale di Metafisica* 7 (1952): 661-668 (Cornelio Fabro); *Gregorianum* 35 (1954): 176-178 (G. Vass); *Journal of Classical Studies* (Kyoto) 5 (1957): 154-157 (Oga) – in Japanese; *Journal of Hellenic Studies* 73 (1953): 159 (L. Minio-Paluello); *Journal of Philosophy* 50 (1953): 161-168 (J. Antonopoulos); *Modern Schoolman* 30 (1952-1953): 146-151 (H. Veatch); cf. ibid., 34 (1956-1957): 247-263 (L. J. Eslick – no. 208); *Museum, Maandblad voor Philologie en Geschiednis* 59 (1954): 42-44 (G. L. Muskens); *New Scholasticism* 26 (1952): 229-239 (J. F. Anderson – cf. no. 193); *Personalist* 36 (1955): 179 (D. S. Robinson); *Philosophical Review* 62 (1953): 577-589 (A. Gewirth – no. 209); *Philosophical Studies* (Maynooth) 2 (1952): 97-109 (J. M. Heusten); *Philosophisches Jahrbuch* 64 (1956): 419 (H.D.); *Philosophy and Phenomenological Research* 13 (1952-1953): 254-256 (R. Taylor); *Review of Metaphysics* 6 (1952-1953): 257-264 (W. H. Walton – no. 222); *Revue philosophique de la France et de l'étranger* 78 (1953): 473-477 (J. Moreau); *Revue philosophique de Louvain* 50 (1952): 471-478 (G. Verbecke); *Revue Thomiste* 54 (1954): 397-399 (A. Forest); *Scholastik* 27 (1952): 409-410 (W. Kutsch); *Speculum* 27 (1952): 576-578 (V. J. Bourke); *Theological Studies* 13 (1952): 165; *Thomist* 16 (1953): 300-301; cf. ibid., 21 (1958): 29-43 (J. D. Beach – no. 196); *Wissenschaft und Weisheit* 19 (1956): 66-68 (T. Barth).

6   *The Doctrine of Being in the Aristotelian* Metaphysics. *A Study in the Greek Background of Mediaeval Thought.* With a preface by Étienne Gilson. Second printing: corrected edition with an added index of Aristotelian texts and a bibliographic supplement. Toronto: Pontifical Institute of Mediaeval Studies, 1957. xi, 478 p. Bibliography, pp. 425-446. Repr., 1961.

7   *The Doctrine of Being in the Aristotelian* Metaphysics. *A Study in the Greek Background of Mediaeval Thought.* With a preface by Étienne Gilson. 2nd rev. ed. Toronto: Pontifical Institute of Mediaeval Studies, 1963. 535 p. Bibliography, pp. 475-501.

> *Ciencia Tomista* 92 (1965): 339 (R. de D.); *Dialogue* 4 (1965-1966): 260-263 (V. Décarie); *Gnomon* 40 (1968): 139-147 (H. Kuhn); *Gregorianum* 45 (1964): 414 (J. de Finance); *Heythrop Journal* 5 (1964): 233-234 (T.C.); *Philosophisches Rundschau* 14 (1966-1967): 62-64 (E. Treptow); *Review of Metaphysics* 17 (1963-1964): 308

(W.G.E.); *Revue philosophique de Louvain* 68 (1970): 249-250 (C. Lefèvre); *Sapientia* 88 (1968): 159 (E. Colombo); *Studium* 4 (1964): 397-398 (B. Turiel).

8 *The Doctrine of Being in the Aristotelian* Metaphysics. *A Study in the Greek Background of Mediaeval Thought.* With a preface by Étienne Gilson. 3rd rev. ed. Toronto: Pontifical Institute of Mediaeval Studies, 1978. xxx, 538 p. Bibliography, pp. 475-503. Includes an addendum to the introduction.
   Revue philosophique de la France et de l'étranger 105 (1980): 90-92 (A. Reix); *Revue philosophique de Louvain* 78 (1980): 138-140 (S. Mansion); *Speculum* 54 (1979): 412-413 (V. J. Bourke).

9 *An Elementary Christian Metaphysics.* Christian Culture and Philosophy Series. Milwaukee: Bruce Publishing Co., 1963. xiv, 384 p. Includes bibliography.
   Aquinas 7 (1964): 133-134 (G.G.); *Catholic School Journal* 64 (Jan. 1964): 70 (W. May); *Heythrop Journal* 5 (1964): 198-199 (T. Murphy); *Modern Schoolman* 41 (1963-1964): 292-297 (L. Azar); *New Scholasticism* 38 (1964); 270-273 (T. C. O'Brien); *Sciences ecclésiastiques* 17 (1965): 561-564 (J. Anglois).

10 *A History of Ancient Western Philosphy.* New York: Appleton-Century-Crofts, 1959. xv, 434 p. Includes bibliography. Map on lining papers.
   Catholic School Journal 61 (Sept. 1961): 50; *Cross Currents* (Spring 1961): 145 (J. Collins); *New Scholasticism* 35 (1961): 391-396 (F. M. Cleve).

11 *An Interpretation of Existence.* Milwaukee: Bruce Publishing Co., 1968. vii, 153 p. Bibliographic footnotes.
   Dialogue 9 (1970): 120-124 (D. Binnie); *Modern Schoolman* 48 (1971): 184-185 (R. Teske); *Thomist* 34 (1970): 151-152 (W. H. Kane).

12 *The Philosophical Tradition of St. Michael's College.* Toronto: University of St. Michael's College Archives, 1979. 40 p. Bibliographic notes pp. 28-40. Includes reproductions of textbook title pages.

13 *Saint Thomas Aquinas, 1274-1974. Commemorative Studies.* Edited by Armand Maurer, Étienne Gilson, Joseph Owens, Anton C. Pegis, John F. Quinn and James A. Weisheipl. Toronto: Pontifical Institute of Medeiaeval Studies, 1974. 2 vols; 488, 526 p.

14 *Saint Thomas and the Future of Metaphysics.* The Aquinas Lecture, 1957. Milwaukee: Marquette University Press, 1957. 97 p. Repr. 1973.
   Ciencia Tomista 86 (1959): 328 (R.); *Ciencia y fe* 13 (1957): 376 (M. Petty); *Convivium,* no. 15-17 (1963): 224-225 (J. E. B.); *Gregorianum* 40 (1959): 387 (J. H. Wright); *New Scholasticism* 32 (1958): 264-266 (W. N. Clarke); cf. ibid., 33 (1959): 68-85 (J. Bobik – no. 199); cf. ibid., 37 (1963): 213-219 (J. L. Yarden – no. 223); *Nouvelle revue théologique* 80 (1958): 427-428 (A. Hayen); *Pensamiento* 16 (1960): 248 (J. Gerardo); *Philosophical Studies* (Maynooth) 7 (1957): 199-200 (J. D. Bastable); *Recherches de théologie ancienne et médiévale* 27 (1960):

187-188 (F. Vandenbroucke); *Revista de filosofía* 17 (1958): 316-317
(D. Díaz); *Revue philosophique de Louvain* 57 (1959): 474-475 (F. Van
Steenberghen); *Scholastik* 32 (1957): 440 (de Vries); *Sciences
ecclésiastiques* 9 (1957): 193 (J. Langlois); *Studies* 46 (1957): 361;
Thomist 21 (1958): 215-220 (J. De Beach); *Zeitschrift für Katholische
Theologie* 80 (1958): 459 (E. Coreth).

15 *St. Thomas Aquinas on the Existence of God.* Collected papers of Joseph
Owens edited by John R. Catan. Albany: State University of New York
Press, 1980. xii, 296 p. Selected bibliography pp. 231-232.
Religious Studies Review 7 (1981): 146 (D. C. Langston).

16 *The Wisdom and Ideas of Saint Thomas Aquinas.* Edited by Joseph Owens
and Eugene Freeman. Greenwich, Conn.: Fawcett Publications, 1968.
160 p. Notes and references pp. 159-160. A collection of writings by
Aquinas.

II. Articles

17 "Abstract" of *The Doctrine of Being* ..., 2nd ed. (no. 7). *Monist* 49 (1965):
670.

18 "Abstract" of *An Elementary Christian Metaphysics* (no. 9). *Monist* 50
(1966): 304.

19 "The Accidental and Essential Character of Being in the Doctrine of St.
Thomas Aquinas." *Mediaeval Studies* 20 (1958): 1-40. Gilson Anniversary
Studies. Repr. No. 15 (Catan), pp. 52-96.

20 "Actuality in the *Prima via* of St. Thomas." *Mediaeval Studies* 29 (1967):
26-46. Repr. no. 15 (Catan), pp. 192-207.

21 "Analogy as a Thomistic Approach to Being." *Mediaeval Studies* 24 (1962):
303-322. Repr. Bobbs-Merrill Reprints in Philosophy, 151 (Indianapolis:
Bobbs-Merrill, 1969).

22 "The *Analytics* and Thomistic Metaphysical Procedure." *Mediaeval Studies*
26 (1964): 83-108.

23 "Anton Charles Pegis." *Royal Society of Canada. Proceedings and
Transactions* 4th series, 16 (1978): 101-104.

24 "An Appreciation of Brand Blanshard's Views on Catholicism." In *The
Philosophy of Brand Blanshard*, ed. Paul A. Schilpp, pp. 1015-1039.
LaSalle: Open Court, 1980.

25 "Aquinas and the Five Ways." *Monist* 58 (1974): 16-35. Repr. no. 15
(Catan), pp. 132-141.

26 "Aquinas and the Proof from the 'Physics'." *Mediaeval Studies* 28 (1966):
119-150.

27 "Aquinas as Aristotelian Commentator." In *St. Thomas Aquinas. 1274-
1974. Commemorative Studies*, ed. Armand A. Maurer et al. (no. 13), 1:
213-238. Repr. no. 15 (Catan), pp. 1-19.

28 "An Aquinas Commentary in English." *Review of Metaphysics* 16 (1962-
1963): 503-512.

29 "Aquinas – 'Darkness of Ignorance' in the Most Refined Notion of God." *Southwestern Journal of Philosophy* 5/2 (Summer, 1974): 93-110. Rept. in *Bonaventure and Aquinas*, ed. R. W. Shahan and Francis J. Korach (Norman, Okla.: University of Oklahoma Press, 1976), 69-86.

30 "Aquinas – Existential Permanence and Flux." *Mediaeval Studies* 31 (1969): 71-92.

31 "Aquinas on Cognition as Existence." *Proceedings of the American Catholic Philosophical Association* 48 (1974): 74-85.

32 "Aquinas on Infinite Regress." *Mind* 71 (1962): 244-246. Repr. no. 15 (Catan), pp. 228-230. Cf. no. 210.

33 "Aquinas on Knowing Existence." *Review of Metaphysics* 29 (1975-1976): 670-690. Repr. no. 15 (Catan), pp. 20-33.

34 "Aristote – maître de ceux qui savent." Trans. Bernard and Roger Carrière. In *La philosophie et les philosophes*, pp. 45-68. Montreal: Éditions Bellarmin, 1973. Cf. no. 49.

35 "The Aristotelian Argument for the Material Principle of Bodies." In *Naturphilosophie bei Aristoteles und Theophrast*, Proceedings of the 4th Symposium Aristotelicum, Göteborg, Aug. 1969, ed. Ingemar Düring, pp. 193-209. Heidelberg: Stiehm, 1969. Repro. no. 2 (Catan), pp. 122-135.

36 "The Aristotelian Conception of the Sciences." *International Philosophical Quarterly* 4 (1964): 200-216. Repr. no. 2 (Catan), pp. 23-24.

37 "Aristotelian Ethics, Medicine, and the Changing Nature of Man." In *Philosophical Medical Ethics; Its Nature and Significance*, ed. S. F. Spicker and H. T. Engelhardt Jr., pp. 127-142. Dordrecht: D. Reidel, 1977. Repr. no. 2 (Catan), pp. 169-180.

38 "Aristotelian Soul as Cognitive of Sensibles, Intelligibles and Self." In no. 2 (Catan), pp. 81-98.

39 "An Aristotelian Text Related to the Distinction of Being and Essence." *Proceedings of the American Catholic Philosophical Association* 21 (1946): 165-172.

40 "Aristotle." In *The Catholic Encyclopedia for School and Home*, ed.-in-chief John H. Harrington, 1: 388-393. New York, 1965.

41 "Aristotle." In *New Catholic Encyclopedia* 1: 809a-814a. New York, 1967.

42 "Aristotle – Cognition a Way of Being." *Canadian Journal of Philosophy* 6 (1976): 1-11. Repr. no. 2 (Catan), pp. 74-80.

43 "Aristotle – Motion as Actuality of the Imperfect." *Paideia*, Special Aristotle Issue (1978): 120-132.

44 "Aristotle on Categories." *Review of Metaphysics* 14 (1960-1961): 73-90. Repr. no. 2 (Catan), pp. 14-22.

45 "Aristotle on Common Sensibles and Incidental Perception." *Phoenix* 36 (1982): 215-236.

46 "Aristotle on Empedocles Fr. 8." In *New Essays on Plato and the Pre-Socratics*, ed. Roger A. Shiner and John King-Farlow, Canadian Journal of Philosophy supplementary volume 2, pp. 87-100. Guelph: Canadian Association for Publishing in Philosophy, 1976.

47   "Aristotle on God." In *God in Contemporary Thought: A Philosophical Perspective*, ed. S. A. Matczak, Philosophical Questions Series 10, pp. 415-444. New York: Learned Publications; Louvain/Paris: Nauwelaerts, 1977.
48   "Aristotle on Leisure." *Canadian Journal of Philosophy* 11 (1981): 713-723.
49   "Aristotle – Teacher of Those Who Know." In no. 2 (Catan), pp. 1-13. Originally published in French; cf. no. 34.
50   "Aristotle's Definition of Soul." In *Philomathes. Studies and Essays in Memory of Philip Merlan*, ed. Robert D. Palmer and Robert Hammerton-Kelly, pp. 124-145. The Hague: Martinus Nijhoff, 1971. Repr. no. 2 (Catan), pp. 109-121.
51   "Author's Abstract – of *An Interpretation of Existence* (no. 11). *Monist* 56 (1972): 144-145.
52   "Being in Early Western Tradition." In *The Question of Being*, ed. Mervyn Sprung, pp. 17-30. University Park: Pennsylvania State University Press, 1978.
53   "The Causal Proposition: Principle or Conclusion." In *Readings in Metaphysics*, ed. Jean R. Rosenberg, pp. 188-199. Westminster: The Newman Press, 1964.
54   "The Causal Proposition – Principle or Conclusion?" *Modern Schoolman* 32 (1954-1955): 159-171, 257-270, 323-339. Cf. nos. 55, 201, 202.
55   "The Causal Proposition Revisited." *Modern Schoolman* 44 (1966-1967): 143-151. Cf. nos. 54, 201, 202.
56   "'Cause of Necessity' in Aquinas' *Tertia via*." *Mediaeval Studies* 33 (1971): 21-45.
57   "The Christian Philosophy of the *Aeterni patris*." Unpublished in English; cf. Spanish version no. 79.
58   "Comment" on "The Concept of Matter in Presocratic Philosophy," by C. Lejewski. In *The Concept of Matter*, ed. Ernan McMullin, pp. 57-58. Notre Dame, Ind.: University of Notre Dame Press, 1963. Repr. in paperback: *The Concept of Matter in Greek and Medieval Philosophy*, NDP 46 (1965), pp. 37-38.
59   "Comment – Effects Precede Causes." *Technology and Culture* 14 (1973): 19-21. Comment on a paper by Marshall McLuhan.
60   "Comments on Mr. Anderson's Theses." *Review of Metaphysics* 5 (1951-1952): 467-469. Comment on James F. Anderson's views on analogy. Cf. nos. 194, 195.
61   "Common Nature: a Point of Comparison Between Thomistic and Scotistic Metaphysics." *Mediaeval Studies* 19 (1957): 1-14. Cf. no. 3. Repr. in *Inquiries into Medieval Philosophy*, ed. James F. Ross (Westport, Conn.: Greenwood, 1971), pp. 185-209.
62   "Concept and Thing in St. Thomas." *New Scholasticism* 37 (1963): 220-224. Cf. nos. 135 and 217.
63   "The Conclusion of the *Prima via*." *Modern Schoolman* 30 (1952-1953): 33-53, 109-121, 203-215. Repr. no. 15 (Catan), pp. 142-168.

64   "The Content of Existence." In *Logic and Ontology*, ed. Milton K. Munitz, pp. 21-35. New York: New York University Press, 1973. Cf. no. 211.

65   "Critical Notice of John M. Cooper, *Reason and Human Good in Aristotle*." *Canadian Journal of Philosophy* 7 (1977): 623-636.

66   "Dewart's View of Christian Philosophy and Contemporary Man." *The Ecumenist* 5 (1966-1967): 19-22. Discussion of the views of Leslie Dewart.

67   "Discussion" with Wilfrid Sellers. In *The Concept of Matter*, ed. Ernan McMullin, pp. 275-276. Notre Dame, Ind.: University of Notre Dame Press, 1963. Repr. in paperback: *The Concept of Matter in Greek and Medieval Philosophy*, NDP 46 (1965), pp. 279-280.

68   "The Dissolution of an Eclecticism." *Pacific Philosophy Forum* 5/1 (Sept. 1966): 80-84.

69   "Diversificata in diversis – Aquinas *In I. Sent*. Prol. 1, 2." In *La scolastique – certitude et recherche, en hommage à Louis-Marie Régis*, ed. Ernest Joos, pp. 113-129. Montreal: Éditions Bellarmin, 1980.

70   "Diversity and Community of Being in St. Thomas Aquinas." *Mediaeval Studies* 22 (1960): 257-302. Repr. no. 15 (Catan), pp. 97-131.

71   "*The Doctrine of Being in the Aristotelian* Metaphysics ... Abstract" (no. 5). *Sophia* 20 (1952): 375.

72   "The Doctrine of Being in the Aristotelian *Metaphysics* – Revisited." In *Philosophies of Existence, Ancient and Medieval*, ed. Parviz Morewedge, pp. 33-59. New York: Fordham University Press, 1982.

73   "Elucidation and Causal Knowledge, Rejoinder to J. Bobik." *New Scholasticism* 37 (1963): 64-70. Cf. nos. 135, 197, 198, 213.

74   "The Ethical Universal in Aristotle." *Studia Moralia* 3 (1965): 27-47.

75   "Existence and the Subject of Metaphysics." *Science et esprit* 32 (1980): 255-260.

76   "Existence as Predicated." *New Scholasticism* 53 (1979): 480-485. Cf. article by Barry Miller, no. 216.

77   "Existential Act, Divine Being, and the Subject of Metaphysics." *New Scholasticism* 37 (1963): 359-363.

78   "Faith, Ideas, Illumination, and Experience." In *The Cambridge History of Later Medieval Philosophy*, ed. Norman Kretzmann, Anthony Kenny and Jan Pinborg, pp. 440-459. Cambridge: Cambridge University Press, 1982.

79   "La filosofía cristiana de la *Aeterni Patris*." *Revista de filosofía* (Mexico) 13 (1980): 229-246. Translation of no. 57.

80   "Foreword." In *Aristotle: The Collected Papers of Joseph Owens*, ed. John R. Catan (no. 2), pp. vi-vii.

81   "Foreword." In Richard P. Geraghty, *The Object of Moral Philosophy According to St. Thomas Aquinas*, pp. ix-x. Washington, D.C.: University Press of America, 1982.

82   "Foreword." In Giovanni Reale, "The Concept of First Philosophy and the Unity of the *Metaphysics* of Aristotle," trans. John R. Catan, pp. xi-xii. Brockport, N.Y.: State University of New York, [1976].

83   "Foreword." In Giovanni Reale, *The Concept of First Philosophy and the Unity of the* Metaphysics *of Aristotle*, trans. John R. Catan, pp. xv-xvi. Albany: State University of New York Press, 1980.

84   "Foreword." In *St. Thomas Aquinas and the Existence of God*, ed. John R. Catan (no. 15), pp. vii-viii.

85   "Foreword." In Leo Sweeney, *Infinity and the Presocratics, A Bibliographical and Philosophical Study*, pp. xvii-xix. The Hague: Martinus Nijhoff, 1972.

86   "Form and Cognition in Aristotle." *Ancient Philosophy* 1 (1980): 17-28.

87   "La forma aristotelica como causa del ser." Trans. Adelina Manero and Gonzalo Ituarte. *Revista de filosofía* (Mexico) 10 (1977): 267-287.

88   "The Future of Thomistic Metaphysics." In *One Hundred Years of Thomism*, ed. Victor B. Brezik, pp. 142-161. Houston, Texas: Center for Thomistic Studies, University of St. Thomas, 1981.

89   "God in Philosophy Today." In *God, Man and Philosophy*, ed. Carl W. Grindel, pp. 39-51. New York: St. John's University Press, 1971. Cf. comments by John E. Smith, no. 219.

90   "Greek Philosophy." In *New Catholic Encyclopedia*, 6: 732a-736a. New York, 1967.

91   "The Grounds of Ethical Universality in Aristotle." *Man and World* 2 (1969): 171-193. Repr. no. 2 (Catan), pp. 148-164.

92   "The Grounds of Universality in Aristotle." *American Philosophical Quarterly* 3 (1966): 162-169.

93   "The Grounds of Universality in Aristotle" – Abstract. *Review of Metaphysics* 19 (1965-1966): 830.

94   "Heraclitus." In *New Catholic Encyclopedia*, 6: 1046a-1047a. New York, 1967.

95   "'Ignorare' and Existence." *New Scholasticism* 46 (1972): 210-219.

96   "Immobility and Existence for Aquinas." *Mediaeval Studies* 30 (1968): 22-46.

97   "The Intelligibility of Being." *Gregorianum* 36 (1955): 169-193. Cf. no. 212.

98   "The Interpretation of the Heraclitean Fragments." In *An Etienne Gilson Tribute*, ed. Charles John O'Neill, pp. 148-168. Milwaukee: Marquette University Press, 1959.

99   "Interrogation of Paul Weiss." In *Philosophical Interrogations*, ed. Sydney and Beatrice Rome, pp. 266, 287-288, 301-302, 311. New York: Holt, Rinehart and Winston, 1964.

100   "Jacques Maritain – Toronto Recollections." *Notes et documents* (Institut International "J. Maritain"), 7 (April-June 1977): 12-15.

101   "Judgment and Truth in Aquinas." *Mediaeval Studies* 32 (1970): 138-158. Repr. no. 15 (Catan), pp. 34-51.

102   "The καλόν in the Aristotelian Ethics." In *Studies in Aristotle*, ed. Dominic J. O'Meara, pp. 261-277. Washington: Catholic University of America Press, 1981.

103   "Knowledge and *Katabasis* in Parmenides." *Monist* 62 (1979): 15-29.
104   "The Limitation of Being by Essence." In *Readings in Metaphysics*, ed. Jean
      R. Rosenberg, pp. 276-278. Westminster: The Newman Press, 1964.
104a "Maritain on Aristotelian Ethics." *Notes et documents* (Institut International
      "J. Maritain"), 27 (April-June 1982): 20-23.
105   "Maritain's Three Concepts of Existence." *New Scholasticism* 49 (1975):
      295-309. Cf. Spanish version no. 147.
105a "Material Substance – Temporal or Eviternal?" *New Scholasticism* 56
      (1982): 442-461.
106   "Matter and Predication in Aristotle." In *The Concept of Matter*, ed. Ernan
      McMullin, pp. 99-115. Notre Dame, Ind.: University of Notre Dame Press,
      1963. Repr. in paperback: *The Concept of Matter in Greek and Medieval
      Philosophy*, NDP 46 (1965), pp. 79-95. Repr. no. 2 (Catan), pp. 35-47. Cf.
      nos. 207, 215.
107   "Medalist Address – A Non-Expendable Heritage." *Proceedings of the
      American Catholic Philosophical Association* 46 (1972): 212-218.
108   "Metaphysical Separation in Aquinas." *Mediaeval Studies* 34 (1972): 287-
      306. Cf. German version no. 109.
109   "Metaphysische Trennung bei Thomas von Aquin." Trans. Wenzel Peters.
      In *Thomas von Aquin*, ed. Klaus Bernath, 2: 339-365. Darmstadt: Wissen-
      schaftliche Buchgesellschaft, 1981. Trans. of 108.
110   "Naming in Parmenides." In *Kephalaion, Studies in Greek Philosophy and
      its Continuation Offered to Professor C. J. De Vogel*, ed. J. Mansfield and L.
      M. de Rijk, pp. 16-25. Assen: Van Gorcum, 1975.
111   "Nature and Ethical Norm in Aristotle." *Proceedings of the XIVth
      International Congress of Philosophy*, 5: 442-447. Wien: Herder, 1970.
      Repr. no. 2 (Catan), pp. 165-168.
112   "Natures and Conceptualization." *New Scholasticism* 56 (1982), 376-380.
113   "A Note on Aristotle, *De anima* 3.4.429b9." *Phoenix* 30 (1976): 107-118.
      Repr. no. 2 (Catan), pp. 97-108.
114   "A Note on the Approach to Thomistic Metaphysics." *New Scholasticism*
      28 (1954): 454-476.
115   "The Notion of Actuality in Aquinas." *Proceedings of the PMR Conference.*
      Annual Publication of the Patristic, Mediaeval and Renaissance Conference
      (Augustinian Historical Institute, Villanova, Penn.) 4 (1979): 13-23.
116   "The Notion of Catholic Philosophy." *Antigonish Review* 1 (1970): 112-140.
117   "The Number of Terms in the Suarezian Discussion on Essence and Being."
      Modern Schoolman 34 (1956-1957): 147-191.
118   "Our Knowledge of Nature." *Proceedings of the American Catholic
      Philosophical Association* 29 (1955): 63-86.
119   "Parmenides." In *New Catholic Encyclopedia*, 10: 1027. New York, 1967.
120   "Philosophy – *An est* and *Quid est.*" *Proceedings of the American Catholic
      Philosophical Association* 54 (1980): 37-48.
121   "Philosophy's Role in Thanatology." In *Philosophical Aspects of Thanato-*

logy, ed. Florence M. Hetzler and Austin H. Kutscher, pp. 163-170. New York: MSS Information Corp.; dist. Arno Press, 1978.

122   "The Physical World of Parmenides." In *Essays in Honour of Anton Charles Pegis*, ed. J. Reginald O'Donnell, pp. 378-395. Toronto: Pontifical Institute of Mediaeval Studies, 1974.

123   "Presidential Address: Scholasticism – Then and Now." *Proceedings of the American Catholic Philosophical Association* 40 (1966): 1-12.

124   "The Primacy of the External in Thomistic Noetics." *Église et théologie* 5 (1974): 189-205. Cf. comments, no. 206.

125   "*Quandoque* and *Aliquando* in Aquinas' *Tertia Via*." *New Scholasticism* 54 (1980): 447-475.

126   "Quiddity and Real Distinction in St. Thomas Aquinas." *Mediaeval Studies* 27 (1965): 1-22. Cf. German translation, no. 154.

127   "The Range of Existence." *Proceedings of the Seventh Inter-American Congress of Philosophy* 1: 44-59. Quebec City: Presses de l'Université Laval, 1967. Cf. no. 218.

128   "The Real Distinction of a Relation from its Immediate Basis." *Proceedings of the American Catholic Philosophical Association* 39 (1965): 134-140.

129   "Realism." In *The New Encyclopaedia Britannica*, 15th ed., 15: 539-543. Chicago, 1974.

130   "Reality and Metaphysics." *Review of Metaphysics* 25 (1971-1972): 638-658. Presidential address of the Metaphysical Society of America. Cf. nos. 200 and 220.

131   "The Reality of the Aristotelian Separate Movers." *Review of Metaphysics*, 3 (1949-1950): 319-337. Repr. in *Readings in Ancient and Medieval Philosophy*, ed. James Collins (Westminster: The Newman Press, 1960), pp. 75-81.

132   "Recent Footnotes to Plato." *Review of Metaphysics* 20 (1966-1967): 648-661.

133   "The Relation of God to World in the *Metaphysics*." In *Études sur la Métaphysique d'Aristote*, Actes du vi⁰ Symposium Aristotelicum, pp. 207-228. Paris: Vrin, 1979.

134   "Report of a Recent Thesis Defended at the Pontifical Institute of Mediaeval Studies – The Doctrine of Being in the Aristotelian *Metaphysics*..." (no. 4). *Mediaeval Studies* 11 (1949): 239-245.

135   "St. Thomas and Elucidation." *New Scholasticism* 35 (1961): 421-444. Cf. comment by Bobik (no. 198), rejoinder (no. 73), response by Bobik (no. 197) and comment by La Plante (no. 213); and comment by Nielsen (no. 217) and response (no. 62).

136   "St. Thomas Aquinas and Modern Science." *Royal Society of Canada, Transactions* ser. 4, 1/sect. 2 (1963): 283-293.

137   "Scholasticism and Metaphysics." In *The Future of Metaphysics*, ed. Robert E. Wood, pp. 14-31. Chicago: Quadrangle, 1970.

138   "Soul as Agent in Aquinas." *New Scholasticism* 48 (1974): 40-72.

139   "The Special Characteristic of the Scotistic Proof that God Exists." In *Studi*

filosofici intorno all'"esistenza" al mondo, al Transcendente, Analecta Gregoriana 67, pp. 311-327. Rome: Universitas Gregoriana, 1954.

140   "Stages and Distinction in *De ente*: a Rejoinder." *Thomist* 45 (1981): 99-123.

141   "The Starting Point of the *Prima via.*" *Franciscan Studies* 27 (1967): 249-284. Repr. no. 15 (Catan), pp. 169-191.

142   "The Study of Knowledge – Natural Philosophy or Metaphysics?" *New Scholasticism* 42 (1968): 103-106. Re G. P. Klubertanz, "The Nature of Philosophical Enquiry – An Aristotelian View," *Proceedings of the American Catholic Philosophical Association* 41 (1967): 27-38.

143   "Teleology of Nature in Aristotle." *Monist* 52 (1968): 159-173.

144   "Theodicy, Natural Theology, and Metaphysics." *Modern Schoolman* 28 (1950-1951): 126-137.

145   "This Truth Sublime." In *Speaking of God*, ed. Denis Dirscherl, pp. 128-156. Milwaukee: Bruce, 1967.

146   "Thomistic Common Nature and Platonic Idea." *Mediaeval Studies* 21 (1959): 211-223. Repr. Bobbs-Merrill Reprints in Philosophy, 152 (Indianapolis: Bobbs-Merrill, 1969. Cf. no. 205.

147   "Los tres conceptos de existencia en Maritain." *Revista de filosofía* (Mexico) 14 (1981): 399-414. Trans. of no. 105.

148   "Unity and Essence in St. Thomas Aquinas." *Mediaeval Studies* 23 (1961): 240-259.

149   "The Unity in a Thomistic Philosophy of Man." *Mediaeval Studies* 25 (1963): 54-82.

150   "The Universality of the Sensible in the Aristotelian Noetic." In *Mélanges à la mémoire de Charles de Koninck*, ed. Lucien Zérounian, pp. 301-315. Quebec City: Les Presses de l'Université Laval, 1968. Repr. in *Essays in Ancient Greek Philosophy*, ed. John P. Anton (Albany: State University of New York Press, 1971), pp. 462-477; repr. no. 2 (Catan), pp. 59-73.

151   "Up to What Point is God Included in the Metaphysics of Duns Scotus." *Mediaeval Studies* 10 (1948): 163-177.

152   "Value and Metaphysics." In *The Future of Metaphysics*, ed. Robert E. Wood, pp. 204-228. Chicago: Quadrangle, 1970.

153   "Value and Person in Aquinas." In *Atti del Congresso Internazionale Tommaso d'Aquino nel suo VII centenario*, 1: 56-62. Naples: Edizione Domenicane Italiane, 1979.

154   "Wessen und Realdistinktion bei Thomas von Aquin." Trans. Wenzel Peters. In *Thomas von Aquin*, ed. Klaus Bernath, 2: 239-265. Darmstadt: Wissenschaftliche Buchgesellschaft, 1981. Trans. of no. 126.

III. Book Reviews

155   Julia Annas, *Aristotle's Metaphysics, Books M and N* (Oxford, 1976). In *Review of Metaphysics* 31 (1977-1978): 310-311.

156   A. H. Armstrong, ed., *The Cambridge History of Later Greek and Early Medieval Philosophy* (Cambridge, 1967). In *Phoenix* 22 (1968): 177-180.

157   Pierre Aubenque, *Le problème de l'être chez Aristote, Essai sur la problématique aristotélicienne* (Paris, 1962). In *Gnomon* 35 (1963): 459-462.

158   Karl Bärthelein, *Die Transzendentalienlehre der alten Ontologie*, 1: *Die Transzendentalienlehre im Corpus Aristotelicum* (Berlin, 1972). In *Archiv für Geschichte der Philosophie* 57 (1975): 217-222.

159   Enrico Berti, *Aristotele: dalla dialettica alla filosofia prima* (Padua, 1977) In *Review of Metaphysics* 31 (1977-1978): 471-472.

160   F. Bossier et al., ed., *Images of Man in Ancient and Medieval Thought*, Studio Gerardo Verbeke ab amicis et collegis dicata (Louvain, 1976). In *Archiv für Geschichte der Philosophie* 61 (1979): 112-115.

161   Franz Brentano, *On the Several Senses of Being in Aristotle: Aristotle, Metaphysics, Z.1*, trans. Rolf George (Berkeley, 1975). In *Review of Metaphysics* 30 (1976-1977): 122-123.

162   Karl Brinkmann, *Aristoteles: allgemeine und speziale Metaphysik* (Berlin, 1979). In *Review of Metaphysics* 33 (1979-1980): 414-416.

163   R.-T. Caldera, *Le jugement par inclination chez saint Thomas d'Aquin* (Paris, 1980). In *Review of Metaphysics* 35 (1981-1982): 369-370.

164   Angelo Capecci, *Struttura e fine. La logica della teleologia aristotelica* (L'Aquila, 1978). In *Review of Metaphysics* 33 (1979-1980): 622-623.

165   W. Charlton, *Aristotle's Physics, Books I and II* (Oxford, 1970). In *Phoenix* 25 (1971): 279-282.

166   Anton H. C. Chroust, *Aristotle: New Light on his Life and on Some of his Lost Works*. 2 vols. (Notre Dame, Ind., 1973). In *New Scholasticism* 49 (1975): 244-246.

167   Felix M. Cleve, *The Giants of Pre-Socratic Greek Philosophy: an Attempt to Reconstruct their Thoughts*, 2 vols. (The Hague, 1965). In *New Scholasticism* 41 (1967): 132-135.

168   Victor Coutant, *Theophrastus De igne* (New York, 1971). In *Classical World* (1973): 468-469.

169   J. De Vries, *Grundbegriffe der Scholastik* (Darmstadt, 1980). In *Review of Metaphysics* 35 (1981-1982): 380-381.

170   Josef Endres, *Der Mensch als Mitte* (Bonn, 1956). In *Modern Schoolman* 34 (1956-1957): 144-146.

171   O. N. Gariglia, *Quellenkritische und logische Untersuchungen zur Gegensatzlehre des Aristoteles* (Hildesheim/New York, 1978) In *Review of Metaphysics* 35 (1981-1982): 390-392.

172   Eberhard Jungel, *Zum Ursprung der Analogie bei Parmenides und Heraklit* (Berlin, 1964). In *Modern Schoolman* 43 (1965-1966): 78-80.

173   Paul Oskar Kristeller, *Le thomisme et la pensée italienne de la Renaissance* (Montreal/Paris, 1967). In *Dialogue* 6 (1967-1968): 455-459.

174   Walter Leszl, *Aristotle's Conception of Ontology* (Padua, 1975). In *Journal of the History of Philosophy* 15 (1977): 331-334.

175   A. C. Lloyd, *Form and Universal in Aristotle* (Liverpool, 1981). In *Review of Metaphysics* 35 (1981-1982): 395-396.

176   Geoffrey E. R. Lloyd, *Aristotle. The Growth and Structure of his Thought* (London, 1968). In *International Philosophical Quarterly* 9 (1969): 299-301.

177   William F. Lynch, *An Approach to the Metaphysics of Plato through the Parmenides* (Washington, 1959). In *New Scholasticism* 34 (1960): 134-136.

178   Werner Marx, *Introduction to Aristotle's Theory of Being as Being*, trans. Robert S. Schine (The Hague, 1977). In *Classical World* 73 (1979-1980): 190.

179   Battista Mondin, *St. Thomas Aquinas' Philosophy in the Commentary on the Sentences* (The Hague, 1975). In *Review of Metaphysics* 30 (1976-1977): 532-533.

180   Paul Moraux, *Der Aristotelismus bei den Griechen*, vol. 1 (Berlin/New York, 1973). In *Classical World* 69 (1975-1976): 489-491.

181   Walter M. Neidl, *Thearchia* (Regensburg, 1976). In *International Journal for Philosophy of Religion* 9 (1978): 124-125.

182   Whitney J. Oates, *Aristotle and the Problem of Value* (Princeton, 1963). In *New Scholasticism* 39 (1965): 376-379.

183   Thomas C. O'Brien, *Metaphysics and the Existence of God* (Washington, 1960). In *New Scholasticism* 36 (1962): 250-253. Cf. nos. 221 and 223.

184   John Herman Randall Jr., *Aristotle* (New York, 1960). In *New Scholasticism* 34 (1960): 520-523.

185   Giovanni Reale, *Il concetto di filosofia prima e l'unità della metafisica di Aristotele* (Milan, 1961). In *New Scholasticism* 38 (1964): 254-256.

186   Frederick J. Roensch, *Early Thomistic School* (Dubuque, 1964). In *International Philosophical Quarterly* 6 (1966): 144-145.

187   *San Tommaso e il pensiero moderno*, ed. Pontificia Accademia Romana di S. Tommaso d'Aquino (Rome, 1974). In *Thomist* 40 (1976): 153-160.

188   Friedrich Solmsen, *Aristotle's System of the Physical World: a Comparison with his Predecessors* (Ithaca, 1960). In *New Scholasticism* 39 (1965): 545-547.

189   Thomas Aquinas, *Commentary on the Metaphysics of Aristotle*, trans. John P. Rowan, 2 vols. (Chicago, 1961). In *Review of Metaphysics* 16 (1962-1963): 503-512.

190   Hermann Weidemann, *Metaphysik und Sprache* (Freiburg/Munich, 1975). In *Review of Metaphysics* 32 (1978-1979): 373-374.

191   Ursula Wolf, *Möglichkeit und Notwendigkeit bei Aristoteles und Heute* (Munich, 1979). In *Review of Metaphysics* 34 (1980-1981): 625-626.

192   Harry Austryn Wolfson, *Studies in the History of Philosophy and Religion*, vol. 2, ed. I. Twersky and G. Williams (Cambridge, Mass., 1977). In *International Journal for Philosophy of Religion* 9 (1978): 260-261.

IV. Criticism

193   James F. Anderson. "A Notable Study of the Aristotelian Metaphysics." *New Scholasticism* 26 (1952): 229-239. A review article about *The Doctrine of Being* (no. 5).

194   ——. "Response III. On Fr. Owens' Comments." *Review of Metaphysics* 5 (1951-1952): 470-472. A discussion of Owens' comments on theses re analogy. Cf. nos. 60 and 195.

195   ——. "Some Basic Propositions Concerning Analogy." *Review of Metaphysics* 5 (1951-1952): 465. A discussion opener followed by comments by Owens and others; published in a section entitled "Explorations." Cf. nos. 60 and 194.

196   J. D. Beach. "Aristotle's Notion of Being." *Thomist* 21 (1958): 29-43. Discusses *The Doctrine of Being...* (no. 5).

197   Joseph Bobik. "Some Disputable Points Apropos of St. Thomas and Metaphysics." *New Scholasticism* 37 (1963): 411-430. Cf. nos. 73, 135, 198, 213.

198   ——. "Some Remarks on Fr. Owens' 'St. Thomas and Elucidation'." *New Scholasticism* 37 (1963): 59-63. Cf. nos; 73, 135, 197, 213.

199   ——. "Some Remarks on Father Owens' *St. Thomas and the Future of Metaphysics*." *New Scholasticism* 33 (1959): 68-85. Cf. no. 14.

200   Karel Boullart. "Metaphysische Problemen – Metaphysische Methoden." *Philosophica Gandensia*, no. 10 (1972): 90-96. Includes a discussion of Owens' "Reality and Metaphysics" (no. 130).

201   John C. Cahalan. "On the Proving of Causal Propositions." *Modern Schoolman* 44 (1966-1967): 129-142. Cf. nos. 53-55, 202.

202   ——. "Remarks on Father Owens' 'The Causal Proposition Revisited'." *Modern Schoolman* 44 (1966-1967): 152-160. Cf. nos. 53-55, 201.

203   F. F. Centore, "Atomism and Plato's *Theaetetus*." *Philosophical Forum* 5 (1973-1974): 475-485. Touches briefly on Owens' writings.

204   C. J. Chambers. "Prime Movers and Prim Provers." *Thomist* 31 (1967): 465-507. Discusses many of Owens' writings.

205   Ralph W. Clark. "St. Thomas Aquinas's Theory of Universals." *Monist* 58 (1974): 163-172. Discusses, inter alia, Owens' "Thomistic Common Nature..." (no. 146).

206   Jacques Croteau. "Comments" on "The Primacy of the External in Thomistic Noetics" (no. 124). *Église et théologie* 5 (1974): 207-211.

206a   Lawrence Dewan. "Being *Per Se*, Being *Per Accidens* and St. Thomas' Metaphysics." *Science et esprit* 30 (1978): 169-184. Cf. nos. 7, 27.

206b   ——. "St. Thomas, Joseph Owens, and Existence." *New Scholasticism* 56 (1982): 399-442. Cf. nos. 1, 11, 30, 55, 70.

207   Discussion of "Matter and Predication in Aristotle." In *The Concept of Matter*, ed. Ernan McMullin, pp. 120-121. Notre Dame, Ind.: University of Notre Dame Press, 1963. Repr. in paperback: *The Concept of Matter in Greek and Medieval Philosophy*, NDP 46 (1965), pp. 100-101. Cf. nos. 106, 215.

208   Leonard J. Eslick. "What is the Starting Point of Metaphysics?" *Modern Schoolman* 34 (1956-1957): 247-263. Discusses in part *The Doctrine of Being* ... (no. 5).

209   Alan Gewirth. "Aristotle's Doctrine of Being." *Philosophical Review* 62 (1953): 577-589. Review article about *The Doctrine of Being* ... (no. 5).

210   J. F. M. Hunter. "Note on Father Owens' Comment on Williams' Criticism of Aquinas on Infinite Regress." *Mind* 73 (1964): 439-440. Cf. no. 32.

211   Martha Husain. "The Question 'What is Being?' and its Aristotelian Answer." *New Scholasticism* 50 (1976): 293-309. Comments on, inter alia, Owens' "The Content of Existence" (no. 64).

212   G. B. Klubertanz. "A Comment on 'The Intelligibility of Being'." *Gregorianum* 36 (1955): 194-195. Cf. no. 97.

213   Harry La Plante. "The Characteristics of Existence." *Philosophical Studies* (Maynooth) 17 (1968): 95-109. Comments on the Owens-Bobik debate on elucidation – cf. nos. 73, 135, 197, 198.

214   Walter Leszl. "Knowledge of the Universal and Knowledge of the Particular in Aristotle." *Review of Metaphysics* 26 (1972-1973): 278-313. Discusses in part Owens' *The Doctrine of Being* ... (no. 7).

215   N. Lobkowicz. Comment on "Matter and Predication in Aristotle." In *The Concept of Matter*, ed. Ernan McMullin, pp. 116-119. Notre Dame: University of Notre Dame Press, 1963. Repr. in paperback: *The Concept of Matter in Greek and Medieval Philosphy*, NDP 46 (1965), pp. 96-99. Cf. nos. 106, 207.

216   Barry Miller. "'Exists' and Other Predicates." *New Scholasticism* 53 (1979): 475-479. Elicited response by Owens, no. 76.

217   Harry A. Nielsen. "Father Owens on Elucidation – a Comment." *New Scholasticism* 36 (1962) 233-236. Cf. 135, and 62.

218   W. V. O. Quine. "Thoughts on Reading Father Owens." *Proceedings of the Seventh Inter-American Congress of Philosphy*, 1: 60-63. Quebec City: Presses de l'Université Laval, 1967. Cf. no. 127.

219   John E. Smith. Comments on "God in Philosophy Today." in *God, Man and Philosophy*, ed. Carl W. Grindel, pp. 51-64. New York: St. John's University Press, 1971. Cf. no. 89.

220   F. Sontag. "Reality and its Expressions." *Modern Schoolman* 54 (1976-1977): 259-269. Cf. no. 130.

221   William A. Wallace. "Metaphysics and the Existence of God." *New Scholasticism* 36 (1962) 529-531. Discusses Owens' review (no. 183) of O'Brien's book, *Metaphysics and the Existence of God*.

222   William H. Walton. "Fr. Owens and the *Metaphysics* of Aristotle." *Review of Metaphysics* 6 (1952-1953): 257-264. Reveiw article about *The Doctrine of Being* ... (no. 5).

223   John L. Yardan. "Some Remarks on Metaphysics and the Existence of God." *New Scholasticism* 37 (April 1963): 213-219. Discusses *St. Thomas and the Future of Metaphysics* (no. 14) and Owens' review (no. 183) of O'Brien's book, *Metaphysics and the Existence of God*.

List of Subscribers

Ashley Crandell Amos
Thomas C. Anslow, CM

Basilian Fathers
  of the Institute House
Enrico Berti
Rev. Petro B. T. Bilaniuk
William Boyle
David Braybrooke
Barry F. Brown
Jerome V. Brown
Norman J. P. Brown
Virginia Brown
Kenneth A. Bryson

John C. Cahalan
Venant Cauchy
F. F. Centore
E. James Crombie
Jacques Croteau, OMI
Michael J. Cummings

Joseph G. Dawson
Vianney Décarie
Louis Aramis de Courty
Alan Donagan
John P. Doyle

Desmond J. FitzGerald
Cardinal George B. Flahiff, CSB

Constantine Georgiadis

Holy Redeemer College,
  Waterford
M. Husain and P. Seligman jointly

Institut d'études médiévales,
  Université de Montréal

Edouard Jeauneau
Harold J. Johnson

Antoine Kaluzny
Bill Kelloway
  in memory of William E. Carlo
Dr. and Mrs. John F. X. Knasas
  and family

Yvon Lafrance
Maurice Lagueux
T. J. Lang
Thomas Langan
Michael J. Lapierre, SJ
Herman Henri Lau
R. James Long
Thomas A. Losoncy
John E. Lynch, CSP

E. M. Macierowski
William C. Marceau, CSB
E. J. McCullough
K. L. McGovern
Alastair McKinnon
Robert J. McLaughlin

Francis P. McQuade
Jeff Mitscherling
Jacques Monet, sj
Edmund W. Morton, sj
John Anthony Murray

E. P. W. Nash, sj
M. Frances Nims, ibvm
John H. Nota, sj

Jean T. Oesterle
Peter O'Reilly
James J. O'Rourke

Pierre J. Payer
James V. Penna

L. M. Régis, op
James P. Reilly, Jr.
Herbert Richardson
John O. Riedl
Don D. Roberts
T. H. Robinson
J. Joseph Ryan

James D. Scheer

Edgar Scully
Société de Philosophie du Québec
Francis Sparshott
J. T. Stevenson
Andrzej-Bobola Stypiński
Peter Swan, csb
Edward A. Synan

John Thorp
Emmanuel Trépanier

University of Dallas,
    Department of Philosophy
University of King's College,
    Halifax
University of Toronto,
    Department of Philosophy

Lenke Vietorisz

Laura Westra
Albert Wingell
Douglas White
Judy Wubnig

Richard W. Yee

Index of Greek Terms

References to Works of Aristotle, Plato, Plotinus and Thomas Aquinas

A. Aristotle

Categoris: **1.1a6-7**, 117n; **2.1b6**, 85; **4.2a-13-15**, 85; **5.2b3-6**, 83

De anima: **1.5.411a14-15**, 105; **2.1.412b6-9**, 88; **3.4.429b29-31**, 69n; **3.5.430a10-25**, 207; **3.5.430a11-13**, 236; **3.5.430a-14-18**, 69n

De caelo: **1.4.271a33**, 103; **1.8.277b4-5**, 107; **1.9.278b20-21**, 102n; **1.9.279a21**, 108; **1.9.279a29-30**, 103n; **1.10.280a1**, 171; **1.10.280a22**, 102n; **2.2.285a29**, 102; **2.2.285a30**, 102n; **2.8.289b27**, 110n; **2.9.291a23**, 108n; **2.12.292a21**, 102; **2.12.292a23-24**, 102; **2.12.292b1-2**, 102; **3.2.301b17**, 61n; **4.3.310b16-19**, 107; **4.4.311b14-15**, 107

De generatione et corruptione: **1.2.316a-14ff**, 17; **1.2.316a23-24**, 110; **1.3.319a-32**, 110n; **1.4.320a2-3**, 110n; **1.6.322b-16-18**, 105n; **1.7.324b18**, 110n; **1.10.-327b25-26**, 106; **1.10.328a7-14**, 113n; **1.10.328a28-31**, 106; **1.10.328a34**, 107n; **2.2.329b24-26**, 105-6; **2.2.329b-26-30**, 105; **2.3.330b25-26**, 105n; **2.3.-331a4-6**, 106; **2.4.331a22-23**, 107n; **1.10.328a24-26**, 106; **2.4.331a26-29**, 106; **2.6.333b13-15**, 103n; **2.9.335b9-31**, 110; **2.10.336a15ff**, 212; **2.10.-336b27-28**, 108; **2.10.336b32-7a7**, 108; **2.11.338a18-19**, 102n

De generatione animalium: **1.18.724b5-7**, 111; **1.19.726a9-12**, 111; **1.19.726b15-19**, 109, 111; **1.19.727a2-4**, 111; **1.20.-729a9-11**, 111; **1.20.729a29-30**, 111; **1.22.730b19-22**, 104n; **1.22.730b29-30**, 104n; **2.6.744b16-17**, 104n; **4.6.-775a18**, 105n

De motu animalium: **8.708a10-11**, 103

De partibus animalium: **2.1.646a14-20**, 105, 105n; **2.2.649a18-19**, 105n; **2.9.-654b29-32**, 104n; **4.2.677a10-15**, 104n; **4.5.681a12-17**, 103n; **4.10.687a-10-12**, 104n

Eudemian Ethics: **2.9.1224a18**, 103n

Historia animalium: **8.1.588b4-7**, 103n

Metaphysics: **1.1.981b28-2a1**, 337; **1.2.-982a25-b4**, 56n; **1.2.982b9**, 229; **1.3.-983a26-32**, 229; **1.3.984a27-29**, 110; **1.6.987a33-b10**, 79; **1.6.987b12-13**, 93; **3.1.99b9-10**, 234; **3.2.997a5-10**, 337; **3.2.997a20**, 337; **3.2.997b20-21**, 123n; **3.1.1003a22**, 82; **4.1.1003a17**, 340; **4.1.1003a33**, 230; **4.2.1004a28**, 333; **5.2.1013a29ff**, 188n; **5.4.1014b-32ff**, 230; **5.4.1014b36-5a1**, 103n; **5.4.-1015a10-11**, 103n; **5.12.1019a15**, 58, 61n; **5.12.1019b35-20a1**, 109; **5.12.-1020a4**, 61n; **5.23.1023a9**, 103n; **6.1.-1025b18-21**, 206; **7.1.1028b2-4**, 82, 229; **7.3.1029a29-32**, 87; **7.7.1032a24**, 230n; **7.9.1034a30-32**, 108n; **7.10.-1035b16-18**, 110n; **7.10.1036a8**, 59n; **8.1.1042a25-32**, 59n, 64; **8.2.1043a26**, 112; **8.5.1044b27**, 59n; **8.6.1045a30-34**, 110n; **8.6.1045b18-19**, 110; **8.6.-1045b20-21**, 110; **9.1.1046a4**, 57n; **9.1.1046a9-11**, 57n, 61n; **9.1.1046a10-13**, 58; **9.1.1046a11-13**, 109; **9.2.-1046b4**, 61n; **9.3.1046b33-7a4**, 63; **9.3.1047a1-2**, 63; **9.3.1047a4-6**, 64, 64n; **9.3.1047a7-10**, 64n, 65n; **9.3.-1047a12-17**, 65; **9.3.1047a19-20**, 61; **9.3.1047a24-26**, 67n, 109n, 110; **9.3.-1046b29-32**, 61; **9.3.1047a30-31**, 58, 110; **9.5.1044b27**, 66n; **9.5.1047b31-35**, 58; **9.6.1048a37**, 230n; **9.6.1048b7**, 230n; **9.6.1048a32-35**, 109; **9.6.1048a-35**, 57; **9.7.1049a8-18**, 60; **9.7.1049a-15**, 111n; **9.8.1049b7**, 61n; **9.8.1049b-10-17**, 55; **9.8.1049b16**, 56; **9.8.1049b-24**, 57n; **9.8.1050a1**, 57n; **9.8.1050a16-23**, 110; **9.8.1050b2**, 112; **9.8.1050b28-29**, 108n; **9.10.1051b1ff**, 231; **12.1.-1069a30-36**, 206, 206n; **12.3.1070a11**, 230n; **12.4.1070b34-35**, 215; **12.5.-**

B. PLATO

C. Plotinus

Enneads, Bk. I: **1.8.9**, 145n; **1.12**, 141n; **4.10**, 146-147; **8.5.30-34**, 139; **8.14**, 173
—, Bk. II: **4.5.24-28**, 172; **9**, 136, 140; **9.4.1**, 136; **9.6.2**, 138n; **9.8.10ff**, 190n; **9.10.19**, 138; **9.11**, 136; **9.13**, 30ff, 139; **9.15.39f**, 225; **9.18.4**, 145n
—, Bk. III: **7.11**, 137, 138, 139; **7.11.15ff**, 137; **8.1.14ff**, 183, 188n; **8.1.20-31**, 183-184; **8.4.30ff**, 188n; **8.5.1-3**, 165; **8.5.27-31**, 170n; **8.5.27-30**, 166; **8.5.30**, 172; **8.6.1ff**, 188n; **8.7.1ff**, 188n; **8.7.1-2**, 172; **8.7.21-22**, 170n; **8.7.21**, 172; **8.8.1-30**, 164; **8.8.11**, 168; **8.9**, 154n; **8.10**, 187; **8.10.3ff**, 185; **8.10.3-10**, 186; **8.11.2**, 168; **9**, 149; **9.3**, 144; **9.3.5**, 136; **9.5.1-3**, 169
—, Bk. IV: **2.1.44-45**, 171n; **3**, 140, 143, 145; **3.6.25**, 145; **3.7.16ff**, 145; **3.9.29-30**, 145; **3.12**, 145; **3.12.35**, 145; **3.13.17ff**, 145; **3.16**, 135; **3.17.21**, 145; **3.18**, 145; **4.2**, 146; **4.4**, 148; **4.4.17-18**, 148; **4.17**, 148; **4.17.11**, 149; **4.17.14-15**, 148; **8**, 141; **8.1.40**, 141; **8.2.17-18**, 141; **8.2.27**, 141; **8.2.28**, 141; **8.2.33**, 141; **8.2.41-42**, 139n; **8.2.46**, 141; **8.2.49**, 141; **8.3.5**, 142; **8.4.**, 136; **8.4.5**, 142; **8.5.1**, 140; **8.5.8-9**, 142; **8.5.16**, 142; **8.5.27ff**, 139; **8.5.28**, 150; **8.6.1-18**, 171; **8.7**, 137; **8.7.4**, 143; **8.7.11ff**, 139n; **8.7.15ff**, 150; **8.8.**, 143, 148; **8.8.22**, 143f; **8.8.24**, 141
—, Bk. V: **1**, 138, 144; **1.1**, 137, 138, 143, 145; **1.3.**, 154n; **1.3.7-24**, 166; **1.3.12-20**, 169; **1.3.15-16**, 169; **1.6**, 158n; **1.6.15ff**, 190n; **1.6.53**, 138n; **1.7.5ff**, 190n; **2**, 140; **2.1**, 187; **2.1.1ff**, 190n; **2.1.3**, 185; **2.1.5-11**, 186n; **2.1.7-14**, 164; **2.1.8**, 186; **2.1.13-18**, 186n; **2.1.18-21**, 186n; **2.1.19ff**, 144; **2.1.25-27**, 171n; **3.5.21-23**, 168; **3.7.18-25**, 165; **3.10.14-16**, 168; **3.11.1ff**, 190n; **3.11.1-18**, 168; **3.5.11.5**, 168; **3.11.8**, 168; **4.1.20ff**, 190n; **5.9**, 154n; **5.12**, 1ff, 190n; **5.6.4-5**, 175n; **8.7.18-25**, 170n, 174
—, Bk. VI: **2.21.45-48**, 182; **4.11.9**, 138n; **4.24**, 138n; **5.3**, 154n; **5.12.16ff**, 189n; **7.16.9-22**, 164n; **7.17.18**, 40, 175n; **7.20.16ff**, 190n; **7.33.30-31**, 174; **7.35.29**, 171; **8.7**, 160; **8.7.46-54**, 160; **8**, 158n; **8.10.32-35**, 173; **8.12.19**, 160; **8.13.7-8**, 160; **8.13.8-9**, 160; **8.13.43-45**, 160; **8.13.50-55**, 160; **8.15.1**, 160; **8.16.12-16**, 160; **8.16.18-21**, 161; **8.16.18-24**, 167; **8.16.24-26**, 167; **8.16.25**, 160; **8.18.38**, 161; **8.20.9-11**, 161; **8.20.17-27**, 161; **9.1**, 182; **9.1.1-8**, 182-3; **9.3.39ff**, 190n; **9.3.49ff**, 190n; **9.5**, 154n; **9.5.29**, 137; **9.11**, 146; **9.11.36ff**, 189n

D. Thomas Aquinas

Compendium theologiae: **1.15**, 390; **98-99**, 263
De aeternitate mundi: (ed. Leon.) ll. **67-71**, 254n; ll. **77-80**, 254; ll. **88-157**, 254-255; ll. **158-210**, 255-257
De articulis fidei: 269
De concordantiis: 31, 246n
De ente et essentia: 387
De malo: **3.2. obj. 13, ad 13**, 347
De potentia Dei: **q.3.a.5**, 269n; **q.3.a.14**, 259, 264; **q.3.a.17**, 263n, 266; **q.7.a.1**, 287; **q.7.a.5**, 273n, 288, 289, 290, 291, 296; **q.7.a.5, ad 2**, 292; **q.7.a.6**, 274n; **q.7.a.7**, 296n
De quattuor opositis: 270n
De substantiis separatis: 269-270
De veritate: **q.2.a.1, ad 9**, 277-278n, 298n; **q.3**, 217n; **q.10.a.12, c**, 355n; **q.16.a.1, ad 12**, 347n; **q.16.a2, c**, 345-347; **q.24.a.5, c**, 347; **q.28.a.7, obj. 6, ad 6**, 347
De unitate intellectus: 248
De virtutibus in communi: **a.6, ad 1**, 359
Expositio in librum Boethii De hebdomadibus: 355n
Expositio et lectura super Epistolas Pauli Apostoli: **c.12, lect. 2**, 352
Expositio super librum De causis: 299n; **lect. 6, n. 175**, 236
Expositio super primam et secundam Decretalem ad Archidiaconum Tudertinum: **35.432-434**, 270n

General Index

absolute essences, 86

action, primary and secondary ends of, 358

actual infinity, 246-248

Albert the Great, 191ff, 244, 260, 262, 266-267, 355n, 362, 364; divine attributes, 195-197; divine causality, 197-201; *esse primum creatum*, 199-200; God, agent intellect, 196, 199; knowledge of God, 193-195; *Liber de causis et processu universitatis*, 192ff; Neoplatonism, 192-201; participated being, 198; views on Avicebron, 198n

Albertinus, F., 404n

Albinus, 204n

Alcuin, 353

Alexander Aphrodisias, 13, 118-119

Algazel, 247n

Al-Kindi, 208

analogy of being, 322

analysis by principles and elements, 351ff

analysis, ontological, 322

Anselm of Canterbury, 256

Antiochus of Ascalon, 203-204

Araujo, F., 403; criticism of Suarez, 412; criticism of Vasquez on eternal truths, 405-408; doctrine of eternal truth, 408-415; relation to Aquinas, 405

Aristotle: doctrine of act/potency, 55-73, 110-112, 213; doctrine of being, 206, 229-230; criticism of Plato, 66; criticism of Presocratics, 59, 101, 104, 110; doctrine of elements, 104-108; epistemology, 207-209; doctrine of eternity, 260; doctrine of generation, 107; genetic interpretation of works, 334; interpretation of *Metaphysics*, Book 5, 333-335, 342; doctrine of motion, 108; doctrine of natural powers, 114; optics, explanatory science of, 118, 121, 123-125, 130; physical principles, 205-206; *pros hen* equivocity, 336; doctrine of rainbows, 118-122; doctrine of scientific knowledge, 116ff, 123-127, 128-129, 337-338, 342; substance, essence

identified with, 82, 84, unmoved movers, 209-216, 382; doctrine of weight, 107

Armstrong, H., 178

Arnou, R., 157

ascent to God, threefold, 304-307, 313-314

Aubenque, P., 219n

Augustine of Hippo, 217, 223, 251-252, 256-257, 353

Averroës, 218, 247n

Averroism, 237

Avicenna, 218, 247n, 398

Bacon, Francis, 316, 325

Bacon, Roger, 260

Baldner, S., 259n

Balme, D., 102n, 104n

bare particulars, 92, 93n, 97

Barker, S., 333

Barnes, J., 3, 25n, 116, 120n

being, 232-237; criteria of, 83-84

Bergmann, G., 80, 89, 94-95, 98

Blumenthal, H. J., 180-181

Boethius, 257, 355n

Boethius of Dacia, 243

Bonaventure, 261-262

Bourke, V., 243

Brady, I., 248-250

Bukowski, T., 249-250

Calcidius, 259

Calogero, G., 3, 10

Capreolus, 409n, 410n, 415-416

Carneades, 203

Carteron, H., 106n, 107n, 112n

Cassiodorus, 353

Chenu, M.-D., 243

Chrysippus, 135

Cilento, V., 157

Clark, M., 180n

conceptual distinction, 326

Covotti, A., 157

creation: *ab aeterno* and *de novo*, 377;